FAMILIES

CHANGING
TRENDS IN
CANADA

2ND EDITION

FAMILIES

CHANGING

TRENDS IN

CANADA

2ND EDITION

MAUREEN BAKER, PH.D.
GENERAL EDITOR
McGill University
Director, Centre for Applied Family Studies

ANNE-MARIE AMBERT
York University

PAT ARMSTRONG
York University

CHAD GAFFIELD
University of Ottawa

BRIGITTE KITCHEN
York University

MARLENE MACKIE
University of Calgary

MILDRED MORTON
Employment and Immigration Canada

EMILY NETT
University of Manitoba

JOHN PETERS
Wilfrid Laurier University

ALICE PROPPER
York University

SUSANNAH J. WILSON
Anaheim Hills, California

McGRAW-HILL RYERSON LIMITED

Toronto   Montreal   New York   Auckland   Bogotá   Caracas   Hamburg   Lisbon
London   Madrid   Mexico   Milan   New Delhi   Paris   San Juan   São Paulo
Singapore   Sydney   Tokyo

FAMILIES: Changing Trends in Canada
Second Edition

ISBN: 0-07-549795-6

6 7 8 9 0 W 9 8 7 6 5 4 3
Printed and bound in Canada

Care has been taken to trace ownership of copyright material contained in this text. The publishers will gladly accept any information that will enable them to rectify any reference or credit in subsequent editions.

COVER DESIGN: STEPHEN A. MACEACHERN

Canadian Cataloguing in Publication Data

Main entry under title:
Families : changing trends in Canada

2nd ed.
First ed. published under title: The Family :
changing trends in Canada.
ISBN 0-07-549795-6

1. Family – Canada. I. Baker, Maureen. II. Ambert, Anne-Marie. III. Title: The Family :
changing trends in Canada.

HQ560.F3 1990   306.8′5′0971   C89-095210-8

Statistics Canada information is used with the permission of the Ministry of Industry, as Minister responsible for Statistics Canada. Information on the availability of the wide range of data from Statistics Canada can be obtained from Statistics Canada's Regional Offices, its World Wide Web site at http://www.statcan.ca, and its toll-free access number 1-800-263-1136

Contents

Preface

Much has changed in family studies since the first edition of *The Family: Changing Trends in Canada* was published in 1984. For one thing, Canadian family law has been revised, new reproductive technologies have been developed, and the 1986 census has been partially analysed, providing new statistics relating to family life. In addition, several new textbooks have been written reflecting the legal and social changes in family life, some shifts in theoretical perspective, and changing fields of research and student interest. And finally, family studies appears to have become a more popular subject within universities, colleges, and secondary schools.

The first edition of this book was an attempt to provide a Canadian textbook with a historical, cross-cultural, and structural focus, at a time when few such books were available to university professors in Canada. Six years later, we have retained the historical and structural perspective and the Canadian focus, but have enlarged the size and scope of the book by adding material on mate selection, marital dynamics, the family life-cycle approach, the effects of children on their parents, and cross-cultural comparisons. The second edition has also been updated to include the most recent policy issues and statistics relating to family life.

This text has been prepared by eleven different contributors, most of whom are sociologists. In order to broaden the discussion, however, we have included chapters by professors of social work and history and by a lawyer involved in legal and social-policy analysis. We have maintained the Canadian perspective and focus on structural change but have added more emphasis on interpersonal relations. Each chapter was written from the author's own theoretical perspective, but was prepared specifically for this volume with the other chapters in mind. As with the first edition, this is not intended to be a book of readings, but rather a multi-authored textbook.

In preparing this volume, I have been inspired by the continuing enthusiasm and co-operation of all the contributors, who were expected to meet what sometimes appeared to be unreasonable deadlines. I am also indebted to sponsoring editor Susan Erickson from McGraw-Hill Ryerson, to the anonymous reviewers of the manuscript, to my ever-patient spouse, David Tippin, and to the wonders of computer technology.

MAUREEN BAKER
OTTAWA
JANUARY 1990

chapter one

Introduction: Theories, Methods, and Concerns of Family Sociology

INTRODUCTION

Most of us have personally experienced family life, which tends to make us think that we are knowledgeable in the sociology of the family. Yet, if we have only our own families and those of our friends to observe closely, generalizing from this experience is a poor basis for scientific research. It is tempting to assume that others behave the way we do, sharing our moral values and our lifestyles. However, when we discover that other societies prefer arranged marriages, allow more than one spouse, offer men the best food, or practise female infanticide, it is easy to become moralistic and judgmental.

Knowledge of cultural and historical variations in family structure and relationships may provide us with valuable insights about the relativity of family behaviour to a specific culture. These variations illustrate the importance of socialization and cultural values in influencing personal life. While social scientists talked about "maternal instincts" and "natural sex differences" fifty years ago, they are now more likely to argue that personality, aptitudes, and mannerisms may be affected by genetic inheritance, but are substantially learned within families according to cultural and class prescriptions. While the earlier biological theories of instincts meant that altering social structure and behaviour would be impossible, or at least very difficult, sociological theories suggest that behaviour is largely learned and therefore is subject to change. Sociobiologists have cautioned, however, that we do not yet know the relative importance of nature versus nurture in the development of human behaviour.

The fact that the family is an ancient institution with so many structural variations provides sociologists and historians with an opportunity to trace changes over time and to uncover social and economic factors leading to these changes. The relationship between the family and the economy is a complex one. Sociologists, economists, and historians have tried to understand how behaviour inside the family has been influenced by such factors as the separation of home and work during industrialization, the expansion of the service sector of the economy to include women workers, and the trend toward non-family child care. Further, they have studied how these changes have led to the development of ideologies about "proper" family behaviour. The analysis of the interaction between the economy and the family encompasses a variety of topics, including social policy decisions relating to the family, the importance of domestic labour to society, and variations in birth rates by social class.

Some sociologists who have studied the family as an institution have often referred to it as a "microcosm of society." While it would be exaggerating to say that *all* forms of human behaviour and social relationships exist within the family, we could certainly say that many basic relationships and social processes have been found in the various stages of family life throughout history. The study of variations in family life may provide us with some disturbing insights, however. If change is possible and values are relative to a particular culture, then our own way of life could be challenged. If monogamy is not

Knowledge of cultural and historical variations in family structure and relationships may provide us with valuable insights into the family behaviour of a specific culture.

MILLER COMSTOCK INC.

universal, for example, maybe it is not intrinsically "wrong" to want more than one spouse. If some societies allow premarital sex, maybe we should too. It is difficult not to take the study of family sociology personally, not to think of our own lifestyle and moral values while reading about others' (see below). We may be forced to rethink biological limitations of behaviour as well as the strength of social control. Furthermore, ethical or moral issues may interfere with our attempts to study personal relationships and family life as objectively as possible.

DEFINING THE FAMILY

In this book, we will discuss some of the changes that have taken place in Canadian family life, focusing on economic and ideological changes, legal reform, and recent research trends within the discipline of family studies. But before we do this, we need to define the term *family*. Arriving at a definition is not an easy task, however, due to the many variations in family structure.

In Canada, the popular conception of the family could involve two different social groups: either one's own entire kin group related by blood or marriage, or the immediate household of siblings and parents or spouse and children. The Canadian census comes close to the second group by defining a census family as "a married couple with or without never-married children living in the same dwelling, or a lone-parent living with one or more never-married children" (Statistics Canada, 1979:1). While a childless couple may be considered a family by the Canadian government, sociologists generally suggest that a couple has to have children to make them a family (see page 4).

In 1949, the American anthropologist George Murdock provided a definition of "family" that has been widely used in sociology. According to Murdock, a family is "a social group characterized by common residence, economic co-operation, and reproduction. It includes adults of both sexes, at least two of whom maintain a socially approved sexual relationship, and one or more children, own or adopted, of the sexually cohabiting adults" (Murdock, 1949:1).

FOR INTEREST

WOMEN GET WARNING IN IRAN

NICOSIA – Iranian authorities have warned women that they may be punished by up to 74 lashes if they wear makeup or see-through stockings in public. A notice by the State Security Council printed in Iranian newspapers this week warned that laws punishing violators of *hijab* (Islamic covering) would be strictly enforced beginning Friday. The notice listed eight types of violations, including exposing the hair in a vulgar way, using lipstick and eyeshadow in a provocative manner, wearing clothes that accentuate body curves, and wearing see-through stockings not covered by trousers.

/Reuter

FOR INTEREST

FAMILY DEFINITIONS

Economic Family:

Refers to a group of two or more persons who live in the same dwelling and are related to each other by blood, marriage or adoption. Persons living common-law are considered, for census purposes, as now married regardless of their legal marital status; they accordingly are counted as married couples in the economic family figures.

Census Family:

Refers to a husband and a wife (with or without children who have never married, regardless of age), or a lone parent of any marital status, with one or more children (who have never married, regardless of age), living in the same dwelling. For census purposes, persons living in a common-law type of arrangement are considered as now married, regardless of their legal marital status; they accordingly are counted as a husband-wife family in the census family figures.

Source: Statistics Canada, *Canadian Social Trends* (Ottawa: Supply and Services Canada, Summer 1986), p. 8. Reproduced with permission of the Minister of Supply and Services Canada, 1989.

While not all sociologists agree on how the concept of family should be defined, part of this problem has been resolved by delineating the type of family under discussion. In most of the North American sociological literature from the past fifty years, the *nuclear* or *conjugal* family has been presented as both the statistical norm and the ideal. The nuclear family has been defined as a husband and wife and their children sharing a residence, dividing their labour, and co-operating economically. According to this definition, however, a decreasing number of Canadians are living in nuclear families now compared to twenty years ago, with a later mean age of marriage, more common-law relationships, higher divorce rates, more one-parent families, and more blended families with children from previous relationships.

Sociologists also make a distinction between *family* and *household*. While family members are related by blood or marriage, they do not necessarily share a dwelling place. A household refers to those living in the same dwelling, and this could include roommates who are unrelated, a family, a single person, or a family with a boarder or a domestic servant. Over the past century, the size of households has declined as more people live alone, servants are expensive to maintain, and fewer children are born.

Emily Nett (1980:354) suggests that a family is "any group of people *considered* to be related to each other by blood or marriage." She extends the definition beyond those who share a dwelling place to include a wider network of related persons. She argues that the family is an abstraction involving ideal, expected, and observed behaviour.

Most research on families has focused on nuclear families, despite the fact that about 10 percent of Canadians never marry, about 15 percent of married people never produce children, and many spouses do not remain together. In fact, some people have suggested that the nuclear family, as it has been presented in sociological research, was merely an idealized version of reality and never did exist for many Canadians. Certainly, there has never been one type of family, but in North America sociologists have not made enough effort until recently to delineate the variety of family structures (Eichler, 1983:9, 10). Although cultural variation has been discussed in previous textbooks (such as Ishwaran, 1980), these ethnic families are often compared to some idealized notion of the Canadian family.

While there seems to be an increasing awareness that the nuclear family with mother at home and father at work is becoming a minority phenomenon, less emphasis has been placed on the fact that many Canadians spend at least a portion of their lives outside the nuclear family. An increasing number of Canadian adults are living alone. In 1986, for example, 21 percent of all private households contained only one person (Statistics Canada, 1987). This is largely due to the increase in the elderly widowed population, but it is also the result of higher rates of separation and divorce and older children living independently from their parents before marriage.

It is clear that lifestyles are changing rapidly and that not all adults marry or spend their entire adult life in a nuclear family setting. First of all, not everyone sees marriage and family life as desirable. Some people prefer to live alone or to live with a homosexual partner. Second, marriages sometimes end unexpectedly because of separation or premature death. Third, elderly parents in need of care may come to live with their children, creating a temporary extended family. And finally, not everyone is able to find a suitable marriage partner. For all of these reasons, the nuclear family is only one way of living.

Despite these changes, family plays an important part in many of our lives, even if we are unmarried or childless. We tend to rely on our families – especially our parents and siblings – in times of crisis, obtaining a variety of services from them. For example, adults often depend on their families for emergency child care, loans of money (especially to buy a house), and for emotional support during marriage dissolution or personal tragedy. Women and working-class people, in particular, maintain close contact with their parents and siblings, telephoning when they live too far away to visit regularly (Irving, 1972; Baker, 1983). Although social and economic changes have transformed our society, families remain central in most people's lives.

In recent years, the need to broaden the definitions of "family" has become more obvious as an increasing number of couples remain childless, avoid legalized unions, maintain separate households, dissolve their marriages, and live in one-parent households. Present sociological definitions do not adequately cover this variety of living arrangements. We need to add a prefix or an adjective to clarify our terms: blended family, one-parent family, commuter family, or common-law family.

CHARACTERISTICS OF CANADIAN FAMILIES

Most Canadian adults marry, produce children, and gain considerable satisfaction from family life. Although an increasing number of people are divorcing and postponing marriage, a greater proportion of adults now marry than at the turn of the century. Combined with the fact that the remarriage rate has increased, we can only conclude that family life is not on the decline. It is merely changing.

One noticeable change in Canadian families is their size. Since the 1850s, the birth rate has gradually declined, as Table 1.1 indicates. Some of the reasons for this decline include the increasing cost of raising children and their decreasing economic value to parents. Since children are expected to stay in school until the age of sixteen, parents cannot send them out as servants or apprentices as people did a century ago. Technological advances in birth control and the widespread acceptability of contraception have allowed couples to plan their ideal family size. An increasingly urbanized population finds that ideal to be smaller than a century ago, as shelter, food, education, and general living costs have increased. A rising number of married women are entering the labour force and planning their pregnancies around work and other non-family activities. Finally, the ideology of individualism and the importance of upward mobility have discouraged couples from having more children than they can adequately support.

The rise in life expectancy brought on by improved nutrition, sanitation, health care, occupational safety, and living standards has been particularly noticeable for Canadian women. While the gap in the life expectancy between men and women was about two years in 1931, it increased to about seven years in 1986 (Statistics Canada, 1987). Since men tend to marry younger women (about two years younger in first marriages and four years younger in second marriages) and since women outlive men, most men die before their wives. Many of these widows are left with low incomes, since

Table 1.1   Birth Rates in Canada, 1851-1986

Year	Births per 1,000 Population
1851-61*	45
1861-71	40
1871-81	37
1881-91	34
1891-1901	30
1901-1911	31
1911-1921	29
1921	29.3
1931	23.2
1941	22.4
1951	27.2
1961	26.1
1971	16.8
1981	15.3
1985	14.8
1986	14.7

*Rates for 1851 to 1921 are estimates.

Source: Dominion Bureau of Statistics, *Canada Yearbook 1967* (Ottawa, 1967), p. 241; Statistics Canada, *Births and Deaths*, Cat. 84-204 (annual) (Ottawa: Supply and Services Canada). Reproduced with permission of the Minister of Supply and Services Canada, 1989.

fewer women than men have been employed, have earned high wages, or have acquired employment pensions.

Longer life expectancies have probably also affected divorce rates. "Till death do us part" is simply longer than it used to be. But rising divorce rates have been accompanied by a steady stream of remarriages. The high rate of remarriage and a lower average age of marriage during the 1960s and 1970s have contributed to a higher percentage of married people in the population now than at the beginning of this century. In 1901, for example, about 52 percent of Canadians over the age of fifteen were ever married compared to 73 percent in 1986 (Statistics Canada, 1979; Devereaux, 1988).

Throughout this century, the average age of first marriage declined until the 1970s, when it began to rise again. This decline was related to several economic and ideological changes in Canadian society. For example, urbanization, geographic mobility, and women's participation in the labour force increased opportunities to meet potential mates. Religious and cultural barriers weakened to allow more intermarriage. Greater personal freedom allowed young people to mix more freely with the opposite sex and marry without parental consent. Because of working wives and improved birth control, men no longer need to postpone their weddings until they can support a wife and child. Married women are now in the labour force and tend to delay childbearing for several years until they are psychologically and financially ready. All these factors contributed to the increase in the married population in Canada and lowered the age of marriage. Since the mid-1970s, however, the average age of first marriages has risen slightly, reflecting the greater independence of women, more non-legal unions, economic uncertainty, and some disillusionment with traditional marriage. Furthermore, as more women attain post-secondary education and become self-supporting, an increasing number delay or decide against legal marriage.

Increased personal freedom has also encouraged more people to live outside of the nuclear family. Children leaving home before marriage, high rates of separation and divorce, unmarried mothers raising their children alone, and increasing numbers of widows who maintain separate households have changed the composition of many Canadian households. At the same time that adolescence has been prolonged by higher educational standards, more students are maintaining separate apartments from their parents through part-time work or student loans. And finally, social benefits such as unemployment insurance and mother's allowance may have enabled more people to become financially independent from their families.

Over the past century, we have also witnessed a decline in patriarchal authority in the family. As more women become educated and enter the labour force, their financial independence tends to increase their psychological independence. For example, fewer wives are now willing to quietly accept abuse from their husbands as a "cross to bear," and more are reporting this unacceptable behaviour to the authorities or are initiating divorce proceedings. People have become more conscious of inequalities that have typically existed between parents and children and husbands and wives and have pressed for legal and social change.

Despite the weakening of a husband's authority over his wife, many wives remain powerless in major family decisions. Financial dependence often means abiding by a husband's decision about where to live, what standard of living to maintain, and what to buy for personal use. Despite the fact that over half of Canadian wives are in the labour force, as Table 1.2 shows, most wives retain responsibility for housework and child care. This "double burden" helps to keep women in "pink ghetto jobs" with low pay and few possibilities for promotion.

The increased labour force participation of wives has augmented family income, but has led to a reluctance to raise large families. While some religious leaders have suggested that a major purpose of marriage is to reproduce, families are becoming smaller, and more couples are choosing not to have any children. While there were always couples who remained childless, it was not always a choice, but often a health problem. At the same time that medical technology is allowing more couples to bear children, a growing minority are postponing pregnancy until it is too late, or openly choosing a child-free alternative. Yet, men and women who prefer to remain childless are still treated with some suspicion and contempt. In addition, there continues to be pressure to reproduce only inside legal marriage. Most couples abide by these expectations and have their first child within five years of the wedding (Veevers, 1980:220). However, there has been increased tolerance of out-of-wedlock births in Canada.

Working wives have also reduced the family's ability to move with the husband's job and have increased the number of "commuter marriages" among the middle class. While miners, forestry workers, and other itinerant labourers have always spent portions of the year away from their wives, we are now seeing more couples with professional jobs commuting weekly or monthly. Because of the difficulty of finding two professional jobs in the same community, the decision to move can no longer be unilateral, and husbands are occasionally refusing transfers because of their wives' work. While the lives of most women have expanded considerably, however, most men have not made equivalent changes in their lives. Continued pressure on men to be

Table 1.2 Participation Rates of Married Women in the Canadian Labour Force, 1941-1988

Year	Participation Rate (percentage)
1941	4.5
1951	11.2
1961	20.8
1971	33.0
1981	51.0
1988	59.1

Source: Statistics Canada, *The Labour Force*, Cat. 71-001 (annual) (Ottawa: Supply and Services Canada); Statistics Canada, *Historical Labour Force Statistics 1988*, Cat. 71-201 (Ottawa: Supply and Services Canada, January 1989), p. 257. Reproduced with permission of the Minister of Supply and Services Canada, 1989.

"successful" in their work lives has discouraged them from giving equal priority to their wives' jobs and sharing responsibility for child rearing and housework.

Despite structural changes in Canadian families, most childbearing and child rearing takes place within a family unit. Values education and moral training are still seen as the responsibility of the family, even though some schools are also teaching this material. Parents are also expected to act as an agent of social control, by instilling in their children respect for authority and by encouraging them to work hard and obey school and societal rules.

Private property is also accumulated, protected, and inherited through families. Although educators perpetuate the idea that education and hard work will lead to wealth and high status, in actual fact some people receive many advantages from their families that nearly guarantee wealth and status. Some parents provide invaluable assets for their children through special schooling, cultural experiences, personal contacts, money, and property. Parents also expect that their children will maintain or increase their property and social standing through a "good" marriage.

While we like to think that our behaviour is unique, sociologists assume that patterns in family behaviour can be identified and related to economic, political, and social variables. For example, the duration of childhood has varied with fluctuations in the value of children's labour (Parr, 1982:15). Age of first marriage is related to the socio-economic status of the family of origin, with wealthier people marrying later. Studying the relationship between family interaction and structure and the economic and political structure of society can lead to a better understanding of the social organization of human life.

OVERVIEW OF CONCEPTUAL FRAMEWORKS IN FAMILY SOCIOLOGY

Researchers decide which aspects of family life to study depending on their personal and professional interests, available funding, research assistance, what topics are considered to be important by other researchers, and how well a topic has been researched in the past. All studies in social science are based on certain underlying philosophical assumptions about how society is organized, what motivates human beings, which behaviours are biologically based, and the "best" way to discover patterns in human behaviour. These assumptions cannot be proven or disproven, but serve as starting points for the research. Some of the more popular perspectives or conceptual frameworks from which to study the family are structural functionalism, the systems approach, the conflict or political economy approach, symbolic interactionism, exchange theory, the developmental approach, and the feminist perspective. The basic premises of each of these perspectives are explained below.

STRUCTURAL FUNCTIONALISM

Since the nineteenth century, the structural functionalist approach to social analysis has been used by anthropologists and sociologists to explain variations in family structure and adaptive changes in preliterate cultures (Murdock, 1949). However, it has also provided the framework for studies of modern industrialized societies. Within this perspective, the structures of society, which include laws, the political system, educational institutions, and the family, are the focus of study, rather than interpersonal relations or unique individual behaviour.

The basic assumption of structural functionalism is that people's behaviour is governed not by personal choice, but by laws, rules, regulations, and expectations of behaviour that help to maintain a cohesive and stable society. Individuals cannot behave any way they want, but must abide by social expectations and rules learned within the family early in life. Although structural functionalists do not deny the existence of free will, they argue that a person's family and cultural upbringing to a large extent determines future attitudes and behaviour.

Within this perspective, the family is an important contributor to the maintenance of social order because it provides individuals with emotional support and companion-ship, protection from outsiders, economic co-operation, and a setting for sexual expression, reproduction, and the socialization of children (Goode, 1964). Furthermore, individuals often relate to the outside world through their families and are controlled and disciplined by them. If a child gets into trouble with the law, for example, the police and social workers go to the parents, who are then expected to discipline the child.

The structural functionalist view of the family is essentially a conservative one because behaviour is viewed as largely determined by social expectations and family upbringing. Using a circular argument, structural functionalists have also implied that a certain type of family structure (such as husband as breadwinner and wife as homemaker) was maintained throughout history because it was "functional" for society (Thorne, 1982). Feminist critics have pointed out that this division of labour, which benefited men far more than women, was actually maintained through coercion and ideology, rather than because it was "functional."

Within structural functionalism, change is seen as disruptive rather than normal, progressive, or beneficial, and individual opposition to social pressure has been viewed as "deviance." Consequently, the functionalists have not dealt with conflict and change as well as other approaches, nor have they focused on the dynamic nature of interpersonal relations.

SYSTEMS APPROACH

First developed in the 1950s, the systems approach views the family as a system of relationships and interactions. Anything that happens to one member affects all others. The focus in this approach is on recurring behaviour, triggered by similar situations or responses. For example, researchers have studied family violence within the systems approach and noted the cyclical nature of this behaviour. A boy is physically abused by his parents, for example, and when he grows up, he beats up his wife and children. The behaviour may be triggered by low self-esteem and heavy drinking. Although he later regrets his actions and vows that he will never again mistreat his wife and children, he continues to do so. They lose respect for him, which accentuates his feelings of worthlessness. When his children grow up, they also express their feelings of inadequacy and aggression by abusing their children.

Social work practitioners have used the systems approach in treating clients to show how the entire family can become involved in an apparently personal problem

The structural functionalist view of the family is essentially a conservative one because behaviour is viewed as largely determined by social expectations and family upbringing.

such as being an abusive parent or an alcoholic. Since a person's life is interrelated with the lives of other family members, dealing with the individual's problem may involve treating the entire family.

The family can be viewed as an open or closed system, depending on how much input is received from friends, neighbours, social workers, employers, or the outside world in general. Although viewing the family as an open system takes into consideration social and economic influences on family interaction, the systems approach is generally ahistorical and limited to one culture. It has been most useful in psychiatry, psychology, and social work in focusing attention on how the behaviour of individuals is interrelated with that of other family members.

CONFLICT OR POLITICAL ECONOMY APPROACH

The conflict or political economy perspective is also a structural approach, but emphasizes the link between economic trends in the larger society and historical change in family and personal life. This theoretical approach was originally derived from the work of Karl Marx, but has been modified and amplified over the years. The basic thesis is that attitudes, values, lifestyles, and relationships are largely determined by how people make their living. Trends in the national and international economy affect the kind of work people perform, how well they are paid, their conditions of work, and their standard of living. These experiences colour their entire life, including their family relationships and the division of labour in their home.

Political economy studies of families have examined the effect of industrialization on personal life and found that the industrial revolution in the eighteenth and nineteenth centuries led to major changes in the family. When husbands left farm work to labour under gruelling factory conditions, they came to see the family as a personal refuge from an impersonal world (Zaretsky, 1976) and expected their wives to maintain this sanctuary. Furthermore, many of the goods and services that people used to make at home for their own consumption were eventually made more cheaply in factories, and families became less units of production and more units of consumption.

As more wives and mothers enter the labour force during this century, the division of labour in the family is continuing to evolve. Housework and child care are no longer the exclusive domain of mothers, divorce is more feasible economically, reproductive control is being seen as a right, and women are demanding equality both within the family and the labour force.

While structural functionalists have discussed the family as though it existed in a political and economic vacuum, political economists have de-emphasized interpersonal relations, stability, and social cohesion. Instead, they have examined trends in family life as the economy changes, social class differences in family interaction, the effect of the economy on domestic labour and women's roles, and the effect of government policies on personal choices. Interpersonal relations and family dynamics are studied only from the viewpoint of how they are influenced by work patterns and the family's economic situation.

Some Marxist scholars, however, have been blind to the societal importance of women's unpaid work in the home, focusing instead on men's paid work. However, many feminist scholars have adopted the political economy perspective to analyse changes in gender relations. While feminists have accepted social class as a basic division in society, some have theorized that patriarchy, or male dominance, predates capitalism and will not necessarily disappear in a classless society.

SYMBOLIC INTERACTIONISM

The family has also been studied by sociologists and social psychologists as a small group, in which each individual influences all others. In this approach, it is assumed that we are all "actors" who play a part in "creating social reality." Life does not just happen to us, but we make things happen by exerting our free will. While the structural functionalist approach assumes that people are, at least to some extent, passive recipients of societal rules and regulations, symbolic interactionism emphasizes the active participation of people in their own destiny. How people define and interpret reality affects their behaviour, and this process of interpretation is aided by non-verbal as well as verbal cues. People modify their behaviour depending on how others react to them, but may also influence the behaviour of their friends, family members, and co-workers.

Symbolic interaction studies often take place in a small-groups laboratory, using simulations of family behaviour. Researchers observe from behind windows, which appear to the "subjects" as mirrors. Interaction between mothers and their children, among children in a play group, and between husbands and wives has been studied in this kind of setting. Sometimes researchers will ask the subjects to comment on their own behaviour, and will compare these remarks with their own observations. In a Canadian laboratory study of family decision making, for example, Turk and Bell (1972) found that husbands overestimated and wives underestimated their own power, compared with the observations of the researcher.

While symbolic interactionism does not focus on historical or cultural change, it can explain social interaction within families and provide considerable insight into the dynamics of marriage and marital satisfaction. The interactionist approach became popular in the United States with the work of Charles H. Cooley (1902) and George Herbert Mead (1934) and has formed the basis of research on topics such as childhood socialization and marital adjustment.

EXCHANGE THEORY

Researchers have also studied the family through exchange theory, derived from symbolic interactionism. Using economic analogies from cost-benefit analysis, marriage and family relationships are assumed to involve a process of negotiation and bargaining (Scanzoni, 1972). Social behaviour is influenced by the anticipation of a reward such as social approval, an improved standard of living, or freedom from responsibility.

Recently, exchange theory has been used to explain why some relationships break up and others last. When one partner contributes more time or emotional energy than the other to a relationship, he or she may become resentful and start looking elsewhere for gratification. For example, Huber and Spitze (1980) found that among a variety of subject groups, married women who worked for pay and whose husbands did not share the housework were most likely to consider divorce.

DEVELOPMENTAL APPROACH

The developmental approach began in the 1930s in an attempt to incorporate several perspectives into one. Within this approach, family life is seen as ever-changing, influenced by psychosexual development and social events such as marriage, divorce, child launching, or retirement. With these stages of development, roles shift, the division of labour may change, relationships are modified, and levels of satisfaction fluctuate. The developmental approach shares with structural functionalism the idea that certain prerequisites must be met for continued maintenance of family life and that events such as unemployment will influence other aspects of family relationships. The developmental approach does not view the family as a static institution, however, but as a series of relationships that grow and develop over time.

One criticism of the developmental approach is that it has tended to view the family as a unit that is separate from the political, economic, and social world. While some researchers have used this perspective in cross-cultural and historical studies, most have focused on only one society in modern times. Another criticism is that this approach falsely assumes that all family members are passing through the same stage of development at the same time. It often happens today that a divorced man, with children from a previous marriage, remarries a younger woman who is at quite a different stage in her personal and family development. Furthermore, many people never marry, and others marry but never produce children. Therefore, not everyone passes through the same stages.

FEMINIST PERSPECTIVE

Also an eclectic approach, the feminist perspective focuses on women's experiences of social reality, inequalities between men and women, and the ways in which these inequalities are perpetuated. Some feminist theorists use a structural approach and emphasize the economic bases of women's inequality or focus on ideological pressures, such as biological determinism, sexism, or traditional socialization. Others concentrate on interpersonal relations, examining non-verbal communication, attitudes, and values (Mandell and Duffy, 1988:vii).

Within the past ten years, the feminist perspective has grown within many disciplines, especially sociology, history, and literature. In part, this has been a reaction by the increasing number of female university students and professors, who found that previous theories sometimes excluded women's experiences. While some social scientists have suggested that this perspective is "ideological" or a passing "fad," a considerable amount of scholarly research has been produced within this framework that has revolutionized the way scholars are now seeing family life and the entire social world.

The different theoretical perspectives outlined here both enrich family studies and cause rifts among researchers. While some people argue that accepting one perspective implies that others are rejected, the approach used in this book is eclectic. While different chapters are written from an author's own preferred perspective, most have emphasized structural changes in Canadian families rather than interpersonal relations, and several have highlighted gender differences. As students, an awareness of the various theoretical perspectives is part of understanding sociology and can enrich our study of families.

METHODS OF STUDYING THE FAMILY

Social scientists have drawn upon many different research methods in their attempt to understand family life. How one studies the family, however, depends on many practical concerns, such as available money, research assistance, and expertise. The personal preferences of the researcher will also affect the choice of research methodology because some researchers have more experience or faith in different types of research. Social scientists choose their research topics and methods from their understanding of the way society works and individuals function, as well as their judgment of the best way to do research. But many researchers use more than one method in any particular project. We will discuss five major methods of research in the following pages.

HISTORICAL DOCUMENTS

Both historians and sociologists have drawn upon historical documents to provide information on family life in different eras. Documents such as church registers, municipal records, wills, and letters have formed the basis of many past studies (Ariès, 1962; Shorter, 1975; Tilly and Scott, 1978; Gagan, 1981). Although official records can provide information about dates of birth, marriages, deaths, the age and occupations of marriage partners, and the structure of families and households, they cannot tell us much about the quality of family life. Letters, diaries, novels, and personal accounts, however, can supplement the information in official records to shed some light on family life in the past. In recent years, more sociologists have been drawing upon historical accounts to gain a broader understanding of changes in family life (Laslett, 1972; Lee, 1982; Wilson, 1986; Zaretsky, 1982). For example, some researchers have been interested in how fluctuations in the need for children's and women's labour have influenced conceptions of childhood and femininity.

OFFICIAL STATISTICS

Vital statistics have been collected in Canada since 1821, and since 1851 we have had a regular census. Provincial and federal governments collect information about births, deaths, marriages, employment, family and household income, and family composition. In recent years, Statistics Canada and other government departments such as Health and Welfare Canada and Labour Canada have collected, analysed, and compiled statistical data of interest to scholars and students of family life. One has to remember, however, that these figures have been gathered according to certain definitions of "family" that have changed over time in response to societal changes and government needs, and these definitions may not have been consistent with sociological ones. Answers given to government representatives may also differ from those offered to non-government researchers. Furthermore, the way in which these statistics are analysed may be less useful to students than to bureaucrats, because the figures are gathered with some other use in mind, such as planning for schools or government benefits.

Although we do not have reliable data prior to 1851, statisticians sometimes estimate past figures as well as project into the future. With these data, social scientists can study the structure of families over a long period of time and, with the help of computers, can prepare complex analyses of family life in the past, at the present, or in the future. Statistical information on the family can only reveal the structure of family life, however, and can provide no understanding of the quality of relationships. If we wanted to probe into the quality of family life, we would have to rely on other methods of research, such as interviews or personal observation.

SURVEY RESEARCH

If we wanted to go beyond official statistics but still gather brief answers from many people, we would use survey research techniques. Survey researchers first generate a hypothesis, or a statement of a relation between variables, that they want to test. They then create a sample, or a representative subgroup from the entire category of people they want to study. Then they send these subjects questionnaires or hire people to interview them by telephone. This method implies that the questions must be simple, unambiguous, and conducive to short answers. The responses are usually coded or categorized by numbers that can be analysed by computer to see if the hypothesis can be rejected. If this sample is representative of the population, researchers can generalize to the larger society.

The value of survey research is that large numbers of people can be questioned about their behaviour, attitudes, or opinions in a relatively short time period. It is not possible, however, to obtain in-depth material through this method because people are usually unwilling to provide long and intimate answers to a questionnaire, either in writing or by telephone. Furthermore, if they mail back their answers, the researcher cannot be sure that the designated individual actually answered the questionnaire. In addition, the response rate is often relatively low with a mailed questionnaire (usually less than 50 percent and sometimes much lower). While a large amount of information can be gathered in a short period of time using survey research methods, subtle or detailed issues are usually studied by in-depth interviews.

IN-DEPTH INTERVIEWS

While conducting large numbers of in-depth interviews can be costly and time consuming, a greater knowledge of lifestyles and personal feelings can be gained from this research method. Through the use of systematic questioning and probes, personal histories or other detailed information can be obtained that are either recorded on tape or written on an "interview schedule" (a list of questions with appropriate spaces for the answers). Interviewers do not always ask direct questions in interviews, however, but may encourage subjects to talk at length about the topic of the study (see, for example, page 17).

If rapport can be developed between the interviewer and the subject, interviewing can uncover valuable information. Yet, it is sometimes difficult to establish rapport, especially for interviewers who cannot empathize or who are socially very different from their subjects. The interviewer's personal characteristics may also influence the answers, especially if approval or disapproval is shown for certain types of responses. Bias can be reduced by using several carefully trained interviewers who ask the same questions in the same way and who do not bias responses by showing how they feel about the interview subjects.

DIRECT AND INDIRECT OBSERVATION

Family interaction can also be studied through direct or indirect observation. While the presence of the observer may influence the behaviour observed, there are ways of minimizing this form of bias. One way is to employ several well-trained observers who are not aware of the hypotheses of the study, so that they cannot be accused of seeing only what the chief investigator of the project expects to find. Another way to minimize bias is to observe subjects inside a laboratory from two-way mirrors. A third way is for

FOR INTEREST

A TYPICAL DAY IN THE FUTURE

I'd get up at 6:45, get ready, and have breakfast. Then I'd go to work. But I don't know where. If I'm a journalist, it could be in a foreign country. I don't have to have a stationary home. I intend to do quite a bit of travelling. Maybe I'll live with a male, or alone – with a dog. I probably won't be married, and I probably won't have kids. I don't like kids particularly, and I don't like the idea of living in one place with one person. I want to travel and write. I don't want to have children and ship them off to a day care centre . . . . I might share an apartment, too . . . . I might be an archaeologist or a writer.

After work, I'll do what I do now. Either go out to the theatre with friends, or write, or read, draw or go out somewhere. I'll go to bed around 11:00 . . . . [What do you want most in the future?] Enjoying what I do! Even if I end up being married with two kids, I hope I enjoy it!

Julia: 15 years old, Montreal

Source: Maureen Baker, *"What Will Tomorrow Bring . . . ?" A Study of the Aspirations of Adolescent Women* (Ottawa: Canadian Advisory Council on the Status of Women, 1985), pp. 149-50.

Observations of children's play activity have helped social scientists to develop theories of learning and socialization.

MILLER COMSTOCK INC.

the researchers to disguise themselves as group members and to become so familiar with other members that their presence is barely noticed. This method is called participant observation and has formed the basis of several famous sociological studies, including William Foote Whyte's American study of gang behaviour called *Street Corner Society* (1943).

Content analysis has also been used to uncover attitudes or values in magazine articles, television programs, or textbooks. This form of analysis requires the establishment of concrete definitions and categories before the research begins and often involves more than one observer to help eliminate bias.

Although we have discussed the various methodologies separately, we should be aware that most research projects include a combination of methodologies. For example, a researcher studying the issue of child care in Ontario may first read previous studies on this topic, then consult official statistics about working mothers and the availability of child care spaces, visit several types of child care centres to gain an understanding of the issues, and then interview parents, child care workers, and operators of child care centres. Few modern studies would rely simply on a single research method.

From reading magazines, watching television, or even reading the newspaper, one can get a very distorted picture of family life because unusual cases rather than typical family activities are dramatically portrayed. For example, many portrayals of family life on television show families with above-average incomes living in large homes. Recently, a large proportion of programs show divorced people, implying that most people's marriages no longer last. Similarly, one might think that young people do not want to have children anymore because the media so often shows "DINKS" (couples with Double Income and No Kids). Before we assume that we know about family life, we need to move beyond personal experience and media features to social science research. Most studies make a real effort to investigate people who are representative of those in the general population, thus providing a more accurate view of family life.

RECENT TRENDS IN FAMILY RESEARCH

Although sociologists have been studying family life in North America since the 1890s, most of the research prior to the 1920s was reform oriented and closer to social work than sociology. The gradual separation of academic research and social work practice began after the First World War (Adams, 1974:5). Since then, many of the issues studied by academics have followed discernible trends. From the 1920s to the 1940s, anthropologists studied cross-cultural variations in family life in many societies, including native people and other ethnic groups in North America. Mainly using the structural functionalist framework, they looked for universal behavioural patterns and related variations to the entire culture. Margaret Mead (1935), for example, investigated the influence of culture and learning on family life and the roles of men and women. Although American social scientists of that time thought that gender roles were largely a product of biology, Mead showed that among certain tribes in New Guinea these roles were reversed and therefore a product of culture.

During the 1930s and 1940s, American researchers began to investigate their own cultural patterns and small group behaviour. Romantic love and personal attraction were analysed, as well as social patterns in sexual behaviour. The famous Kinsey studies of male sexuality that were published in 1948 revealed a widespread disregard of societal norms such as sexual exclusivity, monogamy, and the disapproval of premarital sex.

During the postwar period of rising marriage rates, high fertility, and the suburbanization of North American cities, family researchers began to investigate marital satisfaction and happiness and continued their interest in patterns of mate selection. When the work of Sigmund Freud was translated into English and became available to the North American reader, research into early childhood development and maternal behaviour became popular. The English child psychologist John Bowlby synthesized earlier studies on the importance of mothering and began his controversial work on maternal deprivation. This kind of research continued into the 1950s and explored bonding between mother and infant in non-humans as well as humans. These research findings appeared to reinforce the expectation that mothers would become homemakers rather than work in the labour force.

Until the postwar period, there were few Canadian studies specifically on family life, largely because sociology was not taught as a separate discipline in Canadian universities until the 1960s. In 1941, Enid Charles made extensive use of census data in her monograph entitled *The Changing Size of the Canadian Family*. However, most analysis of Canadian families was found within community studies such as the Crestwood Heights study by Seeley et al. (1956), rather than in separate projects on family life (see page 20). In French Canada, family research focused on rural and religious traditions (Garigue, 1962), but studies of social mobility and urbanization also made reference to family life as one of the factors influencing patterns of mobility (Elkin, 1964:68).

As the proportion of married women in the labour force increased, many studies of the 1950s and 1960s investigated the relationship between working mothers and the behaviour of their children. Researchers also continued their studies of "problem families" or those affected by absent fathers, alcohol, or delinquent children. In the studies of sociologists such as Parsons and Bales (1955), the ideal family was implicitly portrayed as a two-parent, one-income family, with father as breadwinner and mother as homemaker, and with two or three children. All other family forms were seen as "deviant."

As more women entered the labour force, however, the "dual-career family" emerged as an important concept. Later, it was acknowledged that the two-income family was a more appropriate concept because many people worked at jobs rather than careers. Early research on two-income families contained a strong middle-class bias as researchers focused on professional couples rather than working-class ones. The fact that working-class wives had always worked for pay was passed over, and researchers saw the two-income family as revolutionary and likely to be detrimental to children and marital relationships.

Toward the end of the 1960s, several new themes became important: the concept of open marriage in which partners operated as separate individuals and explored their "full potential," possible alternatives to the nuclear family such as communal living or a series of non-legal intimate relationships, and concern about the death of the family as

FOR INTEREST

THE FAMILY AS A VEHICLE FOR UPWARD MOBILITY

It is all too common to find in Crestwood Heights that many children are driven towards unrealistic goals. A child who is not academically inclined, or who is mentally dull, may be forced by extra tutoring and parental badgering into competing unsuccessfully for university entrance. Or a plain daughter may be pushed by an ambitious, pretty mother into social situations which she cannot handle . . . . It may well be that a child's failure to achieve is the greatest threat to family integration in Crestwood Heights (p. 221).

. . . .

Some Crestwood residents select a private school taught by British "masters," in a pattern borrowed directly from the British public schools. Even the vast majority of parents who send their children to the tax-supported schools of the Heights proudly approve the word "Prep" which tags each elementary school name (p. 8).

. . . .

Mobility in society, as a motivating drive, probably operates, like social change, to widen the gulf between generations, creating disharmony within the family, if not partial or complete disintegration. However oriented the family may have been originally towards the values of the social class into which it is moving, it seldom, if ever, feels completely at home when it finally arrives in Crestwood Heights. Frequently there is confusion within the family because of the new social behaviour to be learned (p. 217).

Source: J. Seeley, A. Sim, and E. Loosley, *Crestwood Heights* (Toronto: University of Toronto Press, 1956).

an institution (Cooper, 1971). The changing role of women and its implications for family life were also the subjects of many studies. The egalitarian family was viewed as the new emerging form, despite the fact that little evidence was available that equality actually existed between husbands and wives.

In the mid-1970s, several studies destroyed the myth of the egalitarian family. Although decision-making studies indicated that many household decisions were shared, especially in two-income families, Canadian time-budget studies showed that the husbands of working wives did about six minutes more housework per day than the husbands of housewives (Meissner et al., 1975; Clark and Harvey, 1976). Divorce rates soared in Canada and other industrialized countries, leading to more mother-led families, working mothers, and family poverty. Research began to focus on separation and divorce, domestic labour, child care, and family violence as these became controversial topics in the media.

By the 1980s, the family was seen less as a haven from commercialism and violence and more as a complex institution closely tied to the economy and prevalent ideologies. In an attempt to improve family policies and social services, governments sponsored studies of child abuse, wife battering, division of matrimonial property after divorce, and child custody, which all reinforced a negative view of the family. At the same time, feminist scholars revived the sociology and history of the family by adding a more critical and female point of view to the study of family life. They argued against the ideology of the monolithic family (Eichler, 1988), emphasizing that there has never been only one major type of family structure in North America. Feminists also legitimized certain research topics that had previously been overlooked, such as housework, widowhood, and child care. While functionalists had treated the family as a unit, implying that all members experienced life in the same way, feminist scholars encouraged the view that the individual rather than the family should be the unit of analysis.

Researchers are now less likely to see the family as a unit and to ask one member to answer questions about family life on behalf of other members. It is now recognized that husbands and wives often have different perceptions of family life and sometimes have separate goals. In fact, feminist scholars are now showing that legal and social policies on family-related issues have different consequences for men and women (Morton, 1988; Baker, 1988a). Family law reform, for example, appears to have hastened the "feminization of poverty," as more mother-led families now live below the poverty line. Researchers are also examining the implications of the new reproductive technologies for women (Eichler, 1988), as well as family networks among elderly persons.

Family research of the next decade will probably focus more on interconnections among families, the law, politics, and economics. The consequences of divorce and remarriage for family structure and interaction will also be further explored, with more emphasis on blended families, step-parenting, and family networks. Social scientists will likely present a much more analytical and critical picture of family life, law, and policy than researchers have provided in previous decades.

Rather than analysing the complexities and variations of family life, early family researchers based their studies on a monolithic model of the family. Researchers now acknowledge that family experiences differ for men and women, for different social classes, and for various cultural groups. Furthermore, family interaction is psychologically complex and difficult to study because people try to protect their privacy and their egos and cannot always articulate their feelings.

CONCLUSION

Like much of social science, the sociology of the family has reflected the ideological concerns and assumptions of the mass media and the educated public. The topics that have been researched have changed over the past few decades and now focus on interrelationships between family structure and the economy, domestic labour, marriage dissolution and remarriage, the consequences of family law reform, family violence, and family life in an aging society. As families change and respond to the fluctuating demands of the labour force, shifts in the economy, an aging population, and policy changes, sociologists must rethink some of their previous assumptions about the importance of the family to individuals and society.

In the following chapters, a number of specific topics within family studies are examined in detail. In each chapter, the major theoretical and research issues are outlined, and empirical studies are discussed. Each author has retained his or her own theoretical perspective, yet has focused on structural changes in Canadian families.

DISCUSSION QUESTIONS

1. What is the basic difference between the way the Canadian census has defined ''family'' and the way the term is used in common usage?
2. If family life is studied from different theoretical perspectives, how will this affect research methods and conclusions?
3. What does the study of family patterns in other societies tell us about the normality or naturalness of certain marriage patterns?
4. Discuss the various ways in which family background might affect future opportunities, lifestyle, and attitudes.
5. Prepare a research plan (including your theoretical framework, method of research, and sampling plan) to study each of the following topics:
   a. the effects of non-parental day care on children;
   b. *in vitro* fertilization (medical policy decisions, success rate, and why couples participate);
   c. changes in men's working patterns throughout this century;
   d. remarriage rates after divorce.
6. How do funding arrangements and possibilities for publication influence what is studied in family sociology?
7. Why are future trends in personal and family life so difficult to predict?
8. If we had a solid understanding of family life over the past one hundred years, would this help us to formulate better family policies in the present and future?

chapter two

The Social and Economic Origins of Contemporary Families

INTRODUCTION

The social and economic changes of the nineteenth and early twentieth centuries had a dramatic impact on the character and structure of families. During the past twenty years, many scholars have studied this impact in terms of the industrial revolution. Their research has shown that urbanization and the replacement of handicraft production by machine production in factories altered considerably the family's position in society. In the pre-industrial setting, the Canadian economy was in many ways the sum of family economies in which men, women, and children all played distinct but productive roles. With industrialization, Canada's economy became increasingly a collection of factories and agricultural businesses staffed by men whose wives were at home and whose children were at school. This development represented a profound reorganization of society affecting both private experience and public policy. The industrial revolution contributed to new ideals, new legislation, and new institutions, all of which related to the place of families in society.

At the same time, however, recent research has found that the structure and character of families also changed considerably in rural areas at the time of the industrial revolution. The direction of this change was often parallel to the urban experience. For example, as early as the mid-nineteenth century, rural families began to limit the number of their children and increasingly sent them to school. In certain cases, industrialization may explain these changes since the proliferation of sawmills and other rural industries was a central component of the evolving Canadian landscape. The majority of rural residents, however, were not directly affected by such developments, and scholars have now suggested that the origins of modern families actually preceded the industrial revolution. Specifically, studies indicate that many of the characteristics associated with twentieth-century families emerged from processes of adjustment and innovation within rural society. This finding has particular importance in Canada since more than half of the population lived outside even small cities as late as the First World War.

Researchers have also demonstrated that any examination of change must take into account the considerable continuity of the family as a patriarchal institution. While the decades before the 1960s witnessed dramatic transformations in the structures, functions, and ideologies of family life, the legal, cultural, and economic position of women remained remarkably consistent. In formal ways from land-owning rights to schooling, Canada has been a gendered society in which men have held more power and enjoyed more rights than women. Important changes have occurred since the mid-nineteenth century (especially in the past fifteen years), but the general framework of patriarchy has certainly not been fully dismantled as of the late twentieth century. Thus, change in the history of the family should be interpreted as involving alteration to, and a general weakening of, the patriarchal form rather than its complete rejection (Clio Collective, 1987; Prentice et al., 1988).

This chapter examines the relationship between social and economic change and the history of the family, especially during the nineteenth century. The basis of this examination is those studies that have substantially revised established views not only about industrialization, but also about the extent to which modern families differ from those of the pre-industrial period. For example, contemporary discussion often assumes that families have traditionally been stable units, pillars in a society otherwise undergoing constant transformation. In this view, families have been until recently an important element of continuity within larger social changes. Similarly, observers usually juxtapose a historical image of a single family form with the wide variety of contemporary family patterns. Current diversity in marriage forms, childbearing decisions, and living arrangements is judged with reference to an imagined time of conformity and standard behaviour. In both myths, contemporary families are seen as radically different from those of former times, and critics often interpret this difference as evidence of unprecedented crisis.

Such assumptions about the history of the family are accurate to a certain degree. However, recent research indicates that images of stability and conformity cannot be fully applied to Canadian families of the past, especially during periods of substantial social and economic change. This research has shown that current instability and diversity in family patterns are not simply modern phenomena and that the perception of crisis in the family has a long tradition, which was particularly important in the nineteenth century. Similarly, families have historically been nuclear, fragmented, or single parent in various times and places. The implications of these findings extend to the major themes of Canada's social, economic, and intellectual history, and they suggest quite different ways of assessing the families of contemporary society (Anderson, 1980; Soliday, 1980; Parr, 1982; LaRose, 1977 to present; *Journal of Family History*, 1987).

The following discussion begins with a description of the ways in which the rapid development of both rural settlement and cities affected the economic position of men, women, and children. The changing productive roles of family members provide the key to examination of the structural alterations and new ideals for the family that characterized the late nineteenth century. In turn, these developments were related to a social reorganization most dramatically represented by the expansion of formal education. The creation of school systems became part of a new emphasis on public institutions and professional "experts," many of whom considered families (especially those of immigrants and the working class) to be in need of constant surveillance and supervision.

Two concepts are particularly helpful to understanding these complex changes that together engendered the families of the late twentieth century: *family strategies* and *family reproduction*. Historians use the concept of family strategies to emphasize the extent to which individuals lived their lives as part of family and kinship networks. The birth of modern society has traditionally been associated with a new sense of individualism considered to have replaced the communal ties of earlier times. However, scholars have now found that what may appear to be individual decisions and behaviour were, in fact, usually part of larger family and kin-based strategies. Studies of migration, for example, have revealed that, in most cases, the timing, direction, and process of relocation occurred within the context of family connections. Most individuals were not simply free to stay or leave; rather, their decisions were reached with reference to the impact of migration on other family members. In this sense, historians now explain individual experience in the emerging modern era more in terms of family strategies than new levels of personal autonomy.

It should be noted, however, that, like all analytic terms, "family strategies" does not do justice to the complexity of family relations. In particular, the concept downplays tension and conflict among family members as individuals and as parts of collectivities. Decisions about issues such as migration, childbearing, or economic activity were not reached in a context in which all family members had equal power and compatible ambitions. Distinct positions associated with age and gender gave specific family members more or less ability to define what would be the collective strategy. Consensus was undoubtedly obtained at times, but conflict was also certainly present at other moments. Similarly, the term family strategies should not be interpreted to mean that all families could in fact control their destinies. Rather, the choices available to any specific family were defined by material circumstances; the number of possible strategies ranged from many to few (Moch et al., 1987).

The concept of family reproduction is closely linked to the notion of strategies and, not surprisingly, must also be used with care. The concept concerns the ways in which one generation biologically, culturally, and materially creates the next. In this sense, the process of family reproduction varies according to different family strategies and different historical circumstances. Historians are increasingly focusing on inheritance patterns as a key aspect of generational change and continuity. In this research, the origins of modern families can be traced to profound alterations to the context within which families sought to reproduce themselves. At the same time, research shows that this process was not always characterized by a consensus among family members, but rather reflected the larger influence of norms related to age and gender. Thus, in discussing the history of the family in terms of strategies and reproduction, it is important to remember the internal complexity of specific families (Rapp et al., 1979).

FROM DOMESTIC TO FACTORY PRODUCTION

The process of industrialization is often described as a revolution, since an urban industrial society differs so markedly from a rural pre-industrial community. However, the term revolution implies a sudden event and, in this sense, is misleading, since industrialization occurred over many decades and involved several transitional stages. In the same way, the impact of industrialization on the family cannot be understood in "before and after" terms; rather, family alterations paralleled each stage of the transition to urban industrial society. An appreciation of the complexity of these developments is the first step toward understanding the origins of the modern family.

In the *pre-industrial economy* that predominated in Canada until the nineteenth century, most productive activity took place in individual households. Homes were both places of residence and places of work. Production was very small scale and exceedingly labour intensive. The vast majority of the population lived on farms and engaged in some combination of agriculture, fishing, lumbering, and the fur trade, according to the seasons of the year and the region in which they lived. In addition, these settlers had to produce their own clothing, and thus most households included a spinning wheel and a loom. Cities such as Montreal and Quebec were primarily commercial and administrative centres, although they did include craftsmen such as blacksmiths and coopers. These craftsmen set up shops in their own households and worked by hand with very basic tools to produce their goods. The pre-industrial economy was, therefore, relatively small scale, labour intensive, and domestically focused (Dechêne, 1974; Porter, 1985) (see below).

During the first half of the nineteenth century, rural society was transformed by the spread of agrarian capitalism and the emergence of rural industries. Increased domestic demand and new export markets fuelled agricultural expansion, especially in the area that later became Ontario. Gristmills soon dotted the countryside, and small towns and villages grew, as did the larger commercial cities. Canada's extensive forests also became the object of concerted development as the result of both British and American market

FOR INTEREST

The greater part of the labour of the farm is performed by the farmer himself, his wife, his sons and daughters, the former managing all the outdoor operations, and the latter the dairy and domestic departments. Herein indeed lies all the secret of his success. Whatever qualification the farmer should have, mental or physical, all are agreed on this one point — that a good wife is indispensable, and what it is the aim of the husband to accumulate, it becomes the province of his wife to manage, and whenever we hear of a managing wife, we are sure to find a money-making farmer, and *vice-versa*.

Source: Upper Canada Board of Agriculture, *Transactions of the Board of Agriculture and of the Agricultural Association of Upper Canada, 1860-1863* (Toronto: Printed for the Board of Agriculture, at the "Guardian" Book and Job Printing Establishment, 1864), 5:25.

demand. Sawmills were built at almost every well-located source of water power, with massive establishments on the major rivers. These opportunities encouraged families to expand their economic activities, often by combining agricultural endeavour with lumber industry participation (Gaffield, 1982).

The first stage of industrialization is termed the *manufactory stage*, in which handicraft production still predominated but manufactories increasingly brought together various craftsmen into one operation. Carriage makers joined wheelwrights, blacksmiths, carpenters, and other skilled workers. At the same time, these new establishments also increased the trend toward specialization. Shoemaking, for example, now involved cutters, fitters, and other more specialized occupations (Kealey, 1980). In certain economic sectors, this division of labour also involved *proto-industrialization*, in which traditional domestic work patterns combined with new forms of labour in manufactories. In the proto-industrial system, domestic activity was responsible for part, rather than all, of the production process. In the case of textiles, for example, households began producing cloth for sale to dressmakers and yarn for sale to weavers. As a result, households became less self-reliant and more integrated into an emerging cash economy. The overall scale of production increased, although the manufactories were still small operations. This system thus reflected the past and anticipated the future of the production process. Domestic activity continued to be important, but production outside the home was increasingly significant (Medick, 1976).

The emergence of manufactories and proto-industrial activity affected only a minority of the Canadian population for most of the nineteenth century. A large export market and the availability of land encouraged settlers to concentrate on agriculture and lumbering. One crucial change, however, was the spread of wage labour that accompanied the expansion of wheat and lumber production. Shantymen and millhands worked in the lumber industry, agricultural labourers toiled for established landowners, and navvies built the canals and railways that facilitated commercial activity. These workers were often young men who hoped to accumulate enough capital to settle on a farm of their own (Darroch, 1988). Until the later nineteenth century, the extent of land availability made this ambition quite realistic, although restrictive land policies, the activity of speculators, and the irregular nature of employment worked against aspiring young adults in certain regions. By the 1870s, however, the frontier in central Canada had been pushed to its limit, and as land prices rose, wage labour became a way of life for an increasing proportion of the population. The shift from farmers and craftsmen in the pre-industrial economy to propertyless wage labourers in the emerging industrial economy is termed *proletarianization*. This process combined with the spread of manufactories and, to a lesser extent, with proto-industrialization to provide the context for rapid urban and industrial growth in the late nineteenth and early twentieth centuries (Gagan, 1981).

The proliferation of machines and steam engines after the 1870s heralded the beginning of a full *industrial economy* in Canada. The increased use of sewing machines transformed the shoe industry, while hydraulic presses allowed the Canadian tobacco industry to prosper during the Civil War in the United States. Such industrial growth was certainly not reflected in all types of production, but the trend toward mechanization is evident in the rapid growth of large factories. In Hamilton, Ontario, for example, in

1851, only 24 percent of the labour force worked in establishments employing ten or more individuals. Just twenty years later, a full 83 percent of all employees in Hamilton worked in such establishments. Moreover, just over one-half of workers in manufacturing held positions in firms with fifty or more employees. Hamilton's industrial development at this time was unusual for Canadian cities, but the pattern was certainly not unique. In Toronto, slightly more than two-thirds of the city's factory workers in 1871 were employed in establishments with thirty or more workers (Katz, 1975; Kealey, 1980).

Mechanization and centralization of production affected various economic sectors at different times and in different ways (Heron and Storey, 1986). The general transition from production at home to workshops and factories was uneven, with some industries continuing to rely on household activity even as machines were proliferating. In the clothing trade, for example, work in factories and work at home expanded together during the nineteenth century, with each activity representing a different phase of the production process. Factory machines made and cut cloth from which women and older daughters then made garments in their own households as employees of the clothier. This example illustrates that the impact of industrialization on the production process was not always abrupt or complete, but rather took place gradually over many decades (Bradbury, 1979).

The transition from pre-industrial to industrial modes of production redefined the economic role of the family and forced adjustment and innovation in family strategies. In the pre-industrial economy, families operated as economic units in which individual members performed tasks associated with age and gender. Women and children were active producers within family economies, and material security could only be achieved through collective labour. The contributions of all able-bodied family members were necessary in the labour-intensive rural economy of the time. As a result, the European traditions of apprenticeship for boys and work as domestic servants for girls were not fully maintained in Canada, where economic opportunity meant that children could often be most useful to parents by working at home. From an early age, children would be integrated into productive activity by learning to help with land clearing, seeding, and domestic work such as spinning. Similarly, women were responsible for cooking, making clothes, and farm work such as vegetable gardening. The pre-industrial setting was composed, therefore, of *family economies* in which family members laboured in the context of household production (Gaffield, 1979; Gagan, 1981).

The manufactory stage signalled the beginning of the separation of production from the household. The growth of manufactories, an increased division of labour, and the trend toward centralized production made household production an increasingly supplementary aspect of the economy. Moreover, these developments encouraged the spread of wage labour in the later nineteenth century, a process with roots in activities such as lumbering and canal building. Employment outside the home redefined the extent to which productive activity characterized family life, and consequently, this alteration transformed family economies into *family wage economies.* Centralized production and wage labour meant that certain families began pooling the wages rather than the actual labour of various family members. The key to material security for families in this new situation involved employment outside the home for as many family

In pre-industrial society, a great deal of economic activity took place in the home, and family members contributed according to a division of labour associated with age and gender. Mothers taught daughters skills such as weaving, while sons learned from their fathers. The first responsibility of children was often to care for young siblings. This photograph from the early twentieth century indicates that the industrial revolution did not immediately transform all Canadian households, particularly those in remote areas.

members as possible, especially older children. A single wage was rarely sufficient to provide for a family, and the general irregularity of employment maintained the traditional interdependency of family members. Therefore, families continued to be economic units, although the appearance of the family wage economy represented an important departure from the traditional strategies of family activity and organization (Tilly and Scott, 1978).

The replacement of collective household labour by individual wage earning did not always have a simple or immediate effect on the family. In the early phases of this economic change, there was a considerable number of job opportunities for youth, especially teenage boys, and in certain cases family members continued to work together through collective employment in mills and factories. In fact, some employers advertised to attract families, recognizing both the profitability of cheap child labour and the value of having parents to supervise young workers. Employers would sometimes provide dwellings for families working at their establishments. The quality of such accommodation was generally very poor, but the provision of dwellings did reflect the fact that the family could still function as an economic unit despite the new modes of production (Bradbury, 1979; Katz, Doucet, and Stern, 1982; Gaffield, 1982).

Recent studies have also found that while many families needed more than one income, they also wanted to maintain contact among family members. The employment of children was consistent with the tradition of families working together, and thus parents did not hesitate to seek work for their children. Established workers pressured employers to hire younger family members, sometimes by threatening to quit if additional employment was not provided. Of course, such threats were only effective in times of severe labour shortages, but the attempt of family members to work together shows that the traditional concept of collective family labour still operated during the process of industrialization (Kealey, 1973; Harvey, 1979).

The emergence of a wage-labour economy and the growth of manufactories are often described as the beginning of the separation of home and work. However, this description implies significant narrowing of the definition of work to mean wage labour only. In earlier times, the contributions of all family members were considered work, and cooking and cleaning were recognized to be an important part of the family economy. However, the wage-labour economy expropriated the concept of work for paid employment. Thus, the "separation of home and work" must be understood to mean the "separation of home and place of wage labour" (Bourne, 1985).

While early industrial expansion included employment for women and older children, the number of job opportunities for these family members did not match the number of available workers, and in fact these opportunities decreased rapidly over time. In Toronto, for example, the 1880s were a decisive decade in the dislocation of young teenagers from the labour force. Industrialization in the boot and shoe, printing, and tobacco sectors encouraged a sharp decline in the proportion of workers who were under the age of sixteen; this proportion fell from 11 percent in 1881 to 5 percent in 1891 (Kealey, 1980). Economic change especially transformed the position of young women, for whom there were fewer and fewer employment opportunities in cities and no jobs that paid a wage sufficient for material independence. Women continued to gain positions as factory workers or elementary school teachers in the nineteenth century and as nurses and secretaries in later decades. But in keeping with the established patriarchal framework, married women were often excluded from these jobs, and their wages were substantially less than those offered to their male counterparts. In the late nineteenth century, a female teacher received about one-half of the average salary of a male teacher (Danylewycz, Light, and Prentice, 1983). In this context, the economic role of women within families became increasingly confined to domestic chores that were not considered "productive" in the new sense of the word. This new definition of work trivialized both implicitly and explicitly the important activity that continued in the home and that made possible employment outside the home. Moreover, the value judgments that distinguished between home and work must be recognized as contributing factors in the development of contemporary attitudes toward domestic activity.

In stylized terms, the separation of productive activity from the home and the economic dislocation of many women and children changed the affected families from units of production to units of consumption. In the new *family consumer economy*, family life involved decisions and activity related to the purchase and use of goods produced in specialized workplaces. The ideal roles of various family members became much more sharply differentiated, with men as producers, women as homemakers, and children as dependants. This differentiation became increasingly evident among

Canadian families as higher wages in the twentieth century (most notably in the 1950s) made single-income families a viable possibility, at least for the expanding middle class. In this way, the family consumer economy became a characteristic feature of urban industrial society in Canada. The implications of this development extended beyond economic changes to include important changes in the size and structure of families. An examination of these changes provides the next link in understanding the historical development of modern families.

FAMILY STRUCTURE AND KINSHIP

Recent studies have re-examined the ways in which the changing economic role of the family related to the size and structure of households. The traditional version of the transition describes a radical shift during the period of industrialization from large extended households to small nuclear units. This shift is said to have involved a decline in fertility and a decrease in kinship attachment beyond parents and children. However, research in different settings suggests that this traditional interpretation of the impact of industrialization needs to be reconsidered, both with respect to structural changes in the family and to the importance of kinship.

Throughout Canada, the size of families steadily declined after the mid-nineteenth century, thereby considerably changing the biological aspect of family reproduction. Until this time, a marriage was soon followed by the birth of the first child, and children continued to be born every two or three years, with the gap between each birth increasing as the parents aged. By the mid-1800s, however, this natural fertility began to be inhibited by the attempt to limit further pregnancies after a certain family size was achieved. The trend continued to grow in the late nineteenth and early twentieth centuries before reaching a plateau at the modern average of somewhat less than two children per family (Henripin, 1968; McLaren and McLaren, 1986; Gagan, 1981; Katz, Doucet, and Stern, 1982).

While recent studies consistently emphasize the general importance of the fertility decline, scholars have also discovered considerable diversity within the overall pattern. The most surprising finding has involved rural areas where families began limiting family size as early as their urban counterparts. Historians interpret such limitation as a response to increasing difficulty after the mid-nineteenth century of acquiring land, which was the basis of rural family economies. However, the intensity of this decline was less than that of cities where families altered considerably the traditional pattern of natural fertility. Studies also have found that literacy levels and cultural values such as religion were associated with adjustment and innovation in demographic behaviour. Until the 1960s, fertility rates in areas of francophone settlement, for example, declined more slowly than in those of predominantly anglophone regions (Henripin, 1968; Tepperman, 1974; Beaujot and McQuillan, 1986).

Historians are not yet able to explain fully the reasons for such diversity, although the evidence makes clear that different families devised different strategies for dealing with their changing circumstances. Many factors undoubtedly contributed to the fertility decline, including technological developments such as the production of better contraceptives. However, a key phenomenon may have been the gradual redefinition of children as consumers rather than producers. This redefinition first became apparent in more privileged families (often in urban areas) who were not dependent on their children's labour. Their fertility rates decreased more quickly than did those of less advantaged families. Over time, however, the increasing dislocation of children from productive activity, both in agricultural settings and in the urban working class, encouraged even less materially secure parents to similarly limit family size in order to minimize expenses (Stern, 1987). A study of the 1931 census showed that the families of wage earners had, in fact, become on average considerably smaller than those of employers or those who were self-employed. The authors of this study suggested that "limitation in family size for many people is the only alternative to poverty and misery" (Pelletier, Thompson, and Rochon, 1938:19). Thus, the dominant trend has been toward smaller and smaller families throughout the social structure, although distinct motivations and family strategies have always been very evident, especially with respect to ethnocultural values and economic circumstances.

The changing ways in which families reproduced themselves biologically did not mean, however, that families became isolated nuclear units. Families continued to function within kinship networks throughout the transition from the family economy to the family wage economy and to the family consumer economy. The continuing importance of kinship is related to the fact that the stability of families has never been absolute at any point in the past. While contemporary instability due to the high incidence of separation and divorce is unprecedented, families have always faced uncertainty, especially with respect to health and material welfare. In the past, traditionally high rates of mortality meant that the disruption of marriage by the death of a spouse was not uncommon. Partial evidence from France and England in the seventeenth and eighteenth centuries suggests that about one-third of all children younger than age fourteen had lost one or both of their parents. One study in England indicates that one out of every five children was an orphan during these centuries (Tilly and Scott, 1978:28-29). While mortality rates declined in the New World as a result of better nutrition and lower population density, the stability of family units was constantly undermined by warfare and natural disasters, as well as by epidemics such as those of cholera. The important productive roles of both men and women made remarriage both common and necessary in pre-industrial Canadian society, but new unions could only follow an inevitable period of family disruption. Thus, the history of orphans and single-parent families in Canada begins at the time of first settlement and not in recent years (Dechêne, 1974:107-9; Charbonneau, 1975:183-88).

Declining land availability, wage labour, and industrialization ensured that families would face even more serious challenges to their stability, and they relied on kin to help in the search for employment and housing and to support them in times of need. Kin could be instrumental in aiding resettlement in a newly developing agricultural region, or in securing employment for relatives at the same mill or factory where a family member already worked. Relatives could facilitate migration to a new area by providing temporary accommodation or information about land or available dwellings. Historians have found that even the great transatlantic migrations of the nineteenth century were characteristically based on the chain migration of related individuals and families (Elliott, 1988). Such family and kin-based migration was also characteristic of movement within North America, including the settlement of the Prairies. The insecurity of farming as well as employment and the need of many families for more than one income meant that kinship networks represented a welfare system in which the hardships of certain families might only be somewhat balanced by the relative well-being of others (Dickinson and Russell, 1986:113–49). This type of support became very crucial in industrializing cities, where there was little formal assistance in the struggle to survive (Hareven, 1982).

The growing cities developed major sanitary problems, urban housing was very inadequate, and the workplaces had inadequate ventilation and dangerous machinery. Illness, accidents, irregular employment, and low wages placed families in precarious positions if kin were unable to lend support. Even two-parent families were sometimes unable to care for their children. In nineteenth-century Montreal, for example, some working-class parents dealt with family crises by temporarily placing their children in orphanages in the hope that they might at least receive some food and shelter. When and if the situation of the parents improved, they planned to bring the children home again, perhaps to contribute to the family's survival by seeking employment themselves (Bradbury, 1982). Conditions in nineteenth-century orphanages were rarely ideal, however, and studies indicate that mortality rates were often exceptionally high. Unwed mothers, for example, who gave up their children to the foundling hospital of the Grey Nuns in Montreal could not anticipate that they would be adopted by a deserving couple; between 80 and 90 percent died in the institution (Gossage, 1987).

In the modern industrial economy, the responsibility of the family for the material welfare of its members declined with the professionalization of health care and the slow emergence of state aid for those in need. The traditional pattern of home births, home remedies, and informal kinship support systems was increasingly replaced by hospitals, clinics, and publicly funded welfare offices. In this sense, the general direction of the twentieth century has been toward the building of public institutions to support individual existence (Strong-Boag, 1979; Struthers, 1983). Nonetheless, these institutions do not fully respond to individual needs, and families have maintained an important support role for family members as well as for kin. The processes of social and economic change may have encouraged some sense of individualism, but family and kin still provide an important framework for personal welfare in the late twentieth century much as they have since the seventeenth century.

The instability of the family during the urban growth and industrial development of the mid-nineteenth century caused considerable concern among politicians and other public leaders, who feared that widespread social disorder would result from the rapid pace of social change. These leaders believed that the family was in peril as a social institution, and so they promoted new ideals for family members, especially for women and children, who were most affected by the new modes of production. The major development for children was the establishment of schooling as a dominant experience in growing up. For women, the result was a definition of their responsibilities that limited them to the home and to the roles of wives and mothers.

THE ESTABLISHMENT OF COMPULSORY SCHOOLING

The redefinition of the family as a unit of consumption rather than one of production paralleled the development of formal education as a major social institution. Over time, childhood and youth became an extended period of dependency when schooling was a characteristic experience. From the time of early settlement, schoolhouses appeared throughout Canada, but the need for children within family economies meant that formal education was limited to certain periods of the year, to certain age groups, and generally to a small elite. In the pre-industrial economy, families were the dominant institutions for education, transmitting habits and values as well as vocational training. Childhood involved productive activity rather than reading and writing, and children learned practical skills from parents, older siblings, and relatives. In this context, age groups often intermingled in both work and play. The children of the elite were a partial exception to this pattern, and among them both boys and girls received some training by religious orders. However, most children learned at home within the framework of the family unit (Gaffield, 1982; Moogk, 1982).

The pattern of learning at home continued during the early nineteenth century, when schooling was still limited to children (especially boys) from families with both the interest and the affluence to arrange privately for individual or small group instruction. However, attitudes toward formal education changed rapidly, especially during the 1840s and 1850s, when public concern mounted about the present and future behaviour of unoccupied children. The increasing removal of productive activity from the home left many children without time-consuming responsibilities within the family. Public leaders believed that the phenomenon of "idle youth" boded ill for the maintenance of social order in the major cities. This belief encouraged them to promote the building of schools where children could not only be supervised, but also could be taught the values and habits considered essential in the new social context (Houston and Prentice, 1988).

The promotion of schooling by educators and politicians was facilitated by the construction of better roads and the growing population density, both of which made attendance much easier than in the scattered rural settlements of earlier times. Similarly, many parents came to see formal education as a necessary condition for successful participation in the new developing economy. Literacy and arithmetical skills, for example, seemed to be high priorities in an increasingly complex society. Instead of aiming to transmit land and material goods to their children, more parents began considering the need to also provide their children with formal education. Interestingly, parents sent both sons and daughters to elementary schools, while young men were considerably favoured for more advanced learning, especially in universities, where females were not even admitted until the later nineteenth century. Thus, general support for schooling emerged rapidly during the mid-nineteenth century, and within several decades all the Canadian provinces had comprehensive education systems (Stamp, 1982; Wilson et al., 1970). However, in keeping with the gendered society of the time, males and females experienced this development in quite different ways (Gaskell and McLaren, 1987).

As with other features of historical change within families, considerable diversity

FOR INTEREST

Despite the creation of public school systems and the increasing promotion of attendance, the material needs of many families and employers' desire for cheap labour meant that working-class children often laboured rather than studied in the late nineteenth century. The terrible working conditions of the infamous young cigar-makers were somewhat exceptional, but the character of child labour confirms the importance of always distinguishing between the rhetoric and reality of family life.

Theophile Charron, Journeyman Cigar-maker, aged 14, of Montreal, sworn.
By Mr. Helbronner:

Q. When you call yourself a cigar-maker, you mean that you have served your apprenticeship, do you not?
A. Yes, sir.

Q. How long?
A. Three years.

Q. You began working at 11 years?
A. Yes, sir.

(. . .)
Q. What wages did you get during your apprenticeship?
A. One dollar a week for the first year, $1.50 for the second year, and $2 for the third. . . .

(. . .)
Q. Did you have any fines to pay during your apprenticeship?
A. Yes, sir.

Q. Many?
A. A good number.

(. . .)
Q. How many hours did you work a day?
A. Sometimes ten hours, other times eight hours. It was just as they wanted it.

Q. Do you remember why you paid these fines?
A. Sometimes for talking too much; mostly for that.

Q. You were never licked?
A. Yes; not licked so as any harm was done me, but sometimes they would come along, and if we happened to be cutting our leaf wrong, they would give us a crack across the head with the fist.

Q. Was it usual to beat children like that?
A. Often.

Source: *Report of the Royal Commission on the Relations of Labour and Capital in Canada: Evidence Quebec* (Ottawa: Printed for the Queen's Printer, A. Senecal, 1889), Vol. 3, Part 1, pp. 24-25.

accompanied the general expansion of public school systems. Not all parents easily accepted the control and intervention represented by teachers, school inspectors, and other education officials. Conflicts emerged immediately over questions of language of instruction, religion, corporal punishment, and many other issues associated with the establishment of a public institution for children. These conflicts exposed the basic contradiction between the idea of uniform schooling and the reality of diversity among

JOHN SPOTTON / NATIONAL ARCHIVES OF CANADA / C-37334

With the development of a wage-labour economy, social leaders promoted school attendance as the only appropriate activity for children between the ages of seven and twelve. However, working-class families could not survive without the economic contribution of their children, and thus many children spent more time as producers than as pupils despite official opposition to child labour.

families. In some cases, at least partial resolutions were achieved (such as with the establishment of separate schools in most provinces), but other issues (such as language of instruction) remain stubbornly on the agenda of the late twentieth century (Gaffield, 1987; Curtis, 1988).

The pattern of increased school attendance occurred throughout the social structure, although it was less pronounced among materially disadvantaged social groups where youth remained associated with the search for productive opportunities. The continued need for some families to rely on child labour was actually reflected in the Ontario compulsory school attendance legislation of the early twentieth century, which stipulated that the officially accepted age of school leaving could be reduced by two years to age twelve if parents were able to demonstrate a need for income from their children. The 1911 census showed that children in Hamilton, for example, did in fact contribute substantially to the survival of working-class families. Employed children from the families of general labourers contributed just over 44 percent of total family income. This proportion varied among different working-class families, but the trend was consistent (Synge, 1979). The ideal of children as students was simply inappropriate for materially insecure families. Overall, however, children have spent a greater number of years in school and have been dependent on their parents for longer periods since the mid-nineteenth century. The result is that education outside the home has become a characteristic mechanism of family reproduction, and a more important vehicle of cultural transmission. To a greater and greater extent, each generation has transmitted values, skills, and traditions to the next generation through the medium of standardized books, certified teachers, and public school systems. The question of whose values, whose skills, and whose traditions remains very problematic, however, for many families.

THE NEW IDEAL OF WOMANHOOD

The redefinition of children as students was part of a new ideal for families that included a considerable narrowing of the ideal economic role for females within the patriarchal society. Separation of production from the home encouraged what historians have called the *cult of true womanhood*, which defined women primarily as reproducers and creators of havens from the hustle and bustle of the productive world. The ideal woman was pure, pious, and submissive, but also capable of effective nurturing and efficient household management. Despite the transformation of the family's economic role in society, the woman's "proper" place was still in the home. New attitudes to cleanliness, child rearing, and marriage led to a complex array of prescribed female duties to replace women's traditional participation in a family economy. The goal of these duties was to counterbalance the negative aspects of urban industrial development, which had moral and spiritual flaws since it was created by men, who were believed to be naturally less sensitive to the non-material aspects of life. The ideal role of women was to raise children and support husbands in ways that would offset the heartless nature of the marketplace. By the late nineteenth century, the ways to create a proper family environment were specified in an extensive prescriptive literature that included books, pamphlets, and magazines describing the path to "true womanhood." This view was also institutionalized in the development of domestic science as part of the public school curriculum and as the accepted course of advanced study for women (Welter, 1966; Stamp, 1977).

The most vigorous challenge to the exclusive definition of women as mothers and wives came from certain middle-class women who decided that the new ideal of

FOR INTEREST

The social welfare legislation of the twentieth century has been directed toward the support of the family as the basic unit of social order and organization. The extent of this support, however, has never been equal to the material needs of many families. Moreover, the legislation has often assumed a belief in an "ideal" family characterized by male breadwinners and female nurturers.

The Mothers' Pension Act aims to protect the home as the center of human life and activity. We hold that the family ties, deeply embedded as they are in the laws of nature and life, are the greatest source of the strength, morality and stability of the social order, and should not be broken. . . . Nations have risen to power and eminence and have fallen, because the children, mothers and homes of the masses were not taken into account, and nations will again rise and fall until we recognize that no nation can be great until built on the stable foundation of good, strong men and women. That foundation must be built in the home; by the motherhood and childhood of the nation.

Source: Mrs. Rose Henderson, "Pensions for Mothers," *Social Service Congress, Ottawa 1914, Report of Addresses and Proceedings* (Toronto: Social Service Council of Canada, 1914), p. 112.

womanhood could be effectively extended beyond the family and into the larger society. These women agreed (at least publicly) with the basic concept of natural female virtue, but argued that these "feminine" qualities had to be exercised not only in private, but also in public spheres. And so middle-class women formed groups to speak out on temperance, child welfare, sanitation, and similar social issues that attracted concern in the late nineteenth century. The same beliefs motivated the suffrage movement, which helped women gain the vote at most levels of government by 1920. By modern standards, these early challenges to the cult of true womanhood may not seem very radical, since they operated within a framework of accepted gender distinctions. However, the behaviour of at least some of these early feminists may in fact have represented a quite profound critique of patriarchal society. For certain women, the apparent acceptance of a gendered order may have simply been a strategy to achieve more immediate goals such as the right to vote (Gorham, 1979). However interpreted, the activities of these reform groups do demonstrate that women continued to be active agents in the historical process, despite the image of passivity and the attempt to restrict them to the home.

CONCLUSION

The extent to which the economic changes associated with the emergence of modern society altered families varied with social class. In general, the alterations were less extensive for working-class families than for middle-class families during the formative decades of the nineteenth and early twentieth centuries. Despite the ideal family pattern of husbands as sole breadwinners, wives as mothers, and children as students, the concept of a family wage economy remained important as a result of insecure employment and low wages. The economic growth of Canadian society from the late nineteenth century made the ideal of single breadwinners increasingly realistic, but many families still had to rely on supplementary income, and they thus followed strategies more appropriate to their own circumstances. In such families, the strong stigma against married women in the paid labour force placed a large economic burden on other family members, even young teenagers. In comparison to the general trend, a large proportion of working-class children continued to pursue job opportunities, and many of them did not attend school on a regular basis. At the beginning of the twentieth century, the majority of working-class children in Hamilton, Ontario, for example, were already wage earners by the age of fourteen. Some children from single-parent families worked full-time in local mills and factories (Synge, 1979; Brandt, 1981; Coulter, 1982; Strong-Boag, 1988).

Similarly, the ideal of women as domestic nurturers has never been applied or accepted equally by all social groups at all times. In the twentieth century, married women have been seen as a reserve labour force to be called upon when the supply of male workers did not match the number of job opportunities. During both world wars, married women worked in munitions factories, textile mills, and other establishments considered vital to the war effort. In these years, the prejudice against employed wives was only suppressed out of concern about the war effort (Pierson, 1986).

The concept of women as a reserve labour force was extended after the Second

The concept of the family consumer economy is evident in this photograph, which depicts a happy and supportive wife in the kitchen welcoming her approving husband home after another day at the office. The inherently unequal and sexist nature of this concept has become a major focus of public debate since the 1960s.

World War to include employment to supplement family income during periods of high expenses, such as when older children were in university. More recently, our society has accepted in principle the idea that women should share equally with men in opportunities for vocational training and financial independence. In this perspective, women's employment is equal rather than supplementary to men's work. However, many aspects of the nineteenth-century ideals of womanhood continue to characterize the reality of contemporary family life, and the legacy of the family as a partriarchal institution is clearly evident. Employed women are still paid less than their male counterparts in many cases, and they remain disproportionately responsible for most duties within the home (Luxton, 1980). The current position of men and women within families must therefore be evaluated with an understanding of the past, which reminds us that social ideals and social realities have only converged at particular points in time and among specific groups in society.

The evidence examined in this chapter emphasizes that a historical perspective should inform discussion of the current state of families and their futures. The history of the family reveals the ways in which the decline of land as the basis of households, the development of a wage-labour ecoromy, and the process of industrialization affected the roles of men, women, and children, and thereby transformed social organization. The changing character of family strategies and family reproduction emphasizes the ways in which factors of age, gender, ethnicity, and social class have contributed to a diverse range of individual experience during this transformation. Within the general trends, family patterns have included elements of both change and continuity, stability and instability, cohesiveness and fragmentation.

It is not obvious that the historical trends describe either a prelude to the final rejection of the patriarchal family or proof that this family form is a truly resilient social institution. Serious research on the history of the family has only been undertaken during the past two decades, and many basic questions have yet to be explored (Stone, 1977; Lasch, 1977; Flandrin, 1979; Anderson, 1980; Parr, 1980; Sutherland, 1976). Moreover, the variety and amount of evidence available for research is not unlimited, since all societies view routine family experience as unexceptional and thus not always worthy of documentation. One inescapable conclusion, however, is that families must be analysed within a larger social and economic context. The character and structure of families relate directly to the pressures and possibilities of the external material environment. In this sense, questions about the future of the family actually represent questions about the future of modern society.

DISCUSSION QUESTIONS

1. What is meant by the concept of *family strategies*? What are some of the strengths and weaknesses of this concept?
2. What is meant by the process of *family reproduction*? What are the specific components of this process?
3. What are the similarities and the differences among the activities of *family economies, family wage economies,* and *family consumer economies*?
4. Why have historians criticized interpretations that see an industrial revolution as responsible for the transition from "traditional" to "modern" families in Canada?
5. Why was instability a common characteristic of many nineteenth-century families?
6. How has the role of kinship changed during the course of the social and economic changes after 1850?
7. How was increasing school attendance related to the changing context of families in the late nineteenth century?
8. How are contemporary ideals of men and women similar to and different from those associated with the cult of true womanhood?
9. Why do many historians now insist on using the expression "the history of families" rather than the "history of the family"?
10. Do you think families have become less important with the development of major institutions of business, health, education, and welfare? Or are families today simply important in different ways?

chapter three

Mate Selection and Marital Dynamics

INTRODUCTION

While social pressure and economic necessity have encouraged both sexes to marry, different connotations have been placed on the importance of marriage for men and women. Men's social status has generally been defined by their education, occupation, and income, rather than through their marital partners. Sons tend to be granted more independence in their personal lives, but pressure is placed on them to obtain education and employment skills so that they can support a future family. For women, their choice of husband has largely determined both their economic and social status. For this reason, parents have been concerned about their daughters' marriageability and have restricted their relationships and behaviour so that they would not be considered "damaged goods" from the point of view of the families of potential suitors (Nett, 1988:201). Although greater emphasis is still placed on social skills, looks, and marriage possibilities for female children, North American parents are now becoming more conscious of the need for schooling and employment preparation for their daughters.

In the past three decades, relations between the sexes, and sexual attitudes and behaviour, have changed considerably. It has become possible, for example, to be sexually active outside marriage with less social disapproval and less concern about pregnancy. While birth control has been practised for thousands of years, it was not legally possible to advocate it publicly in North America until the 1960s because of efforts to raise the birth rate and because of religious doctrines. Although there were many periods in which these laws were not enforced, the American family planning advocate Margaret Sanger was arrested in the 1920s and threatened with a prison sentence for writing pamphlets on contraception. The development and marketing of the birth control pill, the rise of feminism, and the sexual liberation movement in the

1960s helped to challenge existing laws in both the United States and Canada. In 1969, after years of lobbying, the Trudeau government passed legislation legalizing the dissemination of birth control devices and allowing hospital abortions, if a hospital committee concluded that the woman's life or health was in danger.

Increasingly, it has become possible for women to maintain a healthy social and sexual life outside of marriage and to support themselves through paid work rather than dependence on a husband's income. Yet, the single population did not increase, but rather decreased until the 1950s. This is because the reasons to delay marriage diminished when couples could remain childless until they were ready to start a family, and when government loans became available for married students. Furthermore, after divorce laws were liberalized in 1968, marriage was not necessarily a life commitment. The decision to marry or not became less consequential when it was legally possible to divorce. In addition, increased geographic mobility and women in the work force created more occasions to meet potential partners. It is not surprising, then, that the married population increased during the first half of this century, but has declined since the 1960s, as Table 3.1 indicates. In the last few years, there has been a slight decrease in the married population due to delayed marriage, rising rates of common-law relationships, and high rates of divorce. The percentage of divorced people in the population has increased, yet it is not as high as the media portray. Most divorces are granted to younger couples, and about three-quarters of divorced people remarry.

Statistics Canada's Family History Survey of 1984 found that 22 percent of adult Canadians between the ages of twenty and twenty-four had been a partner in a common-law union. In comparison, fewer than 1 percent of those born before 1940 had been involved in such a relationship when they were in their early twenties (McKie, 1986). At the time of the 1986 census, about 12 percent of men and 11 percent of women were living in common-law relationships, most of whom were under thirty-five years of age (Turcotte, 1988). Living common-law has been referred to as a new phase of

Table 3.1   Marital Status of the Canadian Population Aged Fifteen and Over, 1901-1986 (percentage)

	1901	1956	1966	1976	1986
Single	40.4	27.3	28.0	27.9	27.2
Married*	53.9	65.8	65.0	64.2	63.0
Divorced	0.1	0.3	0.5	1.8	3.5
Widowed	5.6	6.5	6.5	6.1	6.3
Total	100	100	100	100	100

* The ''married'' category includes all those legally married, whether or not they are living together. In 1986, 3 percent of ''married'' people were separated.

Source: Statistics Canada, *Historical Statistics of Canada*, 2nd ed., edited by F. H. Leacy (Ottawa: Supply and Services Canada, 1983), p. A110-124; Census of Canada, 1986. Reproduced with permission of the Minister of Supply and Services Canada, 1989.

Table 3.2 Percentage of Women Who Are Never Married by Age Forty-five to Forty-nine, Canada, 1881-1986

1881	11.3
1891	9.4
1911	12.0
1921	11.1
1931	10.3
1941	11.2
1951	11.7
1961	9.5
1971	7.0
1981	5.8
1986	5.8

Source: Ellen M. Gee, "The Life Course of Canadian Women: An Historical and Demographic Analysis," *Social Indicators Research* 18 (1986): 266; Statistics Canada, *The Nation: Age, Sex and Marital Status*, Cat. 93-101 (Ottawa: Supply and Services Canada, September 1987), calculated from Table 5-3. Reproduced with permission of the Minister of Supply and Services Canada, 1989.

"courtship" because 46 percent of men and 43 percent of women who lived in a common-law union later married their partner. By the age of forty-five to forty-nine, only about 6 percent of women have never been legally married, as Table 3.2 reveals.

Parents generally assume that their adult children will want to leave home, to marry, and to create their own family of procreation. Yet, parental attitudes and relationships and the family environment are important factors affecting their children's attitudes about independence, the desirability of childbearing, normal marital dynamics, effective child-rearing methods, and what is important in life. More than young people would like to admit, their choice of friends, "dating" partners, and later their mate selection has been influenced by their parents' behavioural patterns and attitudes, as well as the family's socio-economic status.

MATE SELECTION

In the sociological literature, a distinction is always made between "dating" and "mating." Dating involves socializing with the opposite sex to have fun, to develop social skills, and to explore potential relationships. Mating implies a search for a more permanent relationship or marital partner. While young people may "date" people from a variety of socio-economic backgrounds, with different looks and personalities, they tend to be more selective when choosing a marital partner.

Mate selection, however, does not always follow a period of social experimentation with the opposite sex. In countries with arranged marriages, dating is discouraged because it inevitably leads to personal choices that could conflict with family decisions about mate selection (see page 44).

FOR INTEREST

MATE SELECTION IN OTHER CULTURES

Tepoztlan, Mexico

I was eleven years old when a boy came from Gabriel Mariaca to ask for my hand. He came with his parents and a jar of silver money. But my grandmother became angry and told them I was still a child, and she didn't want to see me going about carrying babies yet. When I was twelve my mother took me home again. Then a boy of sixteen came to ask for me, and my mother said yes. She told me that she wanted me to marry before something bad happened to me. I did not want to marry, especially because I did not know who the boy was. My mother said that if I did not say yes to the priest in the church she would throw me from the top of the church. I was afraid and did what my mother told me* (Lewis, 1955:399). University of Illinois Press © 1955.

Pukapuka, Polynesia

A man set on marrying a girl who at first refuses him makes frequent and regular presents of fish, nuts, taro, even fish-hooks, to her parents, and helps them at every opportunity in house building, canoe making, etc. The parents soon realize his object. They talk to their daughter, telling her she ought to marry the man. If the girl refuses, they give her a thrashing, saying that as they have accepted all the presents, they will be shamed before the whole island if she does not pay this indebtedness. Willing or unwilling, the girl is thus taken to the man. If she later runs away, she is dragged back to her husband. If she remains recalcitrant, girl, husband, and parents fight it out until one or the other decides to give in (Beaglehole and Beaglehole, 1938:296).

*In Tepoztlan courtship is a recent innovation. Arranged marriage was the old custom.

ARRANGED MARRIAGES

Parents, elders, or marriage brokers select marital partners for young people in many countries of the world, such as parts of Indonesia, Japan, and many African and Middle Eastern countries. This selection is based on a number of important considerations, including kin obligations, family wealth, and reputation. Educational background, potential economic productivity, and health are considered important for the groom, while health, physical appearance, ability to produce children, personality, and increasingly, education are important for the bride. Also included in this list are rules of endogamy and exogamy, which indicate whether it is appropriate to marry inside or outside the cultural group. In cultures that accept polygamy or plural marriage, for example, rules of endogamy (or marriage within the group) may specify that a man should marry his wife's sister if she becomes a widow. This provides some means of support for widows in a society where women do not work for pay.

In all societies, there are rules of exogamy called incest taboos, which state that people cannot marry other family members. Who is defined as a family member varies somewhat from culture to culture, but most agree that parents, siblings, and first cousins are not suitable marriage partners because they are too closely related by blood or consanguinity. In Canada, there is a long list of those legally ineligible for marriage, including some relations by marriage or adoption (ties of affinity). These rules are intended to prevent potential conflicts within the family as well as genetic problems in the offspring of blood relatives.

In societies with arranged marriages, romantic love is considered to be a poor basis for marriage. Some cultures have tried to prevent love attachments from developing by arranging betrothals or engagement contracts before or shortly after children reach physical maturity. Personal fulfilment is de-emphasized in these arrangements, and young people are taught that betrothal is a legal contract between two families and requires conformity to the wishes of older family members. Love is also controlled through gender-segregated schools, the separation of young people from ineligibles, and institutionalized chaperonage (Goode, 1959). Parents encourage their offspring to anticipate marriage and childbearing, which helps to establish their adult status and produces heirs to continue the family line.

In societies or segments of societies where kin lines, inherited wealth, or family name are important, arranged marriages or partially arranged marriages tend to predominate. Marriage is the predominant adult lifestyle and the major way for young people to gain more independence from parents. Some immigrants to Canada from Egypt, Lebanon, Japan, and India, for example, still try to arrange marriages for their children. In some cases, however, young people raised in Canada expect to choose their own partners, and resist their parents' suggestions. Other young immigrants temporarily return to their native country to participate in an arranged marriage, and then return to Canada with their new partner.

With industrialization, there seems to be a trend toward monogamous nuclear families (Goode, 1963), and young people in many countries now expect more choice in marital partners. Where arranged marriages continue to be the custom, many young people want the right to veto parental decisions. Furthermore, polygamous marriages have been outlawed in many Middle Eastern and African countries, because these unions are viewed as oppressive to women or benefiting mainly the rich.

FREE CHOICE MARRIAGES

In free choice marriages, many of the same considerations enter mate selection, yet they are often disguised by the expectation that "love" is the primary motive for marriage. In actual fact, people marry for a variety of reasons, including companionship, sex, children, and additional financial support. Getting away from home and establishing a separate identity is often a subconscious reason for marriage, as a wedding is still an adult rite of passage or an indication of adult status, even when the couple is already living together. In other words, people marry for more than love, both in North America and in other societies.

North American young people usually choose their own spouse, but they are often introduced to potential partners by parents, siblings, other relatives, and friends. Yet, there are sociological patterns involved in these introductions and choices. The literature and music of Western cultures are filled with stories of people who fall in love with an inappropriate person (such as Romeo and Juliet) and marry against their parents' wishes. This folklore indicates that there are implicit social rules governing mate selection, which people violate at their own peril.

Several theories exist about how mate selection occurs when young people make their own choices. The social homogamy theory suggests that people from similar socio-economic and cultural backgrounds tend to marry because they have more opportunity to meet and get to know each other, and are likely to share a similar "world view." Marital partners are generally of the same race, within three or four years in age, often have similar education, and usually come from families with about the same social status and income level. Although the popular media pays considerable attention to interracial marriages, marriages between older women and younger men, and examples of poor employees marrying the boss's daughter, these situations are relatively rare.

Despite the acceptance of social homogamy, researchers have noted that men tend to "marry down" in social status. By this we mean that North American men tend to marry women about two years younger at their first marriage and about four years younger if they remarry. Men also tend to marry women who have similar or less education, lower incomes, and who are physically shorter. There appear to be unwritten rules against men marrying women who are substantially older, more educated, from a wealthier family, or physically taller. This tendency has been called the "marriage gradient" (Bernard, 1982), and implies that poorly educated and low-income men may experience difficulty finding suitable partners, as do highly educated women earning above-average incomes. In actual fact, women with graduate degrees and high-level jobs not only have low marriage rates, but also experience high divorce rates, especially if they marry men with lower income and education (Spreitzer and Riley, 1974; Glick, 1984).

While social homogamy and the marriage gradient may explain which category of people are considered to be eligible for marriage, they cannot explain why individuals within those categories are attracted to each other. While some attractions may be based largely on sexual appeal or "chemistry," ongoing relationships are generally based on much more. Psychologists have created theories that look at both subconscious psychological needs and more explicit ideals.

The theory of complementary needs suggests that people are attracted to those whom they think will complement their psychological needs. For example, men with dominant mothers may subconsciously look for a "mother substitute," people who were abused as children may marry someone who continues to abuse them, and people who feel insecure may marry someone who flatters them and bolsters their ego. These needs may not be conscious, and attraction may be based more on an intuitive feeling of compatibility rather than any explicit recognition of needs. Furthermore, needs may change throughout the relationship, making couples less compatible over time.

Another theory stresses the developmental aspects of relationships. The development of "courtship," according to this theory, is predetermined by neither social nor psychological variables. Instead, it is the end product of a series of interactions characterized by advances and retreats, changing definitions of the situation, bargaining, and the resolution of tensions. Initial choice of partner may be based on a physical attraction, chance, or similar interests, but the path to marriage has been portrayed as an escalator – once you get on, it is difficult not to ride to the top. One of the partners may negotiate for greater commitment. Friends and family make assumptions about the relationship and apply subtle or explicit social pressure for the couple to move in together or marry. In some cases, circumstances may encourage an already committed couple to live together or break up, such as a job opportunity in another city.

The ideal mate theory suggests that, based on parental role models and past dating experience, we form impressions of an ideal marital partner. This ideal may involve physical attributes, personality type, attitudes, occupation, or interests. Throughout adolescence or early adulthood, we continue to look for a mate with these characteristics and eventually choose the person who best approximates this ideal. The ideal mate theory certainly makes the process of mate selection sound more rational than the developmental theory or the theory of complementary needs. Yet, these theories are not necessarily mutually exclusive.

From a pool of socially similar eligibles, people may choose a partner whom they think will fulfil their needs or will best represent their ideal mate. After the relationship is established, they may move toward commitment tentatively, negotiating new arrangements when they approach roadblocks. They may be propelled toward marriage by parents, friends, or circumstances. These theories suggest that some chance factors may be involved in mate selection, yet the type of person who subjectively appears attractive follows a pattern.

MILLER COMSTOCK INC.

Although we think we marry for "love," most Canadians choose their marital partners according to certain unspoken rules.

Computer dating services and marriage brokers rely on portions of these theories when they look for potential partners for their clients. They are particularly likely to match age, height, education, race, and religion. In countries with arranged marriages, marriage brokers may also focus on social standing, family reputation, and income. Although we usually rely on our friends and families to introduce us to eligible partners, North Americans are increasingly turning to newspaper "companion ads," dating services, and singles' clubs to assist them when they no longer are meeting those they find interesting. This may be the case for women who have postponed marriage to further their education or career development and who later find there is a shortage of eligible men. Others who have recently moved to the city or who work in a place with no potential partners may also turn to "companion ads." Advertising for a mate is not a new idea, however, as it has been used for decades by certain immigrant groups looking for a partner from their own culture (Baker, 1982).

Although we think we marry for "love," most Canadians choose their marital partners according to certain unspoken rules. For example, young people tend to marry at a similar time, generally in their early to mid-twenties. The groom is usually older than the bride by a year or two and has slightly more education and a higher income. Seldom is the groom shorter than the bride. The daughter of a supreme court judge typically does not marry the son of a garbage collector. We may fall in love, but we usually do so selectively.

Many Canadian couples perceive the decision to marry as an indication of greater commitment, even when they already live common-law. The wedding ceremony itself is frequently perceived as a "rite of passage" to adult status, involving considerable symbolic and traditional behaviour as well as expense. The romantic view of marriage is perpetuated by the media, with magazines devoted to brides and weddings and considerable attention given to wedding protocol, attire, rings, receptions, and honeymoons. Furthermore, many families save for years and spend considerable sums on wedding clothing and receptions, even though the event lasts only a day or two. Although some couples choose to bypass a traditional wedding, most see the ceremony and the reception as an essential step marking the beginning of a new life.

MARITAL RELATIONSHIPS THROUGHOUT THE FAMILY LIFE CYCLE

Marriage has historically been the normal living arrangement in adult life. Although some people always remained single through choice or circumstance, entering convents or monasteries or caring for their aging parents, the majority of men and women married and produced children. As we have seen in Chapter Two, even in Canada marriage was not always seen as a vehicle for personal fulfilment and romantic love, but rather as a way to survive economically, to be socially acceptable, to have sex and to bear children legitimately. Although marriage was particularly crucial for women when they could not legally own property or earn their own living, it was also important for men. Since so many worked at least a twelve-hour day, men needed someone to prepare food for them, to clean their houses, to make and maintain their clothes, and to care for their children. Marriage was therefore viewed as a mutually necessary partnership. With economic, legal, and social changes, it gradually became possible to exist without marriage, but most people prefer to live in an intimate and socially acceptable relationship.

Modern marriages are usually based on economic co-operation, shared residence, companionship, a sexual relationship, childbearing, and child rearing. Before children are born, both partners tend to work full-time and to share at least some of the housework. However, Canadian and international studies show that although marital roles are changing, wives tend to accept responsibility for performing most of the routine household tasks (Meissner et al., 1975; Clark and Harvey, 1976; Luxton, 1980; Mandell and Duffy, 1988; Nett, 1988). Research also indicates that relationships are likely to be more egalitarian in the early years of marriage, before children are born. Leisure time and household chores are more likely to be shared by childless couples, making this stage in the family life cycle more companionate than later stages.

NEWLYWEDS

Recently married couples need time to establish a division of labour, sexual intimacy, and the effective means of communicating and resolving conflicts (see below). Urban dwellers are likely to live in an apartment, with a minimum of cleaning and no outdoor chores, enabling them to engage in leisure activities on an impulse without carefully planning their privacy and their recreation. Without babies to interrupt their sleep or their sexual activities, they can enjoy more spontaneity and privacy than in later stages of the family life cycle.

FOR INTEREST

MARITAL ADJUSTMENT: A DEFINITION

Marital adjustment is the process of resolving conflict and achieving need fulfillment to the satisfaction of both partners. If both are able to meet most of their needs most of the time in interaction with each other, and to deal to their mutual satisfaction with the conflicts which inevitably arise, they can be considered to be well adjusted. If one or both are frustrated in fulfilling their needs most of the time or dissatisfied with their attempted solutions to conflict, their adjustment is poor. This definition avoids the value trap which so many fall into. The values implied in "good" and "poor" adjustment are those of the participants, and not of the definer or observer. If persistent conflict is mutually satisfying, for example, and meets the needs of both partners, as

seems to be the case in the comic strip "Andy Capp," the adjustment is good. Looked at another way, marital adjustment is the process by which two people define their relationship to each other (and others). They must work out the rules of their marriage, including (1) the rules for living together (or apart in the case of commuter marriages), and (2) the rules for making the rules. In societies in which there is only one role pattern, these rules are part of the scripts to be followed by the role players and the process of marital adjustment is somewhat simpler. It is never entirely automatic, however. Even when the script provides the rules which should be followed — for example, that only the husband/father has the legitimate authority to make the rules about the rules – informal negotiations occur between some couples for deciding who actually does make them. Furthermore, as two people define their relationship, not only do they establish the rules, but they also define themselves and evaluate their identities. Communication is the means by which rules are made and identities are established and maintained.

Source: Emily M. Nett, *Canadian Families: Past and Present* (Toronto: Butterworths, 1988), pp. 233-34.

Increasingly, young married couples each have full-time jobs and feel they require expensive labour-saving devices to enable them to acquire leisure time. Furthermore, couples with two incomes and no children enjoy a higher standard of living than same-aged couples with children, especially if they remain childless and receive income increases with employment seniority. Professional couples can spend their earnings on extras, such as holidays, luxury housing, home renovations, house-cleaning assistance, restaurants, movies, expensive cars, or sports equipment. Even for those in poorly paid jobs, their expenses are less than for couples with children. In fact, the two-income family has heightened the economic disparity between one-parent and two-parent families, because the majority of two-parent families now have two earners.

CHILDBIRTH

At the time of their first pregnancy, most young wives are now in the labour force and must make important decisions about whether to take maternity leave or resign from their job and stay home to care for their child. If they take leave, they will have to make suitable child care arrangements for their return to work. Regardless of this decision, the couple will need to modify their division of labour to accommodate a heavier workload. Becoming parents will dramatically change the lifestyle of most young couples. Their work, their sleep, their sex life, their leisure time, and often their housing will be affected by the new baby, as we will see in Chapter Seven.

Increasingly, young women with full-time jobs are taking a maternity leave from work rather than resigning from their jobs and caring for their own children. This is usually primarily an economic decision, for wages have not kept up with inflation over the years and two incomes are necessary to maintain the same living standard of a generation ago (Maynard, 1988). If a woman is eligible for maternity leave, the federal unemployment insurance program pays a portion of her former wages for about four months, although some employers top up this amount to approximate lost income more closely.

The actual experience of childbirth varies with the woman's physical and emotional health, the presence or absence of the father, and social conditions surrounding the birthing process. In the past few decades, feminists and health care reform advocates have argued that childbirth has been "medicalized" by physicians. While births used to take place at home with the assistance of midwives or experienced married women, most now occur in impersonal hospital environments, where doctors sometimes treat pregnant women like sick people and use various interventions such as anesthetics,

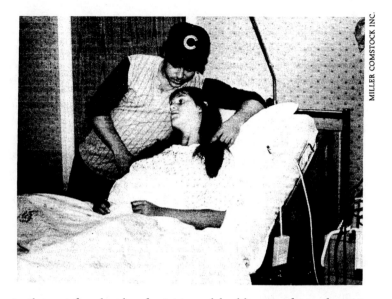

In the past few decades, feminists and health-care reform advocates have argued that childbirth has become "medicalized" by physicians.

episiotomies, and caesarian sections. Doctors argue that sterile conditions and medical procedures are necessary for the safety of the birth. However, Canadian infant mortality rates are still higher than other industrialized countries that allow home births, license midwives, and have lower rates of caesarian births (United Nations, 1988).

These controversies have led to several provincial investigations about the licensing of midwives, the safety of home births, and the development of more pleasant birthing rooms in local hospitals. Recent government reports have recommended greater use of midwives, partly to reduce rising health care costs (see page 52). Yet, Canadian physicians have historically attempted to maintain control over childbirth and to discourage home births.

While a generation ago, fathers were discouraged from participating in the birthing process, they are now encouraged to be present in the operating room. Some people have suggested that participating in their child's birth creates a stronger bond between men and their babies, a bond that can last a lifetime. However, many fathers are not able to take off much time from work either during or after the birth of their children because of the lack of paternity or parental leave.

The first few months after childbirth are typified by the sheer fatigue of parents engaging in twenty-four-hour care of their infant. Parents who must get up and go to work after feeding, changing a baby, or caring for a sick child during the night undoubtedly experience mixed emotions about the "joys" of child rearing. But the amount of physical care subsides when the baby no longer requires night feedings, and later when he or she is toilet trained.

Some mothers find it difficult to return to work after the birth of their child because they are reluctant to leave the baby with anyone else. The lack of high-quality and

FOR INTEREST

PRENATAL CARE BY MIDWIVES EQUAL TO DOCTORS, STUDY SAYS

By Ann Rauhala

Nurse midwives provide care equal to, if not better than, that provided by family physicians, a Canadian study has found.

Using medical records of 132 pregnant women, the researchers found that in 84 per cent of cases handled by midwives, pregnant women received adequate or superior prenatal care.

Among those cared for by family doctors, only 40 per cent received adequate or superior care, leaving 60 per cent receiving inadequate care.

When the distinction is made between adequate and superior care, nurse midwives' performance rates as superior in 77 per cent of cases while doctors' performance was found to be superior in 24 per cent of cases.

"Nurse midwives provide more adequate and comprehensive care to pregnant women than family physicians do," the researchers conclude in their report.

"We weren't surprised that the nurse midwives did so well," said Dr. Samuel Sheps of the department of health care and epidemiology at the University of British Columbia and one of three authors of the report.

The study was partly financed by Health and Welfare Canada.

"What we were surprised by was that the family physicians didn't do as well as we thought, especially since the measures were adapted and altered to reflect current thinking among family practitioners," Dr. Sheps said yesterday.

The researchers also conclude that, with appropriate support, nurse midwives can provide safe and adequate prenatal care to low-risk women.

"It's not that they're so much better," Dr. Sheps said. "It's that they're unlikely to be a whole lot worse."

The researchers compared midwives to family doctors by studying and ranking routine medical records showing what kind of attention patients received during their pregnancies.

The charts were rated against a set of criteria reflecting minimal standards of care. The criteria were checked with 20 family physicians who did not know about the study to make sure they were relevant to ordinary practice. The scorer did not know which chart came from which kind of professional.

To rate as adequate, a doctor or midwife would have had to perform 10 specific tasks pertinent to pregnancy, for instance, recording of weight or measurement of blood pressure at each visit.

The study involved women with low-risk pregnancies who sought care at an outpatient clinic of Grace Hospital in Vancouver or from family doctors in the Vancouver area between 1982 and 1984.

The new study stands in some contrast to a Canadian Medical Association survey released last year that found 95 per cent women were satisfied with the prenatal care they received. That study, however, involved more than 2,000 patients and included those who received prenatal care from obstetricians.

Dr. Sheps said that the new study did not necessarily contradict the CMA survey.

"Measuring patient satisfaction says nothing about quality of care," he said.

"People can say they're satisfied with what is really appalling care. The advantage of our study was that it had explicit criteria of good care."

The study, published in last month's Canadian Medical Association Journal, is the first of its kind in Canada, Dr. Sheps said.

Source: *The Globe and Mail*, October 12, 1988.   **Reprinted With Permission of The Globe and mail.**

affordable child care services for infants complicates this decision. Other young mothers are anxious to return to work to escape the routine of diapers and feedings, to enjoy more time with adults, and to earn some money. But regardless of the wishes of individual mothers, most families require two incomes to meet their daily expenses, and most mothers feel they must resume employment.

DECISION MAKING AND THE DIVISION OF LABOUR

For several decades, researchers have examined decision making in marriage and have tried to identify factors most influential in determining which partner retains more power. Early studies asked wives to report the number of decisions made by them and their husbands and concluded that decision making was shared (Blood and Wolfe, 1960). But these studies also suggested that higher-income husbands held more power in their families, suggesting the "power of the purse" theory. These studies were later criticized for relying on women's views about family decision making when research has indicated that men and women often perceive their relationships quite differently. Furthermore, decisions were counted and all were treated as equal (Duffy, 1988) when it is evident that some decisions are more consequential than others.

Research on family power and decision making indicates that a number of factors influence who has the final say when husbands and wives cannot agree. A number of "personal resources" help to establish bargaining power, including higher education, social skills, youth and physical beauty, high income, inherited money, or a combination of factors. Furthermore, the "personal resource theory" (Blood and Wolfe, 1960) suggests that power may shift from one spouse to the other in different circumstances. If a wife is very knowledgeable in one area, her husband may defer to her, but his voice may hold more weight in another area of decision making.

Brinkerhoff and Lupri (1983) found that although the number of decisions made by each spouse might be roughly equal, the areas in which wives make decisions are considered to be less important by both spouses. Other authors have argued that the "decks are stacked" against women because they often marry men who are older, more educated, more experienced on the job, have higher incomes, and are physically larger than themselves (Gillespie, 1971; Kandel and Lesser, 1972). Although personal resources may give individuals power in specific interpersonal situations, we live in a society in which men have more opportunity to acquire these resources simply because they are male. If women want egalitarian marriages, advocates of this "patriarchal society theory" argue that they should marry younger men with less job experience, education, and income. This might counteract some of the effects of patriarchy. Yet, despite the professed desire in egalitarian marriage, many young women still want to marry a man they can "look up to," in terms of height, experience, expertise, and income (Baker, 1985).

Some studies have found that wives increase their relative power when they are employed, especially if their earnings approach or exceed those of their husbands. Decisions about major purchases are often made jointly because part of the money comes from each pay cheque. Yet, the relationship between family power and wives' earnings is ambiguous (Duffy, 1988:122). Most wives earn less than their husbands and on average contribute about one-third of the family income (Statistics Canada, 1985).

Many young women now have their own bank accounts and can make purchases with their own money without consulting their husbands. Their financial situation could differ substantially from their parents' generation, when wives had to ask permission to buy something with money earned by their husbands. Although some housewives undoubtedly controlled the family finances, most husbands retained the power of the purse when they were sole earners. Recent studies have confirmed that employed wives are less willing to move with their husbands' jobs, and more likely to make demands on their husbands to share the housework (Harrell, 1985).

If the mother becomes a full-time homemaker when the baby is born, the previous division of labour may change dramatically. While some household tasks might have been shared when the couple was childless, the homemaker/wife is now likely to take over the cooking and cleaning as well as child care. The longer she stays home, the more traditional the division of labour tends to become. The husband may feel that he is now able to work late or to go out occasionally with his friends, but this may aggravate his wife's feelings of isolation, overwork, and lack of contact with adult activities and labour force requirements. Many homemakers are able to overcome these feelings with community activities, volunteer work, play schools, baby-sitting co-operatives, a part-time job, a mothers' support group, or continuing education courses.

Women who care for their own children at home have historically provided a vast amount of volunteer work benefiting their communities. Homemakers have raised money and volunteered services for religious, community, cultural, and charitable organizations. In addition, some women have taken in piecework from factories, cared for other people's children, made clothing for extra money, or taught music lessons at home. Other women have cared for foster children, even when remuneration was low and barely covered their expenses. Increasingly, however, families need a second income, and women are less often available for volunteer work or underpaid positions.

Although few men stay at home to care for their children while their wives work, those who do may actually experience more problems than women because they do not fit into traditional women's groups geared to homemakers. Lack of a job also seems to lower a husband's decision-making power in the family (Brinkerhoff and Lupri, 1983). Neighbours may criticize a "house-husband" because he is not fulfilling the traditional masculine role of breadwinner and family head. Few men have remained homemakers for more than short time periods because of financial need and social pressure from friends and family.

Considering the structure of the labour force, continuing high unemployment, and rapid technological change, it is no longer easy to leave the labour force for child-rearing purposes and expect to return several years later. For those with higher-level jobs, their training, education, and experience are soon considered outdated. Parents (usually mothers) who have remained at home to care for their children might be expected to retrain and start at the bottom of the hierarchy again.

Many women enter "pink collar" jobs, such as secretary, teacher, hairdresser, or nurse, which enable them to move in and out of the labour force for family reasons. But women have paid a penalty for this flexibility. Traditionally, they have occupied relatively low-level jobs, earned about two-thirds of men's wages, and have been less likely than men to be protected by unions or to enjoy fringe benefits such as pension plan membership. Furthermore, women are much more likely than men to work part-time, usually in order to care for young children.

Increasingly, however, women are unwilling to stay at the bottom of the job hierarchy and are joining labour unions with the hopes of protecting their jobs, raising their wages, and obtaining more fringe benefits, including maternity and parental leave. Largely through necessity, women's attitude toward work has become more committed, since it is no longer easy to move in and out of the labour market. Yet, many parents and policy makers still worry about how children will cope with long hours of non-family care while their parents work.

Despite the fact that so many mothers have entered the labour force either full-time or part-time, most have remained responsible for housework and child care (Northcott, 1983; Coverman and Sheley, 1986). Some parents feel that mothers can best care for and socialize their own children, and do not want to trust their children to hired baby-sitters or child care workers, many of whom have low levels of education and high turnover rates. But remaining at home reduces the family's income and may deny children certain costly opportunities, limits women's activities, and reduces social contact for children. These dilemmas cause some mothers considerable anxiety.

CHILDLESSNESS

Many countries such as Canada and the United States have promoted pronatalist values, encouraging people to reproduce to maintain the population. Yet, there has always been a certain percentage of the population that remained childless. In the past, people assumed that childlessness among married couples was due to physiological problems, but there undoubtedly were people who disguised their lack of interest in reproduction because it was not socially acceptable to admit it. Historically, childlessness among married people was stigmatized and was viewed as an indication of ill health, sexual inadequacy, immaturity, gender identity problems, or selfishness (Veevers, 1980). Sex without procreation also violates some religious beliefs. The presence of children in a marriage not only confirms adult status, but is also seen as an indication of social responsibility and mental and physical health.

As birth control technology has advanced, more married couples have postponed childbearing or have decided to remain childless. The percentage of childless couples has not increased dramatically, however, because medical technology has also enabled low fertility couples to reproduce. If some women who previously could not become pregnant are now having children, and others are deciding not to have children, the two groups cancel each other out in the statistics. However, there has been a slight rise in childlessness in Canada in the past decades. In 1984, for example, about 17 percent of ever-married women were childless compared to about 14 percent in 1961 (Rao and Balakrishnan, 1986:26).

Although the percentage of married couples who remain childless has never been very large, there were always some couples who could not bear children. Without the available technology to test fertility, it is usually assumed that the woman is infertile. In fact, having an infertile wife has been a suitable reason for a man to take a mistress or concubine, or to obtain a divorce in some countries.

In developing nations where fertility is important for both sexes, childless couples are pitied. A childless woman may be expected to care for her relatives' children or to take on community work. In industrialized countries such as Canada, where involuntarily childless women have a career, there may be slightly less social pressure to bear children. Yet, most people feel that having and raising a child is such an integral part of life that they do not want to miss the experience. Some couples spend years trying to get pregnant or to adopt, and thousands of dollars on medical interventions, such as *in vitro* fertilization.

Contrary to the claims of doctors at some fertility clinics, only about 10 percent of women who undergo *in vitro* fertilization actually produce a baby (Eichler, 1989). Furthermore, the technique is extremely expensive for hospitals and for the patient. Months and years of fruitless waiting may also be involved. Some Canadian feminists called for a Royal Commission on reproductive technology because they felt that important moral and policy decisions were being left to a small group of mainly male physicians.

A very small but growing number of childless couples have contracted fertile women to bear children for them. These "surrogate mothers" are usually poor women who see childbearing as a relatively easy way to earn a living, while the childless couple is often financially well off. In addition to the moral problems that may exist in paying poor people to produce children for the rich, legal complications are also ever-present (see page 57).

In 1988, the "Baby M" case was widely publicized in North American newspapers and provides a good example of the potential legal complications. The surrogate mother, who was artifically inseminated, decided after the birth that she wanted to keep the child she produced rather than give her to the biological father and his wife as the contract stated. After a prolonged court battle, the father and his wife won custody of the child. This American court case has underlined the need in both the United States and Canada for public policy on the legality of surrogate motherhood, the role of women in reproductive technology, the acceptability of profit making or the use of public funds for infertility clinics, and the changing definition of paternity.

Despite pronatalist values, some childlessness was always voluntary, and contraception and birth control knowledge has been available for thousands of years. Married and unmarried couples practised celibacy or infanticide to control the population, regulate the sex ratio, or curb their family size. Mechanical methods of birth control, such as condoms and diaphragms, have been available for decades. Yet, childlessness was not really a viable option for many Canadians until the development of more

FOR INTEREST

STUDY UNDERTAKEN FOR LAW REFORM BODY TURNS UP 118 SURROGATE-MOTHER CASES

By Dorothy Lipovenko

An unpublished report prepared for the Law Reform Commission of Canada has found at least 118 cases of surrogacy contracts for the production of babies involving Canadians.

Although suggesting its figures err on the low side, the report, a copy of which was obtained by The Globe and Mail, provides the first comprehensive national data about "preconception contracts" to produce children for couples with fertility problems.

Most of the cases involve Canadian couples who hired U.S. women through U.S. agencies, or employed a Canadian surrogate, to bear them a child. In most instances, the husband's sperm was used to impregnate the "contractual mother."

Because surrogacy is fraught with legal uncertainty in Canada, some contractual mothers have given birth in a Canadian hospital using the name and health insurance number of the women to whom they will eventually relinquish the children.

While many surrogacy contracts are between people with no ties, the report found that some women agreed to carry a child for a sister or close friend.

The 118 cases "constitute a minimum which probably underestimates the real incidence by an unknown, considerable factor," noted the report's authors, Toronto sociologist Margrit Eichler and researcher Phebe Poole.

In the summer, the authors canvassed lawyers, social workers and judges across Canada and in the United States and learned that:

● One couple kept secret the fact that they had adopted a baby at the same time the husband impregnated a surrogate mother. The two babies were born within six weeks of each other and are being raised as twins despite the different dates on their birth certificates.

● A couple with adopted twin daughters wanted a boy, so in addition to applying for another adoption, they tried infertility treatment. The wife was unaware she was three months pregnant as a result of test-tube fertilization when the husband impregnated a surrogate mother. In the end, the wife bore twins, (one of which was a boy) and the surrogate mother also had the man's child, which the couple kept.

● A divorced woman agreed to become pregnant with her brother-in-law's sperm to give her sister a child.

● One couple engaged a close friend on two occasions to have children for them.

● One couple found a surrogate through a newspaper ad.

● One social worker reported that a colleague gave birth to a baby in a contractual arrangement for friends in the United States.

Delving into the backgrounds of clients and surrogates, the study found information that reinforces the belief that a surrogate and her family are likely to come from a lower social and economic rung than the couple who hired her.

By comparison, couples who contracted for a child tended to be in professional occupations; the men included lawyers, engineers and doctors, while the women were teachers, or worked in medicine or business.

· · · · · · ·

A woman who agrees to be inseminated with the sperm of a man to whom she is not married may or may not be paid under the agreements. Some surrogates received $10,000 and medical expenses, while others charged nothing if the couple involved were friends or relatives.

"The major finding of this study is that preconception contracts involving Canadians are a phenomenon of very moderate scope but considerably more frequent than (was estimated by) all of the people with whom we talked and who considered themselves knowledgeable in the area," the report says.

The authors said they were confident the 118 cases they found "represent a very conservative estimate which probably greatly underestimates the real extent of the phenomenon."

Source: *The Globe and Mail*, February 10, 1989. **Reprinted With Permission of The Globe and mail.**

effective birth control technology in the 1960s and until abortion was legalized in 1969. Furthermore, women lack positive role models of childless women. By age fifty, for example, about 94 percent of women have been married (Gee, 1986), and about 85 percent of married couples eventually bear children.

Although motherhood has been portrayed as the major role for women throughout Canada's history, there have always been women who have rebelled against these expectations. In industrialized countries, low marriage rates and childlessness have been correlated with high education, continuous employment, and high career involvement for women (but not for men) because of the difficulty of balancing children and career.

Veevers (1980) found that childless couples tended to perceive that their parents, especially their mothers, had lived unsatisfying lives because they had to sacrifice other activities for child rearing. These childless couples also associated pregnancy with illness and lack of erotic appeal, and saw motherhood as synonymous with dependency and incompetence. They felt that having children would interfere with their career plans, travels, or marital stability. Childless people often lacked child care skills because they were an "only child," or alternatively, were first-borns and experienced too much child care responsibility as children (Veevers, 1980).

Childless couples reported various satisfactions with their lifestyle in Veevers's study, including spontaneity and avoidance of routine, time to seek out new experiences and develop skills, and opportunities to travel. While childless women reported strong commitment to their careers, men tended to emphasize the freedom from having to work to support children, low career involvement, or a varied career history. These couples also had a more egalitarian division of labour, the incomes of husbands and wives were more similar than among couples with children, and husbands tended to encourage their wives' outside interests and career development. Other studies have found that childless married couples, and especially men, report more satisfaction with their marriages than married couples with children (Veroff and Feld, 1970).

At the same time, we know that childless couples have higher rates of divorce than couples with children. This can probably be explained, however, by the practical difficulties of divorcing when children are involved and the relative ease of divorcing in a childless marriage. Now that couples have more lifestyle options, more may choose a childless marriage. Yet, there remains considerable social pressure, especially from older relatives and policy makers, to reproduce in order to perpetuate the family line or to counteract the dwindling birth rate.

MID-LIFE AND OLDER CHILDREN

Parents with older children may find that rearing adolescents is a complex task involving patience and understanding, because adolescents are experiencing both physical and emotional changes and attempting to define their personalities. Their children may be wrestling with what kind of person they want to be, what kind of life they want to live, and what they believe in. While many young people are physically mature, they are not educationally and socially prepared to live independently and to earn a living. As dependants of their parents, some adolescents resent restrictions on their personal freedom and demand more rights and independence than parents are prepared to give.

Parents with older children may find that rearing adolescents is a complex task involving patience and understanding.

MILLER COMSTOCK INC.

Although life with adolescents may be trying for some parents, others enjoy their children more as they grow up. Many parents can feel proud of the children they have raised and derive considerable satisfaction from watching them develop new interests, talents, and unique personalities. In fact, some parents become remotivated and adopt some of their adolescent's interests or hobbies. They may also enjoy a kind of companionship not possible in earlier stages of the family life cycle when their children were less mature.

If adolescents are financially dependent on their parents, as most are, they may make economic demands that parents cannot or will not meet. Adolescents often feel that they require certain types of clothing, footwear, and entertainment to conform to peer standards. These expenses frequently violate parental standards of what young people really need or what the family income can afford. Furthermore, young people often want to be different from their parents, both in lifestyle and ideas, while parents usually expect their children to adopt their values. Disputes about physical appearances, clothing, musical taste, choice of friends, and leisure activities often cause considerable friction between parents and their adolescent children.

Rollins and Feldman (1970) found that having older children tends to have a negative impact on the general life satisfaction of married people. Using four different indexes, including general marital satisfaction, positive companionship, satisfaction with the present stage in the life cycle, and the absence of negative feelings, they found that scores were the lowest between the time when couples have school-age children and young adults. Fathers seemed to be more positive about teenage children than mothers. Yet, the concept of marital or life satisfaction has been criticized because it is influenced by expectations and socialization to gender roles. The conclusion that men find teenage children more satisfying than women do may relate to men's socialization to derive more satisfaction from talking to and sharing activities with children, especially their sons. Women, on the other hand, may be encouraged to enjoy breast-feeding, cuddling infants and young children, and teaching basic skills to preschool children before they demand more independence.

Children who have been adopted are likely to ask many questions about their biological parents during their teen years. While many adoptive parents readily tell their children what they know of their past, provincial adoption records have not been open to them. A recent federal government study has recommended that these records be made available to adopted children when they are twenty-one years old.

Although adolescence is often a time of psychological and parental conflict, young people may later find that they have more in common with their parents and siblings than they initially thought. Family experiences create a solid bond and lasting impressions about desirable lifestyles and acceptable values. In fact, children often unknowingly pattern their behaviour and their relationships after their parents'.

CHILD "LAUNCHING"

When the last child leaves home, parents could be alone for the first time in years. Since their wedding, they have enjoyed years of common experiences and suffered through numerous tribulations, but their years of child raising probably brought them closer together. Now that they are alone, they need to re-establish themselves as a couple, rather than seeing each other mainly as parents. Some couples make this transition easily, but others continue to interact as parents, even calling each other "dad" or "mother."

Dealing with the children now that they have left home requires a new form of interaction. When adult "children" visit, they may spend time chatting about their activities and exchanging news, but parents soon realize that they now have little control over their children's behaviour and activities, unless they continue to support them financially. They cannot continue to discipline these adults as if they were still children, or even expect them to abide continually by parental ideas of appropriate behaviour. On the other hand, they can still set house rules that must be followed while their children are in the parental home. This readjustment of parental roles may require some practice and involve a period of negotiation between parents and their grown children.

For women who have not remained in the labour force or re-entered at a younger age, child launching may require some re-evaluation of educational or employment plans. In most Canadian homes, however, mothers have already re-entered the labour force by the time their children have left home, or have never left the labour force at all during their childbearing years.

At a stage when many people are beginning to feel free of parenting responsibilities, their own parents, if they are still alive, may be becoming frail and in need of personal assistance. Longer life expectancy may mean that more middle-aged parents will need to bring their own parents home to live with them or help them find suitable care and accommodation elsewhere.

After the children have left, parents' financial responsibilities may decrease, and it may be possible for some to consider early retirement. With improvements in employment-related pensions and social security programs, more people are now able to retire before the age of sixty-five. In fact, a Gallup Poll from February 1984 found that 47 percent of Canadian workers intended to leave the workplace before the age of sixty-five.

MIDDLE AGE AND UNMARRIED PEOPLE

Some of the behavioural patterns of married people during middle age also pertain to unmarried people, such as concerns about the accomplishment of career goals, physiological aging, and disabled parents. However, there are also some important differences in life patterns of married and unmarried people. Throughout the life span, unmarried people tend to maintain closer relationships with their parents and siblings than do married people, who are often preoccupied with their children (Connidis, 1989). Especially among the present generation of older unmarried women, some feel that they jeopardized marriage or other opportunities to care for disabled parents. While unmarried people, especially women, used to be expected to reside with parents or other relatives rather than alone, they are now more likely to rent an apartment or to buy a house or condominium. While some live with friends of the same or opposite sex, others live alone. The former stereotype of the maiden lady living alone with her cats is certainly an image of the past; many unmarried women maintain active social and sexual lives and generally hold full-time jobs.

Unmarried women tend to have more stable career patterns and higher incomes than married women. This may reflect the fact that single women have often acquired more formal education than married women, and also did not take time off work for child rearing. In fact, single women's occupational commitment is similar to men's, although they are less likely than men to have achieved a high-status or well-paid position. While well-educated men have higher marriage rates than men with lower education, the opposite is true for women (Glick, 1984). In fact, sociological studies have shown that higher levels of intelligence, education, and occupational achievement are associated with singleness among women (Scanzoni and Scanzoni, 1988:208). These women may have postponed marriage while they were developing their careers and thereby reduced the probability of later finding a partner. Alternatively, they could have consciously decided to focus on a rewarding career or an independent life rather than marriage.

Although some middle-aged single people of both sexes have always remained celibate, we can no longer assume that this is the case. Many maintain permanent relationships that are either heterosexual or homosexual. Sometimes these relationships are open and public, but often they are covert because their partner is married or because they are homosexual and want to protect themselves from public disapproval. Some unmarried people have a series of relationships throughout their lives, but never settle into a live-in arrangement. Others live as husband and wife, but never legally marry. While 8 percent of all heterosexual couples were living in a common-law union in 1986, this arrangement was more typical of people under thirty-five rather than older couples (Turcotte, 1988).

The reported life satisfaction of unmarried people tends to be lower than for married people. While unmarried women tend to rate themselves as less happy than married women, unmarried men score the lowest (Bernard, 1982). Unmarried men also show more psychiatric symptoms and higher premature death rates than married men and all women. While this could be interpreted as proving that men need wives to keep them happy and healthy, it could also indicate that men with lower levels of mental or physical health are less likely to marry.

The presence of intimate relationships and the perception of social support are correlated with high levels of satisfaction for both unmarried and married people. Yet, we cannot assume that unmarried people lack intimate relationships. Many are more gregarious than married people and have a wide network of friends and acquaintances. However, there is still considerable pressure to marry even in later life, and well-meaning friends and relatives sometimes treat unmarried people as less fortunate and in need of assistance or matchmaking. These attitudes could reduce the life satisfaction of unmarried people.

By mid-life, many single people who wanted to marry have probably come to terms with their present situation and created a satisfying lifestyle outside the nuclear family. Marriage rates have declined in recent years and divorce rates remain relatively high. These factors make the single life more visible and probably create more tolerance toward alternative lifestyles by the general public.

Although most divorced people remarry, about one-quarter to one-third do not. Men are more likely than women both to remarry and to remarry soon after divorce. One reason for this is the fact that men are supposed to propose marriage and typically choose younger women. This often leaves older women without partners, and these women have fewer opportunities to meet potential husbands. The probability of remarriage tends to be higher for widowed than divorced women, and for younger rather than older women. In all cases, however, men's probability of remarriage is higher than women's, and men tend to remarry faster than women after divorce or the death of their spouse (Kuzel and Krishnan, 1973).

In studies of the probability of remarriage, we cannot discount the idea that middle-aged women who are divorced or widowed may prefer to remain unmarried. In *The Future of Marriage* (1982), Jessie Bernard argued that the experience of marriage varies for men and women and that marriage is more advantageous for men. When women marry, they usually take on more housework and child care, continue their paid jobs, and "look after" the social, emotional, and physical needs of their husbands. Men, on the other hand, rarely take as much responsibility for housework and child care, and seldom are as supportive to their wives as women are to men. Increasingly, men are not totally responsible for earning the family income, as most wives also work for pay. Bernard suggests that women are more frequently rejecting traditional marriage because it means taking on two full-time jobs.

In the male gay community, those who have permanent partners may pass through mid-life as heterosexual couples, except for the necessity to keep their personal situation discreet and without the presence of adolescent children. Unattached gay men, however, may be disadvantaged in the pursuit of casual sex, as so much emphasis seems to be placed on youth and physical attractiveness in the gay community. In a study of aging among gay men, however, Lee (1987) argues that the theory of accelerated gay aging is based on stereotypes and may pertain more to unattached men prior to gay liberation. He claims that the same factors influence life satisfaction for both gay and heterosexual men: perception of health and adequate income, higher educational levels, and meaningful relationships.

Some of the social pressure on homosexual adults may diminish with age, either because they have learned how to cope with it or because they have developed a network of friends with similar values and lifestyles. Furthermore, pressure to marry and bear children tends to lessen as homosexual people, especially women, pass the customary age of marriage and childbearing. Lesbian mothers who have experienced custody problems may find it easier to live their lives after their children have grown up. By mid-life, many single people have created alternatives to traditional family living that they feel are more satisfying, spontaneous, and sophisticated than the way most others live. Many feel that their present lives more than compensate for the absence of marriage and children, although some may regret that they did not marry and have a family of their own.

RETIREMENT AND OLDER COUPLES

At the time of retirement, a new division of labour may need to be established. If the woman never had an outside job, she may enjoy the companionship from her husband during the daytime. Yet, despite the fact that her husband is retired, the housewife continues to be responsible for domestic chores. While her retired husband may now share some of these tasks with her, he is unlikely to accept equal responsibility.

Furthermore, he may have more discretionary time and may disrupt her household routine.

If both were in the labour force, their household division of labour is more likely to have been egalitarian than a couple with complementary roles, yet a new division of labour still needs to be renegotiated. Wives are usually persuaded to retire when it is convenient and feasible for their husbands, however, and not when it is best for them (Atchley and Miller, 1983). This may mean that the wife may not be psychologically ready for retirement. Since fewer women work in jobs that include pension plan membership as a fringe benefit, the wife is also less likely to have a full pension when she retires.

Because most people marry and bear children, the majority of parents eventually become grandparents. Relationships with grandchildren seem to be particularly important to women rather than men, especially women without paid employment and those from lower-income families (Baker, 1988:23). Since each generation is having fewer children, the number of grandchildren will become fewer in the future.

In the later years, the marital relationship tends to become a greater source of satisfaction than during the middle years. Sharon Abu-Laban (1978) has compared the post-retirement family to recently married couples experiencing the honeymoon period. Both are times of relative leisure, a more egalitarian division of labour, and emotional intensity. In the honeymoon period, the relationship is new and exciting; in old age, the imminence of death means that each moment becomes important. Furthermore, communication problems have probably been worked out after many years of marriage, and the couple has developed some form of conflict resolution.

Because women usually outlive their husbands, most women must experience widowhood. The death of the husband often means a reduced income, moving from the family home, and increased dependence on their children, their grandchildren, and their widowed friends for companionship and advice. Most elderly people maintain their own households even after widowhood and choose to live independently from their children. The building of more seniors' apartments has assisted elderly people to maintain their independence and also provides a ready-made support group. The development of more home care programs may further enable more disabled elderly people to stay as long as they choose in their own homes.

The time may come, however, when elderly people require more assistance in their daily lives. They may need help with their finances, their housework, their home maintenance, or personal care. Coming to terms with failing health and dependence is difficult for most people, especially if they have also suffered the loss of their spouse and some of their friends. Yet, more elderly people today are able to maintain financial independence due to improvements in public pensions and community services for seniors. Furthermore, the growing percentage of elderly people in the population has given new credence to their concerns.

CONCLUSION

Throughout this century, family size has continued to decline as women bear fewer children and more parents separate and divorce. Most demographers project that declining birth rates will continue in the near future, because children are increasingly costly in modern urban environments. Furthermore, working in the labour force and caring for children in the evenings and on weekends is very tiring for parents, especially for mothers who perform most of this domestic work. People now expect to enjoy some time to themselves and are less willing to make major sacrifices for children than in previous generations.

Employers and governments could make it easier for parents to work and have children by allowing more generous maternity leaves and benefits, by developing parental leave so that either parent could take some time off to care for sick children or other family responsibilities, and by providing flexible work hours or shared work without loss of benefits. Governments and employers could also assist working parents by providing more child care spaces in neighbourhoods or in the workplace. Parents would then be relieved from the burden of transporting their children to and from day care centres that are often distanced from home and work.

Pronatal values, or values that encourage childbearing, were dominant during the 1950s. Yet, Canadians in the 1980s have been almost overwhelmed by negative publicity concerning family life. This has included detailed media coverage of child abuse, the high cost of raising children, the probabilities of birth defects after a certain age, and women's difficulties in juggling family life and job. After romanticizing family life in previous decades of research, we are now focusing on the negative aspects instead of simply presenting a more realistic picture of the satisfactions and the anxieties of being married and raising children.

Although Canadians are bearing fewer children and finishing childbearing at younger ages, their children are dependent on them longer than in previous decades because of greater educational requirements and the high cost of living. While this prolonged dependency could lead to more companionate relationships between parents and their adult children, it could also encourage adolescent rebellion and cause parents to be caught between the demands of two generations: their aging parents and their children.

Marital relationships tend to vary in strength throughout the life cycle and appear to be stronger in old age than in middle age. In fact, several studies have found that satisfaction tends to peak at the beginning of marriage, to decline in the middle years, and to rise again after retirement (Rollins and Feldman, 1970; Lupri and Frideres, 1981). While earlier research suggested that most couples reported lower levels of life satisfaction when their children were adolescents, more recent research indicates that the difference in reported satisfaction does not vary much throughout the family life cycle (Scanzoni and Scanzoni, 1988:532). Higher rates of divorce, however, might have eliminated some older couples from recent studies of marital satisfaction. With continuing high rates of separation and divorce, some people in middle age leave unhappy marriages and establish a new life in another relationship. Yet, these new relationships do not always improve life satisfaction, as we will see in Chapter Nine.

Because of rising life expectancies, young people often anticipate a more active old age than their parents' generation. With the aging of the baby boom generation, there will certainly be a larger proportion of elderly in the future who could acquire the political power to demand improved housing, pensions, health services, and consumer services. On the other hand, a continuing low birth rate will mean that fewer children will be available to assist frail elderly. Consequently, formal support services or friends might take over some of the support presently offered by adult children.

DISCUSSION QUESTIONS

1. Why are there fewer single people in the population now compared to 1901?
2. What criteria do parents use in selecting mates for their children in countries with arranged marriages?
3. Why is romantic love considered to be a poor basis for marriage in many societies?
4. Discuss four theories of mate selection in societies where young people choose their own mates. Do you think that one theory explains mate selection better than the others?
5. What do we mean by the "mating gradient"?
6. Look through the "companions" advertisements in a daily newspaper in your region. Why would people need to advertise for a partner?
7. What factors affect the decision of whether or not to marry, and the timing of marriage?
8. How has the experience of childbirth changed over the past century?
9. Do the husbands of working wives share the housework with their wives any more than the husbands of housewives? Why or why not?
10. What factors are causing couples to delay childbearing or to decide to remain childless?
11. What are some potential social or legal problems relating to surrogate parenting?
12. Why did Jessie Bernard, in *The Future of Marriage* (1982), conclude that marriage was more beneficial to men than to women?

chapter four

Economic Conditions and Family Structures

INTRODUCTION

Although we often talk about the traditional family, suggesting that there has been a single family form that remained the same throughout most of our history, a variety of family structures and practices have always existed. Moreover, families have changed significantly over time.

Writing in the seventeenth century about Quebec's Montagnais society, Jesuit Paul Le Jeune complained that "the young people do not think that they can persevere in the state of matrimony with a bad wife or a bad husband. . . . They wish to be free and to be able to divorce the consort if they do not love each other" (quoted in Leacock, 1986:12). He objected as well to their acceptance of sexual freedom after marriage (Leacock, 1986:11). But divorce and open marriages were not the only seemingly modern practices that were evident from the earliest period of European settlement in Canada. Lone-parent families headed by women were not uncommon, especially among the native women who had married "a la façon du pays" to fur traders who returned to Europe, or among the European women married to men who went to seek furs. Nor were blended families – ones based on a second marriage and involving children from more than one marriage – uncommon, given the high death and remarriage rates. And many women and men avoided marriage entirely, lived communally, and took vows as nuns or priests.

While variations in family forms have existed throughout Canadian history, the frequency, acceptability, structure, and meaning of the variations have changed significantly over time. These changes reflect the complex interaction of economic conditions, ideas, biology, technology, and collective actions. Consequently, family experiences vary not only with historical periods and from country to country, but also with region, ethnicity, and class. And they are different for women and men.

This chapter examines the recent and dramatic developments in the economy, in women's labour force participation, in fertility, and in mortality patterns that have marked the transformation of the structures, activities, and meanings of family life in Canada. It begins with a brief examination of the economy because it is assumed that what happens in the market sets the conditions for, but does not determine, what happens in households. Women's movement into the market has reflected emerging household requirements at the same time as it has influenced these requirements. Similarly, declining fertility rates are both cause and product of women's movement into the market, and they, too, have an impact on family life as well as on the market. As more people survive through the early years and live well into old age, both households and economy are affected. In the process, marriage patterns have been altered. So have the laws related to the establishment and dissolution of families.

In tracing these developments, this chapter also presents some comparisons with Australia. It is, of course, most common to compare Canada to our closest neighbour, the United States. While it is true that the American economy and the American culture have a profound influence on structures and practices in Canada, it is also the case that there are very important differences between the countries that often disappear in texts that focus on the United States. The United States had a revolutionary break with Britain; it is a leading world economic power that depends on resources from countries such as Canada; it has a much more limited social support system and fewer restraints on some aspects of private enterprise; it has a higher poverty rate, a higher female labour force participation rate, and a higher divorce rate. In many ways, Canada shares at least as much with Australia as it does with the United States. Like Canada, Australia has a huge land mass, few people, a British colonial past, and a resource extraction-based, foreign-dominated economy. It has had, however, a different history of collective action and state legislation. The contrast between Canada and Australia is designed to illustrate how the two economies have encouraged similar patterns and how collective strategies have created somewhat different results.

ECONOMIC CONDITIONS

The economies of Australia and Canada have been restructured since the Second World War. While some jobs have disappeared, others have been created. New products, technologies, and services have been introduced. Old means of satisfying needs have been eliminated. These developing economic trends have produced new conditions for family life and have in turn been influenced by emerging patterns within households. Since the 1970s, deteriorating economies in both countries have placed additional pressures on family structures and relationships.

The economic boom that followed the war was characterized by the growth of giant, mainly foreign-owned corporations and by the virtual disappearance of small, family-owned enterprises. The family farm and the family store became memories in most areas of Canada and Australia. As they entered the 1980s, few people worked together as a family in order to acquire the necessities of life, and few lived in rural areas. Contrary to much popular myth, Australia and Canada are now highly urbanized and suburbanized countries.

The economic boom also created new urban jobs and helped keep unemployment low; so did union successes in winning better job security, vacation, work hours, and pensions. Demands from unions and other groups contributed as well to the expansion of state programs for health care and education, for welfare and unemployment insurance, for family allowances and pensions, and to the reduction of the standard work week to forty hours. These developments also helped to maintain relatively full male employment. The combination of income security programs, low unemployment, and rising real wages contributed to the high family consumption levels. Reflecting these trends, jobs in health, welfare, and education and in clerical and sales work grew dramatically while the standard of living rose. The demand for female workers increased, as did the demand for workers with many years of formal education. Taxes also increased, as the state extended both regulation and services.

In Canada, differences in rates of unionization, in provincial governments, and in resources meant that the benefits from this economic boom were not evenly distributed across regions, ethnic or racial groups, and classes. Lower minimum wages for women, along with the sex segregation of work, meant that rewards were not equally distributed between the sexes. Nevertheless, most Canadians experienced improved material conditions and better educational and employment opportunities for several decades after the war. In Australia, the boom created similar tendencies, although there were some important differences. Because half of Australian workers, compared to a third of Canadian workers, were unionized, and because many wage settlements were applied nationally, differences were smaller among industries and regions. However, state sanction of a family wage, which set minimum male pay at what was argued to be sufficient to support a man and his family, helped keep women out of the labour force and helped to maintain large pay differences between women and men.

Seeking to increase sales and to maintain wartime production levels, companies introduced a wide array of new products, appliances, and services in the years following the war. Cake mixes and other partially prepared or frozen foods appeared for the first time, often at prices that made them cheaper to purchase than the raw materials required to make their equivalents at home. Automatic dishwashers, clothes dryers and washing machines, no-iron fabrics, self-polishing floors, oil and gas furnaces, and power lawn mowers became available on the market. Fast-food restaurants multiplied, as did dental services and television programs. Post-secondary educational institutions offering specialized training appeared overnight. New contraceptive techniques were developed, and the rapid expansion of medical technology encouraged the growth of hospital-based health care.

Many of these "luxuries" rapidly became necessities as their usefulness was demonstrated and as their alternatives disappeared. For example, Canadian winters and regulations restricting clothes lines mean that few people are willing or able to forgo the use of a clothes dryer. Television not only provides a less expensive alternative to many forms of entertainment, it also disseminates enormous amounts of information, much of which is now assumed by teachers. Consequently, those without access to television are often left behind in school. Once medical technologies and specialized educational institutions are developed, they become integral parts of the system. Automatically regulated gas or oil furnaces have become essential in Canadian households, because wood and coal are no longer delivered to the door and because they are much more convenient than constantly stoking a stove. With rising real incomes, households were able to purchase many of these new goods and services, in the process abandoning many of the alternatives and losing many of the required skills.

But by the end of the 1960s, there were clear signs that the boom was coming to an end. Seeking to reduce costs, employers introduced more technology and used more part-time workers. Unemployment rates began to rise significantly in the mid-1950s, and they continued to grow. "Before 1958, postwar unemployment never reached 5.0 percent; since 1970, it has never been that low" (Armstrong, 1979:70). Although Australian unemployment rates grew later and more slowly than those in Canada, they followed a similar, if less rapid, progression. Prices, too, continued to rise and to rise more quickly than wages. The largest increases were in loan and mortgage rates, in housing and heating prices, in taxes and in transportation costs. There are few alternatives to these goods and services, they are difficult to do without, and they have to be paid for in cash. Like the benefits from the boom, the losses from the developing recession have not been evenly distributed across regions, ethnic and racial groups, classes, or sexes, but few people in either Canada or Australia escaped feeling the pinch.

FEMALE LABOUR FORCE PARTICIPATION

These developments in the economy have set the stage for rising female labour force participation rates. More than four out of five people in both Canada and Australia are classified as belonging to families. For most of them, the family represents an economic collective, even if the economic resources are not evenly distributed or equally controlled (see Dulude, 1984; Edwards, 1981). In the 1950s, the majority of families depended on income received by the male "breadwinner" in order to purchase most of their market goods and services (Armstrong and Armstrong, 1984:Table 23). By the 1980s, this was the pattern in only a minority of households. A mere 16 percent of Canadian families had a husband as the sole income recipient in 1982 (Statistics Canada, 1985:64), while in the previous year, 22.5 percent of Australian families had one adult income earner, one adult not in the labour force, and some children at home (Institute of Family Studies, 1985:4). The trend away from what is often referred to as the traditional family continues. In 1986, only 20.2 percent of Australian families conformed to this old ideal (calculated from Australian Bureau of Statistics, 1986:25). Canadian figures for the following year indicate that 12.1 percent of women in families had an employed husband, children under sixteen, and no labour force attachment (calculated from Statistics Canada, 1987c:Table 61A).

The cause of this fundamental change in the family's economic base was, of course, the massive movement of married women into the labour force. With the boom still evident in the early 1960s, only 17 percent of married Australian women and 21 percent of their Canadian counterparts were in the labour force. By 1986, 48 percent of married Australian women and 55 percent of married Canadian women were counted as having a paid job or actively searching for one (Australian Bureau of Statistics, 1986:23; Statistics Canada, 1986a:Table 56). In recent years, even women with small children have been entering or staying in the market. Forty percent of Australian women with preschool children (calculated from Australian Bureau of Statistics, 1986:26) and almost 60 percent of the Canadian mothers with children under five were participating in the labour force by 1987 (calculated from Statistics Canada, 1987c:Table 61A).

Women responded to the rising demand for female workers primarily because their families needed the income. Few of the new goods and services that were becoming increasingly necessary could be produced by women working at home, and women's possibilities for making money within the household or of reducing family need for income were declining. With inflation and rising unemployment, their economic needs became even more pressing. Research in both countries has demonstrated the consistent link between husband's income and wife's labour force participation, concluding that "the wives of men earning below or about average weekly earnings have a higher labour force attachment than the wives of men with higher earned incomes" (O'Laughlin and Cass, 1984:5). As one married woman explained: "All of a sudden . . . you found your husband's pay cheque wasn't adequate. Especially when the family was younger, there was always so many things they needed. When the necessities became hard to come by,

MILLER COMSTOCK INC.

By 1986, 48 percent of married Australian women and 55 percent of married Canadian women were in the labour force.

then you knew that you had to go out to help" (Armstrong and Armstrong, 1983:36–37). Women married to men in higher income groups have also been entering the labour force, but the Australian research indicates that such women are more likely to work part-time or intermittently and when attractive jobs are available. At the same time, economic pressure pushes other women to take any job and to take full-time employment if possible (O'Laughlin and Cass, 1984).

New domestic technology and products not only increased the need for cash income in most households, especially as wages failed to keep up with prices; they also made domestic work both easier and more boring. Some women responded by raising their standards and by undertaking other complex tasks in the home. For many, it became more possible and more desirable to leave their homes in search of a paid job.

At the same time, more accessible higher education and the increasing demand for workers with more years of formal training encouraged women to stay longer in school. With more education, women had more employment opportunities and different attitudes about remaining in the home to do domestic work. Males, too, were staying in school longer. As a result of prolonged formal education, children of both sexes were spending more years as dependants in their parental homes, increasing the economic pressures on their families and making it necessary for many mothers to take paid work.

Different rates of female labour force participation in Australia and Canada may be primarily explained by differences in wage rates and male unemployment levels. In Australia, strong unions representing the majority of workers helped maintain the purchasing power of male wages for a longer period of time. The economic boom lasted longer in Australia as well, ensuring more men had stable employment. Male attitudes may also be a factor in varying female labour force participation rates. It has been argued that Australian men display "suspicion, hostility and fear of women who step out of an essentially domestic role" (quoted in Dixson, 1976:22). But other research suggests that men's attitudes toward their wives working in the labour force depend more on family need than on traditional values (Brewer, 1983:10).

DOMESTIC WORK

Although a growing number of women are working outside the home, and although new technology has helped reduce the domestic workload, there is still a large amount of work to be done in the home, and it is still mainly done by women. Most of the personal service work for the majority of Canadians and Australians is performed within the domestic sphere. An Australian study published in the early 1980s found that the "average homemaker spent 69 hours per week 'on the job' of which 38 were spent devoted to housework and 31 hours to childcare" (Gowland, 1983:36). The amounts of work done by women working full-time in the home varied little with family income or with women's education. In Canada, Meg Luxton found that housewives averaged twenty-eight hours a week in food preparation alone (1980:Table 153). When women take on a second job in the market, they reduce their hours of domestic work by working faster when they are at home, by doing some chores less often, and by purchasing more goods and services. But Canadian women with paid work still spend an average of four hours a day providing child care, doing housework or household maintenance tasks, and shopping, even when they also work for pay in the market (Statistics Canada, 1985:Table 20).

While 70 percent of Canadians and 85 percent of Australians think men should help with the housework, men in both countries have increased their contribution only slightly as more of their wives enter the work force and as male hours spent in paid employment decline (Gowland, 1983:42; Boyd, 1984:39, Table 3). One Canadian study found that in families with children, husbands' contributions to regular housework increased by an hour a week when their wives obtained paid employment (Meissner et al., 1975:436). Another study reported that the total time men devoted to child care, housework, household maintenance, and shopping averaged about half as much as their employed spouses (Statistics Canada, 1985: Table 20). A third study found that wives do three times as much domestic work as their husbands. "In families where the wife has a part-time job, this ratio is approximately 5 to 1, and it increases to 6.7 to 1 when the wife is employed full-time" (Michelson, 1985:65). Husbands are helping more with household chores, especially with the more enjoyable tasks related to child care, but they are not equally sharing the burden of domestic work (Luxton, 1983).

Women's responsibility for domestic work reinforces, and is reinforced by, their segregation in the market. In both countries, the majority of women do clerical, sales, or service work, and more than a quarter of them have only part-time jobs, mainly in these fields (Armstrong and Armstrong, 1984:Table 5:15; Eccles, 1984:Table 5.4). As Table 4.1 indicates, over 70 percent of employed women in Canada and Australia do what has been defined as traditional female work. Table 4.2 shows the significant difference

Table 4.1 Distribution of Employed Women, Selected Occupations, Canada and Australia, 1986

Occupations[1]	% of All Female Workers	
	Canada	Australia
Clerical	30.9	32.6
Service	17.7	12.7[2]
Sales	9.7	14.9
Medicine and Health	9.1	7.2
Teaching	6.3	7.2

Note: 1. These occupational categories are not precisely comparable due to the different definitions of occupations used in each country.
2. Included in this category are those classified as personal service workers, cleaners and miscellaneous labourers and related workers. The numbers probably underestimate those who would be counted as service workers if Canadian definitions were used.

Source: Calculated from Australian Bureau of Statistics, *Labour Statistics of Australia* (Canberra: Australian Government Publishing Service, 1986), Table 3.8 and from Statistics Canada, *The Labour Force* (Ottawa: Supply and Services Canada, 1986), Table 71.

Table 4.2 Part-time Employment by Sex, Canada and Australia, 1986

Sex	% Part-time	
	Canada	Australia
Females	26.5	38.9
Males	7.8	6.6

Note: Some of the differences between the figures from Canada and Australia may be attributed to somewhat different definitions of part-time employment.

Source: Calculated from Australian Bureau of Statistics, *Labour Statistics of Australia* (Canberra: Australian Government Publishing Service, 1986), Table 2:13 and from Statistics Canada, *The Labour Force* (Ottawa: Supply and Services Canada, 1986), Table 82.

between the sexes in terms of part-time employment. Segregated into low-paying, frequently part-time jobs, women do not earn as much as men even when they are doing similar work. In 1987, women in Canada were paid just over 60 percent of what men received, although women employed full-time were paid 66 percent of what men were earning. In Australia, the gap is significantly smaller, with women paid just over 80 percent of the male wage (Burton, 1987:xii). The smaller gap reflects both the abandonment, under pressure from women's groups, of the family wage policy in the early 1970s and the higher rate of unionization that made equal pay agreements more effective than the equal pay legislation in Canada. Only a quarter of Canadian women are unionized. However, as Table 4.3 indicates, the women who are unionized receive significantly higher wages than those who are not.

Table 4.3 Average Weekly Occupational Earnings for Women Employed During the Year, Canada, 1986

Occupation	Union Job	Non-union	Total
Managerial & Professional	$459	$349	$399
Clerical	353	248	277
Sales	265	192	198
Service	277	153	175
Primary Occupations	390	206	223
Processing, etc.	331	237	271
Construction	523	–	319
Transportation	361	204	243
Materials Handling, etc.	354	236	269

Source: Statistics Canada, *Canada's Women: A Profile of Their 1986 Labour Market Experience* (Ottawa: Supply and Services Canada, 1988), Table 20. Reproduced with permission of the Minister of Supply and Services Canada, 1989.

IMPLICATIONS FOR EQUALITY

The combination of higher male wages, female segregation, and traditional attitudes toward men's labour force work means that men's jobs in the market take precedence over those of women. When families have to decide who will leave the market in order to care for children or elderly relatives, to handle emergencies, or to do the regular domestic work, they usually choose to forgo the earnings of the person with the lowest wage and least interesting work.

Although the number of house-husbands may be growing slightly, Australian research indicates that this practice "is confined to professional couples drawing good salaries. In keeping with the majority of decisions about dual-working in lower income families the need to guarantee economic sufficiency is paramount" (Brewer, 1983:7). Canadian research also suggests that few men interrupt their paid work in order to fulfil domestic responsibilities or in order to accommodate a partner's job (Burch, 1985:26). However, Bassett's (1985) research indicates that a quarter of the Canadian women who have highly paid careers would not relocate in order to accommodate their husband's job and that an increasing number of their spouses would not move unless their wives could find employment in the same location.

Women's access to any wage does mean some increase in power. As two incomes become more and more necessary, women's paid jobs must also be taken into account. Moreover, women with paid work seem to be healthier and happier than other women. Eichler (1988:214) concludes that "all indications are that in terms of mental health, self-esteem, and marital happiness wives with paying jobs fare better than house-wives."

Acquiring a wage often means acquiring more power and more assistance in the household, but lower female wages help ensure that domestic labour and domestic power are still not equally shared. Some women do manage household finances, but this is most likely to happen in low-income households where there are few choices to be made about paying relatively fixed expenses. In households with higher incomes where there are more financial decisions to make, husbands tend to manage the money if their wives do not have paid work. When wives in such families are employed, "either a joint management system or an independent system" is more likely, but it should be remembered that these wives very often have relatively high professional salaries (Edwards, 1984:151).

Lower female wages, combined with women's domestic responsibilities and the limited public support for child care services (see Task Force on Child Care, 1986), also mean that women usually "have a greater financial stake in marriage than do men" (Ehrenreich, 1984:8). Those Canadian mothers without access to a male wage have a one in two chance of being poor. "More than half of single-parent families led by women – 56.0 percent or 233,000 – had incomes below the poverty line" in 1986 (National Council of Welfare, 1988:32). Although the risk of poverty for families headed by women was somewhat less in 1986 than it was in 1980, and although the reverse is true for male-headed families, the poverty rate for lone-parent women remains very high and continues to be much higher than the rate for men (National Council of Welfare, 1988:41). In Australia, as well, the number of female-headed lone-parent families has

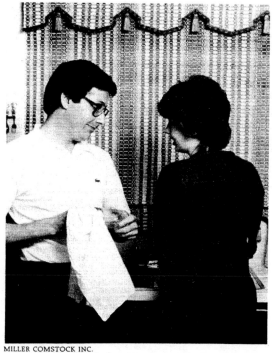

Acquiring a wage often means acquiring more power and more assistance in the household, but lower female wages help ensure that domestic labour and domestic power are still not equally shared.

MILLER COMSTOCK INC.

been growing, and they "are the family type most likely to be suffering economic deprivation" (Institute of Family Studies, 1985:11). However, Australian government programs in the early 1980s helped keep the proportion of such families living below the poverty line lower than the proportion of lone-parent families in Canada who live below the poverty line (Institute of Family Studies, 1985:14).

Although women's low wages make them more financially dependent on marriage, falling real wages and rising unemployment have forced many men to rely more on female earnings. Estimates in both countries suggest that poverty in husband-wife families would have increased by at least 50 percent if women had not entered the labour force (National Council of Welfare, 1979:Table 3; Edwards, quoted in Cass, 1984:10). Between 1971 and 1981, the income of Canadian wives "was the significant factor in preventing family income from declining in real dollars," and family economic resources continue to deteriorate. "By 1979–81, increases in wives' income were no longer able to offset the decline in husbands' average income" (Pryor, 1984:102). Reflecting these changes, poverty among couples with children has been rising sharply in both countries during the 1980s (Institute of Family Studies, 1985:14; National Council of Welfare, 1985:18). At the other end of the scale, the real economic gains made by some women and their marriage to men with professional or managerial jobs have helped to at least maintain the position of high-income families and to ensure that inflation does not reduce their purchasing power (Rashid, 1986).

MARRIAGE RATES

Rising female participation in the labour force and in higher education has done more than shift the economic base and the allocation of power and tasks within households. It has also contributed to changing patterns in age at first marriage. While in 1971 close to two-thirds of Australian women between the ages of twenty and twenty-four had been married, less than half of this age group had been married by 1981 (Institute of Family Studies, 1985:5). In Canada, the 1984 average age of brides and grooms who were marrying for the first time was twenty-five and twenty-seven respectively, a full year older than the average age recorded for both sexes in 1971 (Statistics Canada, 1985:Table 8).

Rising female labour force participation may also have contributed to the greater decline in female than in male marriage rates. With jobs, women have more choice about marrying. In 1980, the Canadian marriage rate was 9 per 1,000; by 1986, it had dropped to 6.9 (Statistics Canada, 1988:35). The number of marriages registered in Australia declined steadily throughout the 1980s, dropping from 44,088 in 1982 to 39,548 in 1987 (Australian Bureau of Statistics, 1988:2). Similar patterns appear in Canada. The decline in marriage rates reflects both the increase in the number of couples living together without marrying and the smaller number of people in the age group most likely to marry. The decline for both sexes may also reflect the growing scepticism about the benefits or stability of marriage and the increasing possibility of purchasing many of the services previously provided mainly in the home (see Breton, 1984). The greater decline in female marriage rates reflects the higher proportion of men who do not remarry after divorce.

FERTILITY PATTERNS

Rising female labour force participation is related as well to declining fertility rates. While participation rates have been going up, fertility rates have been going down. "Canadians now have fewer children, later in their lives and more may choose to forgo parenthood altogether" (Romanuic, 1984:7). Similar patterns appear in Australia. In both countries, most families now have only one or two children. Most mothers are in their mid-twenties when their first child is born, and if they have a second child, it is usually born before the mother is thirty. There has been a slight increase in the fertility rates for women in their early thirties, however. As we moved into the 1980s, 15 percent of Canadian families had never had children (Statistics Canada, 1985:4), and it seems likely that 20 percent of the Australian women born in the 1950s will remain childless (Institute of Family Studies, 1985:7). While more unmarried Canadian women are having babies, the fertility rates in Australia for unmarried women have been declining slightly (Cass, 1983:178). But in both countries, the number of children born outside marriage remains small and does little to make up for the decreasing numbers of children born within marriages (Romanuic, 1984:60).

"It is well documented that there is an inverse relationship between female educational attainment, labour force participation and occupational status, on the one hand, and fertility, on the other" (Romanuic, 1984:66). The evidence indicates that general economic conditions influence fertility rates as well. During the Great Depression of the 1930s, for example, birth rates in many areas matched those of the 1980s. Although it is clear that all these factors play a part in determining whether or not women have children and how many they have, their relative importance is difficult to determine.

THE HIGH COST OF CHILDREN

At the same time as more and more women have been moving into the labour force, the time and money involved in rearing children has been steadily increasing. According to one estimate, a single child will cost, in 1986 Canadian dollars, more than $115,000 before reaching age eighteen. Sending that child to a local university for four years would add at least another $6,800 in books and tuition alone (Clayton and Swift, 1986:182). Two children would cost nearly a quarter of a million dollars to support through graduation, at a time when average yearly income for one-earner families was $34,460 and for two-earner families was $44,840 (Task Force on Child Care, 1986:13).

Raising children puts severe economic pressure on most families in both countries. Australian data indicate that "individual provision for children's needs results in the significant impoverishment of families at the lower levels of the income distribution, significant impoverishment of families excluded from the labour market, significant impoverishment for single-parent, mother-headed families and significant impoverishment for children who live in families" (Cass, Keens, and Wyndham, 1983:34). In Canada, "families with children have experienced a substantial increase in poverty in the mid-1980s although childcare costs have of course not been the only factor involved in this increase" (National Council of Welfare, 1985:18). Although young families with children were more likely to be poor than they were in 1980, the poverty rate has declined somewhat in recent years for families headed by persons aged thirty-five to sixty-four (National Council of Welfare, 1988:35).

Moreover, children's economic dependency in both countries has increased not only with lengthening periods of schooling, but also with continuing high rates of youth unemployment. It is much more difficult for children to help pay their own way when summer jobs are scarce and costs are rising. Furthermore, it is difficult for them to leave or stay away from home when unemployment is high or rents are exorbitant and state support through welfare or unemployment insurance is low or inaccessible. An Australian survey conducted in 1981 found that a high proportion of young people frequently returned home for economic reasons (Institute of Family Studies, 1985:6). In Canada, more than half of the children between twenty and twenty-four and a tenth of those twenty-five and over were living in their parents' homes in 1985 (Burch, 1985:22). While in both countries children are now more likely to leave home and live independently before they marry, this does not necessarily mean that they are no longer a financial burden. Especially those who are continuing their education may still be receiving money from home.

Not only do modern children cost more money, they take more time. Fewer children do not necessarily mean less work. Researchers in Canada and Australia have documented the rapid growth of professional advice on child rearing and the emergence of a new emphasis on the crucial nature of parenting (Reiger, 1985; Strong-Boag, 1982), as we will discuss in Chapter Six. As early as the 1920s, women were counselled to devote more time, energy, and skill to mothering (McLaren and McLaren, 1986:27). In recent years, the pressure has intensified with the proliferation of child care manuals, advice columns, and professional services, and with the rising educational attainment levels of women. Child care is becoming more time consuming as well, with more complicated educational programs and after-school activities. Older children spend six hours a day for about two hundred days a year in school, but the increasingly complex demands children face in learning about everything from computers to AIDS are often brought home for parents to handle. While older children at home may require less physical care and may even help with the household chores, the tensions resulting from their struggles for independence may require enormous amounts of time and energy.

Although most experts agree that child care requires dedication and a wide range of resources, little public support has been provided for this job (see page 80). Canadian and Australian governments assume that children are primarily the responsibility of families and that the state should support children only when they are handicapped, when they have broken the law, or when families have clearly demonstrated economic need (see Task Force on Child Care, 1986; Sweeney, 1983). In both countries, very few men are allowed to take leave from their labour force jobs in order to stay home with their children. While most employed women in these two countries are eligible for brief maternity leaves, such leave merely provides time for women to recover physically from childbirth, and does not provide time to offer continuing care for children. While not attending school, most Australian and Canadian children spend at least some time each week being cared for by someone other than their mother, but only a small proportion of this care is provided in publicly funded or supervised centres. In Canada, a couple with two young children could in 1984 "expect to pay approximately $6,970 for full-day licensed child care" (Task Force on Child Care, 1986:15), if they could find space in such a centre. In 1988, the cost of infant care in a licensed space was $5,419 a year in Ontario. Not surprisingly, given the shortage and expense of child care facilities as well as the emphasis on the value of family care, the majority of families make do with relatives or neighbours and juggle their work hours to provide care at home. The result, all too often, is exhausted and less than high quality care in or out of the home and high levels of tension between parents (Johnson, 1986; Johnson and Abramovitch, 1986).

The problems related to the time demands of raising children are often particularly acute for female-headed lone-parent households. Although such families do receive some state support for child care services and other economic needs, it is seldom enough. In both Canada and Australia, one-parent families headed by women are the fastest growing family type, and they are also the family type facing a dramatic decline in their economic status (Institute of Family Studies, 1985:11). These women have no husbands to share the daily parenting tasks. While state subsidies for day care help when the children are young, there is little public support for substitute care at other times, and little money to purchase it.

FOR INTEREST

DAY-CARE WORKER TURNOVER HIGH BECAUSE OF POOR PAY

By Laurie Monsebraaten

Day-care centres hire staff according to the number of children they serve.

Provincial licensing requirements say there must be one worker for every three infants or five toddlers or eight pre-schoolers.

But chronically low wages mean worker turnover is high and keeping qualified staff is tough.

A day-care worker in Metro earns from $18,000 to $26,000, while a kindergarten teacher earns between $24,000 and $45,000.

Hiring day-care workers with two-year college degrees in early childhood education is half the battle, says Valerie McInnis, supervisor of the Birchcliff Heights day care centre in Scarborough.

If a centre is lucky enough to get staff to work for those wages, the next hurdle is finding families who can afford to pay fees.

If families take their children out of day care because of rising cost, or new children don't replace those who graduate, centres are forced to lay off those staff members they fought so hard to find.

"It's a Catch-22 situation. We try to stay open to provide the service, but the cost of the service is beyond most family's ability to pay," says McInnis, whose centre is licensed for 32 children but has only 24 kids.

"What we need are more subsidies."

Source: *The Toronto Star*, April 9, 1989. Reprinted with permission.

In spite of women's rising labour force participation and the increasing amount of time spent with others, and perhaps because of the limited public support for child care, mothers are still the primary caregivers for young children. Moreover, men continue to play a major role in shaping their children's lives. Indeed, this influence may be growing as offspring remain in and dependent upon the parental home for more and more years. As in earlier decades, family income in particular is "a major determinant in life-chances of the next generation" (Brewer, 1983:7), and children are still learning many of their basic values and skills at home.

CONTRACEPTIVES AND SEXUAL RELATIONSHIPS

Of course, even if the rising costs and time demands of child rearing and the growth in female labour force participation are encouraging people to have fewer children, the reduction in fertility would have been more difficult to accomplish without relatively easy access to birth control techniques. Birth rates began to decline in Canada well before public pressure from doctors, women's groups, and the obvious widespread contravention of the law forced the 1969 changes in the Canadian Criminal Code that ended the ban on the advertising and sale of contraceptives. Birth rates had even started to drop before the pill became generally available on the market in the early 1960s (McLaren and McLaren, 1986:134). However, now that information on birth control is readily available in both countries, contraceptive methods not requiring a prescription can be easily purchased in pharmacies, the state offers some financial support for family planning, and legal abortions are possible for broadly defined health reasons, it is much easier for women and men to reduce the number of unplanned pregnancies. While a 1968 Canadian survey found that 16 percent of couples had an unintended child, a 1971 study uncovered only 11 percent, and when the study was repeated in 1976, only 7 percent reported unintended births (reported in Romanuic, 1984:61). Increasingly, couples are deciding that one or two children complete their families. Many are having tubal ligations and vasectomies, in most cases permanently ending the possibilities for more pregnancies (McLaren and McLaren, 1986:134).

Because contraceptives cost money and take time and information to master, birth control is not equally available to all groups, however. In Canada and Australia, the data indicate that poverty tends to increase with the number of children, or put another way, the poor are likely to have more unplanned children (Institute of Family Studies, 1985:14; National Council of Welfare, 1985:18-19). Education also makes a difference. The "number of unplanned pregnancies among married women declines as their level of schooling increases" (Breton, 1984:5). Cutbacks in state funding underway in both countries and attacks on abortion legislation may make the distribution of birth control even more unequal.

Improved birth control techniques and better access to them have done more than help reduce fertility rates. They have also contributed to changing sexual practices and attitudes. Better access to birth control may be a factor in the increasing number of Australian and Canadian couples who live together without a formal marriage. Between 1981 and 1986, the number of couples in Canada living together without being married increased by 37 percent, compared to a 2.7 percent increase in the number of married couples over the same period. As the Australian National Population Inquiry points out, "de facto unions are usually associated with effective contraception and therefore, with no children or with a very small family" (reported in Cass, 1983:178). A 1982 Australian study indicated that as many as 40 percent of Australian couples had lived together before marriage (reported in Institute of Family Studies, 1985:7). Research in Canada found that about a sixth of both women and men had been involved in non-marital cohabitation by 1984 (Burch, 1985:13).

But it should not be assumed that cohabitation necessarily means a rejection of marriage. Although in 1981 over three-quarters of the Australian young people interviewed thought it was acceptable to live together without marrying, about 90 percent of them expected to marry at some time (reported in Institute of Family Studies, 1985:7). In Canada, "common-law partnerships are as much a prelude to marriage as a substitute for it." A quarter of ever-married young men and a fifth of the women reported that they married a live-in companion (Burch, 1985:15). Birth control allows both women and men to discover whether or not they are sexually and socially compatible before they commit themselves to marriage or children. In addition to trying out marriage, couples also live together without formalizing the relationship because their marital or economic situation prevents them from taking this legal step even though they define the relationship as a permanent one (see Fels, 1981:34-38).

It is difficult to tell whether or not better access to birth control encourages more short-term, extramarital sexual relationships or discourages marriage based on the desire for more sex. Indeed, it is difficult to determine whether or not extramarital sexual activities have increased. There may simply be a greater willingness to discuss sexual activity today. As Breton (1984:6) points out in his study of marriage markets, however, "the more efficient the birth control devices, the lower the price that would have to be paid for unfaithfulness." On the other hand, better contraceptives may induce some women to marry because they have greater control over pregnancies (Breton, 1984:6). While better birth control may encourage some people to avoid marriage altogether and others to have a variety of sexual partners, it necessarily provides women with more choices in all areas; for "when contraception is inefficient, the terms of trade ruling in the marriage market for the various services traded in that market are likely to be unfavourable to women." However, women's choices in the marriage market are likely to increase "with improvements in birth control technology" (Breton, 1984:6).

In helping to separate sexual relationships from reproduction, contraceptives not only allow more sex outside marriage, they also help make sex within marriage more possible and pleasurable. Fewer couples need practise abstention as a means of avoiding an unwanted mouth to feed and personality to nurture; more women can enjoy sexual intercourse without fearing an undesired pregnancy. In her study of three generations of Canadian women, Luxton (1980:61) found that older women "described sex as a duty a

MILLER COMSTOCK INC.

In helping to separate sexual relationships from reproduction, contraceptives not only allow more sex outside marriage, but also help make sex within marriage more possible and pleasurable.

woman is obliged to provide for her man," while younger women "described a considerably wider range of sexual activities." Here, too, there are class and sex differences, however. Women with high levels of formal education have better access both to contraceptives and to information on their sexual functioning. They may therefore have improved possibilities for a satisfying sexual relationship. However, women continue to bear the greater burden of responsibility in spite of better birth control. Many of the working-class women Luxton (1980:59) interviewed are "ignorant about their own sexual needs and are terrified of getting pregnant," while new attitudes push them to "become more active, take the initiative and either have orgasms or fake them, still mostly to satisfy men" (Luxton, 1980:63).

That sexual relationships constitute an integral and central aspect of marriage even with more accessible contraceptives is demonstrated by the large number of divorce petitions that are justified on the grounds of sexual transgression or incompatibility (see McKie, Prentice, and Reed, 1983:133). For the Canadian state, a sexual relationship is an essential ingredient of a legal marriage: "A persistent and unjustified refusal of sexual relations by one spouse may constitute 'cruelty' as a basis for divorce" (Kronby, 1986:21). When a woman allows a man to stay overnight, it may be used as the basis for withdrawal of state support payments, on the assumption that this practice indicates the existence of a form of common-law relationship.

The fear of exposure to AIDS may be transforming sexual relationships in and out of marriage. Various surveys reported in the popular press suggest that some people are becoming more cautious about selecting and changing sex partners. Monogamous relationships may become an increasingly attractive way of avoiding the syndrome (see Statistics Canada, 1988c:2-5).

At the same time as female labour force participation rates have been rising, better birth control has become more accessible and the costs of raising children have been growing. So too has the time required for each child. As more women enter the labour force, they have less time and energy to devote to children, and they are receiving little extra help from the state or from men. This is particularly the case for the growing number of women who parent alone. Values have also been changing. Couples want to give each child more and to avoid the negative consequences of large families. Women want more choices in their lives. With birth control, both men and women have more choices, not only about children, but also about marriage. Their attitudes related to sex are changing. Not surprisingly, birth rates have been falling and sex outside marriage has become more acceptable. In spite of these developments, however, most women and men still marry, most have at least one child, most of these children receive a significant amount of their early care from their parents, most are raised in the homes of their biological parents, and sexual relationships continue to constitute an important ingredient in the marriage bond.

COMPANIONSHIP

Rising female labour force participation rates are related as well to changing patterns of non-sexual relationships in families. As more women enter the market, the possibilities both for more tension and for more egalitarian, companionate relationships increase.

Comparing generations, Luxton (1980:52) found that women's household load had lightened and men's hours in paid work had decreased, leaving them more time to devote to each other and to their children. Describing their marriages as partnerships, women "seemed to share more activities with their husbands and they expect to be 'friends' with them." Affection was more visibly demonstrated and problems more openly discussed. With women increasingly entering the labour force, they also share more of the financial burden of supporting the family and more of the experiences of going out to work for pay. Women's employment may ease economic pressures on the households as well. In addition, their income may make more leisure activities, domestic technology, and substitutes for domestic labour possible, thereby freeing time for more pleasurable family pursuits.

Increasing longevity and declining birth rates also create conditions that may encourage more companionate marital relationships. Research in Australia suggests that couples now may spend several years adjusting to each other's habits, setting up house, travelling, and experimenting with different lifestyles and division of tasks before they have their first child (Richards, 1985:134). During this period, the economic pressures on the family are often not extremely heavy, especially when there are two full-time salaries coming into the household.

With pregnancies more likely to be planned, gestation and birth may also contribute to the feeling of partnership. Fathers increasingly are participating in childbirth classes and attending the birth. In her study of Australian-born, once-married, and largely middle-class families, Richards (1985:134) found that pregnancy "was almost unanimously remembered as bringing the couple closer together," and for some, childbirth "was also a significant experience, drawing them again closer." Child rearing, too, may offer many opportunities for shared pleasure. With fewer children, parents may have more leisure to watch together their child take that first step, score the first goal, fall in love for the first time. As children move through adolescence and young adulthood, they may not only allow parents more time together, but also provide some companionship for them as well.

Moreover, as couples have fewer children born closer together and as people in both Australia and Canada live well into old age, there are more and more years spent together as a couple after the children have become independent. Even if children born to mothers who are thirty and fathers who are thirty-three stay home until they are twenty-five, parents still have a good twenty years to live together without the social and economic pressures of parenting and often with more free time from work once their position in the market is firmly established. Unlike past generations, they have many years to enjoy the pleasures of grandparenting. Retirement, common at age sixty-five in both countries, permits couples to spend even more time together and with their grandchildren.

Increasing female labour force participation and fewer children may also mean that both women and men are freer to leave tension-filled marriages. The children, as a result, may grow up with more complicated lifestyles, but in less tension-ridden homes.

STRESS

On the other hand, these processes may increase stress levels within the household and make companionship and more egalitarian relationships difficult to attain. Tension from work is often brought home and may explode into violence against spouses and children. As Chapter Twelve indicates, the reported cases of violence (within families) against women, children, and the elderly have been rising steadily in recent years. It is difficult to tell whether or not this reflects an actual increase or mainly the greater public awareness resulting from efforts of the women's movement to expose it and provide alternatives. Nevertheless, it is clear that far too many families are not havens in a heartless world (see Guberman and Wolfe, 1985; Windschuttle, 1980).

When women enter the market, they have two jobs to perform, less energy to handle the stress created by others, and little help in managing their own stress. Sheer exhaustion may push women to demand assistance with household tasks, while male attitudes, lack of training, and tension from their paid work may push men to resist. Even before children arrive, the division of tasks may create problems. One Canadian study revealed that, for newlyweds, issues related to responsibility for housework were a major cause of disputes (reference in Proulx, 1978:13). Low female wages also mean that, in many families, women's wages do little to relieve economic pressures or to provide domestic appliances or substitutes for domestic chores.

The tension and fatigue created by work in and out of the home may also mean couples are too tired or upset for sex (Luxton, 1980). Moreover, couples may juggle their paid work time in order to accommodate child care and in the process eliminate time for each other. Interviewed for a Canadian study of working families, one woman explained that her "husband works evenings, from 5 p.m. until 1:30 or 2 a.m. My work hours are from 7 a.m. until 4 p.m. We avoid child care expenses and it gives the kids enough time to spend with both parents" – but, it could be added, little time for parents alone (Johnson, 1986:18). A Melbourne study revealed that "decisions to do shift work were often made so that one of the parents could always care for the children," making it much more difficult for the entire family to spend time together at core periods during the day or week (reported in Brewer, 1983:25).

While Richards (1985:134) found that pregnancy often brought Australian couples closer together, the early years of parenting are by many "remembered as one of maximum strain." Time and financial demands increase, often when economic resources decline with women withdrawing from the labour force or reducing their paid work hours. It is still common in both countries for women to drop out of the labour force in order to care for young children because many want to be the primary caregiver, because many cannot afford or find quality alternative care, because it only makes sense for the person with the lowest salary to withdraw from paid work, or because maternity leave is only available for a short period of time to women. But for a substantial number of the women who do quit paid work, "it is a shattering experience, bitterly remembered, to be home by yourself with a very young child" (Richards, 1985:134). Moreover, it often means that housework becomes more their responsibility. For the growing number of women who either cannot or do not want to stay home with their child, the price in the overwhelming majority of cases is the taking on of two jobs, competing demands, often guilt, and certainly fatigue.

As a woman in Richards's study explained, the problem "doesn't stop there, it goes on" (1985:286). Children growing up may also be a major source of strain and cause of disputes. In addition to the usual struggles caused by children testing their indepen-dence, tensions generated by an uncertain social and economic situation "are expressed through conflicts between mothers and their children" (Luxton, 1980:87). Fathers, too, may find their knowledge and authority challenged. And, although the children leaving home may reduce these conflicts, they may leave behind parents who find they have little in common except their children.

The growing number of single-parent households face additional tensions. Time management often has to accommodate two families and two sets of relationships. Economic pressures are frequently more severe as well.

Although retirement offers greater freedom and leisure for couples to spend time with each other and their children, in both Australia and Canada it all too often means poverty, ill health, and dependency. In both countries, poverty among the elderly has not been increasing in recent years, due largely to state support programs. However, the "elderly unattached still run a very high risk of being poor," and one in ten elderly families still lives below the poverty line. Moreover, elderly women are twice as likely as elderly men to be poor (National Council of Welfare, 1988). In Australia, 9 percent of the aged income units were counted as very poor in 1981–82 (Cass, 1983:17). Poverty increases tensions in these households, which are at the same time coping with the strain caused by adjusting to new retirement patterns and ill health. Poverty in old age also frequently means dependency on others and a loss of dignity, another source of strain.

"Although Australia is reputed to have one of the highest rates of institutional care in the world, 55 percent more elderly people live with adult children than in nursing homes or other institutions" (Kinnear and Graycar, 1983:77). Those living outside of institutions also frequently require additional help from families. A survey conducted by Statistics Canada indicates that one in five of the people aged fifty-five years or over living outside institutions "have trouble with or are unable to do heavy housework" (1987b:175). State cutbacks in Australia and Canada are placing increasing pressure on younger families to bear the responsibility for their elderly parents. Research in both countries (Heller, 1986; Kinnear and Graycar, 1983) indicates that family care means care by women. Married to men often much older than themselves, outliving men by several years, women frequently face many years caring for sick husbands and then have no one to look after them in their widowhood. When elderly parents of either spouse move in, it is the women who take on the extra load. Both the work and the changed social relationships may cause rising tensions, as children and grandparents spend too much time together and as dependency relations are reversed. The situation is further exacerbated by rising female participation rates, which leave women with less and less time or energy to do the work.

Finally, continuing unemployment and the threat of unemployment may place additional pressures on families, inhibiting the maintenance of companionable partner-ships. A Canadian study concludes that men without jobs feel "that their unemployment has taxed their relationships within the family – particularly the marital relationship. Relationships with parents and in-laws are also placed under strain as a result of paternal unemployment and the resulting shifts in roles and responsibilities within families" (Johnson and Abramovitch, 1986:ii). For some couples with a strong initial relationship, there may be benefits from additional time together. For most, however, the result is often conflict. Given men's higher wages, male unemployment means a drastic decline in living standards. It also often means poor health not only for the men, but also for their families who must live under increased stress and reduced incomes. As one unemployed Australian father of three explained to researchers: "My wife and I have never argued before, but lately we don't seem to do anything else. There's a lot of tension because we're worried about the kids. They've got hardly any clothing left" (Windschuttle, 1980:80). According to Australian investigations, domestic violence and divorce accompany high levels of unemployment (Windschuttle, 1980:81).

Women's unemployment may affect family tranquillity as well, particularly in the many households where women's income is essential to family survival. This may be the case not only in female-headed lone-parent households and in those that hover around the poverty line, but also in families that have committed themselves to monthly payments on houses and cars. Without the second income, the family's entire way of life may be under threat. Moreover, women suffer from stress and depression with job loss as well, placing additional strains on family relationships.

Both tensions and possibilities for closer family relationships arise with different phases in family development, with marriage breakdown, and with changing economic conditions. Rising female labour force participation, falling fertility rates, and increasing longevity have helped to reduce some strains and to lower tensions in some households while exacerbating them in others. In most households, the benefits and strains have been different for women and men.

MILLER COMSTOCK INC.

Rising female labour force participation, falling fertility rates, and increasing longevity have helped reduce some strains and lower tensions in some households while exacerbating them in others.

MARRIAGE AND THE LAW

In both countries, changes in the law related to marriage have reflected and influenced the changing patterns of female–male and parent–child relationships. In Canada, Judge Abella (1985:13) has pointed out that the basis of the law has "shifted from the need to preserve marriages to the need to preserve families – serially if necessary. It has come from a recognition that saving a marriage may in fact be destroying members of the family." As Chapter Ten indicates, there has been a movement away from assigning fault in marriage breakdown and from distinguishing between children born in or out of wedlock. At the same time, there has been a movement toward equalizing rights and responsibilities within marriage. Both countries have made marital rape and violence punishable under the law.

Under the various provincial statutes that cover marriages in Canada, spouses now have a mutual obligation of financial support, a shared responsibility for children, the right to cohabit and to expect a sexual relationship (Kronby, 1986:21). According to the Australian federal law that governs marriages, men and women have equal rights and responsibilities in maintenance, in child custody, and in living as well as in sexual arrangements (Scutt, 1983:237). As a result of pressure from feminists in both countries, a woman's economic contribution through her work as mother and homemaker is recognized as equal to the contribution made by a man working outside the home. Generally, in Canadian marriages "each spouse is entitled to do what she or he wants with the property she or he personally acquires." Exceptions include "two sorts of provisions: those intended to protect the spouse's future rights and those enacted to protect the matrimonial home" (Dulude, 1984:13). Assets acquired in the marriage are shared. Similarly, in Australian law, property purchased with personal earnings or other money coming to that person alone is individually controlled, while family assets are equally shared. This legislation based on the assumption of spousal independence and equality is, however, not equally beneficial to women and men.

Although new divorce laws in Canada and Australia are also based on a laudable principle, that is, the assumption that both spouses are "equally innocent victims," they too have different, and unequal, consequences for each sex. According to the 1981 amendments to the Australian Family Law Act, the only ground for divorce is "irretrievable breakdown of marriage." The main requirement is that the couple live apart for a year. Custody may be awarded to either parent or may be granted to both jointly (Morgan, 1984:61). Economic need is a major factor in the list that the law provides to guide judges in the determination of maintenance. As of June 1986, Canada has a very similar law. The federal Divorce Act "establishes only one ground for divorce: marriage breakdown, which arises as a result of adultery, cruelty or separation for a period of one year" (Kronby, 1986:xiii). Custody is now based on the doctrine of "best interest" of the child (Abella, 1985:170). In both laws, there is a new emphasis on self-sufficiency.

When Canada in 1968 and Australia in 1975 introduced the first legislation to broaden grounds for divorce, the annual divorce rate jumped dramatically as many people rushed to leave marriages that had long ceased to function. But divorce rates have not been growing significantly in recent years, although Canadian rates did rise in 1986, as will be discussed in Chapter Nine. Estimates in both countries suggest that two out of five marriages may end in divorce (Institute of Family Studies, 1985:9; McKie, Prentice, and Reed, 1983:60), but only "about one in ten of ever-married Canadian males and about one in eight of ever-married females have had a legal marriage end in divorce" (Burch, 1985:ii). In other words, predictions indicate high divorce rates, while in practice the overwhelming majority of Canadians and Australians stay married to the same person throughout their lives.

As Scutt (1983:239) has pointed out for Australia, in the new laws women "are viewed as responsible to the same degree as men for their own upkeep and for that of their children, yet are not granted the social and economic equality that would allow them to fulfill that responsibility." Or as Abella (1985:15) has said of the Canadian legislation: "It is hard to be an independent equal when one is not equally able to become independent." It is men who have higher earnings that permit them to acquire the personal property described in the law. It is women who have the children. When marriages break up, women in both countries suffer severe economic setbacks. Women's setbacks are more severe than those faced by men because women usually have custody of the children, because support payments are usually very low and are often not paid at all, and because women's employment opportunities are more restricted as a result of the segregation in the market and of women's child-rearing responsibilities now and in the past. Perhaps because they do not have custody of the children and because they are left in a better financial position, men in both countries are more likely than women to remarry after divorce.

FOR INTEREST

RIGHT OF GAYS TO BE FAMILY UNIT CARRIES OBLIGATIONS, ACTIVISTS SAY

By Ann Rauhala

Homosexual couples must accept that, along with their newly recognized right to be treated as a family unit, they could acquire the same obligations as heterosexual couples – such as child support, alimony and "palimony," gay activists say.

A tribunal of the Canadian Human Rights Commission ruled last week that the Treasury Board discriminated against a civil servant when it denied him bereavement leave to attend the funeral of his male partner's father. It said gay couples may constitute a family and the couple, who have a long-standing relationship,

had been discriminated against on the basis of family status.

Les McAfee, executive director of Equality for Gays and Lesbians Everywhere, said he was thrilled with last week's decision, but he said gay couples will have to assume increasing obligations.

"There's a flip side to this that the gay and lesbian community will have to come to terms with," he said in a telephone interview from EGALE's Ottawa headquarters. "For every benefit, there's a responsibility. What gay couples have to do if they identify themselves as a couple is take on responsibilities – palimony suits, child care and child support – the same way heterosexual couples would."

Lesbian couples who had a child by artificial insemination, for example, could find themselves in dispute over support payments or custody orders.

The tribunal did not explicitly say that same-gender couples should be treated as spouses.

But Max Yalden, chief commissioner of the human rights body, said the ruling may have cleared the way for future decisions. "We may be heading for a time when the courts will be asked whether two people of the same sex will be in a spousal relationship – and that will have far-reaching implications."

Married and common-law heterosexual couples enjoy a wide range of potential advantages that gay couples do not receive – tax breaks, employment perks, parental and family leave and medical and pension benefits.

Jim Egan, a pensioner who is challenging the Old Age Security Act under the Charter of Rights and Freedoms, said gays and lesbians contribute to these programs through tax dollars.

"The dinosaurs on the back benches say we want special treatment. There is nothing special being asked for. What's being asked for is equal treatment."

Mr. Egan, who lives in Courtney, B.C., is trying to obtain spousal pension benefits for John Nesbit, his partner of 41 years. When one member of a married or common-law couple turns 65, his or her spouse may receive spousal benefits provided he or she is 60 and has an income of $16,000 or less.

The act, however, defines spouse as a member of the opposite sex and the couple will argue that the definition violates the Charter.

Karen Andrews, a Toronto lesbian, is waging a similar battle to obtain family coverage for her partner and her partner's children under the Ontario Health Insurance Plan. She is appealing an Ontario Supreme Court ruling that legally a spouse is someone of the opposite sex.

The Canadian Human Rights Act does not explicitly prohibit discrimination on the basis of sexual orientation, but the human rights codes of Ontario, Quebec, Manitoba and the Northwest Territories do.

Source: *The Globe and Mail*, April 19, 1989.   **Reprinted With Permission of The Globe and mail.**

With the increasing number of couples living together without going through an official marriage ceremony, "all Canadian jurisdictions have adopted measures that deal expressly with common-law spouses." If they conform to the criteria established in the various provincial laws, common-law spouses qualify for many of the same rights and responsibilities as a married couple (Boivin, 1985:181). In Yukon and in four provinces, the distinction between legitimate and illegitimate children has been abolished, and in all provinces children born to unmarried women have some right to support from their parents (Boivin, 1985:181). In Australia, children of common-law marriages are legally in the sole custody of their mother, although there is now some protection for women whose common-law marriages break up. Children born out of wedlock have full rights (Morgan, 1984:61). Although there is a more visible presence in both countries of homosexual unions, neither country legally recognizes such relationships or permits same-sex marriages. In Canada, however, a tribunal of the Canadian Human Rights Commission ruled in April 1989 that a gay couple may constitute a family (see page 89).

Laws in both countries have changed along with the emergence of a new economic reality and new family structures. Provisions reflect the growing economic strength of women, the avoidance by some of the legal marriage tie, and the large number of marriages that end in divorce. They both assume and legislate equality; however, while women have pushed for and benefited from these changes, the results still frequently favour men.

CONCLUSION

As always, economic conditions, family structures, family values, and the marital system are changing. Female labour force participation rates have been rising, fertility rates have been falling, and both women and men are living well into old age. Marriage and childbirth are being delayed. Fewer people are marrying, more are divorcing and living together without formalizing the union. Extramarital sexual relationships and homosexual unions are more openly practised. Children are living longer in parental homes before they marry. As a consequence of some of these changes and of women's greater longevity, there are a growing number of single-person households. Divorce and separation also mean that more people of both sexes, but especially women, parent alone. Remarriage at the same time means a growing number of blended families.

However, the overwhelming majority of Australians and Canadians marry; increasing longevity means most stay married to the same person for much longer than ever before because they live longer; most have at least one child, and raise that child for many years in their homes. The predominant pattern is one of marriage in the mid-twenties, with women marrying men a few years older than themselves, of children born a couple of years later, and of childbirth completed by the time the woman turns thirty. While women are increasingly staying in the job market throughout their childbearing years, the scarcity of public and private support as well as preference means that a high proportion drop out of the market or take part-time work in order to care for their children. This pattern, the continuing segregation of the market, women's and men's training, skills, and values combine to ensure that women bear primary responsibility for domestic work and take a secondary place in the labour force. As a result of this inequality and the failure of the state or men to provide adequate support, lone-parenting for women often means poverty.

After partners nurture their children through the early years, adolescence, and young adulthood, they often still have many years together as an employed and then as a retired couple. Longevity makes grandparenting more possible; in the absence of adequate pensions, it also makes poverty more likely. And because most women outlive men and marry men who are older, widowhood is almost inevitable.

Significant class differences remain and may be exacerbated by women's labour force participation. Women's wages have, however, been the major factor in keeping even more couples out of poverty. Rising female labour force participation has also increased women's strength, allowing them to demand more rights and choices in and out of marriage. It has, in addition, helped couples abandon unhappy marriages and has encouraged women to expose abuse. It should be noted, however, that the majority of women are not abused by their spouses, and men have had to make many adjustments, too, as more and more women enter the market.

Few of these patterns are new, except perhaps for the growing number of retired couples and single-person households, and these patterns may reflect more a restructuring than an abandonment of marriage and family life. Their meanings and consequences are, however, constantly changing. While marital systems and economic conditions are very similar in Australia and Canada, differences reflecting human choices and actions remain.

DISCUSSION QUESTIONS

1. Do declining marriage rates necessarily mean a rejection of parental values?
2. What factors could contribute to lower female labour force participation rates in Australia?
3. What are the consequences of university-age children remaining in the parental home?
4. Do modern appliances and services eliminate housework?
5. Who should take the primary responsibility for children, and why?
6. Why do women "have a greater financial stake in marriage than do men"?
7. Will AIDS help eliminate the double standard that now applies to female and male sexual practices?
8. Does "living together" mean couples reject marriage?
9. Does the fact that most women now have paying jobs mean that most marriages are egalitarian?
10. Why are unattached elderly people more likely than others to live in poverty?

chapter five

Alternatives to Traditional Marriage

INTRODUCTION

"Although most persons still marry, have children, live in single-family households, prefer heterosexuality, and wish for permanence and sexual exclusivity, increasing numbers choose other lifestyles at some point in their lives, and even more acknowledge the right of others to do so" (Macklin, 1987:342). The nature of family life and the living arrangements experienced by those born in the 1970s will be very different from the experiences of their parents or grandparents. A typical twenty-year-old woman today reaches sexual maturity earlier, stays in school longer, marries later, has a smaller family later in life, retires earlier, and lives longer than her grandmother. When this young woman marries, both she and her husband will be gainfully employed. Approximately 40 percent of the marriages of this generation will end in divorce after an average of nine years. During the course of their lives, those now in their twenties will experience many different family arrangements. They will likely spend part of their adult lives living singly, cohabiting, being married, or living as single parents, and may also experiment with some sort of communal living or joint property ownership. If estimates are correct, 10 percent are homosexual, although part of this group will marry and some will become parents. In certain cases, living arrangements will represent active choices. Others will simply find themselves in situations that are more or less to their liking, and these arrangements may be short or long term.

The distinction between households (defined as people who live together under the same roof) and families has become blurred with the rising incidence of single living, cohabitation, and reconstituted families created by remarriage, and there is as much variation among household types as between them. Shifts in household and family composition have been accompanied by more tolerant attitudes to what have been called alternative lifestyles.

In different ways, the protest movements of the 1960s and the human potential movement of the 1970s contributed to an atmosphere conducive to experimentation with what have been described as alternate lifestyles (Chilman, 1983). According to one American pollster (Yankelovich, 1981:39), as many as 80 percent of Americans were involved in a search for self-fulfilment in the 1970s, and 17 percent of these were deeply committed to the search. While these people did not invent the alternatives, the duty-to-self culture (to use Yankelovich's term) encouraged involvement by more people than ever before. But as Chilman (1983) points out, we do not know the extent to which these movements accompanied the economic prosperity of the period and will die with it. On the other hand, demographic evidence makes it clear that alternative lifestyles, both in and outside of marriage, are well established.

Two other important social changes in the 1970s had an impact on family life. The first was the rapid movement of women, particularly mothers of young children, into the labour force. At the same time, the women's movement began to give voice to growing concerns about sexual inequality. Across the country, grass-roots organizations developed to meet women's needs, and umbrella organizations such as the National Action Committee on the Status of Women worked to document and publicize issues and to lobby for legislative changes. Public opinion polls and attitude surveys document the extent to which attitudes to women, especially women's family roles, responded to these two changes (see Boyd, 1984).

Although attitudes have become more liberal, and non-traditional family arrangements more accepted, most Canadians marry and most become parents. Certainly, social and religious customs dictate that marriage is an important event for the individual and a fundamental part of our social structure. Most Canadians, whether happily married or not, continue to believe in the ideal of monogamous marriage. Married people generally define themselves as happier than unmarrieds, although young married women increasingly voice frustration about the difficulties of combining employment and family responsibilities. Most young people anticipate marriage positively. In Baker's (1985) study of Canadian adolescents, 75 percent of the girls and 64 percent of the boys expected to be married by age thirty. Most expected to marry eventually, although some thought they might live alone or cohabit first.

The benchmark implied by the phrases "non-traditional family arrangements" or "alternate lifestyles" is the nuclear family. When we refer to the traditional family, we usually envision a husband, wife, and children living in the same place. In the 1950s, variant family forms were described by social scientists as deviant. In the 1960s and 1970s, with the impetus of the human potential movement, sociologists began to think of non-conformists as living alternate lifestyles, while continuing to identify marriage as the ideal and the norm. Now it seems more fruitful to assume that throughout adult life we will move in and out of various living arrangements, all of which will be perfectly "normal" to us at that point in our lives.

The traditional literature on the family has not given us the framework to consider alternate lifestyles in this light. Eichler (1988) has criticized the literature on the family as suffering from four pervasive biases, one of which is the monolithic bias. This bias "expresses itself in a tendency to treat the family as a monolithic structure and in an emphasis on uniformity of experience and universality of structure and functions rather than on diversity of experience, structures, and functions" (Eichler, 1988:1–2). We do not have a systematic model of intimacy that encompasses alternatives to marriage.

In this discussion of alternatives to marriage and the nuclear family, the following points should be emphasized. First, most of us will at some point in our lives live in one or more of the situations discussed. In other words, all household arrangements (including marriage) vary in permanence and duration. Second, none of the alternatives can be treated homogeneously. Singles, for example, are not one but many groups: old, young, never married, previously married, gay, and heterosexual. For this reason, any categorization of non-traditional families, including the one used in this chapter, is problematic. Third, although some people have always lived in non-traditional family relationships, attitude changes in recent years have paved the way for more freedom of choice and more openness about relationships. Clearly, for women there are more opportunities to make active choices concerning education, employment, marriages, and childbearing than was ever the case before. Women can choose to postpone or reject marriage, childbearing, or both. Some choose marriage without children, some choose children without marriage. Nevertheless, we cannot assume that life circumstances necessarily reflect life choices. As Epstein (1974:650) pointed out, to suppose that people do things because they want to is a peculiarly American bias in sociology. Current living arrangements are often consequences of other life events (e.g., divorce) and so do not necessarily reflect an active choice on the part of individuals. Finally, the sociological interest in non-traditional households and families has little to do with the numbers of people involved. About 2 percent of the population is involved in swinging, and yet swinging has received lots of media and academic attention. Twice as many couples have celibate marriages, yet these have received very little research attention. (In Canada, 4 percent of married men and 2.7 percent of married women have never had coitus (Eichler, 1988:16-17).)

ALTERNATIVES TO MARRIAGE

This section describes several alternatives to marriage: singlehood, cohabitation, and homosexuality. Statistically, the largest group is singles.

SINGLE LIVING

Because approximately 90 percent of North Americans marry at least once, we tend to think of singles as a relatively small group. But if we add to the never-married group those who are widowed, separated, or divorced, the single population becomes a substantial and growing one. In 1986, 27 percent of Canadians over age fifteen were single. Another 3 percent were married and separated; 4 percent were divorced; and 6 percent were widowed. In other words, 40 percent of Canadians over fifteen were *unmarried.* In 1981, the unmarried category included 41.3 percent of women in this age group and 37.9 percent of men (Harrison, 1981). These figures are similar to corresponding ones for the United States, where about 34 percent of men and 40 percent of women were unmarried in 1980 (Macklin, 1987).

Two demographic trends have led to an increased number of singles in the

Table 5.1   Probability of Marrying for Never-married Men and Women, by
Age, 1971, 1976, and 1981

	Men 1971	1976	1981	Women 1971	1976	1981
At age			%			
15	95.3	92.7	89.1	95.1	92.8	89.7
20	94.9	92.3	88.2	93.3	90.8	88.1
25	88.1	85.2	81.7	79.6	77.8	75.0
30	70.6	68.7	63.8	58.3	57.3	52.2
35	51.0	50.4	44.1	37.2	39.4	33.4
40	36.3	35.5	29.1	27.0	25.8	21.5
45	25.4	24.9	20.0	17.6	17.2	13.9

Source: D. Nagnur and O. Adams, "Tying the Knot: An Overview of Marriage Rates in Canada," *Canadian Social Trends* (Autumn 1987):5. Reproduced with permission.

population: later age at first marriage and high divorce rates. The age of first marriage has increased in the last two decades as it has become more common for young people to live apart from family of orientation before marriage. There seems to be an increased willingness for men and women to postpone marriage to get an education or establish a

Two demographic trends have led to an increased number of singles in the population: later age at first marriage and high divorce rates.

MILLER COMSTOCK INC.

career. The longer young adults postpone marriage, the more likely they are to remain single for life. "There was only a 52% probability that a 30-year-old never-married (Canadian) woman in 1981 would eventually marry, while the probability for a woman aged 35 was just 33%. For never married men, the probability of marrying was 64% for those aged 30 in 1981 and 44% for those aged 35" (Nagnur and Adams, 1987:5).

The unmarried population varies by age and sex in predictable ways. Because women marry men older than themselves (and also live longer), there are more young single men. However, the proportion of singles in the total population and the male–female differences decline with each age cohort. Older unmarried women far outnumber men. *Hypergamy*, or the tendency for women to marry older (and higher-status) men, has important implications for the growth of the single population (see below).

Highly educated women marry less, later, and divorce more frequently than their less well educated counterparts. Better-educated men marry earlier and stay married longer. That women marry older men who are more highly educated than themselves leaves two groups of unmarrieds: the better-educated and more highly skilled women and the poorly skilled and unskilled men. "The result . . . is that never married men tend to be 'bottom of the barrel' and the women 'cream of the crop' " (Bernard, 1972:36).

FOR INTEREST

THE "REAL" MARRIAGE SQUEEZE

Typically, young women marry men who are two to three years older than themselves. In later life the age differences may be as great as ten to twenty years. According to Veevers (1988) the norm of hypergamy (the tendency for women to marry older men) is the most important factor influencing mate selection for mid-life men and women. Veevers referred to this as the *"real" marriage squeeze*. Using Canadian census data, Veevers calculated an *availability index** to determine how much discrepancy exists, and how much it increases with age. She defined the availability index as "the number of eligible persons of the opposite sex potentially available for every 100 unmarried persons" (p. 176).

Although young women have a slightly larger "pool of eligibles" from which to select marriage partners, men are favoured from mid-life to old age.

At age 20 marriage norms predict that there will be 46 available unmarried women for every 100 unmarried men and 104 available men for 100 unmarried women (see Figure 5.1). At age 30 availability indices are approximately equal: 75 for men and 73 for women. From age 40 on, the index favours unmarried men. By age 70 there are only 20 available men for every 100 unmarried women compared to 261 available women. As Veevers points out, the index has not considered cohabitors, homosexuals, or others including religious celibates or vol-

*Veevers's availability index was based on an assessment of the age range of potential eligibles (defined as the age range within which 80 percent of all marriages occur for each age) and a "fair share" ratio that takes into account competition for available spouses by individuals of various ages (see Veevers, 1988:176–81).

untary singles who do not desire marriage. We could assume that cohabitation
and voluntary singlehood will have a
roughly equal effect on the availability
index for men and women. On the other
hand, since it is estimated that there are
more male than female homosexuals in
the population, the availability index for
women would be further reduced if the
influence of this group were measured.

What are the implications of these
imbalances? Veevers predicts the following outcomes: an increase in the proportion of singles and in ideologies supporting single living, increased divorce, an

increase in the number of female-headed
households, more out-of-wedlock births,
and greater female independence. She
also expects to find definitions of eligible
mates broadening (i.e., women marrying
younger men), greater innovation in mate
selection, including marriage bureaus,
and an increased acceptance of man-
sharing (p. 185). However, within marriage, ''what is involved in the 'real'
marriage squeeze is a *reaffirmation of
the double standard*'' (p. 186; emphasis
in original). In mid-life, men have more
power in relationships because there are
so many available women.

Figure 5.1

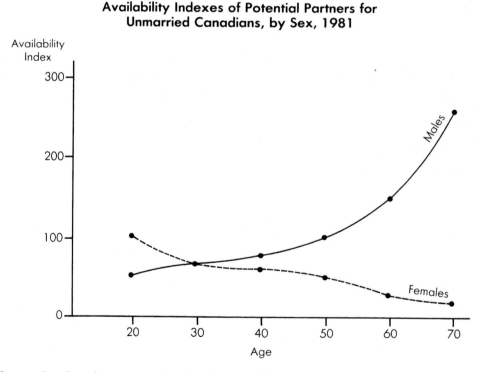

**Availability Indexes of Potential Partners for
Unmarried Canadians, by Sex, 1981**

Source: Based on data presented in Jean Veevers, "The 'Real' Marriage Squeeze," *Sociological
Perspectives* 31, no. 2 (1988): 169–89.

Attitudes to Single Living

Historically, attacks against unmarried women "have ranged from aspersion and mockery to deliberate genocide, including the burning and torturing of millions of widows and spinsters during the witch persecutions of the fifteenth, sixteenth and seventeenth centuries in Europe, and the practice of suttee on widows in India" (Rich, 1980:635). More subtle mechanisms of social control have encouraged marriage in North America, although as recently as 1957, four out of five Americans described never-married individuals as neurotic, selfish, and immoral (Shostak, 1987:366). Single living has always had more negative connotations for women than for men, which may explain why single men over thirty describe themselves as happier than their female counter-parts (Shostak, 1987:258). Two Australian researchers asked respondents to complete the sentence "I think of single women as . . . ." More than half of their sample used pejorative terms such as "spinsters" or "old maids" in their descriptions. Men were far more likely than women to characterize single women negatively (Stolk and Brotherton, 1981). In a study of single women in Ontario, Peters (1983) found that 64 percent of the sample felt that there was a greater stigma for single females than for single males.

While marriage continues to be an important life goal, there is evidence that single living is becoming more accepted and that young people who choose to remain single may find support for their choice. Thornton and Freedman (1982) asked eighteen year olds and their mothers a number of questions about married and single living. Neither group saw marriage as necessarily preferable to remaining single. Both mothers and their children "considered the decision to marry or remain single as a real and legitimate choice between acceptable alternatives."

Not all people who remain single have necessarily chosen this alternative. Shostak (1987:356) categorized singles as falling into one of four groups: *ambivalents, wishfuls, resolveds,* and *regretfuls. Ambivalents* are typically younger men and women "who are temporarily postponing marriage in favor of the pursuit of higher education, career building, self-development and the like." Some in this group may be cohabiting. *Wishfuls* prefer marriage and hope to marry soon. *Resolveds* have chosen singlehood over marriage. While this group includes priests and nuns, and some single parents, it is mostly made up of people who live alone by choice. Some were previously married. *Regretfuls* include people who did not marry, but for whom marriage was a desirable option. The largest proportion of this group are mid-life women, caught in what Veevers referred to as the "real marriage squeeze." While this typology may describe many singles, it does not capture the life events that led women described in the following study to remain unmarried.

When Allen and Pickett (1987) interviewed single women who entered adulthood during the Great Depression, they found that most did not choose single status. Many were only or oldest daughters whose responsibilities to their families of orientation took precedence over other choices. While most of their cohort married, these women remained at home, where their incomes or their care-giving was needed. They cared for aging parents, or for the children of siblings. For these women, the close ties to their family of orientation continued throughout their lives. Far from controlling their own destinies, the lives of these women were "shaped by influences of historical circum-stances, social class, family composition and gender" (Allen and Pickett, 1987:523).

The number of singles in the population has increased in part because of an older age at first marriage and increased marital breakdown. For some, single living is a transition stage; for others, it is a chosen lifestyle. Increasingly, attitudes have become more accepting of those who choose single living. Other factors that affect the increased acceptance of single living include changing sexual mores; safe, available birth control; more opportunities for intimacy; and an increased number of singles' apartments, clubs, and vacation options. The pressure to marry decreases as the facilities and services for singles increase.

For women, having a choice about single versus married life may depend more on financial considerations than attitudes or services. Increases in female labour force participation mean that more women have the financial opportunity to live independently. Nevertheless, women with full-time, well-paid, secure jobs are a minority. Most women work in sectors of the economy characterized by part-time, part-year employment, low security, or low pay.

UNMARRIED COHABITATION

Unmarried cohabitation has not been as widely accepted or practised in Canada or the United States as it has been in some other societies. However, fourfold increases since 1970 (Glick, 1984) in the United States and similar increases in Canada indicate that, here too, cohabitation is becoming an accepted prelude to marriage. In Scandinavia, it is quite customary for couples to live together and often parent before making the decision to marry. In Sweden, an estimated 19 to 20 percent of *all* couples cohabiting in 1980 were unmarried. Estimates for 1975 suggest that *all* persons married and under thirty years of age had cohabited before their marriages (Trost, 1981). For Swedish couples, the marriage ceremony is a *rite of confirmation*, rather than a *rite of transition* (Lewin, 1982).

In 1981, the Canadian census counted cohabiting relationships for the first time. In addition, a 1984 Labour Force Survey asked 14,000 respondents about their marital histories, including previous cohabiting relationships. The 1986 census found 487,000 common-law partnerships – 8 percent of all couples (Turcotte, 1988:35). This was a dramatic increase over five years. In 1981, 350,000 unmarried couples constituted 6 percent of all husband-wife families (McKie, 1986:40). Most people living in common-law unions are young, and the tendency to live together rather than marry declines with age. Sixty percent of couples aged fifteen to nineteen were in common-law unions. This drops to 30 percent for twenty to twenty-four year olds, and declines in each successive age group. However, as Table 5.2 shows, the increased tendency to live in common-law relationships holds across all age groups, including those over sixty-five. The proportion of married Canadians has declined as the proportion cohabiting has increased (Turcotte, 1988:36).

Because cohabitation is not usually a permanent alternative to marriage, the number of couples who have *ever* cohabited is far greater than the number currently living together. The 1984 Family History Survey found 16.5 percent of adult Canadians *had ever* lived in a marriage-like relationship. Twenty-two percent of those born between 1960 and 1964 had ever cohabited, compared to only 1 percent of those born before 1940 (McKie, 1986:40).

Table 5.2   Common-law Partners as a Percentage of All Persons Living as Couples, by Age Group, 1981 and 1986

Age group	1981	1986
15–19	49.5	59.6
20–24	23.1	32.9
25–29	11.3	16.6
30–34	6.8	10.3
35–39	5.1	7.4
40–44	3.9	5.9
45–49	3.0	4.5
50–54	2.4	3.5
55–59	1.8	2.6
60–64	1.5	2.1
65 and over	1.0	1.5
Total	6.4	8.3

Source: From P. Turcotte, "Common-law Unions: Nearly Half a Million in 1986," *Canadian Social Trends* (Autumn 1988):36. Reproduced with permission.

North American cohabiting couples are less likely than Scandinavian couples to have children. In the United States, only three in ten unions included children (Spanier, 1983). In Canada, 38.7 percent of unmarried couples had children living at home in 1986 (Turcotte, 1988). However, it is impossible to know how many of these are children of that union, since 40 percent of Canadians who cohabit are, or were, previously married.

Using 1980 American census data, Macklin (1983:50–51) divided unmarried couples into three categories: "those composed of two never-married persons (37 percent), those composed of one never-married and one currently or previously married person (31 percent), and those composed of two persons currently or previously married to others (32 percent)." Less than 2 percent of Canadians have ever been involved in two or more common-law relationships (McKie, 1986:41). In Canada, more than 40 percent of those who had ever lived in a common-law relationship married their common-law partner (Turcotte, 1988). In Great Britain, 21 percent of recently married couples entering first marriages cohabited with their spouse before marriage. However, for marriages where one or both partners had been previously married, cohabitation is much more common. Sixty-seven percent of this group cohabited with their spouse before marriage (Goldthorpe, 1987:246). Presumably, more individuals in this group cohabit because they are not free to legally marry. In Spanier's study, about 8 percent of unmarried couples were legally married to someone other than their current partner, and half of the individuals in the sample had been previously married. As Spanier (1983:280) explains: "Since divorce disproportionately affects younger adults, there is a growing pool of previously married individuals with the options of living with someone as a unmarried couple or remarrying."

Findings of studies using other data sources indicate that cohabitation is much more common than census data suggest. Gwartney-Gibbs (1986:427) used marriage licence applications to estimate increases in the proportion of cohabiting couples in Lane County, Oregon. In 1970, 13.2 percent of all marriage licence applicants gave identical home addresses and so were assumed to have cohabited before marriage. In 1980, the figure was 52.7 percent. Previously, divorced people were more likely to cohabit than never-married persons, although generally cohabitors were drawn from all demographic subgroups. Watson's (1983) study of Victoria, British Columbia, couples who had been married approximately a year found that almost two-thirds had experienced some form of cohabiting immediately before marriage. However, Watson's definition of cohabiting was less stringent than the one used by Statistics Canada.

Attitudes to Unmarried Cohabitation

In general, researchers have found increased acceptance of the idea of non-marital cohabitation, especially among the young (Macklin, 1980:907). As with other social inventions, including the custom of casual dating, initial negative reactions relax in time. As attitudes become more liberal, greater numbers of unmarried couples may be willing to cohabit more openly than in the past, and more will be willing to admit to cohabiting. A 1981 Canadian public opinion poll conducted by the Canadian Institute of Public Opinion indicates a dramatic change in attitude during the 1970s. Predictably, support is greater among younger people, although older people expressed more favourable attitudes in 1981 than they had a decade earlier.

Early research on cohabitation focused on young adults, particularly students. The results of this research left the impression that cohabitation was a short-term and sometimes part-time arrangement. Data from the Canadian Family History Survey found unions of considerable duration, indicating perhaps that cohabitation is becoming more institutionalized. In Canada, first unions at the time of the Family History Survey had lasted an average of 4.3 years. Among couples who had previously cohabited, 63 percent married after an average of 2.3 years together; 35 percent separated after an average of 3 years. The remaining 2 percent of unions ended with the death of one of the partners, and this group had been together an average of 9.4 years (McKie, 1986).

Legal institutions are beginning to recognize the status of non-marital unions. "Issues have included protection against discrimination, the legal rights of children and cohabitors, the effect of cohabitation on custody and alimony decisions, extension of insurance benefits, and the division of property at termination" (Macklin, 1983:69). In Canada, non-marital cohabitation is covered by provincial legislation, and thus legal rights vary from province to province. New Brunswick and Ontario have the most progressive legislation to protect the rights of cohabitors and their children. However, as Eichler (1988:5) has pointed out, the law is not consistent. Income tax legislation does not recognize a common-law relationship, yet social welfare disentitles a woman (except residents of Ontario) from benefits if she lives with a man.

Effects on Marriage

Will these trends change the nature of marriage in North America? Macklin's (1987) review suggests not, at least for the United States. There seems to be no effect on the marriage rate. It also seems unlikely that divorce rates are affected. In short, "mate selection has not improved, marriages are not significantly better, and divorce has not been reduced" (Macklin, 1983:70). However, the effects on Canadian marriages might differ because Canadians marry later, stay married longer, and are less likely to divorce. Watson (1983) found lower marital adjustment scores among couples who cohabited immediately before marriage, although the difference was not statistically significant. A study of Swedish women (Bennett, Blanc, and Bloom, 1988) found a strong negative relationship between cohabitation and marital stability. Women who cohabited immediately before marriage were much more likely to separate than those who did not cohabit. This effect was most pronounced for women who cohabited for three years or more. The authors suggest that this reflects a weaker commitment to the institution of marriage by cohabitors.

To summarize briefly, the first part of this chapter has discussed two of the most common alternatives to legal marriage: singlehood and unmarried cohabitation. While it is unlikely that rates of unmarried cohabitation in Canada or the United States will ever equal the Scandinavian rates, there has been a recent increase of some magnitude. Most readers, and most Canadians, will spend part of their adult lives living singly, and an increasing number will cohabit. If Macklin (1983:70) is correct, as many as three-quarters of Americans will cohabit at some point in their lives. For most, cohabitation will be a prelude to marriage; it is less often a long-term alternative to it.

HOMOSEXUALITY

The foreword to the book *Lesbianism: A Study of Female Homosexuality* (Rosen, 1974) begins by raising the question: "Is female homosexuality a psychiatric disorder or a way of life?" The question was timely because in 1974 the American Psychiatric Association was debating whether to remove homosexuality from the *Diagnostic Manual of Psychiatric Disorders*. Evidently, there has been considerable change in the study of homosexuality, and this change has come about in a very short period of time. In sociology, we have moved from defining homosexuality as deviance to defining it in terms of a *lifestyle perspective*. In psychology, the emphasis has shifted from etiology to the study of intimacy (Peplau, 1982). Although a preoccupation with sexual practices persists, the research questions now concentrate less on explaining homosexuality and more on reaching an understanding of the nature and implications of gay relationships. What accounts for this change in orientation? Quite likely it is a response to the gay and women's movements (Harry, 1983). In addition, presence of gay and feminist caucuses within professional organizations provides opportunities for debate and discussion (Peplau, 1982).

In the Kinsey tradition, Bell and Weinberg (1978) carried out detailed interviews with a large sample of gay men and women in the San Francisco Bay area. Research such as this has helped to debunk many of the myths and stereotypes concerning homosexuality and homosexual relationships. Bell and Weinberg described two types of relationships. *Closed-coupled* relationships most resembled heterosexual marriages. Yet, as the researchers pointed out: "We resisted the temptation to call this group 'happily married,' although some of its members described themselves that way, because we did not want to imply that heterosexual relationships and marriage in particular are standards by which to judge people's adjustment" (1978:219). These couples lived together in a mutually satisfying, sexually compatible relationship. They were happy and well adjusted as individuals. *Open-couples* lived together, but were less satisfied with the sexual or emotional aspects of their relationship than close-coupled partners. These relationships were not likely to be sexually exclusive. This was the most common type of relationship for gay males. More lesbians were part of a closed-coupled pair. Long-term fidelity seems to be more characteristic of lesbian relationships, and sexual variety appears to be more important for gay men. The best estimates from empirical studies suggest that 75 percent of lesbians and 50 percent of gay men are currently in a steady relationship, and many share a residence with their partner (Peplau and Gordon, 1983).

In short, gays differ from one another in much the same ways as heterosexuals do. Some are happy, well adjusted, and fulfilled; others are not. Furthermore, it makes no more sense to view homosexual men and women primarily in terms of their sexual orientation than to view heterosexuals this simplistically. Many gay men and women dislike the term homosexual because it places too much emphasis on one aspect of life. Gay (for both sexes) or lesbian are the preferred terms (Peplau and Gordon, 1983).

In a study comparing various aspects of the relationships of lesbians, gay men, heterosexual men, and heterosexual women, Peplau (1981) found gender to have a more important influence on relationships than sexual orientation. Women's goals in intimate relationships are similar whether the partner is male or female. The same is true of men. All couples experience similar kinds of problems in maintaining relationships. Homosexual couples scored as high on relationship adjustment as heterosexual couples (Peplau, 1982).

It is difficult to estimate the stability or longevity of gay unions. Part of the problem is that empirical studies have focused on young, educated, middle-class, white respondents. Long-term relationships are thus underrepresented. The few studies of older respondents find that relationships of twenty years' duration are not uncommon. It is certainly true that there are fewer barriers to ending relationships for homosexuals. "There are rarely legal formalities to negotiate, children to worry about, or as much encouragement from family and friends to work out differences. There is also less likelihood that one partner is financially dependent on the other" (Peplau, 1981:34). Lack of financial dependence is one reason why gay relationships are generally more egalitarian than heterosexual ones (Harry, 1983:219). The stereotyped picture of homosexual relationships mimicking male-female roles is simply not true. Most homosexual couples feel strongly about maintaining a flexible division of labour.

Canadian sociologist John Lee recently studied life satisfaction among fifty- to eighty-year-old gay men to look at the combined effects of aging and sexual preference. Two keys to high satisfaction for gay men were living with a sexual partner and having gay friends. Other factors that contributed to high satisfaction were health and income. Lee reported that, "except in respect to problems arising from social stigmatization of homosexuality, older gay men seem much like older nongays" (1987:144).

The most serious issue facing homosexual men in the 1980s is the threat of AIDS (Acquired Immune Deficiency Syndrome). Because three-quarters of those who have developed AIDS in North America have been bisexual or homosexual men, the gay community as a whole is stigmatized. A decade ago, the gay movement was concerned primarily with sexual liberation. Now, attention is focused on support services for those suffering with AIDS and political action to deal with the epidemic (Risman and Schwartz, 1988:141). Individuals face the very real possibility that they, or someone to whom they are close, will die from this devastating disease. Many gay men have responded by changing their sexual practices – becoming monogamous or celibate. If this reaction becomes more widespread, the nature of the gay community will change significantly.

According to Bell and Weinberg (1978), about 20 percent of gay men and 35 percent of gay women were previously married. About half of these are parents. Gay fathers who remained with their spouses did so primarily because of their children. In a very few cases, children have been adopted by American gay couples, but Canadian adoption agencies do not permit adoption by gays. While child custody is always an issue for homosexual parents, it is a greater problem for gay men. Even visiting rights have been contested. According to Harry (1983:225): "In contested custody cases where a parent's sexual orientation is an issue, lesbian mothers win in about 15 percent of the cases, with gay fathers winning less frequently."

Concerns about custody usually revolve around the unfounded concern that children will become homosexuals and the worry that they will be harassed by their peers. "The evidence suggests that, while the lives of the children of gay and lesbian parents are not problem free, harassment is not common and seems typically manageable" (Harry, 1983:200). In a study of American gay fathers, Bozett (1980) found that most had close relationships with their children. Many shared the fact of their homosexuality with their children. The reason for doing so was to enable the children to understand their fathers' social and personal (not their sexual) worlds. Generally, the fathers prepared their children for disclosure by teaching them tolerance for individual differences and by demonstrating tolerance themselves.

ALTERNATIVE FAMILIES: NON-TRADITIONAL HOUSEHOLDS

Some variations in household structure stem from the increased involvement of women in the paid labour force. Three decades ago, it was unusual for mothers of infants and young children to be gainfully employed; now it is the norm. In the 1950s and 1960s two-income couples were unique; now it is the full-time housewife who is the statistical minority. Granted, most employed women work in "pink collar" occupations for which they receive low pay relative to equally educated and talented men. Nevertheless, an increasing number of women are finding employment in the once exclusively male professional and business fields. It is these better-educated women in highly paid jobs who are less likely to marry, and if they marry, to do so later in life. They are also more likely to remain childless. Despite strong pronatalist sentiments in North America, the number of women who are voluntarily childless is increasing, as discussed in Chapter Three. Bloom (1982) predicts that as many as 29 percent of white American women born in the 1950s may never have a child. As career commitments for women increase, we may expect to see equally high rates of childlessness in Canada. Now, between 15 and 20 percent of married women remain childless (Eichler, 1988:228). Career commitments have other consequences for traditional family living as well, including the likelihood of couples living in different geographic areas for periods of time. So-called commuter marriages usually represent a short-term accommodation.

The following sections describe two types of non-traditional households: single-parent and communal households. Most lone-parent families are created by marital separation or divorce, or the death of a spouse. Communes and intentional communities redefine the concept of family to include a wide group of adults and children.

LONE PARENTS

Since 1970, there has been a dramatic increase in the number of lone-parent households in Canada and the United States. In the United States, half of all children will live in a fatherless home before they reach age eighteen (Glick, 1984). The increases in the number and proportion of lone-parent households are directly related to birth and divorce rates. Although birth rates have dropped for all women, the percentage of births to unmarried compared to married women has increased. In Canada, more children are born to unmarried than married adolescents, but the United States has the highest rate of unmarried teenage pregnancy in the developed world. In Canada, divorce rates increased dramatically following the 1968 liberalization of divorce legislation. These increases continued throughout the 1970s and declined in the early 1980s. By 1986, the divorce rate had risen again. One-third of divorces under the 1985 Divorce Act involved children compared to over half of divorces granted under previous legislation (Statistics Canada: 1988b). Because divorced mothers retain custody of their children 75 percent of the time, most lone-parent households are female-headed. In Canada, the majority of female heads of lone-parent households (56 percent) were separated or divorced, 33 percent were widowed, and the rest never married (Statistics Canada: 1985). An increasing number of divorced women do not remarry, although it is possible to determine whether this represents choice or force of circumstances. Beginning in the 1970s, a small but growing number of single women have chosen to adopt or give birth to children without marriage.

Too many female-headed lone-parent families live without the emotional or financial support of the child's father. In Canada, over half of these families have incomes below the poverty line. Nonetheless, without ignoring this economic reality, we should be careful not to make the assumption that lone-parent households are necessarily single-parent families. To compare single-parent and two-parent families may create a false dichotomy. For example, in some two-parent households, one parent may be absent (either physically because of employment, military service, hospitalization, or imprisonment; or psychologically) for long periods of time. In contrast, some divorced parents are equally involved in the care and nurturing of their children, although they retain separate households. From a child's point of view, these two situations may be more similar than different. "Despite marital status and household arrangements, we cannot assume that the noncustodial parent is interactively and/or psychologically absent" (Gongla and Thompson, 1987:409).

A small but increasing number of divorced couples have made a commitment to shared parenting, whether or not it has been formalized by a joint custody agreement.

Since 1970, there has been a dramatic increase in the number of single-parent households in Canada and the United States.

MILLER COMSTOCK INC.

Joint custody under the 1985 Divorce Act is an agreement to share responsibility for decisions affecting the children of a divorcing couple, regardless of which parent the children live with. In 1986, 12 percent of divorces involved a joint custody arrangement (Statistics Canada: 1988a). While shared parenting is too new to have been studied extensively, the few published studies find that it can be a positive experience for both parents and children, despite the practical difficulties. "Shared parenting offers to men and women the opportunity to take on new roles or modify old ones, and it offers families an alternative to the adversarial principle which often creates and maintains destructive and costly conflict between parties involved in divorce" (Morris, 1988:33).

COMMUNES AND INTENTIONAL COMMUNITIES

Perhaps communes more than any other household arrangement reflect the counter-culture of the 1960s and 1970s. More communes developed in the ten-year period between 1965 and 1975 than at any other time in American history (Macklin, 1987:339). In the mid-1970s, it was estimated that about three-quarters of a million people in the United States lived in communes (Macklin, 1980). Communes of the 1970s differed from earlier experiments in that "they were smaller, were more likely to be urban, were less authoritarian, placed more emphasis on individualism and personal freedom, had more unrestricted admission and less long-term member commitment, and subsisted more on wages earned by members at outside jobs" (Macklin, 1987:339).

Those who have studied communes and intentional communities distinguish them in terms of the locus of control and the extent of economic co-operation. For commune members, the group takes precedence over the nuclear family or the individual, and resources are pooled. Members join because they wish to experience living in a unique type of household without the relationship barriers characteristic of most living situations. Child care and other domestic responsibilities, as well as income-generating pursuits, are shared by all members regardless of age or sex. Maintaining a gender-indifferent division of labour is difficult. Inevitably, members fall into traditional patterns, particularly regarding child care and other domestic tasks.

Communes typically consist of between five and twenty-five people; collectives, or intentional communities, can sustain larger numbers. Members of intentional communities live in households, but make a commitment to the emotional and economic well-being of a larger group. Communes and intentional communities have in common a commitment to humanism and egalitarianism, sharing of responsibilities, and a general concern for other members of the group.

Religious communes tend to be far more stable than secular communes, which for the most part are short-lived experiments. Some religious communities, including the Hutterites in western Canada, have survived for several generations. Hutterites, who are

In the mid-1970s it was estimated that about three-quarters of a million people in the United States lived in communes.

CANAPRESS

FOR INTEREST

A TORONTO COMMUNE

Schlesinger and Marshall (1979) studied a commune consisting of eight couples, five with children, and several single people, living together in Toronto. Families lived separately (and monogamously) under the same roof. An important uniting influence for the group was a political ideology described by one member as Christian radicalism. Like the Hutterites, the Toronto group (including the single adults) shared economic and child care responsibilities. Unlike the Hutterites, they were committed to sexual equality. To earn money, members of the group worked in a collective doing carpentry and general house repairs. As part of their effort to eliminate gender inequalities, their goal was to have everyone gainfully employed on a part-time basis, allowing time for child care and leisure. At the time of the study this was proving to be difficult. In the first place, the men were more skilled at carpentry and so were able to earn more money. Second, the children were all young, and most of the women were more active than the men in parenting.

---

descendants of sixteenth-century Anabaptists, hold property in common. Colony members have few personal possessions, and the proceeds from their agricultural pursuits are pooled. The system is supported by a rather complex bureaucratic (and patriarchal) structure. Self-discipline and devotion to community rather than individual goals are required of all members. Children are socialized (and disciplined) by all members of the community.

ALTERNATIVES FOR THE ELDERLY

With the gradual aging of the population, there has been some speculation about alternatives for older people, including communal living, non-marital cohabitation, and even polygyny. However, perhaps because these ideas seem so novel, there has been little empirical investigation of them. While polygyny (the marriage of one man and several women) might solve the problem of an unbalanced sex ratio, loneliness, and a declining standard of living for some older people, it remains an unlikely possibility in our society. There have been a few examples of shared housing arrangements for the elderly in North America. Some groups have agreed to pool their resources and share responsibilities. But unlike communes for younger people, these are often arranged *for* the elderly, without the foundation of an ideological commitment. Such collectivities are chosen as the most practical available alternative, not as the preferred one. Those most willing to share housing are people in poor health and with income difficulties. For women, a history of interrupted paid employment coupled with low pay in a segregated labour force means that lifetime earnings, and consequently pension benefits, are low. Yet, Canadian women live an average of eight years longer than men. Not surprisingly, "unattached" elderly women are among the poorest Canadians.

As people who have grown up in the 1970s age, we may see changes in remarriage patterns that include older women marrying younger men. Non-traditional housing may also become more accepted as attitudes change and choices increase (because of increased labour force participation of women). Kyriazis and Stelcner studied the living arrangements of older Canadians and found that differences in tastes were more important determinants than differences in income. These authors argue (1986:401) that variations in living arrangements for this group "may be a function of the emergence of tastes for alternate lifestyles characteristic of the more highly educated, professional sectors of our population which, in turn, may have generated greater demand for privacy and living alone."

ALTERNATIVES WITHIN MARRIAGE: SEXUAL NON-EXCLUSIVITY

Perhaps the non-traditional patterns described below would be more appropriately called alternative lifestyles. Unlike the alternatives described so far, open marriage and swinging are the structural equivalents of traditional nuclear families. Group marriages are similar to small communes. All three are unique in that they call into question one of the most fundamental ideas about Western marriage – sexual exclusivity. Although extramarital sexual activity has probably always accompanied marriage, and proposals for loosening the bonds of marriage have been made in the past, the "duty-to-self" culture of the 1960s and 1970s created an atmosphere of sexual freedom. During this period, attitudes became more liberal and sexual restrictions loosened as the power of the state, community religion, and family/kin groups to sanction non-marital sexuality became less keenly felt. The important factors became individual choice and reference group support (Whitehurst, 1985:263-64).

Attitude surveys indicate that most North Americans disapprove of extramarital sexuality, although attitudes are more conservative than behaviour. It seems that about 70 percent of North Americans disapprove of extramarital sexual activity (Weis, 1983), but approximately 50 percent of men and almost as many women have extramarital involvements (Thompson, 1983). Most of these are short term and without spousal approval. Approval is strongly related to past behaviour, particularly premarital sexual permissiveness. Involvement is determined by opportunity, predisposition, and perceptions of costs and benefits. The non-exclusive relationships discussed below are based on an assumption shared by spouses that extramarital sexuality will enhance personal growth without jeopardizing the marital relationship.

SEXUALLY OPEN MARRIAGE

The term "open" relationship is popularly used to refer to consensual extramarital sexual relationships. Proponents see open marriage as a way to overcome the sexual and emotional restrictions of monogamous relationships. The term is borrowed from the book *Open Marriage* (O'Neill and O'Neill, 1972), although the authors originally used the term more broadly to characterize trusting, egalitarian marital relationships. In fact, *Open Marriage* was less about sexual non-exclusivity than about developing new rules for marital relationships. Blumstein and Schwartz's *American Couples* (1983:585) found that 15 to 26 percent of couples "have an understanding that allows nonmonogamy under some circumstances."

Typically, couples do not start their marriages as sexually open, but rather they redefine their sexual commitment over time. This has led to some debate as to whether couples seek other sexual contacts because they are unhappy or find their marriages less than satisfactory. What are the long-term effects of a sexually open relationship? Rubin (1982) found little difference in self reports of happiness or marital stability between couples in sexually exclusive and sexually open marriages. When the same couples were contacted five years later, a higher percentage of those in the sexually open group had separated, although the difference was not statistically significant (Rubin and Adams, 1986). The reasons couples gave for marital break-up were not related to sexual openness. Two couples in the sexually open group had become sexually exclusive. One couple in the sexually exclusive group had decided to have an open relationship, although almost 30 percent had had at least one extramarital affair.

SWINGING

Swinging has been defined by Walshok as "the pursuit of sexual activities with extramarital partners by both spouses, at the same time and usually in the same place" (Henshel, 1973:885). Because swinging is not legally or socially sanctioned, it is difficult to determine just how many people are involved. Swinging clubs exist in most major North American cities, and studies of swingers are typically based on samples drawn from these membership lists. The North American Swing Club Association held its first International Convention in Los Angeles in 1982. Now there are 250 member clubs. In Canada, there are active clubs in all major cities. The president of Club Eros, a Toronto swing club with 676 members, estimates that approximately 4,000 Toronto couples are actively involved in swinging (French, 1988).

Participants sometimes learn about swinging inadvertently from friends, but usually they seek out swinging bars or place ads in personal columns of newspapers or swinger magazines. Clubs sponsor get-acquainted social events.

Many couples say they are attracted to swinging because they feel it is preferable to the duplicity of affairs. Typically, husbands initiate swinging, and wives comply, with some initial reluctance. Swingers are predominantly white, well educated, suburban, and middle class. They are drawn from a wide age range, although most are in the thirty-five to forty-five age group. Research results have been less consistent in describing other characteristics of swingers. Because swinging represents such a radical departure from the norm of sexual exclusivity or the secrecy of the affair, researchers have been curious about whether swingers are radical in other ways. Certainly, they are perceived to be "different." Jenks (1985) asked a group of undergraduates about their perceptions of swingers. The students described swingers as unlike themselves in a number of ways. They characterized swingers as disproportionately non-white, politically liberal, frequent drug users, and in need of counselling. All of these are misconceptions. Generally, except for their interest in swinging, swingers cannot be differentiated from the rest of the population. Most seem interested in swinging for the sexual variety it provides, and are not interested in sharing other aspects of their lives or participating in communal or co-operative living.

Because both partners are equally involved and, thus, in a sense women's sexuality is placed on a par with men's, it has been suggested that swinging has the effect of "aiding the decline of the double standard" (Whitehurst, 1975:441). Henshel's study of Toronto couples involved in swinging did not confirm this optimism. She found that swinging was usually initiated by the husbands, and women tended to see it as less advantageous to them. Women are usually the first to want to drop out.

Most swingers drop out within a year, perhaps because swinging does not meet their expectations. A study of ex-swingers found that 70 percent of the men reported sexual dysfunction during swinging. Ex-swingers were concerned about venereal disease, feared discovery, felt guilt and jealousy, and some felt swinging was a threat to their marriage. Many swingers have dropped out, or become more selective and restrictive, as a result of AIDS.

GROUP MARRIAGE

In sexually open relationships or in swinging, commitment still centres on the marriage. Group marriages represent a more radical departure from traditional marriage because commitment is to the group. Group or *multilateral* marriage "consists of three or more partners, each of whom considers himself/herself to be married (or committed in a functionally analogous way) to more than one of the other partners" (Constantine and Constantine, 1973:49). It is no surprise to learn that group marriages occur infrequently and seldom last. What we know about group marriage in North America is based on the work of the Constantines, who conducted a three-year study of one hundred group marriages in the United States. Typically, two couples, with or without children, entered a group marriage for companionship, sexual variety, and personal growth. According to the Constantines (1973:32), what made these marriages unique was that multilateral relationships were sought; they were not "chance results of isolated events." Perhaps because the original-couple relationship was usually stronger than the group commitment, group marriages often dissolved in less than a year. They reported communication problems, jealousy, and interpersonal conflicts.

Canadian sociologist Robert Whitehurst thought that the uneven sex ratios favouring men in urban areas might create opportunities for multiple relationships, especially *triads*, groups in which "three-way sexuality is expressed" (Whitehurst, 1979:177). In an article published in 1975, Whitehurst suggested that triads might become "the modal alternative lifestyle in the urban areas" (1975:439). However, in a later article he conceded that triads were "not of numerical significance."

CONCLUSION

The past two decades have seen a dramatic increase in non-traditional living arrangements. The combined effects of an increase in the average age of first marriage, increased female labour force participation, lower fertility, a high incidence of divorce, and greater longevity have altered the nature of family life. Attitudes and expectations have changed accordingly. The women's movement challenged traditional assumptions about women's family roles, and the human potential movement questioned the nature of marital commitment. In the last decade of the twentieth century, we may see a reversal of the trend toward sexual freedom and experimentation as the effects of the AIDS virus become more widespread.

The non-traditional family types described here do not exhaust the possibilities, for individuals and families continually adjust and accommodate as the conditions of their lives dictate. Some accommodations are temporary; others are long term. Some individuals choose non-traditional living arrangements because of emotional or sexual predispositions and preferences. Others are suddenly thrust into unanticipated situations by divorce or the death of a partner. Still others postponed choices about marriage or childbirth and find for one reason or another that the opportunity has passed. Social class, sex, and age will have an important effect on the nature of commitments and the range of alternatives. Most of us will marry, but we will also experience living in one or more of the alternatives described in this chapter. Some of the alternatives are more radical than others, and so it will remain less common to live communally than to cohabit and far less common to be a part of a group marriage than to live alone. The data presented in this chapter make it clear that traditional family living is one arrangement among many. While it remains the most usual expectation, the two-parent family with children is no longer even the statistical norm for households.

C. Wright Mills has provided a formula for understanding changes in relationships and in the social institution of the family. In his words (1959:10), "What we experience in various and specific milieux is often caused by structural changes." To fruitfully connect the personal troubles of milieu and the public issues of social structure is to possess the sociological imagination. The challenge of the sociological imagination is offered not only to professionals, but to all of us.

DISCUSSION QUESTIONS

1. Using marriage, divorce, fertility, and longevity statistics found in this text, describe possible living arrangements for Canadians born in 1980. Compare scenarios for men and women throughout the life cycle.

2. In investigating attitudes to single women in Australia, Stolk and Brotherton (1981) asked two hundred respondents to complete the sentence "I think of single women as . . . ." Carry out a study like this and compare your results.

3. Why is it still so unusual for women to marry younger men? Are there reasons to believe that age differences will become less important in future?

4. The number of Canadians living in non-marital unions increased significantly between 1981 and 1986. What explains this rise in cohabitation?

5. Over half of all female-headed lone-parent families in Canada live in poverty. Imagine that you have been asked to prepare a list of policy recommendations to alleviate poverty for this group.

6. Do a content analysis of newspaper articles dealing with AIDS. Sample articles from one paper for a period of several months, or compare two papers for a shorter time period. What do these newspaper accounts tell you about social attitudes toward homosexuality? Do you find evidence of increased homophobia?

7. Why do you think most experiments in alternative living (i.e., communes and group marriage) are short lived? What structural and attitudinal variables operate against long-term success?

8. Why has swinging sparked such interest when so few couples engage in it?

9. Interview relatives or acquaintances who are over sixty to find out how receptive they might be to the possibility of alternatives such as house sharing.

10. What evidence suggests that the AIDS epidemic is changing heterosexual practices? Are young people becoming more sexually conservative?

chapter **six**

Socialization: Changing Views of Child Rearing and Adolescence

INTRODUCTION

Contemporary Canadians seem ambivalent about the place of children in our society. We wax sentimental about children as an abstract category. The more fortunate among us recall our own childhoods with nostalgia. Media reports about young victims of poverty, physical abuse, famine, or war move us deeply. Many couples invest enormous emotional and financial resources in an attempt to remedy their infertility problems. However, other reactions betray considerable suspicion and antipathy toward youngsters. Being seated next to a baby in an airplane, discovering preschoolers moving in next door, encountering teenagers skateboarding in a mall, or seeing adolescents kissing at the back of a bus causes some adults to become extremely uncomfortable. Tax support for public day care or for the more than one million Canadian children living below the poverty level does not receive high priority. Canada's current fertility rate, the lowest in history, is insufficient for generational replacement. Mandell (1988:75) suggests that we have now institutionalized so many cultural disincentives to parenting that "adults no longer understand how children fit into their lives."

Those Canadians who do have children are confused about how to raise them. A number of factors diminish parents' confidence in their ability to rear their offspring. Youngsters must be equipped to take their place in a complex, ever-changing society. The knowledge and skills required to function effectively in an urban industrial society such as ours are too complex and extensive for parents to convey to children. Therefore, the family must rely upon other agencies, such as schools. Parents are bombarded with advice from professional experts who disagree publicly with one another. Yet, parents judge themselves and are evaluated by outsiders in terms of standards for successful child rearing that are higher than ever before. Though these standards tend to be inchoate, and vary by social class, successful Canadian parents are those who managed to produce healthy, happy offspring who avoid trouble with alcohol, drugs, sex, and the police; who perform well at school; who enter well-paying, satisfying, useful occupations; who form "suitable," stable relationships with heterosexual mates. No wonder parents frequently feel guilty about their own inadequacies and confused in the face of changing conceptions of motherhood and fatherhood (see below).

FOR INTEREST

THROUGH THE EYES OF CHILDREN

Only sentimentalists have ever considered childhood to be a kingdom of untroubled innocence. Today there is more trouble for children and less time for innocence than in recent generations. The problem is not so much that children have changed. The world has changed. Writes Dr. Robert Coles, a psychiatrist and author who has studied the lives of the young for more than 30 years: "Children have always been, and still are, a mirror to us – ourselves writ small." Ourselves have changed.

It is both the best and the worst of times for children. Their world contains powers and perspectives inconceivable to a child 50 years ago: computers; longer life expectancies; the entire planet accessible through television, satellites, air travel. But so much knowledge and choice can be chaotic and dangerous. School curriculums have been adapted to teach about new topics: AIDS, adolescent suicide, drug and alcohol abuse, incest. Trust is the child's natural inclination, but the world has become untrustworthy. The hazards of the adult world, its sometimes fatal temptations, descend upon children so early that the ideal of childhood is demolished.

Crack, for example, is far more addictive and deadly than marijuana, the drug of a different generation. Strange fragments of violence come flashing out of the television set and lodge in minds too young to understand them. . . .

The messages are powerful and contradictory. Rock videos suggest orgiastic sex. Public health officials counsel "safe sex." Prudence – and morality – would recommend no sex to children, who have no clear idea of what sex is anyway. Oprah Winfrey and Phil Donahue conduct seminars on such subjects as lesbian nuns, exotic drugs, transsexual surgery, serial murders. Television pours into the imaginations of children a bizarre version of reality. But TV has a certain authority in loco parentis. It is there when the kids come home. . . .

Children have lost status in the world. Teachers have endured a long decline in public esteem. Day-care workers rarely earn a living wage. The role of mother is being rewritten, and that of father as well. A generation of children is being raised in the midst of a redefinition of parenting. Childhood has become a kind of experiment. . . .

Perplexed parents, finding their own childhoods seemingly irrelevant to the task, are left to improvise.

Source: *Time* 132, no. 6 (August 8, 1988). Copyright 1988 Time Inc. Reprinted by permission.

The matters discussed above are all interrelated. Family structure has been influenced by the way work is organized and carried out in post-industrialized societies. Images of childhood and parenthood have changed together. As Thorne (1987:97) emphasizes, "in various twists of definition and labelling . . . women and children have been repeatedly defined in terms of one another." As a result of women's increased labour force participation and the influence of the feminist movement, the role of fathers is also being redefined. Questions about who raises children and how they are to be brought up are tied to views about what youngsters are like and what sort of child rearing is necessary in order to maintain a functioning society.

Social scientists are major brokers in ideas about children and parenting. Professional students of children usually begin their work with deeply held personal philosophies about human nature. "These philosophies are influenced by the politics, the economy, and the social structure of the society in which they live" (Kagan, 1984:xi). In time, the work of these experts becomes translated into child-rearing advice for parents. The many and competing theories of social science themselves eventually colour perceptions of childhood. Indeed, childhood has become the most analysed stage of the life cycle.

Socialization is the complex learning process through which individuals develop selfhood and acquire the knowledge, skills, and motivations required for participation in social life. Socialization is essential both for the maintenance of society and the well-being of the individual. From the point of view of the individual, interaction with other people is the means by which human potentialities are actualized. As well, the

Questions about who raises children and how they are to be brought up are tied to views about what youngsters are like and what sort of child rearing is necessary in order to maintain a functioning society.

MILLER COMSTOCK INC.

continuity of Canadian society requires that the thousands of new members born each year eventually learn to think, believe, and behave like Canadians. In short, the socialization of a child "transforms a biological organism into a human being and confronts adults with a new set of experiences and responsibilities" (Peterson and Rollins, 1987:471).

Socialization is characterized by both stability and change. On the one hand, children have probably changed very little over the past three thousand years. Children walked and talked at roughly the same age in classical Greece as they do in contemporary Canada. Parents in ancient times faced the same general tasks (e.g., providing basic necessities, teaching norms and values) as do modern parents in raising their children to be functioning members of their society (Zigler and Seitz, 1978). However, different historical periods have entertained varying conceptions of childhood and adolescence. Also, diverse cultures have placed dissimilar socialization requirements on parents and children. Goals, values, and role definitions all change from culture to culture and over time.

Although any complete account of socialization must come to terms with both continuity and change, this chapter will emphasize change. This emphasis is in keeping with contemporary sociologists' attempts to redress the concentration of previous scholars upon continuity, stability, and conformity (Gecas, 1981). In the past, interest centred on society's need to be perpetuated and "what is 'done' to the child" (Inkeles, 1968:77). In addition, the focus on change in the present chapter seems more congruent with the kind of socialization challenges presented by our society.

This chapter has four tasks: (1) to trace the changing historical views of childhood and adolescence; (2) to analyse the contemporary societal context for socialization; (3) to discuss the evolving social scientific perspectives on socialization; and (4) to outline current issues in socialization theory and research.

CHANGING CONCEPTIONS OF CHILDHOOD AND ADOLESCENCE

Who is the child? What is the child supposed to become (Inkeles, 1968:76)? Are children "pure, bestial, innocent, corrupt" (Jenks, 1982:9)? Are they "little angels" or "little devils" (Synnott, 1983)? Are they priceless or worthless? How shall they be treated?

The answer to this last query depends on our view of children's innate propensities and our vision of the desired outcome of the socialization process. If human beings are by nature selfish beasts, then we must civilize them. If such desirable traits as empathy and concern for others emerge naturally, then we must protect children while they flower into decent citizens (Zigler and Seitz, 1978:740). If children are priceless, they will be cherished. If worthless, they will be neglected, exploited, and abused (Lee, 1982:593).

Historians and anthropologists have taught us that childhood is a social construct. Within limits set by biology, society has great leeway in deciding what childhood is to be and how children are to be dealt with (Berger and Berger, 1975:62). In other words, the manner in which adults think of children, as well as children's relationships with adults, alters from epoch to epoch, and from culture to culture (Jenks, 1982:25). Indeed, the social construct of childhood varies by social class, by gender, by religion, by ethnic group, and by geographic region. We resist acknowledging that childhood is an *idea*, a social invention, rather than a natural state. Our own personal experience seems to have provided us with compelling facts about childhood: "I was a child once, you know" (Lee, 1982:592). Nevertheless, scholars have documented the changing images of childhood through history; anthropologists have depicted various perceptions of childhood in different cultures. Because of space limitations, our discussion here will focus exclusively on Western ideas of childhood across time.

The history of childhood is a challenging area of scholarship. Family affairs are private affairs, and until recently, authentic history was considered to be the record of public events (DeMause, 1982:48). Also, the witnesses and recorders of family life have been adults, not children.

> Crowds and crowds of little children are strangely absent from the written record. . . . There is something mysterious about the silence of all these multitudes of babes in arms, toddlers and adolescents in the statements men made at the time about their own experience (Laslett, 1965:104).

Although the study of childhood has, over the past half century, become routine for the psychologist, it is only beginning for the historian. The family historian is especially interested in reconstructing the lives of ordinary families, rather than focusing on those of celebrated individuals or elites (Hareven, 1987:37). Fortunately, a number of excellent social histories of American and European childhood and family life have become available in recent years (Ariès, 1962; Demos and Boocook, 1978; Gillis, 1974; Laslett, 1965; Stone, 1977; Zelizer, 1985). In Canada, historically oriented sociological research has had a slow start (Brym, 1979:viii). However, the interdisciplinary nature of women's studies has given immense impetus to historical investigations of family life (Nett, 1981:254). Though sparse, some first-rate work is now available (Katz, 1975; Parr, 1982).

MEDIEVAL CHILDHOOD

In medieval European society, the concept of childhood simply did not exist (Ariès, 1962). That is, there seems to have been no awareness of the unique nature of children that distinguishes them from adults. Recognition of a first stage of life, which we now call "infancy," was apparent in medieval times, "but thereafter the dividing line between childhood and adulthood faded" (Suransky, 1982:6). The high infant mortality rate of the time seems to have been partially responsible for a certain amount of indifference toward children. It was risky to get attached to a child who might die, and as soon as the child could live without constant care, it belonged to adult society.

Twelfth-century children, just out of swaddling clothes, were dressed as adults. As soon as they could move about independently, they joined the world of adults, participating in adult work and social life as fully as their physical capacities permitted (FitzGerald, 1983:54). The Middle Ages provided no initiation or education for adulthood and therefore failed to perceive a difference between the world of the child and the world of the adult (Ariès, 1962:411).

That childhood had neither interest nor reality for medieval Europeans is supported by the fact that, until the twelfth century, medieval art did not attempt to portray childhood. Somewhat later, painters depicted children as dwarfed adults, devoid of childish expressions or features. Take, for example, a miniature of the biblical scene where Jesus asks that the little children be allowed to come unto him. Grouped around Jesus are eight small-scale men, without any of the physical characteristics of children (Ariès, 1962:33).

Scholars disagree about the treatment accorded children in the Middle Ages. Philippe Ariès (1962:128) insists that the absence of a construct of childhood in medieval society did *not* mean that children were neglected, forsaken, or despised. However, DeMause (1982:48) argues to the contrary:

> The history of childhood is a nightmare from which we have only recently begun to awaken. The further back in history one goes, the lower the level of child care, and the more likely children are to be killed, abandoned, beaten, terrorized, and sexually abused.

Although the grim picture of cruelty toward children painted by DeMause appears to be accurate, this brutality must be understood as part of the generalized social cruelty of the times (Suransky, 1982:5). DeMause (1982:56) characterizes parent–child relations during the period from antiquity to the fourth century A.D. as the *infanticidal mode*, and says that "parents routinely resolved their anxieties about taking care of children by killing them" (1982:56). Though the destruction of legitimate children was slowly reduced during the Middle Ages, the killing of illegitimate children continued into the nineteenth century. Because of the high value placed on sons within the family, daughters often died through neglect when whole families fell ill. Every effort was made to ensure the survival of sons, at the expense of daughters.

From about the thirteenth century onward, the value placed on children's lives by adult society increased dramatically. Ariès (1962:43) attributes this change to the growing cultural impact of Christianity and its insistence that the child's soul is immortal.

FOURTEENTH TO SEVENTEENTH CENTURIES

During this period, childhood became an acknowledged social fact as certain categories of parents began to realize that children were not simply miniature adults. By the seventeenth century, upper-class children, at least, were given special costumes that marked them out from adults (Ariès, 1962). The fact that age-graded dress was worn by offspring of the nobility and the middle classes (but not the poor), and by sons (but not daughters), emphasizes the point that "childhood emerged first as a male middle-class phenomenon" (Mandell, 1988:59).

Several different conceptions of childhood were popular. DeMause (1982:57) has labelled these parental attitudes as the *ambivalent mode*. On the one hand, the child, because of its "sweetness, simplicity and drollery" (Ariès, 1962:129), became a source of amusement for adults. This gave rise to the coddling attitude toward little children of both upper and lower classes. Children, then, were regarded with a certain amount of fondness. This sentimentality about children was accompanied in the world of art by a proliferation of paintings of Mary, the mother, and her infant, Jesus. On the other hand, the fourteenth century shows an increase in the number of instruction manuals for children. The image of physical moulding was prevalent. Children were seen as "soft wax, plaster, or clay to be beaten into shape" (DeMause, 1982:57).

All this need for control sprung from the idea that children were full of dangerous impulses. The swaddling of infants was congruent with this "moulding" notion of child rearing. Enveloping children's limbs in endless bandages was thought to be necessary because if the child

> were left free it would scratch its eyes out, tear its ears off, break its legs, distort its bones, be terrified by the sight of its own limbs, and even crawl about on all fours like an animal (DeMause, 1982:54).

Swaddling was convenient for adult caretakers. Although it took up to two hours to wrap an infant, thereafter the child could be hung on pegs on the wall or left, like a parcel, in any convenient corner. Swaddled infants were extremely passive, indeed, almost inert: their hearts slowed down, they cried less, and they slept far more (DeMause, 1982:54-55).

Toward the end of this period, treatises on education retained the moulding concept of socialization, but strongly criticized the coddling attitude mentioned above. They found repugnant the idea that children, like monkeys, were to be a source of adult amusement. Instead, it was recommended that children be turned into "thinking men and good Christians." The moralists and churchmen who wrote these treatises saw children as "fragile creatures of God who needed to be both safeguarded and reformed" (Ariès, 1962:133). The Calvinists (including the Puritans) among them regarded children as "little devils," born with original sin and prone to evil (Synnott, 1983:80).

The appearance of schools at the end of the seventeenth century was a landmark event in the evolution of childhood. According to Ariès (1962:412), the concept of formal education for children was a consequence of the ascendancy of churchmen who stressed the moral, ethical aspects of religion over theologians who emphasized the afterlife. Over and above its religious implications, the development of formal education meant recognition that children were not ready for life, that they had to be subjected to a special treatment, a sort of quarantine before they could be allowed to join adult society (Ariès, 1962:413). School lengthened childhood for those who attended, namely, males from privileged classes. The content of schooling comprised Christian doctrine and "a little classics" (Laslett, 1965:105). An emphasis on discipline and control continued the moulding theory of child rearing.

The *property paradigm* has been used to characterize the socially constructed reality of childhood in pre-industrial society. Children were the chattels of adult males "who had the right to beat them, confine them, and dispose of their labour" (Lee, 1982:593). Gillis (1974:11) says that "children were to preindustrial society what pensions and disability insurance are to our own." They represented an investment in the parents' old age. Indenture to guild masters, marriage arrangements, and education all were property investments. Children always remained firmly subordinate in status to adults (Lee, 1982:593).

THE EIGHTEENTH CENTURY

Several new eighteenth-century developments augmented the coddling and moulding concepts of childhood from the previous period. For one thing, parents developed an interest in conquering the child's mind. DeMause (1982:57) labels this parental conquering of will the *intrusive mode*.

> The child raised by intrusive parents was . . . toilet trained early, prayed with but not played with, hit but not regularly whipped, punished for masturbation. . . .

Also, concern with children's hygiene and physical health emerged (Ariès, 1962:133). This new interest accompanied some improvement in mortality rates, though significant declines in these rates for the mass of the population did not occur until well into the nineteenth century (Zelizer, 1981:1040).

In the late seventeenth century, life expectancy was thirty-two years in England and twenty-seven and a half years in Germany. The most vulnerable ages were the youngest. In the French village of Challain during the last third of the seventeenth century, 18 percent of the children died in their first month, 35 percent in their first year, and 53 percent before they reached the age of twenty (Gillis, 1974:10). Understandably enough, parents protected themselves against the pain of a child's death by remaining emotionally aloof (Zelizer, 1981:1040). With fertility rates higher as well, "love was 'spread around' more children, who were more likely to die" (Synnott, 1983:82). But by this time, the child had taken a central place in the family, and every detail of its existence was of great interest (Ariès, 1962:133).

Although the earlier view of children as "little devils" plagued with original sin lived on, it received some challenge from the Romantic idea that children enjoy original virtue, are "little angels," and are intrinsically good (Synnott, 1983:81). The belief that human beings are naturally good was given widest currency by Rousseau in his famous educational treatise *Emile* (1762). The corollary here was that children should be protected by school from the morally corrupting influence of adult life (Lee, 1982:594). Nevertheless, Puritan and Methodist views of the depravity of children, which harkened back to the biblical adage "He that spareth the rod, hateth his son" (Proverbs 13:24), also circulated (Synnott, 1983:82). Obviously, several worlds of childhood co-existed, with considerable variation by religious orientation and by social class (Synnott, 1983:83).

THE NINETEENTH CENTURY

Although industrialization began in the latter half of the eighteenth century, it was not until the next century that the process gained momentum. Industrialization, modernization, and urbanization were associated with great changes in the family. "The labor market created by industrial capitalism tended to drive the family apart and make the individuals in it separate entities in that labor market" (Bridenthal, 1982:226). Class divisions were extraordinarily important as the experiences of bourgeoisie and proletariat diverged (Synnott, 1983). The status of children and women changed dramatically.

One of the most salient features of nineteenth-century childhood was the exploitation of child labour (Synnott, 1983:84):

> Children's labour was not new but the *conditions* of labour were new. Conditions in the British coal mines, the cotton mills and factories were appalling. Investigation after investigation . . . documented atrocities of child labour. (Emphasis in original.)

Many children did not survive industrialization, as infant and child mortality rates soared over the pre-industrial levels. Reform was slow. The first British Factory Act (1833) prohibited child labour, but only for children under six. Children under ten years were limited to sixteen hours of work a day (Synnott, 1983). As crime, ill-health, and alcoholism rose, social reformers proposed stabilization of the family by removal from the labour force of the women who had worked alongside the men and children (Bridenthal, 1982:227). Especially among the bourgeoisie, the concept of motherhood as women's chief vocation and primary identity emerged. This construction of motherhood as serious, full-time responsibility was congruent with the conception of children as fragile, dependent beings in need of prolonged protection and care (Glenn, 1987:359).

Although regional variations existed, a similar situation characterized North America. Here we can begin to comment on Canadian society. "It is only back to about 125 years ago that any image of children in Canadian families, other than their numbers, begins to materialize" (Nett, 1981:251). On the agricultural frontier, families were large and children's labour essential (Parr, 1982:13). As well, children's earnings were vital to family economies in the working-class sectors of eastern Canadian cities (Nett, 1981:251). Some 70,000 homeless British children were brought to Canada as labourers and servants (Sutherland, 1976). The proverb "Children are the riches of the poor" rang especially true in New France (Moogk, 1982:43). In addition to the adult responsibilities they shared with European children, many Canadian children experienced the geographic dislocation and reshaping of kinship networks and traditions (Parr, 1982:10) that accompanied migration from Old World to New World and movements within this continent.

For children of the bourgeoisie, the nineteenth century was quite different: "At the same time as the children of the industrial and agricultural proletariat died in North America and Western Europe . . . this was the Golden Age of Victorian childhood (for the middle class)" (Synnott, 1983:85). Children were idealized. They occupied a conspicuous role in the family. Nineteenth-century authors such as Wordsworth, Dickens, and Twain took great interest in the child as a symbol of innocence (Coveney, 1982:45).

Middle-class Victorian parents began to view child rearing less as a process of conquering the will of the child than one of guiding it along proper paths (DeMause, 1982:57). For the first time a *socialization mode* emerged, as parents thought of training the child to fit into society. This perspective came to fruition at the turn of the century when Christian doctrines of original sin and Romantic doctrines of original virtue were supplanted by the scientific orientation in child rearing (Coveney, 1982:46).

By the end of the nineteenth century, various religious denominations were

The proverb "Children are the riches of the poor" rang especially true in rural areas and in Quebec prior to the 1960s.

operating several hundred day, boarding, and industrial schools for the purpose of inculcating Christianity and European values in Canadian Indian children (Grant, 1984:176ff.). Much criticized today, these schools set out to change the personalities of the "heathen" native children. Many forbade these youngsters to speak their native languages. Such rules were enforced by corporal punishment. "Buildings were drafty and crowded, food scanty and often unappetizing. . . . Parents expressed further dissatisfaction when homecoming pupils offered wholesale condemnation of the way of life to which they were accustomed. The schools seemed to be agencies of alienation more than of education" (Grant, 1984:180-81).

A nineteenth-century development especially worthy of note is the emergence of adolescence as a distinct stage of the life cycle (Gillis, 1974:105; Katz and Davey, 1978). Pre-industrial European and North American societies recognized a stage of life, commonly called "youth," that was different from both childhood and adulthood. This very long transition period lasted from the time the young child became somewhat independent of the family (seven or eight years) to the point of complete independence in marriage, usually in the mid- to late twenties (Gillis, 1974:2). The great majority of young people lived in a state of semi-independence from their families as servants, apprentices, or students boarding away from home. It was "this detachment from family that gave pre-industrial youth its peculiar structure and meaning" (Gillis, 1974:2). The period of youth lacked the distinctions we make today between preteen children, adolescents, and early adulthood. Neither pre-industrial work nor education were as sharply age-graded as is the case in modern society. Since the youth of earlier times were assigned responsible roles at early ages, the onset of puberty was not particularly significant.

Adolescence emerged first among the middle classes. Mortality and fertility dropped earlier among the privileged classes. Families no longer sent their children to live elsewhere. According to Katz and Davey (1978:S117): "The prolonged dependency of young people upon their parents and their increased education in specialized age-segregated institutions formed the basis for adolescence." Demographic variables were also important factors. With increased life expectancy, society could now afford adolescence. When individuals had few years of life remaining after biological maturation was attained, precious years could not be expended preparing for adulthood (Rogers, 1981:12). Social commentators coined a new phrase – adolescence – to correspond to the new stage in young people's lives. This social change spread eventually to the working class as their children began to attend high schools. In sum, the origin of adolescence lay not in puberty, but in dependency (Katz and Davey, 1978:S117).

The social scientific study of adolescence commenced at the turn of the century. In 1904, psychologist G. Stanley Hall published a two-volume set entitled *Adolescence*. Hall introduced the view that adolescence was a distinct stage between youth and adulthood, characterized by *Sturm und Drang* (storm and stress). "The majority of psychologists who study adolescents no longer believe it is valid to view adolescence as a period of crisis" (Santrock, 1984:17).

FIRST HALF OF THE TWENTIETH CENTURY

> The Victorian age ended with the death of the old Queen in 1901, and much of what the age symbolized died with her or on the battlefields of World War I. A new world of childhood dawned with the new century (Synnott, 1983:86).

Two new developments in the early part of this century had far-reaching effects on socialization. The first was the emergence of the "economically worthless but emotionally priceless" child, which accompanied mature industrialism (Zelizer, 1981). Second, the radical idea that the scientific method could be applied to human behaviour produced experts on child rearing whose views had an effect on everyday family life.

A great transformation in children's value occurred as children's lives were gradually divorced from the marketplace (Zelizer, 1981:1037). Eventually, all classes of children lost their economic utility as contributors to family income and security for parents' old age. Children became *sacralized* and were transformed into emotional assets. In return for the cost of raising them, children were now "expected to provide love, smiles, and emotional satisfaction but no money" (Zelizer, 1981:1038).

The state's recognition of children as "citizens who have social rights independent of their parents" (Lee, 1982:595) reflected its changed evaluation of children. Various children's charters provided children with the "right to freedom from cruelty, hunger, lack of shelter, lack of 'appropriate education,' " and so on (Lee, 1982:596). Children became a resource of the state and their education an investment by the state (Lee, 1982:594). Parr (1982:15) notes for the Canadian situation that "by the twentieth century childhood and schooling had become closely identified."

In the modern world, the social roles of the child have become increasingly distinct from those of adults (Boli-Bennett and Meyer, 1978). During the eighteenth century, among the lower classes of France, children and adults dressed alike, worked together, and amused themselves with the same diversions. Similarly, the blending of age groups was evident in pre-industrial New France (Moogk, 1982:35). In the twentieth century, children have become organizationally segregated from many aspects of adult life; schools, recreational and medical facilities, prisons, and so on have been developed for the exclusive use of young people. Institutionally (but perhaps not culturally), they are more insulated from adult life than children in the past. This role segregation occurred under the aegis of the state (Boli-Bennett and Meyer, 1978:797).

Four interrelated reasons can be given for the above changes. First, the success of industrial capitalism at the turn of the century put children out of work and into schools to satisfy the growing need for a skilled, educated labour force (Zelizer, 1981:1039). Second, efficient capitalism meant that a cheap juvenile labour force threatened to depress adult male wages (Zelizer, 1981:1040). To protect the adult male breadwinner from competition during times of economic uncertainty such as the Great Depression, schooling became compulsory in Canada and the United States. Third, the exploitation of children by the industrial system and their mistreatment by their own parents (e.g., street children driven out of poor homes) as they became economically useless brought pressure on the state to protect children (Lee, 1982:594). Finally, the new emotional value of children is related to falling birth and mortality rates in the twentieth century. Declining death rates meant that it was no longer necessary for parents to protect themselves against the pain of a child's death by remaining somewhat aloof emotionally (Stone, 1977). A declining birth rate also makes more resources available for each child (Boli-Bennett and Meyer, 1978). As familial resources (emotional and otherwise) devolved fewer children, each child became more precious.

The second major turn-of-the-century development that had far-reaching effects on socialization was the intrusion of science into the rearing of children, especially middle-class children. Psychoanalytic theory as formulated by Sigmund Freud "tolled the death-knell on the ideology of childhood as innocence" (Synnott, 1983:86). Little angels are not aggressive creatures driven by subconscious motives and sexual urges. Such Freudian ideas as the long-term significance of the child's early years and the crucial importance of the unconscious and of parent–child relations became part of many parents' child-rearing concerns. Such Freudian terms as repression, id, Oedipal complex, and super-ego entered the general vocabulary.

From 1900 until the early 1920s, psychology (including the Freudian variety) was dominated by Darwin's theory of evolution and by biological determinism. Parents looked to inborn instincts and heredity for the roots of their children's behaviour. Then, in the 1920s, environmental determinism and behaviouristic learning psychology held sway. Now parents were impressed with the importance of nurture, environmental influences, and learning. Behavioural psychologist John Watson (1924, quoted in Robertson, 1981:107) boasted:

> Give me a dozen healthy infants, well-formed, and my own specified world
> to bring them up in, and I'll guarantee to take any one at random and train
> him to become any type of specialist I might select – doctor, lawyer, artist,
> merchant, chief and, yes, even beggar and thief, regardless of his talents,
> penchants, tendencies, abilities, vocations, and race of his ancestors.

The end of the First World War heralded the "age of the expert" (Synnott, 1983:88). Canadian mothers were deluged with advice from experts, who "contrasted their superior professionalism with parental amateurism" (Strong-Boag, 1982:161). They complained that the Canadian home was the "most mismanaged and bungled of all human industries" and that Canadian women raised their children "by a rule of thumb that hasn't altered since Abraham was a child" (Strong-Boag, 1982:161). According to Ehrenreich and English (1978:183-84):

> The child-raising science which developed was a masculinist science, framed
> at an increasing distance from women and children themselves. It was a
> science which drew more and more on the judgments and studies of the
> experts, less and less on the experience of mothers – until . . . it comes to see
> the mothers not only as the major agents of child development but also as
> the major *obstacles* to it. (Emphasis in original.)

Parents were intimidated by the criticism of pompous experts. The situation was aggravated by Canada's poor international showing in infant and maternal mortality (Strong-Boag, 1982:161). The message to parents: child care is a huge responsibility and failure due to bad handling a distinct possibility (Synnott, 1983:88). However, the experts underestimated the capabilities and common sense of most women and overestimated the value of their own scientific knowledge.

The experts recommended discipline and regularity in eating, sleeping, elimination, and exercise. Indeed, socialization amounted to the efficient running of little machines (Synnott, 1983:87). A Toronto psychologist stated that while "it formerly was believed that mother instinct or mother love was the simple and safe basis for the problems of training, it is now known that a much more reliable guide is the kitchen [clock]" (Strong-Boag, 1982:164). A popular child care manual, Dr. Holt's *The Care and Feeding of Children*, written in 1894 and reissued dozens of times until 1943, dictated minimum emotional involvement: "Babies under six months should never played be with . . ." (quoted in Synnott, 1983:87).

Middle-class parents were most likely to make a "religion" out of this child-rearing advice. Nevertheless, as the story of the Dionne quintuplets illustrates, the homes of the poor had another sort of vulnerability to the care of the child care professionals:

> Up to May, 1934, [their parents] had met the requirements of exemplary
> parenthood according to their faith and their culture: five living children, all
> nourished and housed without recourse to public assistance (Strong-Boag,
> 1982:174).

Nonetheless, with the birth of the famous quints, Mr. and Mrs. Dionne were now found wanting. The Ontario government stepped in and placed the quintuplets under the control of a board of guardians that did not include their parents.

By separating the quintuplets from their family – physically, psychologically, and financially – and by treating the five sisters as royal celebrities, artificially reared, constantly on display, and identically attired, the Ontario government and its appointees had created a schism within the family that could never be healed (Berton, 1977:267).

The rigid disciplinary approach of the 1930s gave way to the new views of the 1940s, which emphasized self-regulation and understanding of the child (Synnott, 1983:87). The new ideas are exemplified by Dr. Benjamin Spock's *Baby and Child Care*, originally published in 1946, revised several times, and a best-seller for several decades. The first sentence reassures new parents: "You know more than you think you do." Page one continues:

> Don't take too seriously all the neighbors say. Don't be overawed by what the experts say. Don't be afraid to trust your own common sense. Bringing up your child won't be a complicated job if you take it easy, trust your own instincts and follow the directions your doctor gives you.

The latest edition of *Dr. Spock's Baby and Child Care* (Spock and Rothenberg, 1985) retains the above wording.

The socio-historical context continued to define the nature of childhood and parenting. The upheaval of the Second World War had challenged the way work was done and the way the sexes related to one another. With the men off to war, women replaced them as workers in the factories and as authorities in the home. In the intensely conservative decade that followed, Rosie the Riveter was sent packing from the factories into suburbia. The feminine mystique centred on home, husband, and "baby boom" kids (Friedan, 1963). Not much had been said about helpless children's need for mothering during the war years. Now, the notion of "maternal deprivation" (Bowlby, 1952) came to mean that mothers who failed to lavish 100 percent of their time and attention on their needy children risked producing neurotics and juvenile delinquents. The myth grew of "the all-powerful, all-giving mother" (Glenn, 1987:361). As Bridenthal (1982:232) points out, advanced capitalist society continues to idealize mother*hood* while isolating and marginalizing mother*ing*. Social childhood and adolescence were prolonged, and responsibility for child rearing was placed in the hands of the female parent, who received sentimental cards on Mother's Day, but little societal support for her trouble.

THE CONTEMPORARY CONTEXT OF CHILD REARING

What ideology of childhood do we embrace today? What does it mean to grow up in the closing years of the twentieth century? Social scientists conclude that the period from the "end of World War II to the present has challenged the culture's fundamental values as profoundly as any coherent set of changes since the Enlightenment" (Brim and Kagan, 1980:18). Small wonder that in this time of rapid social change, Canadians seem confused about the place of children in their lives.

Changes in the larger society present a complex context for socialization. For

Growing up in suburbia differs drastically from the rural, town, or small city upbringing of previous Canadian generations.

example, growing up in suburbia differs drastically from the rural, town, or small city upbringing of previous Canadian generations. The physical layout of suburban housing often isolates families from one another. Long walking distances separate children and teenagers from hockey rinks and playgrounds. As a consequence, kids hang around convenience stores. Suburbanites look to shopping malls for solutions to isolation and boredom. A teenager wrote this letter to the *Calgary Herald* (September 12, 1988) during public debate about the advisability of development of the Alberta Kananaskis mountain area:

> My first childhood memory is that of lying in a stroller, on my back, and being wheeled through a shopping mall. . . . By the time I was 12, I was spending at least 40 per cent of my time hovering around food fairs, clothing shops, parking lots. Can't [the people protesting Kananaskis development] understand that there is a whole generation that due to childhood conditions, really cannot appreciate mountains, fresh air, space? If there was a mall someplace to hang out in Kananaskis, I might visit the place. As it is now, what's the point?

Important influences upon this generation's socialization experiences are outlined below.

TECHNOLOGICAL CHANGE

Historically, science and technology have had profound effects on the family and its socialization of children. For one thing, development of the social sciences was responsible for the ascendancy of the child-rearing experts discussed above. Another important factor was the industrialization of Canadian society. As a result, the family has moved from a production to a consumption unit; most activities defined and rewarded by our society as "work" have been transferred out of the home into the public sphere. Finally, modern contraceptive devices have made possible control of family size.

Technological change continues to affect the family. The symbolic environment, which sociologists see as defining and embracing human life, is rapidly becoming an electronic environment (Ellis, 1983). Young people, surrounded by television, computers, and video arcades, are at the centre of this emerging technological revolution. Television bypasses parents and directs its programming and advertising to children, who watch an average of twenty-one hours a week (Singer, 1986:80). Television "crowds out" other uses of time (Condry and Keith, 1983). Because of its relatively easy availability, television slows down the acquisition of reading skills. Its provision of ready-made ideas dampens creative thinking (Williams, 1986). Advertising promotes hedonistic materialism as a way of life. It peddles harmful products (sugary cereals, alcohol, cigarettes). It creates invidious distinctions between kids who can afford brand name toys and clothes and those who cannot.

Television has been labelled the "total disclosure medium" because information intended for adults becomes readily accessible to children. Youngsters tune in to "incest, promiscuity, homosexuality, sadomasochism, terminal illness, and other secrets of adult life" (Postman, 1982:81). Many parents acknowledge the educational value of television programs such as "Sesame Street" and "Degrassi Junior High," but are appalled by the pervasive mediocrity and violence of the medium.

Computers, "the most powerful yet of the artifacts of this inventive century" (Condry and Keith, 1983:88), are bringing fundamental changes to children's education and recreation. They may even be reaching into people's minds to influence how they think about themselves; users often describe themselves in terms of computer metaphors (Turkle, 1984). Video arcades, with their bluish light and space-age noises, are now being compared with pool halls and condemned as the "latest seducer of the young" (Panelas, 1983:522). Computer games certainly devour a great many quarters. However, in deciphering the logic of the game, in achieving a meeting of mind and computer program, children are preparing themselves to dwell in an increasingly computerized adult world (Turkle, 1984). For the first time, many youngsters know more than their elders and have been instructing their parents in ways that parents have traditionally enculturated children (Williams, 1983:x).

ECONOMIC TRENDS

Closely linked with technology, the economy is another significant influence upon the socialization of young Canadians. Though the family provides a refuge from the stresses of work, "men and women are bound to their jobs out of the family's need for economic survival, and in many ways . . . the nature of paid work shapes the daily experience of families" (Thorne, 1982:16).

The rapid expansion of the economy following the Second World War (especially the availability of service and clerical jobs), along with feminist ideology and improved contraception, was responsible for a dramatic increase in the labour force participation of women (Armstrong and Armstrong, 1984). More than half of Canadian mothers of preschoolers are now in the labour force (Labour Canada, 1986:22). The economic circumstances of the past two decades – first inflation and then recession, combined with rising levels of expectations – have produced the need for two incomes in many Canadian families. For example, a modest bungalow in Don Mills, Ontario, bought for $13,500 in 1954 cost $280,000 thirty-five years later *(Globe & Mail Report on Business Magazine*, August 1988). "In the boom years of the early 60s, 65% of families were couples relying on one income. . . . Just 20 years later, a mere 16% of families consisted of couples with one income earner" (Armstrong and Armstrong, 1988:163). If and when marriages end, women and children often suffer economically, in what has come to be labelled the feminization of poverty.

Economic trends have had a particularly severe impact upon adolescents. Young people are disproportionately represented in jobless figures for this country (Lowe, Krahn, and Tanner, 1988). The youth unemployment rate runs at twice that of the adult population. Regional disparities in the Canadian economy mean that youngsters from economically troubled regions of the country must move to more prosperous regions in order to get work. As economic opportunities for young adults have contracted, older children, instead of becoming independent, are returning to the parental home (Schnaiberg and Goldenberg, 1986). This "crowded nest" phenomenon (or subsidized middle-class lifestyle elsewhere) produces difficulties for both generations. Grown children are a burden on parents' finances and intrude on their privacy. On the other hand, it is hard for dependent members of the younger generation to remain subjected to parental control and to become self-confident adults. Because the work ethic has long been a central motivation for Canadians' lives (Burstein et al., 1984), youth unemployment and the prospect of permanent unavailability of congenial work remain serious concerns in some regions of Canada. Economic insecurity may be one reason why materialism and consumerism as ends in themselves seem to have replaced the youthful idealism of the generation who came to maturity two decades ago (Tausig, 1984).

DEMOGRAPHIC FACTORS

Socialization is influenced by population trends, which in turn are affected by the technological and economic factors discussed above. Decreased fertility, later marriages, and postponed births mean smaller families (see page 132). The average Canadian family now has 1.3 children (Statistics Canada, 1987e). Fewer children per household means more space, more privacy (and probably more isolation), more material possessions, and more educational opportunities for children, especially middle-class children (Eichler, 1983:38). As siblings become less available, the role of other socialization agents, such as parents, peers, and the mass media, is enhanced. In addition, with fewer children, the potential exists for parent-child relationships to increase in emotional intensity. A consensus exists among social scientists that, popular wisdom to the contrary, children without siblings are *not* disadvantaged compared to other youngsters (Hernandez, 1986). Couples without children have become more commonplace. As we have discussed in Chapter Three, although voluntary childlessness is now an acceptable option (Houseknecht, 1987; Veevers, 1979), many currently childless couples would eventually like to have a family. For example, Ramu and

FOR INTEREST

ENCOURAGE MORE BIRTHS OTTAWA TOLD

OTTAWA – The federal government should encourage Canadians to have babies by paying those who have more than two, a Quebec economist says in a report to the federal Health and Welfare Department. Georges Mathews of the Institut national de recherche scientifique says an allowance of $200 a month for each newborn after the second – to be paid until the child is 5 – might be one way of bolstering a declining birth rate. He also calls for better maternity leave, more subsidized day-care spaces and a lowering of the school-entry age to 5 from 6. Mr. Mathews's report is one of 26 research projects commissioned by Ottawa as part of a population study started in 1986.

/CP

Source: *The Globe and Mail*, April 5, 1989.   **Reprinted by Permission of Canadian Press.**

Tavuchis (1986) report that although most Canadian couples accept the proposition that marriage entails parenthood, the timing of childbearing remains problematic. Involuntary childlessness produces role strain for couples who had anticipated parenthood (Matthews and Matthews, 1986; Miall, 1985). In order to establish careers and enhance economic security, some couples are delaying having children until their thirties or even early forties. We speculate that being brought up by older parents produces some unique socialization experiences. While older parents can provide material advantages and are more experienced, their energy and flexibility are probably lower. However, research is not yet available to assess the adjustment of lateborn children.

Socialization is also affected by the "greying" of the Canadian population. For one thing, youngsters are becoming increasingly familar with the elderly. Living in a low-mortality society means lower probability of a child being orphaned or growing up without grandparents (Sullivan, 1983). However, children may find themselves competing with these grandparents for their parents' time, attention, and financial resources. Contemporary middle-aged parents, responsible for both their own offspring and for providing a safety net for elderly needy parents, have been aptly labelled the "sandwich generation." Indeed, as the large numbers of children born in the years following the Second World War become elderly, it seems likely that the attention and resources of our society will increasingly be focused upon these greying baby boomers, and away from the problems of the young. Therefore, shifts in the cultural evaluations and conceptions of childhood may be predicted.

Population immigration into Canada represents a final important contextual aspect of socialization. In the 1960s and 1970s, large numbers of people arrived from Asian, Latin American, and Caribbean countries. These newcomers face the dual challenge of conveying something of their culture of origin to their children, while they and their offspring learn to fit into their new society. Often, the new immigrant family protects its members from stress by a "creative schizophrenia" that allows its members to be "modern" at work and "traditional" at home (Berger and Berger, 1984).

THE CONTEMPORARY CANADIAN FAMILY

The structure of the Canadian family has altered as it adapts to the social and economic conditions discussed in the foregoing section. These sociocultural factors, and structural changes that have occurred in the family in response to these developments, greatly complicate its socialization function. Ironically, parents today are being judged, by their children, by themselves, and by various professional experts, according to higher standards than ever before in history (Becker, 1981). Modern society assumes that if the child develops undesirable qualities, "the practices of the family during the early years – especially parental neglect, indifference, restriction, and absence of joyful and playful interaction – are the major culprits" (Kagan, 1984:242). Children's difficulties are especially likely to be attributed to failures in mothering. Nevertheless, both historical and sociological analyses show the family to be a resilient institution whose perform-ance as socializer of the young has not been seriously compromised (Mackie, 1989).

Changes in the social organization of the family that affect socialization are briefly enumerated in the paragraphs to follow. These matters are explained more fully elsewhere in this book.

As we shall see in Chapter Nine, growing up in a one-parent family influences children's socialization. More than one-third of divorces occurring in Canada involve dependent children (Statistics Canada, 1986b). When families break up, children's lives change dramatically. The impact of these events depends upon children's age, their gender, parents' management of the divorce transition (Spanier and Furstenberg, 1987:426), and the family's social class (Ambert, 1985). In any case, relationships with both custodial and non-resident parents depart from the traditional script of the nuclear family. For example, joint custody often means children shuttle back and forth between two households. One in ten Canadian single parents has never been married (Davids, 1985:3). Though not all children of single parents are in this situation, those exposed to the premature parenthood of unmarried teenage mothers "are often short-changed in their emotional and social development" (Schlesinger, 1985:37). When single parent-hood means single motherhood, as it typically does, children grow up in a family facing financial difficulties, even poverty. However, not all the consequences are deleterious. Empirical studies consistently show "that marital conflict, as perceived by the children in a two-parent family, is more harmful to the children than their living in a peaceful single-parent family (with little or no postdivorce bickering between the ex-spouses or using the children as pawns in the parents' psychological war)" (Raschke, 1987:616).

Many offspring of divorces and never-married parents eventually find themselves part of reconstituted families involving "his" and/or "her" children from previous relationships, and "their" children from the present marriage. A certain amount of role confusion and ambiguity seems inevitable in complex families involving parents, siblings, step-parents, step-siblings, and an assortment of grandparents, aunts, and uncles (Cherlin, 1978). For example, who has authority to discipline children? What kinship terms are to be used? (If a child calls her mother "Mom," what should she call her stepmother?) Does the erstwhile eldest child who has acquired older siblings lose privileges as he descends the pecking order? Although more studies are necessary, American researchers conclude that "the majority of children growing up in stepfamilies appear to develop a reasonably amicable relationship with their stepparents and are not severely handicapped in their social interactions" (Ihlinger-Tallman, 1988:35).

The socialization process has also been influenced by the increased labour force participation of Canadian women. One consequence is that the majority of Canadian preschool children are regularly cared for by someone other than a parent (Eichler, 1983:249). According to the federal Task Force on Child Care (1986), chaired by Katie Cooke, the availability and quality of day care is a national problem. Another consequence of women's work outside the home is the greater emotional involvement of fathers in socializing their children. However, despite a plethora of magazine articles about nurturant "androgynous fathers" anxious for involvement in their children's lives (Robinson and Barret, 1986), a recent Canadian study concludes

> that while men who have children 16 years of age or younger do not completely neglect their share of the parental role, they find their role less taxing and time-consuming, less confining, affording more freedom and discretion, and with a more leisure-like nature (Horna and Lupri, 1987:72).

Now that the majority of mothers are engaged in work outside the home, the question of the consequences of this absence for their offspring has become less controversial than it once was. It is extremely difficult to generalize about the socialization consequences of non-familial child care facilities because these facilities range from nannies in residence, to mothers' baby-sitting co-operatives, licensed child care centres run by highly trained personnel, unlicensed arrangements in church basements, to the neighbours baby-sitting in their homes to make a few dollars. Obviously, social class and income influence the type and quality of non-familial child care experienced by a child. Research shows that children are not adversely affected by a mother's decision to work outside the home or to stay home, so long as she is comfortable with her decision (Task Force on Child Care, 1986:209). Moreover, studies of the development of bonding between mother and child find little difference among children at home with their mothers, day care children, and children cared for by baby-sitters (Gerson et al., 1984:447). Positive effects accrue from *good* child care, especially to children from disadvantaged homes (Task Force on Child Care, 1986:209).

Nevertheless, experts on child development (Suransky, 1982:200) caution that effective socialization requires that one or more adults be "crazy" about the child, that is, be irrationally and unconditionally involved with the child. Effective socialization also requires consistency and predictability in the child's relations with significant others (Berger and Berger, 1984:152). Unfortunately, the shortage of quality day care in this country creates serious problems. The number of children in need outnumbers spaces available in licensed centres by more than ten to one (*Maclean's,* November 10, 1986:48). However, we must also keep in mind that the fact that both parents often have responsibilities outside the home is increasing the role flexibility of family members.

The final task of this section is to comment on adults' imagery of children in contemporary society. The perceived worth of children has certainly risen from its turn-of-the-century level. Though their traditional economic value to their families has declined, those concerned with child welfare have adopted a *human capital* or investment rationale. The idea here is that investment in the welfare of children will eventually yield a rich return to society (Brim and Kagan, 1980:21). Two additional images co-exist upon this substructure or acknowledgment of the children's significance: *children as victims of adults* and *children as threats to adult society* (Thorne, 1987).

The first image of children as victims recognizes what has been labelled the two-edged nature of family life: "One edge is warm, protective, and fiercely loyal while the other edge is destructive, narrow and ultimately violent" (Morgan, 1975, cited in Himelfarb and Richardson, 1982:411). Children (and women) have been vulnerable to family violence (Badgley, 1984). As we shall see in Chapter Twelve, each province and territory of Canada has legislation to protect children against adult neglect, abuse, or exploitation. Indeed, "laws are starting to incorporate the needs of children as affirmative rights expressed by positive standards, and not just to assert negative standards of minimum care" (Tomlinson and Foote, 1987:236).

However, children are also pictured as threats or menaces to adult society (Thorne, 1987). Some potential parents consider them hindrances to their personal growth or career advancement (Lasch, 1977). Raising children is time-consuming and expensive – it now costs at least $100,000 to raise a child from birth to age eighteen (*Royal Bank Reporter*, Spring 1986:18). Children are unwelcome in many restaurants and housing complexes. Adults tend to be especially negative toward teenagers, who "are criticized as people whose chief delights are sexual immorality and attendance at rock concerts, smoking drugs and listening to shocking music" (Friesen, 1986:11).

In sum, considerable ambiguity exists in Canadian society concerning the value and place of children. As a result of the broad factors described earlier – industrialization, economic situation, labour force participation of women, control over fertility, feminist values – adults tend to be confused about parenthood. For example, according to Meg Luxton's (1980:111) observations of women in Flin Flon, Manitoba:

> When groups of mothers with young children get together, their discussion inevitably revolved around their ambivalent feelings about their work as mothers. They liked their children, enjoyed their company and delighted in watching and helping them grow. Yet they felt trapped by the complete dependency of their children and by their own sense of total responsibility.

Sociologist Nancy Mandell (1988:75-76) strikes an optimistic note about the future conceptualization of childhood. She suggests that as the combination of labour force and family roles becomes a lifelong reality for most Canadian women, children will increasingly ease the burdens of household work:

> Rather than being portrayed as frail, dependent and helpless creatures, children [will be] socially constructed as robust, independent and helpful individuals who are more involved in family economics.

She goes on to point out that, although children are indeed financially costly, "women and men still claim that having children provides the greatest happiness, pleasure and job in their lives" (Mandell, 1988:76).

CHANGING SOCIAL-SCIENTIFIC PERSPECTIVES ON SOCIALIZATION

Social-scientific views on socialization evolve over time as changes in the broad social context stimulate developments in scientific thought. In addition, the results of research show some theoretical notions to be promising and others to be dead-ends. In either case, fashions and foibles in scientific orientations have implications for lay child-rearing practices. At any one time, a diversity of perspectives co-exists; for the most part, they are complementary rather than opposed sets of ideas. After all,

> socialization is not a unitary phenomenon, but rather a term for a variety of processes. The relationships among these specific processes are by no means fully worked out and understood; a unified and comprehensive theory of socialization has yet to be achieved (Elkin and Handel, 1984:33).

These theoretical viewpoints are also closely related to the major socialization issues of concern to social scientists. This section will briefly examine some of these theories of socialization.

PSYCHOANALYTIC THEORY

As noted earlier, Freud's wide-ranging ideas about socialization were a pervasive influence in previous years upon both social-scientific and popular thought about child rearing. However, "the passage of time has witnessed a decline in its importance" (Zigler and Seitz, 1978:733-34). Little support now exists for the psychoanalytic position that maternal styles of feeding, weaning, and toilet training shape children's personalities (Peterson and Rollins, 1987:471). A major exception to this generalization – feminist use of psychoanalytic ideas (Chodorow, 1978) to explain the emergence of gender – is discussed below.

Psychoanalytic theorists regard socialization as society's attempt to tame the child's inborn, animal-like nature. Freud believed that the roots of human behaviour lie in the irrational, unconscious dimensions of the mind. He assumed that the adult personality is the product of the child's early experiences in the family. Freud saw the personality as composed of three energy systems: the id, the ego, and the super-ego. The *id* is the biological basis of personality, the *ego* is the psychological basis of personality, and the *super-ego* is the social basis of personality (Shaw and Costanzo, 1982).

Freud held that every child goes through a series of personality stages, each stage marked by sexual preoccupation with a different part of the body – the mouth, the anus, the genital area. Personality development, according to psychoanalytic theory, is essentially complete by five years.

On the positive side, Freud's emphasis on early family experiences stimulated research on cross-cultural variations in child-rearing practices. His solution to the problem of how society gets inside the individual, namely, the identification of children with their parents, was a major insight. His consideration of roles played by the emotions, sexuality, and the unconscious covers aspects of human motivation that no other theoretical approach attempted. Finally, the emphasis of psychoanalysis "on conflicts between individual and society still informs our thinking about human behavior" (Deaux and Wrightsman, 1988:8).

Psychoanalytic theory has also been severely criticized, and these criticisms explain why its popularity has declined. Much of the theory does not lend itself to empirical test, and that is a fatal flaw. In addition, feminists object to Freud's perception of women as defective men, and to his argument that the moral thought of females is inferior to that of males (Gilligan, 1982). Moreover, Freud's biological theory holds that anatomy is destiny. By contrast, sociologists emphasize society's role in moulding personality. Also, his ideas were based on his experiences with middle-class Viennese patients during the Victorian era. Consequently, care must be exercised in generalizing his notions to normal populations and to other cultures and historical periods. Lastly, contemporary social scientists, convinced that socialization occurs over the life span, disagree with Freud's belief that personality development ends with childhood. For example, Freud's disciple, Erik Erikson (1963, 1968), argued that development continues throughout the life cycle from infancy to old age.

Despite telling criticisms such as these, a few scholars have urged reconsideration of the utility to feminists of some segments of Freudian thought. (See Sydie, 1987, for a useful discussion of their work.) These feminist friends of psychoanalytic theory take as their starting point the Freudian assumption of children's identification with parents. However, turning Freud on his head, feminist theorists such as Chodorow (1978) focus upon the mother, the enormous power she exerts over young children, and the consequent fear of maternal figures experienced by relatively powerless children. According to Chodorow, the dynamics of children's separation from the mother to become individuals carries lifelong consequences for both girls and boys. However, other feminists share Lerman's (1987:44) contrary position that Freud's original theories have not served women well: "I see the theory as so fundamentally flawed in its thinking about women that it cannot be repaired, however extensive the tinkering with it."

LEARNING THEORY

Since the beginning of this century, social scientists have debated the relative contributions of biology and environment to human development. From the late 1920s until the last decade, environmentalism and the *nurture* side of the nature–nurture argument prevailed. Since the consensus was that *Homo sapiens* become human through learning, theories that explicated the precise mechanisms of learning became enormously important. For a time, "socialization theory was virtually synonymous with learning theory" (Zigler and Seitz, 1978:737). Also, learning theorists' empirical orientation and experimental tradition were salutary influences on socialization research. Partly because of renewed interest in the genetic foundation of socialization and sociobiology (see below), learning theory has now fallen to the status of "one valuable approach among many" (Zigler and Seitz, 1978:738).

Learning theories focus on three main types of learning: classical conditioning, operant conditioning, and imitation. In the first two types, learning occurs as a result of practice or the repetition of association (Yussen and Santrock, 1978:164). However, since much of what children learn is through observation rather than extensive practice, the last type (associated with Bandura, 1977; Bandura and Walters, 1963) is the most important for socialization. The imitation/modelling approach to learning considers youngsters to be more active participants in their own socialization than the other two types. They "can learn lessons contained in the reinforcement received by others (vicarious reinforcement), provide their own rewards (self-reinforcement), and antici- pate their own futures" (Peterson and Rollins, 1987:478).

How do socialization experts assess learning theory? On the positive side, when they wish to explain the precise mechanisms involved in the internalization of socialization lessons, they turn to these extensively developed and researched psycho- logical theories. Nevertheless, a serious drawback is the assumption of a unidirectional influence from caretaker to child. Below we discuss the increasing appreciation of the role children play in the socialization of themselves and of their caretakers. The cognitive-developmental and symbolic interactionist approaches better capture these aspects of socialization.

THE COGNITIVE-DEVELOPMENTAL APPROACH

Cognitive-developmental theory, associated with Swiss psychologist Jean Piaget (1928, 1932, 1970), has been an extremely influential approach to socialization. However, Piaget's work has been more central to child psychology than to sociology.

As the word *cognitive* suggests, Piaget is interested in thought processes such as reasoning, remembering, and believing. His concern with moral thought, carried on by Kohlberg (1976), is a particularly important dimension of his theory. The term *development* indicated Piaget's interest in the systematic changes that occur over time in children's thought processes.

The theory's central assumption is that the child needs to make sense of his/her cognitive environment. The structure of children's thinking changes in discrete stages until eventually they use the adult rules for reality construction (Kessler and McKenna, 1978:96). Cognitive-developmental theory assumes that intellectual functioning, and hence behaviour, is governed by patterns of cognitive structure called *schemas*. Schemas result from experience and then influence subsequent interpretations of the physical and social worlds (Bush and Simmons, 1981:138). For example, children learn the words "boy" and "girl," and they hear others label them in this way. Once the child learns the implications of the gender schema, it becomes a major organizer and determinant of many attitudes and activities: "I am a boy, and therefore I should act like a boy and do the things that boys do," or "I am a girl and therefore I should act like a girl and do the things girls do." Psychologist Sandra Bem (1983) ponders the problem of feminist parents who wish to raise *gender-aschematic* children in a *gender-schematic* world.

Although cognitive-developmental theory, like psychoanalytic theory, posits a universal sequence of growth changes, the former provides more room for the influence of social interaction. However, the socialization role of parents is played down. Indeed, cognitive-developmental theory has been described as a self-socialization theory, since the motivation and initiative in organizing cognitions come from the child, not from the socializing adults (Maccoby and Jacklin, 1974:364). Lastly, a major difficulty with this perspective is that cognitive development as such is not really explained. Because the underlying mechanisms are not specified, it seems to just happen.

A highly acclaimed book by Carol Gilligan (1982) argues that both Piaget and Kohlberg had based their ideas about moral development on research conducted almost exclusively with male samples. From her observations of both sexes, Gilligan maintains that females and males speak with different "moral voices." The *male justice orientation* is concerned with preserving rights, upholding principles, and obeying rules, while the *female care orientation* speaks of concern for others and connectedness with them. Gilligan's intriguing hypotheses have provoked considerable debate (see Kerber et al., 1986; Walker, 1984).

SYMBOLIC INTERACTIONISM

Symbolic interactionism is the most sociological of the approaches discussed so far. In comparison with the other theories, this perspective emphasizes the importance of social influence and of language. Interactionists, like cognitive-developmentalists and unlike learning theorists, stress the active part played by the child in his/her own socialization. Their perspective is in line with the less deterministic view of socialization that has emerged over the last few decades (Peterson and Rollins, 1987). Children are not the passive recipients of culture, but actively discover and interpret their world (Thorne, 1987:94).

Symbolic interactionists view the individual and society as two sides of the same coin. One cannot exist without the other. Take the case of Genie (Pines, 1981). From the age of twenty months until she was thirteen, this California girl lived in nearly total isolation. She was harnessed to a potty chair all day and caged in a crib all night. She was almost never spoken to. When Genie was discovered, she was malnourished, deformed, incontinent, and "eerily silent." She scored at the one-year-old level on intelligence tests. However, her subsequent development under the tutelage of rehabilitation specialists suggested that her deficiencies were not inborn. Rather, this mistreated child had been deprived of emotional contact with reasonably intelligent, articulate adults in her early years.

Interactionist socialization theories emphasize the development of the self and the linkage between the emergence of self-awareness and the acquisition of language. Cooley (1902) and Mead (1934) saw the genesis of self in the child's intense social experience within primary groups. Cooley's metaphor of the *looking-glass self* illustrates the point made by both early sociologists that the content of the self reflects children's interpretation of others' appraisals of themselves. (Research shows a strong association between what we believe others think of us and our self-concepts, and a weaker association between our self-concepts and what others *actually* think of us (Rosenberg, 1981:597-98).)

Symbolic interactionists often undertake studies of socialization that employ observational techniques in order to see how children define their own situation. For example, Gary Alan Fine (1986) writes about "the dirty play of little boys." Adults thoroughly disapprove of such pre-adolescent pranks as "mooning" cars (pulling down one's trousers while facing away from the traffic), "egging" cars, and ringing doorbells and running away. However, according to Fine, these activities serve as anticipatory socialization for manhood. Males are supposed to be tough, cool, and aggressive. "There is risk involved in throwing eggs at houses or at moving cars; one could get caught, beaten, grounded, or even arrested" (Fine, 1986:66). Boys gain status with their peers for behaviour that adults regard as troublesome. Such behaviour is the antithesis of "girls' play." In short, a boy's identity as a male is enhanced by engaging in "dirty play," partly because it is *dirty* play (i.e., it defies adult authority), partly because it is *not* girls' play.

THE SOCIOBIOLOGICAL APPROACH

Over the past twenty-five years, there has been a new open-mindedness concerning the similarities between human beings and the infrahuman species and an increased emphasis on genetic and constitutional factors in determining the outcome of the socialization process (Zigler and Seitz, 1978:736). Many new ideas have been introduced into sociology from a relatively new subdiscipline called sociobiology, which studies the genetic and biochemical foundations of animal social behaviour (Wilson, 1975). This move away from exclusive environmentalist explanations has stimulated considerable debate (see the May 1985 issue of the *Canadian Review of Sociology and Anthropology*). The most controversial aspect of sociobiology is the extrapolation of its ideas to human social life.

For our purposes, the essential features of sociobiology can be reduced to three:

1. The method is *evolutionary* and the time scale is large. This extension of the Darwinian theory of natural selection holds that all animals act so as to maximize the chances of their genes being propagated and surviving to maturity (Sayers, 1980). It is assumed that any adaptive behaviour has a genetic component and that it has developed so as to maximize the number of genes favouring that behaviour being passed on to future generations (Lowe, 1978:119).

2. Sociobiologists' primary means of determining whether human behaviour is genetically or environmentally determined is to look for *cultural universals* (Lowe, 1978:121). It is assumed that behaviour observable in all societies is adaptive and therefore determined primarily by the human genetic make-up.

3. A large part of sociobiology's data and principles is based on the behaviour of the *lower animals*. Extrapolations to human social life are made from these non-human species (Kunkel, 1977:69). As one critic put it, sociobiologists are "more than willing to leap from ants to chickens to baboons to humans and back again, with only the most casual glance at the intellectual chasms yawning beneath their feet" (Fausto-Sterling, 1985:162). The strategies of searching for universals in human behaviour and analysing animal behaviour are often combined. After a universal human behavioural trait has been identified, sociobiologists then attempt to find similar behaviour in non-human primates in order to strengthen the argument that human behaviour has evolved through natural selection (Lowe, 1978:121).

Sociobiology faces formidable problems, the most serious of which concerns the difficulty of subjecting its hypotheses to empirical test. Sociobiology has been criticized for its conservative values. Nevertheless, sociologists cannot afford to ignore or misunderstand the biological substratum of human behaviour. Alice Rossi (1987:73), an influential proponent of this approach to the family, argues that "neither Marxism nor feminism, to say nothing of mainstream social science, has yet taken up the challenge of the biological component to human behavior, despite the fact that sexual dimorphism is important in both human production and reproduction." Rossi goes on to say that a sociology that does not confront the biological substratum of human behaviour is sterile.

Some of the best examples of the sociobiological approach to socialization are contained in the book *Parenting Across the Life Span: Biosocial Dimensions* (1987), edited by Lancaster et al. As the title suggests, the various articles examine parent–child relationships across species and across time.

CONTEMPORARY ISSUES IN SOCIALIZATION RESEARCH

The current theoretical and empirical work of socialization specialists involves seven central themes. These professional views have some impact on folk theories of childhood and child-rearing practices. Many of these ideas have already been mentioned, implicitly or explicitly, in earlier sections of this chapter.

ACTIVE VERSUS PASSIVE VIEW OF THE CHILD

One authority claims that "perhaps the most significant trend in the area of socialization . . . is an increasing shift from a passive to an active view of the individual" (Gecas, 1981:197). Many years ago, Dennis Wrong (1961) complained that sociology encouraged an "over-socialized conception" of human beings. By this, Wrong meant that sociology depicted people as completely moulded by the norms and values of their society. If it were possible, such thoroughgoing indoctrination would, of course, destroy individuality and render nonsensical the notion of free will and responsibility for one's actions.

Sociologists are now convinced that children are *not* passive recipients of the socialization process. Rather, each child "resists it, participates in it, collaborates with it in varying degrees" (Berger and Berger, 1975:57). Neither are children identical products turned out by an omnipotent socialization factory. The existence of at least some deviant behaviour within every society testifies to the fact that no system of socialization is perfectly efficient. A considerable amount of evidence (much of it collected by symbolic interactionists and cognitive-developmentalists) shows that children play an active role in their own socialization. They select experiences according to their own idiosyncratic styles (Zigler and Seitz, 1978:739). As well, researchers now acknowledge that children begin with differing "biological predispositions which cannot easily be changed by caretakers" (Zigler and Seitz, 1978:739).

SOCIALIZATION AS A TWO-WAY PROCESS

The earlier image of the child as passive recipient of socialization implied that socialization was a one-way process. Socialization theories such as learning and psychoanalytic theories encouraged this idea that parents were on the dispensing end and children on the receiving end (Bush and Simmons, 1981:162).

As the next chapter demonstrates, socialization is now seen to be a two-way process. Just as the parents socialize the child, the child socializes the parents (Rheingold, 1969). This mutual influence extends from infancy, where the effect of an

infant's cry upon the parents is "all out of proportion to his age, size and accomplish-
ments" (Rheingold, 1966, quoted in Peters, 1982:3), through adolescence, and into
adulthood. Interesting changes take place in the socialization functions of the aging
family. As parents enter the last decades of their lives and become more dependent, the
burden of socialization has shifted so that now adult children interpret the world for
their elderly parents (Hagestad, 1987:413). However, the latter teach their children
important lessons about aging and dying.

SOCIALIZATION AS A LIFELONG PROCESS

Earlier research, under the influence of psychoanalytic theory, stressed the first years of
childhood. By contrast, an important new direction in socialization research is the focus
upon individuals in interaction with other family members, across the life course (Elder,
1985). Current work distinguishes between primary socialization (which occurs in
childhood and adolescence) and adult socialization. Although primary socialization lays
the foundation for later learning, it cannot completely prepare people for adulthood. For
one thing, our age-graded society confronts individuals with new role expectations as
they move through life. Moving beyond the family into day care centre and neighbourhood, entering school, becoming an adolescent, choosing an occupation, marrying,
bearing children, encountering middle age, retiring, and dying all involve new lessons to
be learned.

As society changes, people must equip themselves to cope with new situations, for
example, technological job obsolescence, changes in sexual mores, war. Finally, some
individuals encounter specialized situations with which they must deal. Geographical
and social mobility, marital breakdowns, and physical handicaps all require further
socialization (Brim, 1966).

An important issue related to the view of socialization as a lifelong process
concerns the degree of continuity and consistency of personality throughout life (Bush
and Simmons, 1981). Although earlier scholars contended that personality was fixed in
childhood, contemporary social scientists tend to emphasize the malleability of the self
and the possibility of continuing change. Apparently the "consequences of the events of
early childhood are continually transformed by later experience, making the course of
human development more open than many have believed" (Brim and Kagan, 1980:1).

ADOLESCENT SOCIALIZATION

Accompanying the general consensus that socialization is a lifelong process is the rather
recent realization among social scientists that the socialization that occurs between
childhood and the adult years requires special attention. Adolescence has been both
romanticized as a period of irresponsible frivolity and deplored as a time of inevitable
distress and conflict. Results of a national survey of Canadian teenagers by Bibby and
Posterski (1985) contradict the first view. In the words of a sixteen-year-old Ontario
girl:

> Teens are expected to feel happy about themselves while enjoying their
> "carefree" years. These years I find are hard, trying, and painful – it's

basically growing up and coming to terms with the fact that you're now almost an adult and can't depend on any one (Bibby and Posterski, 1985:51).

Sociocultural changes discussed earlier in this chapter complicate growing up. For one thing, the extension of high school and post-secondary schooling means continued dependence for adolescents, while the rise of the market economy implies their independence (Fasick, 1984). A Quebec girl told researchers Bibby and Posterski (1985:159): "Teenagers today are scared. With unemployment, the economy, divorce, and the world's peace situation – we all wonder what will happen."

Although authorities no longer regard the "storm and stress" emphasized by pioneer psychologist G. Stanley Hall (1904) as the hallmark of adolescence, most agree that the years spent in the "uneasy biological borderland between childhood and adulthood" (Berger and Berger, 1984:5) entail important socialization tasks.

The question "Who am I?" (studied by symbolic interactionists) takes on special urgency in adolescence. Pubescent changes (a body growth rate equal to that of early childhood and the new addition of genital maturity) disturb the sense of self established in childhood. Consequently, adolescents face the task of re-establishing identity, of refining their "sense of who they are and what makes them different from everybody else" (Santrock, 1984:425). Gender identity, an understanding of oneself as a sexually

Adolescence has been both romanticized as a period of irresponsible frivolity and deplored as a time of inevitable distress and conflict.

PETER COMSTOCK INC.

and socially mature female or male, is a fundamental component of this refined identity. Research suggests that it is not pubertal change per se that accounts for the turmoil some adolescents experience. Rather, changing biology and altering (and increased) social expectations interact to place pressure on youngsters this age (Petersen, 1987:32).

Socialization to function as an adolescent and the anticipatory socialization for adulthood both involve learning values, skills, and roles. This learning occurs in interaction with significant others who provide the mirror for the adolescent version of self. The family remains influential where values, future goals, and educational aspirations are at stake. However, in matters of current lifestyle (fashion, music, leisure activities), friends take precedence over family (Davies and Kandel, 1981; Fasick, 1984). Obviously, "the stronger the bonds between parents and children, the more central the parents will be as significant others" (Acock, 1984:160).

EXPANDED SET OF SOCIALIZATION AGENTS

Classic socialization theories concentrated on the socialization link between child and parent, especially the mother. However, as mentioned earlier, various social forces have operated to decrease the amount of parent-child interaction and consequently to increase the child's involvement with other socialization agents. Therefore, although the family is still seen to be the primary agent, social scientists have turned their attention to an expanded set of socialization agents – peers, fictive kin, schools, community organizations, voluntary associations, and the mass media. In addition, mothers' recent involvement with activities outside the home has enhanced social scientists' interest in the socialization efforts of other family members, especially fathers. The new apprecia-tion of the lifelong nature of socialization has widened the set of agents to include work settings, self-help groups, counsellors, religious organizations, and prisons.

A very important trend in recent socialization research is recognition of the importance of studying family roles, as well as those of extrafamilial socialization agents, as a network. This systemic perspective facilitates understanding of how these different agencies interact with one another in their impact on the child (and the child's impact upon them). "That is, the parent-child relationship interfaces with schools, peers, work settings, socioeconomic conditions, and the surrounding ethnic environ-ment. All of these settings, including the parent-child relationship, influence each other" (Peterson and Rollins, 1987:496). Fortunately, computer technology has provided the means to analyse this complicated matter of reciprocal interaction.

FEMINIST INFLUENCES UPON THE STUDY OF SOCIALIZATION

The renewed women's liberation movement provoked a fundamental realization: the sociology that had previously been accepted as the science of society was really the male science of male society (Bernard, 1973). In sociology, "we have envisioned our social universe as if men were in the centre and everything and everybody – women, other men, children, social institutions, etc. – revolved around men" (Eichler, 1984:35). Feminist sociologists called for a recentred sociology, a sociology *for* rather than *of* women (Smith, 1975:367). This radical shift in thinking has influenced the conceptual-ization of socialization. The study of the role of power and violence in families, of women's domestic labour, of pregnancy, childbirth, and mothering, of gender socialization, all attest to this "Copernican revolution in scholarship" (Eichler, 1984). The feminist influence is being felt in related disciplines. For example, a provocative book by Belenky et al. (1987) proposes that females and males have distinctive ways of knowing and learning.

Considerable attention is now being given to *gender socialization*, a subtype of general socialization, which involves the processes through which individuals learn to be feminine and masculine according to the expectations current in their society. In particular, individuals develop gender identity and learn gender norms. Especially important is the internalization of norms specifying gender inequality and gender division of labour. In Eichler's words (1980:20), gender socialization is "the systematic teaching of a double standard." Gender socialization has been successful when the double standard seems "natural" to the people affected by it.

The combination of the sociology of knowledge and symbolic interactionism offers a promising avenue to explanation of gender socialization (Mackie, 1987). The sociology of knowledge allows us to understand that the essence of gender is power, that femininity and masculinity are rooted in social structure. "The domination of women by men precedes the emergence of class domination and is structured deeply into the relations of production and reproduction of almost all known societies" (Miles, 1982:9). Symbolic interactionist theory enables "us to link the private and the public, the innermost acts of the individual with the widest kinds of social-historical phenomena" (Gerth and Mills, 1953:xvi). For symbolic interactionists, gender socialization is one aspect of the self-development discussed earlier (Cahill, 1980).

Research suggests that although the thinking of Canadian children about gender is changing, they still entertain traditional sex-typed ideas. For one thing, like children throughout the world, Canadian youngsters continue to demonstrate thorough familiarity with gender stereotypes (Williams and Best, 1982). Moreover, a study of career aspirations of elementary school children reported evidence of both liberated and traditional thought. When asked, "What do you want to be when you grow up?" two-thirds of the girls mentioned a traditionally masculine occupation. Though almost all of these "masculine" choices were learned professions rather than trades, a few girls wanted to be mechanics or truck drivers. Only 1 percent of the boys chose traditionally feminine careers (office worker, nursery school teacher). The boys looked forward to a wider range of future jobs than did the girls. Boys, but not girls, wanted to be astronomers, air traffic controllers, stockbrokers, machinists, plumbers, mathematicians. Closer scrutiny of the girls' responses suggested, however, that many did not apply to themselves their general belief in the equality of the sexes.

> Many of them seemed to be saying, "Yes, women can become doctors, but
> I expect to be a nurse," "Bank managers can be women as well as men, but I
> am going to be a teller," or "Dental assistant is my career goal, although
> I know that women can be dentists" (Labour Canada, 1986:55).

Finally, Baker's (1985) national study of the aspirations of adolescents reported that young Canadian women looked forward to enjoyable work and satisfying family life. However, they are vague about exactly how this is to be accomplished. A seventeen-year-old Toronto girl had this to say:

[At age twenty-two] I'll be owning or managing a clothing store. [At age thirty] At 6:00 I'll get up and get breakfast for my husband and two kids. One is a baby and one is school-age. I'll drive the one kid to school, feed the baby, and play with it. Then I'll put the baby to bed and watch the soaps. . . . [Later in the interview – what happened to your store?] Oh! I forgot about it. I guess someone is looking after it (Baker, 1985:88).

Why does gender traditionalism persist? While it is true that patriarchal authority is not as strong as the historical record indicates it once was, Canadian society remains a gendered society. Females are still culturally devalued, and the male–female distinction is a basic principle of social organization. The gender division of labour children experience at home is a critical determinant of their understanding of femininity and masculinity. A recent study of the headship of Canadian families concluded that "traditional male-dominated authority patterns continue to characterize much of family life" (Rosenthal and Marshall, 1986:195). Despite women's labour force participation, mothers and fathers continue to model traditional division of household work (Horna and Lupri, 1987; Michelson, 1985). Until sex/gender becomes unimportant as a basis of role assignment in the family, children's sex-typed thinking and behaviour will continue.

INTRASOCIETAL VARIATIONS IN SOCIALIZATION

A continuing trend in socialization research is the examination of the ways various segments of society differ in their socialization practices and the outcomes of those practices (Zigler and Seitz, 1978:744). This approach to socialization is especially appropriate for our heterogeneous society. Although many values and norms are shared by all Canadians, differences are found by region, by language, by social class, by ethnic group, by religion, and by place of residence (urban or rural). These variations in social environment bring with them variations in the content of socialization. Social class and ethnicity will serve to illustrate the broader problem of intrasocietal variations in socialization.

Members of different social classes, by virtue of experiencing different conditions of life, come to see the world differently and develop different conceptions of social reality (Kohn, 1977). Distinctive occupational backgrounds are related to parental values. According to a Hamilton, Ontario, study (Pineo and Looker, 1983), white-collar families consider their children's self-direction to be more important and obedience to parents to be less important than do blue-collar families. Working-class parents almost everywhere are more likely than middle-class parents to be intolerant of children's insolence and temper, to restrict autonomy, to insist on good manners, and to wish to maintain male–female distinctions (Lambert et al., 1980). Moreover, social class is a key factor affecting socialization in one-parent families (Ambert, 1985). As noted earlier, single parenthood typically means single motherhood. The end of marriage frequently spells downward economic mobility, even poverty, for the women involved (Boyd, 1977). Single mothers from lower socio-economic levels are especially vulnerable. The class origins of a child remain important throughout life. For example, they are a significant influence upon the occupation that a child will eventually choose (Boyd et al., 1985; Guppy et al., 1984).

Ethnicity is a socialization influence that is often related to social class. Despite Canada's official policy of multiculturalism within a bilingual framework, it is difficult for ethnic groups to maintain their ethnic identity in the face of powerful pressures for assimilation to the Anglo-dominant culture (Zureik and Pike, 1975). As Elkin (1983:149) notes: "Unless a child learns and experiences his basic ethnic identity within his family and other early primary groups, it seems unlikely that he will ever strongly feel it thereafter." Several studies of immigrant Canadian families underline the added complexity of their socialization experiences. A study of immigrant Indian and Pakistani children in a western Canadian city (Wakil et al., 1981) reports that, while parents were willing to tolerate their children's enthusiasm for Western food, music, and festivals such as Christmas, the generations clashed over critical matters such as dating and arranged marriage. A study of Vietnamese families in Victoria, British Columbia, illustrates the reciprocal nature of socialization. Some parents, as yet unaccustomed to Canadian languages or customs, rely upon their children to mediate their contact with the larger society (Woon, 1986).

CONCLUSION

This chapter has considered changing perspectives on socialization in terms of Western culture's historical constructs of childhood, changing socio-historical context, socialization theories, and major research issues. Throughout, we have emphasized the confusion and ambivalence of Canadians about the place of children in our society.

While prognostication is always a risky business, the future study of socialization will likely include:

1. the examination of research questions with multiple methods: quantitative surveys, computer simulations, naturalistic observation, and experiments;

2. increased attention to socialization across the life course, with investment of more time and resources in following the same individuals throughout the life cycle;

3. very intensive (and practical) interest in socialization for the middle and later years of life;

4. study of socialization in the less traditional forms of family organization, such as one-parent and blended families, and multiple step-family networks;

5. enhanced influence of feminist ideas upon socialization research.

DISCUSSION QUESTIONS

1. What do social scientists mean when they say that childhood is a social construct?

2. How did industrialism and capitalism alter conceptualizations of children and childhood?

3. Discuss the basic assumptions behind each of the following theories of

socialization: psychoanalytic theory; learning theory; cognitive-developmental theory; symbolic interactionism; sociobiology.

4. How do the socialization experiences of females and males differ?
5. What impact does advertising have on young people?
6. What are some ethnic group differences in child rearing in Canadian society?
7. How are young people's recreation and education being changed by computers?
8. Discuss the advantages and disadvantages of having older parents.
9. Is Canadian society a violent society? Describe the physical and verbal violence in TV cartoons, sitcoms, and adventure programs; in movies and videos; in sports such as hockey.
10. Why do substantial numbers of young adults now find it necessary to remain dependent on their parents? What difficulties are experienced by returnees to parental "nests" and their parents?

chapter seven

The Other Perspective: Children's Effect on Parents

INTRODUCTION

There is, both in sociology and psychology, a vast literature focusing on parents and children. The emphasis of that literature has been on various aspects of the socialization process and on parent–child interaction. Within the family unit, the concepts of socialization and child rearing have generally focused on the effect that parents have on their children. In this chapter, we will pursue some of the themes developed in the previous chapter on socialization, but we will do so from a complementary vantage point: we will investigate the effect that children have on parents.

In the past, and even to this day, the literature has been very specific: How do parents affect the well-being and the "normalcy" of their children? Or, more specifically and pointedly, what are the characteristics of *parents* of problem children? In other words, what is it that is *wrong* in such children's *parents* that has contributed or even caused these children's problems? Similarly, on the positive side, parents of well-adjusted children are compared with parents of problem children: What does each set of parents do to produce such a difference?

Such studies are individually valid. Indeed, parents are one of the major influences on children's lives. However, *as a group* and representing nearly all that has been accomplished in the field of parent–child relations, such studies represent a *scientific bias*. The totality of these studies leads us to believe erroneously that parents are always and unavoidably *the* major influence, and often the only influence, in their children's lives. This line of inquiry derives in great part from a well-established tradition in the clinical literature that sees the first five years of a person's life as the decisive ones in the shaping of personality. This causality model is far too simplistic. Indeed, there is a growing scientific body of research indicating that childhood is only *one* stage in a person's life and not necessarily an irremediable mould. Or, put differently, there is development after childhood. For instance, many children who are abused grow up to be very loving parents because other circumstances in their later lives have also contributed in shaping their personality. Moreover, there are many children who enjoy a happy childhood, yet are maladjusted as adults. No matter how well their parents treated and raised them, such children mature into problematic adults. In other words, childhood experiences do not necessarily mark a person for life, neither on the positive nor on the negative side.

In addition, this one-sided perspective may have misled generations of parents into believing that they held their children's future in their hands. Eager children, adolescents, and generations of those who service them – that is, teachers, social workers, psychiatrists, and psychologists – have been only too willing to follow this one-sided perspective. Moreover, an entire industry arose in this century with the sole purpose of exploiting this parental mystique. As discussed in the previous chapter, parents were besieged and intimidated by an endless series of ever-changing and often contradictory child-rearing fads. It goes without saying that the collective parental burden has been enormous, and probably even more so on the maternal than the paternal side, as will be explored later in this chapter.

When "socialization" fails or even breaks down and results in delinquency, school drop-out, drug abuse, anti-social behaviour, sexual promiscuity at a young age, or teenage pregnancy, to name only a few of the areas that have been heavily researched within this traditional perspective, the onus is placed on parents. Parents' social backgrounds, personal characteristics, child-rearing patterns, and marital relationships are the "causes" generally targeted. Such a line of inquiry states or implies that the parental variables are unavoidably responsible for the children's problems. Even studies of handicapped and chronically ill children often adopt a clinical and critical attitude toward parents. It is only recently that researchers have started studying the effects of these health problems on the parents themselves (for a review of research, see Philp and Duckworth, 1982).

CHILDREN AND PARENTS IN PERSPECTIVE

There is absolutely no doubt that parents are the primordial influence on a child's development. But this is only so until that child reaches the school system, and this now often includes nursery and day care. Thus, as children have other primary caretakers at an early age, parental influence is likely to be lessened. However, for many children, parents continue to be the major influence in their lives until young adulthood. For parents to remain influential in their children's lives, there has to be a converging set of variables: a conducive mix of parental variables, child (personality/constitution) variables, and perhaps socio-economic variables. In other words, for parental influence to remain strong in a teenager living in an urbanized (as opposed to farm) area of Canada, favourable circumstances have to be present.

In our rapidly changing technological world, we should not take for granted that parents are all-powerful in their children's lives. In fact, it is obvious that our society offers many "distractions" or competitive influences, both positive and negative, that can detract from parental influence. Thus, we have to study how other social forces such as peer groups, neighbours, mass media, popular culture, and religion influence children and, in turn, how these forces push children to affect their parents. Such an analytical model is assuredly much more complex than the simple parent–child causality path. This does not mean, however, that we should accept the fallacy of a simplistic parent–child causality theory that is erroneous from the start. Nor, especially, does it mean that we should fail to inquire into the effect that children exert on their parents' lives.

Bell and Harper preface their book on *Child Effects on Adults* (1977) by pointing out that what is often overlooked is the extent to which children influence their parents and other adults. Belsky et al. (1984) and Lerner and Busch-Rossnagel (1981) go one step beyond and discuss children as "producers of their own development"; they point to the circular interactions that take place between child effect, parental effect, and back again to produce a result on the child. For instance, a good-natured baby who smiles easily when her father picks her up unwittingly rewards the father and encourages him to continue interacting with her. In turn, the father's response to the child's stimulus (smile, babbling) contributes to the development of a healthy interpersonal outlook in the child. Thus, even a tiny infant can induce in its parent a response that in time will contribute positively or negatively to the child's own development. Even the literature on child abuse recognizes the contribution of child characteristics to this syndrome (Belsky, 1980). Thomas and Chess (1980) advance that children's temperament can contribute to negative interactions with their parents (see also Webster-Stratton and Eyberg, 1987). Tyler and Kogan (1977) have found that negative response to mothers on the part of handicapped children led to maternal "affect turn-off." Interestingly, however, even the literature on child effects has dealt almost exclusively with infants and preschoolers rather than school-age children (Bell, 1968, 1971, 1974; Lewis and Rosenblum, 1974), as well as with handicapped children (Blacher, 1984) rather than, for example, older children or even delinquent children.

In the 1980s, a literature of feminist inspiration began examining and criticizing the clinical literature because of its focus on parents as the chief cause in the development of emotional problems in their children. For instance, Chess and Thomas (1982) and Caplan and Hall-McCorquodale (1985;1985a) have analysed mother-blaming in clinical journals and criticized the analytical orientation toward maternal causality (Chodorow, 1978; Konstantareas et al., 1983). Admittedly, such studies are still few (e.g., Spiegel, 1982). Nevertheless, their publication indicates a timely climate that allows for a reorientation of this unidirectional and often biased research on the relationship between parents and children.

It is quite possible that it is only recently that the effects of children on parents could begin to be studied, for the simple reason that, in the past, children were probably less influential on their parents than they are now. Children were an essential resource to their parents whether as farm workers, in the cottage industry, as sitters for younger siblings, or to boost the family's earnings (Nett, 1981; Parr, 1982). As described in the previous chapter, even the conceptualization of childhood has changed over time. Moreover, in our current technological world, parents have to share their children's attention with the media, especially in the form of television, which even infants watch. A very simple example here is that of advertising directed at children, especially before the Christmas season. Most of us will recall incidents whereby, after viewing a particularly attractive toy or game advertised on TV, we badgered our parents until *they* gave in and bought the desired object.

Peer groups are also more influential than in the past because they have greater autonomy and salience. Preteen and teenage subcultures are certainly a new phenomenon that originated in North America and arose after the Second World War. Adolescent behaviour learned via the peer group is frequently at odds with parental expectations and, as such, exerts a great deal of power on the shaping of parent-child relations. For instance, teenagers who abuse drugs as a response to peer pressure may create difficulties in their *parents'* lives – not to omit their own. Furthermore, with universal education, the school system impacts on children for more years and far earlier than in the past. Also, children now rarely work with their parents at a young age. Finally, a growing egalitarianism in family relations, with an emphasis on children's rights, may be an added factor contributing to a greater influence of children on domestic life. All of these recent developments seem to point to a greater child independence and lower parental influence on children than in the past – and a greater potential for child effect on parents.

In this chapter, we will be following a multilevel ecological model (Bronfenbrenner, 1977, 1979; Garbarino, 1982). We are dealing with *interactions* rather than unidirectional causality. One problem, as indicated above, is that circular interactions are difficult to investigate (Lewis and Lee-Painter, 1974; Lerner and Spanier, 1978). While a few other researchers have presented models that overlap with ours (Belsky, Lerner, and Spanier, 1984; Roskies, 1972; Whalen and Henker, 1980), the advantage of our model, however, resides in its specificity. It can be used as a map to guide future research and is amenable to the development of precise research hypotheses. Moreover, it suggests more areas of studies than have been previously suggested in the past literature and opens up new avenues for research.

It should be emphasized that when we talk in terms of child effect, *we include both negative and positive effects* (the pleasures as well as the burdens of parenting). We will first explore some of the areas in which children can affect their parents. In order to achieve this, we present a typology that is not meant to be exhaustive, but that is nevertheless wider in scope than models focusing on broad familial subsystems (parental, marital, sibling subsystems; Minuchin, 1974). We will then examine how children affect their parents depending on three sets of conditions: the characteristics of the children, of the parents, and of the societal response to parents and children.

In this chapter, the term children refers to non-adult offspring, most particularly those still living at home and dependent upon their parents. Adult offspring, and even grandchildren, constitute yet another exciting area of research that has not been well studied. Their exclusion from this chapter stems from practical considerations of space.

AREAS OF PARENTS' LIVES

How children affect their parents is a rather vague and general question. It is important to be more specific and to delineate the areas in parents' lives that can be affected, although there is an unavoidable overlap between them. Below are six major areas in parents' lives from which vantage point child effect can be studied with greater specificity. Each area opens up a multitude of research opportunities.

SITUATIONAL/STRUCTURAL AREA

This area focuses on the *place* and *space* parents occupy in society as well as the *structure* of their *daily* lives. Generally, this area is considered "natural," and is therefore taken for granted and not studied. As a first example, parents may have to move when a child arrives or later on when the child is of school age, either to have more space, or more appropriate space (a "better" neighbourhood in which to raise children). This move may in turn have economic consequences for the parents (a mortgage), may necessitate secondary acquisitions (more furniture), and may limit or enhance parents' activities depending on the new locale (distant suburb as opposed to downtown for urban parents). Basically, children influence where their parents will live and the space they will require.

Parents' *schedule* is altered. Children dictate, because of their survival needs, especially at the infant stage, when parents get up, when the family eats, and so on. Further changes in parents' schedule occur as the child ages so as to meet school, lessons, and peer group requirements. It would be interesting in this respect to speculate whether the schedules of middle-class parents are more or less dependent upon their children's activities than the schedules of working-class parents. In urban areas especially, middle-class children often follow a complete regimen of after-school activities, including lessons, sports, competitions, sleep-overs, and parties. Especially when parents have to chauffeur their offspring to these demands of middle-class upbringing, one would expect considerable effect on their daily schedule.

Parents' *activities* are restructured because of children. Lovemaking may become more discreet, less spontaneous, and less frequent. Parents no longer can leave the home whimsically; their freedom of movement is more limited (Hoffman and Mavis, 1979).

Parents' schedules are dramatically changed by the arrival of children and their survival needs.

Upon the arrival of a baby, one of the two parents, generally the mother, may have to leave employment (Burton, 1975; Baldwin, 1977; Moss and Silver, 1972), find a less demanding job, change field of work, or even relocate.

As parents experience a decline in the number of certain activities or a restructuring of their timing, other activities broaden their horizon. Thus, parents have to visit doctors and teachers, entertain children's peers, play children's games, read children's books, and participate in extracurricular activities at schools, to name only a few examples of activities in which non-parents do not usually engage. When the child is problematic, parents have to seek professional help from a wide variety of resources, including incompetent ones.

The child has to be cared for on several levels. Therefore, parents' *workload* is increased. Studies indicate that this is even more so for mothers than fathers. Even the amount and frequency of cooking (one of the most time-consuming and repetitive chores) can be affected by the child's fussiness, weight, and medical problems (Luiselli et al., 1985; Palmer and Horn, 1978; Traughber et al., 1983). Studies of families with a handicapped child indicate that only 25 percent of the fathers help mothers significantly (Baldwin, 1976; McAndrew, 1976). A workload increase triggers additional effects, whether on health, feeling of well-being, sociability, or quality of martial life. Time management becomes one key priority (LaRossa and LaRossa, 1981). On the other hand, as the child ages, and if the child co-operates, he or she may diminish parental workload by taking on more family responsibilities.

MARITAL AND FAMILIAL AREA

With the arrival of the first child, the couple becomes a family. The effect on the spouses seems to differ by gender. For instance, in a longitudinal study of couples interviewed during pregnancy, then when the first baby was one month old and, finally, eight months old, Miller and Sollie (1980) found that mothers' marital stress increased, but not fathers'. As indicated earlier, the child may inhibit spontaneous sexual expression between the parents. Similarly, the wife and husband have less time to devote to the development of their *marital* relationship as each (particularly the mother) is busy parenting. The marital relationship often is replaced in part by the co-parental relationship. As a result, after a number of years of marital life, certain couples have nothing left in common except for their children. They have become dependent on their children for the contents of their marital life. There is a body of research that shows that married couples with children are somewhat less happy than those who are childless. The evidence points to a negative effect of children on marital quality (Glenn and McLanahan, 1982), well illustrated in the quote below from a student's autobiography.

> It was a difficult time in my life [adolescence]. I was doing drugs, skipping school, I used to talk back, walk out slamming the door behind me. My parents didn't know how to take me, they had to tiptoe around me otherwise I'd have a fit. I was hell to live with and it reflected on their happiness with each other. I'd started fights between them, they'd argue

over what to do with me, my mother used to cry a lot. . . . Now that I've settled down, they're back to normal.

(Twenty-two-year-old male student)

Recently, the literature on remarriage and step-parenting has zeroed in on the effect of stepchildren on the marital relationship (Ambert, 1986; Hobart, 1987; White and Booth, 1985). This literature will be reviewed in Chapter Nine on divorce. However, first, let's hear from a father on this child influence (Luepnitz, 1982:130):

I like my son to meet my dates. But on occasion while he was asleep, there has been a girl out here visiting . . . and then I got . . . thinking, "What if he woke up and found me in bed with a woman?" I could say, "I was a married man; I have my needs." But he could say, "I'm fourteen and I have my needs too." I make some sacrifices for my son.

(Divorced father; son is thirteen)

In the domain of kin relations in general, the child may also contribute to bringing the parents closer to their own families, especially to the grandparents. Or the child may act as a divisive force, whether directly or indirectly. For instance, if grandparents do not agree with parents' child-rearing methods and voice their objections, their adult children may avoid them. Thus, the grandchild will have unwittingly created a wedge between parents and grandparents.

PARENTAL PERSONALITY

The literature generally informs us that, apart from their biological constitution, children derive their personality in the interaction between biological and environmental influences. Since parents are the main environmental influence on very young children, parents are the determining variable. While this may be so, examining the other side of the equation is at least as scientifically valid. What effect, if any, do children have on their parents' personalities and personal development? And how does the effect vary depending on parents' stage of the life cycle? Such questions fall within the new wave of research on adult development (Clausen, 1986). Elder (1984:111) points out that not only should we "allow for the possibility that children can be important influences in the lives of their parents," but that we should do this within the context of "the developmental trajectory of children and parents" over their life course.

Let's consider two couples, both with two children each. The first couple, Paula and Bruno, married at eighteen; by the time they were twenty, they had had their children. In contrast, Michael and Janet married at twenty-one and twenty-four respectively and had their children five and eight years later. Both couples' children are now eighteen and fifteen. But the two sets of parents differ in the stage of their *own* life cycles. Paula and Bruno are thirty-six while Michael and Janet are forty-four and forty-seven. Because Paula was so young when she had her children, she was never gainfully employed and has spent all her life at home until now. In contrast, when she had her first child, Janet had already been employed for six years, took only a brief maternal leave, and is still employed.

Paula depends more than Janet does on her children and her husband for emotional support. She feels secure only as a mother, whereas, for Janet, being a mother is only *one* of her many roles. Paula gets easily hurt when her children are less than perfect, while Janet sits them down for a chat and then goes on to other matters. If asked how much influence the children have on their personality, Paula answers "a lot," although she cannot pinpoint exactly what. Janet answers that her children are important to *her*, but are not determining factors in terms of her personality development. Paula was still a teenager when she had her first child, while Janet's personality had had more time to develop. Becoming a mother so young seems, in fact, to have hindered Paula's development as an independent adult.

PARENTAL HEALTH

The first obvious child effect in this domain resides in pregnancy and childbirth. Currently, because of medical trends, often for the benefit of doctors, up to a third of births are by caesarian section, in itself major surgery. In such cases, the birth of a child becomes as much a medical event as a familial one for the parents. Parents, especially mothers, report fatigue during infancy because of night duty and infant illness.

Several studies of poor families have found that mothers frequently go hungry so as to provide the basic necessities for their children. A mother's health declines in large families, in part because of childbearing and birthing, but especially because of workload, consequent lack of sleep and recreation, as well as worries about children's behaviour and health. Single mothers who shoulder most child-rearing responsibilities alone are especially vulnerable and are consequently among the main consumers of medical resources (Belle, 1980).

Many studies, especially of handicapped children, show that mothering may have a negative impact on the mental health of these mothers (McAndrew, 1976; McMichael, 1971). It should be noted, however, that few studies have used control groups of mothers who do not have a handicapped child (Gath, 1977; Rutter et al., 1970). Characteristics of the mothers that make them particularly vulnerable under such circumstances have also been studied (Bradshaw and Lawton, 1978).

Cook (1988) has shown the high degree of stress from which mothers of mentally ill *adult* children suffer, including even physical violence on the part of these children. During research on divorce, Ambert (1982) encountered two mothers who were frequently beaten by their teenage sons. The literature on violent delinquents seems to indicate that such occurrences are far from rare. Yet, the effect on these unfortunate mothers has not been extensively studied. From these few studies, it is easy to suggest that the health (both physical and mental) of parents of various types of children should be carefully mapped.

HUMAN INTERACTION

Children and parents interact: verbally, expressively (facial expressions and body language), and behaviourally. Children make requests of parents, ask questions, respond, fail to respond, talk back, criticize, and verbally quarrel with their parents. Parents make requests and demands of children, answer and ask questions, fail to respond, scold, criticize, and quarrel with their children. Children, therefore, increase the interactional repertoire of adults in that the parent-child interaction, especially at the infant and preschool levels, is a unique type of interaction. For instance, in observations of normal preschoolers with their mothers, Patterson (1976) found that there was a "rapid escalation in sheer decibels of noise when the mothers' attention was not rapidly forthcoming." Non-parents generally do not get to enjoy/suffer from this pattern of interaction.

> She objects to me talking to someone else . . . she will do her utmost to get my attention – shout, scream, throw things. She *always* spills a drink, sometimes on purpose for attention, which is mortifying. You can't think along the lines of what you're saying. It's distracting. It's very, very hard on your nerves.
>
> (Married mother of two toddlers) (Bolton, 1983:84)

Children may provide company to their parents, especially their mothers. For instance, Bolton (1983) has found that working-class mothers derive more companionable benefits from their children than do their more educated counterparts who find children's conversations less stimulating. As children age, parents may learn new modes of interaction from them and acquire new dimensions of knowledge. This socialization of parents by their children may be especially evident among immigrant parents who are not fluent in English or French: their children learn these national languages at school, and the children frequently have to explain Canadian "facts of life" to their parents.

At the affective level, many parents enjoy a close physical bond with their children. Some parents talk of the calming and soothing effect that holding the hand of a small child has. Yet, the literature rarely addresses the nurturing effect that children can have on their parents (Boulding, 1980; DeMause, 1982). Rather, parental physical affection is one key variable that is said to promote well-being and a sense of self-esteem in children. Why not the reverse as well?

> I'm glad I had my children when I divorced. They've been so supportive. I don't know what I would have done without them.
>
> (Custodial mother, two children)

> Having so many children, that's what I regret most in life. I've done nothing else in my life except taking care of children . . . and most times they've been so nasty to me.
>
> (Custodial welfare mother, five children)

When the child's response is not that which the average mother/father expects, the parent may be negatively affected. For instance, as indicated earlier, Tyler and Kogan (1977) have found that a difficult response to mothers on the part of handicapped children led to maternal "affect turn-off." That is, mothers eventually stopped trying to elicit a response from their non-responsive children, as if the children had taught these mothers a lesson. These mothers, in response to repeated negative reinforcement, became more distant from their children.

COMMUNITY

Persons with children have to develop a network of day care, sitters, schools, and pediatricians, whereas non-parents do not need to have recourse to such persons or agencies. Moreover, parents of special-needs children may be involved with a large number of professional helpers (Kazak, 1987). Similarly, women with children are more likely to be on welfare than childless women. This means that the former become subjected to the requisites of a variety of welfare agencies that may act as agents of social control in their lives. When parents have to have recourse to agencies, their private lives become scrutinized, and as Rubin and Quinn-Curran (1983:89) put it, they have to learn that "their family's boundaries will need to become highly permeable" – more subject to intrusions from non-family persons.

On the one hand, we would like to learn if parents' social networks are more or less *extensive* than those of non-parents. For instance, children bring friends home, and these friends have parents with whom one can become acquainted. Adult children marry and bring with them a set of in-laws. Children who roam farther afield in their neighbourhood return home with observations about the neighbours. On the other hand, we would like to learn if parents' social networks are more or less *positive* (rewarding) than non-parents' social networks. It is possible that, because of the demands of parenting, adults find their social interaction less rewarding. Or, still, the opposite could hold. This question has never been investigated.

Children may act as social facilitators (for instance, as noted earlier, in the case of immigrants who do not know the language of the host country) and as matchmakers. Children may also impede social relations by keeping their parents captive. Other children may push social interactants away from their parents, either because of a restricting handicap or misbehaviour (Kew, 1975; Butler et al., 1976). Parents of school-age children have to form relations and interact with school authorities, as mentioned earlier. This can be a positive experience, but it can also be a negative one, especially when the child deviates from the norm as would be the case for delinquent children. Yet, this possibility has also not been researched.

DETERMINANTS OF CHILD EFFECT

We have presented *some* of the areas and ways in which children may have an effect on their parents. We turn now to the factors that will determine whether and how child effect will take place. There are three sets of characteristics that will determine or influence child effect: the characteristics of the child, of the parents, and of the societal support for the parents and their children. A set of hypotheses covering the direction and the intensity of child effect is presented based on these characteristics.

CHILD CHARACTERISTICS

First, it can be hypothesized or predicted that child effect will be greater on parents or on certain domains of parental lives depending on the following child characteristics.

Child demographic characteristics:

1. age
2. gender
3. birth order (including twinship)

Child personal characteristics:

4. IQ and other capabilities
5. personality traits, mental health, affectivity level
6. physical health, including birth weight
7. physical appearance/handicaps
8. behaviour, including delinquency

More specifically, we propose that the more a child deviates from the accepted average in child traits 4 through 8, the greater the child effect on parents. We will further refine this hypothesis by recognizing a negative and a positive deviation from the average.

The more a child deviates *negatively* from the accepted average in child traits 4 through 8, the more negative the child effect on parents. For instance, studies have shown that "difficult" children, at times called coercive children (a negative deviation), may be so difficult to control that parenting skills break down: the child "replaces the parents as the dominant force in the household" (Loeber and Stouthamer-Loeber, 1986:39). As the mother of a teenage runaway puts it, "It's the most frightening thing in the world for parents to feel if they say or do the wrong thing the child will run away. Beth held running away over us like a weapon" (Chapman, 1976). The negative child behaviour will affect several areas of parents' lives, and will affect certain parents more than others. For example, single mothers may be more negatively affected than married mothers; socially isolated parents may be more negatively affected than parents who have a supportive network to back them up.

Parents of children who deviate negatively from the accepted average cannot take for granted what other parents take for granted and what they themselves expect (Roskies, 1972). They have to readjust their conception of *what* is normal and of what to expect. The discrepancy between parental expectations and child traits and behaviour may be stress producing (Deiner, 1987), and may demand a great deal of adaptation on the part of the parents.

The more a child deviates *positively* from the accepted average in child traits 4 through 8, the greater the positive effect on parents. For instance, parents who have a high-IQ child (a positive deviation from the average) may benefit from an increase in self-esteem and pride.

We could refine this last hypothesis further by stating that the effect on parents will be positive in *some areas* and perhaps even negative in other areas – depending on parental characteristics and societal response. If we return to the example of the gifted child, an insecure parent may actually feel threatened psychologically by such a child while at the same time reaping social praise. Similarly, lower-class parents may not only feel inferior because of the higher learning ability of the child, but the child may actually overtake them intellectually and a certain role reversal may take place. These parents may not know how to cope with such a child and may feel helpless, especially when the school system intrudes. More educated parents may not be so vulnerable to this child characteristic – which leads us into the next section.

PARENTS' CHARACTERISTICS

Child effect will be prevented, mitigated, or magnified depending on certain parental characteristics and situations. In other words, the child's characteristics alone are not usually sufficient to cause *directly* an effect on the parent (Sameroff, 1975) – although there are numerous exceptions to this rule, especially as the child ages. Another way of putting this is that certain parents are more vulnerable to child effect than others because of their own characteristics.

Parents' demographic characteristics

1. age
2. gender
3. SES
4. adoptive versus biological
5. ethnicity and minority group status
6. religion and religiosity
7. immigration status
8. marital status

Parents' personal characteristics

9. IQ and other capabilities
10. personality traits/affectivity levels
11. coping patterns
12. parenting skills
13. parenting expectations
14. commitment to parenting
15. physical health
16. physical appearance
17. overall parental material resources
18. parental social resources (friends, etc., often referred to in the literature as "social support")
19. quality of marriage and kin system
20. other children and their characteristics including their number and how closely spaced they are

For example, children seemingly affect mothers more than fathers (parents' gender) (Kazak and Marvin, 1984). A child with a low IQ (child characteristic) may affect higher-SES parents more negatively than low-SES parents (parents' characteristic). Single parents may be more affected by their children's behaviour than married parents. Immigrant parents may be more affected, both negatively and positively, by their children (who know the host country's language) than non-immigrant parents or immigrant parents who are fluent. Parents who are less committed to parenting (more egotistical perhaps, more self-centred) may be less influenced by their children. In turn, it should be added, their children are more likely to be undersocialized. It should be pointed out here that the concept of commitment is one that is greatly overlooked in the family literature. For instance, studies have found that marital commitment contributes to marital quality. This observation relates to Chapter Nine on divorce (causes of divorce) and applies as well to the effect of children on parents and vice versa.

To pursue other examples, parents who have a developmentally handicapped child may experience less stress if they can afford (material resources) a caretaker and go on a vacation alone. Parents of a delinquent child who have just moved to a new city where they have no friends (social resources) may also be under more stress than other similar parents who are surrounded by a *supportive* group of friends.

We have placed the number and spacing of children among parental rather than child characteristics because child characteristics pertain to *individual* children. Nevertheless, parents who have a large family may be affected differently from parents who

Parents who have a developmentally handicapped child may experience less stress if they have support from other relatives or if they can afford a caretaker and go on a vacation alone.

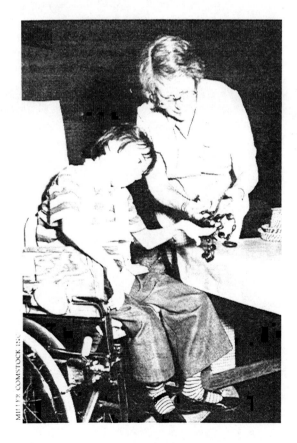

have only one to three children. The effects could be even greater when the children are closely spaced. Indeed, research indicates that parents react to a large family group by adopting more managerial child-rearing techniques; as well, they are less able to devote as much individual time to each child as can be the case in smaller families. The latter has consequences for the children (for example, on average, children from large families do less well in school), but the consequences for the parents are also obvious, although less well documented.

Indeed, large sibling groups may actually be more adept at forming a coalition against their parents, and the latter may be less able to socialize their children as they would see fit. The children, having less individual adult attention, may socialize each other – often both to their own and their parents' detriment. The vast literature in juvenile delinquency, for instance, clearly shows the higher probability of delinquency in larger families than in smaller ones. Parents who have many children may feel less in control of their family life or that their contribution to their children's future is negligible. Such parents may experience a lower sense of self-esteem and, as we have seen earlier, a lower level of physical health, especially among mothers.

These are only a few examples of specific hypotheses and research topics that could be tested and proposed. We need to do for parents what has already been done for children (Felner et al., 1985) – that is, to identify parents who are "at risk" of suffering from a high negative child effect. This is already being done in public health services when nurses visit the homes of very young and uneducated new mothers to teach them parenting skills. The rationale is that by increasing the mother's coping ability, she will react more appropriately to her child – who in turn will develop more healthily.

CHARACTERISTICS OF SOCIETAL RESPONSE

Parents and children interact within a society and not in a vacuum. How society supports or fails to support both parents and children will in great part determine parents' reaction as well as the direction of child effect on parents. Moreover, cultural as well as class demands within various social groups will also contribute to determining whether or not certain child characteristics affect parents (Super and Harkness, 1981; Thomas and Chess, 1980). Important to parents is the help and moral support they receive from society, as well as the resources that society can offer their children to maximize their development and enhance parent-child interaction (see Kazak, 1987).

Societal support refers to the resources that a society places at the disposal of parents in order to facilitate the fulfilment of their role. When a society has few of these resources, or chooses, as a socio-economic and political choice, not to invest into these resources, parents are deprived of societal support.

Characteristics of societal support include the following:

1. adequate housing for families
2. quality and existence of early day care systems
3. quality of schools
4. quality and existence of after-school programs

5. income supplements for poorer families

6. adequate dental, medical, and psychiatric resources

7. quality of the contents of mass media (one adverse quality is media violence and sex role stereotyping)

8. safety of neighbourhoods

9. appropriate recreational facilities for youngsters

10. home and community support for parents who have special-needs children

11. society's open acknowledgment of parental contribution (labour reproduction)

12. fostering of a positive peer group culture among children and adolescents

Any one of these characteristics, or a combination of them, may diminish the potentially negative impact that children with certain characteristics could have on their parents, who in turn show a set of characteristics. Similarly, absence of positive aspects in social support can increase the negative impact of children on parents – as obviously the reverse has also been found: that parents placed in situations of low social support can negatively impact on their children. An example is child abuse, which is more likely to occur in times of stress and isolation of the parents who, as a result, may respond to a negative child trait (such as incessant crying) in an abusive manner (Fried and Holt, 1980).

Parents who have handicapped, difficult, or disturbed children need more societal support than parents of average children. Especially important for them is the availability of special classes, after-school programs, homemakers' helpers – all aspects of societal support that could give them time for themselves while providing for their children. The availability of these services will reduce the negative impact that these children can have on their parents. This would be especially true of parents who themselves are poor, isolated, and in ill health.

Thus, we see how societal response can buffer negative child characteristics on parents who, themselves, also may have negative characteristics that make them particularly vulnerable to child effect. It should be pointed out that there are very few parents who do not have at least one or two negative characteristics that make them vulnerable to child effect. Moreover, one should not presume that negative child effect cannot befall "perfect" parents. Consequently, an adequate societal response and adequate societal resources are a key determinant in parents' welfare – as well as in children's (Eichler, 1988).

Over two decades ago, Rodman and Graves (1967) called for "parent-education television," which would put television at the disposal of parents so that they could learn effective parenting skills as well as more about various child problems. Television is one societal resource that, until now, has not responded to parental needs. Quite the contrary: television submits parents to a barrage of fabricated and artificial child "needs" of the materialistic kind via advertisements, and exposes children to violence, racism, and sexism as well as additional values and lifestyles that are antithetical to most parents' own values.

CONCLUSION

In summary, the *results* of child effect on parents may be positive or negative, and this can be so in any of the areas of parents' lives described earlier. The model proposed in this chapter is interactive. It consists of the interaction of child characteristics with parental characteristics and societal response to produce or not produce an effect in parents, and to produce a negative or a positive effect, and a strong or a mild effect. Certain child characteristics are more likely to produce an effect than others, and this effect will be more positive or more negative depending on the deviation from the accepted average in a given society.

The analytical model described can apply to *any* society. Each society, however, will offer a somewhat different set of societal characteristics. For instance, a tribal society's supportive traits toward parents will obviously bear few similarities to the ones described in this chapter. Thus, it is important to keep in mind the *cultural* context in which child effect is studied. In Canada, this cultural caveat would apply particularly to native and Inuit societies, as well as, for instance, to Amish and Mennonite communities.

We have also seen that certain parents will be more "vulnerable" than others to child effect because of their own characteristics/situation. Moreover, certain parents will be more "vulnerable" in the direction of negative effect, while other parents may be so in the direction of positive effect. In addition, when society's response is inadequate, the negative effect on parents of non-average children is likely to increase greatly. This stands both for problem children as well as children who have certain gifts (intellectual, artistic) and for children who are developmentally behind or ahead of their years whether physically, emotionally, or intellectually.

As early as 1972, Roskies recognized the importance of linkage of this triumvirate of conditions (which, at that time, consisted of the child, the mother, and society). Discussing the birth of a thalidomide child, she pointed out that this birth upset "the delicate network of interlocking needs and obligations – child's, mother's, and society's – on which the successful rearing of a child depends" and, we would add, from which child effect on parents will flow. She continued: "And what makes this event so disruptive . . . is that the failure does not occur on one level, or in one partner. Instead, there is a chain reaction in which the needs of mother, child, and society, rather than working in harmony, become embroiled in a complex conflict of interests" (1972:289). However, Roskies's voice has been a relatively forgotten one. For instance, although Hartup (1982) discusses "effective complementarities between child and caregivers," he does not develop any hypotheses concerning which child traits lead to such complementarities.

The model proposed in this chapter is suited to all types of parents and all types of children. Special-needs children, average children, delinquent children, or gifted children can all be studied within this model in terms of the effect they exert on their parents. In turn, poor or rich, young or old, mentally unstable or healthy parents can also be studied in terms of their vulnerability to child effect – whether positive or negative. Finally, different social responses and institutions, as well as their quality, can be investigated from the point of view of their role as facilitators of positive child effect or, contrarily, of negative child effect.

The model can therefore be utilized from a psychosociological perspective as well as from a larger macrosociological analysis. It has the potential of being interdisciplinary and could be utilized by sociologists, psychologists, clinicians, social workers, and experts in the various domains of special education. This model would be especially appropriate in a multicultural society such as Canada. Indeed, we could assume that child effect will differ depending on the ethnic background of the parents and the societal support offered to, or withheld from, the various ethnic groups. An excellent case in point here, for example, would be the lack of Canadian societal support that native parents receive, not only as a collectivity and as individuals, but as parents. Finally, the model would be particularly helpful in formulating social policies geared toward the family in general and, more particularly, families with special-needs children, as well as with families who are socially disadvantaged because of finances, education, and/or discrimination.

DISCUSSION QUESTIONS

1. Why has the emphasis until now been placed on the effect that parents have on their children, rather than that of children on their parents?
2. Why do all the studies done on parental effect represent, as a group, a scientific bias?
3. In our technological society, why is it that parents' influence on their children may be relatively small?
4. What is meant by children as "producers of their own development"?
5. Can you give an example, not presented in the chapter, of the influence of children on each one of the areas in parents' lives described?
6. Give reasons why mothers are more influenced by their children than fathers.
7. Discuss how children's influence on parents can be different depending on the stage of the parents' life cycle.
8. Why would working-class mothers have been found by Bolton to derive more companionable benefits from their children than middle-class mothers?
9. Sketch a research project to test the hypothesis that "the more a child deviates *negatively* from the accepted average in child traits 4 through 8, the more negative the child effect on parents."
10. What do we mean when we say that certain parents are more vulnerable to child effect than others? Give an example.
11. Take three of the characteristics of societal support and show how each can increase or decrease the possibility of a negative child effect on parents.
12. Why is the model proposed in this chapter called "interactive"?
13. Can you turn back to your own childhood and think of ways in which you had an effect on your parents?

chapter eight

Cultural Variations: Past and Present

INTRODUCTION

We can learn a great deal about Canadian family life by studying the Amerindians and Inuit as well as the distinct political, economic, religious, and social influences on the early settlers. With the coming of the French to Canada in the 1600s, the *habitant* family became the dominant family structure in eastern Canada. Due to the travels of the fur traders into central and western Canada and their intermarriage with the Indians there, Métis families emerged and became significant in the history of the country. The union of the thirteen American colonies to the south and the migration to Canada of those loyal to Britain brought Loyalist families to eastern and central Canada. Anxious to develop the agricultural land in the West, the Canadian government encouraged many European families to emigrate, including Ukrainians, Poles, Scots, Mennonites, and Doukhobors from Russia. Before the turn of the century, the Chinese came to build the railways, and many Japanese farmers and fishermen settled on the West Coast.

In more recent times, war has had an impact on Canadian families, prompting an influx of 48,000 war brides after the Second World War, most of whom were from Britain. Other families were affected because a husband or father was killed or disabled in the war. After the war, Italians, Germans, and other ethnic groups arrived to fill the desperate need for labourers in Canada's expanding economy. Political upheaval in other countries has also had the effect of attracting refugees to Canada because of its relatively generous open-door immigration policy. Hundreds of distressed Czech, Hungarian, Vietnamese, Chilean, Ugandan, and Salvadoran families have taken up residence in Canada. Today, immigration continues, with African, Caribbean, and Indian immigrants adding to the country's rich ethnic heritage (see Table 8.1). Consequently, although the British and French are the dominant cultural groups in Canada, Canadian families form a rich mosaic.

At the time of Confederation, about 60 percent of the population was British, 33 percent French, and 7 percent from other origins. By 1986, 34 percent of the population was British, 24 percent French, and 42 percent from other origins. The ethnic mix varies by province. For example, in Newfoundland 95 percent were of British origin in 1986, while in Quebec the British comprised only 8 percent. Two provinces, Manitoba and Saskatchewan, have populations where the majority are neither British nor French. In other words, Canada remains a country of regional contrasts and ethnic variations.

The majority of Germans are found in Ontario or the Prairie provinces. Chinese and East Indians have settled mostly in Vancouver and Toronto. The Italians are heavily concentrated in Ontario, particularly in Toronto. Nearly 750,000 Canadians report some aboriginal origin, the majority residing in Ontario, British Columbia, Manitoba, Alberta, or Quebec. At least 52 percent of the population of the Northwest Territories is native. The Inuit are located in Yukon and the Northwest Territories. The political and economic development of the country while it was being explored, the immigration legislation of the past one hundred and fifty years, as well as the sponsorship policy of more recent years have all contributed to the geographic distribution of ethnic families.

Whether pioneers or more recent immigrants, most newcomers must attempt to come to terms with an alien land and a social system different from their own. Many must learn a new language and adjust to an unfamiliar culture. Family traditions are often passed on for generations, although usually in a modified form. These traditions involve religious values, language, food and diet, special festive occasions, discipline of children, and even career choices. Some ethnic traits persist through several generations, others may be lost, while still others are modified in each subsequent generation (Elkin,

Table 8.1 Population by Major Ethnic Categories, Canada, 1986

Group	Single Origins	Multiple Origins
British	6,332,725	6,038,760
French	6,093,160	2,030,200
German	896,715	1,570,340
Italian	709,590	297,325
Ukrainian	420,210	541,100
Native (Peoples)	373,260	338,460
Chinese	360,320	53,720
Dutch (Netherlands)	351,760	530,170
East Indian (Asia)	220,630	40,805
Polish	222,260	389,845
Portuguese	199,595	37,590
Greek	143,780	33,530
Total Population	25,309,331	

Source: Statistics Canada, *Profile of Ethnic Groups*, Cat. 93-154 (Ottawa: Supply and Services Canada, February 1989), Appendix XLIII–XLV. Reproduced with permission.

1983). Furthermore, differences between family customs of a particular ethnic group and the dominant culture sometimes create tensions between generations within immigrant families.

The mosaic motif is appropriate for Canada's ethnic groups, as 28 percent reported more than one ethnic origin in 1986. Some groups have a high proportion with multiple ethnic origins, such as the Irish (81 percent) and the Scots (78 percent), while others have a smaller proportion of multiple origins, such as Koreans (7 percent) and Cambodians (12 percent), who are recent immigrants (Statistics Canada, 1987a). About 10 percent speak a mother tongue other than English or French in their homes (Statistics Canada, 1987f), and 4.5 percent speak more than one language at home.

In this chapter we will briefly examine the history of French, British, and native families in Canada. We will then become acquainted with a few of the more than one hundred and twenty ethnic family structures that are representative of the contemporary Canadian family mosaic.

FRENCH-CANADIAN FAMILIES

THE EARLY SETTLERS

The French settlers preceded the British settlers by at least one hundred and fifty years. Today 26 percent of the population of Canada recognizes French as its home language. This proportion includes immigrants from a wide range of countries. The earliest French families were the *habitant* families who, just after 1600, settled near the Bay of Fundy, in the Annapolis Valley, and along the St. Lawrence River. Some forty years later, the regions around Montreal, Quebec City, and Trois-Rivières were settled, and the population of New France reached 10,000 by the year 1680.

As contact with their native land was minimal, the French in New France became increasingly alienated from France. Consequently, it did not take long for these early settlers to develop their own culture. For centuries the *habitants* were fairly self-sufficient, raising their own garden produce and livestock and augmenting their meat supply by hunting. It was not uncommon for families to have ten or twelve children, all of whom contributed to the maintenance of the family within a harsh environment.

Although the family was patriarchal, the mother was the centre of the home. This was partly because the father's search for a suitable means of providing for his family by such activities as trading or lumbering kept him away from home for long periods. The exploration and development of new lands resulted in fewer contacts between extended members.

The early inhabitants of New France had a phenomenal rate of population growth. A typical "almost complete" family would be a husband in his early forties, a wife in her mid-thirties, and eight children between a few weeks and fourteen years of age. Such large population growth differed from that of France. Some women married as early as twelve or thirteen. The Crown encouraged young marriages by financially rewarding brides under age sixteen and bridegrooms under age twenty. Poor families were also assisted by the Crown with dowries for their daughters (Bosher, 1975:2). However, population growth was limited by several factors. Dowry obligations made it difficult for many women to marry young, and the average age of marriage for women through the late 1600s was twenty-two years of age. With the fur trade, men were absent from their families for periods of up to three years at one time. And finally, infant mortality rates were high.

Infants were baptized within four days of birth, and godparents were expected both financially and socially to favour the child in later life. Although children were considered an asset to the settler family, not all children experienced a loving family environment. By the 1700s, poor widows who were incapable of providing food and shelter often sent their children to be servants in wealthy households, where they could serve without pay until the age of eighteen. Many orphans also found employment with well-to-do families, and in fact, most of the servants in New France were children.

Recorded baptisms of illegitimate children climbed markedly between 1701 and 1760, possibly due to the presence of French regular troops in the colony. In the mid-1700s, 12.2 out of every 1,000 births were illegitimate, but not all illegitimate births were recorded. Rather than face social censure, an unmarried *habitant* mother might give her infant to Amerindians, who would raise the child and fully accept it into the native community.

The authority of the priest was evident in the French-Canadian village and family. In schools, which were rare in these rural communities, the boys were taught by priests and the girls by nuns. The key events in life – birth, marriage, and death – were clearly associated with the Roman Catholic Church. In keeping with the doctrines of the church, sex was only permissible within the confines of marriage and for the purpose of procreation, but in reality these religious expectations and social norms were broken. Divorce was not considered an option in an unsatisfactory marital union. Since there was a shortage of women in New France, the king of France further encouraged family life by sending to the colony approximately one thousand "filles du roi," mostly working-class women between the ages of sixteen and twenty-five, who had few opportunities to marry in France. By 1659, celibacy was forbidden by law in New France (Garigue, 1967:337), and widows usually remarried for economic survival.

With a birth rate of 50 to 65 per 1,000 population and an average of five or six children per family, the population of New France had one of the highest fertility rates in the world (see Table 8.2). Sixteen percent of all families had at least ten children. The mortality rate was low by the standards of the time, but high compared to today's standards. In response to the needs of the growing population, the first family allowance was granted in 1676. Any parent with ten legitimate children received a special yearly grant from the French government (Garigue, 1967:338).

Although there were family variations in New France depending upon social class and region, most families were similar in three specific areas: the dominant culture was French; the purpose of the family was procreation; and there was uniformity in the definition of age and gender roles (Garigue, 1967:337). The father ruled, and wife and children were expected to obey. "Children" up to age thirty had to receive permission from their respective parents in order to marry (Moogk, 1982:23). If the parents disapproved, the dowry or a contribution to the newlyweds' household could be withheld. By law, adults who were refused parental approval to marry could make three requisitions begging for their parents' consent. Thereafter a magistrate or other relatives could be consulted about any lawful impediment to marriage.

Table 8.2 Average Number of Children Born to Women Ever-married, by Mother Tongue, Canada, Generations of Women Born Before 1896 up to 1941–1946

Generations	English	Mother Tongue		All Languages
		French	Other	
Before 1896	3.23	6.37	4.70	4.04
1896–1901	2.90	5.58	3.81	3.65
1901–1906	2.69	5.05	3.46	3.39
1906–1911	2.58	4.61	3.17	3.15
1911–1916	2.68	4.33	3.03	3.11
1916–1921	2.87	4.13	2.92	3.19
1921–1926	3.09	4.12	2.90	3.32
1926–1931	3.29	3.92	3.08	3.41
1931–1936	3.25	3.48	3.01	3.26
1936–1941*	2.88	2.83	2.76	2.84
1941–1946*	2.35	2.23	2.43	2.33

*The fertility of these women was not complete in 1981; women born between 1941 and 1946, for example, would be 35–40 years old in 1981.

Source: A. Romanuic, *Current Demographic Analysis: Fertility in Canada* (Ottawa: Supply and Services Canada, 1984), p. 16. Reproduced with permission.

AFTER THE CONQUEST

By the time of the British Conquest (1760), French-Canadian social and family structures were well entrenched. Nonetheless, economic and demographic factors were to greatly influence the *habitant* family at the end of the 1700s. Land for young farmers was no longer available near established family households. Consequently, young men spent many months in the lumber trade far away from home (Verdon, 1980:116), earning money that made them less dependent upon their families' influence. A type of patriarchal *stem family* became prominent in which only the youngest son farmed with, and cared for, his aging parents and eventually inherited the farm. Older sons also received parental assistance when they too married and began farming.

Urbanization, commerce, and the economic rule of the English also had an effect upon French-Canadian society and family patterns. Daughters of the French-Canadian aristocracy were encouraged to marry moneyed English entrepreneurs (McKie, Prentice, and Reed, 1983:24). Often these intercultural marriages did not fare well. Some families stayed intact while extramarital affairs were pursued; other marriages were terminated socially, if not legally, and replaced by common-law unions. As a result of this situation, common-law marriages and illegitimate children were given legal status in Lower Canada in 1801 (McKie et al., 1983:24, 25).

Most of the differences in family law between Quebec and other parts of Canada have their roots in the mid-1800s. While church control loosened in the West, it tightened in the East, partly in reaction to the changes brought about by urbanization. In

Quebec, the Roman Catholic Church's conservative influence on the Civil Code of 1886 was evident in the lack of freedom allowed the French-Canadian woman. A woman had no control over property. Any wages she earned were to be turned over to her husband, and her husband was to represent her in any judicial proceedings. Despite the fact that the society was quickly shifting from a rural to an urban one, a woman's place was still considered to be in the home raising children. It is no surprise, then, that voting rights for women in Quebec were not granted until 1940, whereas in other parts of Canada they were granted much earlier.

With increased urbanization and industrialization, the structure of the family changed. Some of the authority vested in the *habitant* father shifted to the village or civil government. Children experienced greater independence in their activity, and increasingly the mother and oldest adolescent daughter were employed outside the home. Children gradually became a financial liability where once they were an asset. However, family size remained higher than the Canadian average throughout the first half of this century.

AFTER 1950

Throughout the 1950s it has been shown that, in Quebec, the kin network varied with social class and region, and was fostered by social and religious gatherings (Rioux, 1959). Garigue (1956) contributed further to our understanding of the significance of kin in urban Quebec by showing that families chose to live near kin, that visiting between kin was frequent, and that services between kin were common. (These same characteristics are true for working-class families in British and other ethnic groups.) Women were the "integrators of the kin group," arranging visits and keeping in touch. Nepotism, which was seen as family solidarity, was frequently practised with no negative connotations. Although social mobility among French Canadians dislocated families geographically, kin retained contact with one another. However, marriage with a non-French Canadian diminished contact between kin members, particularly if the spouse was non-Catholic and non-French speaking.

Carisse (1975) studied the effect of French and English intermarriages in Montreal after fifteen years of wedded life. She found that 20 percent of English people and 5 percent of French married across ethnic lines. She found such marriages were considered inappropriate, a kind of treason to the French race and language (1975:97). Although the French culture dominated in these intermarriages with regard to home, kin, religion, school, and friends, the English culture was strongest in the mass media (television, newspapers, and magazines), and the English language was used somewhat more frequently than French. Carisse's work further indicated that the higher the social class, the greater the tendency to adopt the English culture (1975:101). The husband's native tongue, whether French or English, more frequently became the language of the family despite the fact that the wife was invariably the social convenor in the kin network.

Since 1967, there has been a dramatic change in Quebec birth rates. Quebec's 1986 birth rate was 13.1 per 1,000 population, the lowest rate in the country, while the national rate was 14.6. In 1988, the Quebec government initiated an additional child bonus in an effort to increase the province's fertility rate. Quebec's marriage rate is also lower than the Canadian average, and this difference has become marked in recent years (6.4 compared to 7.8 per 100,000 population in 1985). The pervasive influence of the Roman Catholic Church has diminished: young women are waiting longer to marry and bearing fewer children, birth control is practised, many young people are choosing not to marry at all, cohabitation in urban areas is common, and there are relatively few restraints for couples to opt for divorce.

Up until the late 1960s, Quebec's divorce rate was extremely low for an industrial society. For residents of Quebec, the only means to dissolve a marriage was one of two difficult options: an annulment through the church or a legal decree of divorce through the federal government. In the nine-year period between 1960 and 1968 there were 4,700 divorces processed through the federal government in Quebec. There were 19,000 actions of legal separation in Quebec's courts in the same period (McKie et al., 1983:93). Adultery was the only grounds for a divorce, but women had to show an additional complaint of at least two years' desertion or extreme mental or physical cruelty (McKie et al., 1983:35). Quebec's divorce rate rose significantly after 1968, the year Canada's divorce laws were liberalized. Since 1977, Quebec's divorce rate has been close to the national figure. In 1985, Quebec's divorce rate was 240 per 100,000 population, while Canada's rate was 243. In the same year, Quebec's marriage rate was 560, while Canada's was 730. These statistics point to a secularization of the Quebec society. Hobart's research on premarital sex confirms this secularization trend; the attitudes of francophone males and females have become much more permissive than the anglophone sample (Hobart, 1989:64-66).

Although the population of Quebec had one of the highest birth rates in the world, there has been a dramatic reduction in birth rates since the mid-1960s.

MILLER COMSTOCK INC.

Remnants of the traditional values of French-Canadian society are seen in current marriages: the real source of wealth is still considered to be land, wealth should be kept within the family, the family must show unity of direction through the husband, and financial assistance must be given the wife, both within the marriage and after divorce. Rural-urban differences are marked. As in other parts of Canada, urban women are well represented in the urban labour force. In general, the traditional religious norms relating to the family have been replaced by the secular norms commonly found in contemporary Western urban societies. Families are smaller, sexual behaviour outside marriage is more acceptable, and divorce is accepted as a viable solution to marital dissatisfaction. Amid these social changes, Québécois families continue to have a unique ethnic identity.

BRITISH FAMILIES

Although British people represented 44 percent of Canada's population in 1986, British families are not as homogeneous as their French counterpart for several reasons. The British settlers engaged in many occupations and lived in many regions across the country. The British were not a homogeneous group in religion, politics, or social status, nor in degree of allegiance to the British Empire. Before Canada's official nationhood in 1867, Britons arrived as early fur traders, others came as Loyalists from America after the Revolutionary War of 1776, and still others emigrated from Britain's industrializing cities or from Ireland during the potato famine of 1845-47. Others came after Confederation.

After securing eastern Canada, the British slowly moved westward, coming first as militia, then as fur traders. Many British men lived common-law with Indian women and married if and when it was convenient, often after the birth of several children. Some remained single.

The accommodation of a European custom such as baptism to frontier family living is seen in records from a Montreal church. In a number of instances, while a father and his children were on a visit to this urban centre, several children of one family are recorded as being baptized on the same day. These records show a disproportionate number of male children, indicating that daughters were often left unbaptized in the hinterland with their mothers. The Hudson's Bay Company made every effort to prevent the marriages of their employees to native people, and the men of the Company were sworn to a seven-year period of celibacy. Indian offspring were not permitted by Company rules to accompany the father to England. However, despite these regulations, many fur-trading men established families with Indian women of the plains and valleys of Canada's interior. Some men remained with their families near a trading post, while others returned to their families in Britain after their years of Company service. Frequently, "half-breed" sons were sent to Montreal to be educated.

During and after the separation of the thirteen American colonies from Britain, the English population in British North America swelled by approximately 50,000 in the brief period from 1775 to 1780. Many of the newcomers were United Empire Loyalists who moved to Canada because the new American government did not appreciate their British sympathies (Acheson, 1974:87). Not only did the emigration from south of the border make the British population larger than the French in Canada, but it further established the English legal system. This "American" presence had an assimilationist effect upon the culture that was being developed by the earlier settlers in Upper Canada (Clarke, 1962:71).

The next large wave of almost one million Britons came between 1815 and 1855, when unemployment forced British citizens to look abroad for work. Though many of these families were not socially mobile, Gagan and Mays (1974:96-122) effectively show that the central Ontario family in the mid-1800s was quite geographically mobile. Not only was this true of landless and unskilled individuals, but also of the professional and the skilled. Land value, which jumped 300 percent in ten years, certainly contributed to such mobility. In the rural community, tenant farmers in particular moved frequently in search of work.

Instead of living alone, transient singles boarded with families, establishing surrogate family relationships. Stable employment for a single male meant long-term social relationships in one geographical area, increasing the probability of marriage, the purchase of a dwelling, and a home environment for parenting.

There were several other peak years of British immigration to Canada: 1906, 1913, 1957, and 1969. Since the first years of immigration, Britons have played an important part in Canada's fishing, lumbering, shipbuilding, and farming industries. Since the Second World War, many professional and technologically trained British immigrants have also contributed to Canada's wealth.

CHILD IMMIGRATION

The story of the Canadian family is not complete without an account of child immigration from Britain to Canada. Thomas Barnardo is likely the best known philanthropist involved in this organized child immigration. In response to the overcrowded living conditions and the number of homeless children in Britain's growing industrial centres, he set up a series of homes for these children in England. At the time, the Canadian government was actively promoting the idea that "Canada needed young immigrants," and that "Canada's northwest suffered from a famine of women" (Corbett, 1981:24, 75). Encouraged by this news, Barnardo organized the emigration of over 25,000 British children between 1882 and 1915. From his point of view, he was providing these children with opportunities for independence and advancement that they never would have had in England.

The children were placed with families in Canada and expected to work for their keep. At age fourteen they were to negotiate their wages with their employers, and all money was to be banked until a boy's eighteenth birthday or a girl's twenty-first. Although it was anticipated that these children, referred to as "little people," would be treated as members of the families in which they were placed, some employers viewed the children simply as a source of cheap labour and seriously exploited them. Between 1887 and 1908, the Barnardo Industrial Farm operated near Russell, Manitoba, where young men between seventeen and twenty developed agricultural skills. Many of these young men became independent farmers in the West.

By 1925, it was estimated that 1.5 percent of all Canadians were Barnardo children or descendants of Barnardo children. Throughout the years of child immigration, there were those who disapproved, seeing these projects simply as a form of cheap labour for the Canadian middle classes and a poor way of relieving overcrowding in England. After the Second World War, the government took two steps that brought about the end of the Barnardo program. The Canadian Adolescent Act of 1921 required all children to attend school until the age of sixteen, and a bill in 1926 stipulated that all immigrants under fifteen be accompanied by their parents. The movement terminated in 1939.

CANADA'S NATIVE PEOPLES

INUIT FAMILIES

The Inuit of Canada's North are indigenous to the Canadian physical environment, but like many immigrants, they are culturally distinct. Our discussion of the Inuit will focus primarily upon family life as it existed at the time of contact with Europeans and the changes that have occurred in the contemporary Inuit family. Some of the early data are of questionable validity because European foreigners chose to record the unusual or the exotic without reference to the frequency of such practices. Early reliable ethnographic data have come to us from Franz Boaz (1888) and Knud Rasmussen (1931). Furthermore, because the Inuit sparsely inhabit a vast tract of land and comprise eight tribal groups, there is considerable variation in lifestyles.

Life for the Inuit in Canada's northland has been arduous, which has had a direct bearing upon social groupings and relationships. Formerly a nomadic people, the Inuit depended on co-operation between husband and wife in their separate roles (Balikci, 1970:103-4). Along with occasionally collaborating with their husbands in fishing activities, the women operated primarily as domestic managers. Among the Netsilik, located in the central Canadian northland,

> she scraped, cut, dried, cleaned, and washed various kinds of skins, sewed all clothes and boots, made tents and skinned containers, covered kayaks. She softened the boots, dried the clothes, and looked after the sleeping skins. Clearly the wife's work was as essential to the well-being and survival of the family as was the husband's (Balikci, 1970:104).

Since it was important for the male hunter to know his hunting territory to maximize the capture of game, marriage was usually patrilocal, meaning that the bride came to live in the groom's community or settlement.

Due to the difficult environment, families were not large. Infanticide, particularly of females, was practised, although there is some dispute over its frequency (Rasmussen, 1931; Matthiason, 1980). Balikci views female infanticide as an adaptive custom that increased the survival chances of the community when food was in short supply. However, from a social point of view, he saw it as harmful, dividing the community into "small, mutually suspicious, unrelated kinship groups" (Balikci, 1970:161). Obviously, the practice of female infanticide affected the sex ratio among the Inuit and thus the availability of marriage partners for men. Monogamy (where the marriage consists of one husband and one wife) was commonly practised, although Rasmussen (1931) and McElroy (1975) both indicate that there were some cases of polyandry (multiple husbands) and polygyny (multiple wives). With a scarcity of women, however, polygynous unions appeared to be uncommon. In such unions the husbands were exceptionally skilled hunters, quite capable of supporting two wives. Rasmussen reports that because there was often a considerable age difference between the two wives, such unions did not provoke unusual marital tension.

Along with infanticide, the practice of adoption helped to reduce family size in this severe environment. Although extensive and detailed information on Inuit adoption is not available, it seems to have been common. The pregnant woman who already had several children would promise her unborn child to a family who had fewer children (Matthiason, 1980:269). A variable price was paid for the infant. Adopted children usually had the same rights as other children, and Matthiason reported that in the northern regions of Baffin Island he often detected an almost privileged position for the adopted child (1980:270). Both Balikci (1970:123) and Rasmussen (1931) recognized the custom of aging Netsilik women adopting small boys or girls, preferably a grand-child, niece, or nephew. Such a child was referred to as their "walking stick," or helper, for their declining years (see page 177).

There were other bonds besides those within the nuclear family. Kinship ties were significant. Among coastal Inuit, the winter sealing camps required more hands than the nuclear family could provide, and therefore two or more families camped together. Since food was not plentiful and not everyone could afford to keep dogs, relatives turned to one another for the loan of dogs or a sled. Balikci reports that relations between the leader and the younger men were not always peaceful (1970:116-17), but the catch was always shared. The closest male relationships were between brothers-in-law, particu-larly if they married sisters. These men hunted and shared together in many ways, even to the point of exchanging their wives.

The transition of the Inuit from the traditional into the modern world can be viewed in two stages. Matthiason refers to the first stage as the contact-traditional period, while Balikci calls it the time of the Arctic troika. During this period, traders, missionaries, and police moved into the North. The Inuit became less nomadic; winter camps became base camps, which meant that contact with, and dependence upon, extended families became common year round. Children grew up with other kin members of their own age, and affective ties were formed in these relationships. Travel via new, larger boats required the sharing of monies among extended family members. The male often became the "boss" of the jointly owned boat. Quick cash could periodically be earned by the men when supply ships arrived. The hunter also became a trapper, and the trading posts of the Hudson's Bay Company played a significant part in the lives of the Inuit. Yet, Matthiason contends that real change was minimal. Foreign personnel were few and sometimes seasonal. The missionaries feared secularization almost more than they feared the continued presence of traditional shamans (witch doctors) (Matthiason, 1980:276). The presence of the Royal Canadian Mounted Police, however, brought a new form of authority to northern Canada: the federal government (Balikci, 1970).

Matthiason refers to the second stage of transition as the period of centralization

FOR INTEREST

INUIT WAY OF ADOPTION CONTINUES TO FLOURISH

By Matthew Fisher

RANKIN INLET, NWT – Everywhere in the tiny winter-bound communities that hug the west coast of Hudson Bay, babies fill the distinctive oversized hooded parkas worn by Inuit women.

But many of the bowlegged infants riding quietly in their "amautit" have not been born to the women happily carrying them.

The Inuit tradition of custom adoption is flourishing. In 1988, about 30 babies in Rankin Inlet, which has only 1,400 residents, were legally given to others by their birth parents.

Peter and Marie Ernerk of Rankin Inlet received a 2-month-old girl called Iquutuq – or the bumblebee – from a young woman in Chesterfield Inlet last April.

"It's hard to describe the feelings we had when we saw her for the first time," said Mrs. Ernerk, a white social worker married to an Inuk for more than 10 years.

"We already had an adopted son and a natural son, but we've always wanted a girl. I felt extreme joy and honor to be given this child. She was a gift."

Although Iquutuq's natural family visits her, "it's not culturally acceptable to seduce the child back," Mrs. Ernerk said.

To make the point that the relationship has changed, birth mothers sometimes tease the children they have given up or are otherwise harder on them than on the children they have kept, she said.

According to local residents such as the Ernerks, as many as 20 per cent of the children in the Keewatin District of the Central Arctic have been informally or formally adopted.

"There is no hard-and-fast evidence, but it would not surprise me if it's true that one in five children there are not with their original families," said Diane Doyle, director of family and children's services for the NWT government in Yellowknife. "There is a very high birth rate – maybe the highest in Canada. A large number of people are taking in the children of friends and relatives. Nobody gets too excited about this, and quite rightly so in my view. The practice is well accepted."

In many cases, the child has been promised to another couple months before it is born. Although often breastfed by their birth mothers, the babies usually are placed with their new parents within a few weeks of birth.

Ruby Arngna'naaq, an interpreter who has been mother to her sister's 2-year-old daughter since the child was born, said the custom discourages abortion and ensures that children are well cared for.

"If someone has too many boys or too many girls or is poor, you take pity on them," she said. "Mothers also often give their first born to their own mother or an older sister.

"All the children know they are adopted and they know their birth mothers, too. When we Inuit look at children adopted in the south who are searching for their real parents we shake our heads. Imagine the situation of those poor children?"

In the 1960s, in an attempt to legitimize what was always a widespread practice, the federal government gave the Northwest Territories Supreme Court the power to approve custom adoptions. The process, which does not cost anything, involves getting an affidavit from the birth mother consenting to the adoption. If the father is known, he must also sign a consent form.

The adopting parents must sign a petition requesting to adopt the child, with a supporting affidavit affirming that at least one of them is Inuit. If one of the parents is not, there must also be a letter from a recognized Inuit leader stating this parent is accepted as a member of the Inuit community.

Once a judge in Yellowknife approves the adoption, it is immediately recognized as final and has the same legitimacy in law as much more complicated private or departmental adoptions in the rest of Canada. Southern adoptions are not final until 12 months after the adopting parents receive possession of the child.

Ms Arngna'naaq, who lived for several years in Ottawa, said: "If I had to follow the western system, I would never have been allowed to adopt a child. First of all, the legal process costs at least $1,500 and I would have to pass a series of interviews. I'm single and I don't have a regular job so I would have been at the bottom of the list.

"My sister knows me. She knows I am a good mother. This is a lot healthier way. The system works well."

Source: *The Globe and Mail*, January 2, 1989.

(1980:276). It began during the Second World War, when "the forgotten people of Canada received considerable publicity, and the Eskimos learned that conditions could be less harsh" (Davis and Krauter, 1971:24). Since that time, a prime agent of change in the Canadian Arctic has been the federal Department of Indian Affairs and Northern Development. Numerous non-Inuit administrators, teachers, and oil exploration crews now live in the Inuit territory, along with the missionaries, former traders, and police, but few are long-term residents.

During this period, the Inuit moved into settlements for two major reasons: "to provide their children with a more secure life than was possible in hunting camps" and "to maintain the cohesion and stability of the family during a period of economic hardship" (McElroy, 1975:380). Children attended day school and went on to high school in larger centres. Men began to find employment that was steadier than the hunting ventures of earlier times. Families moved into new homes and paid a low rent with an option to purchase. The role of the extended family has retained its significance in these settlements, for visiting and business partnerships are common. The workings of the town council have been facilitated by kinsmen or trustworthy hunting companions (McElroy, 1975:393). Some Inuit have become prosperous in the settlements, and sometimes speak of the uemployed Inuit or welfare kin in a disparaging tone.

The role of Inuit women has changed as well. Many acquire cash through employment outside the home, family allowance, welfare, or the sale of handicraft work. In some areas, men are absent from home for several weeks, working with oil companies, and their absence leaves women with the responsibility of socializing the children.

The practice of adoption found in the traditional Inuit family was still practised in the 1970s. At Frobisher Bay and Pangnirtung, McElroy found that women who were widowed, had hysterectomies, or were past menopause adopted children (1975:388). Eighteen to 21 percent of all children were adopted. Children born out of wedlock were given up for adoption, although more recently, unmarried women are keeping their children. In addition, marriage now takes place at a later age than in the traditional period.

Despite the rigours of the physical environment, the Inuit nuclear family and its extended family network remained secure throughout the traditional stage. Social, economic, and political forces now appear to be a greater threat than the physical environment to the stability of the Inuit family. Television and school are strong influences socializing Inuit children into two distinct cultural systems simultaneously – a process referred to as biculturalization (Polgar, 1960). Most Inuit work in a wage economy controlled by Euro-Canadians and therefore no longer have control over their own livelihoods. Some communities have been seriously affected in the recent past by starvation, diphtheria epidemics, tuberculosis, alcoholism, venereal disease, and suicide. Poverty and isolation exacerbated these problems. Although medical aid is now fairly accessible, the infant mortality rate among the Inuit remains high.

Canada's current Inuit population of 25,000 (Romanuic, 1984:20) is in an extremely vulnerable state. The cultural heritage of strong family bonding, coupled with community leadership, could do much to assure stability in the decades ahead. At the same time, the economic interests and political directives of Canada's industrial south and its multinational corporations will have a critical effect upon any family system. Isolation for the Inuit is now history, and controlled or limited contact with the non-Inuit world is no longer possible. The future may see dramatic changes in the Inuit family structure.

AMERINDIAN FAMILIES

It is impossible to depict Canadian Indians as a homogeneous people. The term "Indian" is ambiguous and has distinct categories such as "status," "non-status," "treaty," and "non-treaty." These are legal distinctions, not culturally or ethnically definable entities (Christie, 1986). These social and legal designations comprise a people of fifty distinct languages. The registered or status Indian population is 349,000, of which 71 percent live on one of the 592 reserves in Canada. Twenty-eight percent of all status Indians under age nineteen live off the reserve (Johnston, 1983:58). There are an additional 75,000 non-status Indians and 98,000 Métis (Romanuic, 1984:20). With the amendment to the Indian Act of 1985 to reinstate Indian women who married outsiders, a potential 76,000 women and children could gain Indian status.

Amerindian peoples are the least understood and historically the most manipulated and mistreated (see page 180). Indians vary markedly from one tribe to another, differing because of their historical political structure, economic resources, and geographical habitation. Some of the better known groups or nations are the Algonkian, Cree, Kwakiutl, Micmac, Ojibwa, and Sioux.

At the time of European exploration of what is now Canada, the Huron lived in a matrilineal organization with approximately six families in each long house, five to six such dwellings forming a village. Premarital sex was common, initiated by either sex. The selection of the monogamous marriage partner was done by the female. A mother was considered heroic not to cry during the birthing process. Girls were preferred, and children were breast-fed for two to three years. There was no physical punishment in the disciplining of children. Young men were initiated into adulthood by spending two weeks alone in the forest (Trigger, 1976:45-49).

FOR INTEREST

CULTURAL CONFLICTS

Historically, both Indian and Inuit people exhibited a real fondness for children. In fact, the evidence suggests that Native people treated their children with more kindness and gentleness than did European parents. Furthermore, Native children occupied a more privileged position in society than did their European counterparts. As a result, the use of corporal or physical punishment was virtually unknown. In fact, the Inuit considered it demeaning for an adult to become angered with or annoyed by a child.

A pacifistic approach to child rearing meant that Native families adopted other means of socializing and disciplining their children. It was believed that children learned by imitation, so the concept of the adult-as-role-model was fundamentally important. The development of positive and appropriate behaviour in children was fostered by public opinion and the use of community approval or disapproval. Humour and teasing were employed as a means of discipline in both Indian and Inuit society. . . .

Native people also had a distinct and different concept of the family. Unlike the nuclear family definition most commonly used by non-Native people, the term "family" had a much broader meaning for Native people and included grandparents, aunts, uncles and cousins. The family for Native people was what most people refer to as the "extended family."

Implicit in the Native notion of family was a belief that the responsibility for raising children rests with all the members of a family, not only with a child's parents. Grandparents, in particular, have traditionally played a very important role in child rearing. Even more distinct from Euro-Canadian tradition was the belief that the community as a whole had a legitimate role and, indeed, a responsibility to participate in the rearing and caring of all children.

There are many other examples of distinctive approaches to child rearing that were shared by many Native people. For example, there were children who were born out of wedlock but the concept of illegitimacy was virtually unknown. As one Indian elder explained, in many tribes the mother of an "illegitimate" child had the right to name the father. Even if the male denied it, the mother's word was accepted by the tribe, so that the child had a father. From that point on, the man's family took responsibility for the child, who was accorded the same honour and status as if he or she were the "legitimate" child.

Source: Patrick Johnston, *Native Children and the Child Welfare System* (Toronto: James Lorimer, 1983), pp. 68, 69.

From journals, correspondence, and wills, Van Kirk (1988) has pieced together the life of Indian women in the fur trade society. These women were important to the traders, not only by filling the sexual void, but by performing valuable economic tasks such as making moccasins and netting snowshoes. Such marriages often formed valuable trading alliances and social bonds consolidating economic relations. Van Kirk reports that Indian women often preferred a white partner because the marriage elevated her status (1988:156). Cox (1957:354) reports that Indian women married to whites bore more children because Indian taboos of sexuality were violated, their lifestyle was less fatiguing, their diet was more regular, and their offspring were not nursed as long.

The Amerindian family of a century ago varied by tribe, but was generally self-sufficient, somewhat isolated, often matrifocal (the strongest family bonds were between mothers and children), and kin structured. Sex roles were clearly defined, and older men wielded much authority. Children were treated with respect and were socialized in the traditional ways by older members of the extended family. The contemporary Amerindian family, however, is caught in a vacuum. The extended family is still idealized, but it has been damaged by governments, Western technology, and economic imperialism. Although there has been some movement toward the nuclear family and increased non-familial socialization of the young, the transition to stable new ways is not complete, nor is there convincing evidence that it will ever be completed under present conditions. Some say that change has been too rapid and that dependence on government has been fostered too extensively.

Until the 1900s, some Amerindians were treated as economic equals by non-Indians, and many became acculturated when they took up small-scale farming (Christie, 1983). Since that time, however, with the establishment of the reserve system, the Amerindians' standard of living, sense of identity, and the cohesion of tribe and family have almost steadily declined. Increasing development and urbanization near reserve lands has virtually destroyed the economic viability of traditional forms of employment. Only 20 percent speak their native tongues.

Most of the Canadian Amerindian population are now of low economic status. In comparing living amenities – such as quality of house, electricity, running water, and sewage disposal – with the national average, the Indian population has a marked lower proportion. Forty-seven percent live in housing that fails to meet basic standards of physical conditions (Siggner, 1986). In fact, more than one-half of Amerindian families receive social assistance, and many individuals are unskilled and unemployed. The unemployment rate is two and a half times that of the national figure.

The native family has several distinctive features when compared to the average Canadian family. Twenty percent are lone-parent families, twice the Canadian rate. The average Amerindian family is made up of 4.5 individuals, while Canada's average is 3.7. The Amerindian birth rate is 3.15 births per woman, while the rate for the rest of the Canadian population is 1.7 per woman. Natives tend to have larger families; proportionately, there are five times as many natives with five children or more (White, 1985:24). Although their marriage rate is lower than the Canadian average, the number of births outside of marriage is considerably higher than the national average. The percentage of Amerindians under age five dropped to 13 percent in 1981 from 19 percent in 1961.

Despite high birth rates, an increasing number of native women have no children, and women are giving birth to their first child at a later age. Also, the period for breast-feeding has declined (Romanuic, 1984:19). While 1 percent of all Canadian children were in the care of child welfare authorities in 1980, 4.6 percent of all status Indians were under this authority. This is also true of non-status Indians and Métis (Johnston, 1983:57). Johnston also indicates that 77 percent of all adoptions of status Indian children in 1981 were by non-Indians.

The Amerindian death rate is 50 percent higher than that of other Canadians, although birth and death rates have dropped considerably over the past fifteen years. The infant mortality rate has declined from 79.0 per 1,000 live births in 1960 to 15.0 in 1981. The primary causes of death are accident, poisoning, and violence, all three times the Canadian average. The life expectancy of a male is sixty-two years (seventy-three for Canada) and of a female, sixty-nine (eighty for Canada in 1985) (Siggner, 1986).

After admitting to family breakdown among their people, and in view of the continued threat to the Dene way of life due to pipeline construction, Dene leaders have stated: "We have no assurance of a Dene future of any kind. We have no guarantees; we have no control; and a very good example is this pipeline" (Erasmus, Norwegian, and Andrew, 1980:10). Added to this social and economic peril are the continued environmental threats from oil spills and the chemical pollution of Arctic lands and waters. Yet, increasingly, indigenous peoples are gaining new political power, which in turn may have a positive impact on social structure and family life.

OTHER ETHNIC GROUPS

A child's identity is fostered by the early socialization within the family, where particular values, beliefs, habits, behaviours, and preferences are learned. The degree to which any ethnic family adapts to Canadian culture and the dominant Canadian family model is dependent upon numerous factors. Of prime significance is the symmetry or asymmetry between the Canadian culture in which the child associates and the culture of the ethnic group to which the family belongs. Will Canadian children ridicule the ethnic child's peculiar behaviour, or more important, will the school system question or challenge the behaviour? Another factor in the persistence of ethnic identity is the size and institutional completeness of the ethnic community. Institutional completeness refers to the degree to which a group is economically, socially, religiously, and educationally self-sufficient (Breton, 1964). A more highly concentrated ethnic population with its own services tends to support the retention of ethnic identity. The length of time in the new country and the sex and age of the immigrant are further considerations. Second-generation and younger immigrants modify their lifestyles and values more than older immigrants. Conditions under which the immigrant family left their homeland may further contribute to ease of assimilation into the new culture.

Immigrant families often change as a result of contact with the new culture. Children receive more education than their parents and move away from ethnic neighbourhoods. Children and young people increasingly choose activities that are extrafamilial, and career choices are often made independently of parents. Patriarchy, or the father as final authority in family matters, is viewed as inappropriate.

One particular area in which old and new values may conflict involves marriage and the structure of the family. In Canada today, marriage is seen as the choice of two individuals, primarily for their own happiness within as well as outside the family. The union may be sanctioned by a civil or religious ceremony, but many people choose to cohabit without legally marrying, often for a brief trial period. A couple may anticipate having children, but only when planned, and seldom more than three. Marriage duration is contingent upon compatibility; divorce and remarriage have become increasingly acceptable. However, many immigrants come to Canada with traditional ideas about marriage and family. If their own children begin to adopt Canadian attitudes, there may be intense family conflict before the new family patterns are accepted, if they are accepted at all.

Canadian family patterns are themselves changing, and ethnic families must come to terms with these changes. Some find the new family patterns undesirable and resist them. Others accept them, at least in part, while still others appear to relinquish quickly the old ways and to welcome the more democratic, particularistic, and individualistic norms of present-day Canada. The interplay between emerging forms of the Canadian family and some selected ethnic family patterns is discussed below. Although social class differences exist within each ethnic group, many similarities can be noted among families of the same ethnic origin.

Along with differences in courtship practices, interethnic marriages show differences in wedding preparations. Who is invited, which clergy preside (or whether there will be a non-religious celebration), the dinner menu, type of reception, and kind and quantity of alcohol served are only a few of the considerations.

Statistics Canada does not keep a record of ethnic marriage endogamy, but we have some hint of ethnic endogamy by looking at religious intermarriages. Ethnic identity is more likely to be significant in endogamous marriages. Jewish (72 percent) and Mennonite (63 percent) groups have a relatively high rate of marrying within their own group (Statistics Canada, 1986b).

Fertility rates vary considerably among ethnic groups. Jewish and Asian women show a low rate of reproduction, while Amerindians and Inuit show a high rate. Ethnic populations also vary sharply in their age distribution, which is affected by birth rates, health care, and immigration policies.

Kalbach's earlier work based upon 1971 data shows Jews, French, and the British to have the lowest propensity for ethnic intermarriage, with the highest propensity being among Scandinavians. He also shows regional differences in intermarriage among ethnic groups. While French ethnic intermarriage is low in Quebec, it tends to be high in British Columbia. British ethnic intermarriage is low in the Atlantic provinces and high in British Columbia. Ukrainians show a low propensity to ethnic intermarriage in the Prairie provinces (Kalbach, 1983:43–45). For some groups, a high rate of intermarriage with other ethnic groups simply indicates a lack of available partners to marry from within their own group.

OLD ORDER MENNONITE FAMILIES

Old Order Mennonites have been more successful in maintaining their distinctive lifestyle than other Canadian ethnic groups. They are a religious-ethnic society who fled Alsace and Switzerland four hundred and fifty years ago for Pennsylvania. Two hundred years ago they crossed the Niagara River to farm in southern Ontario. Large numbers left this conservative group for religious reasons at two points in time: 1889 and 1939. The Old Order group of 6,000 (1988) can be readily identified by their simple lifestyle, work ethic, black dress, and the horse and buggy means of transportation. Cars, home telephones, radios, and television are all forbidden. Despite their traditional way of life, they do have contact with the "English" (their term for any non-Mennonite) for economic exchange. They shop in nearby towns or malls, and sell agricultural produce or baked goods on the farm, or at a city farmers' market.

Old Order Mennonites tend to show a satisfaction and pride in their history and traditional ways. Modernity is not seen as successful or even good, but rather as destructive to personhood and disintegrative to society. There is no apology made for their distinct clothing, values, or habits. Compromise or accommodation in these matters is seen as a weakness and as deviance.

The family and the religious institution are the chief agents of socialization. All children attend a parochial Mennonite one- or two-room rural school taught by one of their own members, where instruction in history conforms to the Bible and the curriculum is adapted to their traditional values and goals. Peer group influence is temporary and minimal. At age fifteen the vast majority are happy to leave school and work on the farm, an activity in which they participate throughout childhood. Increasing responsibility comes with age and is continuous rather than abrupt. Males and females serve apprenticeships on Mennonite farms other than their parents'. Females receive about half the value of male wages, yet Mennonite males receive considerably less than

COURTESY OF JAMES HERTEL, WILFRID LAURIER UNIVERSITY

Old Order Mennonite family.

they would receive on an "English" farm. Consistent socialization within the Mennonite community reinforces their distinctiveness (Peters, 1987).

In the home, patriarchy, a spartan lifestyle, hard work, co-operative living, a family focus, and religious values reinforce the advantages of Mennonite life. The home tends to be a place of care and love, though affection is seldom visible except with young children. The leadership of male Mennonites recognizes traditional and religious values as all important. The political-religious structure directed by men at church and in the home reinforces these beliefs.

At age fourteen, the males already ride to church separate from their parents in horse and buggy. After age fifteen and until marriage, young people attend weekly Sunday night singings in a home. As many as one hundred and fifty people may attend these social events, which include the singing of hymns and folksongs and the playing of games. Seating is sex segregated. Some young men engage in dancing, radio playing, or drinking and smoking, despite the fact that these activities are not permissible and cause concern for parents and church leaders. At about 10:30, couples leave and the young women are escorted home by their suitors.

No casual dating is accepted among Old Order Mennonites, but couples are expected to court for two years prior to marriage. The average age of marriage is 23.7 for males and 22.2 for females. Weddings are scheduled for the months before seeding or after harvest. Weddings are all-day events held at home with about seventy guests personally invited by the couple. Following the preacher's exhortations and sermon, pranks are played and a sumptuous meal is served. The couple will likely spend the night in an upstairs bedroom, then drive to their farmhouse in the morning. The bride's family provides the basics for the furnished house, and the bridegroom's parents provide some livestock. The farm is financed by parents or other farmers in the community.

Within two years, couples are expected to bear their first child. Parents do not attend prenatal classes, and doctor's visits during pregnancy are an exception. Most babies, however, are born in hospitals. The average size of the completed Mennonite family is 5.8 children (Peters, 1988). There are one or two separations in the entire group, and no divorces.

Despite the encroachment of urban sprawl, higher costs in farm management, increased government intervention in dairying, and a centralization of education in the larger society, the Old Order Mennonites have been able to maintain their private and collective identity through family cohesion, strict religious socialization, and considerable economic self-sufficiency.

PORTUGUESE AND ITALIAN FAMILIES

Most of the Portuguese immigration to Canada has occurred within the past thirty years. Men generally emigrated first and were followed by their families and extended family members (Anderson and Higgs, 1976). Immigration policies encouraging sponsorship by a relative have perpetuated kin migration among the Portuguese. European Portuguese families tend to be traditional, patriarchal, and Roman Catholic, and there is an extensive communication network among kin members. A man's closest relationship is with another man, usually his brother or father, and not with his wife.

Anderson and Higgs (1976) show several pressures for change in the Portuguese community. Both boys and girls are becoming better educated than their parents and are moving toward a more egalitarian ideal. Although the closely knit traditional families are resisting change, many young families desire more independence from their relatives.

Some similar patterns exist among the Italian-Canadians. Families are close and extended families assist one another (Boissevain, 1975). Upon arriving in Canada, it is common for Italians to live with relatives until they can establish their own home. As time passes, children are encouraged to keep contact by letter with relatives and friends in Italy. In Canada, relatives often live near one another. They frequently meet on the occasion of birthdays, confirmations, weddings, and death. Families also gather to make wine or process meats. The carcass is frequently purchased from a kin or a "peasant" from the same village in Italy. In such activities, the work and product is distributed, a form of exchange in which no cash is passed from one to another.

Within the home, a daughter's domestic role is emphasized. Her good reputation and later her success as a wife and mother add to the family's honour. A son maintains family honour through hard work and in overseeing the behaviour of his sister(s). Children are expected to show gratitude for the sacrifices of their parents, and as adults, to support their aging parents (Boissevain, 1975). Kinship ties imply a series of rights and obligations, whereas among the British such ties are more likely to be instruments of social expression.

According to Boissevain's Montreal study (1975), young Italian women have been fairly restricted in their social activity, with the result that Italian men find freer social exchange with non-Italian women. For Italian men, there is some prestige in finding a French or British partner, since intermarriage is one indication of acceptance into the larger non-Italian community. Consequently, ethnic endogamy is declining, but religious endogamy persists.

GREEK FAMILIES

Perhaps the greatest influence on the family in Greece has been the Greek Orthodox Church. During the Turkish occupation of Greece from 1453 to 1821, the church survived and kept Greek culture alive; it continues to wield great power over family life. Marriage is considered a sacrament, and divorce and remarriage are strongly discouraged. The Greek family in Canada has had a relatively low degree of social integration into Canadian culture, due in part to the fact that Greek family life remains strongly influenced by historical experiences and values. Some important concepts in the Greek family are solidarity, mutual support, and moral obligation to other family members. Kinship bonds are strong, and assistance and co-operation are provided in economic and business matters as well as in time of family crisis and celebration. Many Canadian Greeks continue to send financial aid to relatives in their homeland (Chimbos, 1980).

Greeks in Canada are predominantly endogamous, and a son or daughter who marries a non-Greek is viewed as "lost." The size of the Greek family is somewhat smaller than that of the average Canadian family. The traditional household, where the husband is the head and has absolute authority over the family, is still common. The influence of Canadian institutions and values has modified the familial structure somewhat, however, and wives are beginning to enjoy a higher status and greater freedom.

ARAB FAMILIES

Arabs in Canada number about 80,000, the majority being located in Montreal and Toronto. In the traditional family, marriages are arranged, but in Canada the couple see one another casually before marriage, and women have veto power over any marriage proposal. As with the Greek community, when an exogamous (outside the group) marriage takes place, it tends to isolate the couple from the Arab community. In married life the wife's gainful employment is often a contentious issue, as is the use of birth control. Such strict family regulations place a barrier between the Arab woman and Canadian society (Abu-Laban, 1980:169).

In Arab countries, the extended family is significant in decision making and in social interaction. This is not the case in Canada, where family decisions are usually left to immediate family members and social ties within the extended family are weaker. The Canadian school system serves as a counter-socializing force to Arab norms and values, encouraging children to be more individualistic.

Arabs are by no means a homogamous people. Canadians have become more conscious of variations among Arabs because of the Organization of Petroleum Exporting Countries (OPEC), the lingering tensions with Israel and Jewish peoples, radical Moslem groups such as the Shiites, and the Iran-Iraq war.

CHINESE FAMILIES

Racial prejudice and its effect on Canadian immigration policy are significant in explaining the Chinese family in Canada (Li, 1987). The first Chinese men arrived in Canada during the gold rush in British Columbia in the late 1850s. To fill the need for railway workers after 1880, 17,000 more Chinese men were admitted to the western coastal region of Canada. These labourers, known as "coolies," worked long hours and were never expected to integrate into Canadian society. It was anticipated that they would return to their homeland after their service on the railway was completed, but without government assistance, many could not afford to leave. A head tax (eventually amounting to $500) was levied on each Chinese immigrant after 1885, restricting the immigration of wives and children and resulting in a bachelor society (Verma, Chan, and Lam, 1980). The discriminatory Chinese Immigration Act of 1923 almost eliminated all Chinese immigration for a quarter of a century.

Those Chinese who did manage to enter Canada found a welcome that was far from warm. In western Canada, the Chinese were, by law, forbidden to enter the legal or medical fields, and they could only purchase property in urban Chinese ghettos. Under such discriminatory laws, their incomes remained low. For several decades the Chinese were limited to jobs in businesses such as restaurants, laundries, and retail food outlets. Because of laws restricting non-white immigration, the sex ratio in the Chinese community continued to favour males. Davidson's Toronto study (1952) showed that the lack of normal family relations caused by a surplus of Chinese males in the population led to widespread gambling, opium smoking, and the use of prostitutes.

Chinese immigrants arrived from Hong Kong in increasing numbers after 1962, when Canadian immigration laws allowed more non-white immigrants to enter the country. Today 90 percent of Canada's Chinese live in urban centres of over 100,000 people. Families have become upwardly mobile and have moved out of downtown ghettos into suburban areas. Compared to members of other ethnic groups, the Chinese are currently found in a greater variety of occupations. A higher proportion know English, and families make financial sacrifices so that children can obtain a good education. Chinese families are slightly smaller than the average Canadian family, but 19 percent live in extended family households (Verma et al., 1980). Unlike the situation in some other ethnic families, a high percentage of wives are gainfully employed. Grandmothers play an important role in rearing children as well as in keeping Chinese traditions alive in the family.

Some traits of the traditional Chinese family remain. The extended family as a form of social control remains strong, and this is reflected in a low crime rate (Johnson, 1979) and a low divorce rate in Chinese communities. At the same time, some traditional family practices, such as ancestor worship, are on the decline. The Chinese are more homogeneous than the Japanese, and have a higher birth rate (Halli, 1987). Currently, large numbers of Hong Kong Chinese are applying for Canadian immigration because the colony will be returned to the political jurisdiction of mainland China in 1997.

Many ethnic groups attempt to retain certain family and cultural traditions while becoming a part of the dominant society both economically and politically.

CONCLUSION

There are numerous factors that act against cultural assimilation of ethnic families. Religious socialization and physical separation are the most important factors reinforcing ethnic uniqueness. The degree of contrast with the dominant culture is another factor that affects assimilation. The Doukhobors are a good example of a group whose extreme uniqueness has kept them apart from mainstream Canadian society. And, as already mentioned, the larger the proportion of ethnic families in any geographical area, the greater the likelihood of endogamy, and this, of course, works against assimilation. One exception to this rule is the Jewish community, whose members usually marry within the group, despite their small numbers.

Most ethnic groups in Canada today live in nuclear families. Canadian families bear some resemblance to the families of the United States and Western Europe, but at the same time show evidence of the unique historical and multicultural roots of their members. French-Canadian families in Quebec have had a long history, but in the past two decades have become more like families in other parts of Canada. British families also have been influenced by Canadian history and geography as well as by the social environment, including other ethnic groups. Thus, Canadian families are now distinct from families of fifty or even twenty years ago. They have fewer children, and these children experience less parental control due to the increasing influence of schools, peer groups, and the mass media. The preoccupation of one or both parents with their work and the trend toward greater parental individualism further contributes to the increasing independence of children. Parents are more permissive in allowing children to pursue their own wishes and interests, contributed to in part by the Western ideal of individualism.

There are fewer restrictions on dating and courtship than there were fifty years ago, and most young adults no longer expect male and female virginity at marriage. The double standard of sexual behaviour for men and women is losing ground. Few couples feel compelled to marry because of a premarital pregnancy, as an increasing number of women choose either to abort or to raise their children as single parents.

Some method of birth control is common for most couples, with the exception of Hutterites, Old Order Mennonites, and some Catholics. Not only have birth control devices and a greater understanding of fertility reduced family size, but they have also enabled couples to enjoy more freedom in sexual relations. The belief once held by the *habitants* of New France that sex is exclusively for procreation is far behind us. In fact, some individuals choose to leave their partners or establish a clandestine relationship if sexual satisfaction is not achieved within marriage.

Relations between husbands and wives have changed in other ways. The family pattern where the husband is head of the household and the wife acts as his complement is changing to one where the husband is a senior partner and the wife a junior partner (Scanzoni and Scanzoni, 1981:315, 370). In a few younger families, the husband and wife function as equal or quasi-equal partners. Increasingly, courting and young married couples of all ethnic groups are expecting and experiencing romantic love, defined as a strong emotional attachment. There is a greater tolerance of exogamous marriage in most ethnic communities, and marriage is usually neolocal.

Over 65 percent of Canadian married women with dependent children are employed full-time or part-time outside of the home. Men from some ethnic groups, for example, Arab, Greek, and Italian, feel that their provider role is downgraded if their wives are employed. These husbands also tend to leave household chores and child rearing exclusively to their wives. Employed married women also tend to become more involved in personal and family decision making, including major financial decisions.

Relationships with extended family members in urban families continue, but with fewer individuals and sometimes with less frequency (Ramu and Tavuchis, 1989:143–65). Geographic and social mobility, urban living, single-family dwellings and apartments, individualistic lifestyle, and a lack of social norms that compel contact could inhibit extended family interaction. Yet, commitment to close family members continues, as evidenced by phone calls, the lending of money, or services such as the exchange of baby-sitting. Some ethnic families, such as the Italians, Chinese, and Portuguese, try to keep extended family contact frequent and close, even in urban centres.

In many modern families, child care is a concern for parents, particularly for immigrant women who have higher rates of labour force participation than native-born Canadians. Government funds for public child care services are limited, however, and fluctuate with federal and provincial budget constraints. Because some mothers need to work during their children's early years for economic reasons, parents sometimes work shifts to avoid the need for non-family child care services. A few middle-class couples with flexible work schedules are able to arrange their time so as to integrate work and child care. Hutterite women appear to have the best arrangement for child care and child rearing, for adequate child care is continuously available, allowing mothers time away from their children (Peter, 1987).

Rather than have the elderly in segregated apartments, immigrant groups such as the Chinese, Hungarians, Czechs, Italians, and Greeks have grandparents live with their children in households comprising three generations. In these households, grandmothers often contribute by undertaking child care and housekeeping duties, and their assistance is valued by the younger members of the family. In their rural settings, Hutterite and Mennonite families find appropriate and dignified roles for the elderly: the women in household work and the men in assisting with farm chores, all the while mixing with family and community members.

Although separation and divorce have increased in recent years, as we will discuss in Chapter Nine, many ethnic families have been almost impervious to this trend. Among Chinese, Hungarian, Indian, Portuguese, Amish, Mennonite, and Hutterite families, divorce is very rare. Their religious values and/or their closely knit communities have kept their families intact.

Specific characteristics of ethnic, religious, or cultural groups persist over many generations. For example, most urban centres have restaurants or shops that cater to the traditional tastes of ethnic families. Many of these shops and restaurants are small family businesses in which both parents and their children work together. In some ethnic communities, old customs and traditions are perpetuated by festivals where ethnic songs and dances are performed and ethnic artifacts are displayed or sold. Family ethnicity is also preserved through the use of the ethnic language, through visits to the homeland, or by contact with more recent immigrants.

Because the immigration law of 1967 placed greater emphasis on family sponsorship, immigrants today tend to settle in urban areas that already have a high concentration of their own ethnic group. The Canadian government recognizes the importance of the family in providing social, psychological, and economic assistance to immigrants. Without this assistance from their families, many immigrants would need to rely on public resources in adjusting to Canadian society.

DISCUSSION QUESTIONS

1. What vestiges of the early French family system are still evident in modern French-Canadian families in Quebec?
2. What effect did the absence of men have on families during times of war, fur-trading or hunting expeditions, or out-of-town employment? How did women and children adapt to their absence?
3. Why do native people in North America experience such high rates of illegitimacy, family violence, and suicide?
4. Why was female infanticide practised by the Inuit at the time of early European contact?
5. Explain why most Old Order Mennonite youth adapt to the traditional ways of their parents.
6. What social and economic factors are encouraging young people from immigrant parents to accept the nuclear model of the family?
7. What are some of the ways in which adolescents deal with conflict between their parents' customs and the values of their peer group?
8. What factors influence the different rates of endogamy of the various ethnic groups in Canada?
9. How has discrimination modified the family patterns in Canada of: the Chinese; Pakistanis; West Indians; Germans?
10. How have the Chinese, Greek, and Mennonite people kept their rate of marriage dissolution so low?

chapter nine

Marital Dissolution: Structural and Ideological Changes

INTRODUCTION

Until 1968, divorce was something that did not happen in one's own family – it was an embarrassing situation that afflicted Americans, but not Canadians. Indeed, legal divorce was practically unheard of in Canada before the Second World War. However, one year after the grounds for divorce were extended, the divorce rate in Canada had already more than doubled. A mere ten years later, in 1978, the rate was six times what it was in 1968.

After a steady annual increase, Canadian (and American) divorce rates began declining in 1983 (see Table 9.1). The rates were still relatively high when compared to the 1970s, but the sharp rise seemed to have been contained and even overturned. By 1986, however, we experienced another sharp increase in the divorce rate (see Figure 9.1). It is too early to predict whether this new level will stabilize or whether we will return to the lower pre-1986 rates. Indeed, it is possible that this recent rise has occurred as a result of the new Divorce Act, which came into effect on June 1, 1986. Whenever more liberal laws are introduced, divorce rates rise accordingly.* Whatever the future outcome, one fact is certain: higher divorce and remarriage rates, compared to twenty years ago, are here to stay.

What has been happening to Canadian marriages in the past twenty years? First of all, it should be pointed out that the Canadian divorce rate is still moderate by international standards, as indicated by Table 9.2. Most Western industrialized countries have also been experiencing rising rates of divorce. From 1960 to 1980, the American

---

*Divorce legislation and its impact are discussed in Chapter Ten, "Controversies Within Family Law."

Table 9.1   Incidence of Divorce in Canada by Year: Frequencies and Rates
(per 100,000 population)

Years	Frequencies	Rates
1921	558	6.4
1931	700	6.8
1941	2,462	21.4
1951	5,270	37.6
1961	6,563	36.0
1968	11,343	54.8
1969	26,093	124.2
1971	29,685	137.6
1981	67,671	278.0
1982	70,436	285.9
1983	68,567	275.5
1984	65,172	259.4
1985	61,980	244.4
1986	78,160	308.3

Source: From Statistics Canada, July, 1977. *Vital Statistics*, vol. II. *Marriage and Divorces 1975*, pp. 28-29; Statistics Canada advance bulletins 1984, p. 16, 1985, pp. 2 and 10. See also D. C. McKie et al., *Divorce: Law and the Family in Canada*, 1983, p. 59; *The Daily*, June 3, 1988, p. 8. Reproduced by permission of the Minister of Supply and Services Canada, 1989.

Figure 9.1

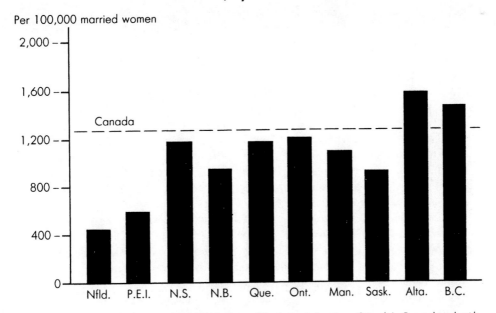

Divorce Rate, by Province, 1986

Per 100,000 married women

Source: Statistics Canada, Cat. 84-205 (Ottawa: Supply and Services Canada). Reproduced with permission of the Minister of Supply and Services Canada, 1989.

Table 9.2 Crude Divorce Rates in Several Industrialized Countries: 1985
(per 1,000 population)

Japan	1.38
France	1.95
Sweden	2.37
Canada	2.44
England and Wales	3.20
U.S.S.R.	3.36
United States	4.96

Source: United Nations Department of International and Economic and Social Affairs Statistical Office, *Demographic Yearbook 1986* (Copyright United Nations 1988), pp. 470-72. Reproduced by permission.

divorce rate in particular has soared to become one of the highest in the world. The divorce rate in the Soviet Union has also risen. The reasons for rising rates of separation and divorce are similar in all these industrialized countries, whether socialist or capitalist.

CAUSES OF HIGH DIVORCE RATES

At a societal level, divorce is a by-product of the individualistic and hedonistic mentality of the technological era. For the "me" generation, the emphasis is on self-fulfilment, personal freedom, and enjoyment. Other-orientation and couple-orientation are values that are not stressed in the family as much as in the past. A climate of moral liberalism has encouraged narcissistic tendencies with such slogans as "Do your own thing," and has contributed to make divorce more acceptable. At the same time, religion has seen its sphere of influence drastically reduced in matters concerning family and personal life. The sanctity of marriage has been eroded and has been replaced by a more personal, legalistic, and secular view of the marital relationship.

Our technological society has also offered us more lifestyle alternatives, from more effective birth control devices to laundromat and catering services. Some of these changes have enabled more women to enter the paid labour force. Indeed, the employment of married women is seen by many moralists as one of the most important contributors to the recent upsurge in divorce rates (Becker, 1981), and it therefore deserves additional comment.

Studies have found that employed married women consider divorce as an option more often than unemployed married women (Huber and Spitze, 1980; Albrecht and Kunz, 1980); moreover, women who can be independent financially initiate the decision to separate more often than women who depend on their husbands' financial support. Ross and Sawhill (1975) have established that women's divorce rates increase with each additional thousand dollars they earn. There are also indications that, once divorced, high-income women are less likely to remarry (Renne, 1971). Ambert (1983) investigated this relationship further and found that high-income divorced women wanted to

The sanctity of marriage has been eroded and has been replaced by a more personal, legalistic, and secular view of the marital relationship.

MILLER COMSTOCK INC.

remarry as often as low-income women; these financially independent women, however, felt less social and financial pressure to remarry. Fairly typical of separated high-income women was a thirty-eight-year-old executive who had been involved in a serious relationship for over a year. Marriage was being considered, but she added that she was "very cautious because I could have so much to lose." Low-income women saw the situation quite differently: they felt they had everything to *gain* by remarrying.

Advocates of the ideology that women should stay home may feel vindicated by these results. We should point out, however, that more women than men had to remain in unhappy marriages in the past because they had no other alternatives. Currently, the choices for both genders are closer to being equalized. This is a negative change only if one operates under the assumption that women should suffer failed marriages more than men should.

Along with these contributory variables, the past decades have witnessed a dramatic shift in the acceptance of divorce as a fact of life. For instance, a Canadian public opinion poll in 1943 showed that only 24 percent of the respondents felt that divorce laws should be more lenient. In 1966, however, 60 percent of the respondents were in favour of relaxing divorce laws (Pike, 1975). It is possible that we have become more accepting of divorce because its consequences are now less catastrophic than in the past. The social costs, and perhaps even the psychological costs, have become less onerous. As Bernard (1971:97) phrased it, "Social costs act selectively; when they are low, they release more people into the divorce population; when they are high, they release few."

Although there is disagreement among researchers on this point, the relaxation of divorce laws could have contributed to a rise in divorce (Stetson and Wright, 1975). However, this probably occurred only because other social circumstances were favourable – that is, the societal variables we have already touched upon increased the demand for divorce, and this, in turn, heralded the introduction of more liberal laws. Both the higher rates of divorce and the less rigorous laws are actually the result of socio-economic forces that we have already described. However, the variables contributing to a high divorce rate create a social climate wherein couples who are not happy together will divorce rather than remain married. They may work even less hard at maintaining their marriage than in a society that is less individualistic, less hedonistic, more family oriented, and where marriage is still viewed as sacred.

In addition to these societal factors, there are personal causes of divorce. For instance, studies have found that couples who marry in their teens, especially if the wife is premaritally pregnant, run a greater risk of being maritally unhappy and of divorcing (Lee, 1977). Other personal variables correlated with high rates of divorce are brief acquaintance before marriage, alcoholism, emotional problems, as well as dissimilarity of social class, education, and age.

DIVORCE AND MARITAL HAPPINESS

Although divorce rates have soared, they do not represent an adequate picture of marital happiness. We cannot know from rates of divorce whether people are more or less happily married than fifty years ago. In retrospect, the social situation up until the Second World War seems to have been less complicated, more regulated by morality, and certainly more bound by religious and social restrictions. Conjugal roles were more clearly delineated, and sexual compatibility was less important than reproduction. There was also far less introspection about the personal aspects of one's marriage. People were more solidly and securely married than today, but we do not know if security necessarily increased happiness.

Do high divorce rates automatically mean that marital happiness is uncommon? Studies of married persons generally indicate that the quality of marriage varies with gender, the stage in the life cycle, the number of children, and the couple's level of education. In a Canadian study of 212 separated and divorced persons, nearly one-third reported that, on the whole, eliminating the last two years of their marriages, their relationships had been above average in terms of happiness (Ambert, 1989). At the other extreme, about 40 percent of the subjects reported unhappy marriages. While there is definitely a relationship between marital unhappiness and divorce, the relationship is far from clear. Many unhappy people stay together while some happily married persons eventually divorce. In the separate research of Ambert (1980) and Baker (1980), in-depth interviews pointed to a few reasons why people who claimed to have had happy marriages eventually divorced.

First, it was apparent that some people divorce for the wrong reasons. These divorces result from circumstances that have little to do with the relationship: problems at work, mid-life crises, or long-term emotional problems. Under such circumstances, feelings of dissatisfaction are generalized to the marriage. The person may even come to believe that the problem lies in the marriage itself and that, by leaving the marriage, things will return to normal. For instance, when asked who was to be blamed for the demise of his marriage, a remarried man in the study said: "Me, no question about that. I threw away a perfectly good marriage. I got out of my marriage rather than reorient my general life goals. I projected onto my marriage my general dissatisfaction – I was so self-centred and distraught by my problems at work."

A separation or divorce follows with a temporary feeling of well-being, which is rapidly replaced, in some cases, by deeper despair as one realizes that the problems are still there. In fact, after the separation the problems may be aggravated by loneliness, loss of financial resources, and estrangement from children.

Another path from a fairly happy marriage to divorce is what could be called "taking a risk," and usually takes the form of adultery. An affair may begin unexpectedly during a business trip or as a result of a long friendship. The person has not been actively seeking the opportunity, but does not turn it down once it presents itself. Because the marriage is secure, the husband or wife sincerely believes that there will be no consequences. But this may be delusional. For instance, the new companion may take up a great deal of time or seems to awaken personal needs that had been forgotten during the marriage. The relationship becomes more involved and a divorce follows. Both ex-spouses are often shocked by the rapidity with which this scenario unfolds, and more often than not, the unfaithful spouse does not remarry the person with whom he or she was having the affair.

Marital unhappiness does not necessarily lead to divorce, nor does marital happiness always guarantee marital stability – a topic that is neglected in the research literature. Nor do we subscribe to the popular belief that to have an affair outside of one's marriage means the marriage is not a good one. To be realistic, any marriage is a human relationship and, as such, is rarely perfect. Something, however small, is therefore always lacking in any marriage, as in any relationship. We have studied marriages that were considered very good and in which adultery took place for no other reason than that the opportunity presented itself: nothing was amiss in the marriage. The idea that this cannot happen is a romantic myth not supported by research evidence. There are, however, marriages in which something is indeed missing, and this lacuna does lead to adultery.

MARITAL STABILITY AND UNHAPPINESS

As there are couples who are happily married but eventually divorce, there are many couples who remain together despite their unhappiness with each other. The reasons why unhappily married couples do not divorce is as interesting a topic as why others seek legal termination of their marriage. Researchers, however, have focused on those who divorce because they are easier to sample and to interview than are unhappily married persons.

Many couples stay together because of religious convictions, since some established religions do not permit divorce or remarriage after divorce. For others, however, the fear

MILLER COMSTOCK INC.

Some couples divorce even though they had a relatively happy marriage, while many other couples who are relatively unhappy remain together.

of social censure seems to be just as compelling a reason to remain married. In particular, those who live in small, cohesive communities may remain married even though they are emotionally divorced from their partner. Unemployed women may stay in unhappy marriages because they cannot afford to live on their own and support their children. Others fear the consequences of a drastically reduced income after divorce. Some men fear the effects of high child-support payments and the division of property on their own lifestyle and business ventures.

Above all, it would seem that many couples remain together because they are used to each other. Separating might actually be more painful than remaining together. Marriage to one particular person has become a habit one cannot abandon. There is the matter of stability and the difficulty of throwing away so much security for the unknown. As well, couples who are unhappy remain together because of a lack of more attractive alternatives. The perceived lack of alternatives may be financial and/or human. As Levinger (1979) has explained it, the external attractions are not sufficiently strong to overcome the internal pull in such situations. During research, Ambert met a couple who had remarried after a three-year separation and a few months of divorce. She was ten years older than he. She explained why she accepted him back:

> In the first place, he had left me . . . not for another woman, but just because he was tired of it all. He is a big child and he found out that he couldn't live with other women because they wanted him to take care of them. He was used to being taken care of. . . . At first, when he left, I was thrown in quite a state of panic. I had never been on my own with four children. . . . The first thing he did was to buy an adult condo and a Ferrari sports car. We had had

money, but with four children and two expensive lifestyles, it was worrisome. . . . I come from a country where people didn't use to marry for love but for familial reasons. He left me and that left me nowhere. Do you think I could ever remarry? No. I am 55. Besides, I prefer to have him here where I can control the finances than having him squander our money away.

Therefore, in contradiction to what we have been taught about marriage, some couples divorce even though they had a relatively happy marriage, while many other couples who are relatively unhappy remain together. These ambiguities stem from the character of the institution of marriage and from the frailties of human nature itself. It is unfortunate, however, that we have no direct research literature on unhappily married couples who choose to remain together.

THE DECISION TO SEPARATE

In the literature on divorce, there has been controversy concerning who makes the decision to separate. In Canada, wives tend to be the petitioners for divorce in approximately 60 percent of the cases. But petitioning for divorce is a legal act that takes place after someone has decided to dissolve the marriage.

In the first study on this topic, Goode (1956) found that ex-wives reported to have been the first ones to suggest divorce. This finding seemed paradoxical since women are often considered to be more marriage and family oriented than men. Women are also more likely to bear total responsibility for the children once the marriage is dissolved. They have less money than men, lower-paying jobs, and fewer alternatives to meet people of the opposite sex (Baker, 1980). Hence, they have more to lose by divorcing. Why, then, would they be the first to suggest divorce? Goode (1956:136–37) provided the following explanation for this apparent paradox:

> We suggest, then, that in our society the husband more frequently than the wife will engage in behavior whose function, if not intent, whose result, if not aim, is to force the other spouse to ask for the divorce first. Thereby the husband frees himself to some extent from the guilt burden, since he did not ask for the divorce. A by-product of this process frees him still more: the wife's repeated objections to this behavior will mean that there are family squabbles, and one almost constant result of repeated family squabbles is a lessened affection between husband and wife. In particular, of course, these squabbles mean that the husband can begin to think of himself as also aggrieved, as also sinned against.

In accordance with the American studies, we found that women were the ones both to initiate discussion of divorce and to keep up the discussion. But, in contradiction to American studies (Goldsmith, 1980), the final decision tended to be more often a masculine or a joint one than a feminine one. In the Ambert study, this was especially so for women older than forty and who were unemployed. Younger women, especially when childless, were as likely as men to be the decision makers in this respect.

Baker's results reinforce Ambert's findings. In Baker's study (1980) both women and men agreed that women initiated the decision to separate. After further probing, however, it became obvious that women had first brought the issue out into the open, but usually in response to what they saw as serious problems in the husband's behaviour or in their relationship. For example, one woman asked her husband to leave after many years of his alcohol and drug abuse. Another asked for a divorce after her husband carried on a blatant affair with her best friend. Wives seemed to be more articulate than husbands concerning problems in their relationships. Husbands were either unaware of the fact that their marriage was dissolving, or unwilling to discuss the decline of the relationship with their wives. Many husbands, however, behaved as though they subconsciously wanted out of the relationship but did not want to take the responsibility for suggesting separation. Instead, they encouraged their wives to initiate the separation.

Husbands may subconsciously reach what Federico (1979) calls the "point of no return" in the marriage earlier than wives do. When this point is reached, the partner stops investing energy in the relationship. The spouse who is unwilling to recognize this point of no return "will engineer the same outcome indirectly" (Federico, 1979:98). This implies that the decision to separate is the result of a complex series of subtle negotiations and often remains subconscious until one partner articulates it as a last plea. After trying various methods of accommodation, such as improving her physical appearance, expressing affection, discussing problems with her husband, using a third party to mediate, withdrawing, and quarrelling, a wife may try the last resort: "If we don't get along we may as well divorce." Separation may follow, even though it is not the wish of the one who first suggested it.

While more women desert now than in the past, our research does not corroborate journalistic impressions that women abruptly leave their husbands and children as often as, or more often than, men do. Women, however, definitely seem to initiate discussions of separation more often than men and become petitioners more often than men.

COPING AFTER MARITAL DISSOLUTION

Once the separation is effected, how do the individuals cope? A great deal could be written on this topic. One finding generally agreed upon is that the first year after separation is usually the most stressful one, and that a rushed decision to separate is related to higher stress levels (Melichar and Chiriboga, 1988). It also seems that women have a more difficult time than men in the first few months, but that men often suffer more a year later. In the first few months after separation, many men throw themselves into a super-charged social life, including much drinking, dating, and a drastic change in lifestyle. This is typically referred to as the "happy bachelor's stage." During the same time, women stay home and try to cope with their children and financial problems. They are often very depressed, but they work at sorting out their problems. Many men, in comparison, ignore or deny their problems, or even drown them. The problems, however, re-emerge at a later stage. At that point, men often suffer from a delayed reaction and may not cope as well as women. To make matters worse, the relationship between the ex-spouses is rarely a friendly one, at best distant, and frequently remains an embattled one for years (Ambert, 1988; Kurdek and Blisk, 1983; Spanier and Thompson, 1984).

One aspect of this coping that has undergone much current study is that of social support. In a Canadian study by Baker (1983), patterns of social and emotional support were examined for one hundred and fifty separated and divorced persons. While men relied on both sexes to help them through the crisis of separation, women turned mainly to their female friends and relatives. Mothers, sisters, and female friends provided companionship, child care, and emotional support that proved invaluable, especially in the early months of separation. Men's helping networks involved friends of both sexes, but male subjects more often praised the assistance of their female friends. In some cases, men relied on a friend's wife rather than on the friend himself and suggested that women were more emphatic and willing to discuss the intricacies of the dissolution of a marriage. Men also changed their friends with greater ease after marital separation, choosing to associate with single or divorced people.

The gender role socialization of women, their training in nurturance, and their greater availability made them important informal resources in assisting people through the personal crisis of separation. Although neither male nor female subjects said that they first turned to professionals for assistance, or even that professionals were most helpful to them, about one-third of the sample sought professional help at the most critical or traumatic time of their marriage dissolution. In Baker's study there were no statistically significant sex differences in seeking professional help; yet, women were far more likely than men to report emotional problems at all stages of marriage dissolution.

Women's closer ties with their families of origin and the fact that they usually receive custody of their children means that they rely more heavily on family for emotional and material support after separation. Custody means that the woman often becomes the link between the children and both the paternal and maternal grandparents (Ambert, 1988b). Men, on the other hand, are more likely to live alone and less likely to need financial assistance from their parents. In addition, half of the fathers do not maintain a regular relationship with their children after divorce.

Women's lower incomes force them to rely on sporadic support payments from their ex-husbands, welfare, or money borrowed from their parents. Reliance on financial assistance from others often increases dependence and reduces self-esteem. Receiving assistance in the form of shared accommodation, help in paying for groceries, free baby-sitting, or borrowed money from parents increases women's obligations to family and makes it more difficult to develop a new self-image and a single lifestyle. By staying within the family or maintaining long-term relationships with friends, women are often subtly pressured into a more conservative, family-oriented lifestyle than separated men. The sexual double standard discourages many women from breaking outside of this closed network and reduces their opportunities to develop new relationships (Milardo, 1987).

Overall, it can be stated that there are certain types of persons who do better after separation than others. For some, it is because they cope better (for instance, they may have more psychological resources). For others, it is because their demographic characteristics place them at an advantage. Generally, the best prognosis for a successful recovery after divorce can be made for those who had been married only briefly, had *no children*, were young, employed, and shared few material possessions. It is much more difficult to be happy after separation when one has children, is older, unemployed, or financially dependent on an ex-spouse who is not too willing to contribute to the support of the children. *Women* with children and who become welfare recipients have a particularly difficult time (Amato and Partridge, 1987).

DIVORCE AND EMOTIONAL PROBLEMS

Studies from various statistical sources unanimously indicate that divorced persons have higher rates of treatment for emotional problems than married, widowed, or never-married persons (Bloom et al., 1979; Gove, 1970). Studies have uncovered rates of psychiatric care as high as 40 percent among divorced men and women (Bloom et al., 1979; Wallerstein and Kelly, 1980).

Rates of psychiatric care, suicide rates, accident rates, and postmarital stress are generally higher for men than for women (Ambert, 1980), although women more readily report emotional problems. (These studies do not contradict the fact that Baker (1983) found no statistically significant sex differences in consultation with professionals after separation. Included in her list of professionals were marriage counsellors, lawyers, and clergy, in addition to psychiatrists.) However, a controversy remains about the differential impact of separation and divorce on men and women. Studies based on self-reports usually indicate that separated and divorced women experience more problems related to depression (Baker, 1980; Belle, 1980), especially low-income divorced women with dependent children (Goldman and Ravid, 1980:49). But depression is only one type of emotional problem, and it is also possible that men fail to report their depression and suffer more from other problems, such as schizophrenia. It has also been suggested that, in men, alcoholism may be a symptom of depression or a response to a depressive state.

Ambert (1984) found that separated and divorced mothers with custody were less happy in their personal role than custodial fathers. The mothers' level of satisfaction was partially affected by financial insecurity. Moreover, the children of low-income mothers were much more difficult to handle at all ages than those of higher-income mothers and even than those of custodial fathers, who generally had higher incomes. Therefore, on a wide range of situations, the daily life of separated and divorced mothers is much more stressful than that of their ex-husbands. Other Canadian studies (Schlesinger, 1979; Nelson, 1981) have corroborated these results.

However, the life of the divorced man is stressful in different ways. Among divorced couples with children, only about 12 percent of the fathers receive custody of their children, and another 11 percent participate in joint custody arrangements (Statistics Canada, 1988). It is also more common for the husband to leave his wife and children in the marital home and thus have to relocate, generally to an apartment that feels very empty. Without his children, the husband often experiences intense loneliness, which he frequently submerges in a series of social and sexual encounters and a rapid remarriage. The fact that men remarry sooner than women after divorce may indicate that they experience more difficulty than they are willing to admit in living on their own (Baker, 1983) – without omitting the fact that men have more opportunities to remarry than women, especially women over forty years of age, as men prefer younger women in remarriage.

Several theories have attempted to explain the high rates of emotional problems among the separated and divorced. The *reaction or stress theory* argues that separation and divorce are emotionally exhausting and highly stressful life events. The loss of a marital partner, the loss of contact with children, reduced financial circumstances, lack of sexual contact, and single parenting severely tax people's emotional resources. One problem with this theory is that it does not adequately explain why men have higher rates of treatment for psychiatric disorders when it is *women* who more often experience a shortage of money, retain custody of the children, must re-enter the labour force, have more problems finding new partners after separation, and report more emotional problems.

Another theory states that emotional problems hinder a marital relationship and may lead to divorce. This is generally referred to as the *social selection theory* (Rushing, 1979). In interviews with 212 divorced persons, Ambert found that more men than women who were in treatment after separation had also been in treatment during their marriage. Moreover, more men than women had had a long post-separation history of treatment, suggesting the presence of long-term emotional instability. The in-depth and longitudinal material in this study led to the hypothesis that men who suffer from emotional problems have more difficulty maintaining a stable marriage than other men or even women with emotional problems. Women's rate of treatment for emotional problems rose sharply immediately after the separation, but levelled off soon thereafter. This could indicate that stress theory may explain post-separation emotional problems among women (as indicated in the previous paragraph) more often than among men, while selection theory may explain the same more often among men than women.

Moreover, a majority (79 percent) of those respondents who had been divorced *more than once* had been in treatment at some point in their adult life as compared to 29 percent for those who had been divorced only once. Again, it could be advanced that the selection theory applies to more people who divorce repeatedly as opposed to those who divorce only once. The multiple-divorced had had a more difficult familial background than the once-divorced, had led a less stable life, had fewer *close* human ties, were less likely to fulfil their parental role after separation, and had had a more erratic employment history – all indicators pointing to personality factors less conducive to smooth social relationships, of which marriage is one type.

CHILDREN AND DIVORCE

What effect, if any, does divorce have on children? Researchers' opinions have fluctuated on this issue. On the one hand, there is evidence that remaining in an unhappy but stable home may be more harmful to children than is their parents' divorce (Hess and Camara, 1979; Johnson and Lobitz, 1974; Ollmanns et al., 1977). But there is also widespread consensus that divorce rarely occurs without at least a temporary trauma for children (Luepnitz, 1982). Many children, however, still suffer after several years of parental divorce (Wallerstein, 1985) and remain less well adjusted in certain dimensions into young adulthood (Southward and Schwarz, 1987). Also, children of divorce grow up themselves to be more divorce prone (Glenn and Kramer, 1987).

Studies indicate that children of divorced parents have a better prognosis when the custodial parent is emotionally stable, provides love and a structured life, and when the non-custodial parent maintains a regular relationship with the children and is supportive of the custodial parent. Unfortunately, the reality is that most divorced parents rarely co-operate in their parental roles (Furstenberg and Nord, 1985). Each parents separately: Furstenburg (1987) has referred to this phenomenon as "parallel" parenting.

Furthermore, Furstenberg (1987) has found that parental contact after divorce was less important than paternal financial support in affecting children's well-being. Thus, it seems that the socio-economic situation of the post-divorce family is a very important determinant of the impact of divorce on children (Colletta, 1979). It is generally agreed that, after separation, the women's standard of living is lower than it had been – especially mothers with the custody of their children (Arnold, 1980; Baker, 1980; Bane, 1976). Indeed, only a minority of fathers regularly contribute to the support of their children after divorce (Weitzman, 1985). Many of the mothers consequently become poor, have to go on welfare, and move to neighbourhoods with substandard housing (Bane, 1986). The family's entire lifestyle is negatively affected. Therefore, it is quite possible that situations that have hitherto been believed to be consequences of divorce are actually consequences of a reduced standard of living. In order to verify this hypothesis, we would need to study and compare families of divorce who lose their standard of living with others who retain it. It may be that it is not so much the father's absence that causes problems, but rather the deteriorated social status that accompanies such an absence.

As indicated previously, Ambert found important differences in the overt, observable behaviour of the children of lower-class and middle- to upper-class custodial mothers. In another study of a large and representative sample of all the in-school

FOR INTEREST

FEWER CHILDREN INVOLVED IN 1986 DIVORCES

Divorces granted under the new law in 1986 were . . . less likely to involve children than those granted under the old law. Of divorces obtained in 1986, children were involved in just one-third (34%) granted under this new Act, compared with more than half (52%) obtained under the old Act.

Under the new Act, as was the case under the old Act, wives are most likely to be awarded custody of the children after divorce. Wives received custody of 75% of the children in divorces granted under the new Act for which there was a custody order. The husband won custody of 12% of the children, while joint custody was ordered for 11%. For the remaining 2%, custody was awarded to someone other than the husband or wife.

Source: Owen Adams, "Divorce Rates in Canada," *Canadian Social Trends* (Winter 1988):19. Reproduced with permission of the Minister of Supply and Services Canada, 1989.

teenagers in Montreal, Ambert and Saucier found that there were many variables on which adolescents from divorced families scored significantly lower than children from intact families, while the scores for adolescents from widowed families were generally intermediate. Some of the differences found were related to academic success and expectations for the future – all of which were lower among children of divorce (Ambert and Saucier, 1983; Ferri, 1984; Keith and Finlay, 1988). Other differences pertained to health and health behaviour (Saucier and Ambert, 1983, 1986) and to the perception of parents – children of divorce were particularly negative about their fathers' honesty (Ambert and Saucier, 1983).

We would expect that one long-term consequence of parental divorce when the custodial parent has a lowered standard of living is a lower educational achievement and reduced employment success for the child. Generally speaking, low standards of living do not promote attitudes that are favourable to learning, school, and schoolwork. Schoolwork benefits from a stable family environment, parental guidance, and space. Overcrowding, improper nutrition, noise, and lack of discipline will tend to lead children into the streets, rather than into the world of books and formal education. On the other hand, one could hypothesize that custodial mothers who are at the poverty level may stress education, especially for their daughters, as they do not want their children to repeat their own mistake. Such mothers also may motivate their children, especially their daughters, as a form of vicarious compensation.

Studies indicate that boys are more adversely affected by parental strife and separation than girls (Hetherington and Parke, 1979; Rutter, 1971). Some of our own results corroborated these findings, although there were many exceptions. How can we explain this gender differential? At the intuitive level, we could expect that girls would be more affected because they are more dependent upon the home environment than boys. Yet, the reverse occurs. One reason may be that children need a same-sex adult role model more than a cross-sex one. Most children live with a custodial mother, and many children of divorce see their fathers rarely or strictly within an artificial context (restaurants, outings, movies). Male children more than female children are deprived of a same-sex role model. Indeed, studies of boys reared by custodial fathers have shown that they had a higher degree of self-esteem than boys reared by a custodial mother, and the reverse occurred for girls (Santrock and Warshak, 1986).

A second and complementary reason for more adverse effects of divorce on male children may be found in results by Wallerstein and Kelly (1980), which showed that custodial mothers were more affectionate toward their daughters and more thoughtful of their needs than they were of their sons'. Daughters were more adequately mothered (or parented) than were sons. Finally, sons often give a more difficult time to their mothers than daughters do, which may explain in part why mothers may be more solicitous of their daughters. Boys may need a stronger authority figure than girls, and the structure of the average divorced family does not always provide this figure.

REMARRIAGE AND STEP-PARENTING

Because three-quarters of divorced men and two-thirds of divorced women eventually remarry, we have to consider remarriage as the most important path after divorce.

Throughout this chapter, it has been obvious that research on divorce is still in its infancy. More questions remain unanswered than have been explored. The situation is even more acute concerning remarriage and familial reconstitution or step-parenting.

While divorce may be a growth experience for the unhappily married couple, we have seen that, in the short run, it can be detrimental to children. Similarly, while remarriage is the goal of most divorced persons, it is sometimes problematic for children, especially for teenagers. The literature indicates that young children suffer more from parental divorce than teenagers do. Children are often too young to understand the situation clearly and less detached from their parents than adolescents, who are striving for independence and are more peer-oriented (Kalter and Rembar, 1981). Thus, they have alternatives that young children do not have (Steinberg, 1982).

On the other hand, if the custodial parent is to remarry, the young child generally adapts better to the step-parenting situation than the adolescent. The young child is more willing to establish an affectionate relationship with the step-parent and more easily fits into the reconstituted family. The adolescent's lifestyle may actually be at odds with the acquisition of a step-parent, who may interfere with freedom and impose a regimen that the teenager is not eager to accept (Hobart, 1987). Friction between step-parent and adolescent is more likely than with a young child, who may eagerly accept one more person to love.

Ambert (1986) has found that the presence of stepchildren in a remarriage is frequently related to the perception that the marriage would be happier if the couple did not have children from a previous marriage. White and Booth (1985) have also found that the presence of stepchildren was related to a lower marital stability. Moreover, stepchildren were likely to leave the parental home at an earlier age than children living with their own two parents. Hobart (1988) has found that the husband's children from a previous marriage were somewhat more marginal than the wife's. In a remarriage, not only do more individuals have to adjust to each other, but the emotional atmosphere itself is more complicated than in a first marriage (Furstenberg and Spanier, 1984). Also, when children are present the ex-spouse probably remains more in evidence than when there are no children, and this often becomes a source of friction for the entire family. This situation may be particularly difficult when only one ex-spouse remarries. This is especially so when the husband remarries first, as his new marriage may bring about a renewal of hostilities with his children's mother. In addition, the new wife and the ex-wife may be competing for the same financial resources. Many men are actually relieved when their ex-wives remarry since they no longer have to contribute to their support, and many even use the remarriage as an excuse for decreasing child support.

Other variables that should be studied in the context of the stability of second marriages are age, social class and financial responsibilities, the age differences between the spouses, the effect of the first marriage, and the social network. A greater proportion of remarriages than of first marriages involve a large age discrepancy, especially men marrying much younger women who have never been married before (Ambert, 1989). Such a situation will lead to a much greater proportion of married couples who are at different stages in their life cycles. The older man is generally established in his work, has had children, and has been married before. In comparison, the younger woman has had no children and may want some later; she may not yet have had a chance to test herself in the labour market and, later, may wish for greater independence to do so. As they age, the woman has to face the likelihood of becoming widowed at a younger age. When they are both older, the man will enter retirement before his second wife. How will they cope with his status as a senior citizen? Might not the younger woman wish for a younger husband at that point? Might not the older man envy his younger wife's employment status?

For instance, when asked to compare his two marriages, one man explained that his first marriage probably had been a better one: "I am concerned about the much younger age of my second wife and the fact that she wants a second child. I only wanted one, no more." He also felt that temperamentally he was better suited to his first wife: "It was easier to get along with one's wife ten years ago because there were fewer ideological pressures from outside the marital unit." He added that he did not feel as secure in terms of raising his daughter from his second marriage as he had felt about his older daughter from his previous marriage.

Statistics inform us that remarriages are somewhat more vulnerable to divorce than first marriages. Certainly, we would expect that the divorce rate would be higher among second marriages because of the simple fact that people who object to divorce on moral or religious grounds are excluded from the sample of remarried people. But, in addition

Many second or subsequent marriages involve a large age discrepancy, especially men marrying much younger women who have never been married before.

MILLER COMSTOCK INC.

to this, the problems of the reconstituted family seem to be somewhat different and potentially more serious than those of first marriages. The presence of ex-husbands and ex-wives can complicate the new marriage. Additional sets of grandparents and other relatives can be intrusive. Many divorced men are sending money to their ex-wives and children as well as supporting their new families. This puts considerable financial pressure on both families. The children from two families are bound to experience problems of adjustment. These different problems of second marriages and reconstituted families are just beginning to receive serious attention from researchers (Ahrons and Wallisch, 1987; Clingempeel et al., 1987; Ganong and Coleman, 1987).

CONCLUSION

In this chapter, we have presented current information on divorce and have emphasized the roles played by men, women, and children. Although marital dissolution is a fascinating realm of study and has many practical implications for social welfare as well as social science theory, research in this field is still embryonic. Nevertheless, many facts have already emerged from recent studies.

Separation is a stressful life event for most people, even more stressful than legal divorce. The decision to separate is usually made tentatively over a long period of time and often culminates when the partner who does not want to separate brings the topic into the open as a mechanism of last resort. Men often leave the marital home first and leave their wives with the children. Women experience particular financial difficulties, not only because their incomes are considerably lower than men's, but because they may be unemployed *and* have the sole support of their children. Although the courts often order ex-husbands to pay child support, a majority of men default after a year or two. This increases the ex-wife's financial difficulties as well as those of her children. A reduced standard of living may be one of the key negative factors in divorce for children. Children are also affected by the emotional state of the custodial parent, their own understanding of the break-up, the relationship between their parents, and the quality of their own contact with the non-custodial parent. Although there has been a recent increase in joint custody after divorce, this arrangement seems to be practised mainly by middle- to upper-class people. Many working-class men give up their children to their ex-wives, not knowing that they have any custodial rights. Despite the fact that the new family law states that custody decisions should not be based on gender, there has been little change in patterns of custody over the past twenty years.

As divorce and remarriage become more common in Canada, attitudinal and social change will also continue in order to adjust to this phenomenon. For instance, recent legal reforms have already brought significant alterations in the division of family assets after divorce. Marriage counsellors include separation and divorce as options in their counselling practices. Feminists are encouraging women to plan their education, careers, pension plans, and even their marriage contracts so as to be self-supporting in the event that they have to live alone. Schools are also becoming more aware of the need for programs oriented to children of working and separated parents.

Research also indicates that a substantial proportion of those who divorce are no happier six to ten years after the divorce than they were when married or even early on during their separation (Ambert, 1989; Hetherington, 1987; Wallerstein, 1988). Generally, divorce benefits *one* spouse more than the other. In at least 25 percent of divorces, *neither* spouse is ever better off in the long run. Let's add to these statistics those results showing that a significant proportion of children are affected by their parents' divorce well into young adulthood. These results are a warning to the effect that divorce is not a cure-all, a panacea, and can even be detrimental to what remains of a person's life span. Thus, while divorce is a solution for most, for many it is a new problem. On the other hand, studies also show that many couples who have been married for ten years or more are unhappy. It is difficult to say if these persons would be happier divorced. In some cases, however, the tense home situation is detrimental to the well-being of the children, who would actually be happier and grow up more normally were their parents to divorce.

FOR INTEREST

WHAT SOME DIVORCED PERSONS SAY

My wife says I have to work at our marriage. I don't agree with her. Marriage is supposed to be pleasant and if it isn't, well, it's not my problem.

(Man in his third marriage)

Surely, you do not expect me to tell you that I see my ex-wife every other day! [Laughs] If you have an ex-wife it's because you don't want to see her!

(Man, business owner)

My ex-husband? We get along better now than we used to while married. I think it is because we are now both independent of each other. We are parents but this does not mean we have to be tied down to each other. It took us a while to understand this.

(Woman, business career)

I never dreamt I would ever be a stepmother. Who thinks about this when growing up?

(Stepmother, housewife)

My previous marriage is merely a footnote in my life.

(Woman, career)

Being divorced is not so hard in itself, it's being poor which is.

(Custodial mother on welfare)

My divorce was a pathetic waste, a waste of time and a psychological waste. We could have stayed together; instead we chose to subject each other to all manners of psychological warfare.

(Man, executive)

Divorce is when I started growing up.

(Woman, graduate student)

I didn't marry my husband to acquire *his* ex-wife or *her* new husband, and my husband certainly does not want to be saddled with *my* ex-husband and his girlfriend . . . we don't socialize . . . no. These relationships are nice on a TV screen but not in real life.

(Woman, secretary)

The high rates of remarriage may be an indication that most people remain optimistic about the desirability of marriage and family living. The remarriage rates suggest that people divorce in order to search for better marriages and not because they despair of marriage altogether. This implies that our standards for the quality of married life may be rising. But high rates of remarriage may also indicate that living alone in a couple-oriented society is socially and financially very difficult. The pressures to remarry are strong, especially for the single parent on a low income or the non-custodial parent who is lonely. Regardless of which interpretation of rising remarriage rates we wish to accept, we cannot fail to come to the conclusion that marriage and family living are still popular and satisfying institutions for most Canadians.

DISCUSSION QUESTIONS

1. Why have divorce rates risen in most industrialized countries in the past twenty years?
2. How can we explain the fact that many persons who divorce had a fairly happy marriage?
3. Why do unhappily married couples stay together?
4. Why do women initiate discussions of separation more often than men?
5. What is meant by the "point of no return" in a marriage?
6. How do the problems after marital separation differ for men and women?
7. What is the relationship between psychiatric problems and divorce? What are the theories explaining the relationship?
8. What is the impact of divorce on both younger children and teenagers? Are boys and girls affected differently, and if so, why?
9. What is meant by "co-parenting" and "parallel parenting"? Can you invent an example of each?
10. Why do women so often become poor after divorce?
11. Why are men more likely than women to remarry after divorce?
12. What is the effect of remarriage on children?
13. What are some of the factors influencing the stability of remarriages that may not be involved in first marriages?
14. What steps could adolescent girls and young women take to protect themselves against some of the detrimental effects of divorce?
15. Does divorce benefit both spouses equally? Explain your answer.
16. Does divorce imply a widespread dissatisfaction with marriage as an institution?

chapter ten

Controversies Within Family Law

INTRODUCTION

In its broadest sense, family law refers to all laws that affect the family. This includes legislation that provides government benefits or supports for the family, such as family allowances, child tax credits, income assistance for families under the poverty line, or child care and parent resource services. There are laws that govern wife abuse and negligent or abusive treatment of children. There are laws that regulate the process of getting married – who can marry whom and at what age. Finally, there are laws that apply when a marriage ends.

This chapter deals only with the law governing marriage breakdown. In part, the choice has been made for practical reasons. It is impossible to cover all relevant legislation in a single chapter. Furthermore, issues surrounding government support to families and child abuse are discussed elsewhere in this text. As well, separation, divorce, and their consequences are what most people think of first in relation to family law.

However, the decision to confine this chapter to marriage breakdown also has to do with the reasons for including a chapter on family law in a sociology textbook. It is this area of family law that has been affected most profoundly by the social and economic changes of the past few decades. Since 1968, divorce law has undergone significant reform. Legislators have had to respond to pressure to make it easier for couples to end their marriage. They have been required to give practical effect to women's claims for equality within the marriage, while recognizing the realities of women's inequality in the labour force. They have had to determine what relationships should exist between divorced parents and their children when the parents themselves cannot agree on what these relationships should be.

This chapter will describe how the law has reacted to the demands that have been put upon it. It is not intended to be a comprehensive survey of the area, nor to provide answers to legal questions. For this reason, many aspects of the law have been glossed over or simply ignored.

There is one last point to be made before beginning. Canada is a federal state, which means that both federal and provincial governments have the power to make laws. In the case of marriage breakdown, the federal government is responsible for the legal dissolution of marriage and for what are called corollary issues to divorce, that is, child custody and support. However, only the provinces are able to legislate on matters concerning the division of property, even if this occurs as a result of divorce. Moreover, the provinces also have the power to regulate all matters between spouses that do not pertain to divorce, including support and custody if the spouses have not yet applied for a divorce, or do not wish to do so. The provinces are also responsible for enforcing support and custody orders, including those made under federal legislation. Thus, we have one divorce law, but separate provincial and territorial laws governing the division of property, support, and custody. As is to be expected, the need to harmonize the various pieces of legislation has its effect on the development of the law.

Laws are not confined to the texts in statute books. They must also be interpreted by judges. As will become apparent, in the area of marriage breakdown, the distinction between the law and its interpretation is a fine one. As one commentator has remarked (Payne, 1988): "The golden rule of a successful family law practitioner is still: 'Know Thy Judge.' "

LEGISLATION RELATING TO DIVORCE AND SEPARATION

INTRODUCTION TO CANADIAN DIVORCE LAW

Our present divorce law, the Divorce Act, 1985, has been in effect since 1986. It is Canada's second federal or nationally applicable divorce law. The legislation continues the divorce reform begun with the passage of the original Divorce Act in 1968.

The earlier divorce legislation can be seen as a compromise between two positions: on the one hand, a marriage should be ended only when one or both of the spouses has committed a serious matrimonial fault; on the other hand, the spouses themselves should determine when the marriage has ended. The earlier legislation contained two separate sets of grounds for divorce: fault grounds and what are often called "no-fault" grounds. The fault grounds included cruelty and certain sexual activity, such as adultery, sodomy, bestiality, rape, and any homosexual act. Proof that one of the spouses had misbehaved in these ways entitled the other to an immediate divorce. The no-fault grounds allowed spouses to end the marriage without having to justify their decision; but they had to pay a price – they were required to wait for a significant period of time before they were able to claim a divorce.

The no-fault grounds were characterized as "marriage breakdown." A couple could be divorced on this basis if they had lived separately for three years before applying for the divorce and they both agreed to be divorced. A spouse could unilaterally separate and obtain a divorce on the basis of the separation, but he or she was not allowed to apply for the divorce until five years had passed since the time of separation. Although this last situation was characterized as "no-fault," the legislation in fact punished spouses who walked out on a marriage by forcing them to wait an extra two years before getting the divorce. As an added protection for the economically dependent spouse in cases of unilateral separation, courts were given the discretion to refuse a divorce if a "granting of the decree would be unduly harsh or unjust or would affect the making of reasonable arrangements for the maintenance [financial support] of the spouse."

A divorce could be granted only after a trial at the intermediate or superior court level, at which one of the spouses, and often a witness, had to be present to provide proof of the fault or the separation. The judge who presided at the trial was required to determine whether it was possible for the couple to reconcile; if there appeared to be such a possibility, the trial had to be adjourned in order to give the couple a chance to come together again. Lawyers acting for the spouses were legally obliged to discuss the possibility of reconciliation with their clients. Finally, the old Act contained provisions for what was called "corollary relief": orders for the custody of the children, and spousal and child support.

In the years that followed, there was great pressure to reform the 1968 legislation. Many believed that it was no longer socially desirable nor practical to have courts deal with issues of marital behaviour. They argued that cruelty and adultery were categories too crude to capture the ways in which spouses could harm each other and the marriage relationship, and that the assumption that marriage breakdown could generally be ascribed to the misconduct of only one of the parties was simply false. Moreover, the argument continued, the adversarial process itself was not an appropriate means of dissecting and assessing the process of marriage breakdown. Critics also felt that divorce legislation should not be used to aggravate already existing tensions between the spouses by reviving an unhappy history and providing them with a public forum in which to continue their quarrel. For all these reasons, they concluded that the sexual conduct of the spouses, or any other fault consideration, should not be a factor on which to base a divorce award.

Others objected to fault grounds because they no longer served their original purpose: to signal society's disapproval of those who disregarded their marital obligations. These critics pointed to the fact that most fault divorces were adultery cases, and that these cases were really consent divorces disguised to allow the spouses to avoid the three-year waiting period. They urged the government to end what they considered to be a charade, an adherence to outmoded ideas. They recommended that as few obstacles as possible be placed in the way of spouses who wanted to end their marriage. Divorces were to be based on the request of one of the spouses and to be readily obtainable and inexpensive.

By contrast, religious groups felt that the old legislation did not do enough to support marriage. They considered the provisions for reconciliation inadequate and proposed that couples asking for a divorce be required to receive marriage counselling. They feared a more liberal divorce law because they felt that once the constraints were off, the family would inevitably be harmed. Still others wanted to reduce the role of lawyers and the courts in resolving disputes between the couple. They believed that couples should be encouraged to talk to each other without legal intermediaries and arrange their separate futures in a way that did not pit them against each other as adversaries. Finally, the provisions for support and custody were heavily criticized for failing to provide judges with any guidance for making these awards.

THE DIVORCE ACT, 1985

The current divorce legislation reflects the influence of all the opinions described above. The legislation accepts the position that divorces should not be awarded on fault grounds, although it retains vestiges of the notion of fault. The law makes it easier to be divorced, but recognizes some obligation to keep marriages together. Some acknowledgment is given to mediation and negotiation as alternative dispute-settling processes.

The Act provides only one ground for divorce – marriage breakdown. However, marriage breakdown is defined in terms of three alternative situations: the spouses have lived separately for one year; one of the spouses has committed adultery; or a spouse has treated the other with cruelty. While fault considerations can be used to obtain a divorce, they cannot be taken into account by the court in making an order for financial support. Marital misconduct is relevant to custody orders only if the behaviour can be shown to affect the child's well-being.

As in the past, proof of fault immediately entitles the spouses to a divorce; there is no waiting period. Those who choose the one-year wait may nonetheless apply for the divorce any time after separation, to ensure that their case is heard soon after the year is up. The previous legislation did not allow the couple to do this.

The current legislation allows evidence of fault or separation to be presented in written form, which means that spouses who divorce on consent and agree on other

MILLER COMSTOCK INC.

The 1985 federal divorce legislation allows evidence of fault or separation to be presented in written form, which means that spouses who divorce on consent and agree on other matters may not have to go to court.

matters may no longer have to go to court. In the past, the process of giving evidence at a court hearing was an unpleasant experience for many. As well, the requirement that there be a hearing increased the couple's legal expenses. The present provision was designed to address these problems. Court procedure is a matter of provincial jurisdiction, however, and some provinces still choose to require a hearing in all cases.

The old provisions regarding reconciliation have been retained and somewhat strengthened. Lawyers are now obliged to inform their clients of marriage counselling or guidance facilities that might help them reconsider their decision to divorce. As well, in response to the demand for a less adversarial process, lawyers are required to encourage a negotiated arrangement instead of presenting litigation as the only way or the most preferable way of resolving disputes in every case. Lawyers are also under a legal obligation to inform their clients of mediation services that could help them arrive at a mutual resolution of their differences. Changes to support and custody provisions will be described in later sections.

SEPARATION

People often describe themselves as being "legally separated." This is not a legal term, and it may refer to a number of situations. In most provinces, separating spouses are not required to appear before a court, to register themselves, or to institutionalize their separation in any other way. However, Saskatchewan, Alberta, and Quebec have long provided for judicial separations, a procedure analogous to a divorce, and continue to do so.

In the western provinces, a judicial separation is granted on fault grounds only. Fault is defined in terms of three categories: adultery, cruelty, or desertion. A finding of fault entitles the legally innocent spouse to claim financial support. Guilty spouses are not entitled to support on their own behalf, although they can claim child support. Current divorce legislation has reduced the impact of these laws, since it allows a legally guilty spouse to apply for a divorce immediately after separation, instead of having to wait for three years. The spouse may then ask for what is called an "interim" support order, designed to span the period between the initial application and the divorce decree. In addition, separating spouses are entitled to a share of the matrimonial property under provincial legislation, an award that does not depend on fault. In Quebec, separation orders have been available on no-fault grounds since 1980.

Provinces that do not regulate separation – that is, the majority – nonetheless have legislation that deals with a spouse's rights to support, custody, and division of property after separation. The legislation usually allows spouses to settle these matters themselves by a contract known as a "separation agreement." In some cases, people will use the term "legal separation" to indicate that they have signed such an agreement. Again, couples who plan to divorce after separating may now choose to ignore the provincial legislation and apply for interim custody and support under the federal law instead. As was mentioned above, that legislation also encourages negotiated arrangements.

To sum up, all provinces have laws that govern various aspects of separation. This legislation will probably cease to be used by many separating couples because the new divorce law gives the court jurisdiction to act in the period between separation and divorce. However, there will always be couples who do not divorce, for religious, economic, or other reasons. The provincial legislation will continue to apply to them.

DIVISION OF PROPERTY UPON MARRIAGE BREAKDOWN

INTRODUCTION

In October 1968, after twenty-five years of marriage, Irene Murdoch left her husband. She went to court and asked for a share of her husband's property, which consisted of four hundred and eighty acres of farmland in Alberta. Mrs. Murdoch argued that she had earned a right to the property because she had worked for it. In the early years of the marriage, she and her husband had hired themselves out as farm hands. They used their savings to purchase successive pieces of property, which Mrs. Murdoch had almost single-handedly helped to develop and maintain.

The trial judge concluded that Mrs. Murdoch had made no significant monetary contribution to the acquisition of any of the properties owned during the marriage, nor any relevant contribution in the form of work. What she had done, according to the judge, amounted to the work to be expected from any rancher's wife; that effort was not enough to create a property claim. Four of the five judges of the Supreme Court of Canada agreed with this reasoning.

The Murdoch case made it clear that existing property law, in the common-law provinces at least, ascribed no value whatsoever to the role of a wife. Even the dissenting judge who wanted to award Mrs. Murdoch a share in the property was forced to argue that she had not acted like an ordinary wife, but had in fact performed a "husband's work." The Supreme Court decision was not in tune with the times. Feminists pointed to the decision as a striking example of society's inclination to discount women's work, to view it as somehow different from "real" work. Others felt it unfair that Murdoch should be unable to share in her husband's property after working hard and making so great a contribution to it.

The Murdoch case was instrumental in bringing about matrimonial property reform in Canada's common-law provinces. These provinces, which at the time had no relevant legislation, began seriously to address the general issue raised by this case: What claims should a spouse be able to make on property acquired during the marriage once the marriage has broken down? By the beginning of the 1980s, all provinces had introduced new laws designed to answer that question. Reform continues. Ontario recently reconsidered the approach it had taken in the late 1970s and introduced different provisions in 1986.

Unlike the common-law provinces, Quebec had always regulated issues of property ownership, as well as other matters between husband and wife, through its Civil Code. The provisions contained in the Code accorded the wife an equal share in the matrimonial property, unless the spouses agreed to hold property separately. However, the right of ownership was far from complete, since only the husband could administer the property – buy it, sell it, or collect the income from it. Wives who had agreed to own property separately were in the same position as Mrs. Murdoch in Alberta: they could not claim what they had not paid for. In 1980, Quebec introduced a new Code for the marriage relationship. The Code contained provisions for the equal sharing of matrimonial property on marriage breakdown, as well as some protection for spouses who chose to own property separately. Since that time, the property provisions have been subject to criticism for failing to provide adequate protection for women on marriage breakdown. In response to these criticisms, the Quebec government amended the Code in June 1989.

FOR INTEREST

JUST SIXTY YEARS AGO, WOMEN WERE TOLD BY THE SUPREME COURT OF CANADA THAT THEY WERE "NOT PERSONS" UNDER THE LAW. THE FAMOUS FIVE

Emily Murphy was appointed the first woman police judge in Alberta in 1916. But on her second case, her authority was challenged. A defence lawyer argued that she was not a "person" in law, therefore whatever decisions she made would not be legally binding on his client.

Under British Common Law, at the time, women were "not persons in matters of rights and privileges" though, like "children, criminals and idiots," they were "persons in matters of pains and penalties." Historically, this had barred women from holding public office.

Judge Emily Murphy decided to take this on. While the provincial government backed her authority, the federal interpretation of the legal definition of persons was unclear. She decided to contest the eligibility of women to sit on the Senate since the *British North America Act, 1867*, said only "qualified persons" could be appointed Senators.

For more than a decade she wrote letters, made speeches and organized petitions from the Women's Institutes and other women's organizations, urging the government to appoint a woman to the Senate. But the government said it did not have the authority without an amendment to the BNA Act.

In 1927, Judge Murphy decided that the next step was to petition Parliament to ask for a Supreme Court interpretation of the BNA Act, which was possible with a petition signed by five people. Nellie McClung, Henrietta Muir Edwards, Irene Palby and Louise McKinney joined Emily Murphy. They became known as the Famous Five.

The Supreme Court of Canada deliberated on the case for five weeks, then ruled on April 28, 1928 that women were *not persons* qualified to sit in the Senate.

The five women resolved to appeal this decision to the Judicial Committee at the Privy Council in England.

They won.

On October 18, 1929, the Privy Council reversed the decision of the Supreme Court of Canada, saying the concept of "persons" being limited to men, which dated back to Roman times, was not relevant to the twentieth century.

It was a great day in Canadian women's history. Women, *at last*, had formal recognition as persons!

Source: *Women's Legal Education and Action Fund Newsletter*, December 1988.

LEGISLATION IN THE COMMON-LAW PROVINCES

The laws that are currently in force in the common-law provinces share important general characteristics. Either expressly or by implication, the legislation proposes a new basis for property entitlement in cases of marriage breakdown – contribution to the marriage and the welfare of the family. On this basis, spouses may claim an equal share of *certain* assets (or the value of the assets) acquired during the marriage. However, in no jurisdiction is a 50-50 division automatic. Courts are given the discretion to order an unequal division of assets, and in some provinces to distribute other assets acquired by a spouse but not included in the 50-50 split. In addition, there may be special provisions for the disposition of the house in which the spouses lived before they separated (in legal terms, the "matrimonial home"). Finally, spouses are able to contract out of the statutory requirement to share their property.

Although they adopt the same approach, provincial laws are not uniform. For example, legislation differs with respect to the assets that are selected for the standard 50-50 sharing, especially the sharing of business assets. In some provinces, the courts are given more latitude to depart from an equal division than in others. There are also differences in the guidelines that govern the exercise of the court's discretion to divide assets in a non-standard way. It would be interesting to know whether or not the various provisions lead to similar decisions in similar cases throughout Canada. However, the data needed to determine this are not available.

It should be stressed that matrimonial property legislation is applicable only in cases of marriage breakdown, with the exception of the protection afforded the matrimonial home. In any ongoing marriage, a spouses's claims are limited to the property he or she has bought or has been given, and spouses can dispose of their property as they please. The legislation usually provides a remedy in cases where someone attempts to avoid the consequences of a separation by selling assets and hiding the proceeds, for example, or by borrowing on the property.

A. Contribution to the Marriage

Certain assumptions about the marriage relationship underlie the new legislation. Most provinces have attempted to express these assumptions in preambles or other statements of purpose. The preamble to Ontario's Family Law Act for example, refers to the need "to recognize the equal position of spouses as individuals within marriage and to recognize marriage as a form of partnership." What the recognition of equality and partnership means in relation to the sharing of property is made explicit in a later section:

> The purpose of this section is to recognize that child care, household management and financial provision are the joint responsibilities of the spouses and that inherent in the marital relationship there is equal contribution, whether financial or otherwise, by the spouses to the assumption of these responsibilities, entitling each spouse to the equalization of the net family properties.

A similarly worded provision is contained in the legislation of Manitoba, New Brunswick, Nova Scotia, Prince Edward Island, and Saskatchewan.

The important elements in the Ontario preamble are partnership and equality. Marriage is seen as an endeavour involving responsibilities on the part of both spouses. Certain activities, which in our society are still identified as the purview of the husband (financial support for the family) or the wife (child care, household management), are singled out by the Ontario statute as being joint responsibilities. The performance of these activities is a contribution to the marriage whose value is to be recognized by a property entitlement.

This is the legislative response to *Murdoch*. The ownership of matrimonial property is not to be determined only by the fact that one of the spouses has paid for it. Nor is it necessary that a wife work "like a man" to acquire or maintain the property. Instead, rights are created by contributions to the marriage, whether this activity is income producing or not, and regardless of the value of the activity in the marketplace.

For some, this justification for sharing matrimonial property is not without problems. What if a spouse is a ne'er-do-well and contributes nothing to the family? Suppose she is an alcoholic or is chronically ill? What about the super-achiever, the workaholic partner in the Bay Street firm; must she share all her assets – including her share in the partnership – with her husband whose salary will never approach her earnings? Would it be fair to the other partners to award the husband an interest in the firm, given that it will allow him a voice in the direction of its operations? Is sexual fidelity a marital responsibility? If an affair has caused the break-up of the marriage, should this be reflected by a reduced property claim?

The principal mechanism that the provinces have used to allow courts to respond to these kinds of consideration is judicial discretion. In addition, certain provinces have chosen to restrict the definition of matrimonial property, which may have been intended as yet another way of handling problems posed by sharing business assets.

B. Matrimonial Property

All provincial legislation provides that certain property be shared equally, subject to judicial discretion. Provinces have made different decisions about what that property is to be, however. They also have adopted a variety of terms to designate property subject to equal sharing: "matrimonial property," "divisible matrimonial property," "marital property," "family property," and "family assets." All are referred to in this chapter as matrimonial property.

Legislation in Alberta, Manitoba, Ontario, and Saskatchewan defines the notion broadly to include most property acquired during the marriage (or the value of that property). Ontario also includes the matrimonial home, regardless of when it was acquired. In contrast, Prince Edward Island's Family Law Reform Act restricts matrimonial property to that "ordinarily used or enjoyed" by both spouses or their children. In addition, the legislation also attempts to preserve property held by a family over a period of time, and so excludes property acquired prior to marriage. What would seem to be an important difference among the various statutes is whether they include business and commercial assets among those subject to equal sharing. Examples of this kind of asset include a farm, a convenience store, or any other type of "mom and pop" operation, a partnership in a law firm, a real estate investment, or stocks and bonds. Legislation in the Atlantic provinces excludes business and commercial assets. Only certain types of business venture are included in British Columbia.

The decision to restrict the definition of matrimonial property, however, does not indicate an intention to protect business assets in all circumstances. With the exception of Newfoundland, courts are given the discretion to distribute business assets or other property not subject to the standard equal-sharing provision if equal sharing proves to be unfair. This is in addition to the discretion to award a greater than equal division of the matrimonial property where there is unfairness.

It would be interesting to know the practical effect of legislation that excludes business assets from equal sharing, but gives courts the discretion to divide them in some cases. How frequently do judges exercise their discretion? Do they tend to award the non-owner spouse a smaller share than judges in provinces where business assets are subject to equal sharing? Are they more inclined to give non-owners a larger share of the matrimonial property? Unfortunately, there are no national studies on the subject of property awards. On the basis of reported cases, however, one writer has noted that courts in British Columbia appear to have been more willing to order an unequal distribution of matrimonial assets than most others. He suggests that this may be due in part to the fact that business assets are excluded from equal sharing (McLeod, 1988).

C. Judicial Discretion

As was suggested earlier, the ability to depart from equal sharing, and in some provinces to distribute non-matrimonial property, has been introduced into legislation in order to deal with cases that appear problematic. All statutes contain guidelines for exercising discretion. In effect, these guidelines reflect the legislators' concerns over equal sharing, and their indications as to where the problem areas lie. Factors included in almost every list are the length of time the couple has lived together and the date at which the property is acquired. This allows dispute over equal sharing in cases of short marriages, where contribution to the marriage itself may be negligible, especially when the property is brought into the marriage by the owner. Ontario is unique in trying to make more precise or even limit the concern underlying equal awards in cases of short marriages. Ontario's legislation allows a discretionary award only if the spouses have lived together for less than five years and one spouse would otherwise receive a "disproportionately large" share of the property in relation to the time the couple lived together.

It is interesting to note that three of the four provinces that include business property in equal sharing do not mention contribution to business assets as a factor relevant to a decision to order an unequal share. Alberta is the exception. This would seem to indicate a firm commitment to ignoring the distinction between business and non-business assets on the part of Saskatchewan, Manitoba, and Ontario. In Saskatchewan during the early 1980s, this aspect of the law was heavily criticized. It was argued that working farms and viable businesses were being destroyed as a result of equal sharing. In response to these criticisms, the legislation was reviewed by Saskatchewan's Law Reform Commission, but was not substantially changed.

Is there discretion to award a spouse a lesser or greater share of matrimonial property on the grounds that he or she has not made a significant contribution to the marriage, or has contributed more than is normally required? A recent Supreme Court of Canada case, *Le Blanc v. Le Blanc* (1988), 47 D.L.R. (4th) 1, dealt with this issue. Mr. and

Mrs. Le Blanc had been married for twenty-nine years. The husband was an alcoholic, who worked very little during the marriage, and Mrs. Le Blanc assumed most of the responsibility for supporting the family and raising the seven children. She managed to buy a restaurant, which she operated with her children's help. The restaurant prospered, and this allowed the family to acquire a house, a car, and a cottage. The Supreme Court upheld the decision of the trial court, which had concluded that because Mr. Le Blanc had made almost no contribution to the welfare of the family, either as provider or manager of the household affairs, he was entitled to a much smaller share in the matrimonial assets.

The *Le Blanc* case may invite further litigation relating to the reasons for failing to contribute to the marriage. What if the spouse is chronically ill and can do very little? Suppose the wife's or husband's inactivity is tolerated by the other partner (the couple may have married knowing that the wife was ill). Should there be unequal division in these cases?

Le Blanc may even justify a claim for unequal division on the basis of adultery or desertion if these activities can be shown to constitute a failure to contribute to the marriage (McLeod, 1988). It is not clear how successful such arguments would be. There are provinces, such as Manitoba and Newfoundland, that expressly prevent courts from taking conduct into consideration in cases of property division. As well, as was pointed out earlier, there has been an attempt to reduce or eliminate litigation that centres around fault in cases of marriage breakdown. However, at least one influential writer argues that it is wrong to separate considerations of matrimonial behaviour from the issue of economic justice on marriage breakdown. He wants to "bring back some form of moral accountability to the domestic unit" (Wilson, 1988). It should be pointed out that this measure would harm offending women as a group more than offending men, since currently women receive more benefit from property division.

By contrast, the last set of factors governing the exercise of discretion reflects concern for the economic position of women on marriage breakdown. Legislation in Alberta, Manitoba, and Saskatchewan allows courts to consider the extent to which the financial means and earning capacity of each spouse have been affected by the responsibilities of the marriage, and to award a greater than equal share of the property on that basis. It should be remembered that in these provinces matrimonial property is broadly defined to include business assets. This factor is clearly relevant to the situation of women who stay home for lengthy periods to care for children, or whose participation in the labour force is otherwise affected by family responsibilities (they may work part-time, for example). It is also relevant to long-term marriages where it has been understood by both spouses that the wife should be at home.

In British Columbia, an unequal share may be awarded on the basis of the needs of each spouse to become or remain economically independent and self-sufficient. In Newfoundland, courts may consider the future financial needs and responsibilities of the spouses, their ages, and the fact that a spouse will have lost the opportunity to share in a benefit (such as a pension benefit) as a result of the separation or divorce. Again, while the language is gender neutral, these provisions are of special benefit to women.

One may argue that these provisions are not entirely consistent with the assumption that the basis for property division is contribution to the marriage. McLeod goes so far as to claim that the provisions indicate that there is another principle underlying property division in matrimonial cases; this is to "provide a capital base to assist the spouses (that is women) in achieving or maintaining economic independence" (McLeod, 1988:1). This is a controversial position. The wording of the statutes referring to the future situation of the spouses, with the exception of British Columbia and possibly Newfoundland, is not that broad. Other legislation makes no explicit reference to the future economic position of the spouses, let alone economic independence. More important, it is unlikely most couples have accumulated enough property to effect a division that would ensure the woman a decent future income, even when it is coupled with her earnings. On this point, it is interesting to note that British Columbia restricts the equal sharing of business assets, and Newfoundland excludes them altogether. If the provinces were really interested in promoting a wife's economic independence, surely they would first broaden the definition of matrimonial property.

Like all factors that make up the legislative guidelines, these provisions identify a source of unfairness and attempt to provide a remedy. While it is true that many women face economic difficulties on marriage breakdown, even after the introduction of equal sharing, it seems clear that provinces do not intend to solve this problem by a greater than equal division.

MILLER COMSTOCK INC.

Many women face economic difficulties on marriage breakdown.

D. The Matrimonial Home: A Protected Asset

Provincial legislation has recognized that the family residence or matrimonial home is a special kind of asset. For one thing, it may be the only property a couple owns, and so the one source of capital available for equal sharing on marriage breakdown. The family home can have emotional significance for family members, especially for children, who may have spent a good part of their lives there, go to school in the neighbourhood, and have close friends nearby. Finally, the home is a source of shelter, which in some areas may be a scarce commodity. The last two factors become relevant when a marriage ends and the wife (or husband) finds that she cannot afford the accommodation she needs for herself and her children unless she stays in the home. All provinces have legislative provisions designed to deal with at least some of these considerations.

During the course of the marriage, provinces try to ensure that the non-owner spouse is aware of any dealings that directly affect the equity of the family home. Legislation prevents the owner of the property from mortgaging or selling it without the formal consent of his or her spouse. All other assets, it must be remembered, may be freely dealt with by the owner.

In most provinces the matrimonial home is subject to equal sharing on marriage breakdown, even when it has been acquired before the marriage. One exception is Prince Edward Island. In order to preserve family farms, spouses are only entitled to share the increase in the property during the period of the marriage. It should be remembered that the province defines matrimonial property in terms of family use, and an exception for property brought into the marriage might well leave very little for equal sharing.

FOR INTEREST

ARMY'S DENIAL OF FAMILY HOUSING TO COMMON-LAW COUPLES VIOLATES HUMAN RIGHTS LAW

By Christian Allard

OTTAWA – A Canadian Armed Forces policy of denying subsidized family housing to officers in "common-law" relationships discriminates on the basis of marital status under the *Canadian Human Rights Act*, the Federal Court of Appeal has concluded in a split decision.

The ruling, according to one lawyer, might conceivably entail the revision of statutes that purport to confer benefits only onto those who fit the traditional definition of marriage.

Overturning a tribunal ruling, Mr. Justice James Hugessen held last month in *Schaap v. Canadian Armed Forces*, that

while a common-law relationship did *not* fall within the definition of "marital status," a denial of housing benefits to a common-law spouse would still be a breach of human rights legislation.

Marital status, the judge said, means "no more than status in the sense of 'married or not married,' " citing *Cashin v. Canadian Broadcasting Corporation et al.*, 86 N.F. 24.

The issue at hand, he said, was whether marital status was "determinative" of the right to obtain "married quarters."

Under the impugned *Queen's Regulations and Orders*, married quarters are provided to married officers. But art. 1.075 says an officer is deemed married only if he has "gone through a form of marriage." Furthermore, common-law marriages are explicitly denied the benefit. . . .

Canadian Human Rights Commission lawyer James Hendry said the court had quite properly looked into the Armed Forces' policy, and had concluded that "the employer requiring marriage goes too far.

"What the employer is entitled to know is permanence," said Mr. Hendry. "What business is it of the Armed Forces to know whether or not they're married, as long as they know that this is the family that this guy wants to be moved around with."

He felt the decision could be a landmark case, and Mr. Hendry told *The Lawyers Weekly* it could have ramifications for other statutes that give benefits to married individuals but not to common-law spouses.

But more thought, he said, would have to be given to dealing with the effects of the case, and its administration.

He carefully noted that the court had diligently stuck to the fact situation before it. He doubted, for instance, whether the court's decision would extend to homosexual relationships.

Source: *The Lawyers Weekly*, January 27, 1989. © 1989 *The Lawyers Weekly*. Reprinted by permission.

A number of provinces recognize that there are times when it is appropriate to allow one of the spouses to remain in the home after the marriage has ended, even though both spouses have a claim on the property. An order of this sort (an order for "exclusive possession") is not automatic, but is made at the discretion of the court. Exercise of discretion is limited: typically, the spouse who wants to remain in the home must show that "other provision for shelter is not adequate in the circumstances," or that it is "in the best interests" of the children to make the order. The notion of the child's best interests in this context is not defined. Ontario legislation refers to two factors: the possible disruptive effects on the child of a move and the child's views and preferences, if they can reasonably be obtained. The spouse who occupies the home may be required to make payments to the other spouse to help cover the mortgage or repairs.

Ontario has been innovative in extending the claim for exclusive possession to rental property. This is important because, in large urban centres in Ontario, the matrimonial home is often a rented apartment. Rent increases in the province are subject to rent control, but vacancy rates for affordable housing are very low in some areas. In this situation, exclusive possession of the apartment once shared by the couple may be the only way to provide adequate shelter for the wife and children.

E. Pensions

Many spouses are members of pension plans. As a source of income after retirement, a pension can be a valuable asset. The maximum benefit payable by the Canadian Pension Plan (CPP), a plan regulated and administered by the federal government, was about $6,500 annually in 1988. The benefit is fully indexed, that is, it increases with inflation.

In addition to the CPP, which is available to everyone in the labour force, there are private or "employer-sponsored" plans. These plans are voluntarily established by employers and are designed to supplement the CPP. The maximum amount paid by an employer-sponsored plan depends on the plan design. In very generous plans the combined CPP and employer pension may equal 70 to 100 percent of earnings prior to retirement. Most non-government employer plans are not indexed, but pressure is being placed on employers to introduce some inflation protection into their plans.

At present, women are not as likely as men to be covered by pension plans. This is true of older women, who generally have little or no history of labour force participation. It is also true of women in the labour force, because of their concentration in the service sector of the economy, where employers are less likely to provide plans. Even when women are covered, their pensions will not be as high as men's so long as they remain out of the labour force for significant periods of time to care for children, and of course, so long as they do not have the opportunity to earn the wages that men do.

For these reasons, pensions are important matrimonial assets. However, many provinces have yet to devise and implement adequate policies for dividing pensions on marriage breakdown. In some of the Atlantic provinces, the courts have not decided whether pensions are matrimonial property, or whether the loss of the pension is a factor to be considered in making an unequal division of matrimonial property (Pask, 1988). As well, courts are often not given clear direction on how to value pensions. Valuation is essential in cases where the plan member has not retired, so that the amount of the benefit payable to him or her can be determined. Uncertainty about valuation prolongs settlement negotiations between the spouses, and may lead to court action that would not have been undertaken otherwise. In either case, uncertainty leads to increased legal costs for the couple.

Provinces do not have legislation that describes when and how a non-member spouse may claim her share of the pension from the employer plan itself. A number of problems arise when this legislation does not exist. If a claim cannot be made on the plan, the pension income must be provided by the member spouse. However, if the member has not retired, he may be in no position to pay, since he does not have the property he is supposed to share. It is possible to wait until his retirement, and have him share the benefit as it is paid out. However, this solution may prove unfair to the non-member: her former husband may have moved to another province or even another country; or he may be unwilling to obey the order to share, so that it will be necessary to go to court to collect the payments. One can also imagine that the former husband would not be overjoyed at having regularly to send part of his pension to a person with whom he has long had no connection.

Currently, the federal government, Manitoba, New Brunswick, and Nova Scotia are the only jurisdictions with comprehensive legislation for dividing the pension benefit (Pask, 1988). In the case of the CPP and all employer plans in Manitoba, equal division of the pension is mandatory; the court is given no discretion to award an unequal division. In Manitoba, the spouse may not contract out of equal division or arrange to trade the claim for property of equal value. Legislation governing the CPP provides for contracting out, but the conditions for doing so are severely restricted.

Couples are generally free to opt out of the statutory provisions, and substitute their own arrangements by contract. Manitoba's provisions for pension sharing are an important exception. Some women's groups have strongly advocated that Manitoba's position be adopted by all provinces. They argue that many women are going to have to depend on their former husband's pension as a source of retirement income because they are unlikely to have any pension, or an adequate pension of their own. They point out that pension plan members cannot themselves bargain away or deal with their pension rights, and that the same rules should apply to the spouse who is given a claim to the pension.

LEGISLATION IN QUEBEC: CONFLICTS AND CHANGES

Provisions dealing with the ownership of property acquired during the marriage are contained in the Civil Code of Quebec. As this section was being revised, significant changes were made to this part of the Code. The changes, which were supported by many women's groups and members of the Quebec bar, elicited heated criticism from other segments of Quebec society, which was echoed in the press. The following paragraphs describe the law as it was and the changes that have been made.

Before July 1989, the Code provided for one system of equal sharing, called the "partnership of acquests." This system continues to exist in modified form. The term "acquest" refers to most property acquired by the spouses during the marriage, including business assets, but not pensions. The system differs from those legislated in the common-law provinces in its restricted use of judicial discretion. Judges are allowed to make a discretionary monetary award to one spouse from the other as payment for the "contribution, in goods or services, to the enrichment [of the other's property]." The award is known as a "compensatory allowance." The allowance was introduced in part to provide some remedy for the Murdoch-like cases that arose in Quebec. However, judicial discretion is foreign to Quebec property law; this fact, together with the circumstances that prompted the introduction of the remedy, seems to have impeded its evolution in the province.

Before the introduction of the present Civil Code it was common for women to contract out of equal sharing because the right had a steep price: the loss of the wife's capacity to deal with any of the property acquired by the married couple during the time of the marriage. While the wife was in theory an equal owner of the property, her ownership had no real effect while the marriage was ongoing. The alternative to equal sharing was separation as to property: each spouse acquires and disposes of property as a separate individual, with the result that neither can make a claim on the other's property on the basis of a contribution to the marriage relationship. However, the important point about the choice of separation as to property in the past was that it conferred on the wife the legal capacity to deal with property. Unfortunately, as more marriages began to break up, the more "Murdochs" were left without property claims.

There seems to have been some hostility to the notion of a compensatory allowance to remedy injustices arising in these cases. It is not clear whether this was due to the problems perceived to be created by introducing a common-law mechanism into the civil law without regard for the differences between the two systems, or to the inability to see a need for a remedy. One commentator has remarked with some asperity that

Quebec wives who had by contract agreed to separation as to property were not in the same situation as the Mrs. Murdochs in the common-law provinces: they had, after all, been the authors of any injustice arising at the end of the marriage by contracting out in the first place (Caparros, 1983:140). In any event, in many cases judges have proved unwilling to make much use of the compensatory allowance (Rayle, 1988).

In 1987, at the urging of groups concerned about the injustices arising from decisions to remain separate as to property that were made in the past, the government of Quebec began a consultation process to reform the legislation. In June 1989, new provisions for property division became law. The legislation creates yet another category of property subject to equal sharing, called "the family patrimony." This category consists of the matrimonial home and any secondary property the family uses, such as a summer cottage, the furnishings, the family car, and most important, entitlements in the Quebec Pension Plan, private pension plans, and RRSPS.

The family patrimony must be shared equally, regardless of whether spouses choose to be subject to the partnership of acquests or separate as to property with respect to other assets. Moreover, what is unique to Quebec legislation, spouses can contract out of equal sharing of the family patrimony only at the time of marriage breakdown; that is, they must be able to set aside the differences that led them to separate in order to divide the property in other than equal shares. There is an exemption for couples married before the legislation was passed: they have eighteen months to withdraw from its provisions.

Finally, the legislation provides for an even wider use of judicial discretion than the previous provisions of the Code. Courts may order an unequal division of the family patrimony where the marriage has been of short duration, the assets have been "wasted," or a spouse has acted "in bad faith." All of these terms are subject to interpretation by judges.

From the point of view of this text, the most interesting criticism of the new legislation is that by making it difficult for a couple to contract out of equal sharing of the family patrimony, the legislation favours wives who remain out of the labour force, and in fact encourages them to do so. The following (translated) quotations from two articles by Lysiane Gagnon, in *La Presse*, are typical in substance and tone of the arguments raised in the Quebec press.

> This so-called feminist bill goes against what ought to be the primary goal of a progressive State, is contrary to what should be done to allow women to enter the labour force . . . and to stay there, and so gain financial autonomy, which is the basis of all freedom (June 13, 1989, "Encore mineures?").

> [The Minister] has her notion of marriage and thinks that we all ought to share it: "To be married," she says, "is to share what a couple builds together." Who is she to say [what marriage is]? Marriage isn't a business enterprise; people marry for intimate and personal reasons. In whose name does the State impose on its citizens a uniform way of dealing with their assets and their family life? If we can sign a contract with a plumber . . . why can't we contract with our own spouses? (June 15, 1989, "Papa l'état).

SUPPORT FOR SPOUSES AND CHILDREN

BACKGROUND

Before the introduction of the Divorce Act in 1968, the determination of support awards for spouses was an "exercise in morality" (Abella, 1981:1). Only a wife could claim support, and she was able to do so if she could be shown to be without fault with respect to the marriage breakdown, where fault was defined in terms of sexual misbehaviour, cruelty, or in certain provinces, desertion. Innocence was rewarded with alimony, the obligation of the former husband to pay the wife a "pension for life," as some judges put it. A legally guilty wife could claim nothing from her husband, whatever her financial situation. The problem of child support did not arise: custody would not be given to a guilty wife, since the finding of fault was considered to be proof of her inability to parent. For the spouses, the consequences of the law were clear:

> Husbands could leave, provided they paid the exit tax in the form of support. Wives could leave, but only if they had emotional, physical or betrayal scars. In the absence of scars, departure meant destitution (Abella, 1981:2).

The 1968 divorce legislation did not adopt the same approach, since it would have been inconsistent with the provisions for allowing divorces on no-fault grounds. But neither did the law propose a new approach, although entitlement to support was extended to both spouses. The legislation left the determination of support awards to judicial discretion, with very little indication of how judges were to exercise it. Judges were instructed by the Act to do what was "fit and just," having regard for the "condition, means, needs and other circumstances" of the spouses and the children.

As was explained earlier, federal divorce law exists alongside provincial family legislation. After 1968, the provinces still had jurisdiction over support in the period between separation and divorce and in cases where the spouses did not wish to divorce. Provincial legislation was also affected by the spirit of reform. Most provinces followed the lead of the federal government in abandoning or restricting fault considerations and leaving support to judicial discretion. However, they tried to give judges better direction by presenting them with a more detailed and much longer list of factors to consider. A typical list, taken from Ontario's Family Law Reform Act of 1978, included the following items:

- the assets and means of the person applying for support, as well as that of her partner;
- the capacity of the person applying for support to provide for herself; the capacity of the other spouse to provide the required support;
- the age and physical and mental health of the applicant and the other spouse;
- the length of time the couple cohabited;
- the needs of the applicant, in determining which the court could consider the accustomed standard of living while the couple lived together;

- the measures available for the applicant to become financially independent and the length of time and cost involved to enable her to take such measures;
- the desirability of the applicant or the husband to remain at home to care for a child;
- a contribution by the applicant to the realization of the career potential of the husband; and
- the effect of having assumed family responsibilities on the earning capacity of the applicant.

Both federal and provincial solutions to the problem of support were strongly criticized. The argument against the legislation was succinctly put in a much-quoted article by Rosalie Silberman Abella, then Judge of the Family Division of the Provincial Court of Ontario:

> Lawyers, clients and judges are victimized by the breadth of discretion sanguinely allocated to the bench. Even when the statute purports to circumscribe the discretion by defining some of the ingredients that should go into a support judgment, reported decisions reflect wide differences in how much of each ingredient goes into a decision. . . .
>
> The problem really lies with an inability to agree on what the purpose of economic adjustments on divorce or separation should be. And this, not surprisingly, derives from an inability to agree on what the purpose of marriage should be (Abella, 1981:1).

In designing the Divorce Act, 1985, the federal government had to confront the demand that the legislation set out guiding principles for awarding support. However, the government was not prepared to develop a legislative policy that would create a sharp break between the federal law and the law that had evolved since the late 1970s through judicial interpretation in the provinces (Department of Justice Canada, 1988:19-20). It would seem that the desire for uniformity – in this case, the wish to follow rather than lead the provinces – had the greater influence on the new legislation.

A few words should be said about the vocabulary of support law. In Canada "alimony" is used to refer to pre-1968 support orders made to a wife on fault grounds. The 1968 Act adopted the term "maintenance" to emphasize that there was to be a break from the past. Subsequent provincial legislation used the term "support," rather than "maintenance," and it has now been incorporated into the 1985 federal legislation.

CHANGES IN THE 1985 DIVORCE ACT

For the first time, the 1985 Act sets out objectives for support orders. The objectives focus on the economic situation of the spouses only, and courts are expressly instructed not to consider marital fault in making awards. Orders for spousal support must recognize any economic advantages or disadvantages to the spouses arising from the marriage or its breakdown, apportion between spouses any financial consequences arising from child raising other than those relating to child support, relieve any economic hardship of the spouses arising from the breakdown of the marriage, and insofar as practicable, promote the economic self-sufficiency of each spouse within a reasonable period of time. Orders for child support must meet two objectives: recognize that the spouses have a joint financial obligation to maintain their children, and divide the support obligation between the spouses according to their relative abilities to contribute financially to their children's support.

The Act holds spouses in blended marriages responsible for child support, regardless of whether the child is their own, if they have acted as parents to the child during the marriage. Support obligations extend to all children under age sixteen and children over that age if they are dependent on their parents because they are ill or disabled, or are "for other cause" unable to support themselves. The meaning of the term "for other cause" is left to judicial discretion, as it was in the previous legislation. In the past, courts have agreed that parents are required to help a child who wants to attend university obtain an undergraduate degree, or whatever other initial training is necessary to help the child get on in life. Again, child support is also determined by ability to pay; parents do not have to put their children through university if they cannot afford it.

In addition to the support objectives, the Act contains a list of factors that the court must consider. Besides the general categories mentioned in the previous legislation, the factors include: the length of time the spouses lived together, the functions performed by the spouses during the time they lived together, and any court order or agreement between the spouses relating to spousal or child support.

The Act makes it clear that support may be ended after a fixed period of time or with a specified event. It is possible to change the terms of a support order if there has been a change in the conditions, means, or needs of either of the former spouses. However, once a fixed-time order has expired, it may be renewed only if the applicant is suffering economic hardship that is related to the marriage. All these provisions are relevant to the objective of promoting self-sufficiency.

Although, in divorce cases, property division and support are covered by separate legislation, the two are obviously connected. If the wife is awarded possession of the family home, the support award will not include an amount for rent. In the rare case where there is a great deal of property, the income that could be generated from the wife's share will be taken into consideration in calculating the amount she requires. The Divorce Act, 1985, appears to acknowledge that a support order can be used as a substitute for a property award, since one of the objectives is to recognize the economic advantages and disadvantages arising from the marriage. Indeed, as a number of writers have pointed out, the most valuable property accumulated during the marriage is usually a spouse's "human capital," his or her ability to earn a living (Bissett-Johnson, 1988:159). This is not a resource that can easily be divided, but it can be reached through a support order.

CONTROVERSIES OVER THE RIGHT TO SUPPORT PAYMENTS

> Some, in my experience, most often middle-aged or older women, are left after a divorce with expectations of self-sufficiency that are totally foreign to their own values and expectations – i.e. that marriage and/or right to support was a life-long thing. These people are trapped – by a value system that was totally legitimate in their formative years and a society that has "changed the rules" (Bissett-Johnson, 1988:158).

Many questions can be asked about what is fair in the payment of support. Should older women as described above be treated differently from others? How long should support last? Should education or upgrading be paid for by former spouses? How much of a former spouse's income ought to go to support payments? What expenses should take priority over support: a mortgage for the supporting spouse's new home, for example, or car payments or investments? How do the answers to all the questions differ if the dependent spouse has custody of the children? The legislation does not provide clear answers to these questions. It is still the judges who decide. At the time of writing, the legislation has been in effect for three years, yet no data have been published on the way in which judges are interpreting the law. However, it is possible to make some comments on the basis of reported cases.

Davies (1988) has studied the effect of divorce on elderly women in Canada. She concludes that the courts are recognizing that self-sufficiency cannot be demanded of older women who have been homemakers throughout the marriage. These women will continue to be entitled to live as they did during the marriage, insofar as this is possible. Their husbands will be required to supplement their income or to support them entirely to bring their standard of living to the desired level. But for young divorcing wives, Davies speculates, the situation will be different. One of the assumptions of the Act, according to Davies, is that a divorce "should ensure the termination of all relations between the parties including, where possible, those that are financial" (p. A-4:6). She observes that limited time orders are becoming increasingly common, and predicts that they will be used to encourage a wife to rehabilitate herself for the labour market within a specified, or at least reasonable, period of time, after which they will end.

An equally authoritative writer, Payne (1988), takes a different view of the support provisions. For him, the statutory objectives are not attempts at formulating a rule or rules about self-sufficiency, but are again guidelines to the proper exercise of judicial discretion. He argues that the fact that the legislation has endorsed four objectives is a way of acknowledging that there is no single principle of support that is applicable to all situations. He describes cases that to him indicate that courts are prepared to be flexible in awarding support under the new Act. For example, a mother who was unable to find work that would generate a reasonable income for herself and her preschooler was awarded an amount that would allow her to stay home with the child until the child was old enough to be in school. By contrast, a young wife with no children, whose economic status was found not to be significantly affected by her short marriage, was awarded a small fixed amount to compensate for any economic loss she might have suffered, but nothing more.

One case in Ontario, *Chadder v. Chadder*, 2 R.F.L. 433, indicates that fixed-time orders will not be awarded where there is no evidence that the wife is likely to obtain full-time employment in the designated period, so long as it is clear that she is trying to become self-sufficient. A British Columbia case, *Elsom v. Elsom* (1987), 10 R.F.L. 234, suggests that the objective of self-sufficiency is to be ignored if the husband is rich enough: support was awarded to a wife of nine years whose share of the family assets amounted to $1.45 million.

At the present time, the courts are beginning to develop the theory that support should only be awarded if the need is causally connected to the marriage. This principle is not contained in the Divorce Act (except with respect to the variation of fixed-time orders). Nor is the meaning of the term "causal connection" clear. It could be interpreted narrowly or broadly. Consider the case of a childless couple who live comfortably but do not acquire any significant assets (*The Lawyers Weekly*, 1988:1). The spouses choose their careers freely; neither is encouraged or restrained by the other, but as is often the case, the wife earns considerably less than the husband. On the one hand, it may be argued that the wife's low earnings are determined by her choices and are not causally connected to the marriage. Since her inequality results from the marketplace, her husband should not be asked to provide for her once the marriage is over. On the other hand, one may argue that the wife's needs have been shaped by the marriage: the couple has lived well on a combined income, an interdependence has been created. The husband should be asked to help finance the wife while she improves her skills in an attempt to become self-supporting.

In practice, however, the narrow interpretation is used, and the outcome is that the wife receives little or no support. It is not yet clear whether this theory will be extended to spouses who have dependent children, and whether child support would be adjusted upwards in these cases. It should be pointed out that the approach has come under attack, and at least one Ontario judge has refused to adopt it (*The Lawyers Weekly*, 1988).

In response to groups who have argued that the support provisions could have a detrimental effect on women and children if the courts choose to interpret the provisions in this way, the federal government has made a commitment to monitor the effects of the support provisions, including the effects on women and children. In June 1988, the Department of Justice began an evaluation of the Act, scheduled to be completed by September 1989. The evaluation addresses many important issues. Has the goal of economic self-sufficiency of each spouse taken precedence over the other objectives of support payments? With respect to self-sufficiency, has reasonable consideration been given to the phrases "insofar as practicable" and "within a reasonable period of time"? Have the numbers of time-fixed support orders increased, and if so, to what extent and under what type of conditions? Are the financial circumstances of women coming out of long-term marriages and of single-parent families improved, the same, or poorer than under former legislation? Is this in any way due to the legislation itself, the success or failure of provincial enforcement systems, and/or economic opportunities and conditions for women in the labour force? The government has indicated that it is prepared to consider changes to the Act if they are needed (Department of Justice Canada, 1988:62-64).

ENFORCING SUPPORT ORDERS

One of the most serious problems in the area of family law has been the failure of parents to comply with court orders or private agreements to pay support. In 1976, the Law Reform Commission of Canada estimated that as many as 75 percent of all orders in Canada were in some degree of default. Subsequent studies have confirmed that the rate of non-compliance is high, although reported rates have varied between 50 percent and 85 percent (Steel, 1988). Throughout the 1980s, the federal and provincial governments have worked together to address the problem (Morton, 1988). This has resulted in a new approach to enforcement.

Before the reforms of the 1980s, enforcement was considered a private matter and was left entirely in the hands of the spouse to whom the money was owed (the payee). If the defaulting spouse (the payor) had no assets, the best course of action was to go to court to "garnish" his wages: that is, to claim the money owed to the payor from his employer. However, there was no provision for a continuing garnishment order: the payee had to go to court each pay day. Moreover, provincial and federal laws exempted governments from garnishment, which meant that the wages of civil servants could not be touched. If the payor had moved, the payee would have to find him. If the payor had left the province, it was necessary to start a court action in the province to which he had moved. Obviously, this process imposed significant costs on the payee, especially in an out-of-province case where the woman's testimony might be required during the hearing. That is to say, the costs were borne by the person least able to do so.

Reform of the system has addressed each of these problems. All provinces have made it easier to gain access to the income of the defaulting spouse through continuing rather than "one shot" garnishment. Legislation has been passed allowing garnishment upon federal and provincial governments. As well, federal legislation is now in force that permits garnishment of various amounts that may be owing to the defaulting spouse by the government. These include income tax refunds, unemployment insurance benefits, interest on Canada Savings Bonds, Canada Pension Plan benefits, Old Age Security benefits, and agricultural price stabilization payments.

Provincial and federal governments have set up agreements that would allow certain organizations such as the courts, police forces, and designated provincial agencies to trace defaulting spouses by searching through specified information banks belonging to the government (Canada Pension Plan records, for example) or independent agencies (motor vehicle or public utilities records). In addition, a few provinces have legislation that gives the courts wide powers to question individuals as to the whereabouts of the defaulting spouse.

Finally, and most importantly, provinces are assuming more responsibility for the enforcement process itself. The model for a comprehensive system that is regulated and operated by government was established in Manitoba in 1980. The system is comprehensive in that it includes federal and provincial support orders, and allows for the enforcement of support provisions in separation agreements, if the spouses agree. The system is initiated automatically, rather than by the payee. This means that payments must be put through the system so that they can be recorded and monitored. When no payment is received, or a lesser amount is sent, the relevant officials are notified and enforcement proceedings are begun. The system is computerized, which is essential if it is to operate efficiently. Spouses can opt out of the system and proceed with their own lawyer if they wish.

The model has variations (Steel, 1988). In the three other western provinces and Ontario, officials are given some discretion as to whether they should enforce and what measures to take. In some provinces the process is an administrative one; in others there must be a court hearing. Quebec is proposing to introduce a system that would enforce payments for one year only (*Le Devoir*, 1988). These differences will clearly have an effect on the amounts that are collected and on the time taken for collection. If the automatic system is to work properly, it must be given adequate resources, yet it would appear that this has not been the case in some provinces (*The Edmonton Journal*, 1988; *The Globe and Mail*, 1988).

CHILD CUSTODY

CONTROVERSIES SURROUNDING CUSTODY, JOINT CUSTODY, AND ACCESS

For many years it has been accepted that custody awards are to be based on the "best interests of the child," as opposed to the rights or the desires of the parents. Decisions have been left to judicial discretion, and not surprisingly, they in turn have responded to changing attitudes to child rearing and parental responsibility. For example, until the 1970s it was accepted without argument that a mother's care was best for a child "of tender years" (generally up to age seven). It is now believed that the "tender years" doctrine is unsound (Holmes, 1987).

Unfortunately, we are far from having evolved comfortable ways for divorced parents to be with their children. This uncertainty is reflected in the state of the law. The debate over joint custody illustrates our dissatisfaction with the law as it is and the difficulties involved in changing it.

One factor that makes discussion of joint custody difficult is that the term is used in a number of ways. The meaning of custody itself is not well understood, either outside the legal profession or within it (Mayrand, 1988). In its widest sense, custody comprises all the rights and responsibilities that parents have with respect to their children. In recent years, courts have begun to distinguish between two more restricted notions of custody. One, "physical custody," involves being in charge of the child on a day-to-day basis. By contrast, "legal custody" is parental authority, the ability to make longer-term decisions about how the child should be raised. The distinction between the two notions is not altogether clear; however, to give an overly simple example, a parent with physical custody is responsible for getting the child to day care, while a parent with legal custody decides which day care to attend.

In U.S. legislation, where the term is frequently used, joint custody means joint legal custody, the sharing of the power to make important decisions about the child by the parents. In these cases, physical custody is not shared. It should be stressed that this is not the only way in which divorced parents can participate in the upbringing of their children. The children may live with each parent for alternating periods of time. When this is done on a weekly basis, the arrangement is often called "co-parenting," and the parents are said to share physical as well as legal custody. When the alternating periods are significantly longer, say part of the year with the mother, the other part with the father, the parents are said to have alternate or divided custody, rather than joint custody (Mayrand, 1988; McQueeny, 1984).

Parents who are not awarded custody are generally given access to their children. Access is yet another legal measure that allows divorced parents to be with their children and exercise some influence over them. For many years, it has been assumed that at common law the right of access allows parents no more authority than that implied in being with their children for the access period. Courts and parents alike have acted on this assumption. However, it is now being questioned. Parents with access who disagree with their spouses about the education of their children, their religious upbringing, or any other serious issue may in the future be able to take the matter before the courts, so long as they are not prevented from doing so by legislation (Mayrand, 1988).

A number of specialists involved in family matters believe that joint custody is the arrangement that is the most responsive to the best interests of children (McQueeny, 1984; Katz, 1984; Mayrand, 1988). The belief is shaped by their perceptions about parents and the relationship between parents and children. Children need continued contact and love from both parents after divorce, they argue. The role of an access parent is an artificial one. For example, having the child every other weekend – a common access order – is not enough to maintain a strong bond between parent and child over time. Parents who have no direct influence over the future of their children and are emotionally cut off from them will also cease to be responsible for them. This will hurt both children and parents. As one writer has put it, perhaps the greatest

A number of specialists in family matters believe that joint custody is the arrangement that represents the best interests of children.

MILLER COMSTOCK INC.

benefit of joint custody to parents is the feeling that they can salvage success as parents
from their failure as spouses (Katz, 1984).

Joint custody is also favoured by certain advocacy groups that represent non-
custodial parents (that is men, for the most part). These groups see joint custody
legislation, among other measures, as a means of redressing what they believe to be
widespread injustices against fathers. They claim that men are often deprived of their
access rights, which the courts do not enforce. They argue that men are discriminated
against in child custody determinations, since as statistics show, less than 15 percent of
divorce decrees that deal with custody contain an award to the father. They take this as
an expression of stereotypical attitudes toward parenting, which joint custody awards
will help eradicate. As well, these orders may help relieve the economic and emotional
burden that sole custody puts on single mothers (National Association of Women and
the Law, 1985).

In the United States, the sentiment in favour of joint custody has given rise to
special custody provisions, but state legislation is not uniform. Joint custody may be
presented as one option to be considered by the court, on the condition that both
spouses agree, or it may be presented as an option with the implication that parents
need not agree. The legislation may contain an express preference for the arrangement,
by a device called a "presumption." In that case, joint custody will be awarded unless
the spouse who opposes the order is able to show why joint custody would not be in the
child's best interests. In a few states, joint custody is automatically granted upon the
request of one of the parents (McQueeny, 1984:12). All fathers' rights groups, including
Canadian groups, support a presumption of joint custody, at the very least. The opinion
of researchers and other specialists on the benefits of a joint custody award that is
imposed on one or both parents is divided (National Association of Women and the Law,
1985).

Organized opposition to any legislation that would allow a court to impose joint
custody on an unwilling parent has been led by women's groups. They are suspicious of
an arrangement that grants both parents the power to make decisions, while only one of
them, usually the mother, has to live with the consequences. A decision about what
school or day care a child should go to also affects the mother's routine. If parents are
hostile, joint custody can be used to make life more difficult for the mother, rather than
to advance the relationship between father and child (National Association of Women
and the Law, 1985).

In general, women's groups ask why so much emphasis is placed on decision
making. Why is this aspect of child care expected to create the bond that access does
not? Will the ability to make decisions really weave the father into the child's life and
the child's into the father's?

To make the last point in another way, it is unreasonable to expect joint custody
legislation to create male mothers. Most of the decisions that result in custody awards to
the mother are not made by a court; they are agreed to by fathers who for various
reasons find it difficult to care for their children on a daily basis. In order for men to be
able to participate in the raising of their children in a meaningful way in the future, it is
argued, the law must turn its attention to changes in the workplace, say, rather than to
custody law. If higher-paying jobs were accessible to more women, the decision that it

will be the father who stays home with the infant would not be as costly to the family as it is now. If the workplace were more adaptable to the needs of parents, male or female, it would be easier for fathers to take time off to care for sick children or to pick their children up from day care without having to worry about missing a meeting.

There are others who are sympathetic to some of the arguments raised by non-custodial parents, but who nevertheless find it difficult to see how a joint custody arrangement can be worked out if one of the parents resists. One solution that is often proposed is mandatory mediation, a legally imposed requirement that parents seek professional help in resolving their difficulties. It is believed that a significant number of parents would be able to reach an agreement with this kind of support.

In Canada, mandatory mediation would not be easy to implement immediately. The profession of mediation is in its infancy; there are not sufficient numbers of mediators available. As well, the requirement would have cost implications for parents, although it may be argued that mediation would reduce legal fees. Mandatory mediation might also impose costs on provincial governments, which would be expected to subsidize fees for low-income families.

LEGISLATION RELATING TO CUSTODY AND ACCESS

There is as yet no Canadian legislation modelled after U.S. joint custody statutes. The issues were thoroughly aired before House of Commons and Senate committees when they reviewed the Divorce Act, 1985. The federal government, in fact, responded to some of the concerns raised at the committee stage by amending the bill. But the thrust of the amendments was as much to strengthen access provisions as to encourage joint custody.

Divorce legislation continues to give courts broad discretion over custody. As in the case of support, guidelines are specified in the Act for the first time. Courts must consider the best interests of the child. In addition, however, courts must give effect to the principle that a child should have as much contact with each parent as is consistent with the best interests test. Finally, courts are not allowed to consider the past conduct of a spouse, unless it is relevant to the person's ability to parent. There are no guidelines in federal legislation for applying the best interests principle, but they do exist in some provincial legislation and will no doubt be applied.

There are a number of provisions that attempt to answer the concerns of parents with access. Would-be custodial parents are put under some pressure to allow reasonable access: a court can consider unwillingness to give access as a reason for denying a custody award, as long as this is consistent with the best interests of the child. Parents with access are given certain specific rights: they have the right to make inquiries and to be given information about the health, education, and welfare of their children; they must also be notified if the custodial parent intends to move. What may be even more important, as part of their general discretion, judges may impose any restrictions on a custody order they think just. There are many ways in which this provision could be used to benefit an access parent. For example, a mother could be ordered not to leave the province or the country, because the move would limit the child's contact with the father.

The Act does not expressly mention a joint custody award. However, it is clear that custody can be granted to more than one person, a provision that leaves room for courts to make this order. The Act also indicates that persons other than spouses, grandparents for example, can apply for custody or access with permission of the court.

The Act contains mediation provisions, which are briefly discussed in the "Divorce" section. At the time the legislation was passed, the federal government felt that it was inappropriate to include a provision for mandatory mediation because the measure would have to be implemented together with the provinces (Rivard, 1988). It is the provinces that have constitutional responsibility in most of the relevant areas: the

FOR INTEREST

TUG OF WAR

By Barb Livingstone

A divorced Winnipeg couple shared custody of their two children.

The woman's employer closed its office in the city but offered her a transfer and promotion to Vancouver. The woman was reluctant to move but decided she would have difficulty finding employment in Winnipeg.

She left for Vancouver, temporarily leaving the children with the father and his new, pregnant wife while she moved. The father then applied for sole custody of the children and the mother cross-applied.

In September, 1987, the court ruled in favor of the father during the school term. The judge said although the mother was the better parent, the children wouldn't have to go to day care if left with the father because they could remain at home with the new wife.

The mother appealed with the aid of the Women's Legal Education and Action Fund (LEAF) and in January, 1988, the court ruled in her favor. The father appealed for leave to appeal to the Supreme Court but was denied.

. . . .

A divorced Calgary husband and wife have a joint-custody arrangement – the children live with the mother while the father has liberal access.

According to the mother's lawyer, she finally got up the courage to apply for an increase in maintenance. The father then counter-applied for sole custody of the children.

The mother, fearful he would succeed, fled with her children to the U.S. where she had family. She did not give the father the 30 days notice required but phoned him to let him know where she was. The father went to court.

A judge ordered the children returned to the father and said the mother can return to Calgary or not. In the process, the father was given custody of the children without a hearing into who was the better parent.

The decision was upheld by the Court of Appeal.

Source: *Calgary Herald*, February 4, 1989. Reprinted with permission.

education and regulation of the mediation profession, provision of the service, and instructions to the court regarding the service. The government has, however, funded four long-term research studies of court-based mediation services in St. John's, Montreal, Winnipeg, and Saskatoon. This is an important project. There is a need for more empirical research on the effects of mediation, and for Canadian data especially. A summary of the study results was published in 1988.

Provincial governments are likely to address joint custody and related issues in the years to come. In 1988, a private member's bill in support of a joint custody presumption was introduced into the Ontario legislature. In the same year, the attorney general of Ontario put forward legislation designed to provide a speedy court remedy for parents who are finding it difficult to exercise their access rights (Bill 124, 1988). The legislation was passed in June 1989. In 1989, an Access Assistance Program was scheduled to begin operation in Winnipeg. This is a three-year pilot project, funded by both federal and provincial governments, that focuses on mediation rather than court proceedings as an enforcement mechanism (Diamond, 1988).

CONCLUSION

At this point in its development, the law that governs marriage breakdown raises more questions than it answers. As long as women continue to earn significantly less than men, legislators will be faced with the dilemma of deciding how much responsibility former husbands have for the economic hardship that many women will suffer on separation and divorce. Since the alternative is some form of government support for these women, either in addition to or as a substitute for assistance from the husband, it is easy to see why the issue has been passed from the politicians to the judges.

Questions raised by custody law do not concern the direction of the law so much as its consequences. It is clear that legislators want to encourage the participation of both parents in the raising of their children; it would appear that the law is flexible only in the means by which this is done. In the highly charged adversarial situation that marriage breakdown can be, one cannot ignore the fact that the practical effect of this objective is to give extra leverage to non-custodial parents. It may be used in the negotiation of a separation agreement; for example, the father may offer to limit access if the mother accepts less support. It may also be used to involve the mother in endless court battles, with financial and emotional costs to her. Mediation and conciliation services are offered as a solution, but it remains to be seen how quickly they are introduced and how effective they are.

Legislators may have done the best they can in the circumstances. It may be impossible at this time to elaborate more definite rules that meet our intuitions about the rights and responsibilities of spouses after marriage is over. However, we are far from being able to say this with any certainty. In fact, we do not even have an adequate understanding of the kinds of decisions judges are making. The federal evaluation study referred to in the above section on support is a good beginning, but only a beginning. It can only be hoped that more researchers will interest themselves in finding out how our laws affect the family.

DISCUSSION QUESTIONS

1. Why do federal and provincial governments need to make laws relating to marriage and marriage breakdown? Could we have laws governing separation, but no divorce law? (This is in fact the case in Ireland.) Would such a law prevent marriages from breaking up?

2. How did legislators use the 1968 Divorce Act to signal disapproval of spouses who disregarded their marital obligations?

3. How did the Divorce Act, 1985, change the grounds for divorce? Why were these changes made? Do you think they ought to have been made?

4. Why did the Supreme Court of Canada decide that Irene Murdoch did not have a property claim? How did this case affect subsequent changes to provincial laws relating to matrimonial property?

5. A wife leaves her husband because he has become boring. He is distraught and wants her back. Is she entitled to half his very lucrative real estate business? Does this depend on the province in which she lives? Can her husband argue that she shouldn't get a 50 percent share, and if so, on what grounds? Suppose a husband left his wife for another woman. His wife is distraught. Can she claim more than half the business, and if so, on what grounds? Should she be entitled to more than half?

6. Should a man who has a high-paying job be expected to make lifelong support payments to supplement the income of his former wife who is marginally employed? Should he be expected to support her retraining? If she does retrain and then finds that there are no jobs for her in that area, should support continue? What do the support objectives of the Divorce Act, 1985, say about this problem?

7. Should there be clear rules for support? What would they be? What rule should apply to a woman with children? What rule should apply to a wife who becomes very ill during the marriage? If a husband leaves his wife because she is sick, should he be responsible for her continued support? For how long?

8. Should a Jewish father who goes with his children to temple on Friday nights be able to stop his Roman Catholic ex-wife from taking the children to mass on Sunday? Suppose the woman had converted to Judaism when she married and has since returned to her original faith. Suppose she never converted.

9. Mary and Bill separated when their son Jamie was three. Mary has custody. Jamie is now six. Bill has had regular and frequent contact with Jamie. He sees Jamie nearly every other weekend and takes care of him for two months in the summer. Bill adores Jamie. Mary and Bill live in Regina, but Mary has decided to move to England because (1) she has been offered the job that will give her the break she is looking for; or (2) she has met the man with whom she knows she will have a happy life. Bill cannot afford to go to England to see Jamie on a regular basis. Is it right for a court to offer Mary the choice of not going to England or giving up custody? Should the answer be different if we are talking about situation (1) or (2)? Why? Should it make a difference if Bill has joint custody or access? What other solutions are there?

chapter eleven

The Family and Aging

INTRODUCTION

Among the many myths about families in today's industrial society is the belief that the elderly are isolated by absent or uncaring relatives from the warmth and love they need. Shanas (1979 cited in Novak, 1988) has called this notion "hydra-headed" because, like the many-headed serpent slain by Hercules in mythology, the idea comes back with doubled force each time it is put into dispute by evidence to the contrary. Critics of the contemporary scene have complained that among the "functions" that the modern family has "lost" is that of providing for elderly members. How often have you heard someone say that not only do adult children and other relatives expect the government to provide income and services for their elderly, but they also tend to abandon older relatives emotionally and leave them to fend for themselves or to be taken care of by complete strangers? This alleged pattern of today is purportedly different from the way things were in the past and from the way they are in other parts of the world where kinship is still the basis for most social relationships.

Statements about the declining role of families in the support of older family members need to be questioned. What do we know about family interaction and helping patterns involving the elderly? What have we discerned about the relationships between the elderly, their families, and the political, economic, medical, and welfare institutions in Canadian society? It is important for citizens to know the facts if they are to make intelligent decisions about public policies involving families and their elderly.

Other questions arise about the lives of elderly Canadians. What are their living arrangements, with whom do they keep in touch, and what satisfactions do they derive from their marriages and their grandchildren and other kin? Understanding the answers to these questions can help elders and their families to cope with aging as it affects their everyday lives.

In this chapter, we examine the aging population and the experiences of older people in families and in society as a whole in the past and at the present time.

THE AGING CANADIAN POPULATION

The aging of Canadian society has been going on since Canada became a nation. In 1851, almost two decades before Confederation, less than 3 percent of the population was over sixty-five years old; by 1901, 5 percent; by 1951, almost 7 percent; and in 1986, 11 percent. Another way of looking at our aging population is shown in Figure 11.1, which describes the trend in the average age of Canadians since 1851 and projects it to the year 2051. In 1901, half of all Canadians were under the age of 22.5 years, and half were older than that. The median age in 1981 was 27.7 years. The estimate is that by 2031, the median age will be 41.6 years.

Figure 11.1

Historical and Future Median Age, Canada, 1851–2051

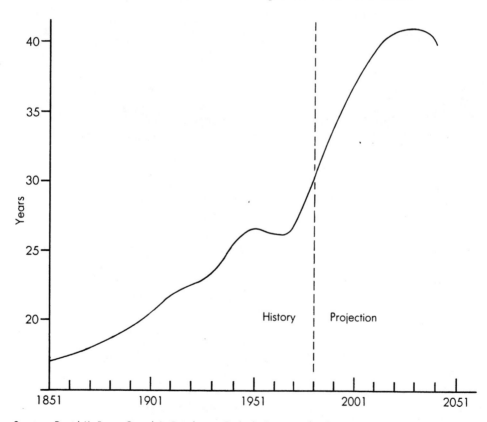

Source: David K. Foot, *Canada's Population Outlook: Demographic Futures and Economic Challenges* (Toronto: James Lorimer & Company, 1982), p. 125.

As with other societal changes, the aging of the population has not been a dramatic overnight affair, but a slow and continuous process going on for over a century with only brief interruptions. Factors involved have been (1) reduced fertility; (2) increased longevity for both sexes; and (3) migration patterns. These in turn are the consequences of numerous changes, sometimes referred to as modernization, in the sociocultural environment. Similar changes have taken place in other Western societies, some of whose populations began to experience the aging trend much earlier than Canada's.

If the total fertility rate (1.6 births per woman in 1986) continues to decrease, reaching 1.4 by 1996 and remaining at that level thereafter, the proportion of older people in the population is expected to reach an unprecedented 29.1 percent by 2051. However, if the birth rate increases to a level of 2.1 births per woman by 1996, the proportion of elderly is not expected to go above 20 percent (Denton, Feaver, and Spencer, 1987).

THE ELDERLY IN FAMILIES OF THE PAST

The more than doubling of the relative size of the older population during the one hundred years ending with 1951 makes it clear that in earlier times very few families had elderly relatives. We know that the idea that large, multigenerational domestic families were characteristic of Canada in the "old days" is part of our cultural mythology (Nett, 1981). In fact, three generations living in one household has been infrequent in Canadian history. Shared households are most likely to occur during periods of financial stress, and even then they do not usually involve related persons or kin. It has never been the custom or the ideal in North America for an older couple to live with their adult married children, or the other way around. However, never-married grown daughters at one time might have continued living with elderly parents, and a widowed elderly parent or other aging relative might have been included in a nuclear family residence. An example of this is provided by Canada's early feminist, Nellie McClung, who described the plight of financially dependent middle-aged spinsters and elderly widows living in the early part of this century (see below).

As for the care of old people by families, there is little reason to believe it was better in the past than today, or that contemporary offspring care less about their parents or other elders than those of the past. The reason for the mistaken belief will become clear as we turn now to a brief description of family types in two kinds of societies and contemplate the roles available to elders in them.

FOR INTEREST

OLD AGE FOR WIDOWS *IN TIMES LIKE THESE* – 1915

There was a rich farmer once, who died possessed of three very fine farms of three hundred and twenty acres each. He left a farm to each of his three sons. To his daughter, Martha, a woman of forty years of age, the eldest of the family, who had always stayed at home, and worked for the whole family – he left a cow and one hundred dollars. The wording of the will ran: "To my dear daughter, Martha, I leave the sum of one hundred dollars, and one cow named 'Bella.' "

How would you like to be left at forty years of age, with no training and very little education, facing the world with one hundred dollars and one cow, even if she were named "Bella"?

To the poor old mother, sixty-five years of age, who had worked far harder than her husband, who had made butter, and baked bread, and sewed carpet rags, and was now bent and broken, and with impaired sight, he left: "her keep" with one of the boys!

How would you like to be left with "your keep" even with one of your own children? Keep! It is exactly what the humane master leaves to an old horse. When the old lady heard the will read which so generously provided for her "keep," she slipped away without a word. People thought it was her great grief at losing such a kind husband which made her pine and droop. But it wasn't. It was the loss of her independence. Her son and his family thought it strange that "Grandma" did not care to go to church any more. Of course, her son never thought of giving her collection or money to give to the funds of the church, and Grandma did not ask. She sat in her corner, and knit stockings for her son's children; another pitiful little broken bit of human wreckage cast up by the waves of the world. In two months Grandma had gone to the house of many mansions, where she was no longer beholden to anyone for "keep" – for God is more merciful than man!

The man who made his will this way was not a bad man, but he was the victim of wrong thinking; he did not realize that his wife had any independence of soul; he thought that all "mother" cared about was a chance to serve; she had been a quiet, unassertive woman, who worked along patiently, and made no complaint. What could she need of money? The "boys" would never see her want.

A man who heard this story said in comment: "Well, I don't see what the old lady felt so badly about, for what does a woman of sixty-five need of money anyway?"

He was not a cruel man, either, and so his remark is illuminative, for it shows a certain attitude of mind, and it shows women where they have made their mistake. They have been too patient and unassertive – they have not set a high enough value on themselves, and it is pathetically true that the world values you at the value you place on yourself. And so the poor old lady, who worked all her life for her family, looking for no recompense, no recognition, was taken at the value she set upon herself, which was nothing at all.

That does not relieve the state of its responsibility in letting such a thing happen. It is a hard matter, I know, to protect people from themselves; and there can be no law made to prevent women from making slaves of themselves to their husbands and families. That would be interfering with the sanctity of the home! But the law can step in, as it has in some provinces, and prevent a man from leaving his wife with only "her keep." The law is a reflection of public sentiment, and when people begin to realize that women are human and have human needs and ambitions and desires, the law will protect a woman's interest.

Source: Nellie McClung, *In Times Like These* (Toronto: University of Toronto Press, 1972), pp. 91-92. (Originally published in 1915 by D. Appleton and Company; distributed in Canada by McLeod & Allen.)

FAMILISM

There is no doubt that social and living arrangements in predominantly agricultural societies are different from those of industrial societies. In rural economies people are involved in a network of kin and community relationships, which have been characterized as *primary groups*. Individuals are identified as belonging to a family, and they communicate with each other as total persons on a face-to-face basis as they play the roles assigned to them by tradition. Domestic family units are all similar in that there is a division of labour by sex and age, and appropriate roles are, ideally, transmitted intact to the next generation. Family households are linked to each other by blood and marriage ties and a set of prescribed exchanges and obligations. Even if related families do not actually share households, they often live close to each other. Such a system has been called *familistic* or traditional. It includes the belief that all family members have a duty to look after each other and to work for the common goals of the wider group. In the context of familism, older people as well as very young ones have a relatively high degree of security. Theoretically, there is always a place for them because extended family solidarity assures that some relative is obliged to help any family member who needs it. Furthermore, the elderly can play portions of their sex-differentiated roles well past maturity, becoming in the process of aging a living symbol of the past and of valued traditions. Their role as carriers of the culture for subsequent generations takes on added value as they grow older.

CONJUGALISM

The social environment in which families function in industrial societies is very different, and so is the place of the elders. In cities, persons participate more frequently in *secondary groups*. Consequently, they relate to others not as representatives of a family, but as relatively unknown individuals who perform segmented tasks within a large-scale organization and communicate very specialized types of information to strangers. They may or may not live in a family household. They are born and die in hospitals, attend school for twelve or more years of their lives, work in offices and factories, and relax in age-segregated commercial establishments such as movie houses, restaurants, bars, and other public facilities. The family system adheres to the type known as *conjugal* or modern. The main unit is ideally depicted as the married pair living in an independent household with dependent children. The group members are voluntarily bonded to intimate kin such as siblings and parents by ties of affection and concern. Children are reared to become independent of the family residence and resources as soon as feasible economically, and cultural differences between the generations are expected, since the social world changes rapidly. *Individualism* is the dominant belief, with the emphasis being on each member's happiness rather than on achieving group goals or solidarity. In these circumstances, the utilitarian value of elders to kin groups is less. As well, the elders themselves value independence and autonomy. The modern family is widespread in both the urban and rural areas of an industrialized society.

RURAL AND URBAN STRATEGIES

The pictures painted of elders as totally integrated into families in agricultural societies of the world today, and in Canada prior to the mid-twentieth century, and of elders as totally isolated and devalued in urban families today are, of course, exaggerations. Synge (1980) interviewed people born before 1908 and still alive in the late 1970s. She has provided descriptions of the coping strategies of older Canadians during the period when her respondents were growing up and becoming young adults. From their recollections, Synge concludes that, contrary to the myth of the past as a golden age for those growing old, there were many problems for families with elders both on farms and in towns and cities. Whereas living space and food generally were more available in rural households, provision of personal services for the old was remembered as often burdensome. The lack of help on the farm could be a major problem for older people, particularly the childless elderly. Synge reminds us that the main character in *Anne of Green Gables*, written in 1908, was a girl mistakenly sent by an orphanage to an elderly sister and brother in Prince Edward Island who needed a boy to help with the farm chores.

In the towns and cities, strategies for coping with aging were different among working-class and middle-class families. Among the working class, the fear of being left destitute or institutionalized gave rise to patterns of (1) saving and economizing throughout life; (2) the acceptance by males of the need to work as long as they were able with no thought of retirement; and (3) the dependence on the income of unmarried grown children by aging parents who tried to make living at home attractive to their youthful income earners. Responsibility for elderly, incapacitated parents was primarily felt by the single daughter or son. Only if there were no unmarried adult children available did married children with their own families take aging parents into already crowded households. Furthermore, there was little expectation of financial assistance from adult children no longer residing in their parents' household. Nor was there a great deal of stability in the lives of the elderly since widows had to rotate among their children's homes. Synge (1980:142) quotes a man who was born in England in 1901 and arrived in Canada in 1902 as follows:

> My father died in 1934. For the next 25 years my mother lived with me or others of her children. We, the family, supported her.

Among urban, middle-class families during the period of early industrialization, the aged had somewhat more financial security. Home ownership was common, and a house, whether sold or kept, provided even widows with some independence. Synge describes the situation in which middle-class sons and sons-in-law were not needed for financial support, but daughters, especially unmarried, were expected to provide emotional support and companionship to aged parents.

At the time of Confederation in 1867, an estimated 7 percent of the population of British North America resided in cities of 20,000 population or over; by 1921 (present-day Canada minus Newfoundland and Labrador), Canada had reached an even balance of rural and urban populations. (According to Kalbach and McVey, 1979:137, this figure is the result of using the 1961 census definition of urban population. If incorporated places are used to define urban, the balance occurred during the Great Depression, or a decade later.)

During the late nineteenth and early twentieth centuries, participation of the elderly in the labour force remained fairly high, despite the fact that the loss of employment opportunities in small businesses and farms due to industrialization and urbanization hit older people the hardest (Bryden, 1974, cited in Synge, 1980). Remember that "retirement" was an unknown word in the late nineteenth and early twentieth centuries. As heads of households in an increasingly urban environment, men expected to work for a wage until they were too disabled or died, in order to provide needed cash for their families. Older married and widowed women kept boarders.

When disability came for elders without familial resources, the ultimate degradation was the poor house, one of several institutions for the indigent that the late-nineteenth-century social conscience had spawned in response to the ravages of early industrial capitalism. Thus, elderly people survived in any number of ways: on the wages or "keep" from their own work, on their life savings, on private charity, on public aid, and on family support. Although organized pressure for social security and government pensions began in the 1920s, universal pensions for those over seventy years were only introduced in Canada in 1951 (Chappell, 1980).

In 1921, 71 percent of men sixty-five years of age and older were in the labour force. By 1966, as Table 11.1 shows, that figure had dropped, with 46.5 percent of men sixty-five to sixty-nine years old and 14.6 percent over the age of seventy in the labour force. The decline has continued, with only 18.4 percent of men sixty-five to sixty-nine years old and 7.6 percent over the age of seventy in the labour force in 1986. The trend can also be observed in the percentage of older women in the labour force. In 1921, 6.6 percent of women over the age of sixty-four were in the labour force. The figure has slightly declined since 1966, the reverse of the trend for younger women.

Table 11.1 Labour Force Participation Rates, by Sex for Selected Age Groups, Canada, 1966–86

	1966	1971	Males 1976	1981	1986
All Ages	79.9%	77.8%	77.6%	78.3%	76.7%
55–64	86.1	83.3	76.7	75.1	68.5
65–69	46.5	32.6	25.4	21.9	18.4
70+	14.6	12.1	9.8	8.9	7.6
	1966	1971	Females 1976	1981	1986
All Ages	33.6%	37.1%	45.2%	51.6%	55.1%
55–64	28.5	30.9	32.0	33.7	33.4
65–69	10.9	9.7	7.8	7.9	7.1
70+	3.2	2.6	2.2	2.5	1.9

Source: Maureen Baker, *Aging in Canadian Society: A Survey* (Toronto: McGraw-Hill Ryerson, 1988).

The relative financial security of seniors today is reflected in changed living arrangements and lifestyles and in different family strategies for coping with the problems of old age in a predominantly urban society.

Compared with a generation ago, older people today are more financially independent of familial assistance. They are able to retire from work in the labour force with some confidence that at least subsistence will be guaranteed. Although the financial situation is often precarious for widows (Dulude, 1978; Gee and Kimball, 1987), women who have not been in the labour force because of full-time homemaking can obtain supplemental income after the age of sixty-five years. The Old Age Security Pension, or oas, is the most basic source of income for elderly Canadians. It is universal because everyone aged sixty-five and over is entitled to it. For pensioners who have little or no other personal income, the oas is supplemented with an additional benefit, the Guaranteed Income Supplement, or gis.

The relative financial security of elders today is reflected in changed living arrangements and lifestyles and in different family strategies for coping with the new problems of old age in a predominantly urban society. To some of these issues, and to the current situation of elders and their families, we now turn.

MARITAL AND PARENTAL STATUS OF ELDERS

The following Canadian census definition of a family household corresponds to the neolocal or nuclear domestic family, as opposed to the extended family household:

A family household is a husband and wife (with or without never-married children, regardless of age) or a parent with one or more children who have never married, living in the same dwelling.

Family households are normally established by marriage (legal or common law) in Canada, and they change in character over the life cycle of the couple. Some, however, begin with the birth or adoption of a child by an unmarried person. If most family households begin with marriage (and between 85 to 90 percent of all Canadians eventually marry), how many couples are still together in old age? Figure 11.2 shows the marital status of persons sixty-five years and over by sex in 1986. With regard to the single (never-married), separated, and divorced, the figures are the same for women and men: 12 percent share this status. The striking feature of Figure 11.2 is the reversal in the proportions of women and men widowed and married in old age. Nearly three-quarters of men over the age of sixty-five years are married, and half of the women in this age group are widowed. Eighty percent of males sixty-five to sixty-nine years old are married; 80 percent of females are widowed by the time they reach eighty-five years of age.

The explanation for the differences in percentages of married and widowed by sex lies in the lower life expectancy of men and the fact that women tend to marry older men. Until after 1951, there were at least one hundred males for each one hundred females aged sixty-five and over. In fact, during the first half of the century, women outnumbered men in the Canadian population only among eighty year olds, but since 1961 there have been more females than males in the older ages, and the difference in numbers has been increasing. In 1986, the over-65 sex ratio was 72.4 males for each 100

Figure 11.2

Marital Status of Elderly Men and Women, 1986

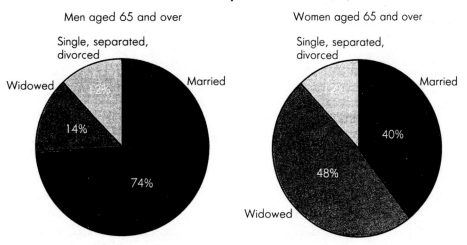

Source: Statistics Canada, *Canadian Social Trends* (Spring 1988):26. Reproduced with permission of the Minister of Supply and Services Canada, 1989.

females or 28 percent fewer males. Women, in 1984, had a life expectancy of 79.2 years compared with 72.5 for men. Widowed men have more opportunities for remarriage due to the excess of older women and the fact that their choice of new partners is not limited to women in their own age group, as is the case with females over the age of sixty-five, who are culturally defined as unattractive to younger males. It is possible that being married makes a difference in how people experience old age, and this is a question that we will raise again later in this chapter.

A high percentage of married women in Canada (approximately 85 percent) have borne at least one child by the time they reach the end of their childbearing years. Furthermore, most elderly persons have children. The figure of 80 percent with at least one living child has been reported in several studies (cited by Rosenthal, 1987). In a study of the ten most common patterns of family and close friendship ties in Canada in 1985, Stone (1988) found very few of the elderly in any age group without a child either in the home or outside. With a decline in the average number of children born into each family, however, there will be fewer children in each older person's family-kin network. Additionally, as the divorce rate increases, non-custodial parents who lose contact with their children may find themselves veritably childless in old age unless they remarry and become a step-parent or start another family. Obviously, marital status and to a lesser extent child status make a difference in the living arrangements of elders. Table 11.2 shows living arrangements of the elderly in 1986.

Three points about the domestic arrangements of elders emerge from Table 11.2.

Table 11.2 Living Arrangements Among the Elderly, 1986

	Male Number	%	Female Number	%
Population in private households	1,050,000	93.7	1,397,000	89.7
Nursing homes and other institutions	70,000	6.3	161,000	10.3
	1,120,000	100.0	1,558,000	100.0
Of Those in Private Households:				
Live with family persons (spouse or unmarried children)	852,000	81.1	770,000	55.1
Live with relatives	26,000	2.5	74,000	5.3
Live alone	154,000	14.7	526,000	37.7
Live with others	18,000	1.7	27,000	1.9
	1,050,000	100.0	1,397,000	100.0

Source: Statistics Canada, *Population and Dwelling Characteristics*, "Families," Part I, Table 7 and "Dwellings and Households," Part I, Table 2 (Ottawa: Supply and Services Canada, 1986). Reproduced with permission of the Minister of Supply and Services Canada, 1989.

The first is that a high proportion of them live in families. Approximately two-thirds resided in nuclear families. Eighty-one percent of males aged sixty-five and over and 55.1 percent of females were members of a domestic family unit that comprised a couple (with or without never-married children) or a parent along with her/his never-married children. Another 2.5 percent of men and 5.3 percent of women aged sixty-five and over lived with relatives. These might be brothers or sisters, aunts or uncles, nieces or nephews, married children, grandchildren, or in-laws. Adding the latter figures to those for living in nuclear families, a total of 84 percent of men and 60 percent of women aged sixty-five and over were living with kin in 1986. Another 1.8 percent of both sexes dwelt in private households with non-related persons, and 27.8 percent lived alone.

The second important point to be noted in Table 11.2 about living arrangements is the large difference in the number of women and men who live alone. In 1986, 14.7 percent of males and 37.7 percent of females over the age of sixty-five dwelt in a household consisting of only one person. These percentages, and the differences between them, have been increasing ever since 1961 when the figures were 9.5 percent for men and 15.2 percent for women. The percentage of women residing by themselves had more than doubled during the twenty-year period.

Finally, Table 11.2 shows that only a small proportion of the older Canadian population is in an institution at any given time. This figure, too, is greater for women than for men, mainly because of women's longer life.

Table 11.2 does not show the number of elderly persons or couples who share a home with their adult children. In fact, most elderly couples maintain their own private residence until one partner dies, after which the widowed spouse generally lives alone. According to the best estimates, only 27 percent of widowers and 30 percent of widows over the age of sixty-five share a household with a child (Statistics Canada, cited in Rosenthal, 1986). In most cases, it is the home of the elderly person, not that of a married or single child, that is being shared.

To the extent that census materials can be relied upon to describe families, these data help us to see elderly persons in relationship to modern families more clearly. To summarize, most elders live in a family, mainly with a spouse or an unmarried child. Those who do not reside in a nuclear family live with other relatives or non-kin or alone, with a higher percentage of elderly females living by themselves than males. Relatively few persons over the age of sixty-five are living in nursing homes or other institutions, and most of them are very old.

However, we must introduce a cautionary note about census data. While probably quite accurate and reliable, they only provide a partial picture. In reality, families are much more dynamic than is implied by the above facts. For example, although 8.9 percent of the older population was institutionalized at the time of the 1986 census, estimates are that twenty out of a hundred will spend some time in a nursing home or other long-term care facility. The period of residence for many is a relatively short one, and the movement is in and out. Gutman et al. (1983) found that 12 percent of those who entered into long-term care facilities in Vancouver in 1978 died within twelve months, and another 14 percent were discharged. Most elderly people are placed in long-term care homes as a last resort if there is no close family or when home care is no longer possible.

Another limitation to official statistics as a source of information about living arrangements of the elderly is that censuses record only those people who live in households. Unfortunately, in many societies today, including Canada, there are significant numbers of homeless people. Estimates of the number of older men and women with no fixed address, the "disaffiliated" (Bahr, 1976), cannot be made, but the presence of "skid row bums" and "bag ladies" in our larger cities and the pressing need for shelters for women are signals that the outcasts in our midst are more numerous than they have been for a very long time. Fischer (1978) described the pitiful old beggars in late-eighteenth and early-nineteenth-century North America, but such scenes have been relatively rare in modern times and have usually not included women. In trying to account for the recent romance that seems to have been built up in magazines, newspapers, plays, and poems around the image of the solitary bag lady (somewhat akin to the idealization in an earlier period of the male hobo), Shulman (1981:12) concludes:

> I think this new, somewhat nervous interest in the lone woman who lugs her mysterious burden through the streets springs from a growing fear many women have for their own old age in a society where the traditional familial sources of women's security are in flux and where so many women can expect to wind up poor and alone.

Disaffiliated women and men are left out – left out of even our censuses, surveys, and most other investigations of the elderly. This omission biases information about the degree of older people's involvement with families.

FAMILY LIFE CYCLE TRANSITIONS

Most Canadians marry at least once, and even if they do not go through the legal procedure, they may enter into common-law relationships that are similar to marriage in many respects (Nett, 1988). Most who marry have children. The timing of these two events and other significant transitions in the life of the average person, however, is not constant over history.

During the first half of the twentieth century, the trend was for the average couple to be younger at the time of their first marriage and the birth of their first child than couples were in the last century. These facts, coupled with the other trend toward having fewer children, meant the pair was also much younger at the birth of their last child than the average nineteenth-century couple was. Since they could expect to live longer, the partners in which the wife was born between 1951 and 1960 would have 23.6 years of remaining together after their last child became independent, if their marriage remained intact. Table 11.3 depicts trends in the family careers of the average woman born at various periods in time.

Since women born in the last cohort displayed in Table 11.3 (1951-60) had only reached the ages of twenty-six to thirty-five by 1986, median ages at marriage and birth of first child are based only on those cases in which these events had already occurred.

Table 11.3 Median Age at Family Life Course Events and Years Spent in Life Stages, Canadian Female Birth Cohorts

| | Birth Cohort | | | |
	1841–50	1901–10	1931–40	1951–60
Median age at:				
– first marriage	26.0	23.3	21.1	22.5
– first birth	28.0	25.0	22.9	24.5
– last birth	40.0	29.1	29.1	26.3
– empty nest*	60.1	49.1	49.1	46.3
– widowhood	59.5	61.3	67.2	69.9
– death of women	64.3	67.3	79.4	82.2
Years spent:				
– between marriage and first birth	2.0	1.7	1.8	2.0
– raising dependent children	32.1	24.1	26.2	21.8
– married, with no dependent children	–0.6	12.2	18.1	23.6
– in widowhood	4.8	6.0	12.2	12.3

*Age of mother when last child is aged twenty.

Source: Ellen M. Gee and Meredith M. Kimball, *Women and Aging* (Toronto: Butterworths, 1987), p. 83. Reprinted with permission of Butterworths Canada.

(A *cohort* is a group of persons who were born or married in the same years.) A well-known fact is that some women (and men) in the baby boom birth cohorts have delayed and will continue delaying both events, compared to an earlier generation. On the other hand, Gee and Kimball (1987) claim that postponing parenthood is only characteristic of very successful middle-class women, whose numbers are too small to influence the overall age at childbearing. Longevity, however, continues to improve for both women and men, so that the projected number of years spent by this cohort in marriage with no dependent children and in widowhood will probably be greater than for previous cohorts.

The increase in the divorce rates since the late 1960s adds other transitions to family careers, especially for persons born after the 1950s. Divorce and remarriage, as well as singlehood and child-free marriage, complicate the concept of a "normal" family life cycle (see Norton, 1983). Divorce and remarriage may or may not significantly alter the years of marriage remaining to couples after the last child has left home, depending on the age difference between the spouses at remarriage and their subsequent fertility. Most divorces occur in the early years of marriage, and most divorced persons remarry within a short time of their divorces. Very few of the elderly experience marital dissolution by any other means than the death of their spouse, and it is the husband who is most likely to die first (see Figure 11.2 for widowhood by sex). The years a woman can expect to spend as a widow have tripled over the past century, from 4.8 years for those born during the years 1841 to 1850 to 12.3 years for those born during the years 1951 to 1960, as shown in Table 11.3.

SATISFACTION WITH MARRIAGE IN LATER YEARS

Couples face many kinds of challenges to satisfaction and happiness throughout their marriages. The changing demands of adult life over time cause substantial alterations in marital partnerships. Occupational demands, the burdens of child rearing, the changes due to children leaving home and adults retiring from the labour force – all involve different tasks and create different stages in the family life cycle. Studies have been made of the marital satisfaction of wives and husbands in these various stages. Although most investigators delineate seven stages, as Lupri and Frideres (1981) have done in Figure 11.3, these can be condensed into four major phases: (1) the newlywed marriage; (2) the parental marriage; (3) the middle-aged marriage; and (4) the retirement or old-age marriage. Figure 11.3 shows the approximate age of the wife in contemporary North America at the time she experiences newlywed, parental, middle-age, and retirement phases of marriage. For example, the so-called "empty nest" (middle-age phase) occurs when she is about fifty years old; retirement (her own if she is in the labour force and her husband's) occurs after sixty-five years.

The results of the study by Lupri and Frideres of Calgary couples, shown in Figure 11.3, reveal the same kind of U-shaped pattern of marital satisfaction for spouses that has been found in studies in the United States. In the *newlywed stage* (phase I) of marriage, the average couple experiences a high degree of satisfaction, despite the fact that they are making many adjustments – to each other, to new roles, and to family and friends as a couple. Perhaps the average newly married couple is so happy because they still enjoy the companionship of the dating period that preceded marriage, because work and careers are not disrupted by the marriage in this stage, and because they have few home responsibilities that clash with self-interest.

With the birth of children, marital satisfaction begins to decline for both partners, and it continues its downward plunge until the end of the *parental stage* (phase II). At least two explanations have been given for this decline: (1) the demands of child care impinge on the intimacy of the couple; and (2) the financial cost of rearing children in urban environments places strains on family finances, and the strains increase as the children grow older. With regard to the first explanation, there is little doubt that as the couple assumes the role of parents their interactions become less person oriented and more structured in terms of roles and obligations. Generally, there is a shift to the more traditional division of household labour, as was suggested in Chapter Three. As for the latter explanation, the marked increase in work outside of the home for Canadian women at the age when they are in the parental phase attests to the *life cycle squeeze* experienced by couples with young children and teenagers in the home. (The *life cycle squeeze* refers to an imbalance between the demands placed on people and the resources available to them at any particular point in the life cycle.)

The third phase in the family life cycle has variously been termed the *post-parental period*, the *launching stage*, the *empty-nest phase*, and *middle age*. It is the time in a couple's life when their children have left home. Historically, it is seen as a relatively new phase, since women born before the turn of the century were usually older at the time their last child married, and since they were widowed younger, the two events might have coincided (Martin Matthews, 1980). In fact, a recent study of "empty-nester" households in Canada concludes that "most families (70 percent of husband-wife families in which the husband is between forty-five and sixty-four years old) never go through a discrete period of empty nesterhood" today either (Miron and Schiff, 1982:5). This is explained by the fact that children leave home over a period of years and at different ages. Furthermore, leaving home may not be a "once only" event. In families with several children, by the time the last one has left, an earlier leaver may return. However valid the concept of an empty nest may be, the proportion of middle-aged wives and husbands in Calgary who reported "very satisfying" marriages began to increase in this phase, as can be observed in Figure 11.3. By the final stage (phase IV), *old age or retirement*, the average couple reported a very high degree of marital satisfaction, almost as high as that of newlyweds.

In the Calgary research, Lupri and Frideres found the wife's participation in the labour force to be a significant factor in explaining fluctuations in marital satisfaction in the middle-age and old-age phases of the marriage cycle. The low point in the percent of

Figure 11.3
Percentages of Husbands and Wives in Each of Seven Stages and Four Phases of the Family Life Cycle Reporting "Very Satisfying" Marriages

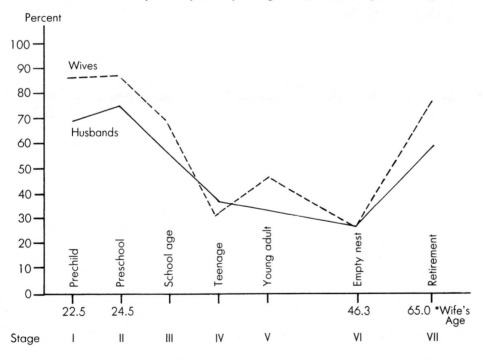

*Except for the age at retirement, the figures are median ages for women in the birth cohort 1951–60, shown in Table 11.3 in this chapter.

Source: Eugen Lupri and James Frideres, "The Quality of Marriage and the Passage of Time: Marital Satisfaction Over the Family Life Cycle," *Canadian Journal of Sociology* 6, no. 3 (1981):289.

In the latter stages of married life, most couples report a high degree of marital satisfaction, almost as high as that of newlyweds.

MILLER COMSTOCK INC.

wives who were very satisfied was for those in the labour force during the years when their children were late adolescents. The corresponding dip for husbands was for those with full-time homemaker wives, and it came in the next stage, when their children had left home. Both of these events, however, occur in the middle-age phase of marriage. After retirement, an increase occurred in the percentages of very satisfied spouses, but the highest rise was for employed wives and the least was for full-time homemakers.

Several kinds of "family theory" can be used to explain these facts. The most obvious explanation for the differential levels of marital satisfaction experienced by wives and husbands in conventional and dual-earner roles in middle age and old age stems from a combination of "developmental theory" and "role theory." Developmental theory (Mattessich and Hill, 1987) is predicated on the idea that the *tasks* required of the partners will vary according to the stage in their marriage and on the *resources* (financial, physical, emotional, etc.) available to the couple, which may or may not be adequate to the demands of the stage. Role theory (Burr et al., 1979) provides the notion of several kinds of *role strains* that may be experienced by persons who, in their interactions with significant others, must negotiate the requirements of the social scripts associated with the positions they occupy in various groups at one time, or at different stages over the life course.

In the middle-age marriage, one kind of role strain is due to the *role overload* that falls primarily on dual-earner wives who are adding to their jobs of homemaking and care for their families a labour force job, in order to cope with the increased costs of adolescent children. The middle-aged husband whose wife is contributing to the family finances in this way obviously benefits from the arrangement, especially if he does not help with the homemaking chores. In the case of the conventional couple (a full-time homemaker wife), it is the husband who (in the next step of this phase of marriage) experiences *role loss* more drastically than the wife when the children are leaving home. He is no longer a father in the sense of providing for dependent children; the wife's role of homemaker remains, and her maternal roles, while altered, continue as she becomes a mother-in-law and grandmother.

In old age many of the *role conflicts* of earlier phases of marriage have been resolved; for example, the different pulls from the marital and parental roles are over. With the discarding of parental and occupational roles, a couple can pay more attention to each other's emotional needs and respond to one another much as they did when they were newlyweds. Marital intimacy among elders has been found to be closely linked with high levels of marital satisfaction (Lee, 1988). The last phase in the family life cycle, depending on the socio-economic circumstances, may be a time of new freedom from many of the responsibilities that earlier tied the couple down and interfered with leisure and companionship. As with other phases, however, adjustments are required. The partners must cope with some physical decline, changed activities, and new identities.

For increasing numbers of couples in the post-parental and early retirement years, a new responsibility will arise in the form of very old parents and parents-in-law about whom they will be concerned and with whose care they will be involved. In fact, the lower percentage of non-employed wives in the Calgary study whose retirement marriages are "very satisfying" may be due to the fact that many are already burdened with such tasks. This task often falls to women who are not employed, or who must leave the labour force to take it on.

Being married has some distinct advantages for the older person. Married couples over sixty-five are better off financially than those who are single (never-married, widowed, or divorced). Widows are the poorest persons among the elderly, mostly because their husbands' private pension payments frequently stop after their death, or are not indexed to the cost of living. Older single women have less money because men generally have a higher lifetime employment income than women and a married man benefits from the contribution that a wife's homemaking makes to his earning capacity. Older women, being less likely than men to be still married (see Figure 11.2), have been found to report more frequently than men that they feel pressure due to their economic situation (Northcott, 1982). A high percentage of older couples own their own home, which gives a degree of economic security.

In other ways, too, marriage provides benefits to elders. Older married persons generally report higher levels of life satisfaction than the widowed or single (Larson, 1978), and they are more likely to be "very satisfied" with their romantic relationship (Statistics Canada, 1980) than persons in any other marital or age status. Older married couples stand a better chance of staying out of hospital or nursing homes if they get sick, of not changing their place of residence (Northcott, 1988), and of not needing social relations outside of home (Novak, 1988). The health of old persons is also related to marital status. For example, unmarried men sixty-five and over are especially at risk with regard to suicide (Canada, 1982, 1982b) and death from other causes.

There is no special magic in marriage that leads to greater satisfaction and higher levels of well-being for the elderly. It is simply that, because of the way our society is structured, older people who are married are more likely to have an intimate companion, a ready-made caretaker, a network of family and friends, and the societal approval that boosts their self-esteem and sense of worth. However, with a good support system of other relatives and friends, older single persons are quite able to manage well even when they live alone (see Norris, 1987, for a more detailed discussion of psychological importance of friends in later life).

KIN NETWORKS: RETHINKING FAMILY STRUCTURE

The obvious effect on families of an aging population is the increase in the number of generations alive at any given time. A study of Canadian university students found that 80 percent have at least one grandparent still alive (Nett and Brown, 1981), and a significant proportion have a great-grandparent alive. Compare this situation with that at the turn of the century, when one out of four sixteen year olds had already lost one or both parents. Today, three living generations in one family are frequent, four are common, and five are not unusual.

By now it has been well established that the kinship system that exists in North America is not the mythical, isolated, nuclear family system, but the empirically discovered *modified extended family system*. The latter is an arrangement in which nuclear family households are bound together in ongoing relationships that are more ego centred and more voluntary and selective than extended family systems, and they are relatively free from normative pressures. Although individualism (self-reliance and financial independence) is emphasized, kin networks beyond the nuclear family household continue to be important for individuals. The social bond between family members who live in separate households is more often affection rather than a compelling sense of duty. Furthermore, in one sense there is no identifiable "family group" other than the household. Because of *bilateral descent* (the inclusion of ego's relatives on both the mother's and the father's side of the family), no one shares the same set of relatives with any other person except for siblings; even they have the same set of relatives only until they marry. In a unilineal system, clear limits or boundaries are established for the family-kin network, since everyone in the group (sometimes referred to as a *clan*) shares the same kin (bloodline relatives from either the mother's or father's side). In North America, distinct extended family *units* exist only as mental pictures of individuals, since each person's set of relatives is unique. There is, of course, an overlapping of the networks of people who are *intimately* related (parents, siblings, and spouses). However, further indeterminacy in group boundaries is introduced because each person has more choice in the matter of kin interaction than one does in a less individualistic culture. Relationships are more voluntary and selective. This is especially the case with more distantly related kin. For this reason, it is *dyadic* (two-person) relationships that assume prominence *between* households.

For the elderly, adult child/parent (and parent-in-law) and grandchild/grandparent are two important kinds of intergenerational family dyads. Other kin also form a part of the lineally extended families of older Canadians, such as aunts and uncles and nephews and nieces. *Collaterals* are brothers and sisters, sisters- and brothers-in-law, and cousins. They are generally age mates or peers. Very few older people are not involved in some kind of two-person or dyadic relationship with kin, whether it be intergenerational or collateral.

ADULT CHILD/PARENT

Most studies of intergenerational ties of elders conducted in Canada deal with the adult child/parent dyad. In a representative community study conducted in Hamilton, Ontario, Marshall, Rosenthal, and Synge (1982) found that approximately 80 percent of respondents over the age of sixty-five had at least one child alive. This figure is somewhat similar to the findings of surveys in the United States and England.

Marshall and Rosenthal (1983) have summarized the findings of their investigations and others into interaction, exchange, and helping patterns found among older persons and their children. They conceptualize as *associational solidarity* the degree to which family members are in contact with each other, engage in shared behaviours, and interact in common activities. They conclude (1983:152) that

> contrary to popular belief, most older people experience high associational solidarity with their children. For example, in countries such as the United States, England, Denmark and Canada, about four of five older people who do have children see a child at least once a week; telephone contact is almost daily. . . . One of the reasons for such contact is that it allows the exchange of help.

Another kind of tie between the generations is the exchange of a broad range of goods and services, including assistance with home repairs, child care, grocery shopping, transportation, and health care, as well as financial assistance and support. Marshall and Rosenthal (1983:152) refer to this aspect of family life as *functional solidarity*. They note the high level of such exchanges as reported in the literature (Shanas, 1981; Chappell, 1981; Marshall and Bengtson, 1983). They conclude: "Contrary to popular images of older people as dependent, these studies suggest a more appropriate image of inter-dependence. Help flows across the generations in both directions, with older people both giving and receiving."

Despite the fact that the organizing principle in our kinship system appears to be marriage (Wallace, 1969), the close child/parent bond that persists through life may be the most important kin tie in industrial societies. Adams (1974) has characterized this relationship as one involving *positive concern*. He would include as manifestations of this active concern both associational and functional solidarity as described above and also "the strong social psychological bond that includes a strong affectional tie and a secondary obligatory element – with the latter subsuming both the general duty to keep in frequent touch and the specific obligation to help out in time of need" (Adams, 1980:329). He notes that when obligation is made the prime factor in continued contact, it may stand in the way of affection, as in the example of a young adult male who has few interests in common with his widowed mother, but feels obliged to visit her often. The balance between affection and duty is always in jeopardy.

Concern about future parental health is a good indicator of the patterning of the adult child/older parent bond in Canada. Health is one of the most important variables affecting the family life of older persons. As an older family member deteriorates either physically or mentally, this may precipitate new kinds of family arrangements and involvements. When the older person is still part of a couple, the involvement of the children is less important. When the person is a widow or widower, intergenerational family interaction is more often required. In fact, Snider (1981) found that elderly women were very likely to rely on kin in a health emergency. In the Hamilton study, concern about parental future health was found to be related to both the age and gender of the child and of the parent. As Table 11.4 shows, by the time a child is fifty years old or over, 47 percent of sons and 60 percent of daughters feel a great deal of concern.

Adult children worry more about their mother's than their father's future health when the parent is middle aged (forty to fifty-nine years), a pattern that continues into old age until seventy to seventy-nine years when father's health becomes the object of more concern than mother's. By the time the parent is very elderly (eighty years and over), the amount of concern felt by the child is the same for either parent.

The higher proportion at all ages of daughters than sons in the Hamilton study who expressed a great deal of concern about the parent's future health illustrates the pattern in our kinship system referred to as *asymmetry*. Despite the bilaterality in the way we

Table 11.4 Concerns about Parent's Future Health, by Age and Sex of Child and Parent

	Percent Concerned							
	Not at all		Only a little		A great deal		Row Ns	
Age	Son	Daughter	Son	Daughter	Son	Daughter	Son	Daughter
Age of child								
50 and older	15.8%	25%	36.8%	14.3%	47.4%	60.7%	19	28
40 to 49	15.2	18	39.4	46	45.5	36	33	50
30 to 39	29.5	6.8	50.8	53.4	19.7	29.7	61	73
Younger than 30	21.3	14.2	51.7	49.3	27	36.5	89	148
Column Ns	45	42	97	139	60	118	202	299
Age of Parent	**Mother**	**Father**	**Mother**	**Father**	**Mother**	**Father**	**Mother**	**Father**
80 and older	30	16.7	20	33.3	50	50	30	18
70 to 79	18.2	8.8	47.7	43.9	34.1	47.4	44	57
60 to 69	22.7	10.5	42.4	68.4	34.8	21.1	66	38
50 to 59	21.2	12.9	45.2	54.5	33.7	32.7	104	101
40 to 49	16.7	27.3	50	54.5	33.3	18.2	36	11
N	60	28	120	118	100	79	280	225

Source: Victor W. Marshall, Carolyn J. Rosenthal, and Jane Synge, "Concerns about Parental Health." Reprinted by permission of the publisher, from *Older Women*, edited by Elizabeth W. Markson (Lexington, Mass.: Lexington Books, D. C. Heath and Company; copyright 1983, D. C. Heath and Company), p. 259.

determine kinship, a matrilateral emphasis exists in North American intergenerational relations. In the average family: (1) women are more involved with kinship obligations and activities than are men; (2) the mother/daughter bond is especially close; (3) the daughter is closer affectionately to both parents than the son is; and (4) the couple tend to be more bound up with the wife's relatives than with the husband's (see Adams, 1974, for a summary of the research in the United States through the 1960s). Within sectors of the society the degree of matrilateral emphasis, or *matrifocus*, must surely vary, but as yet it is unknown from research in Canada how much influence is exerted by region, subcultural background, social class, and other divisions. We will return in a later section of this chapter to social class and ethnicity as factors in kin networks of elders.

The fact that so many elderly persons and couples reside by themselves instead of with adult children reflects a desire by most North American elders for independent living. The excerpt "Intimacy at a Distance" (see below) provides examples of older persons' attitudes. Their preference is for emotional and residential proximity with their children, without actually sharing a home. As for the children's attitudes, some evidence has been found in the analysis of data obtained from the Canadian Fertility Study (Krishnan, 1987) that a relatively high degree of willingness exists on the part of daughters to have parents live with them for an extended period of time, if needed. Information about sons' attitudes is lacking.

FOR INTEREST

INTIMACY AT A DISTANCE

Children and their elderly parents now share what Rosenmayr and Kockeis (1963) call "intimacy at a distance." Young people keep in contact with their parents. Parents and children visit one another, help one another, and keep in touch by phone, but they rarely live with each other.

The National Advisory Council on Aging in 1986 asked seniors living in a seniors' residence why they prefer to live alone. Here are some of their comments:

Albina Tennier: When my doctor advised me that I shouldn't be living alone, my daughter was willing to have me move in with her, but I prefer the independence we have here.

Violet Smith: My son lives in Toronto, and he used to worry about me, but now he knows that someone looks in on me every day. I looked after my mother-in-law for 14 years, and I decided that no one was going to go through that with me.

Hilda Tickell: My son-in-law and grandsons are very supportive, but they respect my independence. They're only a phone call away if I need them, but I wouldn't want to be waiting around for them to call, nor would I ever want them to feel that they have to call. I have my own life to live.

Velma Would: I lived with my granddaughter and her husband and that would have worked out except that I began to feel isolated because they were away at work all day. We didn't live close to public transportation, and I began to feel I couldn't get out, especially in winter. I decided to move here because I'm the kind of person who likes to have other people around.

These comments raise some important questions. How much of older people's desire for independence comes from their feeling that they do not want to become a burden on their children? And how much of their desire for independence reflects the fact that in modern society older people have no place in their children's busy lives? Intimacy at a distance helps to solve this cultural dilemma. It allows older people to keep in touch with their children, but without intruding on them.

Reproduced with the permission of the National Advisory Council on Aging. **Source:** *Expression*, Volume 3, Number 1, 1986.

GRANDPARENT/GRANDCHILD RELATIONS

If you are a young adult or late adolescent, think about what your grandparents were like when you were a small child. Did they fit the stereotype of white hair, wrinkled skin, and rocking chair? It is unlikely. In fact, even if they are over the age of sixty-five now, your grandparents are likely to be relatively healthy, married, living in the community, and fairly active. This is especially the case for maternal grandparents, who on average are younger than paternal ones. It is great-grandparents, aged eighty years or older, who more probably resemble the stereotypical picture of grandma and grandpa.

Not only do demographic trends, such as the earlier age at which the average couple become grandparents today, affect behaviour, but also the fact that older persons are more active and healthier than ever before, a trend that is likely to continue. Furthermore, the roles of grandmother and grandfather are not clearly defined in the modern family as they were in an earlier period. Grandparents might choose to be revered and respected authoritarians, friends, parent substitutes, distant relatives, or "special" and loving persons. The roles they "negotiate" will depend on their own age, social class, and ethnicity, and they will change as the grandchild grows older. Overall, grandchildren expect little from their grandparents materially, but they set a great deal of store on the emotional gratification in the relationship. For grandparents, too, there is a symbolic aspect to their relationship with the third generation. Wood and Robertson (1978) found that the morale of elders is actually more affected by friends than by grandchildren, but the latter are perceived as very important in elders' lives.

Among a select group of youth attending university in Manitoba, Nett and Brown (1981) found that over half felt "very close" to grandparents. This finding corresponds to that of a study of a group of undergraduate women in the United States (Hoffman, 1979). Cross-generational socio-emotional closeness in both groups was significantly related to the grandparents' kin position relative to the grandchild's. That is to say, the youth were closer to the maternal as opposed to the paternal grandparents. The strongest bond was with the maternal grandmother. Thus, the close relationship between adult daughter and mother mentioned in the previous section of this chapter can be seen to extend to grandchildren as well.

MILLER COMSTOCK INC.

Grandparents might choose to be revered and respected authoritarians, friends, parent substitutes, distant relatives, or "special" and loving persons.

Particularly noteworthy in the two studies cited is the fact that the sex of the grandparent does not seem to be as important a variable as one might think. Adult grandchildren are closer to maternal grandfathers than to paternal grandmothers. An example of the emotional linkage made by the grandchild's parents is provided in the words of a nineteen-year-old Jewish woman in Nett and Brown's study (1981:14):

> I am not especially close to my paternal Baba (grandmother), although I see her almost as often as I see my Zaida (maternal grandfather). Over the years, no special relationship had developed between us. Perhaps this is because I was always so much closer to my maternal Baba (now deceased). Probably because I am so attached to my parents, I feel as I do toward most of my relatives. A close parent–son (in-law) relationship developed between my Dad and my maternal grandparents, whereas no such bond developed between my Mom and my paternal grandparents.

Hess and Markson (1980:258) have observed that distinctions between the roles of grandmother and grandfather are hazy. They conclude: "Once one becomes a grandparent, sex-linked expectations for behaviour seem to drop away, perhaps partially because of the asexuality that is erroneously generally accorded the old." Another reason is because of the androgynous features noted in bio-psychological aging: aging women and men everywhere seem to display the psychological traits and take on the physical appearance of the opposite sex (Guttman, 1976) after mid-life to a greater extent than at any previous age except early childhood. Older men show emotions that as youths and young adults they repressed. Nurturance toward grandchildren is an indulgence that grandfathers enjoy as much as grandmothers.

SIBLINGS

It seems logical that with smaller numbers of children born into modern families, older persons should have fewer brothers and sisters and family networks of support will become increasingly fragile. However, although the number of living siblings declines with age, most older adults today have at least one living sibling. In surveys conducted in the United States among persons sixty-five years of age or older, from 75 to 93 percent report at least one living brother or sister (Clark and Anderson, 1976; Scott, 1983; Cicirelli, 1980; Shanas et al., 1968). One recent study in the United States of older white, urban, middle-class adults has concluded that siblings, like grandchildren, were not as deeply involved as children in the social networks of older people, but they did have a visible supportive role (Scott, 1983). The investigators found that more assistance was exchanged as the siblings aged and that the sibling relationship is a more important source of support for the elderly when children of their own are not available. Shanas also found singles had more extensive contact with siblings than did the married or widowed.

The elderly often choose a sister or brother (or friend) as a *confidant* (Strain and Chappell, 1982). Among the widows in Martin Matthews's (1982) research, 50 percent specifically referred to a sister as one of the three people to whom they felt closest either currently or in the year before their husband's death. A high amount of contact between siblings has been found in some studies of elders. For example, Martin Matthews reported that a high 54 percent of the widows in her study had "at least one sibling . . . involved in at least one exchange in the social support system." Harvey (cited in Martin Matthews, 1985) found one out of four widows in her sample had contact with a sibling at least once a week, and one out of ten had contact more than once a week.

Whether sisters or brothers provide more or better support to elderly siblings remains open. Contrary to earlier findings in the United States, Scott (1983) found no evidence to support a stronger sister bond among the elderly; relations with siblings in his study were equally divided by gender. That is, closeness and contact were as likely to be with a brother as with a sister for both women and men. There is no apparent reason why gender equity in sibling relationships of elders should not exist in Canada as well.

The dyadic relationships of elders that have been studied most are the intimate ones reviewed in this section. Only now are relations with cousins, aunts and uncles, and other relatives in support systems of seniors beginning to be investigated. In the next section, we turn to support networks, examining particularly the relationship of kin networks to social class and ethnic background.

MODELS OF KIN NETWORKS

The focus on the married couple by American sociologists goes back to the early studies of the family in the 1930s. The intergenerational model was established about twenty years ago and is now strongly entrenched in the North American study of the family ties of elders. Since a symposium on "The Family, Intergenerational Relations and Social Structures," held at Duke University in 1963, family-kin linkages in which elders are involved have been viewed by gerontologists in terms of old persons being located at the narrow top of a set of overlapping, lineally related conjugal units which broadens at the base.

These lineally linked nuclear family households are normally headed by men; they are ideally financially self-sufficient. This notion of the family-kin networks of the elderly includes mainly (1) the elderly couple or widowed persons, (2) the adult married children and spouses, and (3) grandchildren, all in frequent contact and emotionally close even when living apart. This has recently been termed a *lineage* (Bengston and Cutler, 1976; Rosenthal, Marshall, and Synge, 1980). The validity of conceptualizing the support networks of all, or even most, elders in terms of a lineage is now being questioned.

The concept of lineage, of course, is associated in everyday usage with an elite group, with wealth and succession. Feudalism, with its strict social class divisions, provided fertile ground for great lineages to develop and perpetuate themselves, mainly through the male bloodlines. In modern society, remnants of lineage can be observed primarily in the propertied upper and middle classes. As the major providers and husbanders of family income, male heads in each of the households organize and control money and investments. Although in social matters women form socio-emotional ties between the domestic units, the form of interhousehold relations is largely determined by the principle of succession by younger generations. Consequently, household links take a lineal form. Material aid for children and their spouses and offspring is provided by the older couple. In the research on elders, which is often based on middle-class respondents, financial assistance flows mostly from the older generation to the younger (Cheal, 1983; Stone, 1988), although the situation has been found to be reversed for other kinds of assistance when parents grow old (Adams, 1980; Stone, 1988).

Recently, another model than the lineal one has been advanced to understand the support systems of elders. It was first suggested by the research on working-class and minority families. Rapp (1982) constructed a composite picture of women-centred kin networks from a number of U.S. studies that span the years from the late 1940s to the present. In working- and lower-class families, the task is to produce and distribute the scarce resources of all members of the family-kin network, regardless of bloodlines or residence. The point is to assure the well-being of all persons considered to be related under conditions of relatively constant financial difficulty. The instability in household incomes and the inadequacy of the husband's wages to maintain a domestic unit make it impossible for such families to achieve the cultural ideal of the independent nuclear family household. The realities of their poverty result in pooling, borrowing, and sharing resources between all kinds of households, not just those that are generationally linked. Family-kin networks of working-class people include siblings and their spouses and children to a greater extent than those of the middle class, and also more distantly related persons such as aunts and uncles and cousins, as well as elderly parents. Women are at the centre because they not only perform traditional household services that cannot be purchased, such as child care and homemaking, but they also have more certain employment opportunities in service-connected occupations when their men folk are laid off from their jobs or are unemployed. Older women often provide social security cheques (see Cruiksank, 1971, for parallels among natives in the Canadian North). Households with the least stable incomes shelter fluctuating groups of people who move in and out of each other's homes. *Fictive kinship*, by which friends are turned into family, is taken seriously in these networks.

The concept of lineage obviously does *not* apply to lower- or working-class family organization. This is not because three or more generations do not exist, although the average life span is shorter for poor people than for the wealthy, nor because the tasks of the working-class family are different from those of middle- and upper-class families, since both are charged with child care, socialization, and the physical and emotional well-being of all family members. The concept of lineage does *not* apply because the limited and uncertain resources of working-class, nuclear family households do not allow for *generativity*, or sponsorship, of the second and third generation by the oldest. Instead, the entire family-kin network is required to organize for survival on a day-to-day basis. A more appropriate metaphor than the line for perhaps as many as one-third or more of elderly people with family involvements is an outspread net. Its boundaries are indeterminate, and it can be unravelled and repaired as old lives end and new ones are born or marry into it. The *nodal points* are women, many of them middle aged and older. In fact, lineage may not apply either to the family-kin networks of older middle-class women after widowhood or divorce (see Nett, 1982, for a more comprehensive discussion of problems in the family study of older women).

The analysis of family and social class in Britain, the United States, and Denmark made by Shanas et al.(1968) points to social class as a major source of heterogeneity in the kin networks of the elderly. The number of living children, the kind of living arrangements, distance from and frequency of contact with relatives, and patterns of interaction and help were all found to vary depending on whether the elders were of white-collar (middle-class), blue-collar (working-class), or agricultural background. In fact, for her U.S. sample, Shanas found percentages of people sixty-five and older living in the households of relatives ranged from a low of 15 percent for married middle-class women to a high of 57 percent for unmarried working-class women. Recent research conducted in Canada by Corin (1987), comparing social support networks of elders in the inner city (lower class) with those in an urban suburb (middle class), lends weight to the idea of considerable variation in the form of the family-kin networks of elders. This research uncovered the fact that, compared with the suburb, in the inner city a smaller proportion of spouses and children and a larger proportion of siblings and other kin were mentioned by elders as being present, important, and involved on a day-to-day basis. This picture is more in keeping with the widespread net model than the lineage model of family organization.

Because social class and ethnic background are somewhat intertwined, and so little systematic research has been conducted on their effects on the family life of seniors, clear answers to questions regarding variation due to ethnicity (subculture) are difficult to find. Driedger and Chappell (1987:63–95) have summarized research that has found that elders in various ethnic groups have different marital statuses, preferences for and actual living arrangements, interaction patterns within families, and support networks. Outstanding are the following selected observations: when compared to non-natives, elderly natives are more likely to live with a family member or in extended family households; the most likely to live alone are elderly Chinese (because of restrictions on family immigration in an earlier period); the least likely to live alone are elderly Italians;

Dutch elders are more frequently married than any other group; the French have greater access to relatives; Ukrainians report more frequent interaction with sons than with daughters; the highest proportions of those without children are of British and French ancestry; and elders who do not identify themselves in terms of any ethnic origin do not appear to be significantly different from those who do in regard to the size of their social support network. Table 11.5 shows the great difference found by Bienvenue and Havens (1986) in Manitoba between the amount of help provided to native elders by family and friends (informal assistance), compared to non-natives who receive much more assistance from formal services.

Despite the failure for a clear-cut picture to emerge regarding the importance of ethnic background in family-kin relations of elders, considerable evidence exists that elders in certain ethnic groups, whether they are natives, recent immigrants, or longer-term discriminated against groups, are disadvantaged. They less frequently obtain adequate services for supplementing family support, and their utilization of housing benefits and long-term care facilities is less than that of elders in groups with more power (Driedger and Chappell, 1987; Ujimoto, 1987; Bienvenue and Havens, 1986). Socio-economic status, rather than ethnicity per se, may be the determining factor in how one's family life is affected by growing old. Rural and urban residence, too, is involved in different patterns of living, interaction, and social support for elders of various ethnic origins. Rural elders are just now beginning to be better understood (see Cape, 1987; Corin, 1987; Bond et al., 1987).

Table 11.5 Types of Assistance for Native and Non-Native Elderly (in Percentages)[a]

Help With	Natives		Non-Natives	
	Formal Assistance	Informal Assistance	Formal Assistance	Informal Assistance[b]
Meals	3.2(2)	96.7(60)	20.4(233)	79.6(1,141)
Shopping	3.6(2)	96.4(55)	24.3(258)	75.6(1,057)
Housework	4.8(3)	95.2(60)	25.0(309)	75.0(926)
Repairs	15.7(11)	89.3(59)	58.6(1,033)	41.4(729)
Finances	10.2(4)	89.8(39)	26.0(185)	74.0(526)

Note: N in parentheses.
[a]Percentages based on total number who required assistance. The Total N's differ by item since the number of persons requiring assistance varied by response category.
[b]Informal Assistance refers to services from family or friends. This was assessed on the basis of "who" usually helps with certain tasks.

Source: Rita M. Bienvenue and Betty Havens, "Structural Inequalities, Informal Networks: A Comparison of Native and Non-Native Elderly," *Canadian Journal on Aging* 5, no. 4 (1986):246.

THE FUTURE OF FAMILIES WITH ELDERS

In discussing population projections by age for Canada, Havens (1982) divided her speculations into certainties and uncertainties. We follow her lead as we contemplate the future of families in an aged society. (According to the United Nations definition, a population is considered "aged" when more than 7 percent of it is over sixty-five.)

THE CERTAINTIES

Regarding our already "old" population, Havens (1982:16) foresaw with certainty that "over the next 50 years the population structure will be aging more rapidly." Other trends will no doubt also continue. They include low birth rates, increased longevity for both sexes, and even greater longevity for women. These will co-exist with the cultural trends already in evidence, such as increased labour force participation for women at all ages (which alternatively may have a negative effect on longevity), the strong preference for autonomous living, and the voluntariness in family relationships. As far as families are concerned, more married people will survive middle age and enter the post-parental and retirement phases. Although the trends indicate widowhood at a very old age for the average woman, there will be an increase of widows in the aged population as a whole. Unfortunately, we have not had the space in this chapter to discuss the problems for families of widowhood in old age; however, losing a spouse is a major crisis at any age, and it is best coped with by elders who have the emotional support of family and friends (see Connidis, 1989; Gee and Kimball, 1987; Chappell, Strain, and Blandford, 1986; McDaniel, 1986; Martin Matthews, 1985; and Novak, 1988).

Another certainty for families with elders is that cross-generational and cross-household relationships will become more complicated than they were in the past. Already the problems of the *caught generation* are being discussed. These are people, middle-aged or older, who look forward to experiencing the freedom of the empty nest when children grow up and leave home, but who instead continue to be involved with adult children and grandchildren and at the same time are required to take on the new responsibility of their very old parents and in-laws (Neugarten, 1979; Rosenthal, 1982). Widowed elders and older married couples are now able to remain in the community until they reach extreme old age, but only with considerable assistance and support from family, friends, and community services. It seems likely that middle-aged sons and daughters will continue to be a dependable resource in the care of elderly parents, along with other kin and friends and publicly provided assistance and services.

While middle-aged women particularly will be actively carrying on with their traditional roles of nurturing and caretaking in helping aged parents, new tasks will also confront mid-life and older sons and daughters. They will be intervening in the bureaucracy that now surrounds family life and aging to ensure that their elders receive their old age security benefits, Canada and Quebec pensions and supplements, and other entitlements; they will be dealing with the red tape of hospitals and other service organizations that can confuse an older person. They will also be helping to make decisions, often in conflict with siblings and other relatives, regarding institutionalization, terminal illness, and death. Hess and Markson (1980:266) have concluded:

There is an ironic symmetry here as the child supervises the parent's death in much the same setting as the parent gives life to the child. Although these decisions can bring renewed closeness to family members, they can also become occasions for displays of guilt and grief.

Another irony associated with families is the potential for neglect and abuse of vulnerable members. It has only been since the 1960s that society has acknowledged the risks to children in the home and since the 1970s that spouse abuse has been recognized as a problem (see Chapter Twelve). In the 1980s, domestic abuse and neglect of the elderly finally has been brought to the attention of the public. A review of the research clearly indicates that "the most common causes of neglect and abuse appear to include the consequences of adult caretakers being over-taxed by the requirements of caring for a frail dependent adult" (Douglas, 1983:401). Douglas goes on to say the following:

> A family that is already at the brink of crisis for any reason will only be more quickly thrown into a disastrous chain of events when a frail and dependent parent presents unexpected problems and demands on the family's physical, emotional, and financial resources.

It should be noted that "caring for" one's elderly parents or spouse means different things to different people. One researcher has distinguished between *care providers* and *care managers* (Archbold, 1983). In the middle class and above, family members with frail, elderly relatives are likely to be care managers, arranging for other people to do the actual looking after on a day-to-day, hour-to-hour basis. Providers, generally the spouse and/or the daughter, are more likely to be members of the working or lower class; they suffer more than the arrangers because of decreased freedom in their own lives, a lack of privacy, constant daily irritation, and guilt. Archbold (1983:144) concludes: "Women who care for severely functionally impaired parents are an at-risk and under-served population. They often live under extreme stress and hardship." There is some suggestion that spouses suffer more burden from care-giving than do adult children. They may have health problems themselves and have fewer financial and physical resources. Non-family services to relieve them are not available and are not well distributed in society.

If the presumed present pattern of obligation being subordinate to affection in family-kin relations is permitted to operate, there is no reason to expect that great numbers of old people will be emotionally abandoned by their families. On the other hand, it is possible that the number of elderly who are isolated from kin will increase as the result of smaller-sized families and that the burden of caretaking will increasingly be perceived as an onerous duty, rather than a labour of love.

THE UNCERTAINTIES

In that vast terrain of unknowns about future social life, we can pick out at least two aspects that will probably affect family relations of the elderly. One is the slow but inevitable changes that occur in all family systems as they adapt to societal dynamics; the other, the policies that are formulated in a rationalized society in response to an aging trend and also to profound economic turmoil.

Turning first to policy matters, over the last fifty or sixty years there has been a change in public attitudes regarding family responsibility for the financial support of elders and a growth in government programs providing for the elderly. From the passing of the Old Age Pensions Act in 1927, in an atmosphere where many people in power strongly believed that individual families should "look after their own," Canadians have come a long way to the six layers of provision for the elderly espoused by present-day governments (Chappell, 1980:37). The six layers are: old age security payments, guaranteed income supplements, Canada/Quebec Pension Plan, various provincial supplements, private pension plans and private savings, and hospitalization and medical services. However, as Chappell further points out, recent years have witnessed "an increasing dissatisfaction on the part of the elderly, of welfare organizations, of both provincial and federal governments, and of others" with this patchwork system. Elderly Canadians are becoming increasingly assertive on their own behalf and have exercised increased power over the political arena.

From the perspective of governments, the current programs are costly, and as Baker (1988) says, "with the aging of the baby-boom generation, social benefits, facilities and services for the elderly will have to be expanded at greater cost to the Canadian taxpayer." However, as she further notes, "we can expect little public resistance to expanding services and facilities, since we have now come to rely on these benefits." It is a fact that the average income drops by about half after retirement. It is also a fact that the poorest people in our population are older women and that widowhood is especially impoverishing because of the lack of pension coverage for housewives and dependants. Furthermore, although policy makers view the aged as "service recipients" (Estes, 1980), it is a fact that the families of the elderly, especially the women in them, are "service providers." Even from an economics angle, the cash value of family services at this point in time far exceeds the combined cost of formal services to community-living elderly and to institutionalized elderly (Tobin and Kulys, 1980).

CONCLUSION

Some of the uncertainties with regard to policy that might affect families of the elderly can be summarized as follows: (1) whether the government will try to put more of the financial burden for elders on families, or whether it will reform the present pension system to the point where benefits are more equitable for the poor and for women; and (2) whether the government will favour middle-class and wealthy families by offering tax benefits only to those who provide income assistance for elderly dependent relatives or by offering subsidies and guaranteed loans to build onto houses in order to accommodate elderly relatives, or instead, whether it might also provide compensation and services, such as home nursing and homemaker services, to assist those family members who are caring for their aged. Meals on Wheels, transportation, day care facilities for the elderly, respite care, family counselling, and special housing in the community are important services. Rational policies for the aged would provide the resources to assist families (especially women) in doing what society already socializes its members to want to do – feel and express concern for each other throughout life. They would not require families to do what they cannot do, or what other organizations can do better.

The other set of uncertainties is associated with sociocultural changes. These are extremely difficult to extrapolate from past trends or fluctuations in the economy. Divorce and reconstituted family households, women's higher education and labour force participation, the striking down of the constitutionality of a forced retirement age, and the redefinition of friendship in this part of the century are only some factors that suggest changes in families of the future, with implications for aging. The extension of kin networks through remarriage may cast into doubt our certainty that elders of the future will have fewer kin. New patterns of employment after the age of sixty-five could result in changed ideas of dependency in the later years and give a decided financial advantage to at least some of the elderly; this might also increase their political power within their family-kin networks. The blurring of distinctions between friends and families that Adams (1974) saw emerging in this century may be taking us toward a society in which peer relations, family and non-family alike, assume equal importance with intergenerational relations during old age (Chappell, 1981). Such changes, in turn, will have consequences for both family and old age policies.

DISCUSSION QUESTIONS

1. Why would there have been temporary interruptions in the slow, continuous process of aging that the Canadian population has been undergoing for over a century? At what specific periods in time did they occur?
2. What would lead people today to think that old people were better cared for by families in the past, and what are the facts about family involvement with elders in the past and today?
3. What are the living arrangements of people over sixty-five years of age? Are they more or less likely to be living in families today than in 1961? Why?
4. What percentage of people over the age of sixty-five years are married? Discuss the marital satisfaction of wives and husbands during the last two phases of marriage and some of the factors involved in the pattern.
5. What are some of the new responsibilities that you can see emerging for middle-aged and even older adults in relationship to their very old parents or other relatives?
6. What similarities and differences did Marshall, Rosenthal, and Synge (1982) find between women and men in regard to their concerns about their parents' future health? How do their findings fit in with what you have observed in your own family, or in the families of friends and acquaintances?
7. What difference does social class make in the kinds of family-kin networks with which older people might be involved, and why are there differences? What model of kin network – lineage or net – do you think best fits native families living in the core area of Winnipeg? Italian families in the Italian neighbourhoods of Toronto? Other recently arrived immigrant families?
8. What kinds of policy issues concerning families in an aging society do you think will have to be addressed in the coming years? How will these decisions be made?

chapter twelve

Patterns of Family Violence

INTRODUCTION

Our ideal vision of how the family ought to function emphasizes the love and financial and emotional support family members give to one another. We often think of the family as providing a refuge and a peaceful oasis from the frustrations of the outside world. Many families supply these benefits, yet we are now coming to recognize that some also use force intentionally and repeatedly to injure or kill their own members. Verbal degradation and threatening are frequent and are sufficiently potent to have serious effects on the victim. In addition, husbands and wives assault each other, siblings fight, parents spank children and abuse their elderly parents in various ways. Abuse can be physical, sexual, financial, and emotional.

At times, the types and degree of violence are shocking. Victims have been burned with irons, cigarettes, acid, and scalding liquids; they have had their eyes gouged out and their bones broken; their internal organs have been damaged and their bodies lacerated and mutilated with a variety of objects, including glass bottles, knives, and hatchets. Surgery is sometimes required and victims may even die from the injuries. The detrimental impact of psychological, mental, and financial abuse can also be severe, but these have been more difficult to study. Therefore, physical and sexual abuse are the main topics of discussion in this chapter. Specifically, the goal here is to explain the most injurious forms of physical and sexual assault.

OFFENDER-TARGET PATTERNS OF FAMILY VIOLENCE

Although there are instances where women sexually victimize children, where wives batter husbands, where children beat up on their parents, and where the elderly abuse their caretakers, these are not as pervasive as the assault of women and children. The targets of serious intrafamily violence are not randomly selected. A review of literature by Finkelhor (1983) reveals a pattern wherein the strongest family members victimize the weakest members. Husbands direct their violence at wives, and parents direct their violence at children, in part because the offenders have greater economic and physical power. Historical and contemporary cultural and legal forces support these power differentials.

One study found wife assault was about twenty times more likely in male-dominant families where the husband had more power than in equalitarian families where husbands and wives shared decision making equally (Straus, Gelles, and Steinmetz, 1980). This and a Calgary survey (Brinkerhoff and Lupri, 1988) found that women working full-time were less likely to be beaten than wives who worked part-time or not at all outside the home. These data suggest that economic dependence makes wives more vulnerable to their partners' violence. Alternatively, women who are financially more independent may be more likely to choose non-violent partners.

The most injurious effects of child abuse are suffered by the least powerful children, usually those under the age of six (Gelles, 1979; Kohn, 1977; Maden and Wrench, 1977; Straus, Gelles, and Steinmetz, 1980). The negative results of power imbalances are also apparent in the sexual abuse of children, where most reported cases are of fathers victimizing their daughters (Finkelhor, 1979).

THE RELATIONSHIP BETWEEN VARIOUS FORMS OF FAMILY VIOLENCE

Researchers are just beginning to investigate the relationship between various forms of spouse-to-spouse, parent-to-child, and sibling-to-sibling sexual and physical abuse. The evidence suggests that victims become aggressors and violence begets violence (Chimbos, 1976, 1978; Decima, 1988; Straus, Gelles, and Steinmetz, 1980). An analysis by Straus (1983) finds support for the view that abuse and the widespread use of ordinary physical punishment contribute to the high rate of sibling violence, child abuse, and wife beating. Children who are repeatedly abused (punched, kicked, beaten, or threatened with a knife or gun) by parents and those who experience frequent and severe culturally permissible punishment are far more likely to assault their parents. Wives who have been beaten frequently by their husbands are more likely to assault their children and their husbands.

In addition, parents who are physically punished during their childhood are more likely to employ ordinary forms of physical punishment with their own children, and are also more likely to abuse their children and their spouses. Violence begets violence because children tend to pattern their behaviour after that of their parents who lack non-violent skills to express feelings and resolve conflict. Witnessing assault teaches specific aggressive behaviours, that physical force is a legitimate means of imposing one's wishes upon another, that violence is permissible when other things don't work, that those who love you also hit you, and that you can also hit those you love. MacLeod (1980:14) reports that over one-third of the battered women interviewed in Canadian shelters and over half their husbands had been beaten as children.

The links between love, possessiveness, sex, and violence are just beginning to be researched. Women in many countries are socialized to believe that their partners beat them because they love them. Eisaku Sato, former Japanese prime minister and winner of the Nobel Peace Prize, was not a pacifist at home. His wife reported: "He often used to beat me because he is not the sort of man who can express his affection in words" (*The Toronto Star*, 1980:C1).

The prevalence of violent marital rape (Finkelhor and Yllo, 1985; Russell, 1982; Vallee and Stafford, 1986) and incest (Badgley, 1984; Russell, 1986) is now well documented. Walker's study of battered wives found that most had been raped by their batterers and reported some of the "most unusual kinky sex" that Walker had heard of during her ten years of practice as a clinical psychologist (1979:108). Many wives "stated ashamedly that they had initially enjoyed their lover's possessiveness as proof of his love" (1978:113). Later, the sexual jealousy became oppressive and an excuse to precipitate a battering. The batterer usually accused the woman of having sexual affairs with other men and sometimes even with other women who were kind to her.

As with most findings in social science, the relationship between being a victim or witness of violence and engaging in violence oneself is not perfect. Not all witnesses and victims are abusers. Some abusers have been neither witnesses nor victims. Clearly, many other factors are involved in fully accounting for why some are more likely than others to engage in violent behaviour and why the violence started in the first place.

Our focus in this chapter will be on understanding the combination of economic, psychological, institutional, and cultural factors that maintain the patterns of the most powerful members abusing the least powerful members. Understanding these factors should help us formulate effective policies to reduce the numbers of victims and to make the family a safer place for all its members. Before detailing these factors, it is important to understand that rates of family violence do not seem to have changed much over the decade from 1975 to 1985. It is also necessary to understand some of the problems evident in widely cited research that claims to measure the incidence and patterns of family violence.

FOR INTEREST

UNDERSTANDING THE DIMENSIONS OF ELDER ABUSE

By Elizabeth Podnleks

Most of Canada's 2.75 million elderly enjoy strong, healthy ties with their families, friends and caregivers. But a significant number of older adults aren't happy or safe, and are being victimized in their homes by family members, informal caregivers, friends and landlords, or in the case of the 10 percent of older Canadians living in institutions, by formal caregivers.

Elder abuse is not a new phenomenon, but no one is sure how widespread it is. . . .

Researchers do know that no one is dealing with elder abuse and neglect effectively. No one government, agency or group alone can eliminate it. The majority of cases are criminal offenses, and should be treated as such. . . .

Several provinces, including Newfoundland, Prince Edward Island, Nova Scotia and Alberta, have enacted laws for the protection and guardianship of older people. Only Nova Scotia's legislation provides for mandatory reporting (the legal requirement for professionals to report instances of abuse). It's still a contentious issue. The model for mandatory reporting is based on child welfare laws, and many see the reporting requirement as an infringement on the rights of older adults. Mandatory reporting has severe consequences for both the victim and the abuser when the allegation is disclosed. The result can be premature institutionalizaton – not necessarily the most humane action for the victim. Special protection of guardianship is needed in cases of mental incompetency.

In the United States, where over 40 states have adopted mandatory reporting statutes, needless investigations have been conducted and money has been spent that would have been better used to develop new or additional services.

An encouraging alternative to mandatory reporting is voluntary reporting. . . . However, mandatory reporting of abuse in long-term care facilities is considered essential, because clients are virtually powerless and dependent on their professional caregivers. There is a high incidence of financial exploitation in Canada. . . .

It's essential to document the incidence and prevalence of elder abuse, to clarify terms, and to develop assessment tools and protocols. There is also a pressing need for social and emotional support systems for professional caregivers working in long-term care facilities. Their work is demanding; abuse may be triggered by personal, environmental or economic stress. Caregivers need support, positive reinforcement for their valuable contribution, and help to manage stress before it manifests itself in abuse.

Elder abuse is a complex, hidden problem that won't go away. It occurs oftener and is more grievous than we like to think. Using a collaborative approach, it is everyone's collective responsibility to develop holistic, humanistic programs aimed at the prevention of elder abuse.

Source: *Vis-à-Vis*, National Newsletter on Family Violence (The Canadian Council on Social Development, Autumn 1988): 6, no. 3.

RESEARCH ON PATTERNS OF INTRAFAMILY VIOLENCE

People often speculate about whether the rate of family violence in our society has increased or decreased over time. The media's emphasis upon increased reporting of violence to police and child protective services, such as the Children's Aid Society, often gives the misleading impression that there is more violence now than in the past. In fact, there may be a decline in actual incidence if the increasing population and the professional involvement by police, government, hospitals, and social workers are taken into account. These factors could cause higher rates of reporting, but a decline in actual incidence.

Two similarly designed, large-scale national U.S. studies, the first conducted in 1975-76 and the second in 1985, suggest no major change in the incidence of wife and child assault (Straus and Gelles, 1986). The decline in parental violence toward children and husband-to-wife violence was only 1 percent and not statistically significant. The 1 percent decline could reflect a chance error, rather than a real decrease in violence in the population. It could also reflect differences in the survey methodologies and sampling biases of the two studies. For example, the 1975-76 survey data were collected by face-to-face interview, whereas telephone interviews were used in 1985; also the response rate was lower for the 1975-76 survey (65 percent versus 85 percent in 1985).

In both studies, the researchers measured violence using a self-report instrument known as the Conflict Tactics Scale (CTS). When the scale was first developed in the 1970s, it seemed adequate. In the intervening years, however, there has been an explosion of valid criticism documenting serious inadequacies (for example, Browne, 1987; Dobash and Dobash, 1979; Small, 1985; Smith, 1987; Szinovacz, 1983). The CTS defines violence as the occurrence of at least one of eight items. The first three – throwing something; pushing, grabbing, or shoving; and slapping or spanking – are regarded as "minor" forms of violence even though the consequence might require emergency room treatment. The last five – kicking, biting, or hitting with a fist; hitting or trying to hit with something; beating up; threatening with a knife or gun; and using a knife or gun – make up a "severe" violence subscale because the researchers *speculated* that these behaviours were more likely to cause serious harm (Straus, Gelles, and Steinmetz, 1980:210). No data are collected on the consequences or resulting harm, or the intention of causing harm. All eight items together form an "overall" violence index.

PARENT–CHILD VIOLENCE

Analysis of the 1985 responses of the Straus and Gelles study showed that 63 percent of parents said they had at some time used "overall" violence on a referent child, that is, a particular three- to seventeen-year-old child selected from within the family for the study. Younger children were subject to "overall" violence in higher proportions (97 percent of three year olds) than older children (one-third of fifteen to seventeen year olds). The overall rate of "severe" parent-to-child violence was 14 percent.

SPOUSAL ABUSE VERSUS ASSAULT OF WOMEN

The reports on "spousal abuse" in both the 1975-76 and 1985 U.S. surveys made sensational news. The authors reported that "women are about as violent within the family as men," and also that there is "even greater violence by husbands" (Straus and Gelles, 1986:470, 471). Those two statements are contradictory, and left readers confused.

The CTS scale was imported to Canada and yielded similar results in a survey of Calgary couples (Brinkerhoff and Lupri, 1988:407-34). The sample of both members of 562 couples provided an opportunity to compare husbands' and wives' reports to see if the Conflict Tactics Scale provided valid findings on what the authors call "interspousal violence." The authors state, however, that they decided to ask each partner only if she or he had committed a violent act against her or his partner and to refrain from asking about the wife's or husband's own victimization because they thought that asking both partners about behaviours on the CTS might "incite abuse" among the couples. The speculation seems far-fetched given the voluntary participation of respondents and assurances of confidentiality for any information they provided.

Crime surveys, medical records, police reports, civil and criminal court records, and most people working with victims of spousal assault consistently find that wives are far more likely than husbands to be injured seriously in domestic disputes. A U.S. National Crime Survey (1982) shows that in 91 percent of all violent crimes between spouses, victims were women. Dobash and Dobash (1979) found that women in Scotland were victims in 99 percent of reported cases of spousal assault. A survey of seven major Canadian cities (Solicitor General, 1983) found the wife to be the victim in 90 percent of incidents of spousal assault. In assaults between former spouses, the ex-wife was the victim in 80 percent of cases. An analysis of 606 "assault" and "threatening" reports to the Hamilton police department found 95 percent of the victims were women (Byles, 1980). Kincaid's (1982) study similarly found that of 3,125 cases in Ontario family court records, 95 percent of the victims were wives; when husbands were assaulted, the attacks were generally less severe.

Despite the evidence showing that wives are far more likely to be victims of serious assault, news of "scientific evidence" of "battered husbands" and "spousal violence" is spreading in academic journals and the popular press. Further, the data are often being used – intentionally or not – to protect perpetrators of violence. Regardless of the newsmaker's intent, mutuality statements and terminology tend to create ambivalence toward, if not outright rejection of, theories and public policy that might reduce wife assault. For example, data from the U.S. poll were used by some men's rights groups and others dedicated to protecting male perpetrators to argue against funding more shelters for women, presumably because battered men had as much need for the money. The data were also used to defend male batterers, presumably on the basis of self-defence (Straus and Gelles, 1986). Advocates of mutuality statements too often fail to recognize that the numerous studies finding men and women to be equally violent are all based on the same invalid instrument, the Conflict Tactics Scale. A faulty lens is not going to result in a clear picture – even if that "lens" is used in hundreds of surveys and with thousands of respondents in countries around the world.

PRESSURES TO MAINTAIN MUTUALITY MYTHS AND LANGUAGE

The term "spousal abuse" is misleading because it implies that women initiate violence and injure their victims as often and as severely as men. This is not the case. Using the term "assault" reminds us that this behaviour is *criminal*, and has been acknowledged as such both by Canadian legislators and the public in general. The evidence is, however, that this behaviour is often not treated as criminal and that this enables the behaviour to be perpetuated. A term that reminds us of the criminality of violent behaviour might help to end this pattern. Although the term "abuse" is sometimes used in this chapter because of its widespread acceptance by child protection agencies, it conjures up contradictory images of the forms and seriousness of a wide range of behaviours. Second, it probably does not bring with it images of police intervention befitting its criminal status. And finally, the term "abuse" may subtly suggest that aggressive behaviours can be used so long as they are not abused, that hitting is permissible so long as it does not go "too far." The term "assault" serves to focus the reader on what the law specifies is criminal. In this chapter, laws past and present are discussed in some detail to show how both the wording and enforcement reflect and maintain attitudes that allow assault of women and children to continue.

Mutuality terms, when used, are more accurate when accompanied by numerous qualifying statements. For example, statistics on the nature of "spouse abuse" should be qualified by statements such as "but more women sustain injuries requiring medical treatment," and "but more men tend to initiate the battering." Even when qualified, however, mutuality terms and statements are still misleading. Qualifiers all too often "get lost" and forgotten in summaries of research. Furthermore, research based on the CTS could be manipulated to justify wife battering or to oppose the opening of more women's shelters that are desperately needed for effective prevention of family violence.

A CRITIQUE OF THE CONFLICT TACTICS SCALE (CTS)

The CTS is seriously deficient as an indicator of offender-target patterns. One reason is that behaviours such as choking, throwing a body, dragging by hair or feet, and raping – generally executed only by men – are omitted. A wife who kicks, bites, and struggles with her husband while he rapes and chokes her to unconsciousness scores high on the "serious" violence index, while her husband, who is not explicitly asked about his choking and sexual coercion, does not show up at all. Most proponents of mutuality statements miss this bias entirely on their list of qualifying statements. This limitation of the CTS for studying husband-to-wife violence is documented in Smith's (1987) telephone survey of Toronto women. Self-reports on the CTS yielded data showing 14.4 percent had been victims of violence during the year preceding the survey. Yet, when these women were given the opportunity to report additional abuses that were not specified in the CTS, the violence rate increased dramatically to 36.4 percent for the past year.

A second problem is that the CTS omits scoring information collected on the two items used primarily by men to intimidate wives, thus further biasing the data to give the appearance of mutuality. These two items are smashing or kicking some object, and threatening to hit, a criminal offence in Canada. Small (1985) observes:

> A violent husband often punches holes in the wall, kicks in doors, [and] smashes his fist down on the dinner table to show his wife what might happen to her if she gets out of line. Many women who never actually get hit live in constant fear from threats of this sort.

In in-depth interviews with eighty couples, Gelles (1972) found that no woman threatened her husband, but men often used the threat of violence to control their wives.

A third problem is that the scale is not sensitive to the more injurious, harmful effects of male violence. Again, this biases the data toward the myth of mutuality. The same act – for example, a punch or a slap – is far more likely to cause severe injury and pain when inflicted by a husband than a wife because of his greater average size and strength, yet the CTS treats them the same. Women may experience serious injuries as a result of their husbands throwing something or grabbing them, yet the husbands' behaviour is classified as "minor."

> A man who ... "pushed, grabbed, shoved or slapped" his wife was not considered a wife-beater, for these were defined as "mild" forms of

violence. Yet we know that a single slap from a strong-armed man can draw blood from a mouth and leave a swollen, black eye. A woman I know was shoved so hard against a kitchen cabinet she ended up with a broken nose (Small, 1985:160).

Smith's 1987 study of Toronto women found that behaviours resulting in serious injury were often wrongly classified as "minor" on the CTS.

A fourth problem is that the CTS researchers do not inform their respondents that "violence" is what they are claiming to study. Although the term violence connotes serious, injurious, and unlawful behaviour, the researchers collect no information confirming that the respondents' reports meet such criteria. The scale's lengthy introduction is misleading because it suggests the researcher's purpose is to collect information about normal common activity exhibited by both partners. It implies that all couples use verbal and physical methods when they "disagree," "just have spats because they are . . . tired," or when they "get annoyed," *not angry*, as is implied by the term violence. The respondents are asked to report on their own and their partner's activity in "a dispute," and the list of eighteen activities that follows begins with non-violent activities.

The failures to inform respondents of the scale's purpose and to determine the perpetrator's intent and extent of the victim's injury contribute to a fifth bias. Non-injurious and even mock aggression by women who report that they "hit" their husbands is classified as "severely violent" even if gentle hits or punches were intended and interpreted as non-violent by both spouses.

A sixth problem is that the CTS ignores the motivation and meaning of the acts and treats behaviour initiated by the husband for the purpose of punishing his wife exactly the same as her struggle to fight back in an attempt to end the violence. Research now finds that assaulted women fight back or hit out first in an attempt to stop or prevent a beating (Saunders, 1986). Forty-two percent of abused women in a Toronto shelter said they had "fought back" (Interval House, 1979:20). Walker (1984) found women were more likely to use violence against a violent partner than a non-violent one, and that they were largely motivated by self-defence, even preservation of their own and their children's lives.

Studies show that in homicide, the ultimate form of violence, a large proportion of women who kill their husbands do so in self-defence (Browne, 1987; McNulty, 1981; Vallee and Stafford, 1986). Chimbos (1976, 1978) interviewed five Canadian women who killed their husbands. All five had been victims of long-term beatings. Wolfgang (1957) found that violence was victim precipitated (initiated by the victim) in 60 percent of cases where wives retaliated by killing husbands, and in only 9 percent of cases where husbands killed wives. Husbands' violence is less likely to be in self-defence.

A seventh problem was revealed in a study by Szinovacz (1983) that compared responses of husbands and wives (103 couples). The couples disagreed considerably on the frequency and occurrence of specific tactics. Further, there was a strong likelihood of bias toward wives overreporting their violence (when compared to husbands' reports) and husbands underreporting (when compared to wives' reports) on the CTS, resulting in the false impression of mutuality:

> Not one husband acknowledged to "kicking, biting, hitting" his wife but . . .
> a few wives did report this behaviour on the part of their husbands. . . .
> Wives report more use of violent tactics by themselves than is acknowledged
> by their husbands (Szinovacz, 1983:642).

Experts working with abusive men note that men underreport assaultive violence by minimizing and denying the severity of their behaviour. The men "claim more involvement by the victim in justification of their violence than witness or police reports would support" (Browne, 1987:8).

An eighth problem is that the national U.S. studies using the CTS on men and women not married to each other report a higher refusal rate for men than for women. This could skew the data if the refusers are more violent.

A ninth problem is that although "spousal violence" advocates usually warn that more men initiate violence and more women sustain serious injuries, that message often takes a backseat to the false impression of mutuality.

In light of all these problems with the CTS, it would be foolish to use findings of mutuality as a basis for theorizing and developing public policies on family violence. Reports of "battered" husbands being equal to the problem of battered wives have been met with charges of a "battered data" syndrome (Pleck, Pleck, Grossman, and Bart, 1977-78). There is far more evidence that the abuse of women ought to remain the focus of intervention because:

> husbands had the higher rates of the most dangerous behaviours; husbands repeated their violence more often; husbands are more likely to do more damage because of their size differences; wives are economically trapped in marriage more often than husbands; and many wives may be using the violence to defend themselves (Saunders, 1986:48).

Violence events must be studied in their context, and more caution is needed by writers and academics in reporting simple counts of events and using mutuality labels when the intent and consequence of the event is unknown.

The remainder of this chapter details the main attitudinal and institutional supports for relatively powerful family members abusing relatively weak family members in wife and child assault. Many of the power imbalances that contribute to violence between husbands and wives originate and are tolerated and perpetuated by legal, religious, educational, familial, economic, and political institutions. These institutions support parent and spouse role expectations that often cause abusers to use assault to express anger at behaviour that challenges their power and dominance. Understanding the historical roots of roles and attitudes about spousal and parent-child relationships and how they have evolved helps explain why men hit women and why both parents hit children, both today and in the past. Sexism and ageism are clearly apparent in past and current knowledge, attitudes, and behaviour concerning family violence.

HISTORICAL ORIGINS AND CONTEMPORARY CULTURAL AND LEGAL SUPPORTS FOR WIFE ASSAULT

PAST LEGAL SUPPORT FOR PHYSICAL FORCE

The absence of clear-cut legal prohibitions and penalties for intrafamily violence throughout our society's history is a major reason for our present attitudes and relative lack of interest in punishing wife beaters. Prior to the nineteenth century, it was considered the husband's obligation to control, correct, and manage his wife and children through use of physical force (Dobash and Dobash, 1979; Martin, 1976). Old English common-law doctrines, later adopted in North America, permitted wife and child assault for correctional purposes.

Blackstone, who wrote an influential review of women's legal status in 1765, states that under the old English law a husband's domestic rights included general obedience to and respect for his wishes, conjugal rights, and sexual fidelity. Under the old common law, the husband had a right to *reasonably and moderately* chastise his wife, children, and servants:

> The civil law gave the husband . . . authority over his wife; allowing him, for some misdemeanors to beat his wife severely with scourges and cudgels; for others, only to use moderate chastisement (Blackstone, 1765:444).

References to "moderate" and "reasonable" were intentionally vague to allow individual discretion and enable excesses to be defined in terms of contemporary standards. Although the husband's right and duty to apply "corrections" began to be questioned in the 1600s, it was not until 1891 that the legal right of an English husband to chastise his wife was completely abolished. "Through the seventeenth, eighteenth, and nineteenth centuries, there was little objection within the community to a man's using force against his wife as long as he did not exceed certain tacit limits" (Dobash and Dobash, 1979:56).

Compared with what men were previously permitted to do to women, the now infamous "rule of thumb" was regarded by some as a major humanitarian achievement. In 1866, the Supreme Court of North Carolina declared in *State v. Rhodes* that a husband had a right to whip his wife with "a stick as large as his finger but not larger than his thumb" (cited in Lewis, 1922:416). In other states, wife beating was condemned even more severely, and by 1890 wife beating was illegal in most of North America (Lewis, 1922; Pleck, 1979).

There was a special offence of wife assault in the Canadian Criminal Code from 1901 to 1965 (Small, 1985:173). A man could go to jail for two years for beating his wife, but only if he caused her actual bodily harm. In 1920, Ontario Chief Justice Meridith said that the law that required a wife to be injured in order to get alimony was to be deplored:

> A husband may subject his wife, daily and even hourly, to such treatment as makes her life a veritable hell on earth and she is without remedy if she is robust enough to suffer it all without impairment of her physical health or her mentality (*Bagshaw v. Bagshaw* (1920), 48 O.L.R. 52).

CONTEMPORARY CULTURAL SUPPORTS FOR WIFE ASSAULT

Traditional Gender Roles

Unfortunately, attitudes that tolerated and perpetuated the abuse of women remained long after the laws permitting assault were repealed. Beliefs that wives should honour and obey husbands and that children should honour parents are perpetuated through religious and other socializing institutions. Recently, the practice of asking brides, but not grooms, to "obey" has been changed in most wedding ceremonies. More subtle connotations of possession are still reflected in the traditional nuptial pronouncement of "man and wife." In many marriages, the wife is still expected to be sexually available to her husband, to prepare his meals on time and clean the house properly, to accept his decisions, to keep herself attractive for him and generally make his life more pleasant. If she fails in any of her numerous duties, she may be subject to correction. Thus, a man in the National Film Board documentary "Loved, Honoured and Bruised" (1979) justifies his violence with, "I thought it was my job to discipline my wife and kids." Beating is a way of enforcing a husband's authority over his wife and of parents' authority over their children. Although many beatings happen repeatedly, sometimes all it takes is one to establish the power of the aggressor. Men gain from their use of violence if the result is that the wife tries to placate her husband. She may renew her efforts to please him.

Duty/Discipline

Our societal values and religious and legal practices provide the ideological and cognitive foundations that predispose some people to define violent acts as understandable and even acceptable in the context of the family. Aggressors often defend their actions by calling up positive ideals such as duty, discipline, love, and honour that serve to neutralize the disapproval usually felt when a bigger person hits a smaller one. Because cultural values support the use of a "reasonable" amount of force as long it is applied for the victim's own good, we hear rationalizations such as "She needed it," "I did it to keep her in line," and "It hurt me more than it hurt her." The offenders see themselves as putting the victim on the correct moral path and as being more knowledgeable and better informed than their victims.

Traditional gender-role socialization perpetuates the notion that a man ought to be head of the household and have superior authority, status, and rights. Wives learn to present the image of "Home Sweet Home" to the world and find it difficult to contemplate surviving outside their family role. One woman revealed:

> I felt afraid to go outside the house – afraid that people would find out, afraid of what they would say – that I was a bad wife and deserved it (MacLeod, 1980:29).

Women are still socialized to stay in a marriage, even when the marriage is bad. We say that "a woman's place is in the home," and that "a man's home is his castle." The image of the castle versus the home implies men can expect more from this setting. It also implies that outsiders have no right to interfere, a belief that increases the victim's vulnerability to repeated incidents of abuse.

Intermittent Reinforcement

A woman is also vulnerable when the aggressor is like Jekyll and Hyde. Dr. Jekyll is the part she falls in love with and that friends see. She experiences his transformation into Mr. Hyde alone and may regret promising "for better or worse, till death us do part." She is hooked on the high points (good times) in the relationship and not on the lows (violence), and thus it is incorrect to see her as masochistic. If she is addicted to anything, it is probably the love she wants and sometimes has, and not the violence. The abuser's good qualities act as powerful intermittent reinforcers in keeping the abused victim in a relationship that is not always violent and oppressive.

Some women have been socialized to blame themselves for repeated violence. They may feel that they deserved to be hit or asked for it because they nagged too much, were bad housekeepers, or because they made their husband jealous. Ministers, psychiatrists, and other counsellors may advise women to try to maintain the marriage and placate their abusers (Russell, 1982:210, 293). Husbands may blame their wives for their violence, and wives may believe them:

> He held a knife to her throat threatening to kill her, but instead of apologizing when he cooled down, he told her that she had messed up his life. It is not clear whether or not Mrs. Nelson is able to reject his view (Russell, 1982:211).

The Double Standard

Because large segments of our culture support a double standard, there is a greater expectation of sexual fidelity from the wife than from the husband. Many accounts of wife beating reveal that the husband suffers profound insecurity at even the possibility of the wife's betrayal and takes steps to prevent infidelity. For example, Kincaid's (1982:157-60) analysis of Ontario court records reports the following backgrounds to incidents of wife beating:

- Wife is not allowed to call anyone or go anywhere
- He feels insecure; doesn't want his wife to speak to other men
- Husband monitors wife's friendships
- Husband doesn't want wife to have any girlfriends
- He is jealous of wife getting jobs

These cases reflect the husband's concern about losing control over what (or whom) he has learned is his right to possess absolutely. That feeling of ownership often constitutes a major part of the abuser husband's identity.

Externalizing Blame

Offenders often avoid taking responsibility for their behaviour by blaming someone or something external to themselves – often the victim or the use of alcohol. Although most research finds a high correlation in the use of alcohol and situations of wife assault (Byles, 1980; Chimbos, 1976, 1978; Gil, 1973; Walker, 1979), it is not clear that drinking causes violence. An alternative possibility is that both the drinking and the violence are caused by other circumstances. Also, offenders may drink as an excuse to beat wives and children. Our society tends to excuse negative behaviour when someone is under the influence of alcohol, saying that people who are drunk are "not themselves." In fact, they could be "more themselves" when drunk than when sober. The victim may forgive him because "he was the nicest person when he didn't drink" (Russell, 1982:222). She hopes the beating is an isolated incident and that her often excessively dependent husband will reform. If she accepts her traditional role as a nurturer, she may feel responsible for rescuing him from his excesses.

Victim Dependency

The victims' dependent roles in the family prevent them from escaping their abusers (Gelles, 1976; MacLeod, 1980; Walker, 1979). Even middle- or upper-class women often are dependent economically on their husbands. Without money, the battered wife cannot support herself and her children. Even if she has the skills and experience necessary to get a job, her wages may not be sufficient to provide day care in addition to essentials such as food, clothing, and shelter. Russell's study of marital rape found that all nineteen wives who were the sole income earners at the time of the first wife rape were no longer married to the men who raped them. Russell (1982:222) views this as "powerful evidence that economic resources play a key role in why raped wives stay." The following explanations (MacLeod, 1980:28–29) of why women could not leave their assaultive husbands are typical:

- I was in a trap I couldn't get out of – having no money.
- I put up with not only physical abuse but all kinds of mental abuse also because I had six children to care for and needed a home and food for them which I couldn't provide myself.
- My husband used to beat me for years. Now we're divorced and he remarried. His new wife who has her own money – she controls the money and the man. There's no wife beating in this marriage.

Danger in Leaving

The lack of clear support by potential rescuers – for example, poor police response, non-enforced peace bonds, friends and family who say, "You made your bed; now lie in it" – and the reluctance to allow outside intervention in the home create fear and indecision. If a woman leaves a violent husband, he may pursue her, put her under surveillance, and use threats or physical force to bring her back; or he may threaten her or the children and the friends and family who give her assistance. A battered woman describes the problem (MacLeod, 1980:44):

> I was scared of him – he said he'd get his brother to take the kids away if he ended up in jail and that he'd spend all his time in jail figuring what to do with me when he got out. . . . After all, he is my husband and they are his children, too . . . what else could I do?

Sinclair (1985), who has worked with over seven hundred women and many of their husbands, reports that many are threatened with bodily harm or death if they attempt to leave or report the assault. Many wives told her stories similar to the following:

My husband threatened he would kill me with his bare hands if he ever got wind of my plans to leave him. He says, "If you leave me, I'll find you. No matter how long it takes, I'll track you down. You can't get away from me. When I find you you'll wish you were dead. I'll destroy that pretty face so no one will ever want you. I'll not only kill you but I'll destroy anyone who helps you get away from me. I'll kill you, the children and then I'll take my own life" (Sinclair, 1985:30).

Violence Continues for Separated/Divorced Women

The high rates of violence perpetrated against separated and divorced women by their ex-partners (Lupri, 1989; Smith, 1987) demonstrate the wisdom of women's concerns, as do these quotes:

> I have only raped a woman once and that was my ex-wife. I did not like it. It was recommended by a psychiatrist and I think it was a lousy recommendation (Male respondent, *The Hite Report on Male Sexuality*, by Shere Hite, 1981; cited in Russell, 1982:237).

> We had been divorced for a year. . . . He started slapping me, then pushed me on to the bed and started raping me (Russell, 1982:238).

Francine Hughes, whose story was told in *The Burning Bed* (McNulty, 1981) and in a widely viewed television movie, divorced her husband. This did not stop him from pursuing her and being infuriated by her self-assertion. One night, Mickey Hughes threw his former wife's night-class textbooks and notes about the house and then forced her to burn them. Because he believed that her studies were selfish activities that interfered with her domestic responsibilities, he threatened to take a sledge-hammer to her car to prevent her from driving to school again. He also pulled her hair, punched her repeatedly in the face and head, and threw a glass object at her for challenging his authority. Ex-husbands often believe they have the right to continue to control their ex-wives even when they are living apart or legally divorced. The woman who is faced with protracted court battles over money or custody and who lacks information about, and resources for, enforcing her rights does not always see leaving as a particularly viable alternative.

CONTEMPORARY LEGAL STATUTES AND PRACTICES CONCERNING WIFE ASSAULT

Although Canada's Criminal Code could be used to support prosecution of wife assaulters, most such assault is not reported to the police; therefore, in most cases of family violence the criminal justice system is not involved. Domestic calls make up a large proportion of complaints to the police, second only to motor accidents (Schlesinger, 1980); yet, only a small proportion of abused wives call the police and usually only after they have been assaulted many times before. Police then respond to only a fraction of the complaints and charge only a few offenders, even when there is *prima facie* evidence of an assault. The courts do not always convict the men who are charged, and rarely impose severe punishment.

Current Criminal Code

The assault provisions of Canada's Criminal Code make it an offence for anyone to hit or threaten to harm someone else.* Wives are not excluded from this provision, although caregivers of children are sometimes exempt. According to the Code, assault or violence may be physical or verbal, where the verbal is the threat of physical violence. The exact section of the Criminal Code that can be used to charge an offender depends on the kind of assault, ranging from common "assault" (s. 266 of the Criminal Code) when one person threatens another or acts violently against another's will by applying force, to the more serious charges of "assault causing bodily harm" (ss. 267 and 269) in cases where the victim is seriously injured, and to "aggravated assault" (s. 268) where the victim is wounded, maimed, disfigured, or has his or her life endangered.

An offender can also be arrested for "breach of the peace" (s. 31) or charged with "fearing" (s. 810):

> 810(1) Any person who fears that another person will cause personal injury to him or his spouse or child or will damage his property may lay an information before a justice.

A fearing charge differs from most others in that it need not be shown that a criminal offence has occurred. Persons can lay a fearing charge against their partner if they are willing to prove that they have reasonable grounds for fearing that their partner will injure them or their children. If the judge is convinced of this likelihood, the accused will be required to sign a court order to be on good behaviour and keep the peace and/or have no contact with the spouse and/or children for a specified time up to one year. Police often fail to enforce the orders (MacLeod, 1987:83). Even when they do and a breach results in a conviction, the penalty is relatively light (s. 811). The peace bond or restraining order has not been effective in stopping wife assault.

There are other criminal offences that may apply in rare cases. For example, since 1982 a husband can be charged with sexual assault of his wife whether or not they are living together (ss. 271, 272, 273, and 278). Other possible charges include administering a noxious substance (s. 245); attempting to choke, suffocate, or strangle another (s. 236(a)); causing a person to take a stupefying or overpowering drug, matter, or thing (s. 246(b)); pointing a firearm (s. 86.1); possession of a weapon or imitation (ss. 87 and 90); making harassing telephone calls and sending letters intended to alarm or injure (s. 372); mischief/damage of property/causing danger to life (s. 430); and attempted murder (s. 239).

A double standard of justice exists for all forms of assault. Offenders whose victims are family members are less likely to be charged, convicted, and punished than those whose victims are strangers. Although there are signs that police and the courts are increasingly likely to charge and convict family and *de facto* (meaning in practice, in fact,

---

*All sections in this chapter are taken from *Martin's Annual Criminal Code*, 1989.

or acting as if) family members, such as common-law spouses, step-parents, and foster parents, there is still some ambiguity about when it is appropriate for wives, police, or other social agencies to report, charge, and convict family or quasi-family as offenders.

Studies of North American practices reveal minimal intervention in the home by police and courts. Extrapolating from a number of U.S. and Canadian studies, Dutton (1988) estimates that only 1,400 of 10,000 assaulted women call police, who then arrest only 150 offenders. Seventy-five of these men are convicted, and only thirty-seven are punished with a jail sentence or a fine. If these estimates are correct, then for every one thousand women repeatedly assaulted, less than five men are punished.

Police Discretion

Some police lay charges only when they actually witness the assault (Roy et al., 1982). Even *prima facie* evidence of assault such as visible physical injury does not assure arrest. The underutilization of the arrest option may be unwise in light of the evidence that arrest tends to decrease recidivist assault (Jaffe, Wolfe, Telfor, and Austin, 1986; Sherman and Berk, 1984). In London, Ontario, women were beaten as many as thirty-five times before they called police; injury was evident in 36 percent of women attended by police, with 17 percent requiring medical attention, yet the police arrest rate was only 3 percent (Jaffe and Burris, 1981). A 1974–75 study of 606 assault complaints recorded by the Hamilton police force found injury was evident in 54 percent of the victims, yet Byles (1980) found no record of the police laying any assault charges. Instead, 76 percent of the victims were referred to a court, "presumably with the suggestion that they lay an assault charge" (Byles, 1980:5). Legally married women tended to be referred to family court and *de facto* wives referred to criminal court. By telling the victims to lay the charges themselves, the police put victims at a disadvantage in the likelihood of getting a charge and conviction (Burris and Jaffe, 1983).

> The chances of success in Court are generally higher when the police lay the charge themselves. So it is always better to convince the police to lay this charge, if you can (Backhouse et al., 1980:9).

In Canada, as elsewhere in the world, the police often justify their discretion not to charge by claiming the available evidence would not hold up in court. The victim's account of events can seldom be corroborated by other adult witnesses because beatings are often family secrets that take place behind closed doors. Many also believe that a wife cannot, or should not, testify against her husband. At marriage, the husband and wife are united, and where their opinions differ the husband's view should prevail.

Court Prosecution and Judicial Leniency

Criminal prosecution is particularly complex because the victims are sometimes unwilling to carry through a legal action (Thompson and Gilby, 1980). Their reasons for this are similar to those for not leaving the batterer. Their financial dependence, fear of retribution and being blamed for provoking the violence, and internalized gender-role socialization deter them from laying charges and from acting as witnesses during the trial (MacLeod, 1980). Further, the conviction rate is so low that there is little point in wasting everyone's time in bringing the case to court. Even if a prosecution results, the offender may get only probation, in part because the victim may also suffer if the batterer must serve a jail sentence or pay a heavy fine.

The attendant publicity and the embarrassment of criminal procedures have negative repercussions for the whole family because of our pervasive tendency to blame the victim. Workers in social service and criminal justice agencies may convince the woman that she provoked his violence and that it was therefore justified. If trained to be impartial, they may ask: "Did you do or say anything to provoke him?" Instead, they should assure her: "Nothing you said or did justified his violence. No person ever deserves to be shoved, hit, kicked, or physically.hurt in any way. Everyone has the right not to be perfect."

Since 1982, in some jurisdictions police and Crown attorneys are being directed to encourage vigorous prosecution and investigation of wife-battering cases by their local police chiefs and provincial attorneys general:

> In directives, the police have been instructed that, while they must have reasonable and probable grounds to assume that an assault has taken place, as a result of amendments to the *Criminal Code* proclaimed in 1983, they do not have to actually witness the incident (MacLeod, 1987:82).

Supporters argue that police should lay charges where the necessary grounds exist, to convey that assault is unacceptable and to relieve the victim from the offender's pressure to drop the charges. A parallel logic might be that the victim be required to appear as a witness. She should not be charged with contempt of court if she refuses to testify, however, since such a procedure punishes her twice, first by her offender and then by the court.

Clearly, there are many problems in securing a conviction, and only a few communities (for example, London, Ontario, and Minneapolis, Minnesota) have organized to better utilize the criminal justice system to arrest and prosecute the offender. The criminal justice system remains male dominated, and there are still some judges whose attitudes more closely resemble those of the wife abuser. In such cases, the efforts of dedicated Crown attorneys and police officers who worked hard to make the case prosecutable often become undone through judicial leniency.

CONCLUSIONS ABOUT PRIMARY PREVENTION OF WIFE ASSAULT

Sexist attitudes of some police, Crown attorneys, defence lawyers, and judges are deeply ingrained and widely shared with others in our society. At this time, a policy directed toward the screening of people with such attitudes to prevent them from gaining or being promoted to positions of authority may be more effective than trying to change attitudes. At the same time, the recruitment of people with more egalitarian values to positions of authority is essential. Primary (before the fact) prevention would be further supported by widespread education, using schools and the mass media to change attitudes supporting wife assault. The problem of wife assault will be prevented only when most people believe that no woman ever deserves to be beaten, regardless of her faults and provocation (see page 289).

The agents of our criminal justice system may curtail some of the violence punishable by law, and their practices convey an important symbolic message. Workers

FOR INTEREST

OMA STARTS PROGRAM TO ENCOURAGE DOCTORS TO COMBAT WIFE ABUSE

By Gregory Ip

An Ontario Medical Association program to involve doctors directly in the fight against wife battering has won praise from the Canadian Advisory Council on the Status of Women as the first such move by physicians.

The OMA is distributing brochures and other literature to its members that identify the symptoms of wife abuse and suggest ways of intervening. The material also lists telephone numbers for local shelters and counselling agencies.

In praising the move, advisory council president Sylvia Gold explained that physicians are critical in stopping wife assault because they treat the woman.

"People in the medical profession are often on the front line in dealing with women who are victims of physical abuse. By being sensitive to what the real causes of these injuries might be, they can perhaps stop the abuse at a very early stage."

Her group recommended such a program after a major report last year said as many as one million women are beaten by their partners.

Doctors involved in the program said they are trying to accomplish several things through the program.

They want to inform physicians on the extent of the problem and make them realize there are professional services available, meaning they don't have to tackle it alone.

They also want to help doctors cope with the frustration of dealing with wife battering – a very different situation from routine health problems.

The OMA literature says although conservative estimates indicate one in 10 Canadian women are abused, "physicians unfamiliar with the problem find such statistics startling, and often estimate the incidence in their own practices at 1 to 2 per cent."

As proof of how often abuse escapes the attention of doctors, one physician referred to a U.S. study of emergency room patients that found 24 of 25 abuse cases went unnoticed by the attending physician.

"These things are growing in severity," said Dr. Barbara Lent, a physician in London, Ont., and principal author of the OMA literature.

She said studies have shown that 50 per cent of female murder victims were killed by their partner.

"That puts a woman at more risk from her family than strangers. It's not just slapping somebody on the face. Physicians have not understood this."

Dr. Leonard Hargot, an emergency room physician from Hamilton and a member of the OMA committee that produced the literature, said doctors often feel helpless when dealing with cases of wife assault.

"The tendency of women to go back to the battered situation, even though the family doctor may have tried to intervene, leaves the physician feeling somewhat impotent."

The OMA brochure suggests that bruises, fractures, perforated eardrums and internal bleeding should alert the doctor to the possibility of abuse.

Source: *The Globe and Mail,* July 29, 1989.   **Reprinted with Permission of the Globe and Mail**

in the criminal justice system, however, do little to address the underlying power imbalances that promote or enable the violence in the first place. Only the redistribution of power between husbands and wives, and of men and women more generally, can eradicate wife abuse as a social problem. This would require paying women higher wages, establishing more day care services, providing better economic and social support for victims of abuse through social programs, encouraging husbands to take a share in household and child care duties, vigorously arresting and punishing offenders, and changing sexist attitudes and language to reflect more egalitarian values.

Violence in the home is too often hidden behind terms such as marital violence, domestic violence, conjugal violence, and spouse abuse. Such terms imply that the frequency and the severity of husband-to-wife and wife-to-husband violence are similar. Since this is false, many prefer terms such as wife assault, or wife battering, because they identify women as the main victims of the serious, harmful consequences of spousal violence. Some use the term woman abuse to recognize that many ex-wives and girlfriends are also assaulted. Words reflect, reinforce, and change attitudes and thus should be chosen to portray accurately the most serious patterns of assault.

These societal changes can only be accomplished if people with power are convinced that greater equality and social justice are desirable. For this reason, it is important that men, as well as women, mobilize to prevent men from assaulting their wives, ex-wives, and girlfriends.

HISTORICAL ORIGINS AND CONTEMPORARY CULTURAL AND LEGAL SUPPORTS FOR CHILD ABUSE

Many parallels can be found in the ways that historic practices and attitudes have evolved to affect contemporary ways of dealing with wife assault and child abuse, but there are also some major differences. One difference is that the legal right to chastise women has been abolished. The Canadian Criminal Code, however, explicitly permits the use of physical force against children by socializing agents.

PAST LEGAL SUPPORTS FOR CHILD ABUSE

Child abuse has a long history and was often both common and condoned. Infanticide was common in the ancient world, and if a child was female her chances of death were increased (Bala and Clark, 1981). In ancient Rome, a father's rights included the power of life and death over his offspring and the right to sell them as slaves if he wished. Infanticide and child slavery were common during the Dark Ages, and the father's right to absolute control of his children continued into the Middle Ages.

It was not until the 1800s, when child labour, child prostitution, and baby farming (the boarding out of small children) attracted the attention of reformers, that systematic recognition was given to the rights of children (Radbill, 1980). A landmark English court case in 1893 brought the concept of *parens patriae* into effect and challenged absolute parental authority over children. *Parens patriae* is the right of a court to interfere with biological or legal parental rights by acting as a substitute parent if this is deemed to be in the best interest of the child. It established a legal precedent for removing children from incompetent parents.

Canadian law was very much influenced by such trends in English courts and also by decisions in the United States. Movements to establish the right of children to be safe from physical and sexual abuse gained some momentum in the late 1800s, when the New York Society for the Prevention of Cruelty to Animals was the only agency available to argue that human children deserved the same rights as other members of the animal kingdom (Fontana, 1974). This situation became clear after a church worker became aware that a young girl named Mary Ellen had frequently been beaten by her adoptive parents and was seriously neglected and malnourished. The worker was unable to convince local authorities to take legal action against the parents because the right of parents to chastise their children was unquestionable, and there was no law to protect the child from parental abuse. The church worker therefore appealed to the Society for the Prevention of Cruelty to Animals (SPCA). They took up the challenge and argued that Mary Ellen should be removed from her abusive parents. Because she was a member of the animal kingdom, the laws against cruelty to animals demanded her removal.

The case widely publicized the need for a separate advocate to safeguard human children and led to the founding of the Society for the Prevention of Cruelty to Children in New York City in 1871. Soon after, in 1887, the first Children's Aid Society (CAS) was founded in Toronto. Subsequently, other provinces also enacted child welfare legislation. At the turn of the century in Nova Scotia, however, the SPCA was explicitly empowered to act as a Children's Aid Society in areas that were without branches of the CAS (Rooke and Schnell, 1981).

SECTION 43 OF THE CRIMINAL CODE

Section 43 of the Canada's Criminal Code exempts persons who assault children from prosecution if they are parents, school teachers, or other persons standing in the place of parents (*in loco parentis*), or if the assault is to care for and socialize children. It reads as follows:

> Every schoolteacher, parent or person standing in the place of a parent is justified in using force by way of correction toward a pupil or child, as the case may be, who is under his care, if the force does not exceed what is reasonable under the circumstances.

This provision is controversial because alternative forms of discipline are probably more effective than physical punishment in socializing children, and the term "reasonable" can be given varied interpretations. The law reinforces the widely supported view that the use of physical force is appropriate and necessary with children (Wilson, 1980). No clear-cut criteria exist for determining that elusive point beyond which the quality and quantity of physical force used is to be considered excessive.

In the case of *R. v. Dupperon*, heard in the Saskatchewan Court of Appeal in 1984, a father was convicted of simple assault. In spite of the father's lengthy criminal record, he was given only a $400 fine and eighteen months on probation. *Martin's Criminal Code* (1989) details the multiplicity of objective and subjective criteria our courts should use:

> In determining whether the force used has exceeded what is reasonable under the circumstances, the court must consider both from an objective *and*

subjective [italics mine] standpoint such matters as the nature of the offence calling for correction, the age and character of the child and the likely effect of the punishment on the particular child, the degree of gravity of the punishment, the circumstances under which it was inflicted and the injuries, if any, suffered; *R. v. Dupperon* (1984) 16 C.C.C. (3d) 453, 43 C.R. (3d) 70, [1985] 2 W.W.R. 369 (Sask. C.A.).

The court ruled that the father's use of a leather belt to strap his thirteen-year-old son approximately ten times on his bare buttocks, leaving bruises up to one-half inch wide and roughly four inches long, was excessive, in part because the boy was emotionally disturbed with "several behavioural problems" (16 C.C.C. (3d) 461). In the opinion of the court, the bruises were judged "merely transient or trifling in nature" and not therefore supporting the more serious charge of assault causing bodily harm. The court raised this objection to the defence attorney's justification for corporal punishment:

> I'm aware that some fundamental sects seem to believe that spare the rod and spoil the child gives them the license to practice all kinds of brutality and sadistic practices which cause from time to time the death of the child but I didn't think we were going to argue the benefits of that kind of religiousity or morality in connection with the discipline of children (16 C.C.C. (3d) 459).

The numerous and subjective criteria employed in this precedent-setting case mean that the determination of the appropriate measure of force is effectively left to the discretion of parents, other caregivers, the police, and professional personnel in health, education, welfare, and criminal justice agencies. Our tolerance and our desire to uphold the discretionary right of parents and other caretakers as regards the physical discipline of children is reflected in the difficulties that agencies have in dealing with cases brought to their attention. There is an explicit recognition that the socialization function bestows the right to "use" assault upon the socializers so long as that right is not abused.

Most of the reported decisions about Section 43 of the Criminal Code deal with school teachers or other persons standing in the place of parents. Only a few concern abuse by natural or adoptive parents. Several cases involving non-parents are discussed in this chapter because any use of physical punishment permitted by teachers and other caregivers would probably also be judged as permissible if done by a parent. A criminal case that illuminates these issues is that of a couple who had run a group home and boarding school near Calgary for twenty-two years. They were successfully convicted of several charges of common assault and assault causing bodily harm for severely beating children in their care. The victims suffered bruises, welts, and open sores. A *Toronto Star* editorial argues that the couple's claim that corporal punishment was used for the purpose of discipline to prevent future criminal behaviour was inconsistent with evidence that corporal punishment makes violence more, rather than less, likely:

> Sirhan Sirhan, the convicted assassin of Robert F. Kennedy, was often beaten as a youth. . . . John Wayne Gacy, convicted in 1981 of the grisly murder of 33 young men and boys in Chicago, was frequently beaten as a child. . . . Dr.

Karl Menninger ... in his study, *Murder Without Motive*, found that most seemingly senseless murders were committed by men who had encountered "extreme parental violence during childhood, suffering frequent and severe beatings." Other studies and surveys of criminal behaviour had concluded that from 80 to 90 percent of people convicted of serious crimes against the person were abused as children.

The editorial concludes:

> Because violence tends to beget violence, it's better to avoid corporal punishment altogether and find less violent ways to maintain discipline among our children (*The Toronto Star*, September 25, 1983, p. F2).

Landsberg (1981:H1), in reviewing unpublished evidence, concludes that, historically, Section 43 of the Criminal Code has been used in Canadian courts to defend the rights of child abusers. For example, in 1927 a Saskatchewan teacher was permitted to bruise and welt the buttocks of a ten-year-old girl. In the judge's view, "that part of the anatomy ... has been designed by nature for the receipt of corporal punishment." As recently as 1978, an Ontario teacher used Section 43 to justify four blows to the head of a student who erred by writing a note in class. The judge remarked that the teacher's conduct was "a very slight transgression of the line" and granted her an absolute discharge.

Children have long been "taught to the tune of the hickory stick." It is an anomaly that, in 1958, Ontario banned corporal punishment in provincial correctional institu-

MILLER COMSTOCK INC.

Changing attitudes toward physical punishment are reflected in recent decisions to prosecute parents and professional caretakers who beat children so severely as to cause bruises, welts, and open sores.

tions, but not in schools. A survey of Ontario school boards conducted in 1985 revealed that "only 20% had a policy prohibiting the use of the strap. . . . Further, there is no evidence that the Ministry of Education in Ontario is prepared to take any action provincially, to ban this practice" (Flynn, 1988:3). It took British Columbia until 1973 to ban the use of the strap (Adams, 1974). The other provinces still have not done so, thereby raising questions as to their credentials for teaching courses on non-violence.

CONTEMPORARY CANADIAN STANDARDS ON "REASONABLE" FORCE

Changing attitudes toward physical punishment are reflected in recent decisions to prosecute parents and professional caretakers who beat children so severely as to cause bruises, welts, and open sores. The judge in an Ontario case states that "the formation of child abuse teams at hospitals . . . reflects the distaste of our community for corporal punishment" (61 C.C.C. (2d) 443). Both parents were convicted of assault causing bodily harm after using a belt and extension cord to strike their fifteen-year-old daughter so severely as to cause abrasions, bruising, and disfigurement on her buttocks, back, and left breast [*R. v. Baptiste and Baptiste* (1980), 61 C.C.C. (2d) 438 (Ont. Prov. Ct.)]. This case challenged the father's claim that it was a father's privilege to use such discipline on his daughter. It also rejected both parents' defence claims that beatings of their daughter were acceptable because corporal punishment was normal in Trinidad, the country from which the mother and father had emigrated. The judge explicitly disagreed with this latter justification, stating that the court must consider contemporary Canadian community standards, rather than the customs of the accused persons' former country, in making its determination of whether the force used on a child is reasonable or excessive under the circumstances.

Although recent legal judgments indicate that child abuse is becoming less acceptable, the right of parents to inflict physical punishment with the justification that such "discipline" is for the child's own good is still deeply entrenched in our society. A recent Canadian poll (Decima Research, 1988) of 756 parents aged eighteen to forty-five years living with children under the age of sixteen years reported spanking as being in a different category than other forms of physical striking and slapping. The reason for this was not determined. They were more likely to advocate spanking if they also reported that they were abused as children by their parents. Opinion across the country is basically split between those who agree (51 percent) and those who disagree that spanking is a form of abuse. The French-speaking (68 percent) and Quebec parents (69 percent), however, are more likely to disapprove of spanking in this and a 1979 poll (*Weekend Magazine*, 1979).

ANTI-ASSAULT LEGISLATION: THE SCANDINAVIAN STANDARD

A law prohibiting corporal punishment of all children was recommended by Cyril Greenland, a child abuse expert (Crawford, 1983). Greenland would like to see hitting a child in any way – including spanking by parents – outlawed under the Criminal Code, thus forcing parents to look for ways to spare the rod without spoiling the child. Such a law was passed by Sweden in May 1979. It prohibits "any act which for the purpose of punishment causes the child physical injury or pain, even if the disturbance is mild and passing" (*Weekend Magazine*, 1979). The law carries no penalty (*The Globe and Mail*, 1979); thus its purpose is to signal that beating children is not permitted and to provide encouragement to discipline children in other more positive and more effective ways (Van Stolk, 1983). We could accomplish this in Canada by encouraging the wider use of non-violent parenting skills through community education programs that distribute articles and videos and organize face-to-face discussions on the subject. We could also abolish Section 43 of the Criminal Code.

Pro-Assault Arguments

The Swedish law was initially opposed by many groups in Sweden (*The Globe and Mail*, 1979), and there would be opposition to a similar law in Canada. Some argue that such laws infringe on the freedom of religion of fundamentalist Christians and also on the right to family privacy. Many equate the elimination of corporal punishment with the elimination of discipline and with the extolling of permissiveness. They are either unaware or unconvinced of the effectiveness of alternative methods of discipline that would instill appropriate behaviour and prevent negative, annoying, and socially unacceptable behaviour. Public advocacy of effective non-violent methods of discipline would reflect our growing recognition that being a good parent is less a biological process than a learning process and that constructive discipline is more effective than corporal punishment (Decima, 1988).

Discipline Versus Punishment

The justifications of abusers often emphasize the disciplinary intent of correction, rather than potential physical and emotional injuries. Their unwillingness to reason with a child is probably related to their failure to see the child as a rational person. Our language reflects and reinforces this tendency. We lack a handy term to refer to non-violent teaching and correction, in part because physical punishment has long been perceived as an acceptable and effective form of discipline. In common usage, the words "discipline" and "punishment" are often treated as synonyms. One effect of the failure to distinguish clearly between them is that it is harder for us to visualize non-violent methods of discipline and correction.

Corporal punishment is not synonymous with discipline. Children can be strictly disciplined without resorting to physical punishment. The word punishment itself implies retribution, rough handling, mistreatment, pain, chastisement, and abuse. Such treatment often increases the hostility of the child receiving it, thereby impeding the socializing agent's effectiveness. More positive and constructive methods of discipline have much better results.

Discipline is teaching, guiding, and training that produces moral or mental improvement and controlled behaviour. It involves talking and using reason and persuasion, verbal reprimands, rewarding a child for good behaviour, limit-setting, restitution, sending a child to a quiet place, and withdrawing privileges and imposing specific duties. Discipline is a long process that uses problem situations to motivate and produce maturity, self-control, obedience to rules, and the acceptance of authority. Negative behaviour is not ignored; thus it would be an error to confuse discipline with permissiveness. A positive outcome requires the conscious, consistent use of positive and constructive discipline. It helps if the socializing agent provides a model for the type of behaviour that is expected of the child. For example, if one of the goals is to teach the child respect for others and the unacceptability of physical aggression, bullying, and verbal insults, then parents and teachers also need to avoid such abusive behaviour and provide a role model for appropriate alternatives. Research suggests that hitting children will not teach children that hitting is wrong.

FOR INTEREST

DISCIPLINE

Discipline is a confusing issue for many parents. They wonder if they're being strict enough or too strict – or if they've handled a particular problem correctly.

Part of the confusion arises from what parents mean when they use the term discipline. Often they are really talking about punishment which is but one part of discipline.

Punishment means a penalty inflicted for wrongdoing. It ranges from a mild reprimand or withdrawal of a privilege such as no television for a day, to corporal punishment such as spanking.

The term discipline implies something more positive. It has to do with guidance. It is the training and teaching of your child about desired behaviour, not just the controlling of undesired behaviour. It helps a child learn self-discipline and self-confidence.

Some parents described as strict or disciplinarians may seldom or never use corporal punishment. And some parents who punish often may actually be very poor at maintaining control.

Some parents feel guilty after disciplining children. And some accept behaviour they dislike because they are afraid of causing psychological damage. Some feel it is wrong to be angry with a child – or to show anger. But living with children is not always easy, and it's normal for parents to be angry occasionally.

Here are some generally accepted ways to discipline based on what is known about children.

Consistency

Parents can't, or don't always want to be consistent. But children need to know what is expected of them. Stick by your decisions. If you change your mind, explain why. For example: "You're right, it's not very cold today. I guess you don't need your jacket," or "I've finished my cleaning already so we do have time to read a story."

Some suggestions:

- Consider a request. Don't answer with a hasty yes or no, but once given, make your decision final.
- Establish routines. Young children benefit when they can predict their days. Schedule meals, baths, play periods and bedtime.
- Make rules. Set only rules you feel are important and enforce them consistently. State clearly what will happen. The consequences should be logical and natural. For example, "If you

crayon on the walls, I'll take the crayons away." As children get older, let them participate in setting rules and consequences for breaking them. This will teach them they have rights, and chances are, fewer rules will be broken. Both parents should agree on the rules which should be appropriate for the ages of the children. And both parents should keep in mind that it's natural for children to test rules.

Praise and encourage

Children want to be noticed and continually seek approval from their parents. Tell your child what you expect. For example: "Paint on the paper, not on the table." "You may play in the sandbox but not in the flower garden." Be specific: "Hold on with two hands," rather than "Be careful."

Good behaviour should be praised. Encourage attempts as well as completed tasks: "Good! You put your boots on by yourself."

Speak positively: "If you get dressed quickly we'll go to the park," rather than, "If you don't hurry we won't go."

Smile: A warm smile can also be a reward for good behaviour.

Set examples

Children imitate those around them. If you swear when you are angry, your child will swear when angry. Try to handle situations yourself as you want your child to. If your child says, "#&?*##+##&," a calm reaction is best. Either ignore the remark or tell your child calmly you'd prefer him or her not to talk like that.

Make reasonable requests

Remember that physical development and emotional maturity occur at different times. Before disciplining, consider the following: Perhaps your child is too young to do what you expect. Perhaps there are other factors such as hunger or illness or lack of sleep.

What are your expectations? For instance, most two-year-olds can't fully dress themselves; and most four-year-olds can't sit still.

Perhaps your request is at odds with your child's personality. For example, adapting to new situations may be difficult. A toddler may have trouble sleeping in a new room.

Toddlers need to explore and handle everything. Channel curiosity by providing objects and areas to explore, rather than saying "no" outright.

When children are asked to do the impossible, or are faced with situations they can't handle, it's natural for them to be angry.

DEALING WITH AGGRESSIVE BEHAVIOUR

Aggression is a forceful way of indicating feelings such as frustration, anger or despair. This, of course, is the dictionary definition, a pale reflection of the reality of a frustrated and furious two-or-three-year-old in full voice.

Tantrum-throwers or children who suddenly whack another child on the head sometimes catch parents by surprise. They're seeing a new side of their healthy, usually good-natured child. But it's a side that's always been there. Aggression is a natural part of a healthy child's life.

Babies, for example, thrash and cry when wet or hungry. As needs are met, a pattern begins to form – vigorous movement and crying get results.

By the time a child is three, there's enough strength to hit and kick, and enough co-ordination to connect with a target – a playmate's head or a mother's shin.

Of course, such aggressive behaviour isn't acceptable and children must learn self-control. For some children, learning self-control is a quick and painless process. Others may take years to learn acceptable ways of expressing their emotions.

What can parents do

Be Aware – Keep a watchful eye on your preschooler at play. Frequent supervision, although time-consuming, is essential to help your child learn acceptable ways of expressing feelings and developing self-control.

Anticipate and Act – When you see trouble developing, move in quickly, but remain calm. Gently restrain your child, if necessary. Holding his or her hands while you speak is usually enough. Explain: "I know you're angry, but I can't let you hit. That hurts." There may be a bit of a struggle and some protests, but eventually your child will learn the lesson.

Redirect Behaviour – Explain clearly that screaming and kicking won't get what your child wants. Explain that you under-

stand how he or she is feeling. Listen to your child's side, and come to an agreement on how to solve the problem.

For example, say: "I can't let you hit your friend. It hurts. I know how angry you are feeling. Please tell me what you are mad about." Remain calm and in control and your child will see that his or her feelings are not being denied or ignored.

Children will soon begin to understand that they can get satisfaction by talking about problems rather than through physical force. Redirecting behaviour helps children understand what parents expect.

Disciplining

Children must be shown disapproval of unacceptable behaviour. When speaking, holding or other forms of discipline fail to deal with misbehaviour, other approaches must be considered. Other forms of discipline are removal of a treat or privilege, short confinement to a room and verbal disapproval. Here are some suggestions to help you discipline effectively.

- Discipline should never be used to hurt children physically in order to make them pay for something done wrong.
- Discipline sparingly.
- Be logical and fair. Relate the consequence to the misbehaviour. For example, if your child throws sand at a playmate, remove him or her from the sandpile. Whenever possible, discipline should be a "natural" result of the unacceptable behaviour.
- Follow through on warnings immediately.
- Discipline immediately after the misbehaviour. Don't say: "Just wait until your

father hears about this!'' or "Your mother will be furious when she gets home!''

- Speak sternly but calmly and as little as possible.
- Discipline behaviour: "I know you're angry, but hitting is bad. I won't let you hit your friend." The behaviour, not your child, is bad.
- After disciplining, forgive and forget.

Children may seek punishment if this is the only way they are noticed. This could lead to serious problems, lack of self-confidence, poor self-image and destructive behaviour.

Spanking

Many parents spank their children when other forms of discipline fail. However, spanking is generally not effective in the long term. Here's what is known about spanking.

- Spanking is bad modelling. It teaches a child to hit others.
- It can lead to poor self-image. A child may develop a negative opinion of himself or herself, the idea that he or she is bad.

- Frequent spankings may teach your child to learn ways to avoid getting caught.
- It tends to lose its effectiveness when used too often, and may make your child feel badly and angry toward you.
- If a parent uses spanking often it indicates that he or she lost control of the situation. This may show the child that the parent cannot cope with the problem and this in turn can make the child frightened and insecure.

Self-discipline

Children naturally strive to become independent. Helping children on the road to independence and self-discipline requires that parents become aware of their children as individuals with distinctive personalities and needs. Parents need lots of patience and love to teach their children how to assert and express needs and feelings in acceptable ways. Remember, a preschooler has boundless energy and a relatively short memory. Show your love. Be generous with praise. Love is the key to helping your child learn to express emotions appropriately.

Source: Reprinted courtesy of Ontario Ministry of Community and Social Services from *A Guide for Parents of Young Children.*

POLICIES TO SUPPORT STATE INTERVENTION AND CHILD PROTECTION

Mandatory Reporting

In the past, as now, there were cultural inhibitions about interfering in the affairs of the family. To overcome these inhibitions, most provinces have enacted legislation that makes it mandatory for anyone having knowledge of a case of child abuse to report the information to a child welfare or legal authority, even if the information is obtained by a professional who believes such information is privileged (Ontario Ministry of Community and Social Services, 1988; Robinson, 1976). Immunity from civil and criminal liability is guaranteed to persons making the reports in good faith. Although this mandatory reporting legislation is almost never enforced, publicity about its existence tells parents and other caregivers that abuse resulting in physical injury is unacceptable.

Even with legislation, however, reporting of child abuse remains erratic. This may partially explain the low prosecution rates in parent-to-child homicide. Over a twenty-year period, 185 children in Ontario died at the hands of parents or guardians, yet only 64 people were prosecuted (Crawford, 1983a). Many people do not seem to realize that something like shaking and tossing, which may seem minor, can result in whiplash, brain damage, and death (Crawford, 1983a; Maychak, 1982). Because of erratic reporting, official registers very much underestimate the true incidence and reflect biased sampling patterns of child assault. Greenland's (1973) study of data from Ontario's Provincial Central Registry, from the records of the supervising coroner for Ontario, and from interviews with professionals found that physicians, hospitals, Crown attorneys, and coroners frequently neglected to report abuse cases to Children's Aid Societies. The societies in turn were inconsistent in reporting to the provincial registry and lacked adequate follow-up procedures for the reports of abuse they received (Malarek, 1979). Few cases result in criminal charges and even fewer in convictions: "CAS's [in Ontario] report that of the 50% of cases where charges are laid, only 15–20% of cases result in a criminal conviction" (IPCA, 1988:4). The low rate of convictions tells us that criminal record convictions also provide an inadequate data base for studying victims and offenders in cases of physical and sexual abuse of children.

The registry reports suggest it is the very young who often receive the most serious injuries, but older children are also victimized. In 1986, the Ontario Child Abuse Register recorded over 2,200 cases of child abuse, including approximately 25 cases of emotional abuse, 500 cases of physical abuse, and 1,600 cases of sexual abuse. According to the register:

> In physical abuse, boys and girls are equally likely to be abused until age 13. After 13, more girls are victims. In sexual abuse, more than twice as many girls as boys are abused (Ontario Ministry of Community and Social Services, 1987:10).

The increasing proportion of sexual abuse reports is probably due to the fact that the public is becoming more aware, through popular books, talk shows, films, and numerous newspaper and magazine articles, of the likelihood of incest and its devastating long-term effects on many of its victims. We have less ambivalence in our culture about designating sexual than physical abuse as morally unacceptable. School children are being taught about good, bad, and confusing touching and to "say no and tell someone" if someone is making them uncomfortable. In addition, autobiographies (Allen, 1980; Armstrong, 1978; Brady, 1979; Danika, 1988; Fraser, 1987) and research reports (Badgley, 1984; Finkelhor, 1979; Forward and Buck, 1978; Rush, 1980; Russell, 1986) have helped bring this once taboo subject into the open.

Bill C-15 and New Offences of Child Sexual Abuse

Increased public interest and outrage at sexual assault was reflected by the implementation of new criminal laws specified in Bill C-15 in January 1988. This bill created new offences related to child sexual abuse, revised some existing offences, and created new provisions in the Canada Evidence Act to facilitate prosecutions. The bill tried to protect the rights of the accused adult, while also allowing child victims to tell their story in court. All provisions for a one-year limitation period on bringing charges were repealed. The need to repeal the six-year limitation on civil cases remains (Stewart and Bala, 1988).

The charge of incest remains in the Criminal Code, but is rarely laid because it requires proof of vaginal sexual intercourse. It tends to protect the offender because most abuse involves the child in other activities including oral sex, hand to penis, and other touching that meet the adult offender's sexual needs. By specifying that the offenders can only be blood relatives, the incest law fails to recognize that the breach of trust by stepfathers, uncles, and others also causes physical, mental, and emotional harm to the victim. The incest law reflects the importance placed on "blood," rather than the abuse of power by legal or *de facto* family members.

Bill C-15's new charges of sexual assault, sexual interference (touching the body of a person under age fourteen for a sexual purpose), invitation to sexual touching (encouraging a child under fourteen to touch the offender for sexual gratification), and sexual exploitation (by a person in a position of trust or authority having sex with a fourteen to seventeen year old in a relationship of dependency) will be easier to prove and, therefore, along with sexual assault, will be used more frequently even in incestuous situations. The penalties, however, are not as severe as in the incest legislation.

Bill C-15 tries to provide some protection for the fourteen to seventeen year old from some limited forms of exploitation by persons in authority, but it is most clear that any sexual touching of a child under fourteen years is a criminal offence. Consent is not a defence, and accused offenders cannot argue that they thought the complainant was over fourteen, unless all reasonable steps were taken to ascertain age. The new law recognizes that coercion is not necessarily physical and that age differences limit the young person from providing meaningful consent, particularly if the older person is in authority.

The symbolic message of the unacceptability of these newly defined sexual offences needs to be more widely publicized. To protect victims, we need to publicize that research on over two thousand respondents finds that over 95 percent of the perpetrators of child sexual abuse are male (Badgley, 1984). Many of the offenders are family members, teachers, friends, and religious leaders that the child knows. Russell (1986:60) found, in interviews with a random sample of 930 women, that 19 percent reported being sexually abused by someone in the family at least once in their lives.

Bill C-15 increases the likelihood of successfully prosecuting offenders because it allows a child to provide uncorroborated testimony if she or he has the ability to communicate, can tell the difference between the truth and a lie, understands the necessity of telling the truth, and promises to do so. Lawmakers were convinced by recent studies that child witnesses are *not* inherently as reliable as adult witnesses (Sproule and Wolfe, 1988; Vallance, 1988). A noted authority on the law of evidence, however, concludes that child witnesses should be treated as any other witnesses. Their individual shortcomings and positive attributes can be assessed on a case by case basis.

Rather than parroting such phrases as "Out of the mouths of babes can only come truth," or "It is well known that children fantasize," judges would be better off ... to acknowledge that children can be reliable witnesses (Delisle, 1988:5; cited in Stewart and Bala, 1988:38).

Judges can still comment on the credibility of a particular witness to the jury, but they should no longer cast doubt on the unreliability of particular categories (gender or age groups) of witnesses. This and other recent "sexual assault" legislation was developed in response to criticisms of the way the Canadian courts had traditionally stereotyped children and women as unreliable witnesses in sexual offence cases (Stewart and Bala, 1988), thereby protecting the predominantly male perpetrators. Bill C-15 and new sexual assault legislation are directed to changing this tradition. Offences will remain difficult to prove using the criminal standard of "beyond a reasonable doubt," because they are committed relatively privately.

Bill C-15's Impact

Recent court decisions (for example, *R. v. Khan* (1988), 27 O.A.C. 142) suggest the new legislation may be having the anticipated effect, and that some judges may be more willing to accept the testimony of children abused by trusted adults, in this case a medical doctor. Most observers warn, however, not to expect too much from prosecution of the abuser, which comes after the fact of abuse. An Ontario judge predicts that "if our society is sick enough to have this quantity of incest and abuse in the first place it is not going to be cured in the courts" (Stewart and Bala, 1988:57).

It is vital that we also focus on primary prevention because there will never be enough social workers, police, Crown attorneys, judges, or treatment programs to deal with the real number of children abused in and out of the home. Professionals worry that if the new legislation results in more court cases and convictions, there will be difficulty meeting the demand for treatment. "The availability of such treatment is insufficient and in many parts ... non-existent" (Stewart, 1988:28). Further, we do not have unbiased assessments of its effectiveness.

Unfounded Versus False Allegations

The concern about false allegations has spread far beyond that warranted by the actual incidence. "For example, one Ontario teachers' federation ... recently passed a resolution urging criminal prosecution of children and/or parents where an accused teacher is acquitted" (Stewart and Bala, 1988:56). To some, this punitive response represents a backlash against Bill C-15's advances on behalf of sexually abused children. Better public education on this problem could result in teachers' federations supporting clinical intervention for the reporting child, even if the allegations are unfounded, unsubstantiated, or false. Threats of laying charges of public mischief could prevent children with legitimate grievances from coming forward. Teachers, like the rest of us, need to know that children and adolescents who deliberately lie are usually found out in a thorough investigation before the case goes to court. They may have been abused by someone other than the person charged, and may need therapy to deal with the problems underlying their fictitious report.

Teachers' federations should support any members charged with child abuse. They can also be constructive in preventing child sexual abuse by recognizing that the sexual abuse of children reflects a fundamental malaise in societal attitudes toward power, personhood, and sexuality. Teachers and other authority figures are in a good position to change values that allow for sexual exploitation. Unless they help promote such change, there is little hope that relatively powerful males will stop abusing their less powerful male and female victims in a variety of settings, both in and out of the home.

Distinctions must be made between, first, reports that are "unfounded" or "unsubstantiated" (no charges are laid or charges are dropped) because police and courts feel the evidence does not meet the strict criminal standard of proof and, second, reports that result from false or fictitious allegations that are deliberately fabricated by a vindictive or manipulative child. There are many reasons why an accused might be acquitted, and often it is not because the report was false and maliciously made. Under the Canadian criminal justice system, if there is a "reasonable doubt" as to whether sexual or physical abuse has occurred, the accused must be acquitted regardless of guilt or innocence.

STRAINS ON SOCIAL SERVICE AGENCIES

An unanticipated consequence of the increased reports of child abuse following the implementation of mandatory reporting legislation in the provinces was the strain placed on the capacity of Children's Aid Societies to handle cases. Children's Aid Societies are expected to supervise children at risk in their own homes whenever possible and also to remove them to substitute care if the risk to the child becomes too great. Determining the right balance between a child's welfare and parental rights is a difficult task under the best of circumstances. Thus, the Children's Aid Societies are regularly subjected to criticism for mistakes in judgment that expose children to dangerous situations in the home. This criticism, usually made with the wisdom of hindsight, is particularly common after sensational news stories of infant deaths or critical injuries (Carey, 1981; Lavigne, 1982; Silverman, 1978).

But Children's Aid Societies also come under fire for needlessly taking children out of homes, because their mandate is to give care to a child in his or her own home whenever possible. A report by the National Council of Welfare (1979:1) states that in 1978, approximately 80,000 Canadian children – one in every hundred – were not in the care of their natural parents. Two or three times this number were receiving a variety of supportive services, which included family counselling, day care, and visiting home-makers. The cost was some $750 million a year, shared by municipal, provincial, and federal governments. On a per capita basis, the Northwest Territories and Yukon had the highest proportion, with 3.9 percent (1,100 children). Here, as everywhere, children from low-income, native, and single-parent families are overrepresented. Ontario was the lowest on a per capita basis, with .51 percent, but in terms of absolute numbers it was second only to Quebec in the number of children in care – 13,615. Ontario also had the lowest proportion of children in care among the ten provinces from the sixteen years prior to this survey (Ryan, 1981).

Whatever the balance between children remaining in and being removed from the home, many critics of the Children's Aid Societies in Canada believe better decisions could be made if the societies themselves had fewer serious problems. Many societies lack clear and effectively implemented policies about when a child should be kept at home and when removed to substitute residential care. A CAS worker's goals often conflict when trying to help a family while at the same time trying to investigate and procure evidence for a court hearing to terminate parental rights or to support laying criminal charges to protect the victim and convey society's disapproval (Bodger and McLean, 1977; Garber et al., 1978). Another problem is that children may be left at risk with parents for unacceptably long periods of time because CAS workers are not sufficiently well trained in the preparation of court cases with respect to sexual abuse (Badgley, 1984).

A shortage of good foster homes and group homes also leaves children in high-risk situations. Many Children's Aid Societies are hampered in their ability to help parents and to investigate reported cases because they lack staff with language skills for native Indian and immigrant populations (Garber et al., 1978). Some societies have had problems with high staff turnover. Inadequately trained and inexperienced social workers are given caseloads too heavy to allow them to adequately investigate and effectively prevent child abuse and neglect. Thus, whether supervision of a child at risk is weekly or monthly may depend more upon the social worker's agenda than upon a rational strategy determined in consultation with a supervisor and based on well-developed policy.

CONCLUSION

Our society is experiencing difficulty in dealing with both child abuse and wife battering. However, the media are now drawing attention to the severity of these forms of intrafamily violence, and social scientists are beginning to document the dimensions of family assault and to increase our understanding of these problems by developing empirically supported theoretical analyses of the social conditions that have produced these problems generation after generation. We can now begin to implement solutions because understanding is the beginning of prevention.

Should we not also care about the incidence of battered husbands, raped men, mothers who assault children, and children who hit parents? We certainly should. However, if these problems are seen to be as common as wife and child assault, we will continue to define the problem as one of "troubled" people with individual pathologies who "settle their differences" in ways that sometimes get out of hand. We will not achieve true social justice because we will not see the need for social and political action aimed at preventing the more serious and more extensive forms of assault.

Prevention involves eliminating the social roots of wife and child assault, not just the symptoms. This involves not *merely* giving better assistance to the victims, and arresting, convicting, punishing, and treating offenders, but also providing truly primary prevention programs that prevent the problems. Fundamental social change is required to eliminate the conditions that foster distorted and dysfunctional expectations that physically and emotionally harm a significant proportion of the relatively dependent population. Voluntary compliance with the sexual and physical assault provisions of our Criminal Code will only come if we take action on a variety of fronts – in our personal lives and with institutions in our society – that will change the status quo governing interaction among family members.

Until this kind of widespread, fundamental social change occurs, there will be an increasing demand for proliferation of helping agencies such as shelters, foster homes, child protection services, social workers, counsellors, treatment programs, health care, hotlines for wife assault and child abuse, and the services of police, lawyers, judges, probation, parole, and correctional agencies. Despite the growth of these institutions and any increasingly effective co-ordination of their services, the problems of family violence will continue, in part because many of these institutions are oriented toward maintaining the status quo. This chapter has reviewed evidence showing that police, courts, child protection services, schools, and a variety of religious and other institutions have *not* had a history of initiating or even supporting social reform, or of pursuing those suspected of assault.

We cannot expect legislators, police, researchers, teachers, and workers in various social service agencies to change unless the attitudes they share with the rest of society about victims and offenders also change. A violence-free society with respect for all persons and the equal economic and psychological power between the sexes will require education and resocialization. The problems of family assault can be diminished only if abusers are no longer permitted to justify assault as an act of discipline, concern, or love. Increasing the numbers of violence-free families can be accomplished only if expectations and conditions of equality in economic, psychological, educational, political, religious, and all other institutional spheres prevail, and only if improved detection mechanisms and severe consequences for physical and sexual assault predominate.

DISCUSSION QUESTIONS

1. What social patterns are apparent in family violence?
2. Does the term "spousal abuse" obscure these social patterns? Why or why not?
3. What problems are inherent in the Conflict Tactics Scale (CTS) used to study intrafamily violence?
4. Why have reported rates of family violence increased so much in recent years?
5. Why does the federal Criminal Code accept "reasonable force" against children?
6. Who decides whether or not physical force against children is "reasonable"?
7. What precautions can be taken to protect children against physical or sexual abuse?
8. Why do abused wives sometimes tolerate abuse from their husbands?
9. What services and facilities are available in your community to assist abused women and children; abused elderly people; and abusive parents and husbands?
10. Under what conditions are elderly people sometimes abused?

chapter thirteen

Family Policy

INTRODUCTION

Most Canadians, irrespective of ideological perspective, would consider Canada a country that cares about children and their families. But social policies and practices at many levels in our society seem to reveal subtle biases against certain types of families. The assumptions and principles that determine social policies have not changed to accommodate women's increasing participation in paid employment. Policies affecting families are still designed and implemented on the assumption that women are the dependants of men and carry the primary responsibility for child care. For example, the unemployment insurance program has been known to discriminate against female claimants with parental responsibilities, who have had their claims denied when they cancelled their child care arrangement to look after their children while waiting for another job. Because it is still widely assumed that childbearing and homemaking are the exclusive responsibility of women, it is also believed that women have to find ways of meeting this responsibility when they join the work force. Fathers in the work force already have a system of child care – their wives.

The minimum wage in all provinces is so low that even a two-income couple with one child will have a combined income of less than Statistics Canada's poverty line for a family of three. Wage levels based on individual productivity do not recognize family consumption needs and could be considered inherently anti-family. Existing child benefits are not sufficient to make up the difference between individual earnings and family consumption needs. At the municipal level, landlords are allowed to discriminate against families with children by restricting rentals to adults only.

In divorce and custody cases, our adversarial legal system pits parent against parent. The equal splitting of property between the former spouses ignores the material interests of children who often have to move into a new neighbourhood and a new

306

MILLER COMSTOCK INC.

Although most Canadians would consider Canada a country that cares about children and families, social policies and practices seem to reveal subtle biases against certain types of families.

home, besides experiencing the pain of the break-up of their family and a substantial decline in their standard of living. Why does Canadian family law ignore the interests of children when the parents decide to go their separate ways?

A look at social services also raises questions of whether they really serve the best interest of families. In 1986, 49,000 children were in the care of the various provincial child welfare systems throughout Canada. The absence of affordable child care places some parents, particularly lone-parents, in the untenable position of having to accept child care arrangements that jeopardize the safety and well-being of their children. The six-year-old latchkey child of a single mother working at the minimum wage runs the risk of coming into the care of the state and being moved sporadically between foster homes. In Ontario, for instance, a child under the age of twelve is not supposed to be left alone according to child protection legislation. Children's Aid Societies have let it be known that if they enforced this legislation the number of children in their care would double. But who takes care of the latchkey children while their parents are at work?

The family environment is partly determined by family income. Research has shown the link between low family income levels and the increased risks in infant mortality and poor health (Offord, 1987; Canadian Institute of Child Health, 1988). In 1985, out of about 7.5 million under the age of twenty in Canada, 6,000 died. The child mortality rate was twice as high among families at the lowest income level than among families at the highest income level. Children on welfare had one and half times the rate of chronic health problems compared to children from families not on welfare. Furthermore, being raised on welfare was one of the strongest predicators for childhood psychiatric disorders. These policies and practices would indicate that if Canadian society is not really anti-family and anti-child, it seems basically insensitive to the needs of families, particularly the material needs of low-income families and children and the double burden of work and family for women.

The objectives of this chapter are twofold: (1) to explore the social context against which policies affecting families are shaped and formulated; and (2) to examine specifically the relationships of dependence within the family that are regarded as important and worthy of state support in two particular policy areas – federal taxation and social security provisions. In the space available, it will be possible only to examine the details of the rules and regulations governing these areas to see how the Canadian state defines relations between the sexes and generations. A similar analysis could be made of health care, birth control, housing, and other policy areas affecting families.

THE FAMILY POLICY CONTEXT

Social policies are designed to address specific social problems. Within the last two decades, "the family" has become one of the most controversial problems of our time. Sociologists Brigitte and Peter Berger have declared that we are presently experiencing a war over the family (1984). In Canada, the political agenda over the determination of family policy seems to be divided between two major ideologically conflicting camps. The *monolithic camp* treats "the family as a monolithic structure, with an emphasis on uniformity of experience and universality of structure and function" (Eichler, 1988:2). The *pluralist camp* refers "to a particular, historically and socially specific form of family since no general or essential category can be derived analytically from the many and varied arrangements commonly lumped together as the family" (Barrett and McIntosh, 1982:81). Both camps are pro-family, although they differ in their ideological perspective of the family. The monolithic camp stands for the reassertion of the male breadwinner/ female caregiver type of family. Its supporters could be described as neo-conservatives. The pluralist camp, reflecting a liberal ideology, accepts the changeability and variability of family types. The ideological struggle over a favoured form of the family or a multitude of forms focuses mainly on the social position of women, the issue of the sexual division of labour, and the question of who will care for children.

On the one hand, the monolithic camp insists that women who are mothers of young children belong in the home to personally take care of them. Their position is that the breadwinner/caregiver type of the family, which allows women to be full-time mothers, is best for families and society. This view can, however, be seen as a backlash to a society in transition and in the process of redefining female-male relations. Pluralists, on the other hand, accept that someone other than mothers can take care of children without harm to either children or society, and they argue for state provisions that would enable both women and men to combine family responsibilities with participation in the labour market. This demand stems from the recognition that there is no going back on the trend of increasing economic activity among married women.

So far, Canadian policy makers have not accepted that increasing maternal employment is progress and will improve family life. Supporters of female-male social equality such as George Bernard Shaw saw women's employment as having a positive effect on family life and wrote accordingly (1913:15): "The truth is that family life will never be decent much less ennobling until the central horror of the dependency of women on men is done away with." Earning money gives women a degree of independence from men that in the long run should improve the quality of family life – marriages will be maintained "because of mutual love and pleasure . . . rather than because of economic dependency of one spouse on the other" (Eichler, 1988:56).

An in-between position is taken by those who are concerned that women's personal freedom is limited if mothers, who would prefer to stay at home raising children, have no choice but to take a paying job because of economic necessity. This division separates feminists into two groups, yet both groups reject the biological and social determinism of the neo-conservatives and are committed to making the labour market responsive to family responsibilities. Economic and demographic forces such as the decline in the disposable income of Canadian families with children and the rise in the number of single mothers, who are the main family breadwinners, will ensure that there is no going back on the trend of increasing economic activity among women with children. Both the monolithic and the pluralist camps vie for government action in their areas of concern. The former clamours for a return of the sexual division of labour of the breadwinner/caregiver family, despite the economic and demographic changes that are eroding the material base of this family type. Pluralists recognize that more and more women have to hold a job out of economic necessity and consider it women's right to combine family responsibilities with participation in the labour market. Monolithists regret and disapprove of the changes that have occurred in families since the 1950s. In contrast to pluralists who want to adjust other social institutions such as the labour market, family law, the social safety net, urban design, and so on to the many existing variations in family forms, monolithists attempt to set back the sociological clock of social change. The two sides attempt to influence the state to reflect in its policies affecting families their vision of what should be done about family life.

THE FAMILY AND THE STATE

The state can by no means be considered to be a neutral bystander and arbitrator in the struggle between different ideological positions over the family. Its support and reinforcement of women's care-giving role in the family has been described as alleviating "various political, administrative and fiscal problems confronting the state. Such problems may be partly – but by no means exclusively – attributable to the constraints imposed on the state by the capitalist economy" (Dale and Foster, 1986:60). The costs of child care and care for all those who are unable to look after themselves are high. The care of dependants so far has been carried out mostly within the family by women, without pay, as a "labour of love."

However, improved family incomes since the 1970s have become increasingly dependent on the labour force participation of women, and the state has had to step in to provide public care for children, the sick, the disabled, and the aged. Neo-conservatives have claimed that, through the provision of these new services, the state has not only encouraged the family to abdicate its responsibility toward its dependent members, but also has allowed government expenditures to exceed revenues, thereby causing budgetary deficits. This, they have argued, resulted not only in a staggering national deficit and rising inflation, which contributed to the "fiscal crisis" of the state, but also in a crisis about the role of women. In neo-conservative terms, criticism of the welfare state has to be understood not only as an attack on social spending, but also on women's participation in the labour market (Eisenstein, 1984:68–83).

Fiscally conservative governments at the federal and provincial levels have sought to justify cutbacks on expenditures for social programs and services by attempting to redefine the relationship between the state and the family. Both the Ontario government in 1978 (Ontario Ministry of Social Development, 1979) and the Quebec government in 1984 (Quebec, Minister of Social Affairs, 1984) emphasized the importance of developing a partnership between the state and the family. The political agenda behind this intention was to provide state support to enable families to help themselves. De-institutionalization and community care have become key policy ideas guiding state support to families so that they (read women) can meet their care-giving responsibility toward vulnerable family members (Quebec, Minister of Social Affairs, 1984:49). However, not only is this focus on family responsibility unrealistic in view of the fact that the material base of families is increasingly dependent on two incomes, but it also creates other problems for the state and for families.

A return to the breadwinner/caregiver model of the family and its specific division of labour may mean the revival of the demand by labour for a family wage, that is, a wage that would remove the economic necessity for women to work outside the home for pay to contribute to family finances. Wage increases would, however, raise the production costs of industry and consequently reduce profit rates. These developments are unlikely to be popular with employers. In the past, employers have been able to avoid any responsibility for the reproduction of labour beyond the payment of wages, which are, in accordance with neo-classical economic theory, determined by individual productivity. Any change in wage policy is certainly going to be resisted by employers. At the same time, women may not be content to be reassigned to domestic labour, and low-income men may object to losing their wives' earnings. If women were forced out of the labour market, governments would find themselves in an untenable position not only in relation to employers, who expect governments to curb social spending and are themselves unwilling to raise wages, but also with respect to wage earners.

WHAT IS FAMILY POLICY?

The connection between government social spending policy and its position toward the family raises the question of whether it is possible to identify a particular set of social policies that taken together would constitute a cohesive Canadian family policy. It is undoubtedly true that there are few policy areas that do not affect the family in one way or another. Minimum wage legislation not only determines the standard of living of families, but also that of individuals. Restricting motor vehicle traffic to one direction in a given street helps avoid traffic congestion, but it also protects the physical safety of children walking and playing in the street and reduces the concern of parents about their children's safety. Does this make it a family policy?

Wynn (1972) defined family policy as a process to influence government activities in a way that is beneficial to families. This presumes, however, a commonality of interests between families, which is far from being a reality. Eichler (1988:396) has pointed out that "policy in the name of 'the family' – actually discriminates against some or all families, or against individuals on the basis of their family status." Families differ in composition: there are two-parent and one-parent families, blended families who may have children from previous marriages, and common-law families. And they differ in economic resources: some are well off, others are poor, some have one income earner, others have two and more earners. These differences point to the futility of formulating a family policy that would serve the common interest of different family forms. The family is as illusive a concept as is the concept of "the public good" or "the public interest." Steiner, for instance, pointed out that "when the details are confronted, family policy splits up into innumerable components and becomes many causes with many votaries" (1981:215). However, it has been suggested that a number of social problems that deeply affect the social fabric and the quality of life, such as juvenile delinquency, crime, lack of discipline, and substance abuse, spring from family-related problems such as marriage break-up, child abuse, and inadequate child care arrangements (Morgan, 1975:88). Concern about these issues led professionals, academics, and bureaucrats who make the family their field of expertise to conclude that the "family has problems or even is a problem" (Berger and Berger, 1984:21). Within the context of the welfare state, to define a social problem implies that we believe we can do something about it in some form or another. "We do not have policies about the weather because, as yet, we are powerless to do anything about the weather," wrote Richard Titmuss. "But we do have policies (or can have policies) about illegitimate children because we think we have some power to affect their lives – for better or worse depending on whether you are the policy-maker or the illegitimate child" (1974:24).

The Quebec government proposed to introduce a family dimension into its policies whenever this proves necessary (1984:43). But what constitutes a family dimension? Schorr believed a family dimension could be found as long as there existed a social consensus "on a core of family goals towards the realization of which governments would shape their programs and activities" (1969:143). The notion of consensus is at the heart of modern normative social science and, paradoxically, arises out of the nature of the study of conflict resolution. The emphasis here is on the necessity of a social consensus. However, social consensus in a policy context has to be treated as a variable and not a presupposition (Hall et al., 1975:13). In a class society, government-engendered consensus in the formulation of social policy has to confront the crucial questions: Whose interest is being served? Whose objectives are being achieved for what purpose? These questions are important considering that certain social policies actually encourage or implicitly discourage particular relationships between the sexes and between parents and children.

The fact that a dependent spouse has access to the employer benefits and social insurance coverage of the other spouse seems to encourage marriage. In most provinces, a woman on social assistance moving in with a non-related man is immediately assumed to have a spousal relationship with him (in Ontario, in accordance with family law regulations, after a period of three years) and therefore is no longer entitled to receive assistance. Paradoxically, the man she lives with is not only responsible for her

economic support, but also for the children she might have from another relationship. If
we think of families as a set of legal, economic, and moral obligations and rights, what
implications do the support obligations of a woman's live-in-partner have for the father
of her children? It seems that the state considers him no longer responsible. Is
transferring the support obligations between men moving in and out of intimate
relationships with a woman considered to be family policy? Before we can answer this
question, we first need a useful definition of the family.

DEFINITIONS OF "THE FAMILY"

The problem with defining the family is not with the noun "family," but with the article
"the" (Eichler, 1983:4). The simple question – What is a family? – is not so easy to
answer. Is a parent living with a same-sex partner raising the children from a previous
marriage a family? In Metropolitan Toronto, a homosexual employee applied to have
family coverage for dental care and extended hospital care for her live-in partner. The
application was denied because the employer refused to recognize the couple as a family.
This example would indicate that a family policy that is directed toward the fostering of
a particular family type operates to the detriment of the family types that do not fit the
prescribed mould (Eichler, 1988:132).

The family has been described as "not just a combination of individuals" (Quebec,
Minister of Social Affairs, 1984:20). As an organic entity, it stands over and beyond the
individual. The family is seen as a special kind of institution. It does not matter, wrote
Robert Lowie, "whether marital relations are permanent or temporary, whether there is
polygyny or polyandry or sexual license ... the one fact stands out beyond all others
that everywhere, the husband, wife and immature children constitute a unit apart from
the remainder of the community" (1947:66). The biology of human reproduction is used
to offer a legitimate scientific basis for the family as a "natural" unit. The category of the
"natural" is applied also to other institutions and social situations, but "nowhere is this
category so constantly invoked to strengthen and sanction the existing social arrangement, as in the case of the family" (Barrett and McIntosh, 1982:35). There is, however,
no relationship between the biological phenomenon of mother duck, father duck, and all
the little baby ducks swimming in a pond, and the human mother and father with their
offspring watching them (Kitchen, 1984:12).

Particular forms of human families have varied with the range of kinship patterns
documented by anthropologists and historians. Some anthropologists have argued that
the basic social unit is not the nuclear family, which includes the father, but a mother
and her children (Collier, Rosaldo, and Yanagisako, 1982:27). The family as a small
co-residing group of parents and children does not exist in all societies. "Among the
Mundurucu of tropical South America, for example, the men of a village traditionally
lived in a men's house together with all the village boys over the age of thirteen; women
lived with other women and young children in two or three houses grouped around the
men's house" (Collier, Rosaldo, and Yanagisako, 1982:28). The co-residence of parents
and children is a fairly recent historical development. In Canada, children were sent
away as servants as soon as they were old enough to work for their keep. Thus, we find
that in mid-eighteenth-century New France, for instance, nearly two-thirds of household
servants were children who were generally indentured at the age of five or six with no

other return for their labour but their maintenance (Moogk, 1982:26). These examples indicate that the biological base of the family is transformed through the interaction of its members in society as a whole (Mitchell, 1975:370). In other words, the family is a social construct.

Today, many still see the family only in terms of a couple and their children (Quebec, Minister of Social Affairs, 1984:16). This heterosexual, nuclear unit biologically and legally defined is seen as consistent with its universal function, the raising of children. The function has been translated into a normative imperative that elevated the couple and their children as the only natural and legitimate family form. It is the only family model that is validated and sanctioned by both the state and the church and given unreserved social approval.

The idealized form of the heterosexual, nuclear family also constitutes an attempt to establish a specific pattern of social relations between women and men as well as parents and children. The division of labour by sex, which led to the exclusion of women from the sphere of production in nineteenth-century industrializing countries, created the breadwinner-husband/caregiver-wife type of family. For Herbert Spencer, this type of family represented evolutionary progress:

> Evolution has led to the present division of labour between the sexes: up from the lowest savagery, civilisation has, among other results, caused an increasing exemption of women from breadwinning labour.... In the highest societies they have become most restricted to domestic duties and the rearing of children (quoted in Sayers, 1982:36).

One may wonder why it is so important to social science to identify the family as the fundamental social unit and child raising as its basic function. The significance of this issue seems to be anchored to the paradox of the family as a social institution serving a dual function. It both provides a refuge from an alienated, atomistic world of production and represents a site of repression that is structurally exploitative for women and children. This means, on the one hand, that it is an institution that manages, or is expected to manage, the tensions inherent in the world of work, thus contributing to the maintenance rather than change of the existing social order. On the other hand, it is also a powerful force in maintaining the sexual division of labour into male-breadwinner and female-caregiver that structures women's inequality in relation to men. As such, this division of labour is as important to the continued exploitation of working men as it is to the oppression of women (Leacock, 1981:13).

The sexual division of labour also establishes a relationship of interdependence between the spouses and dependence for children in the family. "Its members, however autonomous and different they may be from one another as persons, live in a relationship of interdependence, and develop together in the family environment" (Quebec, Minister of Social Development, 1984:20). The relations of interdependence between the sexes are most clearly apparent in the breadwinner/caregiver type of family. This division of labour defines a set of social relations between women and men, divides them into hierarchical gender roles, and structures their related duties within the economy and the family.

The wife's contribution in kind (her domestic labour) and the husband's contribution in cash (his paid labour) establish an interdependence between them. It frees him from housework and child care and frees her from the demands of paid employment. The contributions of each of the sexes to family life thus seem to establish a similar status for both partners within the family (Delphy, 1976:79). This is, however, far from being the case. First, since domestic labour is unpaid, it requires the underpinnings of paid labour; and second, men can buy the provision of domestic labour outside the home. "Waitresses serve food and clean tables; nurses tend sick bodies and therapists provide shoulders to cry on" (Brown, 1981:245). Furthermore, the relationship of interdependence in the family leaves women and children economically vulnerable. Family life based on the breadwinner/caregiver sexual division of labour remains structurally, physically, emotionally, and economically exploitative of women. The breadwinner/caregiver type of family involves an economic relationship and division of labour between women and men that has created two spheres of activities that are not only separate, but also unequal.

Criticism of the Family

For almost two decades after the Second World War, women accepted the male dictum that their family was the most important aspect of their life. After the economic turmoil of the Great Depression and the war years, the family seemed indeed a haven from a heartless world. These years have been described as the renaissance of the family. With the new psychology of the human growth movement, however, the individual emerged from the narrow confines of the family (Ehrenreich, 1984:88). The 1960s abounded with severe criticisms and attacks of the often destructive emotional impact of the family on its members, particularly the emotionally damaging effect of women on their children. The economic aspects of family life and its effects were largely ignored. Far from being the fundamental cornerstone of society, the family came to be seen as everything that was wrong in society because of its stifling, sexually and emotionally repressive nature and the emotional stress this placed on husbands and wives, and on parents and children (Laing, 1970, 1976). The family was identified as a threat to individual freedom and as the bulwark of hierarchical class society. Yet, this criticism was not new. In the 1930s, Wilhelm Reich had written that "the cardinal function (of the family) for which it is mostly supported and defended by conservative science and law, is that of serving as a factory for authoritarian ideologies and conservative structures" (Segal, 1983:44-45). Thus, the struggle for a free, unauthoritarian society came to be seen as inseparable from the struggle against "bourgeois values" and the family. And the death of the family seemed imminent because of its threat to individualism (Cooper, 1971).

Throughout the 1960s, the attack on the family focused mainly on intergenerational conflict and the problematic nature of the mother-child relationship, rather than father-child interaction (Spiegel, 1982:95). Family was really a code word for mother. Women's restriction to domestic labour, argues Adrienne Rich, reveals that "the family really means the mother who carries the major share of childbearing, and who also absorbs the frustrations and rage her husband may bring home from work, often in the form of domestic violence" (1976:54).

With the revival of the women's movement in the early 1970s, the emphasis began to shift to the position of women in society and female-male relations. An interesting explanation of women's questioning of their position in society and in the family has been offered by Ehrenreich (1984). Contrary to the widespread assumption that women insisted on changing their gender roles, Ehrenreich argued that the economic basis of family life was seriously undermined by the collapse of the breadwinner ethic. "In the space of a few decades, our culture has inverted the expectations that made the family wage system in any sense justifiable as a means of distributing wealth from those who are relatively advantaged as wage-earner (men) to many of those (women and children) who are not" (Ehrenreich, 1984:12). The revival of the women's movement, therefore, would not be the result of women abandoning the family, but a reaction to men's inability to continue as sole breadwinner.

Despite climbing divorce rates, increasing numbers of lone-parent families, and more women joining the labour market, the majority of people continue to seek personal fulfilment in family life. "Familialism is not a ruling class or patriarchal ideology repressively foisted on an unwilling population" (Barrett and McIntosh, 1982:21). On the contrary, the popularity of the family cannot be underestimated, even though individuals may choose to leave marriage and the family more easily than ever before. This would indicate that the commitment may be more to the institution and ideology of marriage and family, rather than to a specific marriage partner, parent, or child.

Changing Families

It has been estimated that, today, about 14 percent of women and 17 percent of men will never marry (*The Toronto Star*, November 16, 1988:A13). This means that eighty-six out of one hundred teenage girls will get married, and about eighty will have children. With three out of ten marriages expected to end in divorce, about twenty-four of these girls are likely to end up as lone parents. Today, an increasing number of Canadian children born into a nuclear family will live in lone-parent families after the divorce or the death of one of their parents, will re-enter a blended family, and will reside in a non-family household before forming their own nuclear family and repeating the previous cycle (Nett, 1976:75). Whether we like it or not, serial monogamy is happening with increasing frequency, "and to decry this fact will not make it vanish" (Stratham, 1977:41).

Relatively few families weather the storm of death or break-up through divorce without encountering serious and continuing financial hardship. Policies that reinforce women's economic dependency are costly for both women and the state. They are major factors why many women find themselves living in poverty after the loss or death of their male provider. The administrative aspects of the tax system and social programs clearly support the breadwinner/caregiver sexual division of labour that defines women as the dependants of men. The tax system is one of the major vehicles through which the state reinforces the sexual division of labour and women's economic dependency on men in marriage.

TAX POLICIES AND THE FAMILY

THE BASIC TAX UNIT

Despite the fact that the individual is the basic tax unit in Canada, and not the family as in Great Britain or the United States, the Canadian personal income tax system shows a definite bias for the breadwinner/caregiver type of family. This bias is not immediately apparent, particularly because individual taxation avoids two major problems of family taxation. First, it ensures that a wife's income is never deemed to be her husband's even for tax purposes, and second, the illusion cannot be constructed that the income of the breadwinner or the separate incomes of two people are in fact "family income" because of a marriage certificate. Using the individual as the basic tax unit has led to claims, however, that it causes horizontal inequity in the tax system. With an income of $30,000 a year, a wage earner with a spouse and two children pays $3,992 in taxes. By contrast, a two-income couple with two children earning the identical income is taxed $2,169.

To avoid taxing a married couple with both partners in the work force more than a one-income couple, the Royal Commission on Taxation (1966) recommended using the family as the basic tax unit. It argued that a family's ability to pay taxes, rather than that of individual family members, should be taken into account in determining tax liabilities. The Royal Commission on the Status of Women (1970) shared this position on the grounds that the provision of housekeeping services to oneself and one's family adds to the taxable capacity of the individual or family just as the sale of labour services for cash adds to taxable capacity (Hartle, 1971:82). It recommended dropping or at least reducing the married tax exemption, not to disparage the role of homemaking, but to enhance it. The Royal Commission on the Status of Women took the position that women engaged in supplying services to their families should not be considered dependants who reduce the taxable capacity of their husbands when they in fact enhance it (1970:41). While this position seemed to represent an explicit recognition of the value of domestic labour, it also implied support for the sexual division of labour. With more and more women combining their domestic responsibilities with paid employment, the position of the Royal Commission has become unacceptable. Sooner or later, the tax system will have to recognize the dual responsibility of women in the home and in the work force.

The Married Exemption

The Canadian tax system contains a number of generous tax benefits based on marital status rather than parenthood, which implies that the tax system favours marriage more than parenthood. The married exemption clearly indicates that the state is willing to support only the economic dependency of women on men as full-time homemakers in marriage, but denies this tax break to those in common-law or homosexual relationships in which the same division of labour exists. If the marital tax credit were indeed meant as a recognition of the value of domestic labour that stay-at-home partners contribute to their families' overall standard of living, the value of the housework of the dependent partner in a common-law or homosexual relationship would also have to be recognized.

In 1917, when the Personal Income Tax Act was first passed, the married exemption (now the married tax credit) was introduced in recognition of the special legal and moral obligation a husband had to support a wife. In recent years, the tendency has been for this obligation to become reciprocal, and the majority of Canadian families today have two income earners. Yet, the tax system continues to uphold the patriarchal, heterosexual family model.

It seems ironic that women's domestic labour is granted recognition by giving their husbands more money. The value of the domestic labour of the wife of a taxpayer in the 50 percent tax bracket (if federal and provincial rates are added up) is given greater cash value by the tax system than the domestic labour of the wife of a man taxed at a 30 percent tax rate. By replacing tax exemptions with tax credits, the 1987 tax reform has created a more equitable tax system. With a marital tax credit of $850, which provides the same tax reduction for all taxpayers, the domestic labour of women married to men in different income brackets has been equalized.

Dulude (1982) has called the married exemption a relic of the early days of the tax system, when the value of a homemaker's work was considered to be so low that a wife at home was understood by all to be a burden rather than an asset. Differentiating between married and unmarried couples indicates the state's support and endorsement for the breadwinner/caregiver type of family only and recognition of the value of housework for married couples alone.

Despite the many objections raised about the marital tax credit, a major one being its lack of recognition of the domestic labour of married women who are in the labour force, it remains popular and therefore untouched. When a couple has agreed that one spouse (nearly always the wife) is to be a full-time homemaker, this is a private arrangement and of benefit only to them, in contrast to childbearing, which serves the interest of society in producing its future work force. Consequently, there are no grounds for arguing that the state should continue in future to recognize an arrangement that applies to only 17 percent of Canadian families.

The elimination of the married tax credit would not only reduce the after-tax income of childless couples, but also of couples with children. To recognize child care or the care of a dependent adult as an essential public service, the married tax credit could be transformed into a credit for caregivers covering all co-residential arrangements where there is a breadwinner and a caregiver. This would mean the extension of the caregiver credit to all cohabiting couples. Families without tax liabilities, who otherwise could not use the tax credit, would be paid a direct, sliding-scale caregiver allowance. One of the greatest virtues of a universal caregiver credit is to tax care-giving families less so they can keep more of their own earned income. Its cost does not represent a direct government expenditure, except for families without tax liabilities. Instead, its cost is measured in lost government revenue.

The Child Tax Credit

The Canadian state has long recognized that the raising of children entails economic and other sacrifices by parents. The child tax exemption goes back to 1917 and was introduced alongside the marital tax exemption. Like the marital tax exemption, it has been transformed into a tax credit of $65 for the first two children and of $120 for three and more children under the age of eighteen (effective as of the 1988 tax year). This is a considerably lesser amount than the marital tax credit and suggests the notion that marriage seems to require more governmental support than parenthood. Parents of older children who are still dependent on them are no longer given a tax break, increasing the financial hardship of low- and middle-income families who are helping to put their children through post-secondary education. The exceptions are individuals over eighteen who are physically or mentally disabled.

MILLER COMSTOCK INC.

The child tax exemption was introduced in 1917 to recognize economic and other sacrifices made by parents.

The Child Care Deduction

The tax system is also used to compensate partially the costs of child care for parents who need it in order to earn an income from employment, a training course, research, or similar kind of work. In the past, only women could claim the child care deduction, because presumably only women had child care responsibilities. In its National Strategy for Childcare in December 1987, the federal government provided greater assistance to families through the tax system. The maximum child care deduction of $2,000 was increased to $4,000 for a child under the age of six or for a child with special needs. For children over six years, the tax deduction has remained $2,000, but the $8,000 allowable deduction limit per family has been removed (Canadian Day Care Advocacy Association 1988:9).

This is, however, not the best way to direct financial relief to families. Tax exemptions are far from being progressive, equitable tax instruments. Their cash value is always greater for those taxed in a higher tax bracket, since they reduce the amount of taxable income in proportion with the increases in the marginal tax rate by income bracket. Since tax exemptions reduce taxable income instead of tax liability, they are more advantageous to taxpayers in high tax brackets than those in low brackets. Tax credits would have been a fairer and more equitable policy option. They provide proportionally greater relief to families in low-income brackets because tax credits are subtracted after tax liability has been calculated.

The 1987 tax changes allow stay-at-home parents, or parents who pay for child care services but do not have receipts, a $200 supplement a year if they qualify for the refundable child tax credit for children under the age of six. The supplement represents a token recognition of the unpaid child care services provided by the parent and as such supports the breadwinner/caregiver type of family. It provides some additional financial support for low-income families and is the first policy provision that can be considered both a child and a caregiver benefit. The National Action Committee on the Status of Women has raised objections to this child care credit, not because it is opposed to child care benefits for mothers who care for their own children, but because it resists all direct child care subsidies to individuals including the child care tax deduction for mothers in the labour force. Instead, the National Action Committee favours the direct funding of the cost of child care for all parents, since women must have access to these services in order to have a real choice of whether or not to join the labour force (NAC, Family Policy Committee, March 1988:15).

The Refundable Child Tax Credit

A second child benefit delivered through the tax system is the refundable tax credit for low-income families whose net family income does not exceed $24,200 in the tax year. This is the only social security program that bases benefits on family income. Families whose combined net income actually is that amount or less may deduct the full amount of the credit from their tax bill. If they pay no tax, or less than the credit, mothers still receive a payment from the Department of Revenue for the amount owed. In 1988, the maximum credit was raised to $724 from $524 per child through the addition of $200 as noted above. The size of the credit gradually decreases as family income rises, and eventually disappears. A family with two children and a family income of $48,500 would receive no benefit from the credit. If this income was earned by the breadwinner-husband, the caregiver-wife's benefit has been reduced to zero. This effect can be called an attack on intrafamily equity, that is, the objective to provide an income for mothers.

The standard of living of a family is generally measured by the income of the main wage earner. The assumption is that this income is shared equitably among all members of the household since it is considered impossible that women and children in the family can be poor while the husband is affluent. But this is clearly not the case – within marriage there is no law forcing spouses to share their income. A more equitable way of distributing financial resources in parental families is through taxable family allowances. They protect women's access to independent income for their children by increasing the taxable income of men, which has been described as "robbing the wallet to pay the purse." But this cannot be avoided in the breadwinner/caregiver type of family. A 1985 survey in Britain of 2,000 mothers of all income strata found that only 6 percent said the universal child benefit was not important in meeting their children's needs (Henwood and Wicks, 1988:35). It therefore seems crucial to provide women with access to an independent source of income.

Child Support Payment

The prevalent system of individual taxation in Canada has been given a family focus for child support payments from a single, separated, or divorced parent to the custodial parent. The tax system treats child support payments by one parent (usually the father) to the custodial parent (mostly the mother) as "family income." She is taxed on that portion of the father's income that is tax deductible for him. The mother as the custodial parent who carries the actual child care and support expenses is not granted such tax privileges, nor are families in which both parents still live together. The differential treatment of custodial and non-custodial parents by the tax system is hard to explain. It benefits absent parents who can reduce their taxable income, but it hurts custodial parents and the children for whom the value of their fathers' support payments are reduced (Kitchen, 1986:44).

SOCIAL SECURITY PROGRAMS

SPOUSAL BENEFITS

A. The Unit of Benefit

Social security programs, as outlined in the report on *Social Security 1943* prepared by Leonard Marsh for the federal government, were designed with the breadwinner/caregiver model of the family in mind. A woman in the work force, whether married or unmarried, was treated as an individual without dependants. On the other hand, a married man's social insurance premiums against income loss or reduction were to cover not only himself, but also his wife and children. Thus, while the unit of contribution was the individual, the unit of benefit was the family. Initially, unemployment insurance contained a 15 percent benefit differential for men and women, and the survivors' benefits under the Canada/Quebec Pension Plan were restricted to women. Today, unemployment insurance and the two pension plans have become more individualistic in their benefit structure.

However, the unemployment insurance benefit differential did not achieve horizontal equity because it applied to all families regardless of their size. In 1975, the "family provision" was abolished and the individual became the unit of benefit. The earnings-related nature of Canada's two major contributory social insurance programs, unemployment insurance and the Canada/Quebec Pension Plan, is reflected in their benefit structure, which is the same for married and unmarried individuals. This is the counterside to Eichler's concern that "programs earmarking funds or services on the basis of their family status will result in the discrimination of some people in the same objective circumstances" (1988:135).

B. Pension Splitting

Women who have never been in the labour force have coverage under the social security system through their husbands, if they are in the work force. They are expected to share their unemployment insurance or Canada/Quebec Pension benefit with their wives in the same way as they would share their wages or salaries. An interesting, recent policy change is the option for either spouse in a continuing marriage to apply for the splitting of pension credits earned by one or both spouses during their life together. This option was introduced to enhance economic equality in marriage between the sexes, and to give some official recognition to the contribution housewives make to family well-being by making it possible for them to receive their own pension cheques. It is the closest the Canadian pension system has come to earnings sharing between spouses. The same option exists for couples upon marriage break-up.

These options seem to be an attempt to stress the economic interdependence of spouses within the breadwinner/caregiver type of marriage, as well as a recognition of the significantly lower earnings typical of women in two-income families. Credits are divided equally between the spouses, regardless of who paid more into the plan. Couples must have lived together for at least three consecutive years, and the application for the division of credits must be made within three years of the final decree of a divorce. The same provision applies for common-law relationships, but the application for the division of credits must be made within one year of separation.

C. Survivors' Benefits

Whereas unemployment insurance totally ignores the family responsibilities of claimants, the Canada/Quebec Pension Plan only recognizes them after the death of a contributor in the form of survivors' benefits. The patriarchal assumption that husbands are responsible for the financial support of their wives, but wives only in exceptional circumstances for their husbands, found practical application under the Canada/Quebec Pension Plan in the survivors' benefits, which until 1982 were paid only to women (Kitchen, 1980). Widowers whose wives had paid into the plans could only qualify if they were disabled or had been substantially dependent on their wives' income.

Benefit calculations for the surviving spouse are based on age and the presence of children. Widowed spouses under the age of forty-five qualify for the survivors' benefits only if they have dependent children or are disabled. Older spouses receive a pension made up of a flat-rate annually adjusted amount in addition to 37.5 percent of their husbands'/wives' pension entitlement. The maximum monthly survivors' benefits are usually too low to live on. The practice, therefore, is to defer entitlements until the surviving spouse reaches retirement age or becomes disabled.

A surviving spouse over sixty-five whose marital partner had been receiving benefits under the plan qualifies for 60 percent of his or her benefits. Thus, with the death of the pension holder, the surviving spouse loses 40 percent of their previous joint income. As of January 1987, persons receiving survivors' benefits can continue to do so if they remarry (*Canada Yearbook*, 1988). In the case of a woman with no pension entitlement of her own, the continuation of the survivors' benefit provides her not only with a modicum of financial independence from a new husband, but also represents a recognition of the value of the domestic labour she performed in her previous marriage.

D. The Spousal Allowance

The breadwinner/caregiver type of family is given further recognition and support through the federal spouses' allowance benefit. This program was designed to alleviate the income pressure of older couples where the man was receiving old age security and his wife was still too young (under sixty-five) to qualify for a pension in her own right. Since Canadian women tend to marry men who are about three years older and it is difficult for some men to support a wife on a substantially reduced retirement income, the program is essential to guarantee these couples some economic security. Until an amendment in 1980, spouses who became widows between the ages of sixty and sixty-four had their allowances stopped until they qualified for old age security at sixty-five. If they had no other means of support, they had to apply for provincial social assistance. Now both sexes continue to receive the allowance after the death of their spouse of pensionable age.

Linking pension benefits to marital status has its economic disadvantages for never-married or divorced women between sixty and sixty-five. Because they do not qualify for pensions, many of them suffer severe financial hardship, as the following two cases illustrate:

> A sixty-four-year-old woman who had never married has to live on $400 a month. She receives $130 a month from the Canada Pension Plan and the rest from a part-time job in home nursing.

> A sixty-two-year-old divorced woman who left her husband with their eight children after almost thirty years of physical and mental abuse must work at a job that pays her less than $1,000 a month after taxes.

The first woman fails to qualify because she has never been a spouse, and the second woman is ineligible because her husband did not die while she was married to him. The spousal allowance clearly discriminates on the basis of marital status. "There seems to be an attitude that a widow or widower is a superior being to someone who is single or divorced. It really glorifies marriage," charged a woman who met the age and income criterion, but not that of widowhood.

PARENTAL BENEFITS

A. Maternity Benefits

The original 1941 Unemployment Insurance Act did not provide maternity benefits. Canadian women in the work force had to wait thirty years before they could receive an income replacement during a period of rest and recuperation associated with childbirth. To gain support for maternity benefits, the Marsh Report (1943) had referred to such benefits as a desirable corollary to sickness benefits (Marsh, 1975:211). Yet, maternity benefits are a recognition of the fact that women enter the labour market on different conditions from men. The Unemployment Insurance Act of 1971 finally established this fact.

FOR INTEREST

COURT UPHOLDS MATERNITY BENEFITS FOR WOMEN; RECOMMENDS EXPANDED CHILD CARE BENEFITS

In a landmark Federal Court of Canada ruling in June, Justice Barry Strayer decided that existing maternity benefits under the Unemployment Insurance Act must be exclusively available to women to recognize needs relating to childbearing;

and that benefits available to adoptive parents recognizing needs related to child care should also be available to biological parents.

The case was initiated by Shalom Schachter who had applied to the Unemployment Insurance Commission for unemployment insurance benefits to assist his wife while she recovered from childbirth, and so that later she could return to work and he could stay home and look after their newborn. When he was refused, he challenged the Unemployment Insurance legislation under Section 15 of the Charter, on the grounds that he, as a biological father, was denied benefits available to other parents: adopting fathers or mothers had access to 15 weeks child care benefits and biological mothers had access to maternity benefits.

LEAF (Women's Legal Education and Action Fund) intervened in the case to argue that the current 15 weeks maternity benefits are a minimum for biological mothers who may need to be out of the work force prior to birth, and obviously need time off during birth and the recovery period, and to allow for breastfeeding. However, said LEAF, child care benefits should be available equally to biological and adopting mothers and fathers. Justice Strayer accepted LEAF's position.

The Court's decision was very important since it reaffirmed the recognition of women's unique needs relating to child-bearing through maternity benefits and it also recognized the importance of fathers playing a greater role in the care of children. It opened up the possibility for biological mothers and fathers to have 15 weeks of benefits *each* after the birth of a child or of biological mothers to have 30 weeks of benefits, twice as much as before the decision.

Regrettably, the Federal Government appealed the decision. In its Notice of Appeal, the Government took the position that the remedy ordered by Justice Strayer went beyond the Court's jurisdiction and that it provided relief sought by a party other than the plaintiff. (That is, the remedy proposed by LEAF.) The Government suggests that the Court should have struck down child care benefits for adopting parents as a way to eliminate the inequality experienced by biological fathers. If this argument is accepted, child care benefits will be denied both biological and adopting parents, which may technically result in "same treatment," but not substantive equality, and will result in a very narrow remedial authority for the courts under the Charter.

LEAF will continue to intervene in this case in the Federal Court of Appeal, to ensure that women's maternity benefits are safeguarded, and of great significance, to advance a broad and affirmative remedial authority for the Courts to ensure that Section 15 may fulfil its mandate of alleviating disadvantage.

Source: *LEAF Newsletter*, December 1988. The Women's Legal Education and Action Fund is a national organization that promotes equality for women through the support of test cases primarily based on the Charter of Rights and Freedoms and through public education.

Women presently are eligible for maternity benefits if they have been in the work force for at least ten of the twenty weeks prior to the thirtieth week before the expected date of confinement. After a waiting period of two weeks, they qualify for eight weeks of benefit before the confinement, the week of the confinement, and six weeks after it.

Organized women's groups and labour leaders have been pressuring for an elimination of the two-week waiting period and an extension of maternity benefits to seventeen weeks instead of the current fifteen.

B. Parental Leave Policy

Recently, besides the biological mother, maternity benefits have been granted for fifteen weeks for child care reasons to either parent of an adoptive couple. Biological parents, however, are not given this option, which led the Canadian Human Rights Commission to call this omission unfair and administratively inconsistent. To recognize the dual purpose of maternity benefits – giving women not only a period of recuperation, but also acknowledging the intensive care and nurturing required by newborn children – the Commission of Inquiry on Unemployment Insurance (1986) and the Parliamentary Committee on Child Care (1987) joined the Human Rights Commission in calling for a two-tiered system for maternity benefits. The present maternal benefits payable for fifteen weeks for mothers giving birth would be followed by a child care benefit available for another fifteen weeks to either parent, natural as well as adoptive.

There is chance that such a two-tiered system might be achieved in the near future because of a recent amendment to the Unemployment Insurance Act in February 1988. Natural fathers now qualify for child care benefits in the case of the death or disability of the child's mother. This amendment constitutes an important step in the direction of gender equality in family relations. Child care benefits have also been granted to the natural mothers of premature babies who would no longer be able to qualify for maternity benefits by the time the children returned home to them after months of hospitalization (Shifrin, 1988). The recent changes in eligibility indicate that childbirth benefits are meant for more than the recuperation of mothers and that a paternal leave policy will soon back up the birth-related benefit (see page 325).

Universal family allowances are intended specifically to promote the material welfare of dependent children.

MILLER COMSTOCK INC.

FOR INTEREST

SWEDISH MOTHERS, FATHERS WIN 1¹/₂-YEAR PAID LEAVE

STOCKHOLM – Mothers and fathers can look forward to 18 months of paid parental leave after the birth of a child, under Sweden's budget put forward yesterday.

The 1989-90 budget proposed a gradual expansion in already lavish support available to married and unmarried parents, earmarking more for family support than for defence spending.

Parental leave, with the state compensating 90 per cent of lost income, would be extended from nine to 12 months in July, to 15 months next year and to 18 months in July, 1991. The Social Ministry estimated the cost of parental insurance at the equivalent of $2.5-billion for the current budget year.

The budget allocated $7.9-billion for family support, compared with $5.7-billion for defence.

The state pays a monthly child allowance of $107 and heavily subsidizes day-care services. Eighty-five per cent of Swedish women with preschool children go to work.

Parents pay only one fifth of the $9,500 it costs to keep a child in a day-care centre for one year.

The family-support proposal, one of the few expansive items in a tight state budget, is expected to be approved by parliament.

CHILDREN'S BENEFITS

A. Family Allowances

Universal family allowances are intended specifically to promote the material welfare of dependent children. They are paid to mothers to ensure this. Family allowances have been adopted by most Western industrialized countries with the notable exceptions of the United States and Switzerland. In four Canadian provinces (Alberta, Saskatchewan, Manitoba, and Quebec), the universal program is supplemented by a provincial benefit.

Family allowances are a recognition that parents need to have greater financial resources than a childless couple or a childless individual, and are therefore paid for all children regardless of parental income. Second, they are a necessary addition to the present wage system based on the economic principle of individual productivity, which does not take into account the economic costs of parenthood (Child Poverty Action Group, 1986:8). Family allowance was worth $32.38 a month per child in 1988. With the child tax credit and the refundable child tax credit, they constitute the child benefits that cover about 3.6 million Canadian families raising children.

The Canadian government, however, is gradually but definitely withdrawing from its economic partnership with parents in the raising of children. Since the Progressive Conservative government took office in 1984, these benefits have been substantially decreased through partial de-indexation. By the end of 1988, a middle-income family (around $40,000) with two children had their child benefits reduced by about $700 a year (*A Choice of Futures: Canada's Commitment to Its Children*, 1988:4). Since 1973, family allowances have been considered taxable income for the parent who has claimed the child tax exemption. In most cases, this would be the father, to whom the tax exemption is of greater value because of his higher income. To make child benefits more equitable and to ensure that they go to mothers on behalf of their children, it has been proposed that the three programs be combined into one universal, taxable child income benefit (Child Poverty Action Group, 1986).

Several attempts have been made to transform family allowances from a universal into a selective program. It has been argued that universal benefits are made to families who do not necessarily need them, and that by targeting the allowances to those in need, the overall costs of the program could be reduced. The problem, however, is not with family allowances, but with the regressive nature of the tax system, which has been worsened by the 1987 tax changes (Muszynski, 1988:25) (see below).

FOR INTEREST

FAMILY ALLOWANCE: INVESTMENT IN CANADA'S KIDS

By Lawrence J. Nestman
Mr. Nestman is president of the Vanier Institute of the Family in Ottawa.

We are often told that children are Canada's most precious resource. We are also told by those who would shape our opinions and presume to represent our interests that we cannot afford the less-than-$400-a-year family allowance, meant to nourish, protect and enhance the value of this most precious of resources.

Since 1944, Canadians have taken pride in the fact that they have, like almost all other industrially advanced nations with the notable exception of the United States, sought to ensure that all citizens assume some modest responsibility for the well-being of the nation's children. Thus, we have provided parents with a family allowance – a small but not insignificant stipend for sheltering, feeding, educating and nurturing the next generation of workers and citizens, the generation upon which every one of today's adults will grow to depend.

We have done so in the belief that parents should pay less tax and should receive greater benefits than taxpayers without children, precisely because of the costs they bear and the benefits they deliver to society at large.

The family allowance program costs the federal government about $2.6-billion a year. At least one-quarter of that amount is recovered through taxation, and the program has, indeed, served to benefit most those who need it, precisely because the benefits are taxable. At present, it costs each Canadian taxpayer about 47 cents a day to share in the $10 of daily costs incurred by parents.

Recent publicity surrounding extremely wealthy recipients of family allowances threatens to undermine the essential principle of the program. Thus it is the example of the rare but extremely wealthy Canadian who makes $500,000 or $600,000 a year that promises to diminish the support taxpayers provide to the far larger number of families with average incomes.

When it is understood that the

wealthiest recipients of family allowances will return almost one-half of their $400 allowance along with their taxes, their net gain of slightly more than $200 pales alongside the other government benefits available only to the relatively affluent. Whatever its merits, tax reform has ensured that wealthy Canadians will have $2,330 a year more in disposable income in 1991 than they did in 1984, while the working poor and middle-income earners will pay more in taxes by 1991.

Wealthy Canadians also avail themselves of capital-gains exemptions and other investment incentives to ensure a sound economic future. Surely, Canadians still know and appreciate that the future of any society depends, first and foremost, on how willing it is to invest in its children.

Family allowances should not be equated with social assistance and cannot justifiably be thought of as welfare for the middle class. Traditionally, family allowances and child tax exemptions served as the only methods Canadians could use to acknowledge the work par-

ents perform on behalf of themselves, their children and society as a whole. These measures provided that adults with dependent children were taxed less and benefited more than those without.

Few Canadians appreciate that already the value of the family allowance has declined significantly since its introduction and that this erosion will accelerate because, with the decision to reduce the amount benefits increase to keep pace with inflation, they will lose 3 per cent of their value every year. If the government chooses not to eliminate family allowances entirely, there is a good chance that the formula for partial de-indexation, which has already saved the government almost $500-million, will increase another 1 per cent, cutting the cost of benefits by $25-million at the expense of parents and their children.

Moreover, the value of the child tax exemption, the only other tangible benefit received by parents, has been halved since 1984. For all intents and purposes, children have been "factored out" of the taxation system as though they no longer count.

Source: *The Globe and Mail*, April 27, 1989. **Reprinted by Permission of Lawrence Nestman and Vanier Institute of the Family in ottawa.**

B. Benefits for Children of Disabled Persons and Orphans

Under the Canada/Quebec Pension Plan children of persons receiving a disability pension qualify for benefits at the same monthly rate and under the same conditions as those that apply to the children of deceased persons. Benefits are payable until the children reach the age of eighteen, but can be extended to age twenty-five if the children attend school. If education is interrupted, benefits are reinstated as soon as the child resumes full-time school attendance. Benefits for the first four children equal the flat-rate component of the survivors' pension (discussed above). Additional children qualify for half this amount. All children receive the same benefit amount, however, since the total amount of child benefits for a family is divided equally among all children. It is noteworthy that the payments to orphans and the children of disabled persons are continued beyond the age of majority, whereas tax credits and family allowances end at this age level. The assumption seems to be that the living parents of adult children continuing their education have income levels that allow them to support their children's education. This is clearly not the case for many families.

While children could previously receive the benefits of only one parent, since January 1987 they are eligible for the benefits of both parents if the earning power of both parents has been lost through disability or death. This policy change is a reflection of the equality of treatment of contributions that had to be implemented under the Charter of Rights and Freedoms. Benefits continue to be paid even if the children marry. A further benefit for children is the lump sum death benefit payable to the estate of a contributor who dies prior to retirement and who has made contributions to pension or insurance plans for at least three years.

CONCLUSION

Canadian tax and income support policies for families have encountered problems because they reflect the ambiguities about the sexual division of labour and the social position of women. The increasing number of married women in the work force has presented a particular policy conundrum for the state. To overcome the bias for the breadwinner/caregiver type of family, all tax credits and social security criteria on the basis of sex, marital, or family status would have to be removed. As parents are separating and divorcing in increasing numbers, the state seems to be weighing the costs of child care for women in the labour market against the costs of assisting women without a male provider to look after their children at home. Unable to develop a position in either direction, existing policies make one option as difficult and as unpalatable as the other.

The conditions under which women presently qualify for government income support are determined not so much by a desire to reaffirm the breadwinner/caregiver division of labour, but by the state's interest that women will continue their unpaid work of caring for their families. This would explain the preference for the current state of affairs, which offers women limited economic independence by restricting them in the production process to the kinds of jobs that correspond with their domestic role in the family. This role places women in a subordinate position both in family relations and in the social hierarchy of the workplace. As a result, they and their children end up economically worse off than men when the family breaks up. This could lead to the raising of a generation of children who grow up in poverty because their parents separated. It has to be recognized clearly that the poverty of mothers and children is caused by women continuing to shoulder the primary responsibility for child care while oblivious to the economic risks that this involves when they find themselves without a male provider.

The most crucial family policy issue today is the acceptance of gender equality between women and men in the home and in the workplace. This calls for a commitment by the state to employment and pay equity between the sexes. Family policies require an ideological reorientation to provide the services and facilities to enable both women and men to combine family responsibilities with participation in the labour market. This involves universally accessible child care services that are free for all parents, maternity benefits, and parental leave policies.

DISCUSSION QUESTIONS

1. Why does the male-breadwinner/female-caregiver type of family tend to be an economic risk for women?
2. What interest does the state have in the continuation of women's unpaid work of caring for their families?
3. Why does Steiner (1981) believe it is futile to speak about a family policy?
4. Should a one-income couple with two children having the same income as a two-income couple with two children pay the same amount of taxes?
5. Why has the married tax exemption been called a relic of the early days of the tax system?
6. Should the state in its policies favour a particular form of the family, and if so, which one?
7. Is the spousal allowance unfair to people? If so, to whom?
8. What is the importance of a parental leave policy?
9. Why did Bernard Shaw believe that family life could only be decent if the economic dependency of women on men is abolished?

chapter fourteen

The Future of Family Life

INTRODUCTION

Topics of research within family studies have varied with the times, reflecting the concerns and debates of the educated public and the media. In choosing their research topics, social scientists have been influenced by funding decisions, legal controversies, media reactions, demographic trends, and the concerns of popular movements such as feminism or socialism. In the 1950s and 1960s, when increasing numbers of women were entering the labour force and many feared that this would be detrimental to children and the family unit, researchers studied the impact of maternal employment on children and marital stability. In the 1980s, social scientists have been more concerned with issues such as the differential impact of legal changes in divorce and custody laws on men, women, and children; the perpetuation of family violence from one generation to the next; and kin relations in blended families after remarriage. Furthermore, much of the recent research in family sociology has adopted a political economy or feminist approach, requiring an understanding of politics, economics, and the law more than interpersonal relations emphasized in earlier North American research.

In the previous chapters, we have examined various aspects of family life, outlining relevant theories and research results. The issues and research discussed have focused on Canadian families, yet we have compared Canadian family life throughout history to that of other societies. In this last chapter, we will review some of the historical changes in the family life of Western societies and anticipate some future trends in relationships and family structure.

STRUCTURAL CHANGES

THE IMPACT OF INDUSTRIALIZATION ON FAMILY LIFE

As Europe and North America were transformed from agrarian to industrial societies, families had to change to accommodate the work patterns of their earners. Most farm families lived at a subsistence level, growing their own food, making their clothing, and trading their surplus crops or animals for products they could not grow or make. With industrialization, men began to work in offices and factories away from home. This separation of work and home excluded men from child rearing and concerns about household production, leaving these matters to women. When working-class wives also went out to work, non-family child care was needed and less time was available for home production.

While the agrarian family tended to act as a unit of production, the urban family became more a unit of consumption. Yet, family members still pooled their wages and remained an economic unit. Furthermore, wives continued to produce many goods and services for family members within the home.

The expansion of industry depended on unskilled labour, rather than skilled craftsmen, which paved the way for child and female labour. Working-class women and their children were hired in offices, factories, and mines, where the problem of child care was temporarily "solved" by taking children to the factories where they worked alongside their mothers. In other cases, children were left to fend for themselves at home while their mothers worked.

In the gruelling working conditions of early industrialization, female and child

Most pre-industrial farm families lived at a subsistence level, growing their own food, making their clothing, and trading their surplus crops or animals for products they could not grow or make.

labour led to an outcry about the potential decline of the birth rate and the destruction of family life. Middle-class women and trade unions were loud in their objections to child labour, which they saw as inhuman, and organized to have it stopped. Protective legislation was also introduced to limit women's hours of work, restrict the amount of weight they could be asked to lift, provide proper washroom facilities, and improve safety and working conditions. Furthermore, unions were eventually successful in obtaining similar laws to cover male workers as well. Yet, both women and children continued to work for lower wages than men because men were seen as "family heads" who needed a wage sufficient to support their dependants.

While poorer women worked outside the home, middle-class wives maintained the home, supervised servants, or engaged in hobbies or charitable works. As consumer goods were more cheaply manufactured in factories, middle-class wives became increasingly excluded from production and financially dependent on their husbands. Working outside the home was defined as taking jobs away from men and only suitable for poorer women who "had to work." As richer women became idle, an ideology supporting the "natural" domesticity of women was developed and perpetuated. By the early 1900s, wives of wealthier men were encouraged to stay at home and engage in conspicuous consumption and leisure. Husbands tried to protect their wives from the "cold" world of economics and politics, for at that time having a homemaker wife indicated that the husband was a good breadwinner.

After the First World War, women's role as wife and mother was strongly emphasized by professionals and the media, yet women were encouraged to obtain an education in order to become better wives and mothers. Education in home economics legitimized domesticity in a world that was beginning to stress the importance of science and industry. Young women were also expected to acquire an education in order to work before marriage and as a form of insurance, in case they needed to support themselves later on. During the 1920s and 1930s, however, infant and maternal death rates began to fall, birth control was beginning to be practised, and urbanized lifestyles encouraged fewer children. As the cost of labour rose, fewer middle-class families could afford large houses and live-in servants, and households gradually became smaller units.

Although married women's contribution to the war effort during the 1940s showed that women were capable of more than domesticity, they were expected to vacate their jobs for returning soldiers. Many women were pleased to focus on homemaking and child rearing after the lonely war years when their brothers, boyfriends, husbands, or fathers were overseas. Yet, other women, especially those who had worked their way into professional positions or who needed the income, were reluctant to give up their jobs. Consequently, the labour force participation rates for married women increased from 4.5 percent in 1941 to 11.2 percent in 1951 (Statistics Canada, 1989), despite prevailing attitudes about women's role.

Throughout the 1950s, the one-income family was most prevalent, but as the cost of living began to rise more wives looked for ways to raise the family income. Without child care facilities, however, mothers with young children were discouraged from working outside the home. Furthermore, public opinion worked against any real choice; women were still seen as primarily wives and mothers even though they were used as a reserve labour force. Women were encouraged to earn extra money only if it did not interfere with their family obligations.

Since the 1960s, more middle-class women, including the mothers of young children, have entered the labour force. The rising cost of living, expectations of higher living standards, the expansion of the service sector of the labour force and the consequent need for new employees, the development of part-time work, and the relative decline in wages pushed women out of the home. The increasing employment of married women can be viewed as a major impetus to social change, for it has encouraged the development of non-family child care services, household cleaning companies, fast-food outlets, and advancements in household technology. Working outside the home and supplementing the family income has also encouraged family law reform and rising expectations of equality.

The availability of part-time jobs increased quickly from the 1950s to the 1980s. Employer flexibility was the major motive for the creation of part-time work, which meant that non-unionized workers could be hired at low pay rates, without concern about the necessity for promotion or full fringe benefits. Production costs could be reduced, as employers could hire and fire part-time workers more easily than unionized full-time workers. Yet, part-time work has also been considered beneficial for students who need to work their way through school and for married women with young children. Mothers who want to spend the maximum amount of time with their children, but who also need or want to earn some money to boost the family income, enjoy the flexibility of part-time work. Especially with the lack of child care spaces, part-time jobs have been invaluable to women with young children, allowing them to work during school hours, or evenings or weekends while their husbands supervise the children.

The influx of married women into the labour force, however, has also contributed to changes in the job market. "Entry-level positions," which young men formerly used as stepping stones to more responsible work, are now occupied by women. Furthermore, some of these low-level positions are being eliminated with automation and "down-sizing."

The educational requirements for many occupations have recently been inflated. Consequently, it is now more difficult for young people to find permanent jobs without graduating from school and to work their way up in an organization the way people did before the Second World War. This means that young people today are forced to stay in school and to remain dependent on their families for a longer time than previous generations. This creates tensions between parents and adult children, as well as financial burdens for parents who are helping their children pay for their university or college education. These parents may also be providing some assistance to their elderly parents.

The two-income family has undoubtedly raised the average standard of living in Canada. However, it has also widened the disparity between the incomes of one-parent and two-parent families, because most two-parent families now have two incomes. In 1986, 56 percent of one-parent families led by mothers were below the poverty line, compared to 23 percent of one-parent families led by fathers and 10 percent of couples with children (National Council of Welfare, 1988:31).

THE DECLINE OF THE PATRIARCHAL FAMILY

Until the twentieth century, families in Europe and North America were legally patriarchal. By this we mean that the father/husband was legally responsible for his wife and children and spoke on their behalf to the community and government. Furthermore, wives were expected to obey their husbands. Husbands voted for their wives and became owners of their wives' property and earnings upon marriage. Fathers were legal guardians of the children, and had the right to discipline them with corporal punishment and to make decisions about their education and training without consulting their wives.

Women's status of legal minor was questioned when large numbers entered the labour force, performing jobs formerly done by men. In order to compete on the job market with men, women needed and demanded entrance to professional colleges and universities. As wage earners, they felt that they should be entitled to equal pay, the right to vote, and the opportunity to participate in public life.

From the late 1800s to well into the twentieth century, women gradually gained more political and legal rights, but only after many years of speeches, protests, and legal battles. In Britain, the Married Women's Property Act of 1870 was seen as a milestone for women's rights. Similar laws were introduced into the Canadian provinces within the next few years. From 1910 to 1923, provincial legislation allowed mothers to gain legal custody of their children both during marriage and after divorce. In 1918, women gained the right to vote in federal elections, but could not vote in Quebec provincial elections until as late as 1940. These legal changes were precipitated by the participation of women in the labour force, by ideologies of equality emanating from other political movements, and by the determined efforts of the women's rights movement.

Until the late nineteenth and early twentieth centuries, marriage was seen more as a religious union blessed by God rather than a legal contract able to be dissolved by man. While family celebrations and disputes were formerly settled by the church, the state gradually gained more control of the family. Laws were developed that stated that children had to be sent to school until a certain age, that people could not marry until they reached the chronological age that the government decided represented "maturity," and that marital partners could neither physically nor sexually abuse each other or their children. Marriage became a legal contract that could be broken through divorce proceedings. New laws stipulated that property had to be divided according to certain rules, and one parent was usually granted custody of the children. Human rights legislation was developed that attempted to prevent employer discrimination on the basis of gender, marital status, and (in some provinces) sexual orientation. The state has ruled on many aspects of family life, but it has yet to create any laws or rules about which married couples can procreate or when they must do so.

The separation of marriage and reproduction has presented a number of legal problems that have not yet been fully resolved. The rights of biological and legal fathers, for example, have been complicated by rising rates of common-law marriages, artificial insemination, surrogate motherhood, and motherhood outside an established relationship. Increasing numbers of single mothers needing social assistance have provided the incentive for governments to tighten the eligibility rules for benefits. Some provinces still assume that the presence of a man in the house means that a single mother no longer needs financial assistance because the man ought to support her children. But assumptions such as these can no longer be made without the threat of court challenges based on the Charter of Rights and Freedoms. The Ontario government, for example, changed its social assistance regulations in September 1986, abolishing the "man in the house" rule.

As we have seen in Chapter Ten, family law has undergone extensive review in Canadian provinces and in some American states throughout the past decade. In Canada, matrimonial property should now be divided equally in most provinces. Mothers and fathers are supposed to have equal rights to custody of their children, but in fact women more often are granted custody. While part of the justification for this has been that men seldom asked for custody in the past, fathers' rights groups are now demanding equal access to their children. In some cases, they are suggesting that joint custody be assumed by the court, even when parents are not in full agreement. Although women's groups support voluntary joint custody, they argue that men are sometimes using joint custody as an excuse to reduce child support payments when they do not intend to accept the daily care of children. Divorce mediation and joint custody will probably become more prevalent in the future because of the high cost of custody cases in the court system, the damage to children caught in the middle of custody disputes, and the strength of the fathers' rights movement.

Although the rationale for recent changes in family law has been to make the family a more egalitarian institution, the end result has sometimes impoverished wives and children. Part of the problem is that many family policies are based on erroneous models of family life, which either assume that wives are dependent on their husbands' incomes or suggest that they should be fully capable of supporting themselves and their children (Baker, 1988a). In actual fact, most wives contribute to the household income either by providing services or by earning money, but they tend to earn considerably less than their husbands. Without assistance, women generally cannot support themselves and their children after marriage dissolution.

DEMOGRAPHIC AND SOCIAL CHANGES

The decline in infant mortality from improved sanitation, nutrition, living standards, health care, and inoculations is one factor that encouraged people to have smaller families in the early twentieth century. If parents could be reasonably sure that their babies would live to adulthood, they could afford fewer pregnancies. At the same time, industrialization and urbanization made large families expensive and less useful. When children were allowed to contribute to the family income, it was advantageous to have many children. But compulsory education, the abolition of child labour, and the rising costs of urban living discouraged large families. Birth control gradually became more acceptable and effective in Canada, although the Roman Catholic Church continues to object to any mechanical method of preventing conception.

Birth rates have continued to decline in most industrialized countries, which indicates that fewer people are willing to make undue sacrifices for large families. It also suggests that parents feel that each child deserves more attention and family resources than in previous generations. Many people of both sexes still expect women to contribute to the family income and perform all the household tasks formerly done by full-time housewives. Women have responded to this "double burden" by reducing their family size. Families have also purchased labour-saving devices, such as dishwashers, microwave ovens, self-cleaning ovens, frost-free refrigerators, and central vacuum systems, and men have begun to assist with household chores. As long as women work for pay without flexible hours, adequate parental leave, or child care services, birth rates will remain low.

With so much publicity given to family violence, custody disputes, and contested property settlements, we may now be less inclined to think of marriage in romantic terms. We may even be wary about entering the institution. Furthermore, people tend to feel less bound by duty to tolerate parental pressure to marry a particular person or to be willing to stay in an unhappy marriage than a few generations ago. With more opportunities to have sex or to live together without marriage than in the 1950s, people are more likely to get married because they really want to, rather than from social pressure. For the same reasons, they can separate from their spouse or obtain a divorce much more easily than in the 1950s. This implies that marriage is becoming more of a voluntary institution.

Yet, with high unemployment and rising costs of accommodation, some people are entering marriage for openly pragmatic reasons. This is nothing new, however, as many early settlers to North America resorted to "mail-order brides" or advertising in the ethnic press for marriage partners. This pragmatic approach to marriage may be more typical of older divorced or widowed people, or mothers who cannot adequately support their children on their own incomes.

Since the rise in sexually transmitted diseases such as herpes and AIDS, many young people have reverted to a more traditional attitude toward intimate relationships and sexuality. The sexual experimentation of the 1960s and 1970s appears to be over as many people restrict the number of partners or insist on monogamous relationships for fear of sexually transmitted diseases. In addition, with fewer permanent and more contractually limited jobs, employees may be forced to present a more conservative personal demeanour in order to find employment or keep their positions. Appearing too radical may now interfere with one's occupational life.

Conservative governments in several countries have tried to reduce their national deficits by curbing increases in social spending. With cutbacks in social programs in some Canadian provinces and fears of rising costs in others, expectations are being placed on families and communities to care for their unemployed, disabled, and elderly. Rising medical costs and fears of more increases with the aging population have led to the development of home care programs.

Policies of de-institutionalization imply that community facilities and services will take the place of hospital care, but in many regions these programs are not yet in place to assist with the care of sick or disabled family members. Furthermore, these programs assume that someone is at home to look after disabled elderly people; yet, increasingly, both sexes are at work during the daytime (Baker, 1988).

FAMILIES IN THE FUTURE

THE FUTURE OF CHILDBEARING

With the exception of the "postwar baby boom," birth rates have gradually declined over the past century. Reasons for producing large families have disappeared: laws require school attendance and prevent child labour; the cost of accommodation, education, food, and clothing has increased; and more mothers are working outside the home. Most demographers project that birth rates will remain low in the foreseeable future because no change is anticipated in the factors affecting the desire to produce small families.

One-parent families, small families, and childless couples will continue to be more prevalent in the future. While more low-fertility couples will be able to reproduce, a larger number of couples may opt for a child-free lifestyle. Already, some couples have postponed childbearing to the point that conception becomes more difficult and the risks of fetal deformities are higher. Unless major changes are made in the structure of the labour force and the cost of child rearing, more couples will postpone having children, and some may then find that they can no longer conceive.

Technological changes in reproduction may help a small percentage of women to conceive, but the cost of these interventions to society and to the family may surpass the benefits received. Furthermore, as the medical and legal professions intervene more in the process of reproduction, women's groups are becoming concerned about the "medicalization" of childbirth, about women's lack of control over their own bodies, and the lack of public policy relating to new reproductive technologies (Eichler, 1989). In addition, fathers and the foetus may acquire new legal rights that diminish the existing rights of mothers.

At the same time, a growing minority of women are determined to bear children even when they are not married. While some women have always produced "illegitimate" children, they were not usually middle-class "respectable" women. Now a small number of middle-class and professional women are deliberately choosing to become pregnant outside of marriage and to raise their children alone. Women's gains in the labour force, improved social assistance programs, and equal rights for all children regardless of the marital status of their parents have made this possible. Social attitudes have also become liberal enough to allow women to raise their children alone. Similarly, some biological fathers are requesting full or joint custody of their children, even though they are not married to the mother. Yet, single parenting is both emotionally and financially difficult and will likely remain the choice of only a small minority of men and women in the future. Many more, of course, will become single parents involuntarily through divorce.

Increasingly, childbearing occupies a shorter period of most women's lives. Research from the 1950s and 1960s assumed that women would experience depression when their children left home, or when they reached menopause and lost their ability to reproduce. Yet, most studies now indicate that this stage in life can be energizing for women who have interests other than their families, as well as for their husbands. In fact, child "launching" can increase the disposable income of the household, lessen the household workload, and provide a couple with more leisure time and privacy. In cases where the children were all the couple had to keep them together, their marital relationship might suffer. However, most couples have mutual interests and years of common experiences to revitalize their relationship. With more leisure time, they can travel, go out for dinner, entertain, spend time with their individual hobbies, or just relax at home.

FUTURE CHANGES IN PAID AND UNPAID WORK

Since the 1960s, more women have acquired post-secondary education, and increasing numbers of married women have entered the paid work force. At the same time, women's groups have lobbied for political, legal, and economic equality with men. In the last three decades, legislative changes have granted legal equality to men and women, even though much inequality still exists in the labour force. Furthermore, with greater access to jobs and with equal pay for equal work (but not yet equal pay for work of equal value), women are more able to support themselves and to live apart from their parents or husbands. While some critics have feared that greater economic independence would lead to the demise of the family, in actual fact the vast majority of adults still marry and produce children. Yet, the traditional nuclear family, in which husbands and wives occupy separate but complementary roles, is being forced to change now that women are sharing the "breadwinning" role.

Despite these changes, women are still more likely to be offered and to accept jobs that replicate the housewife/mother role – such as nurse, teacher, cleaning woman, child care worker, or secretary. Only recently have women made inroads into professions such as medicine and law. But other occupations such as technical positions, skilled trades, and professions such as engineering and applied science have remained dominated by men. Furthermore, men have not entered female-dominated jobs such as day care worker, nurse, elementary school teacher, or secretary in any significant numbers. This is not surprising, since female-dominated positions have traditionally held low prestige and pay. It makes far more sense to aspire to higher- than to lower-level positions. Yet, when men do enter the teaching or nursing professions, they are more likely than women to take over the administrative or managerial positions.

Just as men have not scrambled to take over women's work in the labour force, neither have men taken equal responsibility for housework and child care. Men are now more likely than a generation ago to perform child care and household tasks, especially if their wives are earning a relatively high proportion of the family income (Harrell, 1985). Husbands with egalitarian ideas about gender roles and those married to women with high-paying jobs tend to do more housework than other men, but few men regularly share equal responsibility with their wives. Instead, men tend to work longer hours at their paid jobs than women do and to take on secondary positions. Women, on the other hand, generally feel greater responsibility for the care of elderly parents and children, and for housework. Women are also expected to maintain relationships in most families, which means buying cards and gifts, writing letters, and phoning relatives. Although women usually perform these tasks willingly, they require time and energy and receive little social recognition.

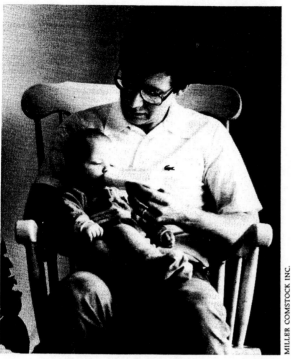

MILLER COMSTOCK INC.

Men today are more likely than they were a generation ago to perform child-care and household tasks, especially if their wives are earning a relatively high proportion of the family income.

Women who work for pay, including those who are not married, tend to carry extra familial responsibilities compared to most men. Although men usually perform maintenance chores around the house, the work they tend to do involves fewer hours and can often be done at their discretion. Women are more likely to perform the routine cooking, cleaning, and child care tasks that have to be done every day – often at a particular time. These domestic responsibilities interfere with women's commitment to paid work, and to their ability to devote extra hours and effort to the job in order to be promoted. As more men become separated or divorced, or receive joint custody of their children, they may inherit some of these domestic responsibilities. If enough employees retained these responsibilities, the structure of paid work would have to change. Employers would be forced to offer flexible work hours and more generous parental leave, for example.

The traditional division of labour, with father as breadwinner and mother as homemaker or secondary worker, has allowed most men to devote more time to their occupations, to reach higher-level positions, and to accrue more financial assets than their wives. Since policy makers and judges tend not to recognize publicly that much of the unpaid labour traditionally done by wives and mothers contributes to men's financial assets, they have not always placed a monetary value on homemakers' contributions to those family assets. Consequently, many divorced women find that they must live in poverty despite the fact that during their marriages they made financial sacrifices to assist their husbands and children.

From the social trends of the past three decades, we can assume that more married women will enter the labour force and that this will gradually change the division of labour in most families. Working hours will probably decrease for paid workers in the future, as more companies computerize. Reducing working hours may also help counteract high unemployment rates and lower employers' costs. Men rather than women will gain more leisure time as a result of such changes, although some may choose to find a second job. The pressures of women's "double workload" of paid work and housework, however, will likely force more men to share child care and housework.

FOR INTEREST

STRESS OF JUGGLING HOUSEWORK, JOB, CALLED HAZARD TO WOMEN'S HEALTH

By Ann Rauhala

The stress of combining housework and paid work may be the No. 1 health hazard for women, a study done for a federal advisory body on women's issues says.

Women, Paid/Unpaid Work and Stress, released yesterday by the Canadian Advisory Council on the Status of Women, suggests that women face a range of stressful situations that are unlikely to occur in men's lives.

"Women's double day of paid employment, child bearing and household work sets up a stressful scenario which few men confront," council president Sylvia Gold said in a statement.

The council, appointed by the government to advise it on issues of concern to women, "is concerned that work stress is a major barrier to women's well-being," Ms Gold said.

The report, by University of Alberta sociologist Graham Lowe, points to research showing that as much as 80 per cent of all illness can be linked to stress.

It reviews research on work-induced stress, noting that more investigation is needed into forms of stress unique to women.

For example, Mr. Lowe points to sexual harassment as a workplace stress that affects more women than men. A human-rights survey cited in the report found that 15 per cent of women and 4 per cent of men received unwanted sexual attention they regarded as harassment.

Other stressful situations which are more likely to occur in women's lives include part-time work, which often tends to be lacking in benefits and job security, and single parenthood, which creates difficulties in finding and keeping a home and a job, the report suggests.

It also argues that wider economic trends create different stresses on men and women.

With less public-sector spending on health care, for instance, the taxing work of caring for the sick and elderly usually falls to women family members. Tough economic times also add to the burden of stretching the household budget.

"The recession of the early 1980s intensified women's domestic roles, as they spent more time bargain-hunting, preparing food, cleaning and repairing clothes and looking after children," a summary of the report says.

The report notes that literature on the subject of stress has too often made generalizations about stress based only on male employees.

The advisory council has called for a number of changes to diminish stress in women's lives.

"Creating work environments which promote well-being, recognizing the value of women's work in the home, and reorganizing child rearing in the family and the community would go a long way toward reducing life stress," Ms Gold said.

Source: *The Globe and Mail*, March 8, 1989. **Reprinted with Permission of the Globe and Mail**

The transition to shared housework will not be easy, however. Women themselves will have to accept more responsibility for outside work and car maintenance. At the same time, mothers will have to teach their children to perform all household tasks formerly assigned only to one sex, and encourage them to expect equality in their future homes. Furthermore, wives will have to encourage their husbands to take on part of the responsibility for cooking, cleaning, and laundry for the family, as well as total responsibility for their own personal care, such as packing suitcases for travel, buying clothing, preparing lunches, and other household tasks wives sometimes do for their husbands.

It is unlikely that many men will want to become "house-husbands" for the same reasons that women are rejecting this job – it is unpaid and retains low status. Yet, it is not possible for women to obtain employment equity if they must also accept full responsibility for child care and housework, as well as partial responsibility for the personal care of their husbands.

Baker (1985) found that in projections into the future, adolescent women talked a lot about the household chores, child care, and the division of labour in their homes. Adolescent men, on the other hand, barely mentioned these activities unless specifically asked, and then they often said that housework should be shared. Furthermore, children of working mothers and those with divorced parents were more likely than the children from one-earner or two-parent families to expect an egalitarian division of labour in their future homes. Girls planning to go to university and girls from families having a higher socio-economic status also expected an egalitarian division of labour. These data suggest that any changes in household division of labour will come slowly, and will be strongly influenced by parental role models.

While most people maintain close contact with their kin, families have a weaker influence over the daily actions of their members than a few generations ago. Now that most people live and work in cities, and both partners often work during the daytime, their work lives and family lives can be very separate. Furthermore, employers are often unconcerned about their employees' private lives and allow little paid leave to care for sick children, for family-related crises, or even for childbirth.

Now that word processors have reduced the need for typists, and electronic mail has allowed better transmission of business messages, more work in the future may be done in home offices rather than in office buildings. Working at home could alter the division of labour between husbands and wives, especially if the husband is at home while his wife works outside. This work arrangement could result in men accepting more responsibility for supervising the children and performing routine household tasks.

As children grow older, parents acquire more flexibility in their own lives. Women who are not already in the labour force are increasingly returning to school or work when their child-rearing duties are over and are finding new challenges at this stage in life. At the same time, decreased financial responsibilities as the children leave home, greater prosperity of the two-income family, and early retirement incentives are allowing employees to retire early or to find more satisfying careers instead of being content with a secure job. Changing careers is not easy, however, because people get locked into pension plans and benefit packages that are hard to transfer or forfeit. Furthermore, employers tend to prefer to hire younger employees, and it is difficult to find a new job after a certain age. Yet, pension plans are becoming more portable and home computers are providing more opportunities to establish self-employed careers. Some employees leave their comfortable positions in mid-life and set up their own business or begin to work as a consultant. This kind of occupational gamble can only be attempted, however, when there are no more children to support or the spouse has a steady income.

At the present time, mid-life career changes may be characteristic of only a small portion of the population of middle-aged people. But such changes may become more predominant in the future as employment competition increases from younger colleagues, as two-income families become even more prevalent, and as home computers allow more people to become self-employed. Higher disposable incomes and generous early retirement programs may encourage others to retire in their fifties and spend more time on leisure activities.

We cannot assume, of course, that both members of the couple are reaching mid-life at the same time. Many men marry younger women, and men may be considering early retirement just as their younger wives are re-establishing themselves in the labour force. This could cause friction in their relationship. Traditionally, married women have retired when their husbands retired (Connidis, 1988:25), but younger wives may have no desire to leave work when they are still under fifty and especially before they are entitled to a pension.

Although an increasing number of families have two incomes, the jobs are not necessarily given equal priority by husband and wife, relatives, or outsiders. For one thing, most wives earn considerably more than their husbands, even with equal qualifications and employment experience. Furthermore, many men have been encouraged throughout their lives to grant priority to paid work, rather than family, friends, or leisure pursuits, and are therefore prepared to work overtime and accept extra responsibilities with the hope of gaining a promotion. Greater expectations appear to be placed on men to "get ahead," by parents, bosses, male colleagues, and often by wives themselves.

Traditionally, many "successful" men have been assisted, both psychologically and physically, by supportive wives. In addition to child care and housework, wives have typed papers for husbands, served as editors and research assistants, and worked as receptionists and bookkeepers. In certain occupations, such as foreign service officer or politician, wives have been expected to perform unpaid duties to further their husband's career, such as entertaining or campaigning (Finch, 1983). Yet, wives have seldom been fortunate enough to receive this kind of support for their own careers. While many of these expectations for wives have diminished in recent years, some men still find it easier than women to "succeed" occupationally because they so often can count on emotional support and domestic back-up. Furthermore, there is little indication that men will provide this for their wives in the near future.

RELATIONSHIPS

Young men and women are now given more freedom than in past generations to get to know members of the opposite sex without parental supervision and intervention. Dating practices also appear to be slightly more egalitarian, less formalized than in the 1950s, and more explicitly oriented toward sexuality (Nett, 1988:181). There is no evidence, however, that young women are more interested in dating or mating with men they see as their social inferiors. Educated young women are still hoping to find partners with equal or higher educational attainment, high intelligence, and good job prospects (Baker, 1985).

As we have seen in Chapters Three and Five, more couples are living together without being legally married, and a slightly higher percentage of couples plan to remain permanently childless (Rao and Balakrishnan, 1986). Living together without being legally married has lowered the marriage rates as well as raised the average age of marriage. Young people who want to continue their education, but who also want to experience an intimate relationship, often choose to cohabit. Furthermore, those from divorced families or adults who have previously been married are often reluctant to enter into legal marriage without some detailed knowledge of their partner's habits and character. Living together will probably become more socially acceptable in the future, both as a "courtship pattern" or preliminary stage to marriage and as an alternative to marriage now that there are few differences between the legal rights of common-law and legally married partners.

There is no evidence, however, that couples who experience this "trial marriage" actually enjoy more stable marriages. The opposite, in fact, is true. People who live together without marriage are often those who question social customs and traditions, and who are willing to oppose authority. Those who for religious or other reasons believe that living together without legal marriage is morally wrong are also likely to think that divorce is wrong. While cohabitation may give potential marital partners a more realistic notion of what they are getting into, it is not a way of ensuring a more stable marriage.

Despite the trend toward more common-law living, marriage remains popular for the vast majority of the Canadian population. Most couples remain married and derive considerable satisfaction from their family life. Despite high divorce rates, Canadian young people usually expect to marry and to remain with the same partner throughout their lives. A slightly larger number are now opting for a child-free marriage. Canadian marriages are changing, but there is no indication that either marriage or "the family" is dying.

Marriage is no longer viewed as permanent by many younger people, especially those whose parents have divorced (Baker, 1985). Legal divorce and single parenting are now more prevalent and more socially acceptable. Because of the financial difficulties of single parenting and the continued popularity of marriage, however, the percentage of marriages in which at least one partner has been divorced will continue to rise. Serial monogamy, or one marriage partner at a time but several over a lifetime, is becoming more prevalent in Canada, as it has been in the United States for over a decade. Yet, we need to keep in mind that the American divorce rate is considerably higher than the Canadian rate (United Nations, 1988).

Despite publicity given to family violence, there is no clear evidence that today's families are more violent than they used to be. Reporting procedures are now stricter, victims are encouraged to notify authorities and to leave an abusive home, police are more likely to arrest alleged abusers, and the public is less tolerant of the physical, sexual, financial, or emotional abuse of family members. Now that this kind of behaviour has become public knowledge, solutions are being sought in the form of transition houses, family and individual counselling, self-help groups, stricter child and elder abuse legislation, and easier divorce laws. Yet, social service agencies are not always able to intervene in family violence situations because of the backlog of cases, staff shortages, and lack of funds. Transitional housing has not increased as fast as the demand, and counselling programs are frequently underfunded.

While working women may not be able to provide personal care for elderly spouses or parents, as they did in the past, they still tend to purchase care and housekeeping services, supervise caregivers, and provide emotional support to disabled family members (Connidis, 1988:50). But in the future, with a smaller number of children per family, middle-aged mothers may suffer from too many responsibilities if they have their own employment, dependent teenaged children, and ailing parents. This may encourage men to become more involved in providing care for aging parents. Provincial governments, municipalities, volunteer groups, and private firms also may provide more home maintenance services, visiting homemakers and companions, and health care services for seniors in the future.

The relative income of seniors has been rising throughout the past twenty years, which has assisted those in need to purchase services. Despite threats of cutbacks to public pensions, government social security benefits will likely remain in place, considering the public acceptance of old age pensions in Canada. Even though the future elderly may have fewer children to assist them in their old age, they may be more accustomed to receiving government benefits and services, better able to purchase services, and possibly more likely to receive assistance from friends or "fictive kin."

CONCLUSION

Throughout this chapter, we have discussed historical changes in family life and made some future projections about marriage and childbearing. Rather than assuming that husbands and wives always form a unit in terms of experiences and attitudes, we have emphasized that both single life and marriage may provide different experiences for men and women because of their socialization and biology, the differences in their personal relationships, and their varying job experiences and earning power.

Although there are different theoretical perspectives that can be used to analyse trends in family life and personal behaviour, no one approach is "correct" because each provides an explanation for some aspect of behaviour. Sociologists have argued, of course, that some theoretical perspectives present a more thorough or realistic view of family life, but these judgments are open to dispute. Furthermore, the family life of one cultural group is not necessarily the same for all groups, and one family member cannot be expected to give valid answers on behalf of the entire family. The student of family studies should now understand that family life differs by gender, social class, and cultural group, and that family structure and relationships have varied throughout history with economic, demographic, and ideological changes.

DISCUSSION QUESTIONS

1. What structural changes have occurred in family life since the 1800s?
2. Why was the Married Women's Property Act seen as a milestone for women's rights?
3. Why were soldiers returning from the Second World War given priority in the labour force instead of married women?
4. List several factors that pulled married women into the labour force after the 1960s.
5. What are some of the legal and social problems presented by the separation of marriage and reproduction?
6. Why have couples reduced the number of children they produce since the turn of the twentieth century?
7. Do you think that more people will remain childless in the coming decades? Why or why not?
8. What impact has the two-income family had on relations between husbands and wives and between parents and their children?
9. Why do married women continue to perform much of the housework when they also work full-time?
10. How might home computers affect family relations in the future?

GLOSSARY

access Refers to the rights that a non-custodial parent has to visit his or her child after divorce.

affect turn-off If a person is constantly ignored, abused, or rejected by another, he or she may eventually show no feeling or response toward that person. For example, a mother with a non-responsive child may eventually deaden or harden her feelings toward this child.

aging population The demographic process involving a relative increase in elderly persons and a decline in children compared to the middle-age groups. This raises the average age of the population.

alimony A term that used to be used in Canada and is still used in the United States to refer to financial support for a separated or former spouse. The 1968 divorce legislation used the term "maintenance" for both spousal and child support, but the term "support" is currently used in Canada.

betrothal A promise to marry; official engagement.

biculturalization The process by which children are socialized in two cultures through the agents of school and home.

blended (reconstituted) family Two people remarry creating a new family with children from both previous relationships. The new relationship may also produce children.

body language Facial expressions, gestures, and bodily movements exhibited in social interaction, often unconsciously, that convey a person's feelings about the social situation.

buffer Something that lessens shock or impact.

caregiver burden Emotional stress, resulting from restricted time and freedom, that affects persons who provide care for a disabled spouse, parent, or other dependent person.

care orientation Gilligan's feminine orientation to morality. The emphasis in moral thinking is upon concern for, and connectedness with, others.

child care, licensed Government-approved care either in child care centres or in private homes.

child launching Assisting a grown child to establish a new home separate from the parents.

circular interaction The behaviour or personality characteristics of each person is affected by the behaviour and qualities of others.

classical conditioning A type of learning that encourages a particular response after the presentation of a certain stimulus. An unconditioned stimulus (ucs) is presented at about the same time as a conditioned stimulus (cs) to an organism in a drive state (i.e., hungry or thirsty), and after several trials, the previously neutral response (cs) alone produces the response normally associated with the ucs.

cohabitation Living together, usually without legal marriage.

common-law (or de facto) relationship Living together as though married, but without wedding ceremony. For those who have shared a life together for a period of time, there are federal and provincial laws that impose responsibilities or give legal rights to partners. For example, common-law partners are generally expected to support their children and may be allowed to claim financial support even when they have not legally married.

commune   A group of families or individuals sharing possessions and responsibilities.

companionate relationship   A relationship in which the emphasis is placed on being friends or companions.

complementary needs, theory of   The theory of mate selection that people tend to marry those they think will satisfy their psychological needs.

complementary roles   A division of labour within marriage in which husbands earn the money and wives look after the household and children; both functions are different, but are mutually beneficial.

compulsory education   The government requires parents to send their children to school until a certain age.

confidant   A trusted and intimate friend in whom one confides troubles and shares joys.

confidential research report   The subjects' names will not be paired with their responses, so that no one, apart from the researcher, will know what they answered in response to a particular item on a questionnaire or in an interview.

conflict or political economy approach   A theoretical perspective that emphasizes the link between historical change in family patterns and economic changes in society.

conflict tactics scale   A series of questions designed to find out how people settle disputes or differences with their spouse, partner, or child.

conjugal roles   Norms or rules that dictate the proper behaviour of married people.

consanguinity   Relationship by blood; kinship.

courtship   The development of a love relationship with the intention of marriage.

cult of true womanhood   Women were redefined primarily as wives and mothers rather than paid workers, and as creators of havens from the world of work.

custody   To be in charge of a child's daily care (physical custody) and to have the power to make major decisions about the child's upbringing (legal custody).

dating   The leisure time two people of the opposite sex spend together for the sake of enjoyment, without any intention to marry in the near future.

de-institutionalization   The policy of discharging disabled or ill people from large residential institutions to live in the community in group homes or with their families.

developmental approach   A theoretical perspective that emphasizes how individuals and family life typically change throughout the life cycle.

developmental theory of mate selection   Neither social nor psychological variables determine who marries whom, but rather the resolution of tensions and conflicts and social pressure on the relationship.

divorce   The formal dissolution of a marriage by a legal process. In Canada, divorce law is federal, which means that there is one law, applicable across Canada.

divorce mediation   Assistance to divorcing couples to help them dissolve their marriage, arrange custody of the children, and divide property with a minimum of antagonism and distress.

double burden   The difficulty most working women experience in working full-time for pay and then coming home to child care and housework in the evenings and on weekends.

double standard   Different standards of behaviour or sexual morality for men and women.

Doukhobors   A small, pacifist sect of Russian dissenters who live in western Canada.

downsizing   Reducing the size of the work force through layoffs or early retirements.

dual-career family   A family in which both adults have careers. (A more correct term would be "two-income family," as most individuals work at jobs rather than careers.)

endogamy   Marriage within the social group.

entry-level jobs   Low-level positions for new participants in the labour force.

exchange theory   A theoretical perspective that sees most social interaction in families as involving reciprocity and negotiation.

exogamy   Marriage outside the social group.

externalizing blame   Placing blame on external circumstances or on someone other than oneself. Accepting responsibility oneself is internalizing blame.

family   A social group comprised of one or two adults of the opposite sex, involved in a mating relationship, and their children (biological or adopted) that generally shares a residence, divides their labour, and co-operates economically.

family consumer economy   Family life involves decisions and activities related to the purchase and use of goods produced in specialized workplaces. Men generally are the producers, women are the homemakers, and children are dependants.

family economy   The pre-industrial setting in which family members laboured together in the context of household production.

family head   The person, traditionally the husband, who has the final say in family decisions and represents the family to the outside world.

family life cycle   The stages people pass through in their intimate relationships, from dating and engagement, the early years of marriage, through childbearing, child rearing, child launching, old age, and bereavement.

family reproduction   The ways in which one generation biologically, culturally, and materially creates the next.

family strategies   The extent to which individuals live their lives as part of family and kinship networks rather than as autonomous individuals.

family wage economy   Family members pool their wages from work outside the home to allow the family to subsist.

family wage policy   A policy (which used to be explicit in Australia and merely implicit in Canada) that a man should be paid enough to support himself and his wife and children. This was used to justify paying lower wages to women, because it was assumed that they did not have dependants.

feminist perspective   A theoretical perspective that examines women's experiences and differentials between the power and status of males and females. The approach assumes that males and females should be treated equally in terms of opportunities and societal rewards.

feminization of poverty   An increasing number of poor people in our society are women.

fertility rates   The number of children a thousand women would have throughout their lifetime if they had children at the same rate that women currently do in each age group.

fictive kin   People who are treated as family members.

gender   Societal definitions of appropriate female and male traits and behaviours.

gendered society   A society that emphasizes distinct roles for men and women.

group (multilateral) marriage   Three or more partners each of whom considers himself/herself to be married to more than one of the other partners.

hedonism   The doctrine that pleasure is the chief goal in life.

household   Those who share a common residence, whether or not they are related by blood or marriage.

Hutterites   An agricultural Anabaptist people who live in Alberta, Saskatchewan, and Manitoba in communities of between one hundred and one hundred and fifty in which finances and property are shared.

hypergamy   The tendency for women to marry older and higher- or equal-status men; marriage to a person of a higher social status.

ideal mate theory People tend to marry those who approximate the ideal they have formulated from their family life and past dating experiences.

ideology A set of beliefs and interests of a group or society that underlies political or social action.

illegitimate children Children born to an unmarried mother.

incest taboo An unwritten rule against having sex with a family member.

individual productivity A measure of the individual contribution a worker or employee makes to national output.

industrial economy Most production is centralized and takes place in large factories using heavy equipment and machinery.

infant mortality Deaths to live-born babies who have not reached their first birthday.

institutional completeness The degree to which a group is economically and socially self-sufficient.

intermittent reinforcement Behaviour that is periodically rewarding. Abused women sometimes stay in relationships because they find their husbands' intermittently good behaviour rewarding or reinforcing.

in vitro fertilization An egg is removed from the ovary of a female and placed with semen in a petri dish where fertilization occurs in successful situations. The fertilized egg is then returned to the ovary of the mother.

joint custody Legal guardianship of the children and decisions about their upbringing are shared between former spouses after divorce, regardless of where the children live.

justice orientation Gilligan's masculine orientation to morality. The emphasis in moral thinking is upon preserving rights and upholding principles.

kin-based migration People move from region to region or country to country as family groups, and then encourage other family members to join them. Family members then help each other find accommodation and work.

labour force participation rates The proportion of people aged fifteen and over who have paid work or are actively looking for work (unemployed).

labour force reproduction A Marxist term referring to the fact that women give birth to children, raise them, and thereby produce the future labour force.

longevity The average length of life; increased life expectancy.

looking-glass self The self as the interpreted reflection of others' attitudes, or the self as we think others see us.

Loyalists American colonists in sympathy with Britain who migrated to Canada because of the American Revolution.

mail-order bride A bride who has been found through advertising in the press.

manufactory stage of industralization Handicraft production still predominates, but manufactories increasingly bring together various craftsmen into one operation.

marital adjustment The relative agreement by husband and wife on issues perceived to be important, sharing similar tasks and activities, and showing affection for one another.

marriage A legally recognized relationship between a man and a woman that imposes certain obligations and confers legal claims upon them.

marriage gradient The fact that men tend to marry "down" in terms of socio-economic status means that low-status men and high-status women are least likely to marry.

marriage (separation) contract Formal agreements made between partners upon marriage that specify marital roles, future support, property division, or child custody arrangements in the event of separation. Courts will not always enforce these agreements, especially aspects relating to marital roles and child custody.

maternal deprivation   The incorrect assumption that children who fail to receive full-time attention from their mothers (for whatever reason) will be developmentally handicapped.

mating   Seeking a sexual partner or a permanent marital relationship.

matrifocus   The tendency for family ties to be created and maintained by women.

mediation   A non-adversarial and non-judicial process to help couples deal with disputes, such as disagreements over custody or support, or to attempt to reconcile differences in attitudes toward their marriage.

Métis   People of Amerindian and French descent.

monogamy   Marriage between one man and one woman.

monolithic family   The bias from earlier family sociologists that there is one major type of family structure that is unchanging; all family members are assumed to experience the same quality of family life.

multilevel ecological model   A theoretical approach adopted by child psychologist Urie Bronfenbrenner that suggests child development is affected by several levels of the environment, beginning with the ecology of the family.

narcissistic   The quality of being self-centred or selfish.

negative reinforcement   Actions meant to discourage unacceptable behaviour, such as verbal reprimand or spanking. The opposite would be positive reinforcement or encouragement.

neo-conservatism   The political view that natural differences justify social and economic inequalities among people in general and between women and men in particular.

operant conditioning   A type of learning whereby the organism gives a number of trial-and-error responses. Those responses followed by reward (positive reinforcement) tend to be repeated on future occasions. Those responses followed by negative reinforcement or no reinforcement tend to be extinguished.

particularism   A doctrine that emphasizes personal or subjective considerations over impersonal or objective considerations.

part-time employment   Work in the labour force for less than thirty hours per week, which is not considered to be full-time work.

patriarchal society theory   Men tend to hold more power than women in families because they have greater access to money and symbols of status in the larger society.

patriarchy   A family form in which the oldest male dominates.

peace bond   An order obtained from the provincial family courts that requires an abusive spouse to keep the peace and be of good behaviour for a specified period of time. It can be obtained if a spouse feels an assault is likely to take place, but does not remove the offender from the home and is difficult to enforce.

personal resource theory   Attributes such as education, skills, physical attractiveness, experience, and income affect family power.

pink collar jobs   Jobs performed mainly by women that tend to replicate maternal or wifely roles, such as teacher, nurse, hairdresser, and secretary.

pluralist view of the family   Recognizes that family forms change and that individuals experience family life differently.

polyandry   Marriage of one woman to more than one man.

polygamy   Marriage to more than one spouse at a time.

polygyny   Marriage of one man to two or more women.

postwar baby boom   The temporary increase in the birth rate after the Second World War, from about 1945 to 1965.

power of the purse theory   The person who earns the money and pays family expenses is most likely to have the final say in family decisions.

pre-industrial economy   A situation in which most economic production takes place in individual homes, and production is small scale, labour intensive, and based mainly on agriculture or fishing.

prima facie evidence   Sufficient evidence to prove an issue if not contradicted and overcome by other evidence. An example would be visible signs of injury on a victim that would enable police to arrest a suspected offender.

prognosis   A forecast or predicted outcome.

proletarianization   The shift from farmers and craftspeople in the pre-industrial economy to propertyless wage labourers in the emerging industrial economy.

pronatal values   Values that promote and encourage childbirth and child bearing.

protective legislation   Legislation that protects certain categories of workers (i.e., women and children) from heavy labour or difficult working conditions.

protocol   Agreements of procedures to be followed. In this book the term refers to written procedures for investigating and treating child abuse or other cases of family violence.

proto-industrialization   Domestic activity is responsible for part, rather than all, of the production process. For example, in the textile industry, households may spin yarn, which is then sold to weavers who make cloth in a small factory.

reproductive technologies   Medical interventions for those experiencing fertility problems that are designed to promote conception or birth.

restraining order   An emergency court order that prohibits an accused offender from doing the threatened act until a hearing can be held.

rite of passage (rite of transition)   A ceremony or formal recognition marking a transitional period in a person's life.

role strain   Emotional stress experienced when a person's qualifications or resources for a position are inadequate (role overload), or when there is a conflict in expectations for different positions occupied by the same person (role conflict).

schema   An organized configuration of knowledge developed from an individual's past experience that serves to influence subsequent interpretation of physical and social worlds.

scientific bias   A distortion, prejudice, or false report in research that results from an inappropriate sample, a failure to control certain variables, or encouragement of a particular response.

separation   The breaking up of a marriage, usually without a legal process. Because a separation may affect the financial status of former partners and their children, there is legislation (provincial) relating to support payments.

separation of home and work   Where one lives and where one earns a living become two different places, as happened during industrialization.

service sector   Occupations in the labour force that provide a service to customers, such as waiter/waitress, child care worker, or public relations officer.

sex ratio   The relative number of males and females in a given population, usually computed as the number of males per one hundred females.

sexual division of labour   The sex-specific assignment of work tasks.

sexual orientation   Whether one prefers an opposite-sex or same-sex mate.

social construct   A set of ideas that emerge out of social interaction, whose connection with empirical reality may be tenuous or non-existent, but is nevertheless perpetuated.

social homogamy   The theory that people tend to marry those who are socially similar.

social interaction   Mutual or reciprocal action or influence between people.

socialization, primary   The learning process during childhood and adolescence that equips individuals to be functioning members of society.

socializing agents   Persons responsible for teaching rules of behaviour or providing motivation to a given social group, including parents, teachers, and other children.

social mobility   Movement to a higher or lower social status or class.

social policy   A government action to address a social problem.

social security system   Publicly financed and administered income support programs to protect individuals and families against job and life risks (such as unemployment and disability in old age) that cause a reduction or loss of income.

social selection   A theory stating that certain individuals, because of their physical or intellectual qualities, are selected to occupy certain social roles.

social support network   Friends, relatives, or professionals having the potential to help or actually assisting a person to maintain basic physical, psychological, and social needs.

sociobiology   Analysis of social behaviour as an outcome of organic evolution.

socio-economic status   The place a person occupies in the social hierarchy, usually based on a combination of income, education, and occupation.

structural functionalism   The theoretical perspective that focuses on social structure rather than individual behaviour and assumes that behaviour is governed by rules and expectations.

surrogate mother   A woman who bears a child for a couple who cannot conceive or cannot continue a pregnancy without miscarriage.

survey research   Research with a large sample, involving mailed or telephoned question-naires.

swinging   The pursuit of sexual activities with extramarital partners by both spouses at the same time and usually in the same place.

symbolic interactionism   The theoretical perspective that emphasizes that social reality is created by people defining and reacting to the behaviour of others.

systems theory   The theoretical perspective that sees the family as a system of relationships and interactions in which behaviour is recurring and sequential.

ties of affinity   Relationships by marriage or adoption.

unemployment rate   The percentage of the labour force that is officially counted as out of work and actively looking for a job. It also includes those who have been laid off and those who have found a job that will start within the next four weeks.

unidirectional research   Research that looks at only one aspect of an issue, such as the effect of parents on children rather than the effect of others on children or of children on parents.

unionization rate   The percentage of employed paid workers who belong to a labour union.

wage-labour economy   Most people work for an employer outside the home for regular pay, as opposed to being self-employed or performing unpaid work for one's family.

REFERENCES

Abella, Rosalie S. 1981. "Economic Adjustment on Marriage Breakdown: Support." *Family Law Review* 4:1-10.

_____. 1985. "Opening Address." In Elizabeth Sloss, ed. *Family Law in Canada: New Directions*, pp. 9-26. Ottawa: Canadian Advisory Council on the Status of Women.

Abu-Laban, Sharon. 1978. "The Family Life of Older Canadians." *Canadian Home Economics Journal* (January):16-25.

_____. 1980. "Arab-Canadian Family Life." In Baha Abu-Laban, ed. *An Olive Branch in the Family Tree*, pp. 158-80. Toronto: McClelland and Stewart.

Acheson, T. W. 1974. "A Study in the Historical Demography of a Loyalist County." In M. Horn and R. Sabourin, eds. *Studies in Canadian Social History*, pp. 85-95. Toronto: McClelland and Stewart.

A Choice of Futures: Canada's Commitment to Its Children. 1988. Ottawa: Canadian Child Welfare Association, Canadian Council on Children and Youth, Canadian Council on Social Development, Canadian Institute of Child Health, Child Poverty Action Group, Family Service Canada, Vanier Institute of the Family.

Acock, Alan C. 1984. "Parents and Their Children: The Study of Inter-generational Influence." *Sociology and Social Research* 68:151-71.

Adams, Bert N. 1974. "Isolation, Function and Beyond: American Kinship in the 1960s." In Carlfred B. Broderick, ed. *A Decade of Family Research and Action*. Minneapolis, Minnesota: National Council on Family Relations.

_____. 1980. *The Family: A Sociological Interpretation*, 3d ed. Chicago: Rand McNally.

Adams, John N. 1974. "Authority or Violence? Flogging the Strap Issue Again." *The Globe and Mail*, October 4, p. 9.

Ahrons, Constance R. and Wallisch, Lynn. 1987. "Parenting in the Bi-Nuclear Family: Relationships Between Biological and Stepparents." In K. Pasley and M. Ihinger-Tallman, eds. *Remarriage and Stepparenting*. pp. 225-56. New York: Guilford Press.

Albrecht, S. L. and Kunz, P. R. 1980. "The Decision to Divorce: A Social Exchange Perspective." *Journal of Divorce* 3:319-37.

Allen, Charlotte Vale. 1980. *Daddy's Girl*. Toronto: McClelland and Stewart.

Allen, Katherine R. and Pickett, Robert S. 1987. "Forgotten Streams in the Family Life Course: Utilization of Qualitative Retrospective Interviews in the Analysis of Lifelong Single Women's Family Careers." *Journal of Marriage and the Family* 49:517-26.

Amato, Paul R. and Partridge, S. 1987. "Widows and Divorcees with Dependent Children: Material, Personal, Family, and Social Well-being." *Family Relations* 36:316-20.

Ambert, Anne-Marie. 1980. *Divorce in Canada*. Toronto: Academic Press.

_____. 1983. "Separated Women and Remarriage Behavior: A Comparison of Financially Secure Women and Financially Insecure Women." *Journal of Divorce* 6:43-54.

_____. 1984. "Longitudinal Changes in Children's Behaviour Toward Custodial Parents." *Journal of Marriage and the Family* 46:463-68.

_____. 1985. "Custodial Parents: Review and a Longitudinal Study." In Benjamin Schlesinger, ed. *The One Parent Family in the 1980s*, pp. 13-34. Toronto: University of Toronto Press.

_____. 1986. "Being a Stepparent: Live-in and Visiting Stepchildren." *Journal of Marriage and the Family* 48:795-804.

_____. 1988. "Relationship Between Ex-spouses: Individual and Dyadic Perspectives." *Journal of Social and Personal Relationships* 5:327-46.

_____. 1988a. "Relationship with Ex-in-laws After Divorce." *Journal of Marriage and the Family* 50:679-86.

_____. 1988b. "Trajectory of Treatment for Emotional Problems Among Divorced/Remarried Persons: An Exploratory Study." Keynote speech at the Conference on Family, State and Society at Crossroads. University of Saskatchewan, March 17.

_____. 1989. *Ex-spouses and New Spouses*. Greenwich, Conn.: JAI Press.

Ambert, Anne-Marie and Saucier, J. F. 1983. "Adolescents' Perception of Their Parents by Parents' Marital Status." *Journal of Social Psychology* 120 (June):101-10.

Anderson, Grace M. and Higgs, David. 1976. *A Future to Inherit*. Toronto: McClelland and Stewart.

Anderson, Michael. 1980. *Approaches to the History of the Western Family*. London: Macmillan.

Archbold, Patricia G. 1983. "Impact of Parent-caring on Women." *Family Relations* 32(1):39-45.

Ariès, Philippe. 1962. *Centuries of Childhood: A Social History of Family Life*. New York: Vintage Books.

Armstrong, Hugh. 1979. "Job Creation and Unemployment in Post-War Canada." In Marvyn Novick, ed. *Full Employment: Social Questions for Public Policy*, pp. 59-77. Toronto: Social Planning Council of Metropolitan Toronto.

Armstrong, Louise. 1978. *Kiss Daddy Goodnight: A Speak-out on Incest*. New York: Pocket Books.

Armstrong, Pat and Armstrong, Hugh. 1983. *A Working Majority: What Women Must Do For Pay*. Ottawa: Supply and Services Canada for the Canadian Advisory Council on the Status of Women.

_____. 1984. *The Double Ghetto: Canadian Women and Their Segregated Work*, rev. ed. Toronto: McClelland and Stewart.

_____. 1988. "Women, Family and Economy." In Nancy Mandell and Ann Duffy, eds. *Reconstructing the Canadian Family: Feminist Perspectives*, pp. 173-74. Toronto: Butterworths.

Arnold, R. 1980. *Separation and After: A Research Report*. Ontario Ministry of Community and Social Services (mimeographed).

Atchley, Robert C. and Miller, Sheila J. 1983. "Types of Elderly Couples." In Timothy H. Brubaker, ed. *Family Relationships in Later Life*, pp. 77-90. Beverly Hills: Sage.

Australian Bureau of Statistics. 1986. *Labour Statistics of Australia*. Canberra: Australian Government Publishing Service.

_____. 1988. *Monthly Summary of Statistics*. Canberra: Australian Government Publishing Service.

Backhouse, Constance et al. 1980. *London Battered Women's Legal Handbook*. London, Ont.: University of Western Ontario Law School.

Badgley, R. (Chairman). 1984. *Report of the Committee on Sexual Offences Against Children*. Ottawa: Government of Canada.

Bahr, Howard M. and Garrett, Gerald R. 1976. *Women Alone: The Disaffiliation of Urban Females*. Lexington, Mass.: Lexington Books.

Baker, Maureen. 1980. "Support Networks and Marriage Dissolution." Unpublished report to the Faculty of Social Work, University of Toronto.

_____. 1982. "Finding Partners in the Newspaper: Sex Differences in Personal Advertising." *Atlantis* 7(2):137-46.

_____. 1983. "Divorce: Its Consequences and Meanings." In K. Ishwaran, ed. *The Canadian Family*, pp. 289-300. Toronto: Gage.

_____. 1985. *"What Will Tomorrow Bring. . . ?" A Study of The Aspirations of Adolescent Women.* Ottawa: Canadian Advisory Council on the Status of Women.

_____. 1988. *Aging in Canadian Society: A Survey.* Toronto: McGraw-Hill Ryerson.

_____. 1988a. "The Perpetuation of Misleading Family Models in Social Policy: Implications for Women." Paper presented to the Annual Meetings of the Canadian Sociology and Anthropology Association. Windsor.

Bala, Nicholas and Clarke, Kenneth L. 1981. *The Child and the Law.* Toronto: McGraw-Hill Ryerson.

Baldwin, S. 1976. *Some Practical Consequences of Caring for Handicapped Children at Home.* University of York, England: Social Policy Research Unit.

_____. 1977. *Disabled Children: Counting the Costs.* London: The Disability Alliance.

Balikci, Asen. 1970. *The Netsilik Eskimo.* New York: Natural History Press.

Bandura, A. 1977. *Social Learning Theory.* Englewood Cliffs, N.J.: Prentice-Hall.

Bandura, A. and Walters, R.H. 1963. *Social Learning and Personality Development.* New York: Holt, Rinehart and Winston.

Bane, M. J. 1976. "Marital Disruption and the Lives of Children." *Journal of Social Issues* 32:109-20.

_____. 1986. "Household Composition and Poverty." In S. H. Danziger and D. H. Weinberg, eds. *Fighting Poverty*, pp. 209-31. Cambridge, Mass.: Harvard University Press.

Barrett, Michele and McIntosh, Mary. 1982. *The Anti-Social Family.* London: Verso Books.

Bassett, Isabel. 1985. *The Bassett Report: Career Success and Canadian Women.* Toronto: Collins.

Beaujot, Roderick P. and McQuillan, Kevin. 1986. "Social Effects of Demographic Change." *Journal of Canadian Studies* (Spring).

Becker, Gary S. 1981. *A Treatise on the Family.* Cambridge, Mass.: Harvard University Press.

Belenky, M. F.; Cinchy, B. M.; Goldberger, N. R.; and Tarule, J. M. 1986. *Women's Ways of Knowing: The Development of Self, Voice, and Mind.* New York: Basic Books.

Bell, A. P. and Weinberg, M. S. 1978. *Homosexualities.* New York: Simon and Schuster.

Bell, Richard. 1968. "A Reinterpretation of the Direction of Effects in Studies of Socialization." *Psychological Review* 75:81-95.

_____. 1971. "Stimulus Control of Parent and Caretaker Behavior by Offspring." *Developmental Psychology* 4:63-72.

_____. 1974. "Contributions of Human Infants to Caregiving and Social Interaction." In Michael Lewis and L. A. Rosenblum, eds. *The Effect of the Infant on Its Caregiver.* New York: Wiley.

Bell, Richard O. and Harper, Laurence V. 1977. *Child Effects on Adults.* New York: John Wiley.

Belle, Deborah. 1980. "Who Uses Mental Health Facilities?" In Marcia Guttentag, Susan Salasin, and Deborah Belle, eds. *The Mental Health of Women.* New York: Academic Press.

Belsky, Jay. 1980. "Child Maltreatment: An Ecological Integration." *American Psychologist* 5:320-35.

Belsky, Jay; Lerner, Richard M.; and Spanier, Graham B. 1984. *The Child in the Family.* Reading, Mass.: Addison-Wesley.

Bem, Sandra Lipsitz. 1983. "Gender Schema Theory and Its Implications for Child Development: Raising Gender-Aschematic Children in a Gender-Schematic Society." *Signs* 8:598-616.

Bengtson, Vern L. and Cutler, Neal E. 1976. "Generations and Intergenerational Relations: Perspectives on Age Groups and Social Change." In Robert H. Binstock, Ethel Shanas, and associates, eds. *Handbook of Aging and the Social Sciences*. New York: Van Nostrand Reinhold.

Bennett, N.; Blanc, A. K.; and Bloom, D. 1988. "Commitment and the Modern Union: Assessing the Link Between Premarital Cohabitation and Sequential Marital Stability." *American Sociological Review* 53:127-38.

Berger, Brigitte and Berger, Peter L. 1984. *The War Over the Family: Capturing the Middle Ground*. Garden City, N.Y.: Doubleday/Anchor.

Berger, Peter L. and Berger, Brigitte. 1975. *Sociology: A Biographical Approach*, 2d ed. New York: Basic Books.

Bernard, Jessie. 1971. *Remarriage: A Study of Marriage*. New York: Russell & Russell.

_____. 1973. "My Four Revolutions: An Autobiographical History of the ASA." *American Journal of Sociology* 78:773-91.

_____. 1982 (1st ed. 1972). *The Future of Marriage*. New Haven: Yale University Press.

Berton, Pierre. 1977. *The Dionne Years*. Toronto: McClelland and Stewart/Bantam.

Bibby, Reginald W. and Posterski, Donald C. 1985. *The Emerging Generation: An Inside Look At Canada's Teenagers*. Toronto: Irwin.

Bienvenue, Rita M. and Havens, Betty. 1986. "Structural Inequalities, Informal Networks: A Comparison of Native and Non-Native Elderly." *Canadian Journal on Aging* 5(4):241-48.

Bissett-Johnson, Alastair. 1988. "Family Law – Judicial Variation of Final Global Settlements: *Pelech v. Pelech, Caron v. Caron, Richardson v. Richardson*." *Canadian Bar Review* 67:153-67.

Blacher, Jan. 1984. *Severely Handicapped Young Children and Their Families*. New York: Academic Press.

Blackstone, Sir William, Knight. 1922 (originally 1765). *Commentaries on the Laws of England in Four Books*, Book 1. In William Draper Lewis, ed. *Lewis's Blackstone*. Philadelphia: Geo. T. Bissell Co.

Blood, R. O. and Wolfe, D. M. 1960. *Husbands and Wives*. New York: The Free Press.

Bloom, B. L.; White, S. W.; and Asher, S. J. 1979. "Marital Disruption as a Stressful Life Event." In G. Levinger and O. Moles, eds. *Divorce and Separation*. New York: Basic Books.

Bloom, D. 1982. "What's Happening to the Age at First Birth in the United States?" *Demography* 19:351-91.

Blumstein, Philip and Schwartz, Pepper. 1983. *American Couples*. New York: William Morris.

Boaz, Franz. 1964 (originally 1888). *The Central Eskimo*. Lincoln: University of Nebraska Press.

Bodger, Joan and McLean, Catherine. 1977. *An Ontario Perspective on the Problems of Child Abuse: A Background Paper Prepared for Interprofessional Training Programs*. Toronto: Ministry of Community and Social Services.

Boissevain, Jeremy. 1975. "Family, Kinship and Marriage Among Italians of Montreal." In S. P. Wakil, ed. *Marriage, Family and Society*, pp. 287-94. Toronto: Butterworths.

Boivin, Suzanne. 1985. "To Marry or Not to Marry? A Study of the Legal Situation of Common-Law Spouses in Canadian Law." In Elizabeth Sloss, ed. *Family Law in Canada: New Directions*, pp. 169-94. Ottawa: Canadian Advisory Council on the Status of Women.

Boli-Bennett, John and Meyer, John W. 1978. "The Ideology of Childhood and the State: Rules Distinguishing Children in National Constitutions, 1870-1970." *American Sociological Review* 43:797-812.

Bolton, Mary G. 1983. *On Being a Mother*. London: Tavistock.

Bond, John; Harvey, Carol D. H.; and Hildebrand, Elizabeth A. 1987. "Familial Support of the Elderly in a Rural Mennonite Community." *Canadian Journal on Aging* 6(1):7-17.

Bosher, John F. 1975. "The Family in New France." In B. Gough, ed. *Search for the Visible Part*, pp. 1-13. Waterloo: Wilfrid Laurier University Press.

Boulding, Elise. 1980. "The Nurture of Adults by Children in Family Settings." In *Research in the Interweave of Social Roles: Women and Men*, vol. 1. Greenwich, Conn.: JAI Press.

Bourne, Paula, ed. 1985. *Women's Paid and Unpaid Work: Historical and Contemporary Perspectives.* Toronto: New Hogtown Press.

Bowlby, John. 1952. *Maternal Care and Maternal Health.* Geneva: World Health Organization.

Boyd, Monica. 1977. "The Forgotten Minority: The Socioeconomic Status of Divorced and Separated Women." In Patricia Marchak, ed. *The Working Sexes,* pp. 47-71. Vancouver: University of British Columbia Press.

_____. 1984. *Canadian Attitudes Toward Women: Thirty Years of Change.* Ottawa: Supply and Services Canada for the Women's Bureau, Labour Canada.

Boyd, Monica; Goyder, John; Jones, Frank E.; McRoberts, Hugh A.; Pineo, Peter C.; and Porter, John. 1985. *Ascription and Achievement: Studies in Mobility and Status Attainment in Canada.* Ottawa: Carleton University Press.

Bozett, F. 1980. "Gay Fathers: How and Why They Disclose Their Homosexuality to Their Children." *Family Relations* 29:173-79.

Bradbury, Bettina. 1979. "The Family Economy and Work in an Industrializing City: Montreal in the 1870s." In Canadian Historical Association *Historical Papers.*

_____. 1982. "The Fragmented Family: Family Strategies in the Face of Death, Illness and Poverty, Montreal, 1860-1885." In Joy Parr, ed. *Childhood and Family in Canadian History.* Toronto: McClelland and Stewart.

Bradshaw, J. and Lawton, D. 1978. *Tracing the Causes of Stress in Families with Handicapped Children.* University of York, England: Social Policy Research Unit.

Brady, Katherine. 1979. *Father's Days: A True Story of Incest.* New York: Pocket Books.

Brandt, Gail Cuthbert. 1981. " 'Weaving It Together': Life Cycle and Industrial Experience of Female Cotton Workers in Quebec, 1910-1950." *Labour/Le Travailleur,* Spring.

Breton, Albert. 1984. *Marriage, Population, and the Labour Force Participation of Women.* Ottawa: Supply and Services Canada for the Economic Council of Canada (Cat. no. E-C22117/1984E).

Breton, Raymond. 1964. "Institutional Completeness of Ethnic Communities and the Personal Relations of Immigrants." *The American Journal of Sociology* 70(2):193-205.

Brewer, Graeme. 1983. *The Impact of Work on Family Functioning. A Review of the Literature.* Occasional Paper Number 3. Melbourne: Institute of Family Studies.

Bridenthal, Renate. 1982. "The Family: The View from a Room of Her Own." In Barrie Thorne, ed. with Marilyn Yalom. *Rethinking the Family: Some Feminist Questions,* pp. 225-39. New York: Longman.

Brim, Orville G., Jr. 1966. "Socialization Through the Life Cycle." In Orville G. Brim, Jr. and Stanton Wheeler. *Socialization After Childhood: Two Essays,* pp. 1-49. New York: John Wiley.

Brim, Orville G., Jr. and Kagan, Jerome. 1980. "Constancy and Change: A View of the Issues." In Orville G. Brim, Jr. and Jerome Kagan, eds. *Constancy and Change in Human Development,* pp. 1-25. Cambridge, Mass.: Harvard University Press.

Brinkerhoff, Merlin B. and Lupri, Eugen. 1983. "Conjugal Power and Family Relationships: Some Theoretical and Methodological Issues." In K. Ishwaran, ed. *The Canadian Family,* pp. 202-19. Toronto: Gage.

_____. 1988. "Interspousal Violence." *Canadian Journal of Sociology* 13(3).

Bronfenbrenner, Urie. 1977. "Toward an Experimental Ecology of Human Development." *American Psychologist* 32:513-31.

_____. 1979. *The Ecology of Human Development.* Cambridge, Mass.: Harvard University Press.

Brown, C. 1981. "Mothers, Fathers, and Children: From Private to Public Patriarchy." In Linda Sargent, ed. *Women and Revolution: A Discussion of the Unhappy Marriage of Marxism and Feminism.* Montreal: Black Rose Books.

Browne, Angela. 1987. *When Battered Women Kill.* New York: The Free Press.

Brym, Robert J. 1979. "Introduction: New Directions in Anglo-Canadian Historical Sociology." *Canadian Journal of Sociology* 4:vii-xi.

Burch, Thomas. 1985. *Family History Survey. Preliminary Findings.* Ottawa: Supply and Services Canada (Cat. no. 99-955).

Burr, Wesley R.; Leigh, Geoffrey K.; Day, Randall D.; and Constantine, John. 1979. "Symbolic Interaction and the Family." In W. R. Burr et al., eds. *Contemporary Theories About the Family*, vol. II. New York: The Free Press.

Burris, Carole Anne and Jaffe, Peter. 1983. "Wife Abuse as a Crime." *Canadian Journal of Criminology* 25(3):309-18.

Burstein, M.; Tienhaara, N.; Hewson, P.; and Warrander, B. 1984. "Canadian Work Values." In Graham S. Lowe and Harvey J. Krahn, eds. *Working Canadians*, pp. 3-14. Toronto: Methuen.

Burton, Clare, with Raven Hag and Gay Thompson. 1987. *Women's Worth.* Canberra: Australian Government Publishing Service.

Burton, L. 1975. *The Family Life of Sick Children.* London: Routledge and Kegan Paul.

Bush, Diane Mitsch and Simmons, Roberta G. 1981. "Socialization Processes Over the Life Course." In Morris Rosenberg and Ralph H. Turner, eds. *Social Psychology: Sociological Perspectives*, pp. 133-64. New York: Basic Books.

Butler, N.; Gill, R.; and Pomeroy, D. 1976. *Housing Problems of Handicapped People in Bristol.* University of Bristol: Child Health Research Unit.

Byles, J. A. 1980. "Family Violence in Hamilton." *Canada's Mental Health* 28(1):4-6.

Cahill, Spencer E. 1980. "Directions for an Interactionist Study of Gender Development." *Symbolic Interaction* 3:123-38.

Canada, Government of. 1982. *Canadian Governmental Report on Aging.* Ottawa: Minister of Supply and Services.

———. 1982b. *Suicide Among the Aged in Canada.* Ottawa: Policy, Planning and Information Branch, Department of National Health and Welfare.

Canadian Day Care Advocacy Association. September 1988. *A Real Canadian Child Care Act: A Reality or Still a Dream?* Brief to the Legislative Committee on Bill C-144, A National Strategy for Child Care. Ottawa.

Canadian Institute of Child Health. 1988. *Child Health Profile.* Ottawa.

Caparros, Ernest. 1983. "La prestation compensatoire dans le droit civil nouveau." *Revue générale de droit* 14:139-65.

Cape, Elizabeth. 1987. "Aging Women in Rural Settings." In Victor W. Marshall, ed. *Aging in Canada*, 2d ed. Toronto: Fitzhenry and Whiteside.

Caplan, Paula J. and Hall-McCorquodale, Ian. 1985. "Mother-blaming in Major Clinical Journals." *American Journal of Orthopsychiatry* 55:345-53.

———. 1985a. "The Scapegoating of Mothers: A Call for Change." *American Journal of Orthopsychiatry* 55:610-13.

Carey, Elaine. 1981. "Huge Workload Puts Children's Aid in Peril." *The Toronto Star*, November 27, p. A10.

Carisse, Collette. 1975. "Cultural Orientations in Marriages Between French and English Canadians." In P. Wakil, ed. *Marriage, Family and Society: Canadian Perspectives*, pp. 97-112. Toronto: Butterworths.

Cass, Bettina. 1983. "Redistribution to Children and to Mothers: A History of Child Endowment and Family Allowances." In Bettina Cass and Cora Baldock, eds. *Women, Social Welfare and the State*, pp. 54-84. Sydney: Allen and Unwin.

———. 1984. "The Changing Face of Poverty in Australia: 1972-1982." Paper presented to the Continuing Education Seminar in the Department of Social Work, University of Sydney.

Cass, Bettina; Keens, Carol; and Wyndham, Diana. 1983. "Child-rearing: Direct and Indirect Costs." In Adam Graycar, ed. *Retreat From the Welfare State*, pp. 13-34. Sydney: Allen and Unwin.

Chapman, Christine. 1976. *America's Runaways*. New York: Morrow.

Chappell, Neena. 1980. "Social Policy and the Elderly." In Victor W. Marshall, ed. *Aging in Canada*, pp. 35-42. Toronto: Fitzhenry and Whiteside.

_____. 1981. "Informal Support Networks Among the Elderly." Paper presented to the Society for the Study of Social Problems. Toronto.

Chappell, Neena; Strain, Laurel; and Blandford, Audrey. 1986. *Aging and Health Care: A Social Perspective*. Toronto: Holt, Rinehart and Winston.

Charbonneau, Hubert. 1975. *Vie et mort de nos ancêtres: Etude démographique*, pp. 183-88. Montreal: University of Montreal.

Charles, Enid. 1941. *The Changing Size of the Canadian Family*. Ottawa: Dominion Bureau of Statistics.

Cheal, David J. 1983. "Intergenerational Family Transfers." *Journal of Marriage and the Family* 45:805-13.

Cherlin, Andrew. 1978. "Remarriage as an Incomplete Institution." *American Journal of Sociology* 84:634-50.

Chess, Stella and Thomas, A. 1982. "Infant Bonding: Mystique and Reality." *American Journal of Orthopsychiatry* 52:213-22.

Child Poverty Action Group. 1986. *A Fair Chance for All Children: The Declaration on Child Poverty*. Toronto: The Child Poverty Action Group.

Chilman, C. S. 1983. "The 1970s and American Families (A Comitragedy)." Prologue to E. Macklin and R. Rubin, eds. *Contemporary Families and Alternative Lifestyles*, pp. 15-24. Beverly Hills: Sage.

Chimbos, Peter D. 1976. "Marital Violence: A Study of Husband-Wife Homicide." In K. Ishwaran, ed. *The Canadian Family*, 2d ed., pp. 580-85. Toronto: Holt, Rinehart and Winston.

_____. 1978. *Marital Violence: A Study of Interspouse Homicide*. San Francisco: R & E Research Associates.

_____. 1980. "The Greek-Canadian Family: Tradition and Change." In K. Ishwaran, ed. *Canadian Families: Ethnic Variations*, pp. 27-40. Toronto: McGraw-Hill Ryerson.

Chodorow, Nancy. 1978. *The Reproduction of Mothering: Psychoanalysis and the Sociology of Gender*. Berkeley: University of California Press.

Christie, Laird. Personal conversation in March 1983.

_____. 1986. "Canadian Indians: Towards the Year 2000." Paper presented at "Indigenous Minorities in Multinational Democracies in the Year 2000: Problems and Prospects." Wilfrid Laurier University, May 10.

Cicirelli, Victor G. 1980. "Sibling Relationships in Adulthood: A Life Span Perspective." In Leonard W. Poon, ed. *Aging in the 1980s*. Washington, D.C.: American Psychological Association.

Clark, M. and Anderson, B. 1976. *Culture and Aging*. Springfield, Ill.: Charles C. Thomas.

Clark, Susan and Harvey, Andrew. 1976. "The Sexual Division of Labour: The Use of Time." *Atlantis* 2(1):46-66.

Clarke, S. D. 1962. *The Developing Canadian Community*. Toronto: University of Toronto Press.

Clausen, John A. 1986. *The Life Course*. Englewood Cliffs, N.J.: Prentice-Hall.

Clayton, Judy and Swift, Diana. 1986. "When the Time Comes, Can You Give Your Kids a College Education?" *Chatelaine*, September.

Clingempeel, W. Glenn; Brand, E.; and Segal, S. 1987. "A Multilevel-Multivariable-Developmental Perspective for Future Research on Stepfamilies." In K. Pasley and M. Ihinger-Tallman, eds. *Remarriage and Stepparenting*, pp. 65-93. New York: Guilford Press.

Clio Collective. 1987. *Quebec Women: A History*, trans. Roger Gannon and Rosalind Gill. Toronto: The Women's Press.

Colletta, N. S. 1979. "The Impact of Divorce: Father Absence or Poverty." *Journal of Divorce* 3:27-35.

Collier, Jane; Rosaldo, Michelle; and Yanagisako, Sylvia. 1982. "Is There a Family? New Anthropological Views." In Barrie Thorne, ed. with Marilyn Yalom. *Rethinking the Family: Some Feminist Questions*. New York: Longman.

Condry, John C. and Keith, Douglas. 1983. "Educational and Recreational Uses of Computer Technology." *Youth & Society* 15:87-112.

Connidis, Ingrid Arnet. 1989. *Family Ties and Aging*. Toronto: Butterworths.

Constantine, L. and Constantine, J. 1973. *Group Marriage: A Study of Contemporary Multilateral Marriage*. New York: Macmillan.

Cook, Judith A. 1988. "Who 'Mothers' the Chronically Mentally Ill?" *Family Relations* 37:42-49.

Cooley, Charles H. 1902. *Human Nature and the Social Order*. New York: Charles Scribner's Sons.

Cooper, David. 1971. *The Death of the Family*. London: Penguin Books.

Corbett, Gail H. 1981. *Barnardo Children in Canada*. Peterborough: Woodland Publishing.

Corin, Ellen. 1987. "The Relationship Between Formal and Informal Social Support Networks in Rural and Urban Contexts." In Victor W. Marshall, ed. *Aging in Canada*, 2d ed. Toronto: Fitzhenry and Whiteside.

Coulter, Rebecca. 1982. "The Working Young of Edmonton, 1927-1931." In Joy Parr, ed. *Childhood and Family in Canadian History*. Toronto: McClelland and Stewart.

Coveney, Peter. 1982. "The Image of the Child." In Chris Jenks, ed. *The Sociology of Childhood*. pp. 42-47. London: Batsford.

Coverman, Shelley and Sheley, Joseph F. 1986. "Change in Men's Housework and Childcare Time, 1965-75." *Journal of Marriage and the Family* 48(May):413-22.

Cox, Ross. 1957. *The Columbia River*. Norman, Okla.: University of Oklahoma Press.

Crawford, Trish. 1983. "Make Child Spanking a Crime, Expert on Abuse Suggests." *The Toronto Star*, March 4, p. A3.

_____. 1983a. "Ontario's Dark World of Child Abuse: Love and Anger Killing Youngsters Shocked Investigators Learn." *The Toronto Star*, March 19, p. A12.

Cruikshank, Julie. 1971. "Matrifocal Families in the Canadian North." In K. Ishwaran, ed. *The Canadian Family*, pp. 39-53. Toronto: Holt, Rinehart and Winston.

Curtis, Bruce. 1988. *Building the Educational State: Canada West. 1836-1871*. London, Ont.: Falmer Press/Althouse Press.

Dale, Jennifer and Foster, Peggy. 1986. *Feminists and State Welfare*. London: Routledge and Kegan Paul.

Danika, Elly. 1988. *Don't: A Woman's Word*. Charlottetown, P.E.I.: Ragweed Press.

Danylewycz, Marta; Light, Beth; and Prentice, Alison. 1983. "The Evolution of the Sexual Division of Labour in Teaching: A Nineteenth-Century Ontario and Quebec Case Study." *Histoire sociale/Social History*, May.

Darroch, Gordon. 1988. "Class in Nineteenth-Century Central Ontario: A Reassessment of the Crisis and Demise of Small Producers During Early Industrialization." *Canadian Journal of Sociology* 13(1-2).

Davids, Leo. 1985. "The Lone-Parent Family in Canada: The Quantitative 1985 Backgrounds." In Benjamin Schlesinger, ed. *The One Parent Family in the 1980s*, pp. 1-12. Toronto: University of Toronto Press.

Davies, Christine. 1988. "Divorce and the Older Woman in Canada." *1988 National Family Law Program*, vol. 1:A-4-1 to A-4-14. The Federation of Law Societies of Canada and the Canadian Bar Association.

Davies, Mark and Kandel, Denise B. 1981. "Parental and Peer Influences on Adolescents' Educational Plans: Some Further Evidence." *American Journal of Sociology* 87:363-87.

Davis, Morris and Krauter, Joseph. 1971. "The Eskimos." In *The Other Canadians: Profiles of Six Minorities*, pp. 24-39. Agincourt, Ontario: Methuen.

Deaux, Kay and Wrightsman, Lawrence S. 1988. *Social Psychology*, 5th ed. Pacific Grove, Calif.: Brooks/Cole.

Dechêne, Louise. 1974. *Habitants et Marchands de Montréal au XVIIe Siècle*, pp. 107-9. Montreal: Plon.

Decima Research. 1988. *Report to the Institute for the Prevention of Child Abuse On a Nation-Wide Survey of Attitudes Toward Child Rearing*, no. 3099, September. Toronto: Decima.

Deiner, Penny L. 1987. "Systems of Care for Disabled Children and Family Members: New Paradigms and Alternatives." *Marriage and Family Review* 11:193-211.

Delisle, D. J. 1988. "Some Notes for a Discussion of Bill C-15: Corroboration, Recent Complaint, Previous Sexual History." *Criminal Code Amendment, Child Abuse Bill C-15*. Toronto: The Law Society of Upper Canada, Department of Education.

Delphy, Christine. 1976. "Continuities and Discontinuities in Marriage and Divorce." In Sheila Allen and Diana Leonard Barker, eds. *Sexual Divisions and Society: Process and Change*. London: Tavistock.

DeMause, Lloyd. 1982. "The Evolution of Childhood." In Chris Jenks, ed. *The Sociology of Childhood*, pp. 48-59. London: Batsford.

Demos, John and Boocock, Sarane Spence, eds. 1978. *Turning Points: Historical and Sociological Essays on the Family*. Chicago: University of Chicago Press.

Denton, Frank T.; Feaver, Christine H.; and Spencer, Byron G. 1987. "The Canadian Population and Labour Force: Retrospect and Prospect." In Victor W. Marshall, ed. *Aging in Canada*, 2d ed. Toronto: Fitzhenry and Whiteside.

Department of Justice Canada. 1988. *Evaluation of the Divorce Act, 1985*. Ottawa: Bureau of Program Evaluation and Internal Audit, May.

Devereaux, Mary Sue. 1988. "1986 Census Highlights: Marital Status." *Canadian Social Trends* (Spring):24-27.

Diamond, Robin Moglove. 1988. "Enforcement of Custody and Access Orders." *1988 National Family Law Program*, vol. 2:E-2-1 to E-2-39. The Federation of Law Societies of Canada and the Canadian Bar Association.

Dickinson, James and Russell, Bob, eds. 1986. *Family, Economy and State: The Social Reproduction Process Under Capitalism*. Toronto: Garamond Press.

Dixson, Miriam. 1976. *The Real Matilda: Women and Identity in Australia, 1788 to 1975*. Ringwood, Victoria: Penguin.

Dobash, R. Emerson and Dobash, Russell. 1979. *Violence Against Wives: A Case Against Patriarchy*. New York: The Free Press.

Douglas, Richard L. 1983. "Domestic Neglect and Abuse of the Elderly: Implications for Research and Services." *Family Relations* 32(3):395-402.

Driedger, Leo and Chappell, Neena. 1987. *Aging and Ethnicity: Toward an Interface*. Toronto: Butterworths.

Duffy, Ann Doris. 1988. "Struggling with Power: Feminist Critiques of Family Inequality." In Nancy Mandell and Ann Duffy, eds. *Reconstructing the Canadian Family: Feminist Perspectives*, chapter 5. Toronto: Butterworths.

Dulude, Louise. 1978. *Women and Aging: A Report on the Rest of Our Lives*. Ottawa: Advisory Council on the Status of Women.

_____. 1982. "The Person Versus the Family." Paper delivered to the Learned Societies. Ottawa, July 8.

_____. 1984. *Love, Marriage and Money . . . An Analysis of Financial Relations Between the Spouses.* Ottawa: Canadian Advisory Council on the Status of Women.

Dutton, Donald G. 1988. *The Domestic Assault of Women: Psychological and Criminal Justice Perspective.* Boston: Allyn and Bacon.

Eccles, Sandra. 1984. "Women in the Australian Labour Force." In Dorothy H. Broom, ed. *Unfinished Business: Social Justice for Women in Australia.* pp. 80-93. Sydney: Allen and Unwin.

The Edmonton Journal. 1988. "Province Delaying Changes – Women." November 23.

Edwards, Meredith. 1981. *Financial Arrangements Within Families.* Research Report Commissioned by the National Women's Advisory Council. Canberra: Australia.

_____. 1984. *The Income Unit in the Australian Tax and Social Security Systems.* Melbourne, Australia: Institute of Family Studies.

Ehrenreich, Barbara. 1984. *The Hearts of Men: American Dreams and the Flight from Commitment.* Garden City, N.Y.: Anchor Books.

Ehrenreich, Barbara and English, Deirdre. 1978. *For Her Own Good.* Garden City, N.Y.: Doubleday/ Anchor.

Eichler, Margrit. 1980. *The Double Standard.* New York: St. Martin's Press.

_____. 1984. "Sexism in Research and Its Policy Implications." In Jill McCalla Vickers, ed. *Taking Sex Into Account,* pp. 17-39. Ottawa: Carleton University Press.

_____. 1988 (1st ed. 1983). *Families in Canada Today: Recent Changes and Their Policy Consequences,* 2d ed. Toronto: Gage.

_____. 1989. "Reflections on Motherhood, Apple Pie, the New Reproductive Technologies and the Role of Sociologists in Society." *Society/Société* 13(1) (February):1-5.

Eisenstein, Zillah R. 1984. *Feminism and Sexual Equality: Crisis in Liberal America.* New York: Monthly Review.

Elder, Glen H., Jr. 1984. "Parent-Child Behavior in the Great Depression: Life Course and Intergenerational Influences." In Paul B. Baltes and Orville G. Brim, Jr., eds. *Life-Span Development and Behavior,* vol. 6. New York: Academic Press.

_____. 1985. "Age Differentiation and the Life Course." *Annual Review of Sociology* 1:165-90.

Elkin, Frederick. 1964. *The Family in Canada.* Ottawa: The Vanier Institute of the Family.

_____. 1983. "Family Socialization and Ethnic Identity." In K. Ishwaran, ed. *The Canadian Family,* pp. 145-58. Toronto: Gage.

Elkin, Frederick, and Handel, Gerald. 1984. *The Child and Society: The Process of Socialization,* 4th ed. New York: Random House.

Elliott, Bruce. 1988. *Irish Migrants in the Canadas: A New Approach.* Montreal and Kingston: McGill-Queen's University Press.

Ellis, Godfrey J. 1983. "Youth in the Electronic Environment." *Youth & Society* 15:3-12.

Epstein, C. F. 1974. "A Different Angel of Vision: Notes on the Selective Eye of Sociology." *Social Science Quarterly* 5:645-56.

Erasmus, Georges; Norwegian, Herb; and Andrew, Paul. 1980. "We Must Control the Land to Have a Future." *Catalyst* (December):10,11.

Erikson, Erik. 1963. *Childhood and Society,* 2d ed. New York: Norton.

_____. 1968. *Identity: Youth and Crisis.* New York: Norton.

Estes, Carroll. 1980. *The Aging Enterprise: A Critical Examination of Social Policies and Services for the Aged.* San Francisco: Jossey-Bass.

Fasick, Frank A. 1984. "Parents, Peers, Youth Culture and Autonomy in Adolescence." *Adolescence* 19:143-57.

Fausto-Sterling, Anne. 1985. *Myths of Gender: Biological Theories About Women and Men.* New York: Basic Books.

Federico, J. 1979. "The Marital Termination Period of the Divorce Adjustment Process." *Journal of Divorce* 3:93-106.

Felner, Robert D.; Gillespie, Janet F.; and Smith, Rebecca. 1985. "Risk and Vulnerability in Childhood: A Reappraisal." *Journal of Clinical Child Psychology* 14:2-4.

Fels, L. 1981. *Living Together: Unmarried Couples in Canada.* Toronto: Personal Library.

Ferri, Elsa. 1984. *Stepchildren: A National Study.* Windsor, England: NFER-Nelson.

Finch, Janet. 1983. *Married to the Job: Wives' Incorporation into Men's Work.* London: Allen and Unwin.

Fine, Gary Alan. 1986. "The Dirty Play of Little Boys." *Society* 24 (November/December):63-67.

Finkelhor, David. 1979. *Sexually Victimized Children.* New York: The Free Press.

_____. 1983. "Common Features of Family Abuse." In David Finkelhor, Richard Gelles, Gerald T. Hotaling, and Murray A. Straus, eds. *The Dark Side of Families: Current Family Violence Research*, pp. 17-27. Beverly Hills: Sage.

Finkelhor, David and Yllo, Kirsti. 1985. *License to Rape: Sexual Abuse of Wives.* New York: Holt.

Fischer, David Hackett. 1978. *Growing Old in America*, expanded ed. Oxford: Oxford University Press.

FitzGerald, Frances. 1983. "A Reporter at Large: Interlude." *The New Yorker* (April 25):54-109.

Flandrin, Jean-Louis. 1979. *Families in Former Times: Kinship, Household and Sexuality in Early Modern France*, trans. by Richard Southern. Cambridge: Cambridge University Press.

Flynn, Sidney J. 1988. "Letter to Advakid, June 21, 1988." *Advakid: A Frank Pro-Child Newsletter for Adult Visionaries Committed to Abuse Prevention*, Fall, p. 3.

Fontana, Vincent J. 1974. *The Maltreated Child: The Maltreatment Syndrome in Children*, 2d ed. Springfield, Ill.: Charles C. Thomas.

Forward, Susan and Buck, Craig. 1978. *Betrayal of Innocence: Incest and Its Devastation.* New York: Penguin.

Fraser, Sylvia. 1987. *My Father's House: A Memoir of Incest and Healing.* Toronto: Doubleday.

French, Carey. 1988. "Sexual Swinging in the Plague Years." *The Globe and Mail*, October 1, p. D5.

Fried, S. and Holt, P. 1980. "Parent Education: One Strategy for the Prevention of Child Abuse." In M. J. Fine, ed. *Handbook on Parent Education.* New York: Academic Press.

Friedan, Betty. 1963. *The Feminine Mystique.* Harmondsworth: Penguin.

Friesen, Bruce K. 1986. "Labelling Youth Cultures Deviant: Traditional Gender Roles in Heavy Metal." Unpublished master's thesis. Calgary: University of Calgary.

Furstenberg, Frank, Jr. 1987. "The New Standard Family: The Experience of Parents and Children after Remarriage." In K. Pasley and M. Ihinger-Tallman, eds. *Remarriage and Stepparenting*, pp. 42-61. New York: Guilford Press.

Furstenberg, Frank, Jr. and Nord, C. W. 1985. "Parenting Apart: Patterns of Childrearing after Divorce." *Journal of Marriage and the Family* 47:893-904.

Furstenberg, Frank, Jr. and Spanier, G. B. 1984. *Recycling the Family: Remarriage after Divorce.* Beverly Hills: Sage.

Gaffield, Chad. 1979. "Canadian Families in Cultural Context: Hypotheses from the Mid-Nineteenth Century." Canadian Historical Association *Historical Papers.*

_____. 1982. "Boom and Bust: The Demography and Economy of the Lower Ottawa Valley in the Nineteenth Century." CHA *Historical Papers.*

_____. 1987. *Language, Schooling and Cultural Conflict.* Montreal and Kingston: McGill-Queen's University Press.

Gagan, David. 1981. *Hopeful Travellers: Families, Land and Social Change in Mid-Victorian Peel County, Canada West.* Toronto: University of Toronto Press.

Gagan, David and Mays, Herbert. 1974. "Historical Demography and Canadian Social History: Families and Land in Peel County, Ontario." In M. Horn and R. Sabourin, eds. *Studies in Canadian Social History,* pp. 96-122. Toronto: McClelland and Stewart.

Ganong, Lawrence H. and Coleman, M. 1987. "Effects of Parental Remarriage on Children: An Updated Comparison of Theories, Methods, and Findings from Clinical and Empirical Research." In L. Pasley and M. Ihinger-Tallman, eds. *Remarriage and Stepparenting,* pp. 94-140. New York: Guilford Press.

Garbarino, J. 1982. *Children and Families in the Social Environment.* New York: Aldine.

Garber, Ralph et al. 1978. *Report of the Task Force on Child Abuse.* Toronto: Ministry of Community and Social Services, Children's Services Division.

Garigue, Philippe. 1956. "French-Canadian Kinship and Urban Life." *American Anthropologist* (58):1090-1101.

_____. 1962. *La Vie Familiale des Canadiens Français.* Montreal: Presses de l'Université de Montréal.

_____. 1967. "Family Life." In *Facets of French Canada,* pp. 335-55. Ottawa.

Gaskell, Jane and McLaren, Arlene. 1987. *Women and Education: A Canadian Perspective.* Calgary, Alberta: Detselig.

Gath, A. 1977. "The Impact of an Abnormal Child upon the Parents." *British Journal of Psychiatry* 130:405-10.

Gecas, Viktor. 1981. "Contexts of Socialization." In Morris Rosenberg and Ralph H. Turner, eds. *Social Psychology: Sociological Perspectives,* pp. 165-99. New York: Basic Books.

Gee, Ellen M. 1986. "The Life Course of Canadian Women: An Historical and Demographic Analysis." *Social Indicators Research* 18.

Gee, Ellen M. and Kimball, Meredith M. 1987. *Women and Aging.* Toronto: Butterworths.

Gelles, Richard J. 1972. *The Violent Home: A Study of Physical Aggression Between Husbands and Wives.* Beverly Hills: Sage.

_____. 1976. "Abused Wives: Why Do They Stay?" *Journal of Marriage and the Family* 38:659-68. Also reprinted in Richard J. Gelles, ed. *Family Violence,* pp. 95-110. Beverly Hills: Sage, 1979.

_____. 1979. "Child Abuse as Psychopathology: A Sociological Critique and Reformulation." In David Gills, ed. *Child Abuse and Violence,* pp. 49-65. New York: AMS Press.

Gerson, M.-J.; Alpert, J. L.; and Richardson, M. S. 1984. "Mothering: The View from Psychological Research." *Signs* 9:434-53.

Gerth, H. and Mills, C. W. 1953. *Character and Social Structure.* New York: Harcourt, Brace and World.

Gil, David. 1973. *Violence Against Children: Physical Child Abuse in the United States,* 2d ed. Cambridge, Mass.: Harvard University Press.

Gillespie, Dair. 1971. "Who Has the Power? The Marital Struggle." *Journal of Marriage and the Family* 33:445-58.

Gilligan, Carol. 1982. *In A Different Voice.* Cambridge, Mass.: Harvard University Press.

Gillis, John R. 1974. *Youth and History.* New York: Academic Press.

Glenn, Evelyn Nakano. 1987. "Gender and the Family." In Beth B. Hess and Myra Marx Ferree, eds. *Analyzing Gender: A Handbook of Social Science Research,* pp. 348-80. Newbury Park, Calif.: Sage.

Glenn, Norval D. and Kramer, K. B. 1987. "The Marriages and Divorces of the Children of Divorce." *Journal of Marriage and the Family* 49:811-25.

Glenn, Norval D. and McLanahan, Sara. 1982. "Children and Marital Happiness: A Further Specification of the Relationship." *Journal of Marriage and the Family* 44:63-72.

Glick, Paul C. 1984. "How American Families are Changing." *American Demographics* (January): 21-25.

_____. 1984a. "Marriage, Divorce, and Living Arrangements: Prospective Changes." *Journal of Family Issues* 5 (March):7-26.

The Globe and Mail. 1979. "Caning to Be Banned in London's Schools." September 2, p. T8.

_____. 1988. "$437,000 in Federal Payouts Are Seized from Men Flouting Family-Support Orders." December 8.

Goldman, N. and Ravid, R. 1980. "Community Surveys: Sex Differences in Mental Illness." In M. Guttentag, S. Salasin, and D. Belle, eds. *The Mental Health of Women.* New York: Academic Press.

Goldsmith, J. 1980. "Relationships Between Former Spouses: Descriptive Findings." *Journal of Divorce* 4:1-20.

Goldthorpe, J. E. 1987. *Family Life in Western Societies.* Cambridge: Cambridge University Press.

Gongla, Patricia A. and Thompson, Edward H., Jr. 1987. "Single Parent Families." In M. B. Sussman and S. K. Steinmetz, eds. *Handbook of Marriage and the Family,* pp. 397-418. New York: Plenum Press.

Goode, William J. 1956. *Women in Divorce.* New York: The Free Press.

_____. 1959. "The Theoretical Importance of Love." *American Sociological Review* 24 (February):38-47.

_____. 1963. *World Revolution and Family Patterns.* Glencoe, Ill.: The Free Press (revised, with new introduction, 1970).

_____. 1964. *The Family.* Englewood Cliffs, N.J.: Prentice-Hall.

Gorham, Deborah. 1979. "Flora MacDonald Denison: Canadian Feminist." In Linda Kealey, ed. *A Not Unreasonable Claim: Women and Reform in Canada, 1880s-1920s.* Toronto: The Women's Press.

Gossage, Peter. 1987. "Les enfants abandonnés à Montréal, au 19ᵉ siècle: la Crèche d'Youville des Soeurs Grises, 1820-1871. *Revue d'histoire de l'amérique française* 40(4).

Gove, W. R. 1970. "Sex, Marital Status, and Psychiatric Treatment: A Research Note." *Social Forces* 58:89-93.

Gowland, Patricia. 1983. *Women in Families: The Sexual Division of Labour and Australian Family Policy.* Melbourne: Knox Community Relations Centre.

Grant, John Webster. 1984. *Moon of Wintertime: Missionaries and the Indians of Canada in Encounter since 1534.* Toronto: University of Toronto Press.

Greenland, Cyril. 1973. *Child Abuse in Ontario, Research Report 3.* Toronto: Ministry of Community and Social Services, Research and Planning Branch.

Guberman, Connie and Wolfe, Margie. 1985. *No Safe Place. Violence Against Women and Children.* Toronto: The Women's Press.

Guppy, Neil; Mikicich, Paulina D.; and Pendakur, Ravi. 1984. "Changing Patterns of Educational Inequality in Canada." *Canadian Journal of Sociology* 9:319-31.

Gutman, Gloria M.; Stark, Annette J.; Witney, Gail; and McCashin, Brian. 1983. "Deaths Within the First Year of Admission to Long-Term Care." *Canadian Journal on Aging* 1:3-11.

Guttman, David. 1976. "Individual Adaptation in the Middle Years: Developmental Issues in the Masculine Mid-Life Crisis." *Journal of Geriatric Psychiatry* 9:41-59.

Gwartney-Gibbs, Patricia A. 1986. "The Institutionalization of Premarital Cohabitation: Estimates from Marriage Licence Applications, 1970 and 1980." *Journal of Marriage and the Family* 48:423-34.

Hagestad, Gunhild O. 1987. "Parent-Child Relations in Later Life: Trends and Gaps in Past Research." In Jane B. Lancaster, Jeanne Altmann, Alice S. Rossi, and Lonnie R. Sherrod, eds. *Parenting Across the Life Span: Biosocial Dimensions*, pp. 405-33. New York: Aldine de Gruyter.

Hall, G. Stanley. 1904. *Adolescence*. 2 vols. New York: Appleton.

Hall, Phoebe et al. 1975. *Change, Choice and Conflict in Social Policy*. London: Heinemann.

Halli, Shiva S. 1987. "Minority Status and Fertility of Chinese and Japanese in Canada." *Canadian Ethnic Studies* 19(2):44-66.

Hareven, Tamara K. 1982. *Family Time and Industrial Time: The Relationship between Family in a New England Industrial Community*. Cambridge: Cambridge University Press.

———. 1987. "Historical Analysis of the Family." In Marvin B. Sussman and Suzanne K. Steinmetz, eds. *Handbook of Marriage and the Family*, pp. 37-57. New York: Plenum Press.

Harrell, A. 1985. "Husband's Involvement in Housework: The Effects of Relative Earning Power and Masculine Orientation." *Edmonton Studies Area/Series #39*. Edmonton, Alberta.

Harrison, Brian R. 1981. *Living Alone in Canada: Demographic and Economic Perspectives. 1951-1976*. Ottawa: Statistics Canada.

Harry, J. 1983. "Gay Male and Lesbian Relationships." In E. Macklin and R. Rubin, eds. *Contemporary Families and Alternative Lifestyles*, pp. 216-34. Beverly Hills: Sage.

Hartle, D. H. 1971. *Taxation of the Incomes of Married Women*. Study for the Royal Commission on Taxation. Ottawa.

Hartup, Williard W. 1982. "Symmetries and Asymmetries in Children's Relationships." In Jan de Wit and Arthur L. Benton, eds. *Perspectives in Child Study*. Amsterdam: Lisse.

Harvey, Fernand. 1979. "Children of the Industrial Revolution in Quebec," trans. by Robert Russell. In J. Dufresne et al., eds. *The Professions: Their Growth or Declines?* Montreal: Société de publication critère.

Havens, Betty. 1982. "Population Projection: Certainties and Uncertainties." In Gloria M. Gutman, ed. *Canada's Changing Age Structure: Implications for the Future*, pp. 1-31. Burnaby, B.C.: Simon Fraser University Publications.

Heller, Anita Fochs. 1986. *Health and Home: Women as Health Guardians*. Ottawa: Canadian Advisory Council on the Status of Women.

Henripin, Jacques. 1968. *Tendances et facteurs de la fécondité au Canada*. Ottawa: Queen's Printer.

Henshel, A. 1973. "Swinging: A Study of Decision-making in Marriage." *American Journal of Sociology* 78:885-91.

Henwood, Melanie and Wicks, Malcolm. 1988. *Benefit or Burden? The Objectives and Impact of Child Support*. London: Family Policy Studies Centre.

Hernandez, Donald J. 1986. "Childhood in a Sociodemographic Perspective." *Annual Review of Sociology* 12:159-80.

Heron, Craig and Storey, Robert, eds. 1986. *On the Job: Confronting the Labour Process in Canada*. Montreal and Kingston: McGill-Queen's University Press.

Hess, Beth and Markson, Elizabeth W. 1980. "The Family in Later Life." In Beth Hess and Elizabeth W. Markson, eds. *Aging in Social Systems*. New York: Macmillan.

Hess, R. D. and Camara, K. A. 1979. "Post-divorce Family Relationships as Mediating Factors in the Consequences of Divorce for Children." *Journal of Social Issues* 35:79-86.

Hetherington, E. M. and Parke, R. D. 1979. *Child Psychology: A Contemporary Viewpoint*, 2d ed. New York: McGraw-Hill.

Hetherington, Mavis E. 1987. "Family Relations Six Years after Divorce." In K. Pasley and M. Ihinger-Tallman, eds. *Remarriage and Stepparenting*, pp. 185-205. New York: Guilford Press.

Himelfarb, Alexander and Richardson, C. James. 1982. *Sociology for Canadians*. Toronto: McGraw-Hill Ryerson.

Hobart, Charles. 1987. "Parent-Child Relations in Remarried Families." *Journal of Family Issues* 8:259-77.

_____. 1988. "The Family System in Remarriage: An Exploratory Study." *Journal of Marriage and the Family* 50:649-62.

_____. 1989. "Premarital Sexuality." In G. N. Ramu, ed. *Marriage and the Family in Canada Today*, pp. 53-75. Scarborough, Ont.: Prentice-Hall.

Hoffman, Edward. 1979. "Young Adults' Relations with Their Grandparents: An Exploratory Study." *International Journal of Aging and Human Development* 10(3): 299-310.

Hoffman, Lois and Mavis, J. 1979. "The Value of Childcare in the United States: A New Approach to the Study of Fertility." *Journal of Marriage and the Family* 44:583-96.

Holmes, Sheila M. 1987. "Imposed Joint Legal Custody: Children's Interests or Parental Rights?" *University of Toronto Faculty of Law Review* 45:300-21.

Horna, Jarmila and Lupri, Eugen. 1987. "Fathers' Participation in Work, Family Life and Leisure: A Canadian Experience." In Charles Lewis and Margeret O'Brien, eds. *Problems in Fatherhood*, pp. 54-73. London: Sage.

Houseknecht, Sharon K. 1987. "Voluntary Childlessness." In Marvin B. Sussman and Suzanne K. Steinmetz, eds. *Handbook of Marriage and the Family*, pp. 369-95. New York: Plenum Press.

Houston, Susan E. and Prentice, Alison. 1988. *Schooling and Scholars in Nineteenth-Century Ontario.* Toronto: University of Toronto Press.

Huber, Joan and Spitze, Glenna. 1980. "Considering Divorce: An Expansion of Becker's Theory of Marital Instability." *American Journal of Sociology* 86(1):75-89.

Ihinger-Tallman, Marilyn. 1988. "Research on Stepfamilies." *Annual Review of Sociology* 14:25-48.

Inkeles, Alex. 1968. "Society, Social Structure, and Child Socialization." In John A. Clausen, ed. *Socialization and Society*, pp. 73-129. Boston: Little, Brown and Company.

Institute of Family Studies. 1985. *Families and Australia's Economic Future.* Submission to the Economic Planning Advisory Council, March.

Interval House. 1979. *Annual Report.* Toronto.

IPCA. 1988. *Institute for the Prevention of Child Abuse Response to the Ontario Child Abuse Register Report.* Toronto: The Institute for the Prevention of Child Abuse.

Irving, Howard H. 1972. *The Family Myth.* Toronto: Copp Clark.

Ishwarin, K. 1980. *Canadian Families: Ethnic Variations.* Toronto: McGraw-Hill Ryerson.

Jaffe, Peter and Burris, Carol A. 1981. "An Integrated Response to Wife Assault: A Community Model." Ottawa: Research Report of the Solicitor General of Canada.

Jaffe, Peter; Wolfe, D. A.; Telfor, A.; and Austin, G. 1986. "The Impact of Police Charges in Incidents of Wife Abuse." *Journal of Family Violence* 1(1):37-49.

Jenks, Chris. 1982. "Introduction: Constituting the Child." In Chris Jenks, ed. *The Sociology of Childhood*, pp. 9-24. London: Batsford.

Jenks, Richard J. 1985. "Swinging: A Replication and Test of a Theory." *The Journal of Sex Research* 21(2):199-210.

Johnson, Graham E. 1979. "Chinese Family and Community in Canada: Tradition and Change." In J. L. Elliot, ed. *Two Nations, Many Cultures: Ethnic Groups in Canada*, pp. 358-71. Toronto: Prentice-Hall.

Johnson, Laura C. 1986. *Working Families: Workplace Supports for Families.* Toronto: Social Planning Council of Metropolitan Toronto.

Johnson, Laura C. and Abramovitch, Rona. 1986. "Between Jobs: Paternal Unemployment and Family Life." Toronto: Social Planning Council of Metropolitan Toronto.

Johnson, S. M. and Lobitz, C. K. 1974. "The Personal and Marital Adjustment of Parents as Related to Observed Child Deviance and Parenting Behaviour." *Journal of Abnormal Child Psychology* 2:193-207.

Johnston, Patrick. 1983. *Native Children and the Child Welfare System*. Toronto: Lorimer.

Journal of Family History. 1987. Tenth Anniversary Commemorative Issue, 12(1-3).

Kagan, Jerome. 1984. *The Nature of the Child*. New York: Basic Books.

Kalbach, Warren E. 1983. "The Canadian Family: A Profile." In K. Ishwaran, ed. *The Canadian Family*, pp. 34-56. Toronto: Gage.

Kalbach, Warren E. and McVey, Wayne. 1971, 1979. *The Demographic Basis of Canadian Society* (two editions). Toronto: McGraw-Hill Ryerson.

Kalter, N. and Rembar, J. 1981. "The Significance of a Child's Age at the Time of Parental Divorce." *American Journal of Orthopsychiatry* 51:85-100.

Kandel, Denise and Lesser, Gerald S. 1972. "Marital Decision-Making in America and Danish Urban Families." *Journal of Marriage and the Family* 34 (February):134-38.

Katz, Michael. 1975. *The People of Hamilton, Canada West: Family and Class in a Mid-Nineteenth-Century City*. Cambridge, Mass.: Harvard University Press.

Katz, Michael B. and Davey, Ian E. 1978. "Youth and Early Industrialization in a Canadian City." In John Demos and Sarane Spence Boocock, eds. *Turning Points: Historical and Sociological Essays on the Family*, pp. S81-S119. Chicago: University of Chicago Press.

Katz, Michael B.; Doucet, Michael J.; and Stern, Mark J. 1982. *The Social Organization of Early Industrial Capitalism*. Cambridge, Mass.: Harvard University Press.

Katz, Sanford N. 1984. "Introductory Comments on Joint Custody." In *Seeking Solomon's Wisdom*, pp. 4-9. New Orleans: Loyola University School of Law.

Katz, Sidney. 1986. "Blame Mother." *Chatelaine* 59 (July):110-12.

Kazak, Anne E. 1987. "Professional Helpers and Families with Disabled Children: A Social Network Perspective." *Marriage and Family Review* 11:177-91.

Kazak, Anne E. and Marvin, R. 1984. "Differences, Difficulties, and Adaptations: Stress and Social Networks in Families with a Handicapped Child." *Family Relations* 33:66-77.

Kealey, Gregory S., ed. 1973. *Canada Investigates Industrialism*. Toronto: University of Toronto Press.

_____. 1980. *Toronto Workers Respond to Industrial Capitalism 1867-1892*. Toronto: University of Toronto Press.

Keith, Verna M. and Finlay, Barbara. 1988. "The Impact of Parental Divorce on Children's Educational Attainment, Marital Timing and Likelihood of Divorce." *Journal of Marriage and the Family* 50:797-810.

Kerber, Linda K. et al. 1986. "On In A Different Voice: An Interdisciplinary Forum." *Signs* 11:304-33.

Kessler, Suzanne J. and McKenna, Wendy. 1978. *Gender: An Ethnomethodological Approach*. New York: John Wiley.

Kew, S. 1975. *Handicap and Family Crisis*. London: Pitman.

Kincaid, Pat J. 1982. *The Omitted Reality: Husband-Wife Violence in Ontario and Policy Implications for Education*. Maple, Ontario: Publishing and Printing Services.

Kinnear, David and Graycar, Adam. 1983. "Non-Institutional Care of Elderly People." In Adam Graycar, ed. *Retreat From the Welfare State*, pp. 74-88. Sydney: Allen and Unwin.

Kitchen, Brigitte. 1980. "The Patriarchal Bias of the Income Tax in Canada." *Atlantis: A Women's Studies Journal* 11(2):35-46.

_____. 1984. "Women's Dependence." In *Sexuality and the State, The Atkinson Review of Canadian Studies* 1(2):11-16.

Kohlberg, Laurence. 1976. "Moral Stages and Moralization: The Cognitive-Developmental Approach." In T. Lickona. *Moral Development and Behavior.* New York: Holt, Rinehart and Winston.

Kohn, Melvin L. 1977. *Class and Conformity,* 2d ed. Homewood, Ill.: Dorsey.

Konstantareas, M. et al. 1983. "Mothers of Autistic Children: Are They the 'Unacknowledged Victims'?" Paper presented to the Canadian Psychological Association. Winnipeg.

Krishnan, Vijaya. 1987. "The Family in Canada: A Support System for the Elderly." *Research Discussion Paper No. 47.* Edmonton, Alberta: Population/Research Laboratory.

Kronby, Malcolm. 1986. *Canadian Family Law.* Toronto: Stoddart.

Kunkel, John H. 1977. "Sociobiology vs. Biosociology." *The American Sociologist* 12:69-73.

Kurdeck, L. A. and Blisk, D. 1983. "Dimensions and Correlates of Mothers' Divorce Experience." *Journal of Divorce* 6:1-24.

Kuzel, Paul and Krishnan, P. 1973. "Changing Patterns of Remarriage in Canada." *Journal of Comparative Family Studies* 4(2):215-24.

Kyriazis, Natalie and Stelcner, Morton. "A Logistical Analysis of Living Arrangements in Canada: A Comparison of the Young and Aging." *Journal of Comparative Family Studies* 17(3):389-403.

Labour Canada. 1986. *When I Grow Up: Career Expectations and Aspirations of Canadian Schoolchildren.* Ottawa: Women's Bureau.

Laing, Ronald. 1970. *The Politics of Experience.* Harmondsworth: Penguin.

_____. 1976. *The Politics of the Family.* Harmondsworth: Penguin.

Lambert, Wallace E.; Hamers, Josiane F.; and Frasure-Smith, Nancy. 1980. *Child-Rearing Values: A Cross-National Study.* New York: Praeger.

Lancaster, Jane B.; Altmann, Jeanne; Rossi, Alice S.; and Sherrod, Lonnie R. 1987. *Parenting Across the Life Span: Biosocial Dimensions.* New York: Aldine de Gruyter.

Landsberg, Michele. 1981. "The Law Condones Abuse of Our Kids." *The Toronto Star,* November 26, p. H1.

LaRose, Andre. *Histoire sociale/Social History* (annual bibliographies on historical demography).

LaRossa, Ralph and LaRossa, M. 1981. *Transition to Parenthood: How Infants Change Families.* Beverly Hills: Sage.

Larson, Reed. 1978. "Thirty Years of Research on the Subjective Well-being of Older Americans." *Journal of Gerontology* 33(1):109-25.

Lasch, Christopher. 1977. *Haven in a Heartless World: The Family Besieged.* New York: Basic Books.

Laslett, Peter. 1965. *The World We Have Lost.* New York: Charles Scribner's Sons.

Laslett, Peter, ed. 1972. *Household and Family in Past Time.* London and New York: Cambridge University Press.

Lavigne, Yves. 1982. "Brockville CAS Failed Job, Court Told." *The Globe and Mail,* April 20, p. 11.

The Lawyers Weekly. 1988. "Family Law Trilogy Reasoning Doesn't Apply Unless Spouses Have a Support Agreement?" August 26.

Leacock, Eleanor Burke. 1981. *Myth of Male Dominance.* New York: Monthly Book Review.

_____. 1986. "Montagnais Women and the Jesuit Program for Colonization." In Veronica Strong-Boag and Anita Clair Fellman, eds. *Rethinking Canada,* pp. 7-22. Toronto: Copp Clark Pitman.

Le Devoir. 1988. "Québec serre la vis aux obstinés." June 18.

Lee, G. R. 1977. "Age at Marriage and Marital Satisfaction: A Multivariate Analysis with Implications for Marital Stability." *Journal of Marriage and the Family* 39:493-504.

Lee, Gary. 1988. "Marital Intimacy Among Older Persons: The Spouse as Confidant." *Journal of Family Issues* 9:273-84.

Lee, John Alan. 1982. "Three Paradigms of Childhood." *Canadian Review of Sociology and Anthropology* 19(4):591-608.

_____. 1987. "The Invisible Lives of Canada's Grey Gays." In Victor Marshall, ed. *Aging in Canada: Social Perspectives*, 2d ed., pp. 138-55. Toronto: Fitzhenry and Whiteside.

Lerman, Hannah. 1987. "From Freud to Feminist Personality Theory: Getting Here from There." In Mary Roth Walsh, ed. *The Psychology of Women: Ongoing Debates*, pp. 39-58. New Haven, Conn.: Yale University Press.

Lerner, Richard M. and Busch-Rossnagel, N. 1981. *Individuals as Producers of their Own Development: A Life-Span Perspective*. New York: Academic Press.

Lerner, Richard M. and Spanier, Graham B. 1978. *Child Influences on Marital Quality: A Life-Span Perspective*. New York: Academic Press.

Levinger, George. 1979. "A Social Psychological Perspective on Marital Dissolution." In George Levinger and Oliver C. Moles, eds. *Divorce and Separation: Context, Causes, and Consequences*, pp. 37-60. New York: Basic Books.

Lewin, B. 1982. "Unmarried Cohabitation: A Marriage Form in a Changing Society." *Journal of Marriage and the Family* 44:763-75.

Lewis, Michael and Lee-Painter, S. 1974. "An Interactional Approach to the Mother-Infant Dyad." In M. Lewis and L. A. Rosenblum, eds. *The Effect of the Infant on Its Caregiver*. New York: Wiley.

Lewis, Michael and Rosenblum, Leonard, eds. 1974. *The Effect of the Infant on Its Caregiver*. New York: Wiley.

Lewis, William Draper. 1922. *Lewis's Blackstone: Commentaries on the Laws of England in Four Books by Sir William Blackstone, Knight*, Book 1. Philadelphia: Geo. T. Bissell Co.

Li, Peter. 1987. "The Economic Cost of Racism to Chinese-Canadians." *Canadian Ethnic Studies* 19(3):102-13.

Loeber, Rolf and Stouthamer-Loeber, Magda. 1986. "Family Factors as Correlates and Predictors of Juvenile Conduct Problems and Delinquency." In Michael Tonry and Norval Morris, eds. *Crime and Justice*. Chicago: University of Chicago Press.

Lowe, Graham S. 1989. *Women, Paid/Unpaid Work, and Stress: New Directions for Research*. Ottawa: Canadian Advisory Council on the Status of Women.

Lowe, Graham S.; Krahn, Harvey; and Tanner, Julian. 1988. "Young People's Explanations of Unemployment." *Youth & Society* 19:227-49.

Lowe, Marian. 1978. "Sociobiology and Sex Differences." *Signs* 4:118-25.

Lowie, Robert. 1947. *Primitive Society*. New York: Liveright.

Luepnitz, Deborah A. 1982. *Child Custody: A Study of Families After Divorce*. Lexington, Mass.: D. C. Heath.

Luiselli, James K.; Evans, Tracy P.; Boyce, Delma A. 1985. "Contingency Management of Food Sensitivity and Oppositional Eating in a Multiple Handicapped Child." *Journal of Clinical Child Psychology* 14:153-56.

Lupri, Eugen. 1989. "Hidden in the Home: Wife Abuse in Canada: Selected Findings from a 1987 National Survey." *Canadian Social Trends*.

Lupri, Eugen and Frideres, James. 1981. "The Quality of Marriage and the Passage of Time: Marital Satisfaction Over the Family Life Cycle." *The Canadian Journal of Sociology* 6:283-306.

Luxton, Meg. 1980. *More Than a Labour of Love: Three Generations of Women's Work in the Home*. Toronto: Women's Educational Press.

_____. 1983. "Two Hands for the Clock: Changing Patterns in the Gendered Division of Labour in the Home." *Studies in Political Economy* 12 (Fall):27-44.

Maccoby, Eleanor E. and Jacklin, Carol N. 1974. *The Psychology of Sex Differences*. Stanford, Calif.: Stanford University Press.

Mackie, Marlene. 1987. *Constructing Women and Men: Gender Socialization*. Toronto: Holt, Rinehart and Winston.

_____. 1989. "Primary Socialization." In G. N. Ramu, ed. *Marriage and the Family in Canada Today*, pp. 101-19. Scarborough, Ont.: Prentice-Hall.

Macklin, E. 1980. "Nontraditional Family Forms: A Decade of Research." *Journal of Marriage and the Family* 42:905-22.

_____. 1983. "Nonmarital Heterosexual Cohabitation: An Overview." In E. Macklin and R. Rubin, eds. *Contemporary Families and Alternative Lifestyles*, pp. 49-74. Beverly Hills: Sage.

_____. 1987. "Nontraditional Family Forms." In M. B. Sussman and S. K. Steinmetz, eds. *Handbook of Marriage and the Family*, pp. 317-52. New York: Plenum Press.

MacLeod, Linda. 1980. *Wife Battering in Canada: The Vicious Circle*. Prepared for the Canadian Advisory Council on the Status of Women. Ottawa: Supply and Services Canada.

_____. 1987. *Battered But Not Beaten: Preventing Wife Abuse in Canada*. Prepared for the Canadian Advisory Council on the Status of Women. Ottawa: Supply and Services Canada.

Maden, Marc F. and Wrench, David F. 1977. "Significant Findings in Child Abuse Research." *Victimology* 11(2):196-224.

Malarek, Victor. 1979. "9,000 Not Told They're Suspects of Child Abuse." *The Globe and Mail*, October 16, pp. 1-2.

Mandell, Nancy. 1988. "The Child Question: Links Between Women and Children in the Family." In Nancy Mandell and Ann Duffy, eds. *Reconstructing the Canadian Family: Feminist Perspectives*, pp. 49-81. Toronto: Butterworths.

Mandell, Nancy and Duffy, Ann, eds. 1988. *Reconstructing the Canadian Family: Feminist Perspectives*. Toronto: Butterworths.

Marsh, Leonard. 1975. *Report on Social Security for Canada 1943*. Toronto: University of Toronto Press (1943 version, Ottawa: King's Printer).

Marshall, Victor W. and Bengtson, Vern L. 1983. "Generations: Conflict and Cooperation." In Manfred Bergener, Ursula Lehr, Erich Lang, and Reinhard Schmitz-Scherzer, eds. *Aging in the Eighties and Beyond, Highlights of the 12th International Congress of Gerontology*. New York: Springer.

Marshall, Victor W. and Rosenthal, Carolyn J. 1983. "Aging and Later Life." In Robert Hagedorn, ed. *Sociology*, 2d ed., pp. 123-25. Toronto: Holt, Rinehart and Winston.

Marshall, Victor W.; Rosenthal, Carolyn J.; and Synge, Jane. 1982. "Concerns About Parental Health." In Elizabeth W. Markson, ed. *Women and Aging*. Lexington, Mass.: Lexington Books.

Martin, Del. 1976. *Battered Wives*. New York: Pocket Books.

Martin Matthews, Anne. 1980. "Women and Widowhood." In Victor W. Marshall, ed. *Aging in Canada*, pp. 145-53. Toronto: Fitzhenry and Whiteside.

_____. 1982. "Canadian Research on Women as Widows: A Comparative Analysis of the State of the Art." *Resources for Feminist Research* 11:227-30.

_____. 1985. "Support Systems of Widows in Canada." In Helena Z. Lopata, ed. *Widows: Other Countries/Other Places*. Durham, N.C.: Duke University Press.

Martin's Annual Criminal Code. 1989. Incorporating R.S.C. 1985. Aurora, Ont.: Canada Law Book.

Mattessich, Paul and Hill, Rueben. 1987. "Life Cycle and Family Development." In Marvin B. Sussman and Suzanne K. Steinmetz, eds. *Handbook of Marriage and the Family*, pp. 437-70. New York: Plenum Press.

Matthews, Ralph and Martin Matthews, Anne. 1986. "Infertility and Involuntary Childlessness: The Transition to Non-Parenthood." *Journal of Marriage and the Family* 48:641-49.

Matthiason, John S. 1980. "The Inuit Family: Past, Present and Future." In K. Ishwaran, ed. *Canadian Families: Ethnic Variations*, pp. 266-97. Toronto: McGraw-Hill Ryerson.

Maychak, Matt. 1982. "More Criminal Charges by Police Urged in Fatal Child-Abuse Cases." *The Toronto Star*, October 26, p. A3.

Maynard, Rona. 1988. "Were They Better Off Than We?" *Report on Business* magazine (May): 39-47.

Mayrand, A. 1985. "La garde conjointe, reéquilibrage de l'autorité parentale." *The Canadian Bar Review* 67:193-228.

McAndrew, I. 1976. "Children with a Handicap and Their Families." *Child: Care, Health and Development* 2:213-37.

McClung, Nellie. 1972. *In Times Like These*. Toronto: University of Toronto Press. The original edition was published in the United States in 1915 by D. Appleton and Company and was distributed in Canada by McLeod & Allen.

McElroy, Ann. 1975. "Arctic Modernization and Change in Inuit Family Organization." In S. P. Wakil, ed. *Marriage, Family and Society*, pp. 379-99. Toronto: Butterworths.

McKie, Craig. 1986. "Common-Law: Living Together as Husband and Wife Without Marriage." *Canadian Social Trends* (Autumn):39-41.

McKie, D. C.; Prentice, B.; and Reed, P. 1983. *Divorce: Law and the Family in Canada*. Ottawa: Ministry of Supply and Services for Statistics Canada (Cat. no. 89-502E).

McLaren, Angus and McLaren, Arlene Tigar. 1986. *The Bedroom and the State: The Changing Practices and Politics of Contraception and Abortion in Canada, 1880-1980*. Toronto: McClelland and Stewart.

McLeod, James B. "Unequal Distribution of Family Property: Valuation of Property." *1988 National Family Law Program*, vol. 2:D-1-1 to D-1-153. The Federation of Law Societies of Canada and the Canadian Bar Association.

McMichael, J. K. 1971. *Handicap: A Study of Physically Handicapped Children and Their Families*. London: Staples Press.

McNulty, Faith. 1981. *The Burning Bed: The True Story of an Abused Wife*. New York: Bantam.

McQueeny, Jane. 1984. "Joint Custody: A Paradigm of Tomorrow's Family?" In *Seeking Solomon's Wisdom*, pp. 10-33. New Orleans: Loyola University School of Law.

Mead, George Herbert. 1934. *Mind, Self and Society*. Chicago: University of Chicago Press.

Mead, Margaret. 1935. *Sex and Temperament in Three Primitive Societies*. New York: Dell.

Medick, Hans. 1976. "The Proto-Industrial Family Economy: The Structural Function of Household and Family During the Transition from Peasant Society to Industrial Capitalism." *Social History*, October.

Meissner, Martin; Humphreys, Elizabeth W.; Meis, Scott M.; and Scheu, William J. 1975. "No Exit for Wives: Sexual Division of Labour and the Cumulation of Household Demands." *Canadian Review of Sociology and Anthropology* 12 (Part 1): 424-39.

Melichar, Joseph F. and Chiriboga, D. A. 1988. "Significance of Time in Adjustment to Marital Separation." *American Journal of Orthopsychiatry* 58:221-27.

Miall, Charlene E. 1985. "Perceptions of Informal Sanctioning and the Stigma of Involuntary Childlessness." *Deviant Behavior* 6:383-403.

Michelson, William. 1985. *From Sun to Sun: Daily Obligations and Community Structure in the Lives of Employed Women and Their Families*. Toitawa, N.J.: Rowman and Allanheld.

Milardo, Roberta M. 1987. "Changes in Social Networks of Women and Men Following Divorce: A Review." *Journal of Family Issues* 8:78-96.

Miles, Angela. 1982. "Introduction." In Angela R. Miles and Geraldine Finn, eds. *Feminism in Canada: From Pressure to Politics*, pp. 9-23. Montreal: Black Rose Books.

Miller, B. C. and Sollie, D. L. 1980. "Normal Stresses During the Transition to Parenthood." *Family Relations* 29:29-35.

Mills, C. Wright. 1959. *The Sociological Imagination.* New York: Oxford University Press.

Minuchin, S. 1974. *Families and Family Therapy.* Cambridge, Mass.: Harvard University Press.

Miron, John and Schiff, Myra. 1982. *A Profile of the Emerging Empty-Nester Household* (Research Paper No. 130). Toronto: Centre for Urban and Community Studies, University of Toronto.

Mitchell, Juliet. 1975. *Psychoanalysis and Feminism.* Harmondsworth: Penguin.

Moch, Leslie et al. 1987. "Family Strategy: A Dialogue." *Historical Methods* 20.

Moogk, Peter N. 1982. "Les Petits Sauvages: The Children of Eighteenth-Century New France." In Joy Parr, ed. *Childhood and Family in Canadian History,* pp. 17-43. Toronto: McClelland and Stewart.

Morgan, D. H. 1975. *The Family and Social Theory.* London: Routledge and Kegan Paul.

Morgan, Robin. 1984. *Sisterhood Is Global.* New York: Anchor Books.

Morris, Cerise. 1988. "The Politics and Experience of Co-Parenting: An Exploratory Study of Shared Custody in Canada," no. 20. Ottawa: Canadian Research Institute for the Advancement of Women.

Morton, Mary E. 1988. "Dividing the Wealth, Sharing the Poverty: the (Re)formation of 'Family' in Law." *The Canadian Review of Sociology and Anthropology* 25(2):254-75.

Morton, Mildred J. 1988. "Divorce, Custody, Support, Enforcement: Transferring and Sharing Jurisdiction." *Current Issue Review* 81-13E. Ottawa: Library of Parliament (archived).

Moss, P. and Silver, O. 1972. *Mentally Handicapped School Children and Their Families.* University of Birmingham, England: Clearing House for Local Authority Social Services Research.

Murdock, George. 1949. *Social Structure.* New York: Macmillan.

Muszynski, Leon. 1988. "Better Help for Single Parents." *Policy Options* (April):23-26.

Nagnur, D. and Adams, O. 1987. "Tying the Knot: An Overview of Marriage Rates in Canada." *Canadian Social Trends* (Autumn):1-6.

National Action Committee on the Status of Women. 1988. "A NAC Discussion Paper on Government Programs for Parents with Young Children." Ottawa: National Action Committee on the Status of Women, Family Policy Committee.

National Association of Women and the Law. 1985. *Bill C-47: Joint Custody, Child Support, Maintenance Enforcement and Related Issues,* vol. I. A submission to the Senate Standing Committee on Justice and Legal Affairs, September.

National Council of Welfare. 1979. *In the Best Interests of the Child: A Report by the National Council of Welfare on the Child Welfare System in Canada.* Ottawa: National Council of Welfare.

_____. 1979. *Women and Poverty.* Ottawa: National Council of Welfare.

_____. 1985. *Poverty Profile 1985.* Ottawa: National Council of Welfare.

_____. 1988. *Poverty Profile 1988.* Ottawa: National Council of Welfare, April.

National Crime Survey. 1982. U.S. Department of Justice.

National Film Board of Canada. 1979. *Loved, Honoured and Bruised.*

Nelson, G. 1981. "Moderators of Women's and Children's Adjustment Following Parental Divorce." *Journal of Divorce* 4:71-83.

Nett, Emily. 1976. "The Changing Forms and Function of the Canadian Family: A Demographic View." In K. Ishwaran, ed. *The Canadian Family.* Toronto: Gage.

_____. 1980. "The Family." In Robert Hagedorn et al., eds. *Sociology.* Toronto: Holt, Rinehart and Winston.

_____. 1981. "Canadian Families in Social-historical Perspective." *Canadian Journal of Sociology* 6(3):239-60.

_____. 1982. "Family Studies of Elders: Gerontological and Feminist Approaches." Paper presented at the Annual Meeting of the Canadian Sociology and Anthropology Association. Ottawa.

———. 1988. *Canadian Families Past and Present.* Toronto: Butterworths.

Nett, Emily and Brown, Catrina. 1981. "Generational Relationships of University Students: Involvement with Aging Family Members." Paper presented at the Annual Meeting of the Western Association of Anthropologists and Sociologists. Winnipeg.

Neugarten, Bernice L. 1979. "The Middle Generations." In Pauline K. Ragan, ed. *Aging Parents.* Los Angeles: The University of Southern California Press.

Norris, Joan. 1987. "Psychological Processes in the Development of Late Life Social Identity." In Victor W. Marshall, ed. *Aging in Canada,* 2d ed. Toronto: Fitzhenry and Whiteside.

Northcott, Herbert C. 1982. "The Best Years of Your Life." *Canadian Journal on Aging* 1(3,4):72-78.

———. 1983. "Who Stays Home? Working Parents and Sick Children." *International Journal of Women's Studies* 6:387-94.

———. 1988. *Changing Residence: The Geographic Mobility of Canadians.* Toronto: Butterworths.

Norton, Arthur J. 1983. "Family Life Cycle: 1980." *Journal of Marriage and the Family* 45:267-75.

Novak, Mark. 1988. *Aging and Society: A Canadian Perspective.* Scarborough, Ont.: Nelson Canada.

Offord, D. R. et al. 1987. *Ontario Child Health Study.* Toronto: Ministry of Community and Social Services.

O'Laughlin, Mary Ann and Cass, Bettina. 1984. "Married Women's Employment Status and Family Income Distribution." Paper presented to 54th ANZAAS Congress. Canberra: Australian National University, May.

Ollmanns, T. F.; Broderick, J. E.; and O'Leary, K. I. 1977. "Marital Adjustment and the Efficacy of Behavior Therapy with Children." *Journal of Consulting and Clinical Psychology* 45:724-29.

O'Neill, N. and O'Neill, G. 1972. *Open Marriage: A New Life Style for Couples.* New York: Macmillan.

Ontario Ministry of Community and Social Services. 1988. *Reporting Child Abuse: Your Responsibility Under Ontario's Child and Family Services Act.* Toronto: Queen's Printer.

———. 1987. *Child Abuse Prevention.* Toronto: Queen's Printer.

Ontario Ministry of Social Development. 1979. *The Family as a Focus for Social Policy.* Toronto: Ontario Ministry of Social Development.

Palmer, S. and Horn, S. 1978. "Feeding Problems in Children." In S. Palmer and S. Ekvall, eds. *Pediatric Nutrition in Developmental Disorder.* Springfield, Ill.: Thomas.

Panelas, Tom. 1983. "Adolescents and Video Games: Consumption of Leisure and the Social Construction of the Peer Group." *Youth & Society* 15:51-65.

Parr, Joy. 1980. *Labouring Children: British Immigrant Apprentices to Canada, 1869-1924.* Montreal: McGill-Queen's University Press.

Parr, Joy, ed. 1982. *Childhood and Family in Canadian History.* Toronto: McClelland and Stewart.

Parsons, Talcott and Bales, Robert F. 1985. *Family, Socialization and Interaction Process.* New York: The Free Press.

Pask, E. Diane. 1988. "Pension Division Across Canada: New Developments." *1988 National Family Law Program,* vol. 2:D-5-1 to D-5-32. The Federation of Law Societies of Canada and the Canadian Bar Association.

Patterson, G. R. 1976. *Families of Antisocial Children: An Interactional Approach.* Eugene, Oregon: Castalia.

Payne, Julien D. 1988. "A Practitioner's Guide to Spousal Support in Divorce Proceedings." *1988*

National Family Law Program, vol. 1:A-1-1 to A-1-42. The Federation of Law Societies of Canada and the Canadian Bar Association.

Pelletier, A. J.; Thompson, F. D.; and Rochon, A. 1938. *The Canadian Family*, Census Monograph No. 7, p. 19. Ottawa: J. O. Patenaude.

Peplau, L. A. 1981. "What Homosexuals Want in Relationships." *Psychology Today* 15(3):28-38.

_____. 1982. "Research on Homosexual Couples: An Overview." *Journal of Homosexuality* 8(2):3-8.

Peplau, L. A. and Gordon, S. L. 1983. "The Intimate Relationships of Lesbians and Gay Men." In E. R. Allgeier and N. B. McCormick, eds. *Changing Boundaries*, pp. 226-44. Palo Alto: Mayfield Publishing Company.

Peter, Karl A. 1987. *The Dynamics of Hutterite Society*. Edmonton: University of Alberta Press.

Peters, John. 1982. "Children as Socialization Agents Through the Parents' Middle-Years." Paper presented at the Canadian Sociology and Anthropology Association meetings in April. Ottawa.

_____. 1983. "The Single Female." In K. Ishwaran, ed. *Marriage and Divorce in Canada*, pp. 107-25. Toronto: Methuen.

_____. 1987. "Socialization Among the Old Order Mennonites." *International Journal of Comparative Sociology* 28(3-4):211-23.

_____. 1988. "Population Study of the Pennsylvania Dutch in Canada." Paper presented at the National Council in Family Relations. Philadelphia.

Peterson, Anne C. 1987. "Those Gangly Years." *Psychology Today* 21 (September):28-34.

Peterson, Gary W. and Rollins, Boyd C. 1987. "Parent-Child Socialization." In Marvin S. Sussman and Suzanne K. Steinmetz, eds. *Handbook of Marriage and the Family*, pp. 471-507. New York: Plenum Press.

Philp, Mark and Duckworth, Derek. 1982. *Children with Disabilities and their Families. A Review of Research*. Windsor, England: NFER-Nelson.

Piaget, Jean. 1928. *Judgment and Reasoning in the Child*. New York: Harcourt.

_____. 1932. *The Moral Judgment of the Child*. New York: Harcourt.

_____. 1970. *Structuralism*. New York: Basic Books.

Pierson, Ruth Roach. 1986. *"They're Still Women After All": The Second World War and Canadian Womanhood*. Toronto: McClelland and Stewart.

Pike, R. 1975. "Legal Access and the Incidence of Divorce in Canada: A Sociohistorical Analysis." *Canadian Review of Sociology and Anthropology* 12:115-33.

Pineo, Peter C. and Looker, E. Dianne. 1983. "Class and Conformity in the Canadian Setting." *Canadian Journal of Sociology* 8:293-317.

Pines, Maya. 1981. "The Civilizing of Genie." *Psychology Today* 15 (September):28-34.

Pleck, Elizabeth. 1979. "Wife Beating in Nineteenth-Century America." *Victimology* 4(1):60-74.

Pleck, Elizabeth; Pleck, J. H.; Grossman, M.; and Bart, P. B. 1977-78. "The Battered Data Syndrome: A Comment on the Steinmetz Article." *Victimology: An International Journal* 2:680-84.

Polgar, Steven. 1960. "Biculturation of Mesquakie Teenage Boys." *American Anthropologist* 62:217-35.

Porter, Marilyn. 1985. " 'She was Skipper of the Shore Crew': Notes on the History of the Sexual Division of Labour in Newfoundland." *Labour/Le travail* (Spring).

Postman, Neil. 1982. *The Disappearance of Childhood*. New York: Penguin Books.

Prentice, Alison et al. 1988. *Canadian Women: A History*. Toronto: Harcourt Brace Jovanovich.

Proulx, Monique. 1978. *Five Million Women. A Study of the Canadian Housewife*. Ottawa: Advisory Council on the Status of Women.

Pryer, Edward T. 1984. *Canadian Husband-Wife Families: Labour Force Participation and Income Trends, 1971-1981*. Ottawa: Supply and Services Canada (Cat. no. 71-X-512).

Quebec, Minister of Social Affairs. 1984. *A Working Paper on Family Policy*. Montreal: Ministry of Social Affairs.

Radbill, Samuel X. 1980. "A History of Child Abuse and Infanticide." In Ray E. Helfer and C. Henry Kempe, eds. *The Battered Child*, 3d ed., pp. 3-21. Chicago: University of Chicago Press.

Ramu, G. N. and Tavuchis, Nicholas. 1986. "The Valuation of Children and Parenthood Among Voluntarily Childless and Parental Couples in Canada." *Journal of Comparative Family Studies* 17:99-116.

_____. 1989. "Urban Kin Networks." In G. N. Ramu, ed. *Marriage and the Family in Canada Today*, pp. 143-65. Scarborough, Ont.: Prentice-Hall.

Rao, K. Vaninadha and Balakrishnan, T. R. 1986. "Childlessness as a Factor of Fertility Decline in Canada." Prepared for the Review of Demography and its Implications for Economic and Social Policy. Ottawa: Health and Welfare Canada, October.

Rapp, Rayna. 1982. "Family and Class in Contemporary America: Notes Toward Understanding of Ideology." In Barrie Thorne and Marilyn Yalom, eds. *Rethinking the Family: Some Feminist Questions*. New York: Longman.

Rapp, Rayna et al. 1979. "Examining Family History." *Feminist Studies* 5.

Raschke, Helen J. 1987. "Divorce." In Marvin B. Sussman and Suzanne K. Steinmetz, eds. *Handbook of Marriage and the Family*, pp. 597-624. New York: Plenum Press.

Rashid, A. 1986. "Labour Market Activities of High Income Families." In *The Labour Force*, pp. 87-113. Ottawa: Supply and Services Canada for Statistics Canada (Cat. no. 71-001).

Rasmussen, Knud. 1931. *The Netsilik Eskimos*. Copenhagen: Reports of the Fifth Thule Expedition, vol. VIII.

Rayle, Pierrette. 1988. "La prestation compensatoire et la Cour d'appel cinq ans plus tard." *Revue du Barreau* 14:225-49.

Reiger, Kerreen. 1985. *The Disenchantment of the Home. Modernizing the Australian Family, 1880-1940*. Melbourne: Oxford University Press.

Renne, K. S. 1971. "Health and Marital Experience in an Urban Population." *Journal of Marriage and the Family* 33:338-50.

Rheingold, Harriet L. 1966. "The Development of Social Behavior in the Human Infant." In H. W. Stevenson, ed. *Concept of Development: A Report of a Conference Commemoration of the 40th Anniversary of the Institute of Child Development, University of Minnesota*. Monographs of the Society for Research in Child Development: 31(5, whole no. 107).

_____. 1969. "The Social and Socializing Infant." In David A. Goslin, ed. *Handbook of Socialization Theory and Research*, pp. 779-90. Chicago: Rand McNally.

Rich, Adrienne. 1976. *Of Woman Born: Motherhood as Experience and Institution*. New York: Norton.

Rich, A. 1980. "Compulsory Heterosexuality and Lesbian Experience." *Signs* 5(4):631-60.

Richards, Lyn. 1985. *Having Families. Marriage, Parenthood and Social Pressures in Australia*. Ringwood, Victoria: Penguin.

Rioux, Marcel. 1959. "Kinship Recognition and Urbanization in French Canada." In *Contributions to Anthropology*. National Museum of Canada, Bulletin No. 173, pp. 1-11. Printed in M. Rioux and Y. Martin, eds. *French Canadian Society*, pp. 372-85. Toronto: McClelland and Stewart, 1964.

Risman, B. and Schwartz, P. 1988. "Sociological Research on Male and Female Homosexuality." *Annual Review of Sociology* 14:125-47.

Rivard, Glen. 1988. "Divorce Mediation: The Federal Perspective." *1988 National Family Law Program*, vol. 5:L-6-1 to L-6-29. The Federation of Law Societies of Canada and the Canadian Bar Association.

Robertson, Ian. 1981. *Sociology*, 2d ed. New York: Worth Pubs.

Robinson, Bryan E. and Barret, Robert L. 1986. *The Developing Father.* New York: Guilford Press.

Robinson, Kenneth et al. 1976. *Child Abuse and Neglect: Report to the House of Commons Standing Committee on Health, Welfare and Social Affairs.* First Session, 30th Parliament, 1974-75-76. Ottawa: Printing and Publishing, Supply and Services Canada.

Rodman, H. and Graves, P. 1967. "Juvenile Delinquency and the Family: A Review and Discussion." In *Juvenile Delinquency and Youth Crime,* President's Commission on Law Enforcement and Administration of Justice. Task Force Report. Washington, D.C.: U.S. Government Printing Office.

Rogers, Dorothy. 1981. *Adolescents and Youth,* 4th ed. Englewood Cliffs, N.J.: Prentice-Hall.

Rollins, Boyd and Feldman, Harold. 1970. "Marital Satisfaction Over the Family Life Cycle." *Journal of Marriage and the Family* 26:20-28.

Romanuic, A. 1984. *Current Demographic Analysis. Fertility in Canada. From Baby Boom to Baby Bust.* Ottawa: Supply and Services Canada for Statistics Canada (Cat. no. 91-524E).

Rooke, Patricia T. and Schnell, R. L. 1981. "The CAS: Starved for Money, Ignored by Public." *The Globe and Mail,* December 3, p. 8.

Rosen, David H. 1974. *Lesbianism: A Study of Female Homosexuality.* Springfield, Ill.: C. C. Thomas.

Rosenberg, Morris. 1981. "The Self-Concept: Social Product and Social Force." In Morris Rosenberg and Ralph H. Turner, eds. *Social Psychology: Sociological Perspectives,* pp. 593-624. New York: Basic Books.

Rosenthal, Carolyn J. 1982. "Family Responsibilities and Concerns: A Perspective on the Lives of Middle-Aged Women." *Resources for Feminist Research* 11:211.

_____. 1986. "The Differentiation of Multigenerational Households." *Canadian Journal on Aging* 5:27-42.

_____. 1987. "Aging and Intergenerational Relations in Canada." In Victor W. Marshall, ed. *Aging in Canada,* 2d ed. Toronto: Fitzhenry and Whiteside.

Rosenthal, Carolyn J. and Marshall, Victor W. 1986. "The Head of the Family: Social Meaning and Structural Variability." *Canadian Journal of Sociology* 11:183-98.

Rosenthal, Carolyn J.; Marshall, Victor W.; and Synge, Jane. 1980. "The Succession of Lineage Roles as Families Age." *Essence* 4(3):179-93.

Roskies, Ethel. 1972. *Abnormality and Normality. The Mothering of Thalidomide Children.* Ithaca, N.Y.: Cornell University Press.

Ross, H. L. and Sawhill, I. V. 1975. *Time of Transition: The Growth of Families Headed by Women.* Washington, D.C.: The Urban Institute.

Rossi, Alice S. 1987. "Parenthood in Transition: From Lineage to Child to Self-Orientation." In Jane B. Lancaster, Jeanne Altmann, Alice S. Rossi, and Lonnie R. Sherrod, eds. *Parenting Across the Life Span: Biosocial Dimensions,* pp. 31-81. New York: Aldine de Gruyter.

Roy, Marcel et al. 1982. *Minutes of Proceedings and Evidence of the Standing Committee on Health, Welfare and Social Affairs Respecting Inquiry into Violence in the Family, Wife Battering.* Ottawa: Supply and Services Canada.

Royal Commission on the Status of Women. 1970. *Report.* Ottawa: Supply and Services Canada.

Royal Commission on Taxation. 1966. *Taxation of Income:* Part A – Taxation of Individuals and Families, vol. 3. Ottawa: Supply and Services Canada.

Rubin, Arline M. 1982. "Sexually Open versus Sexually Exclusive Marriages: A Comparison of Dyadic Adjustment." *Alternate Lifestyles* 5(2):101-8.

Rubin, Arline M. and Adams, James R. 1986. "Outcomes of Sexually Open Marriages." *The Journal of Sex Research* 22(3):311-19.

Rubin, Stefi and Quinn-Curran, Noreen. 1983. "Lost, Then Found: Parents' Journey Through the Community Service Maze." In Milton Seligman, ed. *The Family with a Handicapped Child,* pp. 63-94. New York: Grune Stratton.

Rush, Florence. 1980. *The Best Kept Secret: Sexual Abuse of Children.* Englewood Cliffs, N.J.: Prentice-Hall.

Rushing, W. A. 1979. "Marital Status and Mental Disorder: Evidence in Favor of a Behavioral Model." *Social Forces* 58:540-56.

Russell, Diana. 1982. *Rape in Marriage.* New York: MacMillan.

_____. 1986. *The Secret Trauma: Incest in the Lives of Girls and Women.* New York: Basic Books.

Rutter, M. 1971. "Parent-Child Separation: Psychological Effects on the Children." *Journal of Child Psychology and Psychiatry* 12:233-60.

Rutter, Michael; Tizard, J.; and Whitmore, K. 1970. *Education, Health and Behaviour.* London: Longman.

Ryan, Bruce A. 1981. "Child Welfare" (letter to the editor). *The Globe and Mail,* December 30, p. 6.

Sameroff, A. 1975. "Transactional Models of Early Social Relations." *Human Development* 18:65-79.

Santrock, John W. 1984. *Adolescence,* 2d ed. Dubuque, Iowa: Wm. C. Brown.

Santrok, J. and Warshak, R. A. 1986. "Developmental Relationships and Legal/Clinical Considerations in Father-Custody Families." In M. E. Lamb, ed. *The Father's Role: Applied Perspectives,* pp. 135-63. New York: Wiley.

Saucier, Jean-Francois and Ambert, A.-M. 1983. "Adolescents' Self-Reported Physical Health and Parental Marital Status." *Canadian Journal of Public Health* 74:396-400.

_____. 1986. "Adolescents' Perception of Self and of Immediate Environment by Parental Marital Status: A Controlled Study." *Canadian Journal of Psychiatry* 31:505-12.

Saunders, Daniel. 1986. "When Battered Women Use Violence: Husband Abuse or Self-Defense." *Violence and Victims* 1(1):47-60.

Sayers, Janet. 1980. "Biological Determinism, Psychology and the Division of Labour by Sex." *International Journal of Women's Studies* 3:241-60.

_____. 1982. *Biological Politics.* London: Tavistock.

Scanzoni, John. 1972. *Sexual Bargaining.* Englewood Cliffs, N.J.: Prentice-Hall.

Scanzoni, Letha D. and Scanzoni, J. 1981. *Men, Women and Change.* Toronto: McGraw-Hill Ryerson.

_____. 1988. *Men, Women, and Change: A Sociology of Marriage and Family,* 2d ed. New York: McGraw-Hill Ryerson.

Schlesinger, Benjamin. 1979. *One in Ten: The Single Parent in Canada.* Toronto: Faculty of Education, University of Toronto.

_____. 1980. "Abused Wives: Canada's Silent Screamers." *Canada's Mental Health* 28(2):17-21.

_____. 1985. "The Single Teen-age Canadian Mother in the 1980s: A Review." In Benjamin Schlesinger, ed. *The One Parent Family in the 1980s: Perspectives and Annotated Bibliography 1978-1984,* pp. 35-56. Toronto: University of Toronto Press.

Schlesinger, Benjamin and Marshall, D. 1979. "Communal Family Living." In B. Schlesinger, ed. *Families: Canada,* pp. 14-18. Toronto: McGraw-Hill Ryerson.

Schnaiberg, Allan and Goldenberg, Shelley. 1986. "From Empty Nest to Crowded Nest: Some Contradictions in the Returning Young-Adult Syndrome." Paper presented to the American Sociological Association. New York.

Schorr, Alvin. 1969. *Explorations on Social Policy.* New York: Basic Books.

Scott, Jean Pearson. 1983. "Siblings and Other Kin." In Timothy Brubaker, ed. *Family Relationships in Later Life.* Beverly Hills: Sage.

Scutt, Jocelynne A. 1983. "Legislating for the Right To Be Equal." In Cora Baldock and Bettina Cass, eds. *Women, Social Welfare and the State,* pp. 223-45. Sydney: Allen and Unwin.

Seeley, J.; Sim, A.; and Loosley, E. 1956. *Crestwood Heights.* Toronto: University of Toronto Press.

Segal, Lynne. 1983. "Smash the Family? Recalling the 1960s." In Lynne Segal, ed. *What Is To Be Done About the Family: Crisis in the Eighties.* Harmondsworth: Penguin.

Shanas, Ethel. 1981. "Old Parents: Middle-Aged Children." Paper presented at the Meetings of the International Association of Gerontology. Hamburg, Germany.

Shanas, Ethel; Townsend, Peter; Wedderburn, Dorothy; Friis, Henning; Milhoj, Poul; and Stehouwer, Jan. 1968. *Old People in Three Industrial Societies.* London: Routledge and Kegan Paul.

Shaw, Bernard. 1913. "Preface." In *Getting Married: A Disquisitory Play.* London: Constable.

Shaw, Marvin E. and Costanzo, Philip R. 1982. *Theories of Social Psychology,* 2d ed. New York: McGraw-Hill.

Sherman, Lawrence and Berk, Richard A. 1984. "The Specific Deterrent Effects of Arrest for Domestic Assault." *American Sociological Review* 49:261-72.

Shiffrin, Leonard. 1988. "Maternity Benefits Still Need Overhaul." *The Toronto Star,* March 21:A17.

Shorter, Edward. 1975. *The Making of the Modern Family.* New York: Basic Books.

Shostak, Arthur B. 1987. "Singlehood." In M. B. Sussman and S. K. Steinmetz, eds. *Handbook of Marriage and the Family,* pp. 355-67. New York: Plenum Press.

Shulman, Alix Kates. 1981. "Preface." In Anne Marie Rousseau. *Shopping Bag Ladies: Homeless Women Speak About Their Lives.* New York: The Pilgrim Press.

Siggner, Andrew J. 1986. "The Socio-Demographic Conditions of Registered Indians." In J. R. Ponting, ed. *Arduous Journey, Canadian Indians and Decolonization,* pp. 57-83. Toronto: McClelland and Stewart.

Silverman, Peter. 1978. *Who Speaks for the Children: The Plight of the Battered Child.* Don Mills, Ont.: Musson.

Singer, Benjamin D. 1986. *Advertising and Society.* Don Mills, Ont.: Addison-Wesley.

Small, Shirley Endicott. 1985. "Why Husband-Beating is a Red Herring." In Deborah Sinclair, ed. *Understanding Wife Assault: A Training Manual for Counsellors and Advocates,* Appendix A, pp. 160-64. Toronto: Ontario Ministry of Community and Social Services, Family Violence Program.

Smith, Dorothy E. 1975. "An Analysis of Ideological Structures and How Women are Excluded: Considerations for Academic Women." *Canadian Review of Sociology and Anthropology* 12 (Part I):353-69.

Smith, Michael. 1987. "The Incidence and Prevalence of Woman Abuse in Toronto." *Violence and Victims* 2(3):173-87.

Snider, Earle L. 1981. "The Role of Kin in Meeting Health Care Needs of the Elderly." *Canadian Journal of Sociology* 6(3):325-36.

Solicitor General of Canada. 1983. *Seven Cities Victim Survey.* Ottawa: Ministry of Supply and Services Canada.

Soliday, Gerald L., ed. 1980. *History of the Family and Kinship: A Select International Bibliography.* Millwood, N.Y.: Kraus.

Southworth, Suzanne and Schwarz, J. C. 1987. "Post-Divorce Contact, Relationship with Father, and Heterosexual Trust in Female College Students." *American Journal of Orthopsychiatry* 57:371-82.

Spanier, G. 1983. "Married and Unmarried Cohabitation in the United States: 1980." *Journal of Marriage and the Family* 45:277-88.

Spanier, Graham B. and Furstenberg, Frank F., Jr. 1987. "Remarriage and Reconstituted Families." In Marvin B. Sussman and Suzanne K. Steinmetz, eds. *Handbook of Marriage and the Family*, pp. 419-34. New York: Plenum Press.

Spanier, Graham B. and Thompson, L. 1984. *Parting: The Aftermath of Separation and Divorce*. Beverly Hills: Sage.

Spiegel, David. 1982. "Mothering, Fathering and Mental Illness." In Barrie Thorne, ed. with Marilyn Yalom. *Rethinking the Family: Some Feminist Questions*. New York: Longman.

Spock, Benjamin. 1946. (revised 1976). *Baby and Child Care*. New York: Pocket Books.

Spock, Benjamin and Rothenberg, Michael. 1985. *Dr. Spock's Baby and Child Care*. New York: Dutton.

Spreitzer, Elmer and Riley, Lawrence. 1974. "Factors Associated with Singlehood." *Journal of Marriage and the Family* 36:533-42.

Sproule, Heather and Wolfe, David. 1988. "Credibility of Child Victim Witnesses: A Review of the Literature." Toronto: The Institute for the Prevention of Child Abuse, Newsbrief, March, edition #2.

Stamp, Robert M. 1977. "Teaching Girls Their 'God Given Place in Life': The Introduction of Home Economics in the Schools." *Atlantis*, Spring.

_____. 1982. *The Schools of Ontario*. Toronto: University of Toronto Press.

Statistics Canada. 1979. *Canada's Families*. Ottawa: Supply and Services Canada.

_____. 1980. *Perspectives Canada III*. Ottawa: Supply and Services Canada.

_____. 1984. *The Elderly in Canada*. Ottawa: Supply and Services Canada.

_____. 1985. *Women in Canada: A Statistical Profile*. Catalogue 9-0503E. Ottawa: Supply and Services Canada.

_____. 1986. *Births and Deaths, 1985*. Ottawa: Supply and Services Canada.

_____. 1986a. *The Labour Force*. Ottawa: Supply and Services Canada.

_____. 1986b. *Marriage and Divorces, 1985*. Ottawa: Supply and Services Canada.

_____. 1986c. *Population and Dwelling Characteristics: Dwellings and Households*. Part I. Ottawa: Supply and Services Canada.

_____. 1986d. *Population and Dwelling Characteristics: Families*. Part I. Ottawa: Supply and Services Canada.

_____. 1987. *The Daily*. July 9, 1987. Catalogue 11-001. Ottawa: Supply and Services Canada.

_____. 1987a. *The Daily*. December 3, 1987. Ottawa: Supply and Services Canada.

_____. 1987b. *Health and Social Support, 1985*. Ottawa: Supply and Services Canada.

_____. 1987c. *The Labour Force*. Ottawa: Supply and Services Canada.

_____. 1987d. *The Nation: Age, Sex and Marital Status*. Catalogue 93-101. Ottawa: Supply and Services Canada.

_____. 1987e. *The Nation: Families*. Part I. Catalogue 93-106. Ottawa: Supply and Services Canada.

_____. 1987f. *The Nation: Languages*. Part I. Catalogue 93-102. Ottawa: Supply and Services Canada.

_____. 1988. *Canada's Women: A Profile of Their 1986 Labour Market Experience*. Ottawa: Supply and Services Canada.

_____. 1988a. *The Daily*. June 3, 1988. Ottawa: Supply and Services Canada.

_____. 1988b. *Health Reports*. Catalogue 82-003 (September). Ottawa: Supply and Services Canada.

_____. 1988c. *Social Trends*. Ottawa: Supply and Services Canada.

_____. 1989. *Historical Labour Force Statistics, 1988.* Catalogue 71-201 (January). Ottawa: Supply and Services Canada.

_____. 1989a. *Profiles of Ethnic Groups.* Ottawa: Supply and Services Canada.

Steel, Freda M. 1988. "An Overview of Provincial and Federal Maintenance Enforcement Legislation." *1988 National Family Law Program*, vol. 2:E-1-1 to E-1-62. The Federation of Law Societies of Canada and the Canadian Bar Association.

Steinberg, M. E. 1982. "Une Etude de la Relation entre l'Androgynie Psychologique et l'Adaptation Post-Divorce dans des Familles d'Enfants de Quatre à Sept Ans." Unpublished Doctoral Dissertation, Université de Montréal.

Steiner, Gilbert Y. 1981. *The Futility of Family Policy.* Washington, D.C.: The Brookings Institute.

Stern, Mark. 1987. *Society and Family Strategy: Erie County, New York, 1850-1920.* Albany, N.Y.: State University of New York Press.

Stetson, D. M. and Wright, G. C., Jr. 1975. "The Effects of Laws on Divorce in American States." *Journal of Marriage and the Family* 37:537-47.

Stewart, Catherine. 1988. *Understanding the New Law on Child Sexual Abuse Bill C-15: Implications and Issues.* Toronto: Institute for the Prevention of Child Abuse.

Stewart, Catherine and Bala, Nicholas. 1988. *Understanding Criminal Prosecutions for Child Sexual Abuse: Bill C-15 and the Criminal Code: A Guide for Community Groups and Professionals.* Toronto: Institute for the Prevention of Child Abuse.

Stolk, Y. and Brotherton, P. 1981. "Attitudes Toward Single Women." *Sex Roles* 7:73-78.

Stone, Lawrence. 1977. *Family, Sex and Marriage in England, 1500-1800.* New York: Harper and Row.

Stone, Leroy. 1988. *Family and Friendship Ties Among Canada's Seniors.* Ottawa: Minister of Supply and Services Canada.

Strain, Laurel A. and Chappell, Neena L. 1982. "Confidants: Do They Make A Difference in Quality of Life?" *Research on Aging* 4:479-502.

Stratham, Daphne. 1977. *Radicals in Social Work.* London: Routledge and Kegan Paul.

Straus, Murray. 1983. "Ordinary Violence, Child Abuse, and Wife-Beating: What Do They Have in Common?" In David Finkelhor, Richard J. Gelles, Gerald T. Hotaling, and Murray A. Straus, eds. *The Dark Side of Families: Current Family Violence Research*, pp. 213-34. Beverly Hills: Sage.

Straus, Murray and Gelles, Richard J. 1986. "Societal Change in Family Violence in 1975 and 1985 as Revealed by Two National Surveys." *Journal of Marriage and the Family* 48:465-79.

Straus, Murray; Gelles, Richard J.; and Steinmetz, Suzanne K. 1980. *Behind Closed Doors: Violence in the American Family.* New York: Anchor/Doubleday.

Strong-Boag, Veronica. 1979. "Wages for Housework: Mothers' Allowances and the Beginnings of Social Security in Canada." *Journal of Canadian Studies* XIV(1).

_____. 1982. "Intruders in the Nursery: Child Care Professionals Reshape the Years One to Five, 1920-1940." In Joy Parr, ed. *Childhood and Family in Canadian History*, pp. 160-78. Toronto: McClelland and Stewart.

_____. 1988. *The New Day Recalled: Lives of Girls and Women in English Canada, 1919-1939.* Toronto: Copp Clark Pitman.

Struthers, James. 1983. *No Fault of Their Own: Unemployment and the Canadian Welfare State 1914-1941.* Toronto: University of Toronto Press.

Sullivan, Teresa A. 1983. "Family Morality and Family Mortality: Speculation on the Demographic Transition." In William V. D'Antonio and Joan Aldous, eds. *Families and Religions*, pp. 49-66. Beverly Hills: Sage.

Super, C. M. and Harkness, S. 1981. "Figure, Ground, and Gestalt: The Cultural Context of the Active Individual." In R. M. Lerner and N. A. Busch-Rossnagel, eds. *Individuals as Producers of their Development: A Life-Span Perspective.* New York: Academic Press.

Suransky, Valerie P. 1982. *The Erosion of Childhood.* Chicago: University of Chicago Press.

Sutherland, Neil. 1976. *Children in English-Canadian Society: Framing the Twentieth-Century Consensus.* Toronto: University of Toronto Press.

Sweeney, Tania. 1983. "Child Welfare and Child Care Policies." In Adam Graycar, ed. *Retreat From the Welfare State,* pp. 35-54. Sydney: Allen and Unwin.

Sydie, R. A. 1987. *Natural Women, Cultured Men: A Feminist Perspective on Sociological Theory.* Toronto: Methuen.

Synge, Jane. 1979. "The Transition from School to Work: Growing Up Working Class in Early 20th Century Hamilton, Ontario." In K. Ishwaran, ed. *Childhood and Adolescence in Canada.* Toronto: McGraw-Hill Ryerson.

_____. 1980. "Work and Family Support Patterns of the Aged in the Early Twentieth Century." In Victor W. Marshall, ed. *Aging in Canada,* pp. 135-44. Toronto: Fitzhenry and Whiteside.

Synnott, Anthony. 1983. "Little Angels, Little Devils: A Sociology of Children." *The Canadian Review of Sociology and Anthropology* 20(1):79-95.

Szinovacz, Maxililiane E. 1983. "Using Couple Data as a Methodological Tool: The Case of Marital Violence." *Journal of Marriage and the Family* 45:633-44.

Task Force on Child Care. 1986. *Report of the Task Force on Child Care.* Ottawa: Supply and Services Canada for Status of Women Canada.

Tausig, Christine. 1984. "Class of 84: They Don't Have Dreams." *University Affairs* (March):2-3.

Tepperman, Lorne. 1974. "Ethnic Variations in Marriage and Fertility: Canada 1871." *Canadian Review of Sociology and Anthropology* (November).

Thomas, A. and Chess, S. 1980. *The Dynamics of Psychosocial Development.* New York: Brunner/Mazel.

Thomlison, Ray J. and Foote, Catherine E. 1987. "Children and the Law in Canada: The Shifting Balance of Children's, Parents' and the State's Rights." *Journal of Comparative Family Studies* 18:231-45.

Thompson, Anthony P. 1983. "Extramarital Sex: A Review of the Research Literature." *Journal of Sex Research* 19(1):1-22.

Thompson, Judy and Gilby, Rhonda. 1980. "Correlates of Domestic Violence and the Role of Police Agencies." In Robert Silverman and James Teevan, eds. *Crime in Canadian Society,* pp. 298-306. Toronto: Butterworths.

Thorne, Barrie. 1982. "Feminist Rethinking of the Family: An Overview." In Barrie Thorne, ed. with Marilyn Yalom. *Rethinking the Family: Some Feminist Questions,* pp. 1-24. New York: Longman.

_____. 1987. "Re-visioning Women and Social Change: Where Are the Children?" *Gender & Society* 1:85-109.

Thornton, Arland and Freedman, Deborah. 1982. "Changing Attitudes Toward Marriage and Single Life." *Family Planning Perspectives* 14(6).

Tilly, Louise and Scott, Joan. 1978. *Women, Work and the Family.* New York: Holt, Rinehart and Winston.

Titmuss, Richard M. 1974. *Social Policy.* London: Allen and Unwin.

Tobin, Sheldon S. and Kulys, Regina. 1980. "The Family and Services." In Carl Eisdorfer, ed. *Annual Review of Gerontology and Geriatrics,* vol. 1, pp. 370-99. New York: Springer.

The Toronto Star. 1980. "Feminism's Rocky Road Through Macho Japan." February 28, p. C1.

_____. 1983. "Spare the Rod, Avoid a Thug." September 25, p. F2.

Traughber, B.; Erwin, K. E.; Risley, T. R.; Schnelle, J. F. 1983. "Behavioral Nutrition: An Evaluation of a Simple System for Measuring Food and Nutrient Consumption." *Behavioral Assessment* 5:263-80.

Trigger, Bruce. 1976. *The Children of Aataentsic I*, vol. 1. Montreal: McGill-Queen's University Press, pp. 45-54.

Trost, J. 1981. "Cohabitation in the Nordic Countries: From Deviant Phenomenon to Social Institution." *Alternative Lifestyles* 4:401-27.

Turcotte, Pierre. 1988. "Common-law Unions: Nearly Half a Million in 1986." *Canadian Social Trends* (Autumn): 35-39.

Turk, James and Bell, Norman. 1972. "Measuring Power in Families." *Journal of Marriage and the Family* 34:215-22.

Turkle, Sherry. 1984. *The Second Self: Computers and the Human Spirit*. New York: Simon and Schuster.

Tyler, N. B. and Kogan, K. L. 1977. "Reduction of Stress Between Mothers and Their Handicapped Children." *American Journal of Occupational Therapy* 31:151-55.

Ujimoto, K. Victor. 1987. "The Ethnic Dimension of Aging in Canada." In Victor W. Marshall, ed. *Aging in Canada*, 2d ed. Toronto: Fitzhenry and Whiteside.

United Nations. 1988. *Demographic Yearbook 1986*. New York: United Nations.

Vallance, Ian. 1988. "Interest Groups and the Process of Legislative Reform Bill C-15 – A Case Study." *Queen's Law Journal* 13(1):159-207.

Vallee, Brian and Stafford, Jean. 1986. *My Life with Billy*. Toronto: McClelland and Stewart.

Van Kirk, Sylvia. 1988. "Women in Between: Indian Women in Fur Trade Society in Western Canada." In R. Fisher and K. Coates, eds. *Out of the Background*, pp. 150-66. Toronto: Copp Clark Pitman.

Van Stolk, Mary. 1983. "A Harder Look at the Battered and Abused Child." In K. Ishwaran, ed. *The Canadian Family*, pp. 317-30. Toronto: Gage.

Veevers, Jean E. 1979. "Voluntary Childlessness: A Review of Issues and Evidence." *Marriage and Family Review* 2:3-26.

_____. 1980. *Childless by Choice*. Toronto: Butterworths.

_____. 1988. "The 'Real' Marriage Squeeze." *Sociological Perspectives* 31(2):169-89.

Verdon, Michel. 1980. "The Quebec Stem Family Revisited." In K. Ishwaran, ed. *Canadian Families: Ethnic Variations*, pp. 105-24. Toronto: McGraw-Hill Ryerson.

Verma, Rvai; Kwok, Chan B.; and Lam, Larry. 1980. "The Chinese-Canadian Family: A Socio-Economic Profile." In K. Ishwaran, ed. *Canadian Families: Ethnic Variations*, pp. 138-56. Toronto: McGraw-Hill Ryerson.

Veroff, Joseph and Feld, Sheila. 1970. *Marriage and Work in America*. New York: Van Nostrand Reinhold.

Wakil, S. Parvez; Siddique, C. M.; and Wakil, F. A. 1981. "Between Two Cultures: A Study in Socialization of Children of Immigrants." *Journal of Marriage and the Family* 43:929-40.

Walker, Lawrence. 1984. "Sex Differences in the Development of Moral Reasoning: A Critical Review." *Child Development* 55:667-91.

Walker, Lenore. 1979. *The Battered Woman*. New York: Harper and Row.

_____. 1984. *The Battered Woman Syndrome*. New York: Springer.

Wallace, A. F. C. 1969. "Review of David Schneider's American Kinship: A Cultural Account (see *American Anthropologist*, 1968)." *American Anthropologist* 71:100-106.

Wallerstein, Judith S. 1985. "Children of Divorce: Preliminary Report of a Ten-year Follow-up of Older Children and Adolescents." *Journal of the American Academy of Child Psychiatry* 24:545-54.

_____. 1988. "Women After Divorce: Preliminary Report from a Ten-year Follow-up." *American Journal of Orthopsychiatry* 56:65-77.

Wallerstein, J. and Kelly, J. B. 1980. *Surviving the Breakup: How Children and Parents Cope with Divorce*. New York: Basic Books.

Watson, Roy. 1983. "Premarital Cohabitation vs. Traditional Courtship: Their Effects on Subsequent Marital Adjustment." *Family Relations* 32:139-47.

Webster-Stratton, C. and Eyberg, S. 1987. "Child Temperament: Relationship with Child Behavior Problems and Parent-Child Interaction." *Journal of Clinical Child Psychiatry* 11:123-29.

Weekend Magazine. 1979. "The Weekend Poll: Child Discipline." July 7, p. 1.

Weis, D. L. 1983. " 'Open' Marriage Relationships: The Emergence of Nonexclusive Models of the Marital Relationship." In E. Macklin and R. Rubin, eds. *Contemporary Families and Alternative Lifestyles*, pp. 194-215. Beverly Hills: Sage.

Weitzman, Lenore T. 1985. *The Divorce Revolution: The Unexpected Social and Economic Consequences for Women and Children in America*. New York: The Free Press.

Welter, Barbara. 1966. "The Cult of True Womanhood: 1820-1860." *American Quarterly*, Summer.

Whalen, C. K. and Henker, B. 1980. "The Social Ecology of Psychostimulant Treatment: A Model for Conceptual and Empirical Analysis." In C. K. Whalen and B. Henker, eds. *Hyperactive Children. The Social Ecology of Identification and Treatment*. New York: Academic Press.

White, Lynn K. and Booth, A. 1985. "Stepchildren in Remarriages." *American Sociological Review* 50:689-98.

White, Pamela M. 1985. *Native Women: A Statistical Overview*. Ottawa: Minister of Supply and Services.

Whitehurst, R. N. 1975. "Alternate Life Styles and Canadian Pluralism." In P. Wakil, ed. *Marriage, Family and Society: Canadian Perspectives*, pp. 432-45. Toronto: Butterworths.

_____. 1979. "Non-traditional Family and Marriage." In G. N. Ramu, ed. *Courtship, Marriage and the Family in Canada*, pp. 166-79. Toronto: Macmillan.

_____. 1985. "Alternatives to Monogamy." In H. Feldman and M. Feldman, eds. *Current Controversies in Marriage and Family*, pp. 263-73. Beverly Hills: Sage.

Whyte, William Foote. 1943. *Street Corner Society*. Chicago: University of Chicago Press.

Williams, John E. and Best, Deborah L. 1982. *Measuring Sex Stereotypes: A Thirty Nation Study*. Beverly Hills: Sage.

Williams, Tannis MacBeth, ed. 1986. *The Impact of Television: A Natural Experiment in Three Communities*. Orlando, Florida: Academic Press.

Williams, Thomas Rhys. 1983. *Socialization*. Englewood Cliffs, N.J.: Prentice-Hall.

Wilson, Edward O. 1975. *Sociobiology: The New Synthesis*. Cambridge, Mass.: Harvard University Press.

Wilson, Franklin C. 1980. *A Look at Corporal Punishment and Some Implications of Its Use*. Toronto: Ministry of Community and Social Services, Child Abuse Program.

Wilson, J. Donald et al. 1970. *Canadian Education: A History*. Scarborough, Ont.: Prentice-Hall.

Wilson, Jeffrey. "Conduct, Property, Marriage and Morality: An Exercise in Mixed Metaphors." *1988 National Family Law Program*, vol. 5:M-1-1 to M-1-12. The Federation of Law Societies of Canada and the Canadian Bar Association.

Wilson, Susannah J. 1986. *Women, the Family and the Economy*, 2d ed. Toronto: McGraw-Hill Ryerson.

Windschuttle, Keith. 1980. *Unemployment*, rev. ed. Ringwood, Victoria: Penguin.

Wolfgang, Marvin E. 1957. "Victim-precipitated Criminal Homicide." *Journal of Criminal Law, Criminology, and Police Science* 48:1-11. Also reprinted in M. E. Wolfgang, ed. *Studies in Homicide*, pp. 72-87. New York: Harper and Row, 1958.

Wood, Vivian and Robertson, Joan F. 1978. "Friendship and Kin Interaction: Differential Effect on the Morale of the Elderly." *Journal of Marriage and the Family* 40:367-75.

Woon, Yuen-Fong. 1986. "Some Adjustment Aspects of Vietnamese and Sino-Vietnamese Families in Victoria, Canada." *Journal of Comparative Family Studies* 17:349-70.

Wrong, Dennis H. 1961. "The Oversocialized Conception of Man in Modern Sociology." *American Sociological Review* 26:183-93.

Wynn, Margaret. 1972. *Family Policy.* New York: Pelican Books.

Yankelovich, D. 1981. "New Rules in American Life: Searching for Self-fulfillment in a World Turned Upside Down." *Psychology Today* 15(4):35-91.

Yussen, Steven R. and Santrock, John W. 1978. *Child Development.* Dubuque, Iowa: Wm. C. Brown.

Zaretsky, Eli. 1976. *Capitalism, the Family and Personal Life.* New York: Harper and Row.

_____. 1982. "The Place of the Family in the Origins of the Welfare State." In Barrie Thorne, ed. with Marilyn Yalom. *Rethinking the Family: Some Feminist Questions.* New York: Longman.

Zelizer, Viviana A. 1981. "The Price and Value of Children: The Case of Children's Insurance." *American Journal of Sociology* 86:1036-56.

_____. 1985. *Pricing the Priceless Child: The Changing Social Value of Children.* New York: Basic Books.

Zigler, Edward and Seitz, Victoria. 1978. "Changing Trends in Socialization Theory and Research." *American Behavioral Scientist* 21:731-56.

Zureik, Elia T. and Pike, Robert M. 1975. "Preface." In Elia T. Zureik and Robert M. Pike, eds. *Socialization and Values in Canadian Society,* vol. 1. Toronto: McClelland and Stewart.

INDEX